Deaf World

Deaf World

A Historical Reader and Primary Sourcebook

Edited by
Lois Bragg

NEW YORK UNIVERSITY PRESS
New York and London

NEW YORK UNIVERSITY PRESS
New York and London

© 2001 by New York University
All rights reserved

Library of Congress Cataloging-in-Publication Data
Deaf world : a historical reader and primary sourcebook / edited by Lois Bragg.
p. cm.
Includes bibliographical references and index.
ISBN 0-8147-9852-7 (cloth : alk. paper)—ISBN 0-8147-9853-5 (pbk. : alk. paper)
1. Deaf—United States. 2. Deaf—United States—Social conditions. I. Bragg, Lois,
1951–
HV2545 .D43 2001
305.9'08162—dc21   00-058727

New York University Press books are printed on acid-free paper,
and their binding materials are chosen for strength and durability.

Manufactured in the United States of America

10 9 8

Contents

Acknowledgments

Niko Pfund, editor-in-chief at New York University Press, envisioned a collection of essays on the general topic of Deaf Studies, convinced me to edit it, then handed over editorial control. As we say in the Deaf community about people like Niko, "It's true that he's hearing, but he's got a great attitude." Jane Dillehay, dean of Arts and Sciences at Gallaudet University, made it possible to edit the book, start to finish, in a mere fifteen months by providing everything from reduction of teaching duties to use of her office for videotaping and photocopying.

In the early stages of work, writing the proposal and lining up prospective authors and potential topics, I strove to involve as many experts as I could to help me shape Niko's general idea into an authentic self-portrait of the American Deaf community. Barbara Kannapell, Tom Holcomb, Ted Supalla, Doug Baynton, Barbara White, John Christiansen, Yerker Andersson, Debbie Sonnenstrahl, Willy Conley, Steve Chough, Bernard Bragg, Roz Rosen, Martha Sheridan, Kathy Arnos, Simon Carmel, Melanie McKay-Cody, and MJ Bienvenu each spent many hours talking over the plan of the book and providing me with ideas and contacts, as did Anita Farb and Dawn Bradley at the National Association of the Deaf, which also provided *gratis* photocopies and bibliographical information. In the case of Willy Conley, those hours turned into weeks of networking the Deaf arts community, combing photo archives, and scanning and copying photos for my consideration. Harlan Lane and Cindy Bailes each read the entire manuscript in draft and likewise offered much generous advice.

The hot topics, germinal articles, and important writers *not* included here must surely have been suggested to me by one or another of these kind colleagues, and it was only my own eccentric judgment that excluded them. Readers' comments and suggestions about selections will be gratefully received in anticipation of a second edition.

As the book took shape, my students Ed Hoyt, Kristen Lemire, Jonathan Nash, Randall Noriega, Brian Sipek, Rachel Valentino, Travis Bastow, Jason Caradine, Sacha Klein, Matt Korpics, Susan Luedee, Melissa Malzkuhn, Mickey Posner, Leslie Southwell, Lisa Valenti, and Bridget Woodley diligently read prospective essays and provided copious feedback and pointed observations about what should and should not be included in a reader alleging to portray the Deaf World. In the Gallaudet Archives, Mike Olson helped me locate photos and Ulf Hedberg tracked down many elusive details. Of course, a book such as this would not be possible if it weren't for Gallaudet's Archives and Deaf Collection, the latter selected and maintained by Tom Harrington. The thirteen scholars and writers who contributed fresh work for this book and the two undergrads who researched the authors' biographies probably didn't realize they were also giving me a graduate education in Deaf Studies and are unlikely ever to know how very much I learned from them or how much I enjoyed their camaraderie over the course of 1999.

Back in the hearing world, Bernard Ahouse of Lodi, New York, read and corrected an earlier draft of the dedication to Uncle Charlie.

I thank you all.

In surdam memoriam:
Karl Jaekel

This book begins with a story, really three stories intertwined. One is the life history of my grandmother's Uncle Charlie, to whom this book is dedicated. The second is a story of institutionalized efforts, in Uncle Charlie's day, to prevent Deaf people from marrying each other. The third tells how my grandmother fared in life as a late-deafened woman. The three stories together explain why, despite having been functionally hearing well into my twenties, I live and work in the Deaf World.

Uncle Charlie was born Karl Jaekel in 1872, somewhere in the German state of East Prussia. Königsberg, a Baltic port now in western Russia and called Kaliningrad, features in family lore as our old-country hometown, but the Jaekels had many connections in the village of Schuttschenofen, some sixty miles inland to the south, and American branches of the family that feature deaf members seem to descend from more than one Schuttschenofen line. Young Karl's parents, Karl Jaekel the elder and Dorothea Pliskatt, kept an inn on a coach line near a German-Russian border crossing. Although the Jaekels were German-speaking and German-surnamed (Karl's mother was a Katzwinkel, Dorothea's a Pusch), a history of mixed ethnicity is suggested by their having belonged to the Russian Orthodox rather than the Lutheran Church.

When little Karl and his twin sister, Juliana, were eleven months old, both infants fell ill. Juliana died but Karl recovered, and at some point over the next few years, as his babbling failed to transform itself into the local dialect of German and eventually ceased, his parents and older sister Adelina would look back on that illness and profess themselves convinced that it was the reason the boy was *taubstumm*, "deaf and dumb." For a family to assume that a deaf child became so by accident is not uncommon, as we see in Laurent Clerc's autobiography reprinted in this reader, but American families of this period tended instead to believe that their deaf children simply were born that way. Since it is patently impossible for a family in this era to have known for sure why their little boy was deaf, any explanation offered is of interest for what it tells us about family or community values rather than actual etiology.

Regardless of his family's spin on his story, Karl's life would not have been all that different from that of his six surviving brothers and sisters born in Prussia. None was ever sent to school in the old country, and all must have worked along with their parents in the inn. Decades later, Adelina would tell her children and grandchildren stories about how she and her sisters and brothers were sent across the border into Russia to buy luxury goods, such as hen's eggs, at lower prices and thereby to evade taxes by smuggling them back home for sale to lodgers.

In 1881, when Karl was nine and Adelina sixteen (and engaged to be married), the Jaekels and Pliskatts began emigrating to Luzerne County, Pennsylvania, Karl probably arriving with his mother in 1882. How Dorothea managed to get a deaf-mute boy through Ellis Island is unknown. The family settled on a small farm near Alden, east of Wilkes-Barre, where they could associate exclusively with German neighbors, even joining a German Lutheran church for the sake of the language. Father and sons, including young Karl, found work in the anthracite mines, while mother and daughters worked the small farm. Dorothea bore one more child, Edith, who would grow up to be her Deaf brother's lifelong companion and interpreter, and Adelina waited for her fiancé. Dorothea's brother Adam settled on the west side of the Susquehanna River, founding a family that would include a number of deafened and hard of hearing people. No one learned English.

On 4 January 1886, the Pennsylvania Institution for the Deaf and Dumb in Philadelphia received a completed application form for a fourteen-year-old boy styled "Chas. Yeackel," witnessed by two English-surnamed men in Wilkes-Barre. Whoever filled out the form plainly had no German, spelling "Blissart" for Pliskatt and "Bush" for Pusch. The statements that the family's resources were "[o]nly their daily earnings," that they could contribute "nothing" to their son's support, and that no efforts had been made to cure his deafness because the parents were "poor" are likely to have been all too true. It is interesting to speculate about the family's shifting fortunes based on the adult stature of their children, which shrinks from around six feet or more for the older ones, including Charlie and even Lena (as Adelina was now known), to around five feet for Edith, who was born during this period. In any case, these items on the application form provided for Uncle Charlie's admission as a "State Pupil," that is, one supported entirely by state funds.

Other questions on the form concern the etiology of the pupil's deafness, and the relentless impertinence of these questions demonstrates how far the pseudoscience (or secular religion) of eugenics had penetrated public education in America. The answers tell us that Charlie was not born deaf, that neither of his parents was deaf, that his parents were not cousins or related in any degree, that neither had any deaf relatives, that none of the other children was born deaf or became deaf. We know, however, that Dorothy Yeakel's brother Adam Pliscott (as we must now spell their names) had at least one hard of hearing child. She may have been born and deafened after Charlie's application was submitted, but deaf cousins do not appear without an immediate family history. Of course, in those days, the Pliscotts would not likely have associated the hard of hearing children and deafened youths of the family with a "deaf-mute" like Uncle Charlie, especially if they were all convinced that Charlie had been deafened by the sickness that killed his sister. But that there were indeed

Charlie with his parents and some of his brothers and sisters. Charlie is the big, good-looking guy with the mustache. Lena is on the far left, Edith on the far right. Undated photo from editor's private collection.

deaf family members among the Pliscotts, and perhaps other intermarried families, prior to Charlie's generation is certain, as we can deduce from the pattern of deaf descendants.

Still other items on the form concern language. Charlie had never been "under instruction at any time" and could not read or write. He could read lips but was totally "dumb," without the ability to "utter any intelligible words," and he communicated "by signs intelligible to those with whom [he] ha[d] constant intercourse." Lone deaf children isolated in hearing families can and do invent a lexicon of "home signs," but, as the linguists Ceil Lucas and Clayton Valli show in the excerpt from "What Happens When Languages Come in Contact" (chapter 16), without an earlier generation of signers or a critical mass of deaf peers, a child's home signs do not approach a natural signed language that could form a basis for English literacy training commenced after childhood. Could Charlie's signs have been such a natural signed language? Encouraging us to think so is the genetic heritage clearly present in the family before Charlie's birth, and, given the Yeakel history of marriages over several generations with a small number of families from Schuttschenofen, a small Deaf community may have been present in that village. On the other hand, an inn on a coach line near the Russian border is not a place that would likely support a number of deaf residents, so the question remains open.

Answers to further questions on the form show that Uncle Charlie, like many deaf family members who describe themselves even today as hard of hearing rather than deaf, had quite a bit of residual hearing, and later traditions about him support that conclusion. He is said to have been only "partially" deaf, to have been able to hear "very heavy playing on the Piano," "thunder if very loud," and even "the sound of a voice nearby." This might explain a family memory that always puzzled me: Uncle Charlie's habit of whistling, albeit in a monotone, while he worked. If transplanted to today's culture, provided with hearing aids as a toddler and thus able to acquire some intelligible speech, he might be regarded as hard of hearing.

Finally, one question on the application was approached with what may have been deliberate deceit: the question "Where born?" was left blank. When the application was received in Philadelphia, it was "referred to the Principal to enquire, where the child was born and how long his father has resided in the State." Any response to this inquiry is lost, but the admission form, which otherwise preserves errors from the application form and must have been copied from it, states unequivocally that Charlie was born in Luzerne County. Someone lied, presumably to secure State Pupil status for him.

The form provided no place to indicate any referral or reasons for the parents' decision to begin a son's education when he was almost a grown man. Family tradition has it that sending Charlie to school was entirely his mother's idea and that she was routinely and roundly criticized for it by relatives and neighbors who thought that such a strapping young man should be kept at work for the family, not fitted up with an education that none of the others could hope to have and no one could see the benefit of. It is pleasant to regard Dorothy as a progressive thinker driven by fierce mother love for her deaf boy, but it is far more likely that she sent Charlie to school because the money he made working in the mines no longer covered the expense of feeding him.

The Pennsylvania Institution for the Deaf and Dumb had been established sixty-six years before Charlie's arrival by a well-meaning but rather ludicrously ignorant hearing tradesman who invented a sign language for his first pupils. By 1821, the school had been reestablished with a firmer language base and called on Laurent Clerc to serve as interim principal. Along with his beautiful young wife, Eliza, who was also Deaf, Clerc modeled the nascent American Sign Language (ASL) for the Pennsylvania pupils during his seven-month stay. That the Clercs were celebrities in Philadelphia can be deduced from their having had their portraits painted there by Charles Willson Peale, Eliza posing with one hand cradling her infant daughter and the other flashing her ASL name sign. Two years later, after the Clercs' departure, the school established a progressive vocational education program, the first of its kind, and the next year it moved to a new building at Broad and Pine Streets, the campus it still occupied when Charlie arrived from Alden.

In 1886 the Pennsylvania Institution, with an enrollment of 433 pupils, was still the signing school Clerc had helped shape, but this was soon to change under its new principal, Dr. A. L. E. Crouter, a hearing man who had been trained at the oral Clarke School in Massachusetts. "Articulation" had been introduced at the Pennsylvania Institution in the early 1870s but only as a distinct program at a separate location, a day school known as the Oral Branch that served local hard of hearing and late deafened youngsters. Crouter would begin, gradually but methodically, to turn the state school into an oral outpost.

In 1886, however, Crouter's public position on the new oral instruction was still moderate and quite reasonable, as he urged it only for the hard of hearing and the "semi-mute," a confusing term for people who were deafened after the acquisition of a spoken language and therefore not mute at all. As a "deaf-mute," Charlie was automatically enrolled in the Manual Department. Nearly 50 percent of the new pupils (thirty-six out of seventy-nine) were reported by their parents as born deaf. The *Annual Report* for 1885 had remarked on such high figures for congenital deafness, and of course, these numbers could not possibly have been correct. As mentioned in connection with Charlie's childhood illness, reported etiologies are interesting not for their factuality but rather for what they tell us of the social climate on the issue of congenital "defects," suggesting as they do that American parents of that day were much more comfortable admitting to congenital than to adventitious deafness in their offspring, for which they would presumably have borne more responsibility. This would change as eugenics taught parents to be more ashamed of their genetic heritage than of any negligence in child rearing.

That Charlie was fourteen by no means made him unusual among pupils entering state residential schools in these years, but it was a concern for Principal Crouter and for oralists in general, whose method depended on starting when pupils were too young to object. Among the year's seventy-nine new pupils when Charlie entered the Pennsylvania Institution, forty-nine were older than ten. "It is greatly to be regretted," Crouter wrote, "that parents should neglect sending their children to school until they reach an age when it is almost impossible for them to acquire an education," identifying ten as the cutoff age (*Annual Report*, 1886). One wonders if Charlie knew his education was considered "nearly impossible" before it was even begun.

The vocational training program that had once been innovative was antiquated by 1886, a common failing of Deaf schools decried in 1930 by Albert Ballin in the chapter "The Graduate" in *The Deaf Mute Howls* (reprinted in this book as chapter 24) and still present until vocational programs were phased out in the 1970s and 1980s. Uncle Charlie was enrolled in the shoemaking department, one of three industrial programs open to boys, the other two being tailoring and printing. While records of pupil academic enrollment and progress have not survived to the present, if they ever existed, complete records of attendance and work in the Industrial Department for these years were carefully archived. The *Annual Reports* declare the shops to have been genuine training programs, established to ensure that all pupils would be able to support themselves after leaving school. The limited number of programs was explained by the intention to maintain excellence over variety. Nevertheless, the shops served another important function: they provided the pupils, who were largely state supported, with all their shoes, boots, and clothing, and the school itself with all its bed and table linens. In addition, the print shop earned money for the school by printing a large number of journals that were jobbed out to the

Shoemaking Department at the Pennsylvania Institution for the Deaf and Dumb, *ca.* 1896. Charlie must be among the older boys in the rear. Photo courtesy of the Gallaudet University Archives.

institution. Thus the training programs, whatever they were originally or officially intended to do, saved the state of Pennsylvania a great deal of money by putting the pupils to work for the state.

When Charlie entered the shoemaking program, he was one of fifty-six pupils making and repairing shoes for his classmates (and presumably, for the staff) under foreman George O'Dowd. (We note that the industrial instructors were not teachers.) The boys' shoemaking shop made the soles and assembled the shoes, while the uppers were stitched by a girls' shop that also produced hand-knitted stockings, a craft already obsolete due to the availability of cheap machine-knitted hosiery. Weekly production and evaluation charts were kept by the industrial program foremen and are extant for the years of Charlie's residence. The shoemaking chart kept by Mr. O'Dowd for the weeks of October 1886 shows Charlie near the bottom of the roll, with his name miswritten as "J. Yerkel." During his first week in the shop, the first week of October, he repaired one shoe and was graded, on a scale of one to five, a three for attendance and a five for both punctuality and conduct. By the next week his attendance was up to a five, and like almost all of his shopmates, he continued to earn straight fives through the ten years of his training. There were no grades for actual achievement in the craft.

As was the custom in all schools for the deaf, the day-to-day life of the pupils was governed by a strict schedule that left little time for leisure or private pursuits. The daily schedule from the 1888–89 *Annual Report* shows that Charlie would have risen at 6:00 A.M., breakfasted at 6:30; endured a "morning lecture" from 7:45 to 8:00; attended academic classes from 8:00 to 1:00, with a fifteen-minute lunch at 10:30; dined at 1:15; worked in the shoe shop from 2:30 to 4:45; supped at 6:00; studied until 8:00; endured an evening lecture until 8:30; and retired at 9:30. Saturdays and Sundays were somewhat freer, although they, too, included mandatory lectures, as well as an hour of Sunday school. Meals seem, on paper at least, to have been ample. Breakfast was oatmeal or grits with milk, bread, butter, molasses, and beef. Dinner featured mutton or beef, potatoes, canned vegetables, and stewed fruit or pudding. Supper was milk, bread, butter, and more stewed fruit.

During the summer holidays of 1887, after Charlie's first year in Philadelphia, Lena, who had been waiting for her sweetheart for at least five years, suddenly married a young Schuttschenofen man who had arrived in Luzerne County just weeks earlier, Karl Brösch. One wonders what persuaded Lena to give up her long wait for her fiancé. Could it have been that Karl Brösch knew this other man and brought Lena convincing information that he would never come to claim her? If so it was a lie, for according to what she told her children many years later, Lena's lover eventually in fact came to claim her—too late. Charlie must have attended the wedding as though through a glass wall. While the older Yeakels would have had some signed language of sorts, they were all still essentially monolingual in German, as was the newly arrived bridegroom, whereas Charlie would have been signing ASL and beginning to read English. His future interpreter, his little sister Edith, was still only three years old.

Charlie returned to school and the shoe shop in the fall, now correctly identified on the roll as "C. Yeakel." During the week ending 29 October 1887, Charlie made his first shoe. Meanwhile, Principal Crouter continued to puzzle over etiology statistics:

> It seems to me there can be little doubt that the defect is transmissible from generation to generation. . . . [T]he deaf should be carefully advised in this serious matter. Their future, and the future of their offspring should be prudently considered before entering upon a condition so fraught with possibilities of misfortune and unhappiness. (*Annual Report*, 1887–88)

During the 1888 summer holidays, Lena gave birth to the first of her twelve children, and a young man named Franz Bormann arrived in Luzerne County fresh from Schuttschenofen.

In the fall of 1888, Charlie returned to the institution and its shoe shop, making ten shoes during the month of October. Sometime during that year, Mr. O'Dowd resigned "to engage in business in this city," and the shop was taken over by Joel Openshaw. In the 1888–89 *Annual Report*, Principal Crouter was counting not shoes but rather deaf relatives and reporting that while five new pupils' families admitted to deaf relatives, only three congenitally deaf pupils actually had deaf parents. Noting sententiously that "nothing . . . gladdens the heart of a deaf parent more than the birth of a hearing child," he concluded a long harangue on the subject with the advice to await further research into the perplexing question of heredity.

The 1889–90 and 1890–91 *Annual Reports* saw something of a drop-off in Crouter's interest in heredity, his remarks being limited to statistics on the new pupils and the misstatement that the proportion of the (reportedly) congenitally deaf averaged at around 33 percent, whereas in truth it had been holding steady at around 50 percent for the past six years. It seems that Principal Crouter was not keeping up with his eugenics reading, because in the 28 November 1890 issue of *Science*, an article titled "The Intermarriage of the Deaf, and Their Education" appeared under the byline of a hearing son of a Deaf mother: Edward Miner Gallaudet, the president of the Columbia Institution for the Deaf and Dumb. In this article, E. M. G., as the younger Gallaudet is commonly called, cited the published *Minutes of Evidence* containing testimony from "Professor Bell" (an honorary title, since A. G. Bell was no professor) to the Royal Commission, including a chart under the rubric "Classification of the Deaf into Four Groups as a Guide to Marriage." Using the terms *congenital/non-congenital* and *sporadic/family*, Bell's groups label deaf people as (1) deaf after birth, with no family history; (2) deaf at birth, with no family history; (3) deaf after birth, with family history; and (4) deaf at birth, with family history. Bell, and E. M. G. citing him, realized that deaf people in class 1, who amounted to some 60 percent of the deaf population in those days, did not "manifest a tendency to transmit the defect to their children," whereas classes 2, 3, and 4 did. From these findings, both men jumped to the conclusion that "those in whose person or in whose family [deafness] inheres are bound by altruistic considerations to take care that by no selfish act or course of theirs the aggregate of this misfortune in the world shall be increased"—in other words, that the 40 percent of the deaf population falling into their classes 2, 3, and 4 would best remain celibate for life.

This conclusion was premised on an odd assumption that both writers frequently stated but never bothered to argue, to wit, that deafness "is certainly a grave misfortune." The mothers of both men were highly competent deaf women, and both men had ample opportunity to learn from deaf colleagues and other family members (A. G. Bell's wife, E. M. Gallaudet's sister-in-law and nieces) that deafness was no tragedy but rather "only a serious inconvenience" (a statement from a deaf colleague that E. M. G. cruelly ridicules in his article). E. M. G., in addition, appears to have been maintaining a lifelong love affair with a Deaf member of his faculty, Amos Draper, while entering into marriages with hearing women and fathering hearing children (and exploiting his Deaf mother as an unpaid administrator at the college). Yet these men, who regarded Deaf people as defective unfortunates whose numbers must be reduced, had the power to set policy for the education and even the marriage of those they pitied—or despised. In the years ahead, as Harlan Lane, Robert Hoffmeister, and Ben Bahan explain in the passage of their book *A Journey into the DEAF-WORLD* excerpted here as chapter 50, Bell's research interests and assimilationist zeal would springboard him into a leading role in American eugenics.

Principal Crouter would have found much with which to agree in E. M. Gallaudet's remarks on the intermarriage question, but he could not have been pleased with the second part of the article, on education, in which Gallaudet argued for the "combined system" that included both signing and speech. Hearing people who made it their business to chart the offspring of deaf marriages generally disapproved of sign language and manual education for deaf children. The connection between articulation and eugenics is not so transparent today, but when Charlie was a schoolboy, it was widely believed that Deaf people would cease to marry each other if the sign language that brought them together could somehow be wiped out and they were forced to speak. It makes sense: if a deaf youth taught to speak but not to sign could not communicate with or even meet deaf girls, he might be brought to marry into the hearing world. What is so appalling about the line of thought is not the logic but the cruelty. E. M. Gallaudet's stance against the new "pure oralism" ideology espoused by Bell and Crouter therefore made his position against deaf marriages logically inconsistent, and himself something of a maverick among teachers of the deaf in his time. It is pleasant to believe that E. M. G. allowed himself to be influenced against oralism by his lover, Draper, whose argument for the combined method, "The Attitude of the Adult Deaf towards Pure Oralism" (chapter 22), would be published five years later.

Unswayed by Gallaudet, Crouter was to take a more radical approach to education in 1891. Rather than merely screening out new pupils with any residual hearing and keeping them isolated from the signing pupils at a separate campus, he placed *all* new pupils in the oral program—until they failed and had to be removed to the Manual Department. Meanwhile, in the shoe shop, Charlie may have been only dimly aware of these policy changes affecting the younger pupils as he continued to move up the roll, making all new shoes, rather than repairing, and earning grades of five and even six under the supervision of Mr. Openshaw.

That winter Lena Brösch gave birth to her second child, a daughter named Ida Maria, and the next year she left for Indian Territory with her husband, two young children, her brother-in-law Martin Brösch and his family, and the now ubiquitous Bormann, who had taken to calling himself "Frank." Lena and Karl Brösch named their third child, born in Oklahoma, Charles Frank. Was Frank Bormann Lena's old-country beau, her cold-feet fiancé? Could he have been the father of one or two (or more?) of his friend Karl's children? While the Brösch brothers and Frank Bormann were carrying out their various family agendas, Lena's two children, little Idi and her older brother, had an adventure. They had been sent out to gather buffalo chips—or were they merely cow pies?—for their mother's cooking fire and somehow, on the open prairie, became bewildered and lost. Some passing Indians picked them up, brought them to their village, and fed and amused them until the frantic parents came to reclaim them. It was not long afterward that Lena insisted on returning to Pennsylvania. Frank Bormann went with them.

Meanwhile, back in Philadelphia, the Pennsylvania Institution moved from its longtime quarters at Broad and Pine to a newly built campus in Mt. Airy. The Industrial Building was not finished at the time of the move, so the department was broken up and housed in temporary quarters here and there among the other departments. The shoe shop was in the basement of the primary school. One wonders how

The Main Building at the new Mt. Airy campus of the Pennsylvania Institution for the Deaf and Dumb. The Main Building housed the Advanced Manual Department, where Charlie attended classes. Photo from undated postcard in editor's private collection.

Crouter kept his young oral pupils from being contaminated by the signing cobblers like twenty-year-old Charlie. Bell was still at his eugenics campaign, lecturing at the National College for Deaf-Mutes (the former Columbia Institution for the Deaf and Dumb and the future Gallaudet University) in March 1891, but now with a decidedly paranoid tone. Denying to his audience of Deaf undergraduates that he ever had any "intention of interfering with your liberty of marriage," he argued that the responsibility for policing deaf marriages should lie with deaf people themselves. And while he had to admit that adventitious deafness (that is, class 1) did not appear to be passed on to offspring any more than was "the accidental loss of [an] arm, in battle, for instance," he raised the specter of this occurring anyway by marriage with a partner in class 2, 3, or 4. Besides, Bell argued, many class 1 deaf people could never be absolutely certain that their deafness was indeed adventitious. Thus were young people who had been deafened by disease or trauma as very young children frightened out of marriage. Bell concluded his lecture by asking his audience of Deaf undergraduates to report his statements accurately, as "translat[ed] into the sign language" by his "friend, Prof. Fay." Apparently doubting Fay's agency or worried that the students would intentionally misrepresent the lecture, he added, "I have, therefore, brought with me to-night a gentleman who has taken a stenographic account of all that I am saying to you," and he asked that no reports of the lecture be disseminated until he had a chance to correct his own secretary's work.

It looks as if Bell was pretty uneasy taking his own medicine—having to communicate orally with people who could not understand him. But perhaps, too, he had good reason to doubt his interpreter. Edward Allen Fay was not to publish his "Marriages of the Deaf in America" until 1898, but he lectured on the subject earlier. Lecture notes discovered among his papers after his death demonstrate a novel view of the heritability of acquired deafness. Like Bell, he warns that adventitious deafness may actually derive from a congenital "anomaly or tendency to disease." But he goes further than Bell to posit that even in cases where it is certain that hearing existed and that "diseases and accidents may be counted as true causes" of deafness, "antenatal tendencies" await only the onset of a fall or a fever to trigger deafness. He concludes this lecture on a false note of optimism, saying that "the deaf themselves, now that they are learning what kinds of marriage are liable to result in deaf offspring, show a disposition to avoid such marriages." Of course, hearing members of deaf families, who were known for certain to be a major factor in the birth of deaf children, were free to marry at will, as Bell and the hearing Gallaudets did while preaching abstinence to their deaf relatives, colleagues, and students. It is clear, therefore, that the underlying concern was not the birth of more deaf children, who were, after all, the source of Fay's, Gallaudet's, and Bell's income, but rather the maintenance of social control over a group of people who appeared to be rather aggressively inclined to live as they, not their hearing teachers, saw fit.

At the Pennsylvania Institution, the big news of the 1892–93 academic year was the introduction of electric lighting at the new campus; but Crouter's focus remained on the expansion of his oral program. He boasted that 57 percent of the pupils were now under "pure oral instruction" and that the Manual Department now "discourages sign" in favor of writing, fingerspelling, and "natural gestures" (whatever those might be). Charlie must have been lost in this classroom atmosphere, but at least the Institution was now spelling his name right in the *Annual Report,* and he would have been relieved when the shoe shop moved into the new Industrial Building in April. The next year, however, the steady progress of oralism took a leap forward with the elevation of Principal Crouter to superintendent and his alleged discovery that pupils who failed in the oral program and had to be moved to the Manual Department turned out to be failures there as well. Rather than considering that inappropriate placement had delayed elementary education for too long and had taught misplaced pupils falsely to regard themselves as dull, Crouter concluded that these students in fact were dull, and that therefore the oral method had no real failures. This Orwellian pronouncement would have had a profound effect on the manual pupils, who were now to be regarded as certified dimwits. As if it were not enough to denigrate the older pupils, Crouter attacked the alumni as well, coercing their organization, then called the Pennsylvania Association for the Advancement of the Deaf, into a formal endorsement of oralism and attempting to keep it from joining the National Association of the Deaf (NAD), which was taking a strong stance against the pure oral method. Within twenty years, the NAD became so alarmed about the imminent extinction of the sign language under the onslaughts of the likes of Crouter that it made a huge investment in filming what it feared were the last surviving vestiges, as George Veditz explained in his statement "The Preservation of the Sign Language" (chapter 10).

The new principal, F. W. Booth, seems to have adopted Crouter's paternalistic attitude toward the signing pupils. In his 1893–94 *Annual Report*, he provides us with some insight into how he would have viewed Charlie, if indeed he ever met him. In explaining the rationale for reducing class size in the Manual Department from sixteen to fourteen, he says, "It would seem but fair to the pupils left under manual instruction, especially in cases of those of slow mind, or of those who are over age, that they have the advantages that small classes afford." As for the pure oral method, while there is no reason to believe that Booth opposed it in any way, he took care to show that the latest and most draconian policy change was a direct order from Crouter, reprinting the following letter in full:

To F. W. Booth, Principal of the Manual Department:
Dear Sir:
In accordance with action by the Board of Directors at its meeting held April 4th, you are authorized and directed to take such steps as may be necessary to prohibit, as far as possible, the use of signs on the part of the teachers and pupils in the class-rooms of your department for purposes of instruction, or on the part of the officers and servants for purposes of communication with the pupils outside of school hours, using instead spelled or written English. The same rule is to be observed in the dining-rooms and in the sitting-rooms during study hour. At chapel service signs may be continued. The object of this regulation is to promote the use of English among the pupils. Please communicate it to the teachers, officers, and pupils of your department as soon as convenient, and take such steps as in your judgment may be necessary to carry it into effect.

Very truly yours,
A. L. E. Crouter,
Superintendent

Booth's response to this directive was to ban signs at chapel as well. Charlie was now totally and absolutely cut off from social intercourse at the school, and he left in the spring of 1894, presumably for the typical "time out" after the eighth year of instruction.

Back in Luzerne County, with Lena busy giving birth every two years, the perennial bachelor Frank Bormann married Karl Brösch's cousin Augusta Ksonsek, who appears to have been brought out from Schuttschenofen for just that purpose, since the wedding followed hard on her arrival. The new couple remained close to Lena and her children for the rest of their lives, Gussie Bormann coming to be known as Fat Grandma to scores of distantly related Brösch offspring. And the marriage was prolific, eventually producing a number of deaf and hard-of-hearing grandchildren. Lena's oldest daughter, still monolingual in German, was sent to a public school, where the teacher, monolingual in English, misunderstood her name, Idi Brösch, as Edith Brush. The name stuck. The two years between 1894 and 1896 were all that Edith Brush would live near her Uncle Charlie until a much later, and far less happy, period of their lives, when she, too, was deaf.

Charlie's return to Philadelphia in 1896 coincided with two significant events. One was the long-awaited publication of Fay's flawed research in the *American Annals of the Deaf* and the immediate acceptance of his false conclusions on genetics as "indisputably established," in the words of Superintendent Crouter. The second was the annual convention, held in early July of this year at the new Pennsylvania Institution campus, of the American Association to Promote the Teaching of Speech to the Deaf. Whether Charlie was present in Philadelphia in July is doubtful, and in any case, he hardly would have been allowed to attend, so he must have missed the remarkable spectacle staged for that event: a deaf and blind undergraduate from Radcliffe College reading, in spoken English, a paper titled "The Value of Speech to the Deaf." This uniquely privileged but closely managed young lady, who all her life spurned association with her fellow deaf, was just beginning her career as a crowd-drawing mouthpiece of the oralists and eugenicists, but already her influence was profound. Helen Keller, more than any other single element, clinched public support for charlatans such as Crouter and effectively shut out the Deaf from meaningful education and work—and discouraged them from marriage—for the next seventy years.

Charlie was discharged at the end of his allowed ten years as a State Pupil and would have attended the ceremony in 1898, where twelve pupils were graduated (four of them headed for Gallaudet College) and twenty-four "honorably discharged." The ceremony included a demonstration of "Lip Reading Exercises"; Charlie's discharge certificate misspelled his name. It is doubtful that any family members made the trip to Philadelphia. His sister Edith was only fourteen at the time. The month before, Lena's husband, Karl Brösch, had been killed in a rockfall in the mine, and the other miners had carried his body back to Lena's house and laid it on her front porch. Left with six children and no means of support, Lena took Idi/Edith out of school in the third grade and sent her to work as a child servant in an exclusive girls' boarding school in Wilkes-Barre, where she completed her education by standing in the hallways behind open classroom doors to hear lessons on such subjects as elocution and German literature. Lena soon married Frank Bormann's little brother Leopold, a twenty-two-year-old who had come from Schuttschenofen just the year before, and proceeded to have six more children. That Leo Burman, as he took to calling himself, was nearly young enough to be Lena's son and that Lena continued so prolific despite desperate poverty has been regarded as a double outrage by scores of Pliscotts, Yeakels, Brushes, Burmans, and assorted affines for the past one hundred years. But it seems to have been a genuine love match, or at least to have grown into love. I can still see them now in my mind's eye, Grandpa Burman with his peg leg and tremendous yellow mustaches sitting on a bench just outside the kitchen door, while Grandma Burman, still affecting ankle-length dresses in the 1950s, lays the clean dishes back on the table upside down in lieu of a cupboard, and the kettle steams on the potbellied stove.

With Charlie's discharge from school, he disappears from the Deaf record: he never married and he never joined any Deaf organizations. Rather than stay on in Philadelphia in the Deaf community that had grown up around the school, he went back to live with his parents immediately or shortly after his discharge. They had moved to Sheatown, and their youngest, Edith, would still have been at home, while others of Charlie's brothers and sisters were raising families in the area. Sheatown was not a German community, so the Yeakels must have picked up some English by then. Of course, since they were both illiterate, they still could not communicate with their son in written English. Did they fall back on the signing they had used before he went away to school? A lot would have depended on how they felt about having a grown deaf-mute son at home again, especially in the new neighborhood. Did they despise him as a fool, as P. H. Confer, in his contribution to the discussion on planning a deaf-mute colony reprinted in chapter 1, claims was usually the case? Or did they regard him as a "perpetual pet," as J. J. Flournoy, in the same discussion, asserts was common? We do not know for certain, but there is no reason to believe they behaved much differently than other hearing families, which is to say they let him stay in the house and simply ignored him.

No one is certain when or how it was that Charlie set up a shoe shop and a carpet loom in a small, vacant house. What we do know about his relations with the family and their role in his business comes from a posthumous brother-in-law of Charlie, Uncle Harold Hayes, and is a bit hard to decipher: "The sad part of his position with the Family [is that they] didn't help his trade so he wasn't able to open a shop and Communicate with the public." The picture we have of Charlie's life in Sheatown in the early years of the twentieth century is one of isolation and frustration, the typical life among the hearing described by so many of the authors of the essays collected here. Why did he come back? And why didn't he join the new state Association of the Deaf, where he could have renewed schoolboy friendships and met some nice Deaf girls?

The old alumni group that Crouter had tried so hard to control was now incorporated as the Pennsylvania Society for the Advancement of the Deaf (PSAD), a state member of the NAD, and was keeping careful membership and fund-raising records, especially with regard to its major project, the Doylestown Home for the Aged and Infirm Deaf. PSAD membership rolls show four or five members from Luzerne County through these early years, but Charlie's name never appears, nor does it appear on any of the donation lists for the home. Family assertions that there were no other Deaf people in the area for Uncle Charlie to associate with are clearly mistaken and rather suspect considering the number of deaf Pliscotts, Brushes, Bormans, and Burmans scattered around Luzerne County, a few of whom were deafened young enough to have learned to sign in a residential school (although surreptitiously as signing was increasingly banned, even outside the classroom). Something was keeping Charlie from contact with the Deaf community. It may have been poverty, a sense of obligation to his parents, an ethical refusal to use money for travel or leisure when he was unable to contribute as much as he would have liked to the family income. His parents felt no such obligation to him, however. After enjoying old age in their own home with the two unmarried children, Charlie and Edith, to care for them, they died without having deeded the house to the brother and sister, and so Charlie and Edith lived on there, in the eyes of their siblings, as charity cases. When their brother Simon was down on his luck, he simply moved his family into the house, and Charlie and Edith had to remove to an outbuilding in the rear.

Alternately, the impediment to Charlie's pursuit of a normal social life may have been Edith. Perhaps she appeared to be unmarriageable and Charlie felt some responsibility for her, or perhaps her fluency in ASL made him so dependent on her that he was reluctant to upset the status quo. One generation after Charlie's schooling, deaf schoolchildren were being surgically sterilized in the United States, on the recommendation of their hearing teachers and with the blessings of their hearing parents, but this horror (which Hitler was later to hold up as precedent for his own policies in Germany) was not yet imposed on deaf children when Charlie was at school. The most likely scenario is that Crouter's eugenics propaganda and his establishment of the pure oral method of schooling had scared Charlie off when it came to social relations with other Deaf, especially women. The constant urging of celibacy for the deaf and the bleak future Crouter had decreed for the deaf children of Pennsylvania would together have been enough to discourage from marriage many a Deaf man less intelligent and sensitive than Uncle Charlie. Who in his right mind would want to father children whose happiness would be destroyed and future quashed in a school such as the Pennsylvania Institution had become?

Whatever kept Charlie away from the Deaf community, it certainly was not any physical, mental, or social disability on either his part or that of his sister Edith. Edith was a sprightly and cheerful woman, well read and outspoken, who delighted her grand-nieces and-nephews and their children into her nineties. When I was fifteen, I was certain that Aunt Edith and I were the only members of the extended family to have read Cervantes, and I'm still certain of that today. Charlie was a tall, handsome, robust man of happy disposition and easy sociability who enjoyed family visitors, taught his nieces and nephews and their children to sign, and would whittle a toy for a new baby in the family. One of these children, now Ruth Brooks, a woman almost eighty years old and deaf herself for the past fifty, still has a slingshot he made for her, sanded to a warm glow well beyond the requirements of any ordinary slingshot. In Aunt Ruth's view, however, the really important thing about Uncle Charlie was that he was the only man in the family who never teased or tickled the children. He let his nieces and nephews watch him at work at his carpet loom and from time to time let them try their hands at it for themselves. A hearing grandniece, my mother, now in her mid-seventies but always selectively amnesiac about anything pertaining to the deaf line in the family, recalls the loom as so big and heavy that she thought at the time it was made out of railroad ties. That several of this generation recall only the signs for "No, don't do that" and "Good, I'm pleased with you" suggests that Uncle Charlie was not afraid to make children behave in his home, a rare gift in a bachelor uncle.

Many of these stories date from the years that Uncle Charlie and Aunt Edith lived in Wilkes-Barre on Carlisle Street, repairing shoes and selling Edith's lollipops around the corner from Lena's Edith and her family. After an ill-fated marriage to a sailor in Philadelphia and rapid loss of her hearing, Edith Brush had returned to the area and married a widower from a Danish immigrant family that had Anglicized its surname to Ahouse: a one-armed piano player locally known as Professor but actually a grade-school dropout and notorious drunkard. Trapped in this nightmare marriage with my brilliant but hopeless grandfather, Granny was raising her children and stepchildren on Barney Street, where they could trundle over to Uncle Charlie and Aunt Edith's whenever they liked. In old age, isolated by a life of deafness without fluent sign language, Granny would often reminisce about Uncle Charlie in those days, always coming around to the plain fact that he was much more intelligent than other members of the family. Her evidence for this fell into two parts. One was that he could express and understand anything in sign language—Granny's amazement at this ordinary feat being a good example of what Elizabeth Broecker, in her essay "Who Speaks for the Deaf Community?" (chapter 6), calls the sign language mystique. The other was that he read voraciously, in the view of family members wholly unacquainted with reading for pleasure and knowledge. Virtually everyone who knew him remembered his unexampled habit of taking the daily paper, and several recall his extraordinarily good penmanship. But everyone agrees that Uncle Charlie had more than book learning. Aunt Ruth (of the slingshot) recalls Charlie's "instinctive knowledge of plants" and "an esoteric knowledge of nature" and cites as an example the day he stood back while other members of the family planted a tree at the house in Sheatown. When they were done and had left, Charlie dug it up and replanted it "correctly." (Deaf readers will recognize Aunt Ruth's story as a version of the old Deaf chestnut, the clever Deaf boy who seems to be a fool as he blandly watches the hearing boss or teacher make a dangerous error, then steps in when the hearing are all out of earshot and saves the day anonymously.)

Woven into all these memories of Uncle Charlie's intelligence, competence, friendliness, and basic human decency is the discordant nub of the word *dummy*, a word that is never absent from any story about him. Granny spoke of him often to me during her last years, two deaf women, grandmother and granddaughter, going over and over the old stories in search of our places in history. Granny's take on the whole family picture was that there are two kinds of deaf people in the family: "deaf-mutes" and "the hard of hearing." Deaf as a doorknob herself since early middle age, she was in her own scheme of things one of the hard of hearing. Chats between us were laborious affairs of lip reading, miming, writing with a thick black marker that she could see through her cataracts, slipping into German (*nicht wahr?*) when memories went way back to Alden or to the nearer past when she lived with us in Germany, and fiddling with her old hearing aid. My own state-of-the-art hearing aids I knew for certain were of no practical use for understanding speech, but her aid, who knew? It might have been some help to her if it weren't always shorting out.

Granny's major gripe about the family's treatment of Uncle Charlie was their use of the term *deaf and dumb*, which she found insulting and, more grievous a fault in her view, erroneous. Her oldest son, Bernard Ahouse, recalls that it was neighborhood children who taunted Uncle Charlie, and Aunt Edith as well, from the railroad tracks, calling Charlie a dummy and mocking his signing. But Uncle Harold Hayes, who married Aunt Edith after Charlie's death, placed the blame squarely on the family: "Aunt Edith was a very smart woman there fore [*sic*] was able to communicate with Charlie but for the rest of the family he was just a dummy. Aunt Lena sure didn't help when she married the second time and produced more dummies so to speak, that never recognized Uncle Charlie." Not even the in-laws could let pass an opportunity to condemn that last Schuttschenofen match, but our interest here is in Uncle Harold's pun on the word *dummy*, a recurrent bit of wordplay among the Ahouse offspring as well.

A funny thing about all these memories is that no one can remember exactly when it was that Uncle Charlie died and what he died of. It must have been sometime in the 1930s, they say—he wasn't old—but the cause of death is forgotten. Aunt Edith was left without a home or income but soon met Uncle Harold, who brought his railroad pension to the marriage. Uncle Bernie took Uncle Charlie's shoemaking tools; they're in the cellar of his farmhouse, and he'll fetch them out for visitors (much as Aunt Ruth does with her slingshot) and show you the signs he remembers. The carpet loom somehow ended up in Ted Brush's attic, and no one knows what happened to it when the house was pulled down. Of course, I could find Uncle Charlie's date of death without too much trouble, and probably his grave as well, but I've just somehow never gotten around to it. Plainly, I don't want to know. In my mind, he's still the powerful, handsome man with the handlebar moustache, sign-reading the newspaper to little Aunt Edith or whistling over his carpet loom in a beautiful deaf monotone.

WORKS CITED

Bell, Alexander Graham. "Marriage: An Address to the Deaf." Washington: Gibson Bros., 1891.

Fay, Edward Allen. "Addresses: 'The Classification of the Deaf' and 'Some Indirect Causes of Deaf-Mutism.'" Unpublished, undated lecture notes, with foreword by Helen Fay. Gallaudet University Archives.

Gallaudet, Edward M. "The Intermarriage of the Deaf, and Their Education." *Science* 16, 408 (28 November 1890): 295–99.

Pennsylvania Institution for the Deaf and Dumb. *Annual Reports.* Gallaudet University Archives.

Contributors

Compiled with the assistance of Susan Luedee and Michael Scott Posner.

A. PHILIP AIELLO's autobiographical sketch is included in this book.

MYRNA (ORLECK) AIELLO was born in Providence, Rhode Island, and became deaf at age three from German measles. She had never met another Deaf person until she enrolled in Gallaudet College, where she quickly became an expert signer and was soon instructing faculty ASL classes while still an undergraduate. Ménière's disease caused frequent interruptions in both her education and her careers as an ASL teacher and Vocational Rehabilitation counselor. Unable to work away from home, Mo turned her attention to her husband's part-time computer business, building it up into a full-time enterprise with a shop in Silver Spring.

BOB ALCORN was born in 1946, graduated from the Texas School for deaf and Gallaudet College (1975), and later earned a master's degree at Texas A&M. A devoted advocate of ASL and American Deaf culture, he worked in various capacities as an ASL teacher and interpreter trainer, including positions as coordinator of interpreter training at McLennan Community College in Waco, Texas, and ASL instructor at the University of Texas–Austin. He died suddenly in 1996.

GLENN B. ANDERSON was born in Chicago and graduated from Parker High School before coming to Gallaudet College in 1965, where he majored in psychology and served as literary editor of the student newspaper as well as co-captain of both the basketball and track teams. After earning an M.A. in Rehabilitation Counseling and coordinating a program for Deaf adult education at LaGuardia Community College, he became the first known Deaf African American Ph.D. when he was awarded a doctoral degree from New York University in 1982. Dr. Anderson is currently the chair of the Gallaudet University Board of Trustees and professor at the University of Arkansas.

BEN BAHAN was born to Deaf parents in New Jersey in 1956 and attended the Marie Katzenbach School for the Deaf. After graduation from Gallaudet College in 1978 with a degree in biology, he worked at the Salk Institute and then moved to the Bay Area, where he joined Joe Dannis in setting up DawnSignPress in 1981. Ben can be seen in many videotapes on Deaf folklore and literature, as well as ASL instruction, and he is also known for his humorous essays in English and his much-in-demand live storytelling. Married and the father of two Deaf children, he holds a Ph.D. in applied linguistics from Boston University and presently serves as chair of the Deaf Studies Department at Gallaudet University.

CYNTHIA NEESE BAILES, the only Deaf member of a hearing family from Atlanta, Georgia, is an associate professor in teacher education at Gallaudet University. She holds a B.A. from Gallaudet, an M.A.T. from Augustana College, and a Ph.D. from the University of Maryland; her areas of interest are language arts, reading, bilingual education, and children's literature. Cindy's involvement in the education of Deaf children includes experience as an elementary and a secondary teacher, a curriculum developer, and an administrator.

ALBERT BALLIN was the son of a Deaf German lithographer in New York City and attended the New York Institution for the Deaf. He studied art in Rome for several years in the early 1880s, returned to America hoping to make a living as an artist, married, and became active in New York politics for a time. He later moved to California, hoping to make a career in the new moving-picture industry. Although widely admired in the Deaf community for his signing style and his mastery of several foreign languages, as well as for his writing, painting, and acting, he never succeeded in any of these pursuits and died in 1932, two years after the publication of *The Deaf Mute Howls*, in the Los Angeles County Poor Farm.

SHARON N. BARNARTT is professor of sociology at Gallaudet University, coauthor (with John B. Christiansen) *of Deaf President Now: The 1988 Revolution at Gallaudet University*, and author of *Contentious Politics in the Disability and Deaf Communities*. She has also published widely in the area of socio-economic status and disability/deafness, legal and disability policy issues, and social movements in the deaf and disability communities. She is a former president of the Society for Disability Studies and currently co-editor of *Research in Social Science and Disability*.

MJ BIENVENU was born Deaf in an all-Deaf family in 1952 and is a graduate of the Louisiana School for the Deaf and Gallaudet University, where she earned a B.A. in English and an M.A. in linguistics. She has published widely, in both print and videotape, on Deaf culture and ASL and is the founder of TBC (The Bicultural Center). MJ is presently on the faculty of the ASL, Linguistics, and Interpretation Department at Gallaudet and is pursuing work toward a Ph.D. in applied linguistics from the Union Institute.

EDMUND BOOTH was born in Springfield, Massachusetts, in 1810, became deaf at age eight, and attended the American Asylum in Hartford, Connecticut. After graduation and a short period of teaching at Hartford, Booth pioneered in Iowa, founding the town of Anamosa, where he married, served in various county and state positions, started a successful newspaper, and wrote on a wide variety of subjects, including his experience in California as a forty-niner. He died in Anamosa at the age of ninety-five.

FRANK G. BOWE is professor of Counseling, Research, Special Education and Rehabilitation, as well as Special Education coordinator, at Hofstra University. He holds an M.A. in education from Gallaudet and a Ph.D. in educational psychology from New York University and has worked in various capacities with the federal government and private industry as an advocate for the civil rights of people with disabilities. He is the author of *Physical, Sensory and Health Disabilities: An Introduction* and *Birth to Five: Early Childhood Special Education*.

LOIS BRAGG, professor of English at Gallaudet University, was born in Pennsylvania in 1951, grew up in the Federal Republic of Germany, and gradually became deaf through her teens and twenties. She holds an M.A. from St. Bonaventure University and a Ph.D. from the University at Buffalo and publishes widely on early Germanic languages, literatures, and mythologies. With her four children now grown and gone, she and her border collie associate, Schaefer, are at home in Silver Spring when Gallaudet is in session but otherwise live in Seneca County, New York, with her husband, Will Sayers.

ELIZABETH L. BROECKER graduated from a public school in New Jersey and found Gallaudet College such a culture shock when she enrolled in 1949 that she soon withdrew. Years later, she returned to Gallaudet as a divorced mother of four and graduated at the top of the class of 1968. Since then, while based in New Jersey, she has worked with deaf and hard-of-hearing people all over the country as an advocate, teacher, social worker, and writer, dedicated to increasing personal autonomy among Deaf people.

H. M. CHAMBERLAYNE was born in 1832 and attended the American Asylum in Hartford. He taught for a time at the Central New York Institution for the Deaf at Rome but otherwise worked mainly as a journalist. He died in 1895.

JOHN B. CHRISTIANSEN, professor of sociology at Gallaudet University, was born in Wisconsin and grew up in Utah. He holds a Ph.D. from the University of California, Riverside. John's current research interest is cochlear implants, specifically, hearing parents who have chosen to have their children surgically implanted. He and psychologist Irene Leigh, both of whom are Deaf, plan to complete a book on this subject for publication with Gallaudet University Press in 2001.

LAURENT CLERC'S autobiography appears in this book.

WILLY CONLEY is an actor, photographer, and playwright based in Laurel, Maryland. After attending public schools in Baltimore, he graduated from the Rochester Institute of Technology with a degree in medical photography, toured with the National Theatre of the Deaf as an actor, studied creative writing with Derek Walcott at Boston University, and won many awards for his plays. He is currently affiliated with Center Stage in Baltimore and the faculty of Gallaudet University, where he is assistant professor of Theatre Arts.

VALERIE L. DIVELY was born deaf to hearing parents, raised on a farm in Michigan, and attended the Michigan School for the Deaf. She holds a doctorate in linguistics, with subspecializations in anthropology and translation studies, from the Union Institute in Cincinnati. Val is assistant professor in the Gallaudet University Department of ASL, Linguistics, and Interpretation and serves as coordinator of the interpreting program.

AMOS G. DRAPER was born in 1845 in Vermont and became deaf at age eleven from a high fever he incurred while rescuing a playmate from drowning in an icy creek. He attended the Hartford School for the Deaf, where he studied under George Wing. When the family moved to Illinois, Draper worked for a time as a typesetter, a vocation he had learned at Hartford, but enrolled in Gallaudet College in 1868, where he immediately formed a lifelong friendship with EMG—the college president Edward Miner Gallaudet. After graduation, he began a forty-four-year career of teaching at Gallaudet College, beginning as a tutor and ending as professor of Latin and mathematics at his retirement in 1916. He died, apparently of grief, shortly after attending EMG's funeral the following year.

GILBERT EASTMAN is Professor Emeritus of Theatre Arts at Gallaudet University. He holds a B.A. degree in art from Gallaudet (1957) and an M.F.A. in drama from Catholic University (1963). He was a founding member of the National Theatre of the Deaf (NTD) and has taught courses for NTD's Summer Program. Gil has been an actor, stage manager, translator, or director for more than fifty plays, and his plays *Sign Me Alice* and *Laurent Clerc: A Profile* have been published by DawnSignPress. As host of *Deaf Mosaic*, he received an Emmy Award from the Washington Chapter of the National Academy of Television Arts and Sciences. He is the author of *From Mime to Sign* and *Just a Deaf Person's Thoughts*.

J. J. FLOURNOY was born sometime between 1800 and 1810 in Jamestown, Virginia. What little is known about his life can be gleaned from his letters to the *American Annals of the Deaf and Dumb*, excerpted in this book. He died in 1879.

ERNEST HAIRSTON was born in 1939 in rural West Virginia, became deaf at the age of six, and attended the West Virginia School for the Negro Deaf and Blind, graduating in 1956. At Gallaudet College, he was active with the Modern Dance Group, which toured widely, and was literary editor of the yearbook. He earned an M.A. from California State University at Northridge and has worked in a variety of teaching and Deaf service positions. Ernie now works for the U.S. Department of Education in Washington.

ROBERT HOFFMEISTER is the hearing son of Deaf parents, both of whom were teachers at the American School for the Deaf in Hartford, Connecticut. Bob's interests include ASL acquisition and bilingual education, and he currently serves on the faculty of Boston University, where he founded and now directs the world's first university program in Deaf Studies.

Tom Humphries teaches at the University of California, San Diego, in the Teacher Education Program and the Department of Communication. Deafened in childhood, he holds a master's degree in education from Gallaudet College and a Ph.D. in cross cultural communication and language learning from Union Graduate School. Current research interests focus on the emergence of collective voice in modern life and its impact on the everyday lives of individuals, including their education and aspects of their economic, social, and cultural lives. Tom is the author or coauthor of several books on ASL and the culture of Deaf people, including *A Basic Course in American Sign Language* (T. J. Publishers, 1980), *Learning American Sign Language* (Allyn and Bacon, 1992), and *Deaf in America* (Harvard University Press, 1988).

Katherine Jankowski currently provides leadership to the Pre-College National Mission Program's two demonstration schools—the Kendall Demonstration Elementary School and the Model Secondary School for the Deaf, located on the campus of Gallaudet University. Previously, she was the superintendent at the Minnesota State Academy for the Deaf and the Central North Carolina School for the Deaf. She has also been an assistant professor in the Communication Arts Department at Gallaudet, a program director at a nonprofit organization, a counselor, and a sign communication specialist. Kathy is a Gallaudet graduate and holds a doctorate in public communication from the University of Maryland. She is the author of *Deaf Empowerment: Emergence, Struggle, and Rhetoric.*

Arlene Blumenthal Kelly, born Deaf to Deaf parents, attended a self-contained day school and a private school for hearing children in Baltimore. Presently a member of the Deaf Studies faculty at Gallaudet University, she has published in journals such as *American Annals of the Deaf, Exceptional Children*, and *Disability Studies Quarterly.* Prior to her faculty appointment, she was a research associate in the Gallaudet Research Institute, where she studied mainstreamed adolescents, mother-infant interaction, and language acquisition. With a B.A. in English and an M.A. in linguistics, both from Gallaudet, Arlene is currently working on her dissertation, tentatively titled "How Deaf Women Construct Language, Culture, and Gender: An Ethnographic Study of ASL Teachers," at the University of Maryland's Department of American Studies.

David J. Kurs, from Riverside, California, was born Deaf into a Deaf family and attended public schools, sometimes with interpreters but often without. He earned a B.S. in business administration at Gallaudet University, where he served as SBG (Student Body Government) president, in 1998. David currently resides in Los Angeles, where he works for Jersey Films as an assistant to the story department.

Harlan Lane was born in 1936 and educated at Columbia, Harvard, and the Sorbonne. He is University Distinguished Professor at Northeastern University and research affiliate at MIT. In 1973, Harlan was a psycholinguist who knew very little about sign language and the Deaf World when, as visiting professor at the University of California at San Diego, Dr. Ursula Bellugi introduced him to Deaf people, their language, and their culture; it changed his life. He is the author of *When the Mind Hears: A History of the Deaf* and *Mask of Benevolence: Disabling the Deaf Community*.

JACK LEVESQUE was born in 1945 in Springfield, Massachusetts. He attended Clarke School for the Deaf, a public high school, and two junior colleges and worked in a mill before he learned of Gallaudet College and enrolled in 1966. After graduation, he worked for two years as assistant to Frederick Schreiber at the National Association of the Deaf and then went on to earn a master's degree in administration from the California State University at Northridge and to work for DCARA, Deaf Counseling, Advocacy, and Referral Agency, in San Leandro, becoming its executive director in 1981.

HEATHER LIGHTFOOT was born in 1976 in Seattle, the only deaf child of a hearing family. She is a graduate of Washington School for the Deaf and Gallaudet University, where she earned a B.A. in graphic design, competed in track and field throwing events, and made many oil paintings of historic campus buildings. She currently works as a recruiter for Gallaudet University and continues to paint in her free time, hoping to turn to illustration of children's books in the near future.

TOIVO LINDHOLM, "Man of Mirth," was born in Finland in 1898, became deaf at age two, and emigrated with his family to Minnesota, where he attended the Minnesota School for the Deaf (MSD). He was graduated from Gallaudet College in 1923 and taught at state residential schools in Baton Rouge, Louisiana; St. Augustine, Florida; and Staunton, Virginia, before returning to Minnesota to teach at MSD in Fairbault. Toivo interrupted his career to work as a printer with the *Los Angeles Times* but later returned to teaching at the California School for the Deaf at Riverside. Best known as a humor columnist for various Deaf periodicals, he also served as president of the California Association of the Deaf from 1950 to 1958.

CEIL LUCAS holds a master's degree in romance linguistics from the University of Texas, Austin, and a Ph.D. in sociolinguistics from Georgetown University. She is professor of linguistics in the Department of ASL, Linguistics, and Interpretation at Gallaudet University, where she has taught since 1982. Her main areas of interest include sign language structure and all aspects of sociolinguistics, especially language contact, variation, and discourse analysis.

SUSAN LUEDEE was born in St. John's Newfoundland, in 1966, to Deaf parents. She taught ASL for fifteen years in various capacities, including a four-year period as coordinator of the Bob Rumball Centre for the Deaf (The Ontario Community Centre, Inc.) in Toronto. Presently a freshman at Gallaudet University, Susan plans to major in ASL and work as an interpreter trainer.

ERIC MALZKUHN was deafened at age ten and entered Gallaudet at sixteen, where he originated an ASL version of Lewis Carroll's "Jabberwocky"; covered sports for the *Buff and Blue*; secured permission for the Drama Club to produce a current Broadway hit, *Arsenic and Old Lace*, and then an invitation to perform on Broadway (the first sign-language performance in Broadway's history); and managed the basketball team. After a long stint in Detroit working for the state vocational rehabilitation service, Malz returned to theater in 1967 as a founding member of the National Theatre of the Deaf. He has taught at state residential schools in Flint and Berkeley, as well as at the Model Secondary School for the Deaf (MSSD) on the Gallaudet campus, and holds an M.A. from Catholic University. Honored by the Gallaudet community with an honorary doctorate and the naming of the MSSD auditorium Theatre Malz, he is now theoretically retired and works as signmaster for many Washington-area professional theaters. He and his wife of fifty-four years, Dr. Mary Malzkuhn, professor of government at Gallaudet University, have three children and five grandchildren. He had wanted this blurb to read only "Began working in theater in 1938. Still at it."

SHANNY MOW provides autobiographical anecdotes in his contribution to the present volume. He is a former printer, English teacher, linguistic researcher, and photographer and presently a playwright and theatrical director based in Santa Fe, New Mexico.

JAMES A. NICKERSON, associate professor of mathematics and computer science at Gallaudet University, earned his doctorate in mathematics from the University of Maryland in 1995. Jim lives in Silver Spring, Maryland, with his wife, Jane, and two young daughters, Ellen and Molly. Although he is a Baltimore Orioles fan, his favorite active player is Sammy Sosa.

CAROL A. PADDEN, professor of communication and chair of the Communication Department at the University of California, San Diego, was born Deaf to Deaf parents. With her husband, Tom Humphries, she coauthored *Deaf in America: Voices from a Culture*, widely regarded as the first and still definitive study of the Deaf community as a cultural group. She has also written broadly on language, sign language structure, Deaf culture, and deaf children's reading.

CYNTHIA LOHR PETERS, a self-described DOD (Deaf of Deaf), is a graduate of the Maryland School for the Deaf and Gallaudet College and holds a doctorate in American literature from the George Washington University. An extensive revision of her doctoral dissertation on the carnivalesque characteristics of Deaf American literature is scheduled for publication by Gallaudet University Press in 2000. Cindy is associate professor of English at Gallaudet.

MICHAEL SCOTT POSNER was born deaf on Long Island in 1981, and is a graduate of Longwood High School in Middle Island, New York. He is presently a freshman at Gallaudet University.

B. M. SCHOWE was graduated from Gallaudet College in 1918 and began working for the Firestone Tire and Rubber Company in Akron, Ohio, the following year. In those days, Firestone employed a large number of Deaf workers, and Akron supported one of the largest Deaf communities in America. In 1934, he took a position on the labor relations staff and continued there until his retirement in 1958, penning many articles on labor relations. He is the author of the still-relevant *Identity Crisis in Deafness* and the father of the late Dr. Ben Schowe, Jr., nearly as well known in Deaf America. He died in 1979.

FREDERICK C. SCHREIBER was born in New York City in 1922, the son of a caterer, and became deaf at age six. He attended both Lexington School for the Deaf and the New York School for the Deaf (Fanwood) and went on to Gallaudet College, graduating in 1942. In 1966 he became the first full-time director of the National Association of the Deaf (NAD) and transformed it from an organization with an annual budget of $80,000, run from members' homes, to the $2 million-a-year NAD with thirty employees and its own building in Silver Spring, Maryland, that we know today. Fred was possibly the most universally loved Deaf man since Laurent Clerc, and his untimely death in 1979 is still mourned in the Deaf community.

RALPH SEDANO was born in San Francisco, the son of Mexican immigrants, and became deaf at age five. He graduated from the California School for the Deaf at Berkeley and Gallaudet College, with a B.A. in English, and earned an M.A. in special education from San Francisco State University. After teaching in Maine for many years, he came to New Mexico and developed the nation's first trilingual (ASL, Spanish, English) interpreter-training program.

MARTHA A. SHERIDAN is a member of the graduate faculty of the Department of Social Work at Gallaudet University and is a Licensed Independent Social Worker with over twenty years of combined experience as a clinician, administrator, educator, and advocate. Her pioneering and fund-raising efforts in the fields of social work and mental health with Deaf and Hard of Hearing people have led to the successful establishment of educational, service, and training programs such as community treatment for Deaf adults with mental illness, child abuse and neglect prevention training, programs for Deaf women, and continuing professional education. Martha is believed to be the first Deaf woman to earn a Ph.D. in social work. Her dissertation research, which explores and describes the lifeworlds and perspectives of Deaf and Hard of Hearing children, will be published by Gallaudet University Press in 2001.

WARREN MILTON SMALTZ was born in 1895 at Stroudsburg, Pennsylvania, and became deaf at age nine. He graduated from the Pennsylvania School for the Deaf in 1913 and subsequently from two public high schools, and then, after marriage in 1917, from the Divinity School in Philadelphia in 1922, with a degree in sacred theology. The following year, he was ordained an Episcopalian priest and became vicar of All Souls' Church for the Deaf. Smaltz published widely both in the Little Paper Family and in general-interest periodicals such as *Reader's Digest* but was proudest of his publications in biblical studies. He died in 1954.

LINWOOD SMITH was born in North Carolina in 1943 and graduated from Gallaudet College in 1965. He studied at Howard University and completed a master's degree in education administration from California State University at Northridge. He was killed in a car accident in 1982.

ANGELA (PETRONE) STRATIY, a native signer from a Deaf family, is a graduate of the Saskatchewan School for the Deaf and Gallaudet University, where she earned a B.A. in English, and she holds an M.Ed. degree from Western Maryland College. She taught Deaf students in North Dakota and Manitoba for many years before joining the staff of Grant MacEwan Community College in Edmonton, Alberta, where she serves as a coordinator, curriculum developer, and instructor in the interpreter training program. Angela is a founding member of the Canadian Cultural Society of the Deaf and coauthor of *Deaf Women in Canada*, as well as of videotapes on both ASL and Deaf culture.

THOMAS A. ULMER was graduated from both the Pennsylvania Institute (1927) and Williamsport (Pennsylvania) High School (1930) and earned a B.A. from Gallaudet College in 1934. After marriage to his college sweetheart, he took a position teaching math and science at the Oregon School for the Deaf in Salem and pursued his M.A. by correspondence. In Salem, he was best known as the school's scoutmaster, and he was known nationally for his advocacy of Boy Scouting in the Deaf community.

CLAYTON VALLI was graduated from Austine School for the Deaf in Brattleboro, Vermont, in 1971. He holds an A.A.S. in photography from the National Technical Institute for the Deaf, a B.A. in social psychology from the University of Nevada–Reno, an M.A. in linguistics from Gallaudet College, and a doctorate in linguistics and ASL poetics from the Union Institute in Cincinnati. Clayton is a widely known and respected ASL poet, with several video publications, and an activist for ASL, as well as the author of a number of scholarly works on ASL linguistics cowritten with Ceil Lucas. He is an adjunct professor in the ASL Program at Northeastern University and senior editor for the ASL project at Gallaudet University Press.

GEORGE W. VEDITZ was born in Baltimore in 1861, the son of German immigrants, and attended a German school there before becoming deaf at age eight and transferring to the Maryland School for the Deaf in Frederick, where he was trained as a shoemaker. The family was too poor to send him to Gallaudet, but he worked his way through and graduated in 1884 as valedictorian. After graduation, Veditz returned to Frederick to teach and became very active in Deaf organizations, founding both the Maryland Association of the Deaf and the Gallaudet College Alumni Association. After moving to Colorado Springs with his wife, where he taught at the Colorado School for the Deaf, he served as president of the National Association of the Deaf for two terms (1904–1910) and worked for the rights of Deaf people to hold government jobs, from which they had previously been barred along with criminals and the insane. He died in 1937.

BARBARA J. WHITE was born, raised, and educated in the Washington, D.C., area but had no contact with the Deaf community until she enrolled at Gallaudet, where she earned a B.A. in 1975. She holds an M.S.W. from the University of Maryland (1978) and D.S.W. from Catholic University (1999) and has been on the faculty of Gallaudet University since 1983, where she teaches both graduate and undergraduate courses in the Department of Social Work. Prior to her current position, she was a social worker in the mental health field. Barbara now lives in University Park, Maryland. She is an adoptive parent.

BRUCE A. WHITE was born in Framingham, Massachusetts, and participated in the early days of The Learning Center for Deaf Children, the program for deaf students at Keefe Tech Regional High School, and D.E.A.F., Inc., Allston, before joining the Department of English at Gallaudet in 1978. He holds a Ph.D. in English from the University of Maryland and has scholarly interests in the freethinkers Alice and Elbert Hubbard and in American periodicals from the 1880s to the 1920s. He is married to Barbara (Pollard) White, whom he met at Gallaudet.

TOM WILLARD provides autobiographical information about his childhood in "What Exactly Am I Supposed to Overcome?" He graduated from the Rochester Institute of Technology with a degree in photography and, after working at various jobs in Rochester as a photographer and writer, founded Deaf Artists of America, a national arts service organization. Tom is best known nationally as the longtime editor of *The Silent News*, a position he left in 1996 when he founded his own highly successful monthly, *Newswaves*.

GEORGE WING was born in Maine and attended the American Asylum in Hartford. After graduation, he was employed as a government clerk until 1872, when he joined the new Minnesota School for the Deaf as an instructor and invented a symbol system used for teaching English to Deaf pupils. He also worked in the school's print shop and invented a gauge pin for printers that he patented and that later provided a large part of his income. Wing was lured away from Minnesota by a better offer from the Illinois School for the Deaf in Jacksonville, but he died only a year after his move, in 1890. His early efforts for bilingual education are virtually forgotten today.

KATHRYN WOODCOCK provides autobiographical information in her essay reprinted in this volume. She holds bachelor's and master's degrees in systems design engineering from the University of Waterloo and a Ph.D. in mechanical and industrial engineering from the University of Toronto. She was the first deaf president of the Canadian Hearing Society and a founding member of the Canadian Deafened Persons Association and has coauthored *Deafened People: Adjustment and Support*, forthcoming from the University of Toronto Press. In 1999 she reluctantly underwent surgery for a cochlear implant.

This autobiography of Laurent Clerc, the founder of deaf education in America, was solicited as "an appropriate introduction" to a tribute to his better known hearing colleague, T. H. Gallaudet

Prologue | # Autobiography

Laurent Clerc

1852

I was born in La Balme, Canton of Cremieu, Department of Isère, on the 26th of December, 1785. The village of La Balme lies twenty-six miles east of Lyons, on the east side of the Rhône, and is noted for its grotto, called, "La grottee de Notre Dame de la Balme." My father, Joseph Francis Clerc, a notary public by profession, was the mayor of the place from 1780 to 1814, My mother, Elizabeth Candy, was the daughter of Mr. Candy, of Cremieu, also a notary public. My father died in April, 1816, and my mother in May, 1818.

When I was about a year old, I was left alone for a few moments on a chair by the fireside, and it happened, I know not how, that I fell into the fire, and so badly burned my right cheek, that the scar of it is still visible; and my parents were under the impression that this accident deprived me of my senses of hearing and smelling.

When I was seven years, my mother hearing that a certain physician in Lyons could cure deafness, took me thither. The doctor, after examining my ears, said he thought he could make me hear, provided I would call at his office twice a day for a fortnight. My mother agreed to take me, so we called regularly every day and the doctor injected into my ears I do not know what liquids, but I did not derive any benefit whatever from the operation. And at the expiration of the fortnight I returned home with my mother still as deaf as I was before.

I passed my childhood at home, in doing nothing but running about and playing with other children. I sometimes drove my mother's turkeys to the field or her cows to pasture, and occasionally my father's horse to the watering place. I was never taught to write or to form the letters of the alphabet; nor did I ever go to school; for there were no such school-houses or academies in our villages as we see every where in New England.

At the age of about twelve, that is, in 1797, my father being unable to absent himself from home on account of the duties of his office, at his earnest request, my uncle, Laurent Clerc, took me to Paris, and the next day I was placed in the Institution for the Deaf and Dumb. I did not see the Abbé Sicard, but I learned afterward that he was in prison for a political offense. Mr. Massieu, deaf and dumb like myself, was my first

1

teacher, and when the Abbé Sicard was set at liberty and had resumed the superinten-
dence of the Institution, he took me into his class, and I was with him ever after.

Out of school hours, the Abbé Margaron, one of the assistant teachers, taught me
to articulate together with a few other pupils. We learned to articulate pretty well all
the letters of the alphabet, and many words of one and two or three syllables; but I
had much difficulty to pronounce *da* and *ta, de* and *te, do* and *to,* &c., and although
Mr. Margaron made me repeat these words again and again, I succeeded no better.
One day, he became so impatient, and gave me so violent a blow under my chin, that
I bit my tongue, and I felt so chagrined, that I would try to learn to speak no longer.

I applied myself to other things. I learned to draw and to compose in the printing
office of the Institution till 1805, when I was employed as a tutor on trial, and in
1806 appointed a teacher with a salary of about two hundred dollars. In process of
time, Mr. Sicard thought me capable of teaching the highest class, and I occupied
that place when Mr. Gallaudet came to Paris. But before speaking of him more at
length, let me say how I happened to make Mr. G's acquaintance.

Mr. Sicard, who was a royalist and an adherent to the dynasty of the Bourbons,
sometimes imprudently entertained secret correspondence with the garrisons of the
Comte de Provence (since Louis XVIII) then in England. Napoleon, as every body
knows, being generally well informed of all that transpired both in Paris and throughout France, knew that such correspondences took place; but not considering Mr.
Sicard a very dangerous enemy of his, and thinking him, on the contrary, very useful
to the unfortunate deaf and dumb, he suffered him to remain undisturbed, but
determined to reprove him for meddling with politics instead of attending to his own
business, by never conferring upon him any title of honor he might merit. Mr. S.,
who had the simplicity to believe that Napoleon was ignorant of his intrigues,
wondered why he did not receive the cross of the legion of honor, an honor not
unfrequently conferred upon persons much less entitled to it than himself. He did
not, however, despair of obtaining it at some future time, and for this purpose, he
besought some of his friends whom he knew to have free access and great influence
over Napoleon to prevail on him to visit the Deaf and Dumb Institution, but all
attempts and persuasions failed, for Napoleon constantly refused, not that he did not
feel interested in the deaf and dumb, but on account of Mr. Sicard, whom he wished
to punish by not seeing him. Things went on without any other extraordinary
occurrences till the Allied Powers entered Paris in 1814. Soon after Louis XVIII was
seated on the throne of his ancestors, Mr. Sicard was among the first who went to
congratulate his majesty on his happy return, and it was not long before the cross of
the legion of honor for which he had aspired so much, was conferred on him by the
king himself, and by and by the order of St. Waldimir of Russia, by the Emperor
Alexander, and another order by the king of Sweden. Mr. Sicard was now satisfied
that justice had been done him, and desired nothing more. But when Napoleon
returned from the island of Elba in March, 1815, Mr. Sicard was so afraid that
Napoleon would deprive him of his honors, that he accepted an invitation to visit
England in order not to be in Paris while Napoleon was there. He took Mr. Massieu
and myself along with him. We arrived at London during the last days of May. We

had our first exhibition on the 2d of June.* We gave two a week, and they were generally attended by princes, members of both houses of parliament, and other distinguished individuals of both sexes, among whom were the Duke of Kent, the Duke of Orleans (since Louis Philippe), and her grace, the Duchess of Wellington. Little did I anticipate, at that time, the total defeat which Napoleon was to experience by the combined armies of Europe, under the command of her illustrious husband, the Duke of Wellington. I had the mortification of being present at the house of lords when the prince regent came in person, to announce to both houses the battle of Waterloo and the flight of Napoleon. I also witnessed the illumination of the city in the evening, and the joy that this event caused to the English!

It was at the close of one of our public lectures that Mr. Gallaudet was introduced to me for the first time by Mr. Sicard, to whom he had previously been introduced by a member of parliament. We cordially shook hands with him, and on being told who he was, where he came from, and for what purpose, and on being further informed of the ill success of his mission in England, we earnestly invited him to come to Paris, assuring him that every facility would be afforded him to see our Institution and attend our daily lessons. He accepted the invitation, and said he would come in the ensuing spring. We did not see him any more, as we left London soon afterward. In the spring of 1816, according to his promise, he came to Paris, and glad were we to see him again. He visited our Institution almost every day. He began by attending the lowest class, and from class to class, he came to mine which, as mentioned above, was the highest. I had, therefore, a good opportunity of seeing and conversing with him often, and the more I saw him, the more I liked him; his countenance and manners pleased me greatly. He frequented my school-room, and one day requested me to give him private lessons of an hour every day. I could receive him but three times a week, in my room up stairs in the afternoon, and he came with punctuality, so great was his desire of acquiring the knowledge of the language of signs in the shortest time possible. I told him, nevertheless, that however diligent he might be, it would require at least six months to get a tolerably good knowledge of signs, and a year for the method of instruction so as to be well qualified to teach thoroughly. He said he feared it would not be in his power to stay so long, and that he would reflect, and give me his final decision by and by. In the mean time, he continued coming to receive his lesson, and we spoke no more of "how long he would stay" till the middle of May, when taking a favorable occasion, he intimated to me that he wished very much he could obtain a well educated deaf and dumb young man to accompany him to America. I named two young deaf and dumb men who had left our Institution a few years since, that I knew would suit him, as they both had some knowledge of the English language, whereas I had none at all; but he answered that he had already made his choice, and that I was the person he preferred. Greatly astonished was I, for I had not the least expectation that I should be thought of. After a short pause, I said I would not hesitate to go if I could do it properly. I suggested to him the idea of speaking or writing to the Abbé Sicard on the subject,

* The questions and answers of Massieu and myself at these public exhibitions were published.

as I considered myself engaged to the Abbé. He said he would write, and accordingly wrote; but although his letter was never answered, we both inferred that Mr. Sicard's silence was rather favorable than otherwise. But in order to ascertain his views, I was requested to sound him. Accordingly I called and inquired in the most respectful manner whether he had received Mr. G's letter, and if so, what answer he had returned. I received but an evasive answer to my question; for he abruptly asked me why I wished to part with him. My reply was simply this, that I could without much inconvenience leave him for a few years without loving him the less for it, and that I had a great desire to see the world, and especially to make my unfortunate fellow-beings on the other side of the Atlantic, participate in the same benefits of education that I had myself received from him. He seemed to appreciate my feelings; for after some further discussions on both sides, he finished by saying that he would give his consent, provided I also obtained the consent of my mother, my father being dead. I said I would ask her, if he would permit me to go home. He said I might. Accordingly I made my preparations and started for Lyons on the 1st of June, after having promised Mr. Gallaudet to return a few days before the appointed time for our voyage. I thought I was going to agreeably surprise my dear mother, for she never imagined, poor woman, that I could come to see her, except during my vacation, which usually took place in September; but I was myself much more surprised when, on my arrival, she told me she knew what I had come for, and on my inquiring what it was, she handed me a letter she had received from Mr. Sicard the preceding day.* On reading it, I found that the good Abbé Sicard had altered his mind, and written to dissuade my mother from giving her consent; saying he "could not spare me!" Accordingly my mother urged me hard to stay in France, but to no purpose, for I told her that my resolution was taken, and that nothing could make me change it. She gave her consent with much reluctance, and said she would pray God every day for my safety, through the intercession of La Sainte Vièrge. I bade herself, my brother and sisters and friends, adieu, and was back in Paris on the 12th of June, and the next day, after having taken an affectionate leave of the good Abbé Sicard, who had been like a father to me, I went also to bid my pupils good-by, and there took place a painful scene I can never forget. A favorite pupil of mine, the young Polish Count Alexander de Machwitz, a natural son of the Emperor Alexander, whom I knew to be much attached to me, came over to me and with tears in his eyes, took hold of me, saying he would not let me depart, scolding me, at the same time, for having so long kept a secret my intention to go away. I apologized as well as I could, assuring him that I had done so, because I thought it best. However, he still held me so fast in his arms, so that I had to struggle, to disentangle myself from him, and having floored him without hurting him, I made my exit, and the day following, the 14th of June, I was *en route* for Havre, with Mr. Gallaudet and our much honored friend, S. V. S. Wilder, Esq., who, I am happy to say, is still alive, and now resides some where in Greenwich, in this state. On the 18th of June, in the afternoon, we em-

---

* One of my sons, Francis or Charles, when in France, took a copy of Mr. Sicard's letter to my mother, which was still in the possession of one of my sisters.

barked on board the ship Mary Augusta, Captain Hall, and arrived at New York on the 9th of August, 1816, in the morning.

Owing to adverse winds and frequent calms which usually occur at sea in the summer season, our passage lasted fifty-two days. It was rather long; but on the whole, the voyage was pleasant. A part of our time on board was usefully employed. I taught Mr. Gallaudet the method of the signs for abstract ideas, and he taught me the English language. I wrote my journal, and as I thought in French rather than in English, I made several laughable mistakes in the construction of my sentences, which he corrected; so that being thus daily occupied, I did not find the time to fall very heavily upon me. We formed plans for the success of the institution we were going to establish; we made arrangements for the journeys we expected to undertake for the collection of funds; we reformed certain signs which we thought would not well suit American manners and customs.

The weather was fair when we landed. Our first steps were directed to the store of Messrs. Wilder & Co., in Pearl street, thence to the customhouse, and thence we proceeded to the house of Mr. Gallaudet's father, in John street. I anticipated much pleasure in witnessing his joy at again seeing his parents, brothers and sisters, after so long an absence; but I must acknowledge that I was rather disappointed; for I did not see any greater demonstration of welcome on both sides than the mere shaking of hands; little was I aware, at that time, of the difference between the French and American mode of saluting, especially with respect to the ladies. We staid about ten days in New York. We met, or rather we called on several gentlemen of Mr. Gallaudet's acquaintance, who gave me a cordial welcome to America.

My first impression of the city was admiration of Broadway which appeared to me to be the finest street in the world, and my astonishment was great at seeing so much bustle in the streets, people in so great a hurry and walking so fast.

My second impression was the wearisomeness which the uniformity produced. Men, streets, squares, buildings, every thing was alike; all looked well, nothing appeared magnificent. I noticed neatness without elegance, riches without taste, beauty without gracefulness. I found that the happiness of the Americans was at their firesides with their wives, children and friends. They had few amusements, few spectacles and very few sublime objects capable of arresting the attention of an European; and such a one could not easily appreciate the extent of the private happiness of a people who were secure and not poor.

At length, we left New York for New Haven, where we made a short tarry, which I wished had been much longer; for I found it a delightful place. We called on President Dwight and some of the professors, who welcomed us. We visited the college, the library and chapel. The next day, it being very pleasant, we took the stage for Hartford, where we arrived in the afternoon of the 22d of August, 1816. We alighted at Dr. Cogswell's in Prospect street. We found Mrs. Cogswell alone at home with her daughters, excepting Alice, who was then at school under Miss Lydia Huntley (now Mrs. Sigourney, our lovely poetess). She was immediately sent for, and when she made her appearance, I beheld a very interesting little girl. She had one of the most intelligent countenances I ever saw. I was much pleased with her. We conversed by signs, and we understood each other very well; so true is it, as I have often mentioned before, that the language of signs is universal and as simple as nature. I had left many persons and objects in France endeared to me by association, and America, at first, seemed uninteresting and monotonous, and I sometimes regretted leaving my native land; but on seeing Alice, I had only to recur to the object which had induced me to seek these shores, to contemplate the good we were going to do, and sadness was subdued by an approving conscience.

On the 23d of August in the evening, that is, the next day after our arrival at Hartford, we attended a meeting of the directors of the Asylum at the State House, and I was introduced to them individually. By and by, I made the acquaintance of the principal citizens of Hartford and their families, who all received and treated me so kindly, that I felt quite at home.

On the 3d of September, Dr. Cogswell, Mr. Gallaudet and myself set out for Boston, with many letters of introduction, among which was one from Gov. John C. Smith to Gov. Phillips. The object of our coming hither was soon generally known. I was at the Atheneum upon two days of the week and answered a great variety of questions proposed to me by a large company of gentlemen. On the second day, that is, on the 9th of September, an address was delivered to the gentlemen, which I had written in the morning. It is proper to remark that I had only studied the English language about three months; no apology, therefore, is necessary for the idiomatic expressions discoverable in my style. Here is my address, the first I ever made in this country:

"Gentlemen—You know the motive which has led me to the United States of America. The public papers have taught you it; but you do not yet know, I believe, the reason why I have come to Boston with Mr. Gallaudet and Dr. Cogswell, and why we have invited you to honor this meeting with your presence.

"It is to speak to you more conveniently of the deaf and dumb, of those unfortunate beings who, deprived of the sense of hearing and consequently of that of speech, would be condemned all their *life*, to the most sad vegetation if nobody came to their succor, but who intrusted to our regenerative hands, will pass from the class of brutes to the class of men.

"It is to affect your hearts with regard to their unhappy state, to excite the sensibility and solicit the charity of your generous souls in their favor; respectfully to entreat you to occupy yourselves in promoting their future happiness.

"The celebrated and immortal Abbé de l'Epée invented the art of restoring them to society and religion. It is according to his method that the institutions in Europe have been formed; it is consequently to him that all the deaf and dumb who know how to write and read, owe their temporal and spiritual happiness.

"The Abbé Sicard, my respectable and beloved master, was the most distinguished among the disciples of the Abbé de l'Epée, whom he succeeded. The latter had left some things to be designed, the Abbé Sicard has supplied them; but if there had not been the Abbé de l'Epée, there would not have been the Abbé Sicard; thus glory, honor and eternal gratitude are due to those two friends of humanity.

"I was about twelve years old when I arrived at the Abbé Sicard's school. I was endowed with considerable intelligence, but nevertheless I had no idea of intellectual things. I had it is true, a mind, but it did not think; I had a heart, but it did not feel.

"My mother, affected at my misfortune, had endeavored to show me the heavens, and to make me know God, imagining that I understood her, but her attempts were vain; I could comprehend nothing. I believed that God was a tall, big and strong man, and that Jesus Christ having come to kill us, had been killed by us, and placed on a cross as one of our triumphs.

"I believed many other droll and ridiculous things; but as one cannot recollect what passed in his infancy, I cannot describe them. I am sure that the deaf and dumb who are in your country, think as I once did. You must be so kind as to aid us to undeceive them. We shall cultivate their minds and form their hearts; but as the mind and heart cannot live without the body, you will have the goodness to charge yourselves, with your other countrymen, with the support of their bodies. In Europe, each nation, however small, has an institution for the deaf and dumb, and most of these institutions are at the expense of the government. Will America remain the only nation which is insensible to the cry of humanity? I hope not, gentlemen; I hope that you will busy yourselves with the same zeal as your neighbors, the good inhabitants of Connecticut. If the deaf and dumb become happy, it will be your joy to see that it is the effect of your generosity, and they will preserve the remembrance of it as long as they live, and your reward will be in heaven."

The next day (the 10th of September) we had another exhibition at one of the new court-house rooms for greater convenience. [. . .]

At the close of my address, many ladies came to me, and shook hands with me, and I answered a number of questions, to the satisfaction of the company. A number of generous donations were made to the institution, and the example was followed by all classes in the community to the amount of many thousand dollars.

Dr. Cogswell had left us a few days previous and returned home; and on the 27th of September, Mr. Gallaudet and myself went to Salem, where we obtained several subscriptions.

The address which I delivered at the court-house was published in the newspapers.

Early in October we returned to Hartford, and in a few days we started for New Haven, where the legislature was in session. We had an exhibition before the governor and both houses; at which time I delivered an address and answered numerous questions.

From New Haven we proceeded to New York, but we were not as successful there as we had been elsewhere. It was not that the New Yorkers were less benevolent than their fellow-citizens of New England, but the reason was that at the several meetings held at the City Hall, a majority of those who attended, wished to have an institution established in the city.

In November, the legislature of New York being in session at Albany, we went there, and a few days afterward we had an exhibition at the capital, where I delivered a long address, of which I regret I have not preserved any copy. We obtained something handsome from private gentlemen, but nothing from the legislature. We came back to New York city and made another attempt, but did not succeed any better. We then went to Philadelphia, where we gave an exhibition at Washington Hall, in Third street. The meeting was much crowded, especially with pretty Quaker ladies; but as the Asylum was not to be located there, we did not receive as much as we had anticipated. I called several times on my countryman, Stephen Girard, Esq. I found him very eccentric: once he said he would give something, and the next day he would give nothing, on account of the school not being in Philadelphia, and said the people of New England were rich enough to support the institution. He was very local in his charity.

We returned north by way of Burlington, N.J., and received some very liberal donations.

On the 15th of April, 1817, our school was opened with seven pupils, in the south part of the building now the City Hotel, and on the 20th, Mr. Gallaudet delivered an appropriate sermon on the occasion in the Rev. Dr. Strong's church.

In January, 1818, I visited Washington city with the late Mr. Henry Hudson, to ascertain whether we could hope to obtain something from Congress for our Asylum. I attended the House of Representatives, and the Hon. Henry Clay, who was the speaker, politely offered me a seat beside him. There was a recess of half an hour, and I conversed with several members of Congress, both in English and French. Afterward I visited the Senate chamber. The next day I had the honor of being introduced to President Monroe at the White House, by Mr. Hyde de Neuville, the French ambassador, for whom I had a letter of recommendation from the Duke Mathieu de Montmorency.

The President received me with much affability and bade me "welcome to America," and said among other things, that he hoped I would receive great honor and much gratitude by doing good to the deaf and dumb. I carefully preserved the paper containing our conversation, but have mislaid it. I attended one of the levees with the ambassador and Mr. Hudson, and holding a paper and pencil in my hands, I had the pleasure of conversing with gentlemen and ladies.

In the session of 1819–20, thanks to the exertions of both our Connecticut senators and representatives, Congress granted us a township located in the state of Alabama, and President Monroe, with the benevolence which characterized him, readily sanctioned the act with his signature.

In May, 1818, I prepared an address, and on the 28th, it was delivered, at my request, by Mr. Gallaudet, in the Center Congregational Church, before Gov. Wolcott and both houses of the legislature.

On the 3d of May, 1819, at the house of her uncle, Benjamin Prescott, Esq., at Cohoes Falls, near Waterford, N.Y., I was married to Miss Eliza Crocker Boardman, a very beautiful and intelligent young lady, and one of our earliest pupils, by the Rev. Mr. Butler, then rector of the Episcopal church at Troy, and the father of the Rev. Dr. Butler, the present chaplain of the Senate of the United States at Washington. The grooms were Lewis Weld, Esq., and Hermann Bleecker, Esq., and the bride-maids Miss Prescott and Miss Butler, and the witnesses were Mr. and Mrs. Theodore Sedgwick, the Rev. Mr. Eaton and two or three other gentlemen of Albany.

Toward the close of April, 1820, that is, about a month after the birth of my oldest daughter, Elizabeth Victoria (now Mrs. George W. Beers), I sailed for France on a visit to my friends, and returned to Hartford in a year. We have now four living children, viz: two sons and two daughters, having lost two, viz: a girl and a boy, each at about two years old. My daughter Mrs. Beers has a son, and my younger daughter, Mrs. Henry C. Deming, has also one. My oldest son, Rev. Francis Joseph Clerc, rector of St. John's church, in St. Louis, Mo., is also married and has two children, a daughter and a son, so that I have now four grand-children, all blessed with the sense of hearing, as well as their parents. My younger son, Charles Michael Clerc, is not yet married; he is at New York city, in a wholesale store.

I | "Scattered as we are and lost among the hearing"

Life in the Hearing World

Deaf child/Dead End. © 1986, Perry L. Conley.

1

Separatism has a long and distinguished history in the American Deaf diaspora but is found today only in the narrow sense of support for segregated schooling of Deaf children. For adults, moderate assimilation is the order of the day, as Deaf enclaves everywhere lose critical mass and disappear. Arguments in favor of a Deaf separatist utopia, however, have much to tell us about the quality of life among the hearing. The following are excerpts from letters, articles, and editorial comments published in The American Annals of the Deaf and Dumb.

On Planning a Deaf-Mute Commonwealth

J. J. Flournoy, Edmund Booth, et al.

1858

Mr. Booth to Mr. Flournoy

Anamosa, Iowa, Sept. 6th, 1857.

Dear Sir,—Yours of August 18th is before me, and after waiting a few days for a quiet moment, I now answer.

In regard to a community of deaf-mutes in the West, or any where—supposing you mean a community exclusively or mainly of mutes—let me say candidly that I hold it to be an impossibility, save in the commencement, and that on a very small scale. Just consider a moment. A community of this class would be a mixture of a few well and many half-educated; and among them must be many non-readers and frivolous. And then the general equality claimed with *all* by the latter, would operate to keep the more sensible from joining such community; for we all know that gossip, scandal, backbiting and other diabolisms, are as common among mutes as among hearing persons.

Again: They will need to work at a variety of trades, and a commonwealth of mutes could never exceed 10,000, supposing all in the U.S. were brought in. A sparsely settled State would make nobody rich, and would satisfy few; and no law could be made effectual to prevent their selling their lands, buildings, &c., to hearing persons. Thus the distinct feature of the community would soon be lost. And it would so happen in any event, for their children being mostly of the hearing order, it would become a hearing community faster than the fathers and mothers died out.

I think the wiser course is, to let the mutes remain as they are—scattered and in one sense lost—among their hearing associates. In such situations they are compelled to *read* and *write*, and thus keep their minds under the educational process through life. [. . .]

Yours truly,
E. Booth.

Mr. Flournoy to Mr. Turner

Near Athens, Geo., Oct. 3, 1857.

Rev. Mr. Turner:

My Dear Friend,—This being a free country, where every "smart" man, and his name is legion, has his opinion, whether crude and vulgar, or refined and intellectual, the American community are very unquiet and debatable, and subject to a thousand though not very learned or profound sentiments, political and social. The deaf and dumb have taken a color of character from this disputatious habit, a specimen of which is evinced in the enclosed letter from Edmund Booth, Esq. Instead of meeting my project with a philosophical view, I am met by objections, some of which, like yours and Mr. Booth's, are truly formidable! It would seem then, that without intending to be the great leader and original mind, I am the chief in this cause, and that if I carry it not forward, the idea of a deaf community may prove abortive as to any practical result.

There is always some objection to every project under the sun, and often very cogent ones. What is a man then to do? [. . .]

I do not know what kind of a constitution the mutes may superstruct, whether to make real estate inherent only in the deaf, by that organic law all have to respect and defer to; or in case of default, to escheat to the estate. This, however, is certain, that the *control* of our community over the commonwealth would be strict and universal. This is what we want and for what we may emigrate. *The government of a piece of Territory.* Nothing more or less.

Mr. Booth believes we can do better, and will read more, scattered as we are and "lost" among the hearing. I challenge him to show me twenty deaf-mutes in a hundred, that are constant readers, adequate to comprehending either literature or science, as they now are dispersed among hearing people, who do not read any or much themselves, and who have a sense (auricular) by which they gather in their knowledge, a privilege debarred the deaf, who therefore are the more ignorant *for being thus scattered.* Whereas if convened in a land peculiarly their own, the concentration of reading intellects would set a beneficial example; and preaching and lectures in the sign language, and libraries of suitable books, may improve their minds and hearts, beyond what is attainable in their scattered condition. For this, as a principal cause and source of improvement, this colony is a desideratum.

But the difficulty that meets me on all sides is, how can you keep up the mute population? The children of deaf parents are mostly hearing. These will inherit property and the community will not endure. This reasoning seems to take it that our society is to be organized like that of the hearing, and to be modeled upon the same principles. Now there is no such thing. I acknowledge that the hearing children of deaf parents may not inherit land in that anomalous and contracted community — neither power nor patronage. But the other States are so near, and their parents may supply them with the means to buy real estate in them. When they have a good location, the mutes would come in from all parts of the world. An Asylum for their education may be founded there, as well as other Institutions, so that there will be no lacking of the deaf *materiel*. What then of this visionary difficulty! We will allow such hearing persons as come for trade or residence, to vote with us. *We would give woman that right*. Hence we may always possess a sufficient population to be a State. But even if this be futile, we can remain a Territory of the Federal Government and enjoy its powerful protection under Omnipotence; the General Government guaranteeing to us the peculiar Constitution we may devise: "Republican in form."

If mutes *cannot* do this they are justly held as inferior and *useless* in the world. For they ought not to pretend to be "any body" among hearing men, who do what deaf "*dogs*" shrink from achieving *alone*. But we are men, and have under God only to try, and the thing is a finished work! [. . .]

Even should the contemplated colony fail, as Mr. Booth predicts, one great utility to ourselves will have been derived from a practical experience. We shall have proved to the other nations and our own, that deaf and dumb people are capable of many things; and to our successors in misfortune, offices and employment may be opened. They may be treated as men and women of *some use* to society and to the country, and respected accordingly. And this will to us be a no inconsiderable triumph; and the victory sure, as the deaf now continues to prove his competency and fidelity in other lands and other trusts. And this, we, as accountable beings, who may not bury our talent in a napkin, owe to the long and harmless line of the "pantomimic generations" that are to come after us!

I have now fully, I hope, in attempting something like a reply to Mr. Booth, given what refutation I am able, to the many objects that are ever starting up to confound this project. I hope the Annals will embrace both Mr. Booth's letter and mine. I presume that invaluable periodical will devote some space to this discussion, as relating so closely to the welfare and interests of the community, to whose benefit it is so inseparately devoted.

I am, dear sir, truly and respectfully, your most obliged, obedient, humble servant,

J. J. Flournoy.

Mr. Flournoy's Project

By Edmund Booth, of Anamosa, Iowa

In the January number of the Annals, is a reply to my letter of Sept. 6th to Mr. J. J. Flournoy of Georgia. My letter being a brief answer to a previous letter of his desiring my views on the subject of a community of deaf-mutes, I necessarily took a practical view of the case; and Mr. Flournoy, in his reply of Oct. 3d, characterizes it as "a specimen" of the "disputations habit" which prevails in the American community, and from which he says the deaf and dumb have taken "a color." Well, I am in a most unfortunate position, being put on the defensive.

Let me say to Mr. Flournoy that the idea of a community of deaf-mutes is to me nothing new. In the year 1831, William Willard and five or six others, including myself, formed ourselves into an association with a view of purchasing land in some favorable spot in the west, and so arranging that we might, through life, live in close neighborhood and continue to enjoy the friendships we had formed in Hartford. At that time, we were pupils of the Asylum, and all, except myself, were to leave in a few weeks or months. By election we added a sufficient number of past pupils to make our whole number thirteen. It was a sort of secret society, as we preferred to put it into practical execution rather than have the project dissipate in mere talk. Time went on, and we all found ourselves compelled to attend to the stern realities of life—procuring a self-support—before we could attend to carrying out what Mr. Willard afterwards, in one of his letters to me, called our Don Quixotic scheme. Mr. Willard became a teacher in the Ohio Institution, I in Hartford; the rest of us were scattered over New England, and the project gradually died away. [. . .]

Mr. Flournoy takes too disconsolate a view of the condition of educated deaf-mutes. Out of the three or four thousand who are educated, I am acquainted with at least one thousand; and I have not perceived that they are much more unhappy than, or held inferior to the masses around them. It is true they can not, save in rare cases, hold office, but this is exceptional and consequent on their deafness. It is true, likewise, that they do not enjoy life in its fullness as do their hearing associates. This, too, results from the same cause; and, as regards the kind of happiness, must always continue so in a greater or less degree. The same may be said of the blind, the lame, etc. It is a part of the punishment inflicted for violation of nature's laws, which violation—whether it comes from carelessness, design or ignorance—results in deafness, blindness, lameness, etc., and will so result until man has so far improved, mentally, morally and physically, that diseases and accidents of a severe nature will be unknown.

Again, looking at the condition of the educated deaf-mutes in the Northern states, every year adds to their sources of enjoyment. They reside among a dense population, and that an educated population. Every year sends from the various institutions of the land, better educated mutes, for these institutions are compelled to keep pace with the progress around; and the time allowed their pupils, formerly four years, is already nearly doubled, and must, ere long, be extended further. Then, rail roads are covering the North and West as with a net-work, thus rendering conventions and individual meetings of educated deaf-mutes easy and frequent. The South is more slow in these matters, and it will probably require one or more generations to bring about the same state of things there. Mr. Flournoy need not despair. He is one of the wealthy slave-holders of the South, and, as such, is entitled to hold and utter his own opinions. Instead then of confining his reading and contemplations to the barbarian glories of Greece and Rome, where were three or four white slaves to every freeman, let him discard the ancients and their rude ignorance and vague surmisings, and turn his attention to the writings of the philosophers who have lived and written since the French Revolution of 1789. Let him read the writings of Combe and other philosophers of the progressive school, and the bold, vigorous essays of such periodicals as the Atlantic Monthly, and become hopeful as regards man's destiny; and, thereby, he will be enabled to cast off what appears to be a gloomy misanthropy; and, by so doing, he will increase his own happiness. He is not the only one who has suffered mentally from being endowed with greater capabilities than his fellows. What he most needs is a more complete understanding of men, and the hopeful and more cheerful spirit founded thereon. [. . .]

FURTHER EXPLANATIONS BY MR. FLOURNOY

Jackson Co., near Athens,
Clarke Co. Ga., 20th Feb. 1858.

Samuel Porter, Esq:

Dear Sir: The more I reflect upon the subject the greater is my conviction of the practicability and utility of the scheme of a Deaf Commonwealth. I am not the originator of it—though without being aware of his early promulgation of the same, I had suggested the views of my venerable friend, Laurent Clerc, to the deaf-mutes of America. He is the real father of the idea. To his wisdom and originality belong the project. "Honor is due to whom honor is due." For my own humble part it is sufficient if I be deemed worthy, and receive a call from the deaf and dumb to the post of leader, that I devote myself in the inception and germ of the scheme to its virtual fulfillment. [. . .]

I would, beforehand, warn the intelligent mutes not to expect or anticipate that the government, or the Congress and executive constituting it, would receive, with a good grace, any proposal from us which may look to a *grant of land* to our people. *Congress will certainly give us no land.* It has grudged all former such dispensations. Members of Congress have stigmatized such donations as those to the first deaf-mute Asylum founded in America, as "*unconstitutional*" and to be repressed, and characterized the precedents which anticipate gifts to the insane and other poor people, as perilous encroachments on the compact of our Union, which may finally lead to unwarranted and colossal appropriations. Indeed, it is known that President Pierce, when he vetoed (though unwillingly, as he said) the appropriation of two hundred thousand dollars to the construction and endowment of an Asylum for the Insane in our country, instanced the grant of money and land to the Deaf and Dumb Asylum at Hartford, in or about 1816, as a precedent which should not be approved into a pattern for further legislation. We are by this, therefore, admonished of the futility of any application for a grant of land in personal *fee simple*, to our class of the inhabitants of the country. The only instances in which Congress appropriated grants of money and bounty land-warrants to persons, and which the executive sanctioned, is that to the soldiers of the Revolution, and to those of the last and of all wars.* These were for services in a military capacity done to the country. None, aside from such and collateral services, have ever been granted, for the last thirty years. If any were, I know of none.

Our course, then, is to petition the Congress, so as soon as the deaf and dumb have had the matter laid before them generally, and have arrived at any conclusion, to lay out a small territory, to be reserved for the purchase, settlement and government of the mutes, to whom only the pre-emption will hold valid. Nothing more need be sought or asked. I believe there are mutes in plenitude, who have enough money to take out bodies of land, and thus to create a society and political organization. There will, if untoward events deter emigration, be no lack of a sufficient number to be the governors of the country, or if that happen, there may exist an *interregnum*, in which the auricular may be substituted, by the constitution, to hold the state strictly in trust, until some deaf person approaches. Thus we can perceive that the commonwealth may be perpetuated indefinitely for our special use. [. . .]

We, deaf-mutes, have a sort of abiding melancholy at our unfortunate deprivation, although our sanguine hope in a common and Almighty Father, who as He has led others to establish growing communities, will lead us also, and protect, uphold and prosper those who call on His name with a sincere and relying spirit, induces us to be gay and contented. It is the quiet of deference to our hearing brethren, and of dependence on Providence. We assume no arrogancy in devising this benefiting project; pretend to no superiority, nor do we cogitate a mastery. We indeed do [. . .] complain of rejections and consignments to inferior places or to none, without tests of capacity; but we do not arrogate to dictate, or to accomplish any policy, or to confirm any principle without the guidance or co-operation of our hearing friends, to whom, in some measure, by the order of Providence, we are in a state of pupilage. We feel duly grateful to them for what we know, which is due to their instructions; we are sensible of and grateful for their sympathy, and alike for them and ourselves, commiserate the circumstances of the whole human family upon the earth. But here we all have to live, and here must work and thrive and suffer, until the hour of withdrawal by death; and we ask only for some place, in which, without interfering

---

* Congress gave lands along railway routes to companies on the stipulation to build roads, of utility to government and people.

with their business, we may quietly evince some competency that may tend to the welfare of coming generations of our unfortunate class.

Yours, etc.,
J. J. Flournoy.

Mr. Chamberlain and Others on Mr. Flournoy's Project

South Reading, Mass.,
April 13, 1858.

Samuel Porter, Esq.:

Dear Sir: The articles by Messrs. Booth and Flournoy, in the January number of the *Annals*, on "a deaf-mute commonwealth," have interested me, and I am induced to send you some rough ideas of my own. Like Mr. Booth, I have some objections to Mr. Flournoy's plan, although they may not prove so "truly formidable" as those of that gentleman and Mr. Turner; yet I can not agree with Mr. Booth in some of his ideas. He thinks a community composed exclusively or mainly of *deaf-mutes* "an impossibility"; I think that one *exclusively* of deaf-mutes could not long remain so, but I believe that if a company of mutes, say two or three hundred, more or less, with such of their hearing friends and relations as choose to join them, should go west, settle in some place where there was room enough, and form themselves into a community, governed by suitable laws, and headed by able leaders, such an institution would be both *permanent* and *beneficial*.

As far as my experience goes, I have always found deaf-mutes to be greater readers, better informed and more intelligent, where there are a number of them in the same place, than when *scattered*, as many, if not most of them are, among the hearing. I therefore can not agree with Mr. Booth that "the wisest course is to let them remain '*lost*' among the hearing." It is true, as Mr. Booth says, that deaf-mutes are compelled to *read* and *write* while in this "*lost*" condition, but it is for want of any better mode of communication with those with whom they live. It does not prove them to be better informed or more intelligent than they would be if placed in a body by themselves. A deaf-mute, generally speaking, is not apt to *understand* what he reads, by himself, so well as when he has access to some individuals of the same class. What one does not understand another can explain, and thus they promote each other's improvement.

Mr. Booth says that "scandal, backbiting and other diabolisms" are as common with deaf-mutes as with hearing persons; I do not doubt it, but if he intends it as an objection against the formation of a community, it is a weak argument, for every one knows that other communities flourish in spite of such things.

I do not pretend that a community of deaf-mutes would be without disadvantages, yet when all things are considered, I think the benefits to be derived from one, if well regulated, are enough to render such a community desirable.

Mr. Flournoy wants Congress to grant us the *government* of a "piece of territory" large enough for a *state*; we, of course, to pay government prices for the land: it is not the land that he asks as a gift, but the *government* of the land. He seems to think that the *land* without the *government*, would be undesirable. The extent of territory proposed, "about the size of Rhode Island or Connecticut," is an objection; all the deaf-mutes in the country could not settle it to advantage.

The government of a "state" would be a very undesirable and inconvenient responsibility. There are ability, energy and talent enough among the deaf-mutes of this country to govern a state with credit to themselves and all concerned; but, as I believe that "politics and government, so far from being 'the chief end of man,' are a necessary evil, of which the less we have the better," I propose to try the experiment on a smaller scale. I believe that an application to Congress would be a *failure*, and I do not intend to encourage a movement in that direction. It would be a waste of time, and in case of its failure, discouragements would arise. Our *first* movement must succeed, or many who would otherwise go with us, will not come up to the aid of another and different plan. It becomes us to be prudent, and consider well, which of *all* the plans offered is most likely to succeed.

Mr. Booth would have us remain in our original "*oblivion*." Mr. Flournoy would scatter us over a tract of territory where we should be like angels' visits, "few and far between."

I suggest that when a sufficient number of mutes, with their friends, are found, as I have no doubt there might be, they emigrate to some previously selected spot in the west, and buy up a piece of land six miles square. This would make a township of 23,040 acres, which, bought with land-warrants at present prices, would cost not far from $20,000.* Let them settle it, choose leaders, and make laws to govern themselves, the laws always to be framed in accordance with the territorial laws and the Federal constitution.

There are enough in the States, willing and able to do this, and all they need is a call from some of their more influential unfortunates. Aside from the benefits to be derived from association with each other, there would be no need of applying to Congress, and the *government* of the township would be as much as they would care to be troubled with. They could regulate their own affairs, build and plant, and would no doubt grow to be a respectable colony. They could have their own Sunday schools and churches, where the gospel would be preached in the silent but expressive language of signs, understood by all and felt by not a few. If a mute wishes to sell out, let him do so, and to whom he pleases; let the colony be truly republican in spirit. Of course, advantages would arise from the mutes being in the majority. They could not be kept so by hereditary descent, but let it begin well and be conducted wisely, and deaf-mute emigration will keep up the required number. The motives

* [This would afford *a hundred and forty* or more farms of 160 acres each, and allowing five persons to each family, would support a farming population of *seven hundred*, besides leaving room enough for a large number who might be engaged in mechanical, mercantile and other pursuits. —EDITOR.]

which governs those who go, should be a desire for personal and mutual benefit. Let brotherly love prevail among them, and let them not go because they thirst for power or wealth. These will accrue to the colony in years to come; no one expects to find them in the wilderness without toil and patience.

I may have more to say in future numbers of the Annals. In the mean time, if any of my fellow mutes have any ideas to communicate, I should be glad to hear from them.

Yours, &c.,
Wm. Martin Chamberlain.

[We think that there are not many intelligent deaf-mutes, who share in the feeling expressed by the writer of the following letter, as well as by Mr. Flournoy, viz., that they are despised by the hearing. Mr. Chamberlain writes us that he has seen nothing to warrant Mr. Flournoy in speaking of the deaf and dumb as "a scorned and down-trodden caste," as he does in one of his letters. It would be a pity that any of the deaf and dumb should cherish such a feeling, with no foundation for it in fact.—EDITOR.]

Six Mile P.O., Jennings Co., Ind.
Mr. Samuel Porter:
I saw in the American Annals for January, 1858, letters from E. Booth and J. J. Flournoy, speaking of forming a colony of deaf-mutes, and to that I would say that it would make me happy, as well as many more of my class of people, if such a thing could be brought about,—for a great many reasons. The deaf-mutes would all be happy, as they can not now be, because they have nobody that can or will converse with them, and many people look on a deaf-mute as if he were a fool, because he can not talk, and because to them deaf-mutes look so foolish, just because they can not understand them. If they were by themselves, they could be happy; but as they are separated, they are in many cases despised by hearing men. That I have found out myself, because the hearing man says to the mute, You are a fool and crazy impostor. Therefore, I say, I am for a place where all my deaf-mute brethren could live and be happy; and I would say to J. J. Flournoy, that I like his enterprise, and if it should come so far as to buy the land, I would say, that I would give $5,000 to it in cash, and if all would help, the thing could be done. I am an orphan. I became deaf by sickness. I was then ten years old, and could never since enjoy myself, with all my father left me, a good farm of two hundred and fifty acres, worth $18,000. I am all alone. My father and mother, brother and sister, are all dead, and left me the farm and $2,000 in cash, which I loan out at ten percent. But with all that, I am not happy, with the present condition of the deaf and dumb. I am twenty-four years old and am not married.

This is what I think of the case, and I would like to see it carried out as soon as possible. Please give me a place in the Annals.

P. H. Confer.

[Mr. John Carlin, of New York, in a familiar letter addressed to Mr. Clerc, notes among other things, his impressions in regard to Mr. Flournoy's scheme. Though not designed at all for the public eye, Mr. Carlin will excuse the liberty we take of copying his words, as follows.—Ed.]

I read in the Annals, the January number, the letters of Messrs. Flournoy and Booth, in reference to the "Commonwealth of Deaf Mutes" in some territory, for which I would most respectfully suggest the name of Deaf-Mutia, or, for euphony's sake, Gesturia. They both are ably written, and do much credit to their heads and to their Alma Mater. As to the merits of Mr. Flournoy's theory, all that I can say is, that nothing is more pleasurable to our sensations, as we loll in our arm-chairs by the fire-side, than the building of castles in the air. Without manual labor, we can rear up in the vacuum, structures surpassing Solomon's temple in magnificence and costliness of materials, kingdoms of vast magnitude and power, or ladders of eminence to ascend to the summit of fame. But in practice to ensure success, it requires dollars, eagles and dimes in countless bags, to commence the work with, besides perseverance, patience and industry to keep the work steady; we all would have to lend our shoulders to the wheel, and not to stand looking on or gesturing all the long day.

As regards the founding of a deaf-mute commonwealth any where, the obstacles to its ultimate success are truly formidable. It must be borne in mind that nine-tenths of the whole deaf-mute community in this country can not raise up the wind so as to swell the flapping sails of Mr. Flournoy's scheme; besides, it is a well known fact that the majority of them show little decision of purpose in any enterprise whatever. For my own part, failing to perceive the practicability of the scheme, to which Mr. Flournoy clings with a constancy worthy of a better cause, I am content with my being "lost among the hearing persons," whose superior knowledge of the English language benefits my mind far more than would the perpetual gestures of the thousands of the *bona fide* residents in Gesturia. Drive to the neighboring states our hearing children whom we love so well! I reckon Mr. Flournoy has no little prattlers of his own to cheer the solitude of his plantation.

[The following sportive treatment of the subject, by Mr. John Burnet, will serve to enliven the discussion, and will give offense, we trust, to no one. It is proper for us, however, to advise Mr. Burnet, that Mr. Flournoy would tell him he has hit wide of the mark in one of his points. Mr. Flournoy writes, to Mr. Chamberlain, that he should not feel himself at liberty even to join the colony in person. "I have long been attempting," he says, "to play a sort of moral reformer in Georgia, to induce the deportation of the slaves to Liberia, and I fear, if I should go west now, I should be abandoning a sacred duty I owe to my God and my countrymen, to, feeble as I am, endeavor to save the republic by the expulsion of the national 'bone of contention.' "—Editor]

I wish to offer the tribute of my admiration for the magnificent views put forth by Mr. Flournoy. I hope he will go on and prosper. The government of a territory is the object to which he at present modestly limits himself. I think I foresee his views will soar higher yet, till he and the deaf-mutes of America will be content with nothing less than the control of an independent republic. Will not *President* Flournoy sound better than *Governor* Flournoy? For myself, having a turn for foreign travel, I would rather be an attaché to the embassy to London or Paris (for which post I hope my application may have precedence on file), than a member of the state government; not intending, however, to decline any office in which it may be judged that I may be useful to my country that is to be; provided the acceptance does not oblige me to neglect my own family.

Speaking of family, I would suggest a way of getting over the difficulty raised by Mr. Booth. Let it be provided that the estates of deaf-mutes may pass to their daughters who hear and speak, *provided these daughters marry only deaf husbands.* And if there be no daughters, I would so far respect the paternal feelings of worthy deaf-mute citizens that I would let their hearing sons inherit, provided they would consent, like Ulysses on the coast of the Syrens, to stop their ears with wax. They would then have no advantage over deaf-mutes in public meetings and conversation at least, which is all that can reasonably be required.

I would further suggest, to make the scheme more practicable, that we need not insist on permanent residence in voters. Let all deaf-mutes come, pay tax, and vote, and then *vamos, a la Kansas.* Many would do that, who might not find it for their interest to pitch their stakes in the new promised land.

REPLY TO OBJECTIONS

by J. J. Flournoy, of Georgia

The April No. of the Annals contains the remarks of Mr. Booth, Mr. Chamberlain, Mr. Carlin, Mr. Confer and Mr. Burnet; all, excepting those of Messrs. Chamberlain and Confer, repudiating my scheme. I do not look upon Mr. Chamberlain's suggestion as adverse, it is a substitute, by a diminution. But he should have viewed the project with a more enlarged survey, and observed that as our Commonwealth is to be founded for all coming time, numerous, *eventually*, may be the emigrations of deaf-mutes from all parts of the civilized world; and hence, a six miles square would prove insufficient for them; and this is the *contingency* for which we should sagaciously provide, by the selection of a forty miles square territory. The deaf residing in its contiguous towns and settlements, will never be materially scattered. Still, should the effort to induce this exodus of the deaf be practicable, some such plan as Mr. Chamberlain's may be *tried*, on the principle and policy, "better a little than none."

Mr. Carlin says he does not fancy a confinement among deaf-mutes, listening to their signs, as improving. Mr. Chamberlain has already refuted some of these objections, as to the facility for intelligence by such unions. But I would respectfully say to Mr. Carlin, that any amount of learning we deaf fellows can amass from conversational intercourse with the hearing, is greatly less than what we could derive from a conjunction of, and intercourse with, our own class of people. There is not a hearing man, that, except for occasional novelty and to while away a *tedium*, would *like* to hold written converse with any of us. It is too irksome. I always endeavour to make it a point never to put my neighbors to such *trouble*. They often have complained of the *burden* of conversing *thus* with me. And such hearing people as know the sign language, or alphabet of our class, never make it a point to convey to us one ninety-ninth of the information they constantly impart to each other by oral converse. Our last resource, then, is to have an unity; to read and to mutually impart our knowledge.

The subject of the Editorial remark on the disposition of Messrs. Flournoy and Confer, to consider the mutes as "despised" by the hearing, has two aspects. It is too obvious for denial, that, while by some we are not estimated of any importance at all to society, and encounter insurmountable prejudice where we would assert an equality, by others, we are only regarded *patronizingly*. It is true indeed, that by some few, and these the more philosophical and christian portion of the hearing community, who also are intimate with some of us, we have respectful or affectionate consideration. But how few are these among the mass! The Editor therefore erred, in supposing Mr. Confer's declaration groundless or unmerited by the world. [. . .]

The [. . .] objection of my friend, Mr. Booth, is on the score of the separation of parents and children. He supposes, with another correspondent, that I have no family. I have only a daughter, married, and removed to Wisconsin,—and she left against my wishes. Children we see will not always abide at home, or near their parents. I do not see how this scheme would separate families before the adult age; but adults will disperse of themselves. The deaf and dumb appear to dwell on this subject. The affections of their parents for them in particular, is such as to stand no separation. Mothers and fathers are fond of deaf, more than of any other children. So wrote a deaf-mute of Columbus, Ohio, name unrecollected—Chase, I believe. Now the true philosophy of such a view, is, that parents can follow such adult children to the State of Gallaudet [the proposed name for the commonwealth]. But on what is this extraordinary attachment, forbidding all improvement of the condition of such favorites, founded? Be it founded not on rational affection, but rather on that favoritism that makes a child a perpetual *pet*, very much as some old woman in single blessedness, loves a monkey, a cat, or a poodle dog,—such enfeebling and frustrating attachment to a deaf child *in particular*, does not very much recognize it as an intelligence, and can not be tolerated, against the manifest destiny of its useful citizenship. But I will meet Mr. Booth's philosophy on its very face. He had said that it would not be right (I use his ideas, not words), to part families. Again, he in the next postulate has a flattering picture of the fact that deaf schools may retain scholars fifteen years, "from infancy to twenty-one." And here is a virtual separation of parent and child at the tenderest age of the *pet*. To what then amounts his reasoning, when he infers that after such academical absence, the educated mute, long weaned from such *lap-dog* attachment, is to be retained by the family as a living automaton, a perpetual "darling"—doing nothing but some mechanical endearment all day long!

I respect the affection and sacredness of the family circle, and would forever consecrate such associations. But can not they be perfected equally in the community we wish to form? Nor when an emergency demands, can the energies of rational minds be contracted into everlasting childhood.

I have observed in my intercourse with the world, that if a first sight of me induce a deference of demeanor in the spectator, when he hears that I am deaf, he is at once familiar, even by speech and look; and though this would appear as a friendly disposition, it soon wears off, and attention and respect is given to others, while I am treated with neglect, or only occasional notice. Attention to us is thus exhibited as based upon inferior considerations. When we would claim equality, it offends. Viewing the case this way, I doubt if the estimation of parents for deaf children is as deep and abiding, all things considered, as that for the others. It is but cruelty to them, if adults, thus to contract their resources to the domestic hearth. [. . .]

What do Messrs. Chamberlain and Booth want? A small township of deaf-mutes, like the Shakers at Lebanon, New York, in which even our social organization and habits must conform to rules, in which, from the nature of things, we can have no agency? Our few votes, in our scattered aggregate, have not a jot of influence in the deliberations of capitals. Every law and legal rule is made independent of the wishes of mutes. Often our *peculiar* necessities and such arrangements as may be indispensable to our welfare, are not known or provided for. In our trade and intercourse, in our multifarious concerns, some new regulation is necessary; and if the thing could be re-arranged, many of us could sit on juries, and consequently be impartial, and hold offices of emolument. [. . .]

LETTER FROM H. M. CHAMBERLAYNE

Montrose, near Richmond, Va., June 28th, 1858.

Samuel Porter, Esq.:

Dear Sir,—I read in the January number of the Annals, the articles ably written by Messrs. Flournoy and Booth, on a "Commonwealth of Deaf Mutes," which have interested me. The first named gentleman's project is brilliant, though novel, and if practicable, will, I trust, be carried into effect; his views, expressed in his letter in the April number, meet my approbation. But his idea of allowing women to vote, is ridiculous. Mr. Booth seems to agree with him. This may be a favorite maxim of a majority of the "children of silence." And well it may be, for it is the ladder by which small men climb into office. Experience would exclaim against the suffrage-rights of women, for they, as is natural, are capable of acquiring the ascendant over the mind of men, which their limited knowledge will not enable them to use wisely. It matters not how enlarged a man's experience may be—how eminent his abilities,—how useful his counsels,—these are all to be held as naught, unless he is a favorite with women. But enough about Eve's daughters.

Mr. Booth thinks that the Georgian gentleman's idea of distinction on earth is merely political elevation. So I think. But his aspirations will be nipped in the bud. In short, I would most respectfully advise him to abandon the thorny ways of politics and turn his attention to his rural pursuits.

The more I reflect upon Mr. Booth's second letter, the greater is my amazement at his coolness and indifference toward the project, which, if carried into execution, would be beneficial to mutes.

I can not agree with Mr. Chamberlain that deaf-mutes are greater readers and better informed, when a number of them are living at the same place, than many who live among the hearing. From my own experience, I can say that those in this "last" state are by far the greatest readers.

I suggest that "Gestrina" should be located on a navigable river, as the inhabitants would avail themselves of such a favorable situation, and commerce with adjacent towns might contribute greatly, not merely to enrich their town, but also to encourage their domestic industry.

All the deaf-mutes, who unfortunately cherish such a feeling as Mr. Confer does, should be under vast obligations to Mr. Flournoy, if he could ameliorate their condition. But for my own part, I having never been "so shamefully" treated, would be unwilling to take leave of the neighborhood where I have ever found the utmost kindness and consideration and enjoy all the advantages of society, preferring to be "scattered" among the hearing, to taking up my residence among stumps.

Those who are contented with their present condition, will find it their interest to stay where they are now.

Dr. Franklin says:

> "Dig deep the soil your fathers hold,
> And find therein a mine of gold!"

Yours, &c.,
H. M. Chamberlayne.

2

Before the invention of the talkies, Deaf Americans went to the movies right along with their hearing neighbors, and Hollywood attracted Deaf artists and actors who worked with the hearing stars, albeit not on an equal footing. Today's captioned TV and films, even if universally available, can never restore the access to popular culture that the silent movies provided. This sketch by a Deaf film artist comes from his semi-fictionalized autobiography

Coming to California

Albert Ballin

1930

With high hopes and ambition, I packed what little I possessed in worldly goods into my grip, and boarded the good ship, *Finland,* to sail for California, the home of our beloved Cinema Child.

Some deaf friends came to wave me God-speed on my hazardous venture. Here I must mention a feature that is often seen, but whose significance is seldom considered. As the ship was unmoored, and started on her long voyage, her passengers and their friends on the dock were yelling their parting farewells, using their hands as megaphones; but all their vocal exchanges were drowned by the steam sirens, clanging bells, stentorian orders of the ship-officers, shouts of the seamen, and the general bedlam. My deaf friends and I were never harassed by this ear-splitting clamor. For us it did not exist. We went on conversing, using our fingers and arms, missing not one word. I believe the last message I flashed off on my fingers was:

"You can see that our deafness is a blessing in disguise. Now we have the laugh on the hearing, and can pity their helplessness? What?"

Came the answer:

"Right you are, old man! Bon voyage and good luck to you!"

Our conversation was soon cut short by the warping of the ship around to the other side. We could have gone on talking at a distance far beyond ear-shot. Our system was far better than that of the signal wig-wagging of sailors on a war-ship.

I now propose to plunge into an account of my adventures in the motion picture world.

I received a splendid welcome at the Ince Studio (now Pathe). Mr. Ince knew and appreciated my purpose in coming, and gave me complete freedom of the studio, and facilities to study all details at close range. I visited other studios where I was welcomed and assisted in my work. From that time dates my affiliation with the industry. I served as a writer for periodicals and magazines, teacher of signs to the

27

Albert Ballin teaching Laura La Plante to fingerspell. Undated photo courtesy of the Gallaudet University Archives.

acting fraternity, and as a painter of portraits. At various times I was used as an actor
in minor bits. In fact, were I to permit myself to digress, I could fill several volumes
with accounts of my interesting experiences.

One of the most striking curiosities, a downright anomaly in this industry, is the
utter lack of directors who can talk fluently on their fingers. I searched diligently, and
found only one. He spells slowly and rheumatically on his fingers, and no more. All
the directors I have met are friendly, very fine gentlemen, supremely clever in their
work. Nevertheless, it does look odd from my point of view that they should not
know this sign-language—*the language so necessary to picture-making.*

With the exception of two or three actors, like the late Lon Chaney, who are
children of deaf-mute parents, practically everyone connected with the industry, from
the highest producer down to the lowly sweeper, is blissfully (?) ignorant of the
sign language. Lon Chaney declared in published articles that he was thankful for

his knowledge of signs, and believed that much of his success was due to that knowledge.

In watching the production of pictures, I noticed a great deal of waste in time and money because of this lack of knowledge of signs. The following is an illustration:

I witnessed a scene where the heroine was fleeing in an automobile. She was crouching at the wheel, turning her head every minute or two to watch her pursuers. The car was actually at a standstill. In the background was a canvas with pictures of fields, trees, shrubbery, telegraph poles, turning swiftly on revolving cylinders, to give the illusion that the car was moving. To intensify the illusion, four men, two at either end, jumped up and down on planks attached to the car, making it appear as if the car were driving along a rough road. In front of the car out of camera range, a motor driven propeller blew wind at the car, fluttering the heroine's hair and ribbons in the breeze. The illusion of the car rushing at full speed turned out perfectly on the screen. By an oversight, the girl's hair and ribbons were stuck fast inside her coat. The director bellowed directions through his megaphone, ordering her to loosen her hair and ribbons; but the din created by the aeroplane machine was too deafening for her to hear him. He had to stop the camera, walk up to her, and explain what he wanted; and then make a retake.

At the conclusion, I wrote on my pad. "You are a h—of a director. If you knew how, you could have made signs to the girl to loosen her hair and be spared the retake."

The director, a good-natured friend, glared at me; then his scowling features melted into a broad grin. He nodded admission that I was just in my criticism.

I also saw mob scenes, cow-boys and soldiers shooting guns, houses on fire, battle scenes and other scenes that produced terrific din, drowning all vocal orders. In the handling of such scenes, signs would have been invaluable.

The time may come when we shall have no more use for directors or players who are ignorant of the sign-language than we would for carpenters who don't know the use of a hammer or saw.

At a certain studio, during a dissertation on my favorite topic, I made some remarks, characterizing the bulk of motion pictures as rank bunk, insulting to the intelligence of the American people. One actor laughingly declared that "stories are written by, of, and for dumb-bells." The director retorted, "About eighty per cent of the American people are morons, the class that pays and supports the movies; we have put across some high-brow stuff (naming several truly great stories), and they were financial failures." Another actor nodded gravely and added, "We have to cater to the tastes of the morons or go out of business altogether."

There is a good deal of sense in these remarks, when viewed from the old, unsound theory that most people are low in mentality and tastes. But the accusation is erroneous. I must repeat my conclusions, that the great majority of the people are really intelligent; but too many, about sixty per cent, are "unschooled."

Those who cannot read the words thrown on the screen lose the story—they become disgusted and bored, and, thereafter refuse to see such shows. This has been plainly proved by the crowds that flock to see Charlie Chaplin's pictures. Those he made fifteen years ago are popular today. They are pictures—*not words*. The bunk offered by some producers will always keep away self-respecting spectators who can read. Ignoring the fundamental causes of diminishing boxoffice receipts, many producers have the idea that they can repair the damage by offering pictures that are sillier and more salacious. They act like the man who fell into quick-sand—the harder he struggled the faster he would sink. Hence the poor Cinema is becoming anaemic and sickly.

There has boomed suddenly into our midst an innovation called the *Talkie,* which reproduces the human voice, music and all sounds. The producers and exhibitors have scrambled after it headlong, spending hundreds of millions with a lavish hand. Though far from perfected, the device, like a mother-in-law, is likely to remain with us. Now that oral speech has reached the screen it is expected to help the box office. It may for a time—but will it last? Will the success be permanent? I doubt it. We are still in a hysterical mood; a natural sequence after the Great War. The instant success of the "Talkie" does, however, show the need of a substitute for the endless *words* that formerly were written on the screen. Speech does help a goodly number of the so-called "unschooled." It also succeeds in driving away all the deaf and hard-of-hearing. And how these bemoan the passing of the silent movie. It was counted among their few blessings. It entertained and helped to keep them cheerful. "But it brings in the blind," remarked a publicity man to me. Smart of him, perhaps, but he forgets that the deaf pay admission fees; the blind *don't.*

The "Talkie" restricts theatre attendance to those understanding the one language. It turns away those to whom the tongue is foreign. It may be all right, even commendable, to utilize music and all other appropriate sounds to enhance illusions of reality, but we can very well eliminate monologues, dialogues and all orally spoken words that have to be translated into many tongues to reach the world. At the best, dialogue retards and slows down action, one of the greatest charms of motion pictures. The Cinema will fall short of its ideal if it does not make itself universal; and it can never be universal unless it is understood everywhere on the globe.

We have been living in the jazz age too long; we are exhausted, sick of the incessant clamor worthy only of savages. Does the Talkie threaten us with more just when we are beginning to yearn after repose?

When we sit down to read and enjoy a story, the book in our hands does not shriek from every page with all varieties of type-screaming capitals, italics, copious foot-notes. It would irritate and disgust us and we would throw it into the fireplace. A good story is best when couched in plain, clean type, clearly and simply phrased, leaving plenty of room for imagination. Many of the old silent pictures have been eminently successful; they linger in our memories like good books. It is the kind of work that we ought to preserve and improve.

Charlie Chaplin, the famous comedian, knows a good deal about the signs and makes excellent use of them without making of them a distinct language. You never see him open his mouth to utter one syllable; his sub-titles are few and short. We know he regrets having to use any at all. His pictures are, in consequence, never in need of translation. From them he has made a fortune that he well deserves.

As I was penning the above lines, I came across an article entitled, "Charlie Chaplin Attacks the Talkies." It appears in the magazine *Motion Pictures,* for May, 1929. I am quoting from it:

"You can tell 'em I loathe them," he said. "They are spoiling the oldest art in the world—the art of pantomime. They are ruining the great beauty of silence. They are defeating the meaning of the screen, the appeal that has created the star system, the fan system, the vast popularity of the whole—the appeal of beauty. . . . It is beauty that matters in pictures—nothing else. The screen is pictorial. Pictures . . . I am not using the talkies in my new picture. I am never going to use them. For me, it would be fatal. I can't understand why anyone who can possibly avoid it, does use it; Harold Lloyd, for instance."

Mr. Chaplin knows his subject thoroughly and can speak about it with authority. . . . We need the influence of a few more men like him to help overcome the ignorance and baseless prejudices that handicap progress.

In speaking of the ignorance on this subject, let me separate it from the *indifference* that is responsible for what the deaf-mute is and for woes that pursue him throughout his whole life. To make clear the presence of this ignorance among those supposed to possess intelligence, I will relate an experience in one of the studios where I met many who were most learned, and generous.

When I first met the very charming Miss Betty Compson, she asked me, during an interview:

"Can you read the lips?"

I answered, "No, I can't."

"Why not?" she demanded.

My reply was, "Can you spell on your fingers?"

"No," came the quick response.

I smiled, as I repeated her own words, "Why not?"

"Why should I?" she asked. "I never meet any deaf people."

When I did not answer she continued, "Let me tell you that I have a very dear friend who is a great actress on both the stage and screen. She was so sensitive when her hearing became affected that she learned to read lips so well that nobody knows about her trouble. Her name is Louise D——"

(I felt like saying, Oh, Louise, how can you read the lips when your back is turned, or when the kleig lights are in your eyes? How can you read the lips of your director when his mouth is hidden behind a megaphone? It is difficult enough for anyone to pretend to be a deaf-mute; but for a deaf person to conduct herself as one who hears—well, it has me stumped. But I could not embarrass sweet Betty with inquiries along such lines.)

"That is very fine," I replied, "How old was she when her hearing began to fail?"

"I am not sure. Perhaps thirty."

"You see," I explained, "she could hear and talk like you until she was thirty, and then lip reading was all she had to learn. You don't seem to realize that it takes a deaf child fifteen, twenty, sometimes twenty-five years of hardest labor, and the sacrifice of all other branches of learning to even attempt to talk orally and to read the lips. Even after years of study and work he is likely to fail in the end. All these years are given to save *you and those like you* some thirty minutes of your whole life. Is it fair to ask this of the deaf when a few minutes would enable you to spell on your fingers and communicate with him?"

Betty looked surprised and pained. She turned to speak with her friends. Then she wrote on my pad with tears trickling down the pencil point:

"We never looked at the thing in that light before. I am so ashamed of myself and beg your pardon."

Like most others, she was merely ignorant of this much-slighted subject. I meet others like her every day, innocent and perfectly sincere in asking me the same questions—never suspecting that they are asking a question no less absurd than, "Can you dance blindfolded on a swinging rope in a stormy night?"

It has taken me a year to compile this book, after almost a lifetime of careful thinking. During the years I have repeatedly been asked the question that was put to me by Miss Compson. It is rather discouraging.

When I first met Mary Pickford, she also asked me this heart-breaking question, "Can you read the lips?" I hope to be forgiven for replying, "No, I only kiss them when they are sweet like yours." Of course, she excused me by laughing merrily.

Historically, American churches and synagogues, while preaching tolerance and charity to their hearing congregants, have in practice neglected to include the Deaf in their fellowship—and this despite the religious cast of all early efforts to educate Deaf children. Today in the United States, houses of worship are specifically exempted from compliance with the federal, state, and local civil rights laws that mandate equal opportunity for Deaf Americans. This speech was given at a government workshop by the president of the National Association of the Deaf.

What a Deaf Jewish Leader Expects of a Rabbi

Frederick C. Schreiber

1970

To say what a deaf leader expects of a rabbi is an occasion made for platitudes. I could discuss for hours all the characteristics of a rabbi which are common demands of everyone, whether he is deaf or not. As a matter of fact, the main point here is not what the deaf leader expects of a rabbi, but rather what he thinks the deaf Jew needs and wants from his rabbi, and this is somewhat more complex. Speaking from my own experiences as a deaf Jew, there are a number of things which appear to stand out as strong problems where religious matters are concerned.

The first of these is the lack of an adequate religious education. There are only one or two schools for the deaf in this country that have any relation to the Jewish faith and even in these schools the opportunities available to the child to learn about his own religion are minimal. Being raised in the Jewish faith at home does not do much to solve the problem. The deaf child needs the same opportunity to learn the hows and whys of his faith as does any other child. He needs not only religious instruction, but also explanations as to why things are not always the way they should be. He needs to know why, for example, he does not always go home from school on Rosh Hashonna or fast on Yom Kippur. He needs to know why his food is Kosher at home but not in school. But most of all he needs to feel that his faith has a deep and abiding interest in him and his welfare and that his rabbi is his teacher, his counselor, his source of comfort and advice in times of distress.

Deaf people live in a world that differs vastly from any other because the common medium that binds most people together is communication. Our world is an auditory one, and the inability to learn by auditory methods imposes a heavy burden on the individual which, so far, has proven barely tolerable. Helen Keller once noted that if she had to do it all over again she would devote her time to working with the deaf because "blindness cuts you off from things, while deafness cuts you off from people."

It is this isolation that needs to be broken down and it is in this area that the rabbi can be of most help. A good Christian friend of mine once told me that it is impossible for a deaf person to fully integrate into the world of the hearing. This man had good speech, good lip-reading ability and he said: "I tried this (integration) in my church. I felt that if I could succeed anywhere, that would be the place because in church, people are *consciously* kind."

Whether or not my friend is correct is immaterial for this paper. The point is that there are very few avenues through which any deaf person can get sympathetic understanding and help for his problems. The deaf Jew needs to have someone to turn to in times of stress, someone who can counsel him, comfort him, guide him not only in religious matters, but with secular problems as well.

Most communities have an abundance of social service agencies which cover the entire spectrum of human needs. But if the Washington Community Survey is any indication, none of these agencies are equipped to deal with deaf persons. Few have personnel who can even communicate with deaf people. Even fewer have people whose knowledge of the psychology of deafness, the educational background and childhood development of the congenitally deaf person, is adequate enough for effective counseling.

When the deaf Jew needs help, can he go to his rabbi and get it? Right now the answer must be "no." But he ought to be able to do so. What's more, the concept of seeking help from this source should be instilled in early childhood, so that when one grows older, one will instinctively think of one's rabbi in times of stress.

This, of course, poses problems. Few rabbis are any more familiar with the deaf than are the social service agencies mentioned previously. It may be unrealistic to expect that every rabbinical student be required to familiarize himself with what is an admittedly complex subject when the chances that he will have deaf people in his congregation are minimal to say the least. Still, it is not unreasonable to suggest that such students be advised to seek help from more knowledgeable people before attempting to give guidance, should the need arise. The deaf person can quickly recognize that his advisor is not familiar with the complexities of his disability and turn away, rejecting not only the advice but the advisor and perhaps even the Temple itself.

It does not seem far-fetched to suggest that rabbis be alerted to this problem and advised that the National Congress of Jewish Deaf be contacted as soon as one discovers there are deaf Jews in one's congregation. Then the Congress could provide lists of referral agencies and other sources of information that are available to the rabbis. Such professional help as psychiatrists, interpreters, social workers, etc., is available and can be secured when needed.

Where there are deaf Jews in a congregation the rabbi might assume a major role between the deaf person and community service agencies: in particular, the State's Vocational Rehabilitation Agency and the counselor assigned to the deaf person. While Rehabilitation Agency counselors may know a little more about deafness than the average rabbi, generally this is only a smidgen more and the counselor, over-burdened with a heavy caseload to begin with, cannot give his deaf client the time and attention he needs. But a rabbi could—he has, generally speaking, few handi-capped people in his congregation and even fewer who need the kind of help the deaf individual requires. Thus, working with a Vocational Rehabilitation counselor, the rabbi could do much to help that counselor provide real service to his client. He might be able to ease communication difficulties, help with some of the formalities involved in processing a case, such as making medical appointments, hearing tests, or whatever is needed to help the client.

Religious leadership is another area where one would hope that the rabbis might exert a positive force. In my own community in Metropolitan Washington, there are enough Jews for at least special services on occasions such as Rosh Hashonna, Yom Kippur and Passover. This situation exists in other communities as well, but such services are seldom held. One might wonder why don't the deaf people themselves move in this direction? And that would be a valid question. The answer might be, first, that we have never received any encouragement to do so. Then there is the problem of communication; a deaf Jew can't just pick up a telephone and find a Temple or a rabbi who is willing and able to arrange for such services, nor can he easily reach the other members of his faith to convey the information. Finally, the quality of leadership varies from community to community so that truly effective leadership on the local level is scarce. Most deaf people are underemployed so that even the community leaders are severely restricted in what they can do; all are volunteers with very limited resources.

These are but a few of the things one expects from one's rabbi. Perhaps a great deal of attention should be focused on the children of the deaf. They are seldom considered, but they have a far-reaching effect on Judaism. All evidence has shown that the deaf Jew has been sadly neglected by his religion. How, then, can he be a functioning member of his own congregation and also insure that his hearing children will be brought up in the faith of his fathers?

When I tried to enroll my children in Sunday School in Montgomery County where I live, I was told I had to be a member of the congregation, and despite my pointing out that I would derive no benefit from such membership, I was told "it would make my children feel better" if I joined. So I joined. I asked only that my children's teachers be made aware that I was deaf and did not have the training necessary to fulfill the role of a typical Jewish father. This did no good because my children were continually coming home with questions that their teachers had told them to "ask their father." These questions, of course, I could not answer, which embarrassed both me and my children. So I refused to continue as a member of this congregation and took my problem to a Reformed Temple hoping for more under-standing. Here I was told by the rabbi that he was more interested in me than in my children. But I knew at that time there was little he could do for me, although, if my children had proper training, proper contacts, it was possible, even probable, that when they grew older they could interpret for me at the Services and thus bring me back in the fold. Since this was not to be, I had a private tutor to complete their religious education because it was never a matter of cost but rather of principle that motivated my actions. My sons were Bar Mitzvah but they never really had the social or religious contacts which lead to regular attendance at any Temple. At this time, two of my children have married Gentiles. The other two will probably do the same. This hurts. Whether he attends a Temple or not, whether he is deaf or not, a Jewish boy who grows up in a Jewish household, is still a Jew. And I began to wonder— how many families are there in the same situation as I? If the deaf Jew is not important to the Temple, certainly his children and his children's children should be and their future is worth considering.

Larger cities have deaf congregations. New York, Philadelphia, Chicago, Los Angeles, all boast of congregations of deaf people. All have regular services for deaf Jews and some may even make provision for the children of their members, but not enough is being done, not for the hearing children of deaf parents, not for the deaf children who live in all parts of the country, not just in the big cities and even in the cities where there are deaf congregations; all too often the impact is lost by the use of lay readers, interpreters and the like. The deaf Jew is reasonable enough to understand why an interpreter might be needed where only a few deaf people are involved. We do not really believe that every rabbi should or would learn to communicate with us in our own language, but we do think that where the congregation is large enough this should be done. We should be able to get rabbis who are thoroughly familiar with all aspects of deafness, who can communicate with us in our own language, and who can instill in us a feeling of trust and security.

For our deaf children, there should be a more intensified effort to see to it that they get proper religious training. It is disheartening to note that when reading over the literature on education, there is, if not frequent, at least regular mention of what is available for Christians—and almost nothing—I say almost to be conservative because I have found nothing at all—about programs for Jews. I don't care whose fault this is and I would not even want to speculate on whose responsibility it is to insure that something is done to provide our deaf Jewish children with adequate religious training. It seems to me that if religion is important, then it is the responsibility of those primarily concerned with religion to see to it that the children are not neglected.

It is fairly certain that there is at least one Temple located in those communities that contain residential schools for the deaf. Many of these schools may have only a few Jewish children but they are there. For the most part the children, perhaps, are en route between the school and their homes on Fridays; they generally live too far from the school to return to their homes for the holidays, Jewish holidays that is; so they get no attention at all. Why can't the Temple take the initiative in seeing to it that the children get adequate training? I am sure school administrations would cooperate, and that interpreters could be found to assist the rabbis in this important task if it were undertaken. When one stops to consider that it is not only the deaf child who is being lost to Israel, but also his children and his children's children, the effort necessary appears justified. After all, aren't we *all* the Lord's Chosen People?

The very existence of ordinary Deaf people is a perennially rediscovered marvel for the hearing news media.

4 | How to Write Like a Hearing Reporter

Tom Willard

1993

It's interesting to observe the way hearing reporters write about deaf people. Over the years I've learned a few things and would like to offer this tongue-in-cheek guide to Writing About the Deaf for Hearing Reporters Only.

Let's start with the headline. There are two words that *must* appear in every headline. One is "silence" (or "silent"). For example:

Sounds of Silence
Silent Courage
The Silent World of Joe Jordan

The other word is "signs":

Signs of Confusion
A Good Sign
Theater Signs

If you want to go all the way, you can combine the two:

Signs of Silence

Another popular approach, keeping in mind that deafness is a disability that must be overcome:

Deafness can't stop Jordache
Jameson conquers deafness

When you write your headlines you may use the terms "deaf," "hard of hearing" and "hearing impaired" interchangeably. The important thing is that the headline fits the space.

Once you've written your headline, you may proceed with the article.

Here is a classic lead:

Jane Jetson gets up in the morning, eats breakfast, gets in her car and drives to work.

But Jane is different from you and me.

Jane is deaf.

That three word sentence, "So-and-so is deaf," should always appear by itself in a single paragraph. It is guaranteed to shock your readers after first reading how *normal* the person seems.

There is another kind of lead used when writing about deaf athletes. It goes:

Jack Jones cannot hear the cheers. . . .

The variation for theater reviews is:

Jill Johnson cannot hear the applause. . . .

Don't let it bother you that scores of reporters have already used this lead. Who ever said journalists had to be original?

When writing about deaf people, be sure to talk with everyone around them: their parents, teachers and employers. You will be able to communicate easily with these people. If you are forced to actually talk with the deaf person you are writing about, make sure you include the phrase "through an interpreter" when you quote them, as follows:

"I like my job," said Jack through an interpreter.

This will enable your readers to see that you are illiterate in sign language.

Another tip: Newspapers traditionally use last names when identifying adults, but first names when referring to children. For example:

Jackson said his daughter Jamie loves her cochlear implant.

But when writing about deaf people, it is permissible to refer to them by their first name throughout the article, as if they were children.

One last tip on writing about deaf people. Don't do it too often. Your community may be filled with interesting deaf people doing newsworthy things, but who cares? Once a year is often enough.

5

Many normal, healthy deaf children grow up isolated in families and communities that are desperate to cure what they regard as a pathology. Almost invariably, the mainstream news media ignore the Deaf view that deaf children are perfect just the way they are.

CBS Hurt Deaf Children with "Caitlin's Story"

Jack Levesque

1992–1993

When CBS aired a segment of "60 Minutes" on November 8, the Deaf community won the battle but lost the war.

I knew we were sunk when interviewer Ed Bradley opened the show with these words: "One thing about '60 Minutes,' you get to meet a lot of people. But we don't remember ever meeting one who captivated us quite as much as this seven-year-old charmer."

He goes on to tells about Caitlin Parton and her "remarkable device called a cochlear implant."

We were doomed. Caitlin was about as cute and smart a kid as I've ever seen, and Bradley was blinded by her. He saw a kid that should have been miserable and lonely, because deaf people all are, and here she was bright and bubbly and happy. Must be medical technology!

As I watched that show, I wished I could show Ed Bradley the reality of Deaf lives. I wished I could tell him that when I was Caitlin's age, I could speak, too. I went to school and learned to read and do math, and my parents would have sworn I was doing just fine, just like a "normal kid." But in my heart, I knew things weren't "normal." I believed that speaking well would make me okay, make me popular and smart. I figured I would be able to bluff my way through life and my reward would be to live among the hearing and not be noticed. It was hard work, but I figured it was worth it.

Then I hit the teenage years. I felt a sort of acid anger in my gut, but I pushed it down. My mother wrote down the words of the popular songs so I could "be cool" and know what was going on. I faked knowing the words to songs like I faked knowing what was going on in class.

One day, I got sick of being a fake. I wanted to be just me. Plain old, deaf me.

Ed Bradley and Caitlin's parents don't know it, but someday Caitlin will feel that way too. I know she will, not just because it happened to me, but because it happened to every other Deaf person I have ever known.

"Caitlin's Story" could have been a balanced and fair report on an important and innovative new technology. They interviewed Roz Rosen and Harlan Lane for hours, they read *The Mask of Benevolence*. They apparently even interviewed a Deaf teenager who won't use her implant.

But then they got smitten by this sweet and innocent child, whose life right now is devoid of controversy and failure and rejection. Much easier, they thought, to just give this nice bit of life to our viewers.

So they cut Rosen's and Lane's comments down to five minutes each. They misconstrued Rosen's words and made Lane look like some kind of hearing-traitor. They had two of the finest minds in the country right there ready and willing to share their wisdom about deafness, yet they chose to pat Roz's head and gag Lane.

The real villains here are not Caitlin's loving and good parents nor even the surgeon who drilled into Caitlin's skull.

The real villains are the Federal Food and Drug Administration which allowed this to happen. They approved the use of cochlear implants in children on the advice of an all-hearing committee (which had one "consumer representative": a hearing former teacher of the deaf!) without enough proof that the procedure even works, and without any evidence that the child will be psychologically healthy afterward.

The decision by the FDA, and now this story, fuel a dangerous fire. They reaffirm parents' belief that deafness is a terrible, awful thing, and that their children must function as much like hearing people as possible. Those parents cry into their pillows imagining what emptiness the lives of their children will be if they never hear a bird sing, or the whistle of the wind, or the patter of rain. How can they know that Deaf people "hear" the rustling of stars, the flowing of sunshine, the laughter in eyes? They can't imagine how their Deaf child will ever communicate. How can they know that there are many two- and three-year-old Deaf kids who can tell you, in detail, just how to mix water into dirt so it makes mud that sticks together just right?

All these desperate parents need is the story of one child to let them cling to the belief that their child can somehow become hearing. They will ignore the fact that Caitlin is not typical, that she had been speaking when she lost her hearing, that she spends hours in speech therapy (is that just like a hearing child?). They won't hear the stories of Deaf adults who warn them to accept their child the way he or she is. They will just see this happy, talkative child and they will believe in their fairy tale hopes of their own Deaf child living happily ever after as a hearing person.

Whatever she appears to be, the truth is that Caitlin is hearing-impaired. She will always be hearing-impaired. Some day she might even proudly call herself "Deaf," but the one thing she'll never be is hearing.

In the meantime, how many children will suffer through useless surgery that makes them only an implant patient for life because their parents saw Caitlin? Will any of them be injured or even killed because of complications of surgery? Will any of them wish for deafness and toss their implant microphones in the trash?

You bet they will.

Caitlin, you are perfect in our eyes. We don't care if you can talk or not. We won't test you with directions to tie your shoe or give us the green square. You are a welcome member of our community. Someday, when you're ready, we'll be here, with a language that fills your needs and people who see the sounds of the world just like you do.

6

When Deaf people today live and work among hearing people who don't know how to communicate with them and have no interest in learning, interpreters are often called in where a pad and pencil were once considered adequate. Most Deaf people find this an improvement, and few ever stop to think what we give up when we let hearing people "voice" for us.

Who Speaks for the Deaf Community? Not Who You Would Think!

Elizabeth L. Broecker

1997

• An Examination of Power in American Society

After many years of various employment throughout the United States, it has become abundantly clear to me just who it is that speaks *for* the Deaf Community in the larger America. Working as I have done in various parts of the country and in many different settings, including education, social services, government, and the private sector, I have had the rare opportunity to observe people in action. From these observations have come my beliefs and theories about a certain area of power in America.

To test myself on the validity of my theories, I developed personal criteria to determine just what assets are required to be able to make profound impact on the Hearing Society in which we all live. Those criteria are as follows:

1. One should be highly visible;
2. One should have high credibility;
3. One should have occasion to interact with people in all aspects of American life;
4. One should be able to influence public opinion on a wide-spread basis again and again.

I wanted to test my criteria by informally asking persons who are deaf in various parts of the country as to who they thought spoke for the Deaf Community. Their answers follow, along with an analysis of how these suggestions may or may not meet my established criteria.

43

Deaf Leaders in Higher Education

Not surprisingly, most persons who are deaf in large metropolitan areas such as Washington, DC and Rochester, NY named highly placed deaf leaders in education in their areas. Reviewing our criteria, such leaders are indeed highly visible in their communities and even occasionally on national television. However, they have high credibility only in their special area—academia.

It is extremely doubtful whether the influence of such individuals reaches down to the mainstream of American life, be it to persons who are deaf or those who can hear. Such individuals represent a widely perceived rarity—a person who is deaf in a high position. There is no opportunity to interact regularly with all those who make up the wide spectrum of American society, and being able to influence opinion on a wide-spread basis again and again is negligible at best.

Deaf Actress and Actors

One well-known actress who is deaf was named by a cross section of individuals across the country. This reveals a certain degree of her high visibility in the Deaf Community. Other names of actors and actresses who are deaf were also mentioned as being known to the Deaf Community, as well as to certain segments of the Hearing Society. However, such individuals are more of a novelty rather than credible spokespersons who can influence public opinion again and again.

Deaf Administrators, Teachers, Social Service Workers, and Workshop Leaders

This is an interesting category. Many of those who fit into this category are without question activists attempting to speak for the Deaf Community. However, they reach a relatively small and localized population of those who can be influenced by their views.

National and State Organizations of the Deaf

Only a very few deaf persons named such organizations. They are viewed mainly as special interest groups speaking for the membership only. Often overworked and understaffed and lacking strong volunteers, these groups, although with some influence in certain areas such as politics, are not able to interact with all members of American society.

Heads of Schools for the Deaf

At one time in American history, such individuals were very influential, indeed. But in these days of change and mainstreaming, they are largely perceived as speaking for the preservation of schools for the deaf rather than speaking for the Deaf Community. They are often well known to the deaf citizens of a state, and some have influence with their state government, but usually on behalf of the school for the deaf. They are seen today as relatively "unknown." Not one deaf person named a head of a school for the deaf as a representative for the Deaf Community.

Heads of State Commissions for the Deaf

Some deaf persons felt that in their state, the head of the state commission, usually a deaf person, is quite influential and to some extent, visible throughout the state. Whether they interact in all aspects of state activities is debatable, and they very often have a such small staff that they spend most of their time fulfilling their function within the bureaucracy. Without strong and knowledgeable political action groups, their influence will remain minimal, at best.

- Taking in the Above Comments, Who Does Speak for the Deaf Community?

Let us now examine, using our criteria, a large and diverse group well-placed all over the American landscape. They are out there every single day in every single way speaking with, for, and about deaf persons everywhere.

How Does This Powerful Group Meet Our Criteria?

1. They are highly visible. They are onstage, in front of classrooms, in numerous policy, personal and social meetings and in every conceivable setting all across America.
2. They have high credibility. They share the values and beliefs of the larger community. They possess a certain mystique—an ability to communicate with a relatively unknown population in a language that is not easily mastered. It is standard practice that they are constantly asked, "How did you learn to do that?" Whereas, the deaf person in such settings is rarely, if ever, asked, "How did you learn to use that service?"
3. They interact with people in all areas of American life. They are in our schools, in our courts, in the welfare office, in the Social Security office, in the police station, in the hospital, in mental health settings, in higher education classes, mainstreamed classes, big business offices, public forums—the list is endless.
4. They are able to influence opinion again and again. If they are sorry for the deaf person and want to "help," or if they are on a mission and want to "assist," or they want to express "inner anger" in subtle ways, if they believe the Deaf Community has the right to be heard on their own, if they think

people who are deaf should be the heads of programs for the deaf, if they know with all their hearts, bodies, souls and minds that deaf people are a pitiful lot, always meant to be second class citizens so that hearing people may continue their role—whatever their beliefs are, they will share it with the public at large. They speak for the Deaf Community when they are out on the job and interacting with American people everywhere.

Who Are These Powerful People?

They are *interpreters for the deaf.* Their very title conveys power—*for* the deaf— and the use of the non-personal term "the deaf" reflects that they represent a faceless group of people without significant recognition or perceived power of any kind.

You might ask *why?*

Because—

1. Deaf people have allowed themselves to continue being an oppressed population and have maintained a larger group belief that they are powerless. Their identity is so intense as a suppressed and angry group, that they will shoot down any deaf local and national leaders who are rising above the group so that they can, because of deep-seated needs based on self loathing and anger, demand that everyone must be the same and remain powerless. Without personal and group growth and the exercise of personal freedom, this will continue;
2. Deaf people as a group like the status quo and its rewards, and do not at this time perceive any reward in change. To bring about change, a very large number of people must collectively be educated and collectively believe that a proposed change will personally benefit them;
3. Deaf people as a group think hearing people are smarter than they are, partly because so many hearing people study in Interpreter Training Programs where they learn about Deaf Culture, the history of deafness, famous Deaf Americans, and the linguistics of American Sign Language. They even learn about the Americans With Disabilities Act, which supposedly is a benefit for use by people who are deaf, along with other groups of individuals who are disabled.

Such programs proliferate in the American landscape whereas opportunities for such study are not routinely available to citizens who are deaf. When was the last time you heard of a program that instructed deaf citizens on how to use and manage interpreting services? Do interpreter training programs teach their students that deaf people are always in the driver's seat, even if they have no idea how to proceed in many situations? It is, after all, the basic goal of the interpreting profession to bring people who are deaf and people who can hear together in effective communication.

Deaf people need the freedom of personal action to fight their own battles, and take on their own pain for failure and their own pride in success, and individually and collectively realize they have the power to be. If persons who are deaf are actually given a level playing field, who knows what could happen. It needs to be tried. Without that attempt, it is fair to say that the "Deaf is dumb and hearing is smart" philosophy is alive and well in America today, as a powerful group speaks for the deaf community throughout the land.

Self-assertive Deaf people can find life among the hearing not only exhausting but often humiliating as well.

7 | My Life on Paper

Shanny Mow

1999

"Isn't there anything you do regularly with your left hand?" I wrote.

I was visiting with Dick who worked as a photographer here at the Air Force Observatory on the top of a mountain east of White Sands. He had decided that we could converse quicker and cover more ground, too, if I would teach him sign language. I did not argue. One just does not argue with this kind of request. So we started with the manual alphabet. As I spelled each letter on my right hand, he replicated it on his left hand.

"Why your left hand?" I asked.

He shrugged.

"You write with your right hand, don't you?"

He nodded.

"You eat with your right hand?"

Another nod.

"Throw with your right hand?"

Still another nod.

Finally I asked the question. He thought for a moment and scratched his right hand.

I walk on water better than I lip read. I do, however, read it right every time a hearing person asks: "Can you read lips?" Standard Hearing Opening Line. I would shake my head and produce my pen and pad. Quickly, before he opens his mouth again. Hearing people never take my negative reply seriously. And they are not prepared for my pen and pad, which are my principal means of in-person communication with them. My speech is shaky. I have not trusted it since I was eleven years old, when I asked my brother for a napkin and got instead a bottle of cream and brown bag.

The sight of a writing pad provokes something akin to an allergic reaction. Shock. Fear. Panic. It means you have to take hold of a pen for a reason other than to sign your name on a credit card purchase slip. Maybe the American educational system forgot to teach you how to write. Maybe lawyers have replaced your fear of God; they will hold anything you put in black and white against you. Maybe technology

48

is rearranging your brains in your ear. Maybe your handwriting is better than only your doctor's.

You encounter someone who talks a foreign language. You will check your dual language dictionary. You will make idiotic gestures. Mime a little. Draw a picture in the sand. But you will not write in your own language on paper. Not unless you are also going to lick a stamp.

"Please write down what you wish to say," I will prod as innocently as I can.

As often as not, you will wave my pad away and walk away. As often as not, you will walk off with my pen. Accordingly, I buy them by the dozen. I do not buy the cheapest kind, which would only aggravate your impatience. You do not struggle with a foreign language with peanut butter in your mouth.

Some years ago, in a Rome bistro, I asked for a cappuccino. The man behind the counter read my pad, roared, and showed it to other patrons. Did they find it hilarious that a Japanese tourist wrote in Italian? Actually, I'm Chinese American. In Europe, in America, in my hometown, I am a Japanese tourist, never a deaf person; but that's another story. In Paris a proprietor corrected, with proper Gallic indignation, my spelling when, hungry and jet-lagged, all I wanted was a ham sandwich. In Amsterdam I stopped a passerby for directions to a hotel and got the brush. Personally, I would commit the same breach of civility if a suspicious-looking character stopped me on a dark street, holding out some vague thing in his hand.

An acquaintance swore he once asked a stranger to please write what he wanted to say. This stranger who had been trying to be friendly looked at the pad, frowned, and wrote back: Can you read? No matter what can and will anyway happen, I feel vulnerable without my pen and pad. I did not have them with me at the Juarez International Bridge and was denied reentry into the United States. The midnight hike in Yellowstone was not much fun. Continuously on the move, through trees, up rocks, around the lake, I could not strike up any conversation with my hearing date, much less join the singing. On Waikiki, the pad got wet; at Black's Beach, it looked ridiculous.

Hearing people seem to have trouble accepting the fact that I can be deaf. They find it inconceivable that someone who does not hear through the ear and speak through the mouth can survive in a world of endless public announcements, nonstop music, and gadgets that do not function unless you answer the beep. I was in a Cleveland restaurant one night. I read the menu and, as is my wont, wrote my complete order down: Prime Rib, Chicago style. Baked potato. String beans. House dressing, on the side. Glass of house red. I showed the pad to the waitress when she returned. She read and wrote: You have a sore throat? It did not then occur to me to ask why she wrote back instead of spoke. Did she think if one has a sore throat, he would also have sore ears? I did leave a generous tip.

I have a well-trained family and friends. When they want to say something to me, they grab the nearest writing material in sight, be it a bill, an envelope, a magazine. A dull-point pencil, a crayon, a Mont Blanc. And scribble away. If there is nothing, they gesture Give-Me-Write, and I take my stuff out. My sister-in-law insists that I save every piece of conversation I have with anyone. She cannot bear to miss a word. I try to remember to remove certain parts the morning after. I do remember fondly a dinner party of eight, I being the only deaf person. Everyone had his or her own pad, legal size. The swapping went on all night. I love the left-handed. Right at the first meeting, they reach for my pen as if it is the most natural thing in the world to do. We have the best conversations.

There are times when I get tired of being deaf, tired of paper and ink, tired of frightening the unsuspecting. Play the other fellow's game and make a fool out of myself. Go along with the flow and end up in the wrong room, the wrong building, the wrong town. Nod, nod and miss the train. Let motorists asking for directions think I don't understand English. Ignore the row announcements for boarding the plane, not that it makes any difference as far as I can see, and hope there will still be room in the overhead bin. I might even run into someone brandishing a pen and pad.

As is so often the case in attempts by talented Deaf men and women to step outside the Deaf World for collaboration with the hearing, Deaf theater artists—and art—are caught between the widespread ignorance of hearing professionals and the lowered standards consequent on the Deaf community's linguistic isolation.

8

Away from Invisibility, Toward Invincibility

Issues with Deaf Theatre Artists in America

Willy Conley

1999

Deaf Theatre[1] and its artists in America seem to have reached a stagnant state, stuck mainly in churches, school cafeterias, gymnasiums, community centers, and small rent-a-theatres—performing for hidden, out-of-the-way Deaf communities and those with a special interest in the deaf. As Donald Bangs wrote, "A few Deaf productions have been successful, but, for the most part, theatre for Deaf audiences in America is a vast wasteland" ("New Ideas" 126). As a Deaf Theatre artist who works in both professional theatre and university theatre, I believe that the potential for Deaf Theatre is vast. Watching African American, Hispanic American, and Asian American theatre artists come of age in the entertainment industry, I sense that our time will come, too. That will not happen, however, unless Deaf Theatre artists regroup and make a concerted, driven effort to achieve a standard of excellence that equals or goes beyond the level of professional hearing theatre.

• Inherent Qualities of the Deaf Theatre Artist

Before we look at what standard of excellence needs to be established or what efforts need to be made, we should examine our natural resources. One of them is deaf children, who express the experience of their world through gestures, mimicry, movement based on innate rhythms, drawings, and paintings. In their essay titled "International Visual Theatre Research Community", Jean Grémion and Maurice McClelland noticed that "deaf children can do more precise imitations of people they meet briefly than most trained mimes. It is in fact that through this kind of imitation that they 'describe' who a person is to each other" (33).

51

Grémion and McClelland also observed that deaf people's intense reliance on visual perception is a "moment-to-moment reality" (33). Because subtle facial expressions and body movements are the foundations of sign language, the deaf often have a heightened ability to "read" human relationships, particularly in watching what hearing people's faces and bodies reveal during social encounters, hearing people being more conscious and in control of their voices than they are of their bodies.

Grémion and McClelland also observed that the Deaf have an increased sense of spatial awareness. Therefore, it almost goes without saying that a deaf actor naturally creates a visual theatre environment with the use of the entire body as means of communication, especially when communicating in American Sign Language (ASL). Imagine the theatre space around a deaf actor being filled by arm, hand, body, and face movements. Imagine further exploring this space by exaggerating and heightening ASL the way hearing playwrights would do with the English language; and then, to add stage business or movement in conjunction with ASL—already, a large amount of that empty stage space gets utilized and covered by movement.

I teach at Gallaudet University, the world's only four-year liberal arts college for the deaf. Large numbers of our students have good physical, gestural, and movement skills and the potential to capitalize on them. Many have a natural command of their facial expressions, their bodies, and their language—ASL. Most are quite creative in this respect. But when encouraged to consider a theatre career or take more theatre courses beyond the customary "Introduction to Theatre," most will decline. They say that either Vocational Rehabilitation (VR) or their parents will not support such a decision. The parents or VR counselors must assume that there is no market for deaf theatre artists: if theatre is extremely competitive for hearing people, then the competition has to quadruple for deaf people. Some of our graduates will go on to find nine-to-five jobs, performing skits or one-person shows at Deaf community events during their spare time. Others will just let their natural theatre skills fall by the wayside.

As sad as it is to see all this wasted talent, it is even more discouraging in light of the amazing number of hearing actors who are weak in the use of their faces and bodies but have nevertheless carved out a substantial career in the theatre. What they get by on is standing in costume looking interesting, and having that almost holy ability to speak the English language to those who adore hearing it, never mind how limited or awkward their movements on stage.

• Mining Undiscovered Deaf Territories: Exploration or Exploitation?

In *Johns Hopkins Magazine*, an article by Leonard Siger focused on the use of Deaf actors in classical dramas. Siger wrote that when hearing actors express their emotions, they should rely on attitudes and movements of the body. "Sign language when properly used links emotions to information in a way not possible in spoken language. True, the musical effects of spoken verse are not possible . . . but another kind

National Theatre of the Deaf actors hanging out during a fast-food and refuel stop. ©
Willy Conley.

of beauty is" (2). Siger goes on to say that in this age of "graceless oratory" from the
mouths of "mumbling protagonists" out of Hollywood, "we forget how important
manual gesture was in classical and Elizabethan drama" (2). This statement could be
applied to any drama put on stage. If actors are not going to fill the large stage space
with gestures, movement, or signs, then they might as well stand together in front of
a microphone and spout their oratories on radio.

In one of his many statements to the media about Deaf theatre artists, David Hays,
the hearing founder of the National Theatre of the Deaf (NTD), remarked:

> To me, there is something inexpressive, stilted, and almost boring about the [hear-
> ing] actor opening and closing a little hole in the lower middle of his face. Wonder-
> ful, meaningful noise emerges, but if only he could do that with his arms, his knees,
> his shoulders, his fingers—and have his full face not just "in support" but as
> something read. And with signing, every part of the body works to inflect color, to
> tilt the word towards full emotional meaning. (Qtd. in Baldwin 101)

It is strange that most professional theatres would shy away from the visual
potential of incorporating ASL and Deaf actors on the stage. Is it because of the
predominantly hearing audience? Fear of the unknown, of people who are different?
In her book *Theatre Games for the Classroom*, Viola Spolin, a world-renowned
pioneer in teaching *improvisation*, has an audience involvement exercise called "Deaf

Audience." Its focus is physically "communicating a scene to a deaf audience" (174). It is a wonder that hearing theatres do not take this further and perform plays in such a manner once in a while. It might be good for the hearing audience as well. The idea is not to dumb down the material but to find creative ways to make it visually accessible to all audiences, regardless of language background. And in the process, why not employ some deaf actors who can do this well?

Spolin's "Deaf Audience" ought to be called "Playing to a Global Audience." There must be something inherently intriguing about watching a performance without spoken language. So much of conventional hearing theatre in this country seems to be afraid of exploring this way of performing.

In a *U.S. News & World Report* article, director Peter Sellars made an apt remark: there is "an extra dimension in the work of deaf actors, who are aware of the miracle of getting an idea across" (Sanoff 83). He would know. He is one of those rare and daring directors who are not afraid to collaborate with deaf actors. Not only did he cast a Deaf actor, Howie Seago, in *Ajax* and *The Persians*, but he also collaborated with Deaf playwright Shanny Mow in a 1981 NTD production of *The Ghost of Chastity Past or The Incident at Sashimi Junction* (Kroll 79; R. Cohen 306; *National Theatre of the Deaf* 1993–1994). Regarding this collaboration, Mow, who is of Chinese descent, commented that since Sellars grew up in Japan, he was the perfect collaborator for this play with its Kabuki-Western motif. The men played women, and the women played men. (Incidentally, Seago acted in this production, too.) Mow remarked that he wrote the script in verse even though he did not have the properly trained ear for it, yet to his surprise, Sellars did not change a single word. They went with the script as Mow wrote it, while Sellars developed the lyrics for the storytellers/musicians, which were handled by two hearing actors. In retrospect, Mow seemed to underestimate his thespian abilities: "Did I really write that? Was I that good then? Did Peter take nothing and make something out of it?" A question Mow raised is one that all collaborators might want to face: Did we achieve the ideal collaboration when we couldn't tell who collaborated on what (Mow, E-mail)?

Another bold director, Robert Wilson, has worked with Deaf actors. He cast Howie Seago in *The Forest* in the role of Enkido, the story's hero. This play was based on the *Epic of Gilgamesh* and produced at the Brooklyn Academy of Music in 1988 with collaborators Heiner Muller and David Byrne (Barranger 104, 245).[2] In one of Wilson's early theatre works, he cast a young Deaf, African American actor named Raymond Andrews in *The King of Spain*. Andrews was also Wilson's inspiration for another play, *Deafman Glance*. About Andrews, Wilson remarked that people "thought the child was a freak or an idiot . . . he's developed another sense of seeing-hearing that's very amazing . . . a great knowledge of a mystical—there is—I don't think there's a child who is handicapped" (Brecht 429). Wilson is particularly interested in developing theatre pieces with individuals who have been restricted in their use of verbal language and have "compensated for this by developing awarenesses and sensitivities to non-verbal channels of communication that go unnoticed by people who use verbal language regularly" (Phillips 5).

Mark Medoff is another venturesome hearing theatre artist who has collaborated with deaf actors. After he wrote *Children of a Lesser God*, Medoff created the substantial role of Marieta, a deaf playwright, in *The Hands of Its Enemy* for Phyllis Frelich. As of this date, Frelich and Medoff are developing a new play titled *Gila*, which includes yet another new character for Frelich.

Michael Kahn, artistic director of the Shakespeare Theatre in Washington, D.C., cast several deaf actors for his productions over the past decade. One was Warren Snipes in the role of Puck in a Shakespeare-in-the-Park production of *A Midsummer Night's Dream*. Another was Mary Vreeland as Katrin in *Mother Courage and Her Children*, who went on to win the Helen Hayes Award for Best Actress in 1992. Most recently, for the September 1999 production of *King Lear*, Monique Holt was selected for the role of Cordelia, along with another deaf actor, Stella Antonio-Conley, as her understudy.

It would be nice to find more risk-taking writers and directors who want to work with people who have a unique perceptual sense. It is really wonderful that these well-known artists, knowingly or not, contribute to upgrading the status of Deaf Theatre artists. It is, however, worth noting that not one deaf director or playwright has yet been allowed the opportunity to make such contributions in commercial theatre (that is, if one does not count Mow, who wrote for NTD, a nonprofit theatre company). Certainly, the gold vein of Deaf Theatre and its artists is being quietly and hesitantly chipped into, but no one is rushing in to dig out the mother lode. It is disheartening to see Deaf Theatre artists employed only on one-time, pet projects of hearing theatre artists. A nagging thought persists regarding hearing directors' and writers' use of deaf actors for one-shot deals. The novelty of deafness and American Sign Language tends to wear off quickly. This raises suspicion about whether or not deaf actors are being exploited for mere spectacle.

• Creating Fair Assessment of Works by Deaf Theatre Artists

For Deaf Theatre artists to take advantage of their potential and rise up, they must seriously address some issues and explore possibilities for improvement. Critical and more appropriate standards of evaluation must be applied to their work, particularly when virtually no evaluators or reviewers have any background in sign language or Deaf culture.

Sometimes deaf playwrights wonder what hearing theatres and solicitors of play scripts think when they receive a script that calls for deaf characters. Are they thinking, "Well, not a bad script, but we have no deaf actors or directors in our theatre that can workshop this; none of the actors on file or in our company knows signs"? How many scripts by deaf playwrights have been turned down with this reasoning?

Another matter deaf playwrights wrestle with when submitting plays outside the Deaf Theatre circle is that sometimes their plays have visual nuances in their use of language and cultural allusions that are hard to envision from what is written on the page. How do hearing, nonsigning judges evaluate such plays? For example, Sign-

Willy Conley as Puck in the 1991 Westerly, Rhode Island, Shakespeare-in-the-Park production of *A Midsummer Night's Dream*. Photo from the author's private collection, courtesy of the Colonial Theatre.

Mime, a dying form of storytelling performance in Deaf culture, was used in a play I submitted for a grant. Since Sign-Mime is entirely visual, incorporating ASL elements, it cannot be written. The only way to remotely hint at its quality is to list English glosses to give the deaf actor a direction in which to go when developing a Sign-Mime piece on stage. An example would be something like the following:

1. Warship on the high seas
2. Fat captain looking through binoculars
3. Thin, bumbling sailor at attention next to him
4. Enemy warplanes in the air
5. Captain hands binoculars to sailor
6. Sailor looks through the wrong end, etc.

From this, the deaf actor would enact a visual story similar to the manner of film—a Sign-Mime trademark—using wide shots, medium shots, close-ups, slow motion, freeze-frame, and points of view. In essence, the actor becomes the film screen. On stage, the Deaf playwright's Sign-Mime story would be woven into the context of the play, much as a hearing writer weaves poetry or songs into a play. A Deaf Theatre artist reading the script would readily be able to visualize such a Sign-Mime interlude. A hearing reader of this script who had never seen Sign-Mime, however, would not be likely to grasp what would happen on stage at this point.

Suppose a deaf writer throws in some "signplay" (as in wordplay) in conjunction with the English language. Would a nonsigning judge or reader get it? What about double entendres? "Nice to meet [sign: SCREW] you" is a classic (and classically vulgar) sign example. You cannot appreciate the humor if you do not know signs, which lend themselves to mutual puns. Deaf playwrights put a lot of time and effort into inventing signplay, knowing that signing theatre artists and audiences appreciate the artistry, but it is lost on the reader who knows no ASL.

One way to achieve a fair assessment of works by Deaf playwrights would be to involve a native informant—someone like a Sign Master,[3] who is well versed in Deaf culture and theatre. A Sign Master could also assist in evaluating or reviewing the work of a Deaf Theatre company. Yet this simple expedient is rarely used. Two hearing adjudicators from the American College Theatre Festival (ACTF) came to a Gallaudet University student production that I directed in the fall of 1997. They evaluated the performance without the assistance of a Sign Master or a native informant. The crux of their feedback concerned sound-related issues and problems with the voicing of the deaf characters created by a group of hearing actors situated offstage. It actually did not dawn on the adjudicators that the Gallaudet audience was predominantly deaf. Not one comment was made on the use of ASL, which the cast and I spent many hours translating to as high and precise an art as possible. How could they evaluate the language aspect of the production when they did not know ASL? How can theatre critics in the media accurately review a sign-language production if they do not know ASL? Many try to hide their ignorance with time-worn clichés such as, "the sign language was absolutely beautiful—silent poetry in the air." For all they know a deaf actor could have flubbed some lines and merely moved the hands around in a manual gibberish to make it look as if something significant were being signed. I know—as an actor I have done this, and I have seen others do this, too.

• Creating Better Accessibility

While Deaf Theatre artists are thus denied access to knowledgeable and professional adjudication, they face a more subtle barrier to evaluation when they become intoxicated by the applause of their peers. When a sign language show comes to town, deaf people drink it all in, with little complaint about quality or flavor. It is hard not to be so intoxicated, because deaf entertainment is scarce, but now seems to be the time for Deaf Theatre and its artists to raise the level of mediocrity and stop being too pleased with what they have been doing.

First, we should look at where we have been. Deaf theatre artists seldom get the opportunity to be exposed to works outside their own small circle. This is not entirely their fault, of course, because as an audience member, it is difficult to watch hearing plays—most are completely inaccessible. Inaccessibility narrows the vision of Deaf theatre artists by making them work mostly with one another and view mostly one another's work. As a result, they are prevented from achieving the standard of excellence in their craft that would emerge in a wider field. Hearing theatre artists are relatively advanced in their field because they get to see lots of theatre anytime, anywhere, and accessibly. They do not even have to read a script before seeing a play!

Some hearing theatre performances are visually rich or nonverbal enough to be worth the time and ticket price for a deaf audience. In these cases, however, the problem lies in the deaf community having no way of knowing when and where such shows exist. Many of the deaf have been "burned" time and again by attending highly verbal and visually static performances and have simply stopped following production notices. To address this problem, I propose that theatre marketing administrators latch onto a theatre-savvy Deaf community liaison and use this person to tap into the Deaf network. The theatre can give the liaison a complimentary ticket or entry to a rehearsal for an upcoming show, which that person would then review for the Deaf community. Sign interpretation of spoken plays has been the "most widely known technique for making performances accessible to the deaf in the U.S." (H. Cohen 68). Yet, contrary to popular belief, simply providing sign language interpretation does not create equal access for deaf audiences. Interpreters are usually placed off to the side of the stage, where they sit or stand, immobile in a small spotlight, and translate the spoken text to the deaf audience during performances created chiefly for the hearing audience: that is to say, with a focus on speech rather than movement. For deaf theatre artists and audiences watching a sign-interpreted show is much like reading a script—it is not much help in getting what Philip Cook calls the "total theatre" experience. Cook pointed out in *How to Enjoy Theatre* that the playwright makes a concerted effort to engage all of the human senses in order to communicate with and stimulate a reaction from the audience (13). Technically, this is impossible to achieve for a deaf audience corralled off to a small section on one side of the theatre, their eyes darting back and forth between the interpreter offstage and the actors onstage. The rich language of the playwright gets watered down, and the subtleties in acting, directing, and design become lost.

Imagine watching an interpreter sign a line of dialogue from Caliban in *The Tempest*: "You taught me language and my profit on't is, I know how to curse" (translation: YOU FINISH TEACH-TEACH ME LANGUAGE, ME BENEFIT WHAT? ME KNOW-HOW SWEAR.) Doesn't exactly capture the rich beauty of Shakespeare's language, but at least it is practical enough to deliver the concept. The deaf audience member now has to figure out who said the line—was it Caliban, Prospero, or Miranda? Next, the line needs to be put into context. And then, very quickly, the audience member needs to look over to the group of characters to see what happened as a result of saying that line. Most good actors in Western theatre act on the line, so this bit of action gets finished by the time a deaf person's eyes return to the stage. All these wonderful missed actor-moments add up. It reaches a point where one just ignores the interpreter for a while and tries to enjoy the play on a visual basis. Eventually this becomes frustrating because the hearing audience will suddenly laugh or cry at something indecipherable to a deaf audience member. By the time the person looks over at the interpreter, the line has already passed through the interpreter's hands. In two hour's time the deaf audience has developed a major headache trying to put together a thousand-piece puzzle with a few main pieces already missing. And why would a deaf person bother to remain focused on an interpreter, "reading" signs throughout the whole play, when the reading could have been done in the comforts of home? In *The Essential Theatre*, Oscar Brockett wrote, "Most of us go to the theatre hoping to be fully caught up in the performance . . . too involved to pass judgment on what we are seeing" (23–24). I'd say most deaf people go hoping to be caught up, but end up playing catch-up during a performance. So much for willing suspension of disbelief! Everything becomes "disbelievable," no matter how good the production values.

It must be said in favor of sign-interpreted theatre that it works very well when a play is light in verbosity, has strong visual elements, and the interpreters are in good position in correlation to the stage and the deaf audience, and when they are well coached by a Sign Master.

An important, positive side effect of sign-interpreted performances is that they give the hearing audience exposure to ASL, which spills over to some appreciation of the Deaf and their culture. The downside is that the interpreters sometimes get all the credit for creating this beautiful "language in the air" because they are the ones in that little spotlight off to the side of the stage. Hearing actors have been known to fret over signed shows because they feel the audience is watching the interpreters, who are frequently more animated than the actors. A big controversy surfaced in New York City in 1996 at Jeremy Irons's live reading of *Lolita at 40*. He was bothered that a couple dozen deaf people showed up for a sign interpretation of his performance. He ordered them to go to the back of the theatre where the interpreters would not be a distraction for him and the audience. Irons was astounded that Deaf people would want to attend a reading (Thigpen 73). Interpreter placement is certainly a delicate audience-focus issue, especially for a one-person show—but to be astonished that deaf people have a desire to attend a reading? How many other hearing theatre artists think like this?

Instead of the expectation that theatres provide interpreted shows, it would be great if this money were used instead for rehearsal interpreters to put deaf actors on the stage. This would guarantee a steady subscription from a deaf audience, and not the sporadic attendance we have now. Oftentimes, I have been begged to come to a performance only because no deaf people were expected to show up for a scheduled interpreted show. It is humiliating and a sheer waste of time and money on the interpreters and Sign Masters who have already translated and rehearsed the script. Shanny Mow, former artistic director of Cleveland SignStage Theatre, told me once that the Americans with Disabilities Act should not be about trying to give the deaf access to hearing theatre. It should be the other way around—getting the hearing access to us. Change their attitude, not ours—we're fine (Mow, personal interview). In any case, the more theatre that deaf theatre artists and audiences have opportunities to see, the more sophisticated their aesthetics.

Shanny Mow, former artistic director of America's only professional resident Deaf Theatre, the Fairmount Theatre of the Deaf, now called Cleveland Signstage Theatre. © 1990 Willy Conley.

• Lack of Education and Training

An obviously important aspect of a Deaf Theatre artist's growth is education and training. Theatre conservatories and university programs have to be more open to the idea of allowing enrollment of deaf theatre students. How else can these aspiring theatre artists improve their craft, unless they are to go out on their own and learn on the job?

An example of failure to level the playing field between deaf and hearing theatre artists happened in 1989 when I applied for the M.F.A. Playwriting program at the Yale School of Drama. Several people, including David Hays, renowned former Broadway lighting and set designer, and Dennis Scott, the chair of Yale's graduate directing program, who had gone down to New York City to see my play off-off-Broadway, wrote glowing letters of recommendation to go with my application. They encouraged me because I had the acting background from NTD, could write fairly well, had a play being produced off-off-Broadway at the time, and . . . I was deaf. This last item, I was informed, might be a plus, since it was doubtful that Yale ever had a deaf playwriting student. This potential uniqueness might get them to take me under their wing. After all, Yale had recently established, under then artistic director Lloyd Richards's guidance, a reputation for developing minority playwrights, particularly African Americans.

A letter soon arrived inviting me to meet Milan Stitt, the playwriting chair, for an interview in New Haven. For political reasons, I decided not to bring an interpreter along. It might have made me look too dependent and needy. On the day of the interview, I found Stitt easy to lipread and was comfortable with the way we communicated. Despite some illegal, personal questions such as, "How did you become deaf?" Stitt and I seemed to really hit it off. A few weeks later I received a double whammy of a rejection. One was a form letter from the Drama School, the other a personal letter from Stitt, the principal tenet of which was that "we do not feel you have quite found your 'voice' " (Stitt). What a terrible choice of words coming from a Broadway-produced and published playwright!

Like a good trainer, Hays nursed my wounds. One day after a performance, he came up to me and asked, "How would you like to go to Boston University and try to get into Derek Walcott's graduate playwriting program?"

"Sure," I said. "Who's Derek Walcott?"

Within a year, Walcott accepted me. He shared his phenomenal sense of poetry, playwriting, and humor with me in class and over occasional dinners. Toward the completion of my degree, he produced a one-act play of mine in his Boston Playwrights Theatre. I left the program with a master of arts degree, feeling proud and respected. And Derek went on writing, publishing, teaching, painting, and received a Nobel Prize for literature in 1992.

But the one thing I wished I could have gotten out of Walcott's program was more feedback on inherent poetic and visual elements in my scripts when it came to the use of ASL. Derek was extremely helpful from an aural point of view, having come from a strong background in the oral tradition of literature. Unfortunately, writing for the ear is not one of my strong suits.

It is not hard to imagine the struggles that other aspiring deaf theatre artists face if they want to enroll in a theatre degree program. A few years ago, I received a letter from a lawyer in Florida who represented a deaf client from the University of Miami. The client wanted to study in the theatre program but was rejected because of his deafness. He would not be able to pass crucial classes such as music and voice. As a professor at Gallaudet University, I was asked to be prepared for a deposition in which I would justify the capability of a deaf student to succeed in such a program. Fortunately, I didn't have to. Miami dropped the case and settled out of court in the student's favor. It is dispiriting to wonder if many other theatre programs in this country have this attitude. For those interested, the following universities have been known to accept deaf students into their drama programs: American University, Arizona State University, Boston University, California State University at Northridge, Catholic University, Connecticut College, New York University, SUNY Purchase, Towson University, University of Texas at Austin, and Wesleyan University (Connecticut), as well as Gallaudet University.

Tim McCarty, theatre arts educator and former artistic director of the Model Secondary School for the Deaf[4] performing arts program, has agreed that exemplary theatre programs in this country are not receptive to applications from deaf students, leaving Deaf Theatre artists not only without professional training but also without knowledge of protocol. McCarty, who is hearing, claimed to have heard occasionally from hearing theatres that they were put off by an incoming Deaf Theatre's unfamiliarity with jargon and lack of knowledge regarding theatre protocol, which made them look unprofessional and uncooperative. Also, since Deaf Theatre personnel tend to lack management experience, their productions have a "spit-and-paste" look—the goal being to get the show up and to try to keep it going for as long as the paste holds up. Most end up having a "community theatre feel" to them. Not much thought goes into budgeting, marketing, and long-term planning. If Deaf Theatre is to be accepted in the general population as well as the professional theatre community, there must be consistent productions of quality (McCarty, E-mail).

Dramaturges, script readers, grant evaluators, and new-works festival judges should be more aware and receptive of the cultural and linguistic background of prospective deaf playwrights who submit scripts. It goes without saying that rejection is part of the business, but sometimes it is hard to distinguish whether a rejection was the result of ignorance and discrimination or lack of artistic merit.

Other minority groups, many far less theatrically disadvantaged than the deaf, have access to earmarked grants or set-asides. A look through editions of *Foundation Grants to Individuals, Writer's Market,* and *Dramatists Sourcebook* for awards and fellowships reveals that there is a grant or scholarship for every possible human category except for the deaf—single mothers, the elderly, women, Cubans, Irish Americans, Armenians, Jews, African Americans, Native Americans, Polish Americans, Texans, Asians, Scandinavians, gay men, and lesbians. (A side note—there is an incredible amount of available funds for composers, musicians, and singers.)

Maybe it is time to pull out the affirmative action card. If it is done in the regular workplace, it ought to be done in the artsplace. The *Gallaudet Encyclopedia of Deaf People and Deafness* contains this unfortunate fact: "no play with a deaf theme written by a deaf playwright has been produced by commercial theatre" (Van Cleve 290). That statement was published in 1987 and is still true as I write twelve years later.

• Suppressing Opportunities

If there has ever been a place that needed the gavel of affirmative action to keep the competition fair and square, it is casting. For any deaf role that needs to be filled in theatre or in film and television—cast a deaf actor, not a hearing one. Hollywood has a horrendous reputation for casting hearing actors in deaf roles.[5] David Hays said it succinctly: "casting performers who can hear in deaf roles is like putting a white actor in blackface to play Othello" (qtd. in Sanoff 84). The theatre is guilty of the same thing. At the 1984 American Theatre Association convention, Phyllis Frelich gave an impassioned presentation about hearing actors who were still being cast to play deaf roles in various offshoot productions of *Children of a Lesser God* (Pearson-Davis 15), despite the playwright's insistence that "in *any* professional production of this play . . . the roles of Sarah, Orin, and Lydia [all deaf] be performed by deaf or hearing impaired actors" (8). Yet why do hearing directors still cast hearing actors for deaf roles?

Roles for deaf actors are not publicized like those for the hearing in issues of *Daily Variety, Drama-logue*, or *Backstage*, so deaf actors are not going to be reading the trades, which they gave up on long ago.[6] Besides, casting agents don't want to bother with deaf theatre artists—it's the old saw, "they're not marketable."

In "The Power of Unspoken Words," Alvin Sanoff writes, "Directors and producers who work with the deaf say reluctance to hire them stems from the days when they were regarded as stupid or retarded" (84)—not surprising, since many people still have this stereotype of the deaf. The condescension in hearing theatre is ironic, though, considering that it is supposed to be the most liberal-minded of professions.

Sometimes it is not "them"; it is "us." We Deaf Theatre artists need to take a hard look at how we can move toward more solidarity and networking and away from back-stabbing or shortchanging one another. Such short-sighted acts range from Deaf West Theatre in Los Angeles shying away from new works by deaf playwrights to actors keeping information about an audition to themselves in the hope that they will be the only ones to try out for a deaf role. They end up hurting the rest of us, because casting directors are left with so few choices that they may well end up casting a hearing person.

• The Key of Collaboration

My own experience suggests that the only way to break into the mainstream of professional theatre, gain artistic and management experience, and raise standards for Deaf Theatre is collaboration. There is a growing trend of Deaf Theatre artists being invited to become associate artists with regional theatres, but this has come after these artists were aggressive and aware enough to find the key to the proverbial backstage door. My invitation to become an associate artist with Center Stage in Baltimore stemmed from a connection with a fellow M.F.A. theatre student at Towson University. The graduate student and I were taking a dramaturgy class when one day she announced to the class that Center Stage, where she worked full time, was interested in reading new plays for a possible staged reading of graduate writings. Immediately, I followed up on this by giving her my latest play, which ended up being selected. Irene Lewis, the artistic director, saw the staged reading and was impressed enough to invite me to join the ranks of Center Stage's Associate Artists. This was a turning point that led to my receiving, with Center Stage, a PEW grant from the National Theatre Artist Residency program, allowing me to develop new plays with financial support in exchange for helping the theatre conceptualize new ways of including Deaf theatre artists in their future productions.

Professional theatres should also take the initiative to seek out long-term collaborations with Deaf Theatre artists. New artistic territories could be explored, particularly in visual, movement theatre. This would inevitably expand not only a theatre's subscription lists but also its range.

If more collaborations were to develop and be well publicized through major media sources nationwide, they would serve as models for other theatres in metropolitan areas with a substantial deaf population. Commercial theatres may find that they can boost ticket sales once the deaf community finds out. A theatre's range of play choices could be diversified by incorporating more visual theatre elements, which would naturally develop from working with a deaf actor, director, designer, or playwright. Once this happens, perhaps Deaf Theatre and its artists will move forward and upward to receive the acceptance and support now granted to minority theatre groups such as blacks, Hispanics, Asians, gays and lesbians, and women, rather than remain stuck in their ghetto state or slowly die off.

• Looking Beneath and Beyond

To avoid ghettoization, even extinction, we should turn to our natural resources and devote more attention to nurturing the artistic growth of our Deaf youth and students, especially in the theatre arts. We should do all we can to encourage and support high-profile hearing theatre artists in employing professional deaf theatre artists. And while they are at it, the hearing theatre artists ought to widen that spotlight on themselves so that the Deaf theatre artists are in it, too. If the media want to review the works of deaf theatre artists, they should invite along a native informant, such as a theatre-savvy deaf community liaison. The same should go for adjudicators and script readers. Most states have a deaf association or a deaf school or program with strong connections to the deaf community. Word can get out fast on a need for a theatre liaison, who could serve many functions. As more people see the potential for visual theatre and the capabilities of professional deaf theatre artists, the minds in control of various theatre training grounds will also open up.

Eventually, a more sophisticated deaf and hearing audience will develop that, in turn, will produce a stronger demand for quality signed or visual performances. Deaf theatre artists will need to assume more responsibility by aggressively seeking opportunities at their local professional theatres. These theatres should work harder at supporting fellow deaf artists, knowing that to do so is beneficial for all in the long run. Networking and support within Deaf Theatre and among its artists should become an important priority now that access to the Internet has lowered communication barriers.

If all of this could be made to happen, Deaf Theatre and its artists would surely emerge from their invisible state into one that is invincible. As it stands, it is a shame that this country is overlooking a potential visual theatre gold mine. Right now, it looks like a vast wasteland. If only people looked beneath the surface.

NOTES

1. This generic term tends to be used interchangeably with Sign Language Theatre, Sign Theatre, Silent Theatre, Theatre of the Deaf, Theatre for the Deaf, and Deaf Drama to represent theatre that involves deaf artists and sign language to some extent. For the purposes of this paper, I will simply use this term.

2. Barranger did not identify Seago as being deaf. In some ways, it is a credit to Seago that he has done so well as an actor in his own right, without any mention of his deafness. In other ways, it is somewhat unfortunate that he is not recognized in publications as one of our leading international male deaf actors. Seago was featured in a main role as a deaf father in the 1998 Oscar-nominated German film *Beyond Silence*. Sign language, gestures, and Deaf culture were major contributing factors to the film's success.

3. Sign Masters tend to be Deaf consultants knowledgeable about theatre and sign language translation. They make sure the interpreters' appearance, light levels on them, and their positioning by the stage are all appropriate. Also, they study the play, watch several shows with the interpreters practicing the translations, and provide feedback. A good theatre will hire a Sign Master along with the interpreters to ensure a high-quality sign-interpreted show.

4. MSSD, located on the campus of Gallaudet University, used to have the premier performing arts program of all the deaf high schools in the United States. The most recognized graduate of the program is Terrylene, who was featured in *Cagney and Lacey, Natural Born Killers, Beauty and the Beast*, to name a few. Another successful graduate, Michelle Banks, a Deaf African American, formed Onyx Theatre in New York City. Monique Holt, another

graduate, well known for her silent, ASL-only cornflakes commercial, formed Artists-in-Motion, a theatre arts advocacy and referral group that supports deaf theatre artists. Unfortunately, in 1996 the MSSD administration shot themselves in the foot when, for unclear reasons, they cut the funds for the performing arts program.

5. The list of miscasting is long, going back as far as Jane Wyman in the title role of *Johnny Belinda*. To name a few others: Alan Arkin in *The Heart Is a Lonely Hunter*; Patty Duke in *The Miracle Worker*; Gene Wilder in *Hear No Evil, See No Evil*; Amy Irving in *Voices*; Rob Lowe in *The Stand*; Liam Neeson in *Witness*.

6. Nowadays, casting notices are being disseminated with more advance notice via the Internet from organizations such as the Deaf Entertainment Guild in Los Angeles and Tim McCarty's organization, Quest: Arts for Everyone, in Maryland.

WORKS CITED

Baldwin, Stephen C. *Pictures in the Air: The Story of the National Theatre of the Deaf.* Washington, D.C.: Gallaudet University Press, 1992.

Bangs, Donald R. "New Ideas, New Directions in Deaf Theatre." *Deaf Studies: What's Up. Conference Proceedings, October 24–25, 1991.* Washington, D.C.: Gallaudet University College of Continuing Education, 1992.

Barranger, Milly S. *Theatre: A Way of Seeing.* 3d. ed. Chapel Hill: Wadsworth, 1991.

Brecht, Stefan. *The Theatre of Visions: Robert Wilson.* Frankfurt: Suhrkamp, 1978.

Brockett, Oscar. *The Essential Theatre.* Orlando: Harcourt, Brace, Jovanovich College Publishers, 1992.

Cohen, Hilary U. "Theatre by and for the Deaf." *TDR: The Drama Review* 33, 1 (1989): 68–78.

Cohen, Robert. *Theatre.* Mountain View: Mayfield Publishing Co., 1997.

Cook, Philip. *How to Enjoy Theatre.* Essex: Piatkus, 1984.

Dramatists Sourcebook. New York: Theatre Communications Group, 1989.

Foundation Grants for Individuals. New York: The Foundation Center, 1988.

Grémion, Jean, and Maurice McClelland. "International Visual Theatre Research Community." Paris: International Theatre Institute, 1976.

Kroll, Jack. "Ajax Updated." *Newsweek*, 26 June 1986: 79.

McCarty, Tim. "Re: Deaf Theatre." E-mail to the author. 25 April 1998.

Medoff, Mark. *Children of a Lesser God.* New York: Dramatist Play Service, 1980.

Mow, Shanny. E-mail to the author. 30 April 1998.

———. Personal interview. 21 April 1998.

The National Theatre of the Deaf 1993–1994, n.p.

Pearson-Davis, Susan. "Working with Deaf and Hearing Actors in the Same Cast Even if You Don't Know Sign Language." *Youth Theatre Journal* 1, 1 (1986): 15–19.

Phillips, Jerrold A. "Strategies of Communication in Recent Experimental Theatre." *Proceedings of Speech Communication Association in Convention, 4 November 1978, Minneapolis, Minnesota.* ERIC fiche ED165212, grids 2–16.

Sanoff, Alvin P. "The Power of Unspoken Words (Deaf Actors in Plays and Movies)." *U.S. News & World Report* 101 (1986): 83–84.

Siger, Leonard. "The Silent Stage: Classical Drama and the Deaf." *Johns Hopkins Magazine*, 12, 1 (1960): 11–19.

Spolin, Viola. *Theatre Games for the Classroom*. Evanston: Northwestern University Press, 1986.

Stitt, Milan. Letter to the author. 9 April 1990.

Thigpen, David. "Irons in the Fire." *Time* 148, 3 (1996): 73.

Van Cleve, John, ed. *Gallaudet Encyclopedia of Deaf People and Deafness*. New York: McGraw Hill, 1987.

Writer's Market. Cincinnati: Writer's Digest Books, 1998.

SELECTED LIST OF WORKS CONSULTED

Baldwin, Carol Hart. "An Evaluation of a Theatre Production on the Communication Skills of Post-Secondary Deaf Students." Research Project Report, University of Texas of the Permian Basin, 1985.

Carlson, Susan. "Collaboration, Identity, and Cultural Difference: Karim Alrawi's Theatre of Engagement." *Theatre Journal* 45 (1993): 155–173.

Chaudhuri, Una. "The Future of the Hyphen: Interculturalism, Textuality, and the Difference." In *Interculturalism and Performance*, ed. Bonnie Marranca. New York: PAJ Publications, 1991.

Chin, Daryl. "Multiculturalism and Its Masks: The Art of Identity Politics." *Performing Arts Journal*, 14, 1 (1992): 1–15.

Marranca, Bonnie. *The Theatre of Images*. New York: Drama Book Specialists, 1984.

———, ed. *Interculturalism and Performance*. New York: PAJ Publications, 1991.

Miles, Dorothy May Squire. "A History of Theatre Activities in the Deaf Community of the United States." M.A. Thesis, Connecticut College, 1974.

Tadie, Nancy Bowen. "A History of Drama at Gallaudet College: 1864–1969." Ph.D. diss., New York University, 1978.

Toomer, Jeanette. "Multicultural Theatre." *Back Stage* 37, 34 (1996): 30–32.

Lost among the hearing, who more often than not are our own parents and children, some Deaf people form Deaf adoptive families as both a rescue operation for Deaf children and an amelioration of life in the diaspora.

9

This Child Is Mine

Deaf Parents and Their Adopted Deaf Children

Barbara J. White

1999

- Two couples, one Deaf and one hearing, applied to adopt a Deaf child through the same public child welfare agency. Although both couples met the qualifications of the agency and had a completed home study, the social workers on the case were hesitant about placing the Deaf child with Deaf parents, due to an assumption that the child would not be exposed to spoken language. The Deaf parents had to organize the advocacy efforts of Deaf leaders and organizations to convince the agency that they were the best "match" for the child. The child has been in their family for nearly ten years.

- A hearing couple applied to an adoption agency and an infant child was placed in their home. When the parents discovered the child's deafness, the couple contacted the agency and requested the adoption be terminated. Soon after that, the agency found a Deaf couple who wanted to adopt the child. The child has now graduated from college and become a professional.

If the social workers working on the above cases had knowledge about the competence and abilities of Deaf parents, the credibility of American Sign Language, and more appreciation of Deaf culture, they might have actively sought out Deaf parents from the beginning.

At a meeting I attended some years ago on adoptive families, a social worker told me she thought it would be better for Deaf children waiting for adoptive homes to be placed with hearing parents and siblings so they would be exposed to spoken English and have a better chance for success "in the hearing world." I was stunned by this lack of sensitivity on the part of another social worker. After all, the National Association of Social Workers Code of Ethics obligates the profession to a respect and appreciation for human diversity and cultural competence. I feel strongly that any social worker involved in arranging an adoption of a Deaf child should consult with the Deaf community, or Deaf social workers if they are available, about the placement decision. I told the social worker that I felt spending time interacting with Deaf people and learning more about Deaf culture would put professionals in a better position to make an informed adoptive placement decision for a Deaf child. My response was not what the social worker wanted to hear—most social workers have heavy caseloads and high stress and cannot take the time to go out and learn about the Deaf community or take up ASL in their "free time."

Despite all the societal changes that have taken place in the past decade—the Deaf President Now movement, increased interest in American Sign Language and Deaf culture, and awareness of civil rights laws such as the Americans with Disabilities Act—social workers and other professionals still show their hearing ethnocentric bias when it comes to understanding Deaf people and their culture.

A few years ago I presented a workshop for social workers on Deaf adoptive families at a national adoption conference. In the workshop I brought the "Deaf community" to the audience of social workers in the form of a home video I had taken of a Deaf adoptive family (with their permission) interacting at the dinner table. I decided the best way to explain to hearing people the smooth interaction that can occur when every family member can interact and participate equally in daily family discourse was to let them see for themselves the lively interaction of the Deaf family in the video. I wanted the participants to gain insight into the specialness of communication when everyone in the family is Deaf and shares the same language, and to see that in Deaf-parented families, the Deaf child is fully included in the conversation. The videotape moved me, especially because I grew up in an all-hearing family and my frequent complaint (which is all too common by Deaf folks in hearing families) was that I was either ignored or told that the topic was "not that important." However, I could not tell if the audience was as moved by the video as I was because they became rather passive and did not ask me many questions. Perhaps anecdotal evidence was just not powerful enough to break through their hearing biases. Most professionals still believe that Deaf children should be exposed to spoken language in the family setting at all costs. This belief system among professionals has resulted in too many adoptive placements of Deaf children with hearing families who have no knowledge of ASL or exposure to Deaf culture. More recently, Deaf children are being adopted by well-meaning hearing people who have plans to have their newly adopted Deaf child "cured" by the cochlear implant surgery. This hearing bias has also been at the bottom of a number of unfortunate court cases where Deaf parents have been denied custody and adoption rights of their children by narrow-minded judges (Gilhool and Gran, 1985; Perl, 1994).

Realizing that I had no "hard data" or empirical research to support my position that Deaf adults should be matched with Deaf kids needing adoptive placements, I decided to do my doctoral dissertation by collecting data from Deaf parents who already had adopted Deaf children in the United States. I found fifty-five such families who agreed to participate in the study. The study explored several variables that I thought were important—Deaf parents' perception of social support they got for their adoption (informally from friends and family and formally from the adoption agency), the family's overall functioning, and the sense of entitlement Deaf parents have for their Deaf child. This discussion focuses on the concept of entitlement.

• What Is Adoptive Parent Entitlement?

The concept of adoptive parent entitlement is highly relevant when considering where a Deaf child should be placed, because it illuminates issues related to the Deaf child's "best interest" and the "goodness of fit" between the child and adoptive parent.

Adoptive parent entitlement means that the adoptive parents feel they deserve their child. Even though their child is not biologically theirs, they have a strong belief that they have the social, legal, and emotional right to take full parental responsibility for and to attach to their adopted child. They feel unconditionally that the adopted child is really theirs and belongs in their family (Smith and Miroff, 1987; Melina, 1986; Johnston, 1992; Denhalter, 1994). This may seem like a "given" to many biological parents, but in fact, establishing a sense of entitlement is an extra psychological leap that adoptive parents must take, because the reality is that the child is genetically linked to another set of parents. Indeed, another woman gave birth to their child. In our society, adoption is viewed as a "second best" way of forming a family, and the expression "blood is thicker than water" runs deep. Most adoptive parents not only must deal with their losses associated with infertility but also must cope with the insensitive remarks of others regarding their adoptive status, such as "Is that child really yours?" A strong sense of entitlement is a significant factor in preventing the disruption of an adoptive placement and strengthening family functioning (Smith and Miroff, 1987; Groze, 1996). When the parents have a weak sense of entitlement, they may face a variety of family problems, including weaker bonding, an inability to use discipline effectively, prolonged grief at their infertile status, and an overriding sense of guilt that they somehow "stole" the child from the birth parents.

Because of the strong value the Deaf community places on Deaf children, I speculated that Deaf parents may have a strong and immediate sense of entitlement to their Deaf adopted children. After all, many accounts of Deaf parents hoping to give birth to a Deaf child, and their joy when their child is diagnosed Deaf, are in the literature (Lane, Hoffmeister, and Bahan, 1996). So, in addition to a quantitative survey of Deaf parents nationally (n = 55) that measured social support, family functioning, and entitlement, I conducted qualitative interviews with seven Deaf adoptive mothers to gather richer descriptions of these variables. The finding that entitlement is exceptionally strong among Deaf parents adopting Deaf children did not surprise me. But it did provide empirical evidence that this factor should be given strong consideration by social workers making adoptive placement decisions for Deaf children.

• Themes about Entitlement in Deaf Adoptive Families

There were ten dominant themes that captured the concept of adoptive parent entitlement in my study—communication, bonding and attachment, identification, competence and caregiving, limited opportunities, spirituality, adoption story, and hearing status. The interviews revealed that Deaf parents' sense of entitlement was exceptionally strong and appeared to be reciprocal; both parent and child felt they belonged to each other. The Deaf parents in this study put a priority on establishing bonds with their children, providing role modeling for communication success, and instilling a sense of normalcy as Deaf people in society.

The commitment of the Deaf adoptive parents in this study to provide their Deaf child with a symbolic language system was profound. These parents focused intensely on language and social development to help their children make up for the valuable years they missed in their earlier hearing environments. In spite of the many language delays of their Deaf children, these Deaf parents were determined to help their children catch up by using creative approaches to help their children learn ASL and English simultaneously. For example, some parents used flash cards with printed words and pictures, and then they added the ASL sign to the word. They also made it an important part of their lives to expose their Deaf children to other Deaf friends and relatives and to read and tell stories in ASL. All of the children in the study came from a foster care or orphanage environment where each was the only Deaf child and had no meaningful communication with his or her caretakers. The interviews revealed that although language learning was a slow process, the children were benefiting from a symbolic communication system that they would not have had in their previous environments. Thus, in their new Deaf-centered environments, the messages these children received were positive messages of affirmation—that being Deaf is "normal" rather than "deviant."

The Deaf parents in the study also served as "buffers" from hearing environments (Hughes and Demo, 1989). The hearing environments were not overtly hostile, but the Deaf parents had to negotiate and make them more accessible. These Deaf parents were positive role models for their children, teaching them interaction strategies with hearing people.

All of the Deaf parents assumed a cultural construction of Deafness, they all had Deaf social networks, and they all used and valued American Sign Language. The stories they told reflected their own experience as Deaf persons and had a view of themselves as part of a cultural and linguistic minority group, rather than as persons with "hearing impairments" that should be cured. Although some of the children used hearing aids, the parents placed little importance on teaching their Deaf children to speak. Instead, the parents overwhelmingly placed a high value on ASL in teaching language visually. Because ASL is a defining value in Deaf culture, this is not surprising. All of the parents used ASL to help overcome the many delays their children experienced with language. Given encouragement and time, these parents saw ASL as the best path to language acquisition and opening up cognitive processes that allowed their children to make sense of their world. Some parents reported that after several years of exposure to ASL, their children were able to tell stories about their previous lives in their home countries and about their orphanage experiences, which helped them cognitively and psychologically to work through their sense of loss related to adoption. At the same time, the parents were realistic in not expecting overnight success, given the early lack of language that most of their children endured.

Entitlement was largely enhanced by the strong bond and communication that took place within these families. Deaf parents saw it as their responsibility to nurture their Deaf child in a visual communication environment and almost immediately attached to their child. These parents had a strong commitment to their child's education and often supplemented their education at home by providing structured literacy activities. Some parents moved to be closer to their child's deaf school, even before locating a job. Due to their own problems with special education systems while growing up, these parents were committed to providing their children with the best learning environment. These parents did not need the legal sanction of the courts to feel that their child belonged to their family. Entitlement appeared to be established even before the child arrived home; the parents commonly reported feeling an emotional connection when they first received a photo of their child and learned of the possibility of the adoption. The identification that these parents felt toward their child was also evident; most wanted assurance that their child was in fact Deaf before proceeding with the adoption. In contrast to the literature that reports that adoptive parents feel a tentativeness to their child or feel they "stole" the child (Reitz and Watson, 1992), the parents in this study readily assumed the role of parent, without any hesitation. One parent at first felt guilty about taking the child from his foster mother but quickly confirmed to herself that she was the best person to parent him because she was Deaf herself.

The quotes that follow are selected from the qualitative interviews of seven adoptive parents with an adopted Deaf child and demonstrate, through ten subthemes, the strong sense of entitlement in these "Deaf of Deaf" adoptive families.

Communication

All of the children were adopted from other countries, and all but two were adopted at school age. The children had little exposure to their home country's spoken language or to the sign language used by Deaf people there. The orphanages where they lived prior to placement tended to use an oral approach, so the children did not have exposure to a visual language system. Therefore, most of the children had no formal language system, which resulted in language delays in the majority of the children at the time of placement. Parents in general felt they gave their children the gift of a visual language, and the children absorbed this language input rapidly. This does not mean that the children had caught up totally with language development. Many children still had language delays because of their early language deprivation. All the parents nevertheless persisted in continuing the process of language acquisition through ASL, with the intent of transferring ASL to written English.

> He had no language when I adopted him, now it is very obvious how much he is delayed language-wise, but he is starting to use it more and more. I never gave up. I kept flooding him with experiences and language and stories and sign language, and he is now starting to use it to describe things that happened before being adopted. It's such a surprise, and a pleasure when he comes with these little gems completely out of the blue.

> I think that is the most important thing we've ever done is begin the communication process with her. She didn't communicate at all when we got her, then when we taught her signs, she was able to communicate her needs and wants instead of just crying all the time. That made me feel like I accomplished something as a parent, helping her break through that void, you know.

> She was very curious and inquisitive and asking us lots of questions. But I don't think she knew that we were Deaf, but somehow she knew that we were communicating with her like she had never communicated with anyone. She asked us about our relationship and she saw our hearing aids and asked us about that. . . . The staff [in the orphanage] were amazed that we could understand her so well.

Bonding and Attachment

This theme related to the parents' perceptions of the initial bonding process with their child, including learning about the child and bringing the child home, commitment to the child, ongoing attachment after placement, and feeling they had the authority to be the child's parents even before the adoption was legally finalized. Several parents said they were attached to their child the moment they saw the child's photo. Some of the most poignant discussions with parents concerned their perceptions of the initial attachment experiences, when they met their child for the first time. Some of the parents went to the child's country of origin, and some of the children were escorted by plane; all of the parents reported feeling an instant bond with their Deaf child, at the moment of meeting the child, or shortly thereafter. In most instances, the children were not aware right away that their parents were also Deaf, but they soon discovered this fact. Bonding and attachment processes for these parents and their children were closely related to the need of the child to communicate and the enthusiasm of the parent to provide the child with ASL, so he or she could begin meaningful communication and true symbolic interaction.

> It's hard to explain; for me, the attachment was instant. . . . I belonged to her and she needed me much more like a baby would. I think she needed that bond, she never experienced a mother, so she was hungry. I could not deny her that.

> The positive part is that I love this child to death. He is very difficult to raise, but I feel very attached to him and really love him. I get frustrated . . . but I do feel he is my child and I love him.

Identification

Deaf people strongly identify with Deaf children, even when they are not related to them (Lane and Bahan, 1998), and the data collected from this sample strongly support this. Many of the respondents reflected on their own experiences growing up Deaf, the isolation and loneliness they felt, and their strong desire for providing their child with better communication. Most of the subjects in the sample specifically requested a Deaf child to adopt, although two said they would accept a Deaf or a hearing child. One mother said she felt she was lucky because her agency would only place "special needs" children, and she was glad that deafness fit under this category because she preferred a Deaf child. Other respondents reported that the "perfect Deaf child" is hard to find; it was rare to find a Deaf child with no emotional or physical disabilities other than deafness, and prospective parents should be open to whatever challenges the Deaf child presents. These Deaf parents showed a keen intuitive sense about what their Deaf child needs and responds to, especially regarding communication.

> Well I know that he feels a bond with me because I am Deaf myself. That is clear in his behavior when he signs to me "same, same, Deaf" and [when planning to adopt a second child] he was very clear that he wanted a Deaf brother or sister.

> When we first read about her being available for adoption, the fact that she was Deaf made me feel very connected to her, and because I am Deaf I think that I will be a good mother because I know what her needs will be.

> I was able to share a lot about what it means to grow up as a Deaf or hard of hearing person without support and help the child with their identity.

> All these people around me were chatting in Spanish and I felt they were waiting for the "magic moment" and it did not happen. He sat on the floor. Finally I thought of an idea. I noticed his hearing aids and then pointed to mine so he could see them. I could see him staring at me and his thoughts about us both being Deaf. Finally, we started to bond with the feeling "Deaf like me" coming from him.

Competence and Caregiving

Denhalter (1994) reported in his study on adoptive parent entitlement that the tasks related to caregiving increase the parents' sense of entitlement. This was also found to be true in this sample; the normal processes of socialization, daily caregiving, and parenting responsibilities seemed to enhance feelings of competence. Of particular interest is the observation that these Deaf parents felt they were positive role models for their children, and that the opportunity to share their own experiences growing up as a Deaf person increased their sense of competence. This is reflected in respondents' comments about their role as advocates for their child, knowing about resources that were available to them, making a commitment to their education, and teaching values. Several parents made a point to move close to the residential school for the Deaf so the children could live at home, expressing concern that another institutional environment would be detrimental to their child's sense of permanency. These Deaf parents were sensitive to the child's losses and demonstrated much patience in helping the child adjust to the home environment. The researcher observed as well that all of the parents showed sensitivity to the child's native cultural heritage. Some families had items in their home representing the child's home country's heritage; several had made photo "life books" for their child that described the child's life up to the time of placement and after his or her arrival in the United States.

> I give him communication and I'm constantly teaching him. I teach him interaction and social skills, I teach him manners.

> I think I model for her the need to persevere and reach her goals, to feel proud of who she is, that she is capable, that she has rights the same as others. Also, that reality in some situations is not easy, some situations are not fair.

Limited Opportunities

This theme is demonstrated in respondents' reflections on what their child's life would have been like if they had not adopted the child. It may be typical for American parents who adopt internationally to feel on some level that they are rescuing their child from unfortunate political and economic circumstances, especially if they adopt from third world countries. The parents in the sample, however, talked considerably about oppression, discrimination, and low expectations, as well as the limited educational and employment opportunities for Deaf people in their child's native country. As one parent said, "If you have to be Deaf, it is best to be Deaf in America."

> It is very clear she would not have gotten an education and would have had a life of menial labor. . . . She would be cleaning homes, working in a factory maybe. I doubt she would have become literate.

> Another reason I feel entitled to her as my daughter is the knowledge that opportunities for Deaf people overseas, particularly in that country, are not good.

> I saw where she lived and it was a dismal place. I'm telling you, it was a small room with ten or fifteen other disabled children, and she was the only Deaf child in that room. I thought to myself, "What if we didn't take her?" She'd still be living there. . . . When I saw that, I felt instantly attached to her. I needed to take her home with me. . . . She needed a better life than that.

> We found out that in their country, Deaf people are on the fringes of society, they can't drive a car, they have low-paying jobs. They are really behind, like second-class citizens.

Spirituality

The adoptive parents in this sample were asked about the spiritual aspects of the adoption, or their sense that the match between parent and child was "meant to be" due to their belief in God, a higher power, or fate. The intention of exploring spirituality was twofold. First, Denhalter (1994) found in his qualitative study that adoptive parents' sense of entitlement comes from a feeling that it is "right" to be the parents of their child, and his respondents described this right in a spiritual sense. Second, the researcher's intent was to triangulate this finding with the spirituality factor from the Adoptive Parent Entitlement Scale, which she developed for this study. In general, all the parents in this sample had examples to share about a higher purpose for being matched with their child, either through God, a higher power, or fate. This spiritual connection seemed to strengthened their sense of entitlement to their child and provided them with a feeling of "rightness" to be their child's parents.

> I heard about him through a church . . . and the orphanage was in touch with the church and I think it was like minds coming together that way. I don't think I'm special because I adopted him. But I know God has a purpose for me.

> I almost feel like she was born to another woman who gave birth to her because I was not in the position to do that. . . . It was because I wasn't ready, someone else had to give birth to her. That's how I feel we came together.

> I just felt like it was the right time and the right place and we found her. That's how I would describe the feeling. . . . I am not a religious person by nature, but I do believe in having faith in one's life. . . . So I feel we were meant to be together.

Blood Ties

A question asked of the respondents was whether they had the experience of having difficulty accepting the child as their own because they were not related by blood. This question stems from the literature regarding the social importance in our culture of blood ties and from Kirk's (1981) work on the social stigma of adoptive parenting that challenges adoptive parents' task of establishing a firm sense of entitlement to their child. In this sample, none of the parents reported having strong feelings about the blood tie, and all showed an unconditional acceptance of their adopted child.

> I think of them as my children. I don't think of them not being mine due to blood.

> I never really thought along blood-related lines. It was just that she needed a Mom and Dad, and I felt really connected to her.

Adoption Story

Telling the child about her or his adoption is an important and sometimes difficult task for adoptive parents. Being able to acknowledge the existence of and talk openly and honestly about the child's birth parents, and being able to answer the child's questions about her or his past, allows the child to develop wholeness and an "authentic sense of self" (Lifton, 1994). Many of the adoptive parents in this sample were quite open with their children about their adoption and were prepared to explain their children's past circumstances to them, even though some struggled with whether to reveal painful facts about their child's birth parents, such as prostitution, attempted abortion, and abandonment. That these parents were in touch with this issue and prepared for it is impressive considering that, as a group, they had almost no exposure to educational workshops or conferences where this topic is often discussed. In addition, most of their Deaf children were young and had insufficient language to be able to grasp fully the complexities of adoption.

Several parents shared the photo albums and life books they prepared for their child to aid in telling the adoption story, which is often recommended by adoption experts (Schaffer and Lindstrom, 1989). In this way, adoptive parents act as their child's historian, providing the child with a life record and history.

> I took a lot of pictures of my child's home country so he knows where he comes from, and I have made contact with local people from there on the Internet. I log on to newspapers in that hometown, which have pictures and list events like carnivals.

One mother traveled with her child to her child's native country, visited the orphanage where she lived, and inquired as to whether the child's birth mother had expressed interest in making contact. All of the children had been in an orphanage or foster care before their placement, and this fact seemed to allow the adoptive parents to feel more strongly entitled.

> I was very open and honest with her from the beginning and we had some challenging and difficult discussions about her birth parents and her history even when she had very limited language. . . . One day she says, "Mother and father don't want me, why?" I believe that they probably wanted her very much and couldn't take care of her and that is basically what I have been telling her all along.

> One of the things we do on her birthday is put an extra candle on her cake to honor her birth parents for giving her to us. . . . She is still very young and still developing language, so I won't be able to explain that now. . . . We'll see what kinds of questions she has and move on from there.

Hearing Status

Respondents were asked to describe the "ideal" home environment for a Deaf child and whether they thought the adoptive parents should be Deaf themselves. This question was considered important in establishing a firm sense of entitlement, because research has established that Deaf children with Deaf parents outperform Deaf children with hearing parents on many measures of social and academic success. These parents' views on this subject highlight their beliefs about the unique qualifications of Deaf parents to adopt a Deaf child. In general, respondents conveyed a belief that the best environment for a Deaf child would be one where there was visual communication at all times, preferably with Deaf parents who use ASL. If the placement is with hearing parents, respondents felt that ideally the parents should be fluent in ASL and always use it at home. Additionally, respondents felt the home should be equipped with visual alerting devices, such as flashing phone and door lights and TTYs (teletypewriters), which are already part of a Deaf household.

> Our house is very accessible with flashing lights for the door, phone, fire and emergency procedures.

> Communication is a priority over anything else. If the parent can't sign with them and communicate, then that's no life for them. I've seen Deaf children with hearing parents and their parents don't sign.

> Yes, I feel very strongly it is most important for Deaf kids to be placed with Deaf parents first.

Another respondent who was not supportive of hearing parents adopting a Deaf child raised the issue of income in the cost of an adoption. Research has demonstrated the significantly lower incomes as well as higher rates of underemployment of Deaf compared to hearing people (Schein, 1989).

> I would say always, if other things are equal, it should be a home where at least one of the parents is Deaf, because in this situation there would be accessible communication all the time due to parents' signing. If both parents are hearing. . . . most of the time they won't be signing and the Deaf child would not have an opportunity for incidental learning that hearing children have in the home.

One respondent who felt strongly about Deaf children being adopted by Deaf parents related her sense of pride in being Deaf that she models for her children.

> I come from a Deaf family. I'm confident in my ability to function in both Deaf and hearing worlds. I feel confident when I take my kids out, we sign all the time. And if I can't understand hearing people, we find a way, and it's good my kids see that. When my kids sign in public and use their Deaf voices, even if hearing people make negative faces and show they can't understand them, they look confident and sign on and on anyway. That shows me they are confident about their deafness and their language. So, I'm teaching them coping skills as a Deaf person and functioning in the hearing world.

Finally, there was an appreciation of hearing parents who were willing to adopt Deaf children, as long as the hearing parents were willing to learn to sign, and an acknowledgment that the demand for adoptive homes is too great to dismiss qualified hearing parents.

> I don't think they [hearing parents] should be turned down, because if they are willing to learn sign, it is better than some hearing biological parents of Deaf children who refuse to learn sign.

Discipline

Comfort in handling discipline was identified in the literature as a strong indicator of adoptive parent entitlement (Cohen, Coyne, and Duvall, 1996). From the interviews, it appears that this sample had very little difficulty accepting their role as disciplinarians and felt comfortable with their authority as parents. The special challenge for these parents was explaining proper behavior to their children, who had limited language, and introducing discipline techniques that were new to them, such as "time out."

> I feel comfortable with the fact that I have control of situations or discipline overall without losing my temper, without being negative, without using violence.

> Both kids are from a corporal punishment environment. . . . We talk about appropriate ways of discipline. I've learned to teach my daughter breathing techniques and relaxation techniques to help her with her temper tantrums. . . . I explain my expectation and use time out. I give them choices and tell them the consequences and choose fair consequences. It works, but it's still a process of learning for them.

• Conclusion

Federal law requires that children waiting for adoptive homes must be placed and matched with parents who can provide the child with a healthy and safe environment and promote the child's well-being. Recent legislation now eliminates race and culture as primary factors in matching a child with adoptive parents, but it is my hope that the Deaf child's needs for a rich linguistic and cultural environment also will not be overlooked. These findings can potentially influence adoption policy and practice when Deaf children are involved. Deaf parents provide a rich language and culture for a Deaf child, have a strong sense that they are entitled to their Deaf child, and unconditionally demonstrate that the Deaf child belongs in their family.

REFERENCES

Adamec, C. 1998 (June). Bonding, attachment and entitlement. *Adoption Medical News*, pp. 1–6.

Arcari, T., and B. Betman. 1987. *Hearing impaired children in foster care and adoption: A profile*. Washington, DC: Graduate Studies and Research, Gallaudet University.

Cohen, N., J. Coyne, and J. Duvall. 1996. Parents' sense of "entitlement" in adoptive and nonadoptive families. *Family Process*, 35(4), 441–456.

Denhalter, P. 1994. Adoptive parent entitlement: An exploratory study. Unpublished doctoral dissertation, University of Denver School of Social Work.

Gilhool, T., and J. Gran. 1985. Legal rights of disabled parents. In S. Thurman, ed., *Children of handicapped parents: Research and clinical perspectives*, pp. 11–34. Orlando, FL: Academic Press.

Groze, V. 1996. Social support and the adoptive family. In V. Groze, ed., *Successful adoptive families*, pp. 101–116. Westport, CN: Praeger.

Hughes, M., and D. Demo. 1989. Self perceptions of Black Americans: Self-esteem and personal efficacy. *American Journal of Sociology* 95(1), 132–159.

Johnston, P. 1992. *Adopting after infertility*. Indianapolis: Perspectives Press.

Jones, E. 1995. Deaf and hearing parents' perceptions of family functioning. *Nursing Research* 44(2), 102–105.

Jones, T. 1996. America's first multi-generation deaf families: A genealogical perspective. In *Deafness: Historical Perspectives. A Deaf American Monograph*, 49–54. Silver Spring: National Association of the Deaf.

Kirk, D. 1981. *Adoptive kinship*. Toronto: Butterworths.

Lane, H., and B. Bahan. 1998 (October). Ethics of cochlear implantation in young children: A review and reply from a Deaf-World perspective. *Otolaryngology—Head and Neck Surgery*, 297–313.

Lane, H., R. Hoffmeister, and B. Bahan. 1996. *A journey into the Deaf-world*. San Diego: DawnSign Press.

Lifton, B. 1994. *Journey of the adopted self: A quest for wholeness*. New York: Basic Books.

Melina, L. 1986. *Raising adopted children*. New York: Harper & Row.

Perl, L. 1994 (August 5). Deaf couple says state took their children: Social workers acted without evidence, parents say in suit. *Detroit News*, p. B-1.

Schaffer, J., and C. Lindstrom. 1989. *How to raise an adopted child*. New York: Crown Publishers.

Reitz, M., and K. Watson. 1992. *Adoption and the family system*. New York: Guilford Press.

Schein, J. 1989. *At home among strangers*. Washington, DC: Gallaudet University Press.

Searls, S., and D. Johnston. 1996. Growing up Deaf in Deaf families: Two different experiences. In I. Parasnis, Ed., *Cultural and language diversity and the deaf experience*, pp. 201–224. Cambridge: Cambridge University Press.

Smith, J., and F. Miroff. 1987. Entitlement: Concept and process. In *You're our child: The adoption experience*, pp. 23–40. Lanham, MD: Madison Books.

White, B. 1990. Deaf adoptive parents: An untapped resource. Paper presented at the annual meeting of the North American Council of Adoptable Children, Milwaukee, WI.

———. 1997. Permanency planning for Deaf children: Considerations of culture and language. *Arete: Journal of the College of Social Work, the University of South Carolina* 21(2), 13–24.

II | "The noblest gift God has given to deaf people"

American Sign Language and Its Literature

Chuck Baird, Deaf actor and scenic artist, puts the finishing touch on the National Theatre of the Deaf's touring show title, which was handmade during rest stops with black duct tape and a razor knife. © 1987 Willy Conley.

10

The suppression of minority languages through compulsory public schooling in the majority language is regarded as a culture crime today but was universally practiced in this country against the Deaf minority for some seventy years. "The Preservation of the Sign Language" was delivered in American Sign Language on film in 1913 for the project of the same name, sponsored by the National Association of the Deaf. Intended as a sample of the "signs in their old purity" as used by the "old time masters," Veditz's language (and that of the other men filmed by this project) is not immediately comprehensible to native signers today.

The Preservation of the Sign Language

George W. Veditz

Translated by Carol A. Padden and Eric Malzkuhn

1913

Friends and fellow deaf-mutes,

The French deaf people love de l'Epée. Every year on the occasion of his birthday, they gather for festive banquets to show their appreciation that this man was born on this earth. They journey to his gravesite in Versailles and put flowers and wreaths on his grave to show their respect for his memory. They love him because he was their first teacher. But they love him even more for being the father and inventor of their beautiful signs.

For the past thirty-three years, with broken hearts and eyes full of tears, the French deaf people have watched as this beautiful *language of signs* has been snatched away from their schools. And for thirty-three years, they have striven, struggled, and fought for its restitution. But for these thirty-three years, their teachers have spurned them, refusing to listen to their pleas. Their teachers prefer instead to listen to the hard-hearted demands of people who think they know all about educating the deaf, but who know nothing about their thoughts, souls, feelings, desires, needs.

It is like this in Germany, too. The German deaf and the French deaf look up at us American deaf with eyes of envy, as a shackled prisoner might regard someone free to wander at will. They freely admit that the American deaf are superior in matters of intelligence, spirituality, worldly success, and happiness, and they admit

83

George Veditz. Photo courtesy of the Gallaudet University Archives.

that this superiority can be credited to—what? To one thing, that we may use signs in our schools. The French deaf people base their inferiority on one thing, the fact that the oral method must be used for teaching in their schools. They have eliminated fingerspelling; they have eliminated signs.

But we American deaf are now facing bad times for our schools. *False prophets* are now appearing, announcing to the public that our American means of teaching the deaf are all wrong. These men have tried to educate the public and make them believe that the oral method is really the one best means of educating the deaf. But we American deaf know, the French deaf know, the German deaf know that in truth, the oral method is the worst.

Our beautiful signs are now beginning to show the results of these efforts. These men are trying to remove signs from the schoolroom, from the church—from the earth. Our sign language is deteriorating. Old-time masters of sign such as the Peets, the Dudleys, the Elys, the Ballards are rapidly disappearing. In past years, we loved these men, the masters of sign. When they signed to us, we could understand them.

Fortunately, we have several masters of our sign language still with us. Edward Miner Gallaudet, who learned his signs from his father, Thomas Hopkins Gallaudet, and several others like Dr. John B. Hotchkiss, Dr. Edward Allen Fay, and Robert P. MacGregor are still with us. We want to preserve the signs as these men now use them, preserve them and pass them on to future generations. There are many now alive who have learned their signs from men like these. Many have tried to preserve and pass on their signs. But there is one known means of passing them on: through the use of *moving-picture films*.

Indeed, our National Association of the Deaf has raised a fund of five thousand dollars for this purpose. We have made a number of films. We have films of Edward Miner Gallaudet, Edward Allen Fay, John B. Hotchkiss, Robert P. MacGregor, and many others. I regret that we do not have twenty thousand dollars, for we could have used it all. If we had this amount of money, we could have performances in sign, sermons in sign, lectures in sign. And not only would the American deaf enjoy the benefits, but deaf people in Germany, England, France, and Italy would also see these moving-picture films. Fifty years from now, these moving-picture films will be priceless.

A new race of pharaohs that knew not Joseph is taking over the land and many of our American schools. They do not understand signs for they cannot sign. They proclaim that signs are worthless and of no help to the deaf. *Enemies of the sign language, they are enemies of the true welfare of the deaf.* We must use our films to pass on the beauty of the signs we have now. As long as we have deaf people on earth, we will have signs. And as long as we have our films, we can preserve signs in their old *purity*. It is my hope that we will all love and guard our beautiful sign language as the *noblest gift* God has given to deaf people.

Today, William Stokoe's Sign Language Structure *(1960) and* Dictionary of American Sign Language *(1965) are regarded as the foundation for modern sign linguistics, the establishment of ASL as a bona fide language, and the subsequent renaissance of natural sign languages and their literatures the world over. Ironically, however, because Stokoe was neither Deaf nor a trained linguist, nor even a skilled signer, most Deaf people who knew him when he was engaged in his germinal research considered it folly. This memoir was written for a Stokoe* Festschrift.

11

From Student to Professional

A Personal Chronicle of Sign Language

Gilbert Eastman

1980

• Introduction

Years ago the professionals in deafness gave their full attention to the *disabilities* of deaf people. Then came Dr. William Stokoe, a linguist who studied Sign Language; he gave his full attention to the *abilities* of deaf people.

In this paper I would like to talk about Dr. Stokoe as a college professor (even though he never taught me), as a colleague in the English Department (even though our offices were in separate buildings), and as an advisor on Sign Language. Also, a bit about myself as a college student, Sign Language instructor, stage actor, director, playwright, and professor of the Drama Department at Gallaudet College in Washington, D.C.

This paper will describe actual events at Gallaudet College. While I have relied on my memory for events of the last twenty-five years, throughout this history I quote from articles from *The Buff and Blue*, the Gallaudet student newspaper.

• Remembering . . .

One September day in 1952 I rode on a train to Washington, D.C., from a little town in Connecticut called Cromwell. I was on my way to a new world . . . away from my home, my family and my friends. I arrived at Union Station. On a paper pad I wrote with a pencil, "Gallaudet College," and I handed it to a cabdriver. He took me to the college without looking at a map. I got out of the cab and looked at the famous buildings . . . Chapel Hall . . . College Hall . . . Fowler Hall. The campus was beautiful and quiet. There was a farm behind the great buildings.

Some time later, an issue of the Buff and Blue (our student newspaper) announced . . .

> *This year Gallaudet is given the privilege to boast of its recordbreaking total of eighty-five new enrollees which includes forty-three men and forty-two women.*

I was one of the members of the Preparatory Class. . . . I was fascinated by the upperclass students' signing—there were flying hands everywhere. And I, too, had the opportunity to acquire "refined" Sign Language from college professors, especially Elizabeth Benson. Everything was so different from the American School for the Deaf that I had attended. Leonard Elstad was our college president then.

In the same *Buff and Blue* (*B & B*) issue another article stated:

Four New Members Added to Faculty

> The Buff and Blue Staff is very happy to introduce all of you to our four new faculty members.
>
> Dr. George E. Detmold, our new Dean of Instruction received his B.A. in 1938, his M.A. in 1940 and his Ph.D. in 1943 from Cornell University. He was an English Instructor at the Cornell University from 1939–1942. In 1941 he was called to active duty in the United States Army, where he served chiefly in China, India, and Burma until 1946. Upon completion of his Army career, he returned to Cornell, where he was once again an Instructor of English. In 1947, Dr. Detmold went to Wells College as an Assistant Professor of English. Then, in 1952, he went to Teacher's College, Columbia University as Assistant on Admissions and studied for a professional diploma in the administration of higher education.

I was told that Dr. Detmold was different; I did not understand what they meant. Maybe he was different from other Gallaudet professors. I decided not to bother with him and avoided meeting him. I went on with all of the traditional activities. The following month (November) there was a stirring talk.

STUDENT ONE: Have you read the Buff and Blue?
STUDENT TWO: What will become of Gallaudet College?
STUDENT THREE: I totally disagreed with him.
ME: Him . . . who?
STUDENT THREE: Detmold. D-e-t-m-o-l-d.

The announcement in the *B & B* was:

Dr. Detmold Gives Outline for New Curriculum Plan

Gallaudet College should have a new curriculum by September, 1953, according to Dr. George Detmold, Dean of Instruction. Plans now under discussion with the faculty, provide for a two-year program leading to the degrees of Associate of Arts and Associate in Applied Science, as well as a four year program leading to the Bachelor of Arts and Bachelor of Science degrees. There will also be a graduate program leading to the Master's degree in Education.

Dr. Detmold stressed that present plans are only tentative and are subject to modifications as the faculty work out details. Guiding principles in the construction of a new curriculum have been offered by two recent surveys of the College's offerings: the report of the Federal Security Agency in 1950 and the evaluation report made in 1952 by the Middle States Association of Colleges and Secondary Schools.

The fundamental purpose of a new curriculum, according to the Curricular Prospectus, now under discussion, is that it "should provide all our students with a basic training in the liberal arts, preparing them to assume intelligently, their roles as men and women in modern society and that (as far as our resources permit) it should prepare each of them for the profession or vocation which he is best fitted to follow."

The students' argument about the new curriculum lasted through the rest of the academic year. In the fall of 1953, the Gallaudet Freshmen invaded Dr. Detmold's office to protest his drastic changes in curriculum. . . . We were lost in chaos . . . we had to take brand-new courses that had never been offered before . . . we said that it was not fair to the past students. It was a tough program. We often planned a boycott which never happened. . . . Several months later we became used to the changes but we still did not like Detmold's transformation. Another protest arose when there was another announcement.

Fusfeld, Detmold Get Top Rank Promotions

Dr. Detmold, Dean of Instruction since 1952, has been named to succeed Dr. Fusfeld as Dean of the college. He will have supervision over all instructional activities.

I went through the Sophomore year with Detmold's modern curriculum. We complained constantly. We often threatened to leave the college. . . . I decided not to come back next year. . . . But I returned anyway. I declared art as a major in my Junior year. I began to like the college and became involved in several extracurricular activities. My favorite was the Dramatics Club and I was selected as the President. *The Buff and Blue* of October 1955 announced:

Gallaudet Faculty Boosted to Seventy

Gallaudet College, the world's only college for the deaf, has added twenty-four new staff members, including three replacements, for its ninety-second academic year, it was announced by Dr. Leonard M. Elstad, President.

The faculty now numbers seventy. There are eleven graduate, and 301 undergraduate and special students—the largest enrollment in the history of the Federally sponsored institution. The new staff positions are provided for in the expansion program recently authorized by the Eighty-first Congress.

Among the newcomers was someone named Stokoe:

William C. Stokoe, Jr. becomes Professor and Chairman of the Department of English. Formerly Chairman of the Wells College English Department, Professor Stokoe has a Ph.D. from Cornell.

STUDENT ONE: Wells College? I have heard of the name. Cornell, too.
STUDENT TWO: Detmold's friend!
STUDENT THREE: Not fair! Why did he hire his own friend?
STUDENT ONE: Oh, I see. Stokoe is Detmold's friend.
STUDENT TWO: I don't understand Detmold. He also hired several deaf professors.
STUDENT THREE: Maybe Detmold recognizes the skills of deaf professors but why did he hire Sto———e?
STUDENT TWO: I am not going to take a course under him.
STUDENT THREE: I heard he is a tough teacher.
STUDENT TWO: I prefer deaf professors in the English Department.
STUDENT ONE: Stokoe just learned Sign Language. Why should I waste my time watching him sign slowly and stiffly?

In 1956, the January issue of the *B & B* reported:

During the vacation Dr. Stokoe attended the annual convention of the Modern Language Association in Chicago. Dr. Stokoe has been appointed contributing editor of the forthcoming revised edition of John E. Wells' A Manual of Writings in Middle English.

STUDENT ONE: Why should he go to the convention? He wasted his time. He should have studied Sign Language during his Christmas vacation.
STUDENT TWO: I don't think he will stay here. Gallaudet students are too much for him.
STUDENT ONE: Hey! You know Detmold's new curriculum. Well, have you heard about the new plan for our campus? Elstad and Detmold's plan? (Shows him a ground plan)

STUDENT TWO: Wow! You can't call this Greater Gallaudet.

STUDENT ONE: I don't think E. M. Gallaudet would like it.

STUDENT TWO: I won't be surprised if Stokoe agreed with the Elstad-Detmold Plan.

STUDENT ONE: Let's look at the plan. Look! New classroom and lab building . . . P.E. building . . . Cafeteria . . . women's dorm . . . men's dorm. . . . Oh, no, speech and hearing center . . . even an auditorium.

STUDENT TWO: I can't believe it. Only 300 students here. Why do we need those buildings?

In the fall of 1956 I shouted: "Now I am a Senior! My last year at Gallaudet!" The new library was being constructed—a very modern building as opposed to the Victorian Gothic buildings. I was still in dramatic activities. . . . Several students still criticized their professors.

STUDENT ONE: Do you know why Stokoe has difficulty learning Sign Language?

ME: No.

STUDENT ONE: I don't believe he actually studies Sign Language. I have seen him practicing signing in his office in the basement of Kendall School. He tries hard to put signs in grammatical order.

STUDENT ONE: Maybe he knows signs but not the Sign Language.

ME: Give him time.

STUDENT ONE: Why doesn't he join us in the Reading Room every night? It is the best place to learn Sign Language. We often stay there all night and we sign and sign and sign about everything . . . international news . . . national . . . and of course, campus news. We often have good bull sessions, too. I think it is a good idea to have electricity turned off at 11 p.m. so we will move from our rooms to the Reading Room to talk.

ME: What does that have to do with Stokeo?

STUDENT TWO: (Corrects him) S-t-o-k-o-e.

ME: Stokoe.

STUDENT ONE: I came across an article in the *B & B* about him.

STUDENT TWO: Yes, I've read it.

STUDENT ONE: He joined the Washington Scottish Band.

ME: Scottish?

STUDENT ONE: Yes, and he wrote about Scotland. Read it.

> Dr. Stokoe was a member of a pipe band during the summer, the Clan MacNaughton, in Rochester, New York, and piped during his spare time. He is now piping for the Washington Scottish Band.
>
> He is also writing a bibliography of medieval Scottish literature for the Modern Language Association. He says that playing the pipes is a good change from studying Scottish Literature of 600 years ago and a good way of "blowing off steam." "What I like about playing bagpipes," he adds, "is that

I have to do so many things at the same time that it keeps me in condition for teaching."

ME: Very interesting . . .

STUDENT ONE: No, he's not interested in us. He prefers to learn piping than signing! No wonder he's a lousy signer.

One day in December 1956, I went to one of the art classes. The instructor came up to me and told me that Dr. Detmold wished to see me. I thought, "What have I done?" I was scared to go to the administration office . . . maybe, bad news from home . . . maybe, my courses . . . no, not my courses . . . why did he want to talk to me? . . . So I went to Dr. Detmold's office and he welcomed me, leading me to a chair. I sat down, shaking all over.

DR. DETMOLD: I remember you when you were in *Macbeth* two years ago.

ME: Yes.

DR. DETMOLD: I really enjoyed helping the cast and coaching those two players in fencing. Remember? I saw you perform a small part . . . Seyton. I was pleased with your performance.

ME: Thank you.

DR. DETMOLD: You have always worked in student productions and you were president of the Drama Club. Right?

ME: Yes.

DR. DETMOLD: (Pauses) Well, I have been thinking . . . hmmm . . . for a long time . . . of a person . . . a deaf person, I mean . . . who might be interested in teaching drama at Gallaudet.

ME: Oh?

DR. DETMOLD: Are *you* interested in teaching drama here?

ME: Me???

DR. DETMOLD: Yes.

ME: But . . . but I'm majoring in art.

DR. DETMOLD: Great. You can major in drama at Catholic University.

ME: Me? At a hearing college? Impossible! No. No. I can't.

DR. DETMOLD: Sure you can.

ME: But . . . I already have a job ready for me in Hartford . . . as a commercial artist at the Travelers Insurance Company.

DR. DETMOLD: I see . . . Well, it's up to you.

ME: It's hard to make a decision.

DR. DETMOLD: You don't have to make it now. Come back next month and let me know your answer.

ME: May I ask you a question?

DR. DETMOLD: Sure.

ME: If I stay here, where will I teach? And for which department?

DR. DETMOLD: The English Department. Dr. Stokoe will arrange everything for you.
ME: Oh, I see . . . thank you. I'll be back in January. I'll talk it over with my family.

I went out of his office, thinking, "Stokoe, no, no, no, Stokoe, no, no, no. Should I accept Detmold's offer? . . . or go back to Connecticut? I don't know. . . ."

Gallaudet College was finally accredited in May 1957, and we, members of the Class of 1957, had the honor of being the first to receive our diploma from the "new Gallaudet." I accepted the teaching position the following fall and I took part-time graduate work at Catholic University.

One day in the spring of 1958, several professors were discussing some incredible research.

PROFESSOR: Do you know that Dr. Stokoe is going to study Sign Language?
ME: Yes, he had better.
PROFESSOR: I do not mean that he is learning Sign Language. He actually *studies* Sign Language.
ME: So?
PROFESSOR: He is doing a linguistic research.
ME: Linguistic?
PROFESSOR: Study of language . . . science of language. . . . He will analyze our Sign Language!

Dr. Stokoe Undertaking a Linguistic Research

At the moment, Gallaudet College has three research projects underway; one of them being a linguistic research headed by Dr. William C. Stokoe, Jr. who began it with six weeks at the University of Buffalo last July and August. Its purpose is to make a scientific analysis and description of the structure of the sign language.

In preparation for the research program, Dr. Stokoe attended a workshop on the structural analysis of English at the University of Buffalo. The information derived from the workshop could be applied in studying any language, but Dr. Stokoe was especially interested in applying it to the language of signs.

In his research program, he is applying the principles of scientific language analysis to the study of sign language. This study is being made on the basis that all languages have a systematic structure which can be discovered and described. For example: A professor of English at Oxford and Mexican laborer in the Southwest United States speak the language very differently but both their dialects can be explained in terms of the structure of the English language. Perhaps too, the signing of a Gallaudet graduate and of a deaf person without much schooling, will be seen to be explainable as variations of a central pattern.

One of the aims of the research is to find the relationships between sign language and other languages an individual knows. It asks and tries to answer such questions as: (a) Does using good English damage one's signing and (b) Does using good sign language affect one's spoken or written English in any way?

My colleagues and I laughed at Dr. Stokoe and his crazy project. It was impossible to analyze our Sign Language. One professor reminded me that people used to laugh at Thomas Edison.

Some of us were concerned about the hearing professor's skills in Sign Language. In the same March 1958 issue in which the article on Stokoe's research appeared, another article was published—this one written by a very concerned student, Bert Shaposka.

Is Gallaudet Losing Its Power of the Sign Language?

Gallaudet is supposed to be the center of the language of signs. As deaf students, we are presumably the cream of the crop. We are supposedly capable of assuming many responsibilities and one is certainly the evaluation of our original language of signs.

Unless remedial measures are taken soon, this essential element in the culture of the deaf, the sign language, may become warped. We are the deaf leaders of tomorrow. Who else but us can keep our unique method of communication alive and functioning as an effective medium?

In recent years, the Gallaudet College faculty has undergone numerous changes. There were formerly quite a number of deaf instructors on the staff who knew the sign language by heart. Although a few of them are still around today, many have been replaced by hearing newcomers.

The faculty is no longer the guiding force it used to be in respect to the sign language. Today they are more dependent on the students to confirm its correct use. Formerly the instructors were looked upon as the authorities in the language of signs and they insisted upon correct signs. One of the courses which had an important role in stressing the correct application of the sign language was public speaking. It is no longer given.

A possible answer to this problem is an organization to preserve the language of signs. Membership could include both students and faculty members. Although a large number of students skilled in the language would be most welcome, we would settle for a handful of interested people.

I began to wonder what the language of signs was. What was Sign Language? The teachers at the American School for the Deaf kept telling me to use Sign Language. Now the older professors warned me to preserve the beauty of the language of signs. I remember when I was introduced to Dr. Elizabeth Peet, an authority on Sign Language. I stared at her signing gracefully about the play she recently saw. She advised me to sign properly and clearly. "Always select right signs," reminded the matron. "Each sign has its meaning. When you fingerspell, do it moderately and clearly." I wished I could sign as well as she did.

Whenever I saw a new professor on the campus, he usually signed awkwardly. I always thought it was easy for everyone to learn Sign Language. I didn't understand why they couldn't sign well. Dr. Stokoe was still a "no-good signer," yet he was analyzing our language of signs.

A *Buff and Blue* report about Dr. Stokoe's project in October 1959:

> *Dr. William C. Stokoe, Jr., head of the Department of English, has penetrated further in his linguistic research on the language of signs, it was learned recently.*
>
> *The purpose of this research is to use the methods of the modern science of structural linguistics to analyze all that can be discovered about the sign language.*
>
> *The results obtained so far in this research project are a fairly complete description of the basic symbols of the system called the "sign language" and the principles of their combination into signs. A system of written symbols for their basic visual symbols so that the sign language can be written down for records and for further study is vital.*
>
> *Research on the language of signs began in 1957 with a grant from the college budget along with another grant from the American Council of Learned Societies to Dr. Stokoe, George L. Trager and Henry L. Smith of Buffalo, New York.*
>
> *Dr. Stokoe, with the help of his assistants, Mr. Carl Croneberg and Miss Dorothy Sueoka, plans a study of the grammatical and syntactic principles— how sentences in the language are established and so forth. This study should then prove of value in teaching English to the deaf.*
>
> *This research will continue as long as any other branch of anthropological sciences continues.*

I did not believe Dr. Stokoe would succeed in his project and I thought these two deaf assistants were wasting their time signing before the camera. I had seen one book published in 1918 by Rev. J. Schuyler Long that had many pictures of Long showing signs. That was sufficient. The subject of linguistic research was continuously discussed among the students and professors. In January 1960, Dr. Stokoe was out of town—this time to Los Angeles to attend a four-day meeting on "Machine Translation" at the University of California. I wondered what he was trying to do with our Sign Language. Later, we were surprised to learn of his progress.

Linguistic Research Gets $22,000 NSF Grant for Project

> *Gallaudet College has been awarded a grant of $22,000 by the National Science Foundation for the support of basic research entitled "Linguistic Structure of Sign Language."*

> *The grant will enable a research team headed by Professor William C. Stokoe, Jr., to continue its analysis of the sign language of the deaf in the United States. Professor Stokoe, Mr. Carl Croneberg, and Miss Dorothy Sueoka of the college will investigate the sentence patterns and the dialect difference of the language during the two-year period of the grant.*

More progress: Dr. Stokoe prepared and wrote a new textbook on English composition for Freshman students. It was called *The Calculus of Structure*. This book used symbols to clarify problems of grammar and syntax for those students whose hearing loss prevented them from a natural acquisition of language. The students protested about the strange book. Some of the students refused to take this special English course instructed by Dr. Stokoe. Those who took it had shown me their assignments. They were alien to me and I thought Dr. Stokoe was eccentric.

In the *Buff & Blue* issue of November 1960, it was stated:

"Written" Sign Language Made Possible by Research

In a new book by Professor William C. Stokoe, Jr. chairman of the Department of English, the language of signs acquires linguistic status. This book, Sign Language Structure, *marks the first stage of the continuing research program in linguistics of which Dr. Stokoe is director.*

Coming hard on the heels of the publication of an English textbook The Calculus of Structure, *the new book deals with the basic elements of the sign language used by thousands of deaf people in the United States and Canada. Dr. Stokoe isolates these elements and gives symbols for them, so that for the first time what is "said" in this language can be written down.*

A table of these symbols is included in the book. A new font, designed by Dr. Stokoe and made by the Vari-Typer Corporation, will make possible the preparation and publication of clear and convenient dictionaries, grammars, and textbooks of the language of signs.

Further research in linguistics is being supported by a National Science Foundation grant, and will examine the grammar and syntax of the sign language.

Sign Language Structure *was originally published in a special issue of "Studies in Linguistics" at the University of Buffalo.*

I became close friends with Dr. Detmold because of our work in theatrical productions. Between classes and rehearsals I went to Catholic University. Once I had to write a term paper for one of the drama courses and I went to see Dr. Detmold for advice. He suggested that I see Dr. Stokoe, which I did. After reading my term paper, he got excited and suggested that I do a little more research on the history of the theatre. I followed his advice, did more research on my paper, then handed it in. I got a good grade on my paper! After several meetings with Dr. Stokoe, I began to admire him for the advice he gave me. I respected him for treating me as a human being—not as a deaf person. Sometimes he would stop me and asked me for a specific sign and I signed it to him. He did not discuss his linguistic research. He occasionally went out of town for meetings, giving speeches or doing research. In the spring of 1961, he was out of the country.

Dr. Stokoe Extends Research on Signs to British Isles

To investigate visual communication among adult British deaf persons, Dr. William C. Stokoe, professor of English at Gallaudet College, left the United States on March 21 for a five-month stay in the British Isles.

The particular interest of this study is the British sign language as it differs from and is similar to American sign language and the relationship of visual language structure to the national and regional dialects.

Dr. Stokoe's main centers of work will be with the welfare centers, clubs, and missions for the deaf in London and Birmingham, England; in Belfast and Dublin, Ireland; and in Edinburgh and Glasgow, Scotland.

His research trip is being sponsored by the American Council of Learned Societies and is part of the long-term program of structural analysis of sign language under Dr. Stokoe's direction.

American Sign Language? That was the first name I ever heard for our own language of signs. I was afraid that the new term might be misunderstood for the Sign Language used by the American Indians.

[. . .]

12

American Sign Language once had vibrant regional, class, and ethnic dialects, deriving from the various schools in which Deaf children were enculturated—white or "Negro," private or state, day or residential—and even between state schools in the same region, such as the Midwest, where distances were too great for frequent contact. By the 1970s, however, racial integration and the cultural hegemony of the Gallaudet dialect flattened all but vestiges of these dialects before they could be recorded.

Black Signs

Whatever Happened to the Sign for "CORNBREAD"?

Ernest Hairston and Linwood Smith

1980

Is there a Black sign language?

Do Black people sign differently from white people?

Why can't Black deaf people understand my signs?

These are questions we often hear. To those of us who have acquired the sign vocabulary used by the white majority, we often are subjected to the remark indicative of paternalistic largesse—"I don't want to hurt your feelings and I don't know how to say this, but you are the first Black deaf person whose signs I can understand."

To the first question, our answer is usually preceded by a smile and a polite "No." We maintain that there is no Black sign language. There is, however, a Black way of signing used by Black deaf people in their own cultural milieu—among families and friends, in social gatherings, and in deaf clubs. There are also sign vocabularies peculiar to the region where the Black deaf person came from, i.e. Black signs for cotton, tobacco, whites, tractor, cornbread, biscuits, and peanuts. These signs are still extensively used, in addition to approximately eight different signs for the word "bathroom." It should be pointed out that these signs are not just a regional variation. Many Southern white people do not use the same signs or do not know the signs used by their Black peers. These sign vocabularies may be classified as more or less indigenous to the Southern Black deaf populace.

Dr. James Woodward, a sociolinguist and well known authority on sign languages, published a perceptive study of Black signs. Dr. Woodward focused mainly on signs used by Black deaf children and adults in Georgia. He described variations in grammar, lexical variation, phonological variation, and variations in hand positions.

Historically, the roots of Black sign language developed because of societal attitudes and educational policy, especially in Southern schools for the deaf where dual systems had existed. Southern Black people from Georgia, North Carolina, South Carolina, Florida, Alabama, and Virginia used signs that were common to their respective schools.

As Black deaf people migrated from the South, they found that many of their signs were not widely used or known except among other Southern Black deaf persons who used them or had been exposed to them. Their signs tend to be either more colorful and demonstrative with nonverbal expressions and body language, or shortcut versions of standard signs. For example, the sign for a fancy car (Cadillac) would be formed with two "C" hands meeting and moving apart to form an elongated figure, while the whole upperbody is moving and the cheeks are puffed out. On the other hand, the sign for "mother" is simply formed by the "five" hand shape on the chin and the loose fingers wiggling.

As Black schools for the deaf merged with predominantly white schools, Black children began to sign "white," or as some others would say, "the Gallaudet way." This was more a survival than a social adaptation. Most adopted this way of signing to better themselves and to succeed in their new schools and so as not to appear different. However, among themselves, they retained their signed dialect and signed Black.

As a result, in the newly integrated schools or during cultural events, the sign "cornbread" was rarely used, if at all. Today, one rarely sees it, except when occasionally signed by older deaf persons at Black deaf clubs. In fact, it is rarely seen in any of the recent sign language books. The sign for "cornbread" is made by placing the hands in the praying position and rocking them from side to side. Its apparent death underscores the need to preserve this part of Black deaf culture. It has been said that when one destroys a people's language, one destroys a people. The future of Black signs does not seem promising. As new generations emerge, legacies of the past are forgotten. Today, there seems to be a cultural erosion and a need to preserve the traditions, beliefs, language, and ideals of Black deaf people.

There is no Black sign language, but Black deaf people are proud to communicate in their own special way, using their own special signs.

13

As in all cultural communities, Deaf humor is premised on shared language and experience and is generally not funny to outsiders (who are often the butt of the joke). This piece is an excerpt from a plenary address at The Deaf Way conference.

Reflections of American Deaf Culture in Deaf Humor

MJ Bienvenu

1989

Mainstream American culture teaches that "normal" people are born with five senses: hearing, sight, smell, taste, and touch. Of course, Deaf people can't hear, and this causes many people to view the Deaf as deficient and deprived. But nothing could be further from the truth—we have always had five senses: sight, smell, taste, touch, and a sense of humor.

Humor is one way that people share their perceptions of the world, express different levels of intimacy, and find comfort in knowing that others share their beliefs. I am going to focus specifically on four categories which reflect the values, norms, and belief systems of our American Deaf Culture.

• Visual

As most of you know, Deaf people perceive most things through their eyes. We acquire language visually. It is worth noting that Sign Languages throughout the world adapt to meet the visual needs and comfort of the people who use them. We also acquire world knowledge visually. It should come as no surprise, then, that Deaf humor also has a strong visual base. To many Deaf people, the world is filled with comical sights. But the humor is not always apparent to the majority of hearing Americans.

An experience I had several years ago may illustrate this point: One night while I was coordinating an intensive ASL retreat for a group of non-Deaf people, we gathered together to watch the movie *King Kong* on TV. The volume was off, and for the first time, they realized what Deaf audiences have known all along: the actors' expressions are hysterically funny. As New Yorkers were running for their lives with the shadow of a monster ape looming over their heads, our group was laughing uncontrollably. I asked them what they found so funny. They replied, "Their faces!"

The same people would have felt frightened if they had heard the actors screaming in terror, with threatening music in the background. Instead, they got a glimpse of the movies from a Deaf perspective.

Deaf people find many visual things humorous which aurally dependent people may not. Often Deaf people are quite creative in their descriptions of people and events. This talent is fostered in residential schools where many children learn the art of story-telling, and most importantly, how to vividly re-create events and characters. When I was in school, no one was safe from our stories. Every identifying characteristic of a person would be imitated, right down to the way s/he walked. This intricate detail is a crucial part of the humor, because it reflects how acutely Deaf people perceive the world, and how adept a tool our language is for expressing our perceptions.

Often people who are not members of the culture will respond negatively to this form of humor. This is a common misunderstanding with outsiders. Deaf people are not insulting the individuals whom we describe; we are delighting in the precision of our language to accurately convey these details. Our culture is reinforced through the shared experience of how we, as a group, see the world and translate it into humor.

- Can't Hear

As we all know, deafness is much more than the inability to hear. It is a complete culture, where one's decibel loss is far less important than one's allegiance to the Deaf Community. Yet, a significant amount of Deaf folklore contains jokes and stories which deal with the inability to hear.

There are many stories that have been handed down for generations in Deaf folklore which illustrate the convenience of deafness. The following popular tale shows how Deaf people can solve a problem creatively and humorously: *A Deaf couple arrives at a motel for their honeymoon. After unpacking, the nervous husband goes out to get a drink. When he returns to the motel, he realizes that he has forgotten the room number. It is dark outside and all the rooms look identical. He walks to his car, and leans on the horn. He then waits for the lights to come on in the rooms of the waking angry hearing guests. All the rooms are lit up except his, where his Deaf wife is waiting for him!*

Interestingly, in Roy Holcomb's book *Hazards of Deafness*, the humor does not follow the culturally Deaf tradition, but rather focuses on stories in which Deaf people lament their "condition." This humor is typical of an "outsider's" view of deafness. Here is an example of one of the scenes in the book: *A deaf person is having a difficult time vacuuming the carpet. He goes over the same spot of dirt repeatedly, to no avail. In a fit of frustration, he turns around and notices that the machine is unplugged.*

This is a perfect example of humor that is *not* Deaf centered. Such a situation would never happen because a Deaf person would naturally feel that the motor was not running and immediately respond appropriately. What is most disturbing is the emphasis on hearing and the dependency on sound which the book portrays. Culturally Deaf people are quite articulate in defining the world in terms other than sound, and have adapted to technology as swiftly as non-Deaf people. The fact that the author does not address Deaf people's keenly developed sense of sight and touch is rather significant.

• Linguistic

Another component of Deaf humor can be categorized as linguistic. Production and misproduction of signs is a common way to elicit laughs in ASL. One example, described in Bellugi and Klima's book *The Signs of Language*, is how we can change the root sign, UNDERSTAND, to LITTLE UNDERSTAND by using the pinkie rather than the index finger.

Much of this linguistic humor is lexically based, and the punch lines to many ASL jokes are related to the production of the words. One of my favorites is the "giant" joke. It is funny both culturally and linguistically: *A huge giant is stalking through a small village of wee people, who are scattering through the streets, trying to escape the ugly creature. The giant notices one particularly beautiful blonde woman scampering down the cobble-stoned street. He stretches out his clumsy arm and sweeps her up, then stares in wonder at the slight, shivering figure in his palm. "You are so beautiful," he exclaims. The young woman looks up in fear. "I would never hurt you," he signs, "I love you! We should get MARRIED." Producing the sign MARRY, he crushes her. The giant then laments, "See, oralism is better."*

There are several components which make this joke successful in American Sign Language. First, it is visually active, because the expressions of the townspeople, the beautiful girl, and the giant can be dramatized to perfection. Secondly, it is linguistically funny because of the sign production MARRY which causes the girl of his affection to splat in his palm. Thirdly, it is humorous in its irony. Culturally Deaf people detest oralism; therefore, the irony in the giant's conclusion that oralism would have saved his beloved girl is funny.

• Response to Oppression

It is no secret that Deaf people are an oppressed minority, and one way that minority cultures deal with oppression is through humor. Often this category of humor, sometimes called "zap" stories, features Deaf people getting even.

Often when Deaf people are naturally conversing in public, hearing people will stare at them in disbelief. When they finally gain the courage to initiate conversation with a Deaf person, they will inevitably ask, "Can you read my lips?" Well, of course, Deaf people are keenly aware of the configuration of this one sentence, and will always answer "No!" which is pretty funny, indeed.

Another way Deaf humor fights back at oppression is to show hearing people being outsmarted by a Deaf person. One famous example, which is a true story, provides the required ending: *A group of Deaf people was at a restaurant, chatting away when a group of non-Deaf people at the next table began to rudely mimic their signs. One of the Deaf women decided she'd had enough. She walked to the public telephone, inserted a coin, and making sure she was being observed by the hearing group, signed a complete conversation into the handset, including pauses for the person on the other end to respond. When the Deaf group left the restaurant, they were amused to see the hearing people run over to inspect the phone.*

Deaf people love this one, because we finally have the last laugh. These tales are rich with justice, and always the rude offender is put in her/his place.

In the same way that American Deaf Culture, as well as European Deaf Culture, is oppressed by the majority community, so our language is oppressed. From oralism to Signed English systems and other forms of English/sound coding, Deaf people have suffered under the thumb of hearing educators for many years. From the signs that these "experts" invent, it is obvious they have little knowledge of Deaf Culture or ASL. Often the invented signs already have an established meaning. Many of them look sexual, and are really inappropriate for young children to see, which is ironic, since school systems teach them. It's even worse when they are printed in "sign language" books. Deaf children leaf through these sign-code manuals with delight, snickering at all the "dirty" signs pictured in the textbook.

As one response to these oppressive attempts at linguistic isolation, Deaf people have chosen to incorporate into their discourse some of the artificial codes created from the oral/cued speech/Signed English systems. Coded signs for IS, AM, ARE, WERE, BE, -ING, -ED, etc. have all been reclaimed by Deaf speakers, and used with sarcasm directed toward those who created them. Of course, the humor is most pronounced when a contorted face accompanies the deviant signs—an editorial on the ineffectiveness of these codes.

In closing, let me say that humor is an essential part of our lives. I'm sure you've all heard the expression "Laughter is the best medicine." Well, there is much truth to that, particularly when you analyze minority cultures, and realize that they all incorporate fighting back at oppression into their humor. It is a common response to the frustration of our everyday lives, for in humor, the storyteller determines who will "win." Someone told me this joke the other day, and it seemed like a perfect way to end my presentation: *Three people are on a train—one is Russian, one is Cuban, and one is Deaf. The Russian is drinking from a bottle of vodka. She drinks about half the bottle, then throws it out the window. The Deaf person looks at her, surprised. "Why did you throw out a bottle that was only half-empty?" The Russian replies, "Oh, in my country we have plenty of vodka!" Meanwhile, the Cuban is smoking a rich, aromatic cigar. He smokes about half the cigar, then throws it out the window. The Deaf person is again surprised, and asks, "Why did you throw out the cigar?" He replies, "Oh, in Cuba we have plenty of cigars!" The Deaf person nods with interest. A little while later a hearing person walks down the aisle. The Deafie picks him up and tosses him out the window. The Russian and Cuban look up in amazement. The Deaf person shrugs, "Oh, we have plenty of hearing people in the world."*

Popular notions about the origin, development, and present health of any community's language tell us much about how the community perceives itself, and the Deaf World is no exception. Especially interesting in this respect is the Deaf myth of an original hearing benefactor.

14

Folk Explanation in Language Survival

Carol A. Padden

1990

In very fundamental ways, languages are collective memories. We need only look at cases of language death, when languages are replaced by a more dominant language, to remind us that living languages are those in which the speakers agree to remember them. Dyirbal, a collection of dialects spoken in the north-eastern corner of Australia, is a particularly instructive example of language loss through organized forgetting. Citing a disinterest in Dyirbal and its irrelevance to their increasingly modern lifestyles, younger members of the Dyirbal community not only avoid using Dyirbal with whites and among each other, but they avoid using it with Dyirbal elders. They complain that older speakers further contribute to their disinterest in Dyirbal by correcting or ridiculing the little Dyirbal they do use. For these speakers, English has become the language of choice, representing the generation's shift away from the traditional life of their elders. After a single generation, only older speakers remain committed to the use of Dyirbal and the "collective memory" for that language may be lost to future generations (Schmidt, 1985).

Other languages have been dying less dramatically, although in much the same pattern. The replacement of Scottish Gaelic by English has been taking place for hundreds of years. Various disruptions through the history of the Scottish Highlands, from land clearances carried out in the 1800s to introduce sheep farming to the deterioration of the indigenous fishing industry, have all slowly but inexorably diminished Gaelic in favor of English (Dorian, 1981; 1985). As familiar contexts for Gaelic embedded in traditional fishing communities were replaced by contexts in which English was required, each new generation of children failed to learn more of the language: they failed to contribute to the collective memory of the language for future generations. Today there are very few complete speakers of Scottish Gaelic; most of those who now speak it are "semi-speakers" and can only use it interspersed with English (Dorian, 1977; 1981).

Dramatic change and disruption are not necessarily fatal to languages, as illustrated by the large influx of Latin vocabulary into Old English in the sixth century. The infiltration of Latin brought new possibilities, including concepts ideal for the rise of Christianity throughout Europe (McCrum, Cran and MacNeil, 1986). But what seems to characterize dying languages is loss without replacement or expansion. Instead of the two-term tense system used by older speakers of Dyirbal, in which there is a marked form for future and an unmarked for all other references to time, younger speakers of Dyirbal have lost the future tense marking, leaving only an unmarked form for all tenses (Schmidt, 1985). Modern speakers of Gaelic have lost the masculine gender marking in the language, further reducing the class of gender distinctions.

Crucially, in the case of language death, almost as dramatic as the disappearance of structures is the disappearance of an explanation for why speakers of a language should continue to use and remember the language. As the following report of an English–Gaelic bilingual shows, speakers of dying languages find that the contexts in which they can use the language are shrinking, leaving what Dennison (1977) finds to be the demise of dying languages: the realization that "there is nothing left for them appropriately to be used about."

> See, when you go to the shops, here, or when you meet people on the road, and they don't understand, well, you've got to speak the language they understand and that's the English. There's more English in the parish now than there is of Gaelic, and before we were born it was more Gaelic than English. See, times have changed. People's changed with it. (Dorian, 1981: 104)

Speakers need a tradition of explanation about the language that helps them organize social forces for remembering it. The Gaelic speaker offers an entirely reasonable explanation, perhaps overly reasonable, of pressures that justify non-use of Gaelic. In the case of Dyirbal, not only have younger speakers replaced their parents' language with English, but they seem to have replaced their parents' mythology about the place of Dyirbal in their lives. Today, when younger speakers of Dyirbal and Gaelic talk about their use of their ancestors' language, they do not repeat their parents' references to tribal and language identity; instead they use themes of resignation and dismissal, of futility in face of the dominant language, as in this comment by a Dyirbal speaker about his language: "Talking Duwal [everyday Dyirbal] to a waybala [white man]—it's like singing and you're ashamed of your voice" (Schmidt, 1985: 18). Use of Dyirbal is associated with "backwardness" and a traditional life that is increasingly at odds with their modern practices. In Nahuatl, an Aztecan language being replaced by Spanish, younger speakers do not show shame, but their association of Nahuatl with the ways of the past achieves much the same end: in their explanations about Nahuatl, they position the language remotely from the circumstances of their everyday lives (Hill and Hill, 1977).

American Sign Language (ASL), a natural sign language used by communities of Deaf people in the United States and Canada, has many of the social features of languages under threat like Dyirbal, but unlike Dyirbal, it seems to be thriving.[1] A primary feature in the memory of ASL, one that is perhaps absent in younger-generation Dyirbal and Gaelic, is the community's collective explanation about the central place of the language in their everyday lives. In stories and anecdotes that the group tell about their language, themes of regeneration, preservation and transmission are common currency. Such collectively held explanations can be seen as ways of collectively reminding each new generation of the special circumstances of becoming a native speaker of the language.

As in Dyirbal, there are dislocations across generations of ASL users. Young deaf children, more often than not, do not learn ASL at birth. Only about 10 percent of all deaf children are born to parents who are also deaf. Of this number, most, but not all, have deaf parents who use ASL. This leaves the large majority of other deaf children without access to ASL until later in life, if at all. The ages at which deaf children learn ASL vary widely, from the small number of deaf children who learn at birth to the larger numbers who learn by age six, when they attend school with other ASL users, and there are sizable numbers of teenage and adult learners of ASL. Like Dyirbal, ASL must also co-exist with a powerful dominant language, English. ASL is very rarely the official language of social institutions that govern the early lives of deaf children, notably the school.

But from all indications, ASL has managed to sustain its vitality over nearly two centuries of tenuous transmission, with each new generation learning mostly from non-relatives rather than the family. There are no reliable official counts of primary users of ASL in North America, but based on the number of users known to social-service agencies, a conservative estimate is about 200,000 (Padden and Humphries, 1988).

There may be a good explanation as to why ASL remains tenacious in face of strong pressures from the more dominant English-speaking community. English is a spoken language, communicated primarily by speech. For Deaf people who do not hear, the inability to access speech would appear to make English a difficult, if not impossible, alternative to ASL. However, there have been, over the years, alternatives to ASL for Deaf people. A powerful alternative has been the signed English systems in which ASL is reconfigured in forms which are putatively more reminiscent of English structure (see Ramsey, 1988). Additionally, there are orally based forms of communication among deaf people where sign language is used in a sharply reduced form. While these forms of communication exist, they have not replaced, nor have they displayed a dominance equal to that of, ASL in the North American Deaf community.

Very little has changed over the years in terms of how ASL is learned by new generations of signers; it is still unusually hard to learn. Yet ASL has remained surprisingly durable despite the lack of a strong institutional base for maintenance of the language throughout its history. ASL continues to have currency among Deaf communities in the United States and Canada and is slowly gaining ground in official institutions outside of the Deaf community. One measure of its growing recognition is the number of colleges and universities which now allow ASL to be used to meet hearing students' language requirements (*San Diego Tribune*, 27 January 1989).

Certainly one of the most interesting stories about the survival of ASL has been the community's flexibly changing explanation over time about why the language needs to be remembered. To understand the history of explanations about ASL, a brief history of the mythological roots of such explanations is necessary. Many "stories" about ASL are framed as stories about the uniqueness of the language and how Deaf people came to use it in place of speech. Stories about the earliest use of ASL can ultimately be traced back to a folk tale told in deaf clubs in France about the founder of a public school for deaf children in Paris: the Abbé de l'Epée. Epée, a priest in search of a calling in the late years of his life, was introduced to the deaf daughters of a widow, and decided to organize a small school for deaf children. His initial success with the children attracted funds from the city and a distinguished benefactor, Louis XVI; his school grew to serve seventy-two deaf children by 1785. At the time of his death in 1789, Epée was a minor celebrity and left behind a legacy of several students and disciples who went on to establish additional schools, including a deaf man, Laurent Clerc. With Clerc, the American story of origins begins. In 1816, Clerc traveled to America with a Congregational minister, Thomas Hopkins Gallaudet, to help establish the first public school for deaf children in America. Clerc introduced his native French Sign Language as the first language of the school. Nearly two centuries later, ASL and FSL are no longer mutually intelligible, although they share a common base (Lane, 1984).

The popular version of how Epée came to his calling is still told in dramatic form in deaf clubs throughout France. Described in an account of a trip taken throughout France by myself and my husband (Padden and Humphries, 1988), "the story of the Abbé de l'Epée" is almost always a preface to an official deaf-club event, to remind visitors such as ourselves of the significance of Epée to Deaf people in France. When these stories are told, it is clear that they are not merely anecdotes, but variations on a stylized folk tale, to be rendered in heightened, lyrical form. One version, recorded by us at one such event, appears below:

> The Abbé de l'Epée had been walking for a long time through a dark night. He wanted to stop and rest overnight, but he could not find a place to stay, until at a distance he saw a house with a light. He stopped at the house, knocked at the door, but no one answered. He saw that the door was open, so he entered the house and found two young women seated by the fire sewing. He spoke to them, but they still did not respond. He walked closer and spoke to them again, but they failed again to respond. The Abbé was perplexed, but seated himself beside them. They looked up at him and did not speak. At that point, their mother entered the room. Did the Abbé not know that her daughters were deaf? He did not, but now he understood why they had not responded. As he contemplated the young women, the Abbé realized his vocation.

The theme of the tale is essentially religious as it draws on motifs of a light at the end of a dark road and a warm fire. At the light, Epée is introduced to two deaf women and undergoes a transformation. His transformation was perhaps the most powerful motif of all, one which would acknowledge his role in the formation of a national community of deaf people in France. Officially, Epée founded a school for deaf children but he had also created a community of deaf children who were housed together for most of their formative years, children who would later form a secondary community of adults around the core of the school. In some versions of this tale, Epée is proclaimed the father of sign language, the inventor of the language of deaf people. Although the credit is misplaced—no individual can create a language, only generations of speakers can—Epée is symbolically the catalyst for the formation of a community of deaf people that continues to this day (Lane, 1984; Padden and Humphries, 1988).

The Epée tale is "reincarnated" in various forms in the United States in the person of his student, Laurent Clerc. Each year, deaf children at the American School for the Deaf in Hartford, Connecticut, perform celebrations of the day Clerc and Gallaudet founded their school, the first school for deaf children in the United States. In much the same style of Founding Fathers' mythology, [they also] re-enact how Clerc met Gallaudet and agreed to leave his homeland to sail with him across the Atlantic.

Increasingly, however, this kind of story-telling is being supplanted by a modern variation, one that is much less religious, much less centered around persons such as Epée or Clerc and Gallaudet. The new explanation for the place of ASL in the everyday lives of Deaf people is essentially "scientific," not because it exhibits features of academic or scientific discourse, but because it is self-reflective and driven by references to features of "language" and "culture," vocabulary which until very recently did not belong to the group.

This transition from the religious or the mythical in stories about ASL to the "scientific" mirrors a profound change in the community itself, best summarized in terms of the emergence of a deaf middle class, a professional class of deaf people who now dominate myth-making in the community, including explanations about their language. The new folk explanation about ASL, if we examine it closely, has not lost its mythical roots, but it has taken on new vocabulary and new kinds of representations that cast it in a decidedly modern light. These new representations form the basis for ways of talking about the place of the language in Deaf people's lives, ways that reflect replacements to earlier explanations without loss.

The crucial role of the middle class in myth-making about ASL underscores the relationship between control of social resources and opportunities for remembering. Survival of minority languages is, as Dorian (1981) notes, dependent not on the numbers of speakers but on *who* is using the language. Catalan is a classic example of a stable minority language thriving in what would otherwise be a hostile situation. Used by the political élite in the Catalonian region of Spain (Woolard, 1983), Catalan has maintained its integrity in the face of pressures from the larger nation-state in which Castilian is spoken. Each new generation of Catalan speakers, including the children of merchants and power brokers of the state, are expected to learn the language. By dominating myth-making about their language, the economically established class maintains resources for remembering the language.

The thematic shift in the folk explanation about ASL can best be illustrated by comparing selections taken from two popular Deaf news magazines, one in 1950 and the second in 1989. In 1950, a few issues after the inauguration of a new magazine for Deaf people, the *Silent Worker*, the editor's page featured a stern editorial on the subject of "The Sign Language." The theme was a familiar one to Deaf people: the sign language was in serious danger of deterioration owing to pressures surrounding it. There were "oralists" who demanded elimination of the sign language from schools for deaf children in favor of teaching speech. Readers were exhorted to join forces and work to preserve the language. The vocabulary features the popular explanation for the language of the Deaf community in America: it is known simply as "the sign language," it is characterized by the fact that it is not speech. The editor could not use the word "grammar" in reference to sign language; he instead uses the word "standard" which he argues derives from "custom." And in recognition of good signing, the editor refers to it as "art" because it is carefully constructed and pleasing to see.

> Anyone who has been observant can detect a vast difference between the sign language in use today and that of a quarter of a century or so ago. . . . What has happened will be considered by some as changes due to the passing of time, while others will call it plain and simple deterioration. At any rate, the sign language is in danger of becoming a lost art unless something is done by the deaf to keep it at a standard where it can be considered the medium of conversation of a cultured people.
>
> There is no grammar in the sign language. There is no standard authority by which it is determined that one sign is correct and another is incorrect, but custom has given us a fairly good standard, and we recognize a correct and incorrect form of usage. (*Silent Worker*, February 1950, p. 2)

The themes in this editorial are solidly rooted in older worries about sign language. In a filmed lecture made by the National Association of the Deaf in 1913 [chapter 10 of this book—LB], the president of the organization gives an emotional and rousing speech on "The Preservation of the Sign Language," resounding many of the same themes that appear in this editorial. Users of the sign language must always "protect and guard their language" against larger forces that conspire to eliminate the language. These malevolent forces of seek to "trap and imprison" Deaf people against their will by forcing them to abandon sign language for speech. In his powerful closing, the president invokes the deity as he acknowledges the sign language as "the noblest gift God has given to Deaf people."

In a recent issue of the *Silent News*, a popular Deaf newspaper published monthly, "the sign language" has taken on a new name: it is now called "American Sign Language," popularly referred to in its abbreviated form, ASL. The following article, reporting on a development in a Deaf community in Canada, is filled with quasi-scientific references:

> On the evening of December 6, 1988, a private member's resolution was passed unanimously which recognizes the cultural uniqueness of the deaf community and

ASL as a distinctive language with its own grammar and rules of usage. It is now recognized as the true and complete first language of Deaf Manitobans.

The resolution received the unanimous support of all the parties. . . . Gary Doer, leader of the New Democratic Party, concluded the debate by congratulating the Deaf Community for bringing forward this resolution and spoke of his party's pride in being able to "support their resolution to have their distinct society and distinct culture with their language, the [sic] American Sign Language [recognized]."

Lawrence Zimmer, president of the Winnipeg Community Center of the Deaf, said "This resolution marks the first time a government in Canada has officially recognized ASL and Manitoba leads the other provinces as a model in recognizing ASL." Several American states have also recognized ASL as the language of deaf people, including California, Michigan and Texas. (*Silent News*, February 1989)

As these two selections illustrate, the popular explanation about ASL has changed dramatically, over time as short as a single generation. In 1950, the *Silent Worker* used "the sign language"; in 1965, a book on the structure of the language (Stokoe, Croneberg and Casterline, 1965) added a qualifier and called it "the American sign language" to distinguish it from other distinct, unrelated sign languages of the world, thus broadening the world pertinent to Deaf people to include other nations and other languages. In 1980, at the centennial celebration of the founding of the National Association of the Deaf, their national convention featured public workshops in "the structure of American Sign Language." Not only was the article dropped, but the language achieved final autonomy as all three words were capitalized. The transition from the lower-case to the capitalized, from the generic to the specialized, is but a single example of a profound shift in how Deaf people in the United States refer to their primary language.

What precipitated such a profound change in vocabulary and ways of talking about ASL? Numerous factors have been cited: the popularization of the civil-rights language extending to not only ethnic groups but disabled groups as well and new paradigms for research in deaf children and signed language which draw from disciplines of linguistics and anthropology. But these are frames of explanation which come from outside of the community; what changes took place within the community to cause such a wide-scale appropriation of this vocabulary? What is often overlooked in this critical transformation beginning in the early 1970s is the emergence of new patterns of work life in Deaf communities in the United States and Canada, one that would demand a new vocabulary for their language, one to match the new social contexts in their everyday lives.

Until about the middle 1960s, the primary occupations for deaf people in the United States were either the "solitary" trades (shoe repair, upholstery, printing or factory assembly) or as school teachers or dormitory supervisors (Braly and Hall, 1935; Crammatte, 1987; Cronenberg and Blake, 1966). Teaching at that time had little of the trappings of "professional" life: there were few requirements on type of training other than a college degree, and sometimes not even this was required. Deaf people were insulated from the ranks of management; nearly none were elevated to principals or supervisors in their schools. The working-class standard within the community was so predominant that it was entirely appropriate and common for deaf teachers to moonlight as printers or upholsterers to supplement their small teaching incomes.

Perhaps an important signal of changes in the economic lives of Deaf people was the formation of a National Theatre of the Deaf (NTD) in 1967. Funded initially by a grant from the Department of Health, Education and Welfare, the NTD was awarded enough money to form a permanent theater. They assembled a repertory of deaf actors and accepted national and international bookings for performances featuring deaf actors in revues they had never before performed—in college theaters, city halls and mainstream auditoriums. These actors had long been community performers; they were well known to the community for the folk entertainment they provided at deaf clubs, picnics and conventions, but the novelty of the NTD was the promise of full-time employment as actors. Many left their jobs as school teachers or printers to be thrust in the public light as actors. The popular entertainment they had provided for the small community of Deaf people was now transformed into an expensive spectacle for the hearing public (Miles, 1974). As they traveled to Deaf communities throughout the United States and Canada, the NTD presented an image of the specialized Deaf professional, one who could earn a living at something other than the traditional trades.

The 1970s were remarkable for another change: the professionalization of teachers of deaf children. The expansion of the access mandate for the handicapped (section 504 of the Civil Rights Act, passed in 1974) and the rapid increase in public funding made it economically lucrative for public schools and universities to offer "mainstreamed" programs for deaf children. Colleges and universities began to provide disabled students with support services, including Deaf students with sign-language interpreting. The general trend toward professionalization in teaching extended to teachers working with deaf children. Certificates and master's degrees were required for new positions. New specializations were offered: "counselors for the deaf," "elementary education," "post-secondary education," etc., highlighting the burgeoning industry of special education in the 1970s and 1980s.

The 1970s also marked the appearance of another profession: the ASL teacher. As public interest in ethnic diversity increased, the demand for adult classes in ASL exploded, to an estimated 50,000 new students each year in the language (*San Diego Tribune*, 27 January 1989), with classes in colleges and universities and in increasing numbers, in high schools. The professionalization of ASL teaching has probably more than any other field contributed to the introduction of the disciplines of linguistics and anthropology into mainstream Deaf life. Teachers of sign language became, within a few short years, newly recast as teachers of a language, ASL.

There were several consequences of the emergence of professionalization within the deaf community, the most significant of which was new social tensions between the middle class and the working class within the community. Teachers now no longer moonlighted as printers; they lost interest in the traditional social organizations of the community, especially the segregated deaf clubs, and sought out new affiliations outside of the community. Deaf clubs in the United States today have nowhere near the popularity they once enjoyed in the 1940s and 1950s when the clubs were packed every weekend night. After the Second World War, the Los Angeles Club of the Deaf was at the height of its strength; it owned a building in the center of town and was the political and social center of the deaf community. It is now defunct, its social and political functions distributed elsewhere in the community (DeBee, 1985).

The flight of Deaf people from the traditional club has variously been blamed on television, the video-cassette recorder and the telephone. As the argument goes, Deaf people turn to more private pursuits and they lose interest in the traditional group activities. But again, the new interest in this technology was not uniform within the community, but promoted most heavily by the new middle class. Along with their new economic lives came a desire for the trappings of middle-class life: to conduct one's business by telephone instead of the traditional face-to-face encounter and to participate in the consumption of televised goods.

Their new economic status brought about new types of political agendas, ones that promoted technological expansion in the community. In 1964, Robert Weitbrecht adapted surplus Western Union tele-typewriter machines for use across telephone lines, and a small group of Deaf people purchased for the first time a telephone in their homes which allowed them to use these machines for typed communication with each other. By 1988, Deaf organizations in the States of California, New York and Minnesota had successfully lobbied for free distribution of these machines to any Deaf person subscribing to the telephone service (Telecommunications for the Deaf, Inc., 1988). Bowing to intense political pressure from Deaf social-service agencies, in 1987 the public-utilities commission in California began providing free "relay" services using operators to link calls between a user of a tele-typewriter device with those who did not have one. After six months, the volume of calls rose to approximately 40,000 calls per *week* made to the relay service in the State of California alone (California Public Utilities Commission, 1987). There are now continuing efforts to persuade the federal government to expand this service nation-wide. In 1981, a federally funded private organization began providing "closed captions" on network television which appear only on televisions equipped with a specially purchased decoder. These English subtitles appeared on regularly scheduled network- and cable-television programming. In 1989 an estimated 375 hours of closed captioning per week were featured on network, cable and pay channels provided by at least four independent captioning companies (National Captioning Institute, 1988).

These social and political changes are accompanied by new ways of talking about their language. Deaf people began using a vocabulary that reflected the specialization of their work lives, a vocabulary that included special names for not only ASL but other varieties of signing. What was formerly referred to as "the sign language" was now divided into several different categories, each with distinct labels, reflecting new cultural sensibilities about appropriate and inappropriate language behavior. Forms of signing which depart from ASL and mimic some structural features of English are called "Sign English"; individuals who use this form of signing run the risk of being judged as overly compliant to the dominant language. Another form of signing, called "SEE," an acronym for a pedagogically developed system, Signing Exact English, has much more drastic departures from ASL where many forms are judged as "odd" and ungrammatical. Signing in SEE is highly stigmatized in the community, drawing suspicion and ridicule. With each new label are new types of tensions, new ways of collectively evaluating the language behavior of the group. These tensions are played out in a number of rich ways, reflecting rapid cross-generational change (see Padden and Humphries, 1988, for further discussion).

Deaf people's contexts for learning and living, formerly called "custom," are renamed, as the *Silent News* segment illustrates, as instances of "cultural uniqueness" and "distinctiveness." While the community has always promoted a theme of uniqueness organized around their unusual language, these new ways of referring to the group as a "culture" and a "society" are new ways of acknowledging the group's minority status in the face of pressures to assimilate. Instead of the deity, the traditions of science and pluralist humanism have become the new standards for themes about self-justification.

These thematic shifts are not specific to the Deaf community; other minority languages, notably Navajo (National Education Association, 1987) and Athabaskan (Paul, 1980; Scollon and Scollon, 1979), have also turned to self-conscious enterprises such as linguistic analyses of their languages in an attempt to maintain survival, with varying results. Perhaps this self-conscious appropriation of scientific vocabulary has been successful in the case of ASL because of how it is thematically intertwined with the changing economic and social lives of Deaf people. As the *Silent News* article illustrates, unlike in Dyirbal, younger Deaf people see ASL as a key emblem of their own future, one which lays claim to cultural uniqueness and to co-existence with English.

The survival and maintenance of a language is typically thought of in terms of maintaining access to that language. The argument presented here is that "living" languages also depend on sharing folk explanations that remind speakers of the language's central position in everyday life. Folk explanations are fundamentally ways of collectively remembering the significance of what a language is to a particular culture, of privileging certain explanations above others. The collective memory for a language is embodied in the collective memory that is formed in justifications, explanations, the rhetorical organization of accounting for the necessity of the survival of a language such as ASL. In this way, the "folklore" of a language contributes to the organization of social resources for maintaining the language in the face of pressures from the outside.

NOTES

An earlier version of this essay was presented at the Center for Language, Politics and Culture, University of Chicago, May 1989. I thank David Laitin, David Middleton and Tom Humphries for instrumental suggestions.

1. Lower-case "deaf" is used when referring to the audiological condition of not hearing, and upper-case "Deaf" when referring to a particular group of deaf people who share a sign language such as American Sign Language (ASL)—and a culture.

REFERENCES

Braly, Kenneth and Hall, Percival (1935) "Types of Occupations Followed," in *The Federal Survey of the Deaf and Hard of Hearing*. Gallaudet College Normal Department in collaboration with the Office of Education.

California Public Utilities Commission (1987) *Report on Funding Problems Involving Deaf and Disabled Telecommunications Services*. San Francisco, CA: California Public Utilities Commission.

Crammatte, Alan (1987) *Meeting the Challenge: Hearing Impaired Professionals in the Workplace*. Washington, DC: Gallaudet University Press.

Cronenberg, Henry and Blake, Gary (1966) *Young Deaf Adults: An Occupational Survey*. Arkansas Rehabilitation Service.

DeBee, James (1985) *The LACD Story*. Film distributed by Beyond Sound, Los Angeles, CA.

Dennison, Norman (1977) "Language Death or Language Suicide?" in W. Dressler and R. Wodak-Leodolter (eds.), *Language Death*, special issue of *International Journal of the Sociology of Language* 12: 13–22.

Dorian, Nancy (1977) "The Problem of the Semi-Speaker in Language Death," in W. Dressler and R. Wodak-Leodolter (eds.), *Language Death*, special issue of *International Journal of the Sociology of Language* 12: 23–32.

—— (1981) *Language Death: The Life Cycle of a Scottish Gaelic Dialect*. Philadelphia: University of Pennsylvania Press.

—— (1985) *The Tyranny of Tide*. Ann Arbor, MI: Karoma Press.

Hill, Jane and Hill, Kenneth (1977) "Language Death and Relexification in Tlaxalan Nahuatl," in W. Dressler and R. Wodak-Leodolter (eds.), *Language Death*, special issue of *International Journal of the Sociology of Language* 12: 55–70.

Lane, Harlan (1984) *When the Mind Hears*. New York: Random House.

McCrum, Robert, Cran, William and MacNeil, Robert (1986) *The Story of English*. New York: Viking Press.

Miles, Dorothy (1974) "A History of Theatre Activities in the Deaf Community of the United States," master's thesis, Connecticut College, New London.

National Captioning Institute (1988) *Captioned Newsletter*. Falls Church, VA: National Captioning Institute, Fall.

National Education Association (1987) *Navajos: A Source Booklet for Teachers and Students*. Washington, DC: National Education Association Human and Civil Rights.

Padden, Carol and Humphries, Tom (1988) *Deaf in America: Voices from a Culture*. Cambridge, MA: Harvard University Press.

Paul, Gaither (1980) *Stories for My Grandchildren*, transcribed and ed. R. Scollon. Fairbanks, Alaska: Alaska Native Language Center.

Ramsey, Claire (1988) "Signing Exact English: The Meaning of English in Deaf Education," mimeograph, University of California, Berkeley.

San Diego Tribune (1989) "Educators in Debate on Language," 27 January.

Schmidt, Annette (1985) *Young People's Dyirbal: An Example of Language Death from Australia*. Cambridge: Cambridge University Press.

Scollon, Ronald and Scollon, Suzanne (1979) *Linguistic Convergence: An Ethnography of Speaking at Fort Chipewyan, Alberta*. New York: Academic Press.

Stokoe, William, Croneberg, Carl and Casterline, Dorothy (1965) *A Dictionary of American Sign Language on Linguistic Principles*. Washington, DC: Gallaudet College Press.

Telecommunications for the Deaf, Inc. (TDI) (1988) *International Telephone Directory for TDD Users*. Silver Spring, MD: TDI.

Woolard, Kathryn (1983) "The Politics of Language and Ethnicity in Barcelona, Spain," dissertation, University of Pennsylvania.

15

The sharp increase in prestige among hearing people that ASL has enjoyed over the past thirty years should have been a good thing for the Deaf community. Somehow, however, ASL's popularity has come at the cost of demotion to some kind of craft or hobby, like quilting or aerobics, taught by volunteer enthusiasts in church basements, not professors in university departments of modern languages. The only credentialing body for ASL teachers has no enforcement authority.

Let's Return ASL to Deaf Ownership

Jack Levesque

1990

Every school day of the year, millions of English speaking people study their language. Students from pre-schoolers to doctoral candidates are drilled in correct usage of verbs and pronouns, when to use "me" or "I," and on correct usage of new vocabulary. Books, articles, lectures, and newspaper columns are written bemoaning some "injustice" done to English or rejoicing in some author's creative new use of it. English is protected from misuse by a vast army of teachers, parents, writers, grammarians, and sticklers.

And each of those school days, thousands of people study sign language. Five thousand of them go to Bay Area classes at high schools, adult schools, and colleges each year. In fact, from the time sign language emerged on the American scene in the early 1800s, there have been sign language classes. Since the establishment of the Communications Skills Program under the National Association of the Deaf in the late 1960s and early 1970s, there has been a tremendous proliferation of sign language classes all over the country.

Some of those sign language classes, especially lately, have begun to teach ASL. There are courses on ASL structure, ASL culture, ASL grammar, and Deaf studies.

Who are those students and who are the teachers? I would venture to say that few of the teachers are deaf, and even fewer of the students are deaf.

For deaf people, ASL is not something we learn in a class. No teachers hurried to correct us when we used ASL incorrectly as children (most of our teachers did not sign at all). Few of us have ever "diagrammed" or analyzed the structure of an ASL sentence. Nobody can tell you we got straight "A" in high school ASL. Even today, those thousands who sit in ASL classes are enjoying an education deaf students are left out of.

The result is that sign language among the deaf is, at best, awful. It has been haphazardly infiltrated with so many new ideas, codes, and systems that the true beauty of ASL has been lost in the confusion. Tom Anderson and George Veditz warned us that the future of sign language and signs is in danger. They foresaw what would happen if it "fell into the wrong hands."

At a recent ASL workshop in San Diego, a group of experts in the area of ASL, all deaf, gathered for four days of exhilarating discussions and sharing of experience and hopes. It was evident that only half of the participants had taken valid courses in Deaf studies, ASL structure, or ASL history.

In my own case, I learned ASL via the hybrid system at Gallaudet University, and as a result, I continue to be a bumbling idiot when it comes to using the language I so love and respect.

The fact that schools don't offer ASL classes comes as a shock to many hearing people. It seems to me that until deaf children get this kind of education, training hearing students in ASL is a hypocritical luxury we can't afford to continue.

In most of today's deaf classrooms, the wonderful new shift to ASL still hasn't quite hit home. It seems so clear that deaf students are hungry for self-knowledge, and this must begin with competence in and full access to the language that is their own.

All those organizations that offer ASL classes in the Bay Area and all over the country need to take a good hard look at the direction this kind of education is taking, who is benefiting, and who is teaching. It is time to bring it home to the deaf people who rightfully own it, and offer them retraining. It is time to make deaf people the experts and protectors of this language.

Perhaps we can do this by sponsoring workshops, by discussing it in our clubs and organizations, by making ourselves aware of how ASL is used, and by always proudly claiming it as our own.

Those hearing fourth-graders who are studying English nouns and adverbs may never know what a gift it is they are receiving: learning to use their language in its most clear and expressive way. Our deaf fourth-graders will have to wait, maybe a lifetime, for the same gift.

16

Today, ASL instruction and research seem more and more to be in the hands of those with preservationist or prescriptivist ideologies. While most ASL users are eager to see some decent grammar instruction in our schools and would applaud the purging of ugly initialized signs, one may well wonder whether the "pure ASL" to which we are urged to return ever actually existed.

What Happens When Languages Come in Contact

Ceil Lucas and Clayton Valli

1992

As far as language contact is concerned, it is important to have a clear picture of what the actual communication situation was at the American School for the Deaf at its inception, since it was by no means monolithic and since the school played such a key role in shaping communication in the Deaf community. Consider, for example, the language backgrounds of some of the teachers and students of the very first class: Alice Cogswell, age 11 at the time of the founding, whose language use Lane describes as "a mixture of her own home sign, pantomime, and fingerspelling with the two-handed British manual alphabet" (1984, p. 179); Parnel and Sophia Fowler, two deaf sisters who apparently had a system of home signs; John Brewster, a painter who entered the school at age 51 and of whom it was remarked that he could "write well and converse in signs" (a remark, as Gannon points out, made in 1790, 26 years before the arrival of Clerc, suggesting the existence of at least some small deaf communities in the United States at that time) (Gannon, 1981, p. 359); three young boys—George Loring, Wilson Whiton, and Levi Backus—with apparently no prior contact with singing or deaf people; and of course Laurent Clerc and Thomas Hopkins Gallaudet. Clerc knew French Sign Language and the methodical signs for French, as well as English; Gallaudet was a native English speaker and had learned some French Sign Language as well as methodical signs for written French. And Clerc reports that he and Gallaudet adapted many of the French methodical signs for the instruction of English (Lane, 1984, p. 226). Our point is simply that the communication system at the very beginning of the school was fairly complex. It was not as though there was only one language being used by students and teachers. It is clear that, at the beginning, teachers and students brought with them a variety of linguistic backgrounds, all of which came together to form a system shared by the school community.

Although in the early years natural sign language was the medium of instruction and some of the teachers were themselves both audiologically and culturally deaf (Gannon, 1981), the situation began to change even prior to the Congress of Milan, as the central roles of English and speech were visibly championed and restored in deaf education. The point, however, is that ASL and English were in close contact long before 1880, and that contact was both the natural contact of two languages existing in the same geographical space and the more contrived contact resulting from the quite self-conscious adaptation of a spoken language to visual means. In addition, the contact situation is made even more complex by the fact that even though the methodical signs were abandoned, there remained some signs which had started out as initialized signs in French Sign Language—that is, resulting from the contact between natural French sign language and written French, contact which produced outcomes long before Gallaudet arrived in France—and which made their way into ASL. Examples include the signs SEARCH, GOOD, and DOCTOR, all ASL signs which have hand-shapes that reflect the first letter of the *French* written word—C (*chercher*), B (*bon*), and M (*medecin*), respectively. Furthermore, there is some evidence that some of the methodical signs invented to represent parts of English structure made their way into ASL even though the system of methodical signs was abandoned. For example, Lane (1984, pp. 213, 226) presents evidence that signs were invented for French and English prepositions, words the grammatical function of which is usually fulfilled in ASL by classifier predicates. Now, in modern ASL, there exist signs IN, ON, UNDER, BEHIND, and TO, that is, the phonological forms exist. However, these signs are not usually used in the same way prepositions are used in English or French. The grammatical relationships shown in English with the words *in, on, under, behind*, and *to* are accomplished in ASL with classifier predicates and use of the signing space. So the phonological forms exist but they do not usually occur in prepositional phrases as they do in English. They may have other functions in ASL. For example, the sign BEHIND occurs in the compound MONEYBEHIND, meaning *savings*, and the sign IN can be produced on the chest with the meaning of "integral part of my being." Not that spoken language prepositions never acquire other syntactic functions; they do, as in the expressions "to up the ante" or "to down a cup of coffee." What's interesting in the ASL case is that it appears that signs were invented expressly for English prepositions with prepositional function and are either not used as such or have acquired other functions.

Finally, there is another interesting fact about deaf education in the nineteenth century that may have some relevance for understanding the early ASL–English contact situation. Lou (1988) points out that the minimum age for admission to the Hartford school in 1817 was 14 years, which later dropped to 12 and then to 8 by 1843. Brill (1974) reports that the average age of the last 100 students entering the school in 1893 was 10.8 years. As Lou (1988) states, "throughout this period the students were predominantly adolescents, not young children" (p. 81). Furthermore, she points out that the percentage of *congenitally* deaf children increased and decreased over the years. The percentage of congenitally deaf children at Hartford in 1844 was 44%, as compared to 57.4% in 1880 (based on census reports), 41.5% in

TABLE 1

Causes of Deafness in Students at the American School for the Deaf,
1817–1844*

Category	Student status		
	Former students	In Attendance in 1844	Total
Acquired			
Fever			
Spotted fever	45	1	46
Scarlet fever	20	22	44 (*sic*)
Fever	29	6	35
Typhus fever	11	1	12
Lung fever	1	1	2
Yellow fever	1	0	1
Sickness	76	8	84
Inflammation in head	24	6	30
Ulcers in head	14	8	22
Accidents	10	12	22
Measles	11	1	12
Dropsy	5	0	5
Fits	2	2	4
Smallpox	2	0	2
Palsy	2	0	2
Croup	1	0	1
Total Acquired	262	72	336
Congenital	270	71	341
Unknown	87	9	96
Total	619	152	773

* Adapted from Moores (1987).

1910 (based on census reports), and 69% in 1970, as reported by Ries (1973). As Lou reports, the change in the number of congenitally deaf children had an impact on the structure of educational programs: "The decrease in the proportion of congenital deafness through the early decades of this century . . . appears to have occurred at the same time that pure oral approaches dominated. The recent increase in the proportion of congenital deafness occurs at a time when manual approaches are back in vogue" (pp. 89–90).

What is of interest for the ASL–English contact situation is that, based on these statistics, many of the students in the early years at Hartford may have in fact been adventitiously deaf, and hence native English speakers. Table 1 (adapted from Moores, 1987, who in turn adapted it from Weld, 1844) shows the causes of deafness in students at the American School for the Deaf, 1817–1844. Moores states that "it may be assumed the majority of students in the 'acquired' category had achieved some level of proficiency in speech and English before losing their hearing, leading to the conclusion that the composition of the 'deaf population' of the American School from 1817 to 1844 was different from that of schools for the deaf today, a large majority of whose students either were born deaf or lost their hearing before the acquisition of language" (Moores, 1987, p. 85). Lou reports that many young deaf children were not sent to school in the early years because public state schools were residential and unable to accept very young children, so that may account for part of the situation at Hartford. That is, there may have been students there who were indeed born deaf but simply did not enroll until a later age. But the possible presence of many students who were already English speakers at the time that they became deaf casts an interesting light on the teaching of English, the teaching and learning of ASL, and the interaction of ASL and English.

For one, English was probably being taught to some students who could already speak it. Second, this was at least in part an environment that included native English speakers learning ASL. In addition to adventitiously deaf students, many of the teachers in the early years were hearing. While there were indeed many deaf teachers between 1817 and 1860, Lou (1988) states that "Between 1817 and the 1860s teachers in schools for the Deaf were typically male college graduates who learned to teach their deaf pupils through on-the-job training, with additional special instruction in Sign Language. The faculty at the American Asylum learned Sign Language from Laurent Clerc, and from their ranks came most of the principals and teachers of the other schools for the Deaf" (p. 81). As Harlan Lane points out (personal communication, 1991), the students at Hartford interacted with members of the larger hearing community in the city of Hartford as well. Given all of these factors, it seems reasonable to say that there was extensive natural ASL–English contact, not limited to classroom settings involving the instruction of English, and there may have existed a form of contact signing from the earliest days. In addition, many Hartford graduates themselves went on to found schools for the deaf or teach at schools for the deaf (Gannon, 1981). This means that the outcomes of language contact at Hartford may have been transported to other places, in addition to the ASL–English contact taking place on its own in those locales.

REFERENCES

Brill, R. G. (1974). *Education of the deaf, administrative and professional developments.* Washington, D.C.: Gallaudet College Press.

Gannon, J. (1981). *Deaf heritage. A narrative history of deaf America.* Silver Spring, MD: National Association of the Deaf.

Lane, H. (1984). *When the mind hears.* New York: Random House.

Lou, M.W.P. (1988). The history of language use in the education of the Deaf in the United States. In M. Strong (ed.), *Language learning and deafness* (pp. 75–98). Cambridge: Cambridge University Press.

Moores, D. F. (1987). *Educating the deaf.* Boston: Houghton Mifflin.

Ries, P. (1973). *Further studies in achievement testing, hearing impaired students, Spring 1971.*

Annual Survey of Hearing Impaired Children and Youth. Ser. D, No. 13. Gallaudet College Office of Demographic Studies, Washington, D.C.

Weld, L. (1844). *Twenty-eighth Annual Report of the American Asylum at Hartford for the Education of the Deaf and Dumb* (p. 38). Hartford, CT.

17

Hearing people like to flash the ILY (I Love You) sign when they know Deaf people are watching, but few realize that, in ASL, it is just a jocular Englishism, often used with mild irony.

I've Had Enough of the I-Love-You Sign, Thanks

Tom Willard

1993

I'm glad the U.S. Postal Service has decided to come out with a stamp to recognize American Sign Language. Really, I am. But. . . .

I confess to having mixed feelings about the "I Love You" sign. I realize I run the risk of being tarred, featured and run out of town for expressing this opinion. But I know I'm not alone. The more I talk with people, the more I find that many people have had their fill of the ILY sign. While the sentiment it expresses is a nice one, many seem to think it has become a tiresome cliché.

You know what really gets my goat? When I see a celebrity flashing the ILY sign. Invariably it is the only sign they know. I can't help but wonder, "If you love me so much, why don't you learn more than just that one sign so we can communicate freely and openly?"

Perhaps I am wrong to take the sign literally, and I know that we should not attempt to be like hearing people in every respect, but I can't help but think how bizarre it would be if hearing people went around saying "I love you" to everyone they meet. The constant and repetitive use of the ILY sign dilutes the impact of the sign when we use it with those we really *do* love.

And what is it about the sight of a camera lens that automatically causes people to flash the ILY sign? Can't anyone have their picture taken without producing that sign on their hands?

Enough, already. When the USPS begins selling the two new deafness/ASL postage stamps next August, I'll line up to buy them just like everyone else. After all, how often does our society recognize deaf people? At the same time, I will cringe a little bit each time I affix one of these stamps to an envelope. As a deaf person, this is not how I wish to be recognized.

18

ASL has acquired a large number of English loanwords, just as Japanese and French have done, and some English grammatical structures as well, while American Deaf culture has adopted a great many of the values of the dominant (English-speaking, Protestant) culture in the United States. This situation leaves Deaf Hispanics (and Native Americans) negotiating a very large linguistic and cultural gap.

Traditions: Hispanic, American, Deaf Culture

Which Takes Precedence in Trilingual Interpreter Training?

Ralph Sedano

1997

The Language Department of the Division of Arts and Sciences of the Santa Fe Community College anticipated growth and demand for trilingual interpreters, specifically for Spanish-speaking parents with deaf children and adults in the states of New Mexico, Arizona, Texas, California. A trilingual program that focused specifically on Spanish language, heritage, and culture of the Southwest was developed in response to the anticipated demand. Although the culture and Spanish language can not be limited per se to Mexican culture because it carries an *Iberio-Catholic* tradition inherent of the majority of nations in Latin America, this College had excellent material and human resources related to the Spanish, Mexican, Mexican-American, and Chicano traditions. In the regions of northern New Mexico, it was logical that such cultural traditions invite the focus of interpreter education, especially in a region where there were a few interpreters.

• Development According to Cultural Primacy

Iberio-Catholic traditions are passed down in the spoken and written Spanish forms. We will focus on the American developments, thus the term *Iberio-American* tradition. Noticeably missing was a SL/Deaf Spanish *cultural* tradition. It has yet to surface in the literature of *Iberio-American* history. Concealed is a hole with big questions. Which culture should be given primacy in the program: Deaf American or

Spanish/Hispanic American, and their corresponding cultural values? It seemed obvious that American Sign Language (ASL), English, and Spanish would be balanced, of course, with ASL/Deaf Culture given primacy simply because the clients and/or students receiving services as a result of training would have a deaf perspective. It turned out to be more complicated and complex than we realized in the beginning. Resistance arose from those individuals least expected to do so: Hispanic interpreter students.

• Perceptions in Conflict: Missing Elements

In the years that the writer has coordinated this program, there have always been individuals, both faculty and students, with positive attitudes to its evolution. Their creativity and willingness to be flexible outweighed the many short-comings encountered every year. However, during all those semesters only one ASL teacher besides myself was of Hispanic descent, a Deaf Hispana. This reality would not die; Hispanic aspirants to the ASL teaching profession were, and continue to be, uncommon individuals.

There always was a short supply of qualified teachers and tutors in the community. Turnovers had been constant semester after semester, and qualified mentors for our interns have been in short supply. The College itself has been experiencing a period of transition. Our curriculum is constantly changing to meet all the inconsistencies of growing pains. Consistently intriguing was that Hispanic interpreters and Deaf Hispanic ASL models were rare. In spite of the above factors, the program made headway and became a core program with a core faculty position, established in July 1997. Unanswerable questions continue to linger; fundamental cultural ingredients were absent from program course requirements.

As a Deaf adult, subconsciously I took for granted the fact our program had been evolving on the Deaf perspective and consciousness. The Deaf perspective seemed appropriately dominant, yet perplexing in its presence, somehow. Experience has always been a true master of knowledge in building this program. It taught the writer that regardless of whatever material or human resource available or accumulated for a multicultural/lingual program, development and technical knowledge, of necessity, must undergo prudent scrutiny through a cultural microscope. It is because culture is power, especially by those cultures that have taken root on this continent spanning centuries. My own Hispanic heritage could not realize the power of the *Iberio-American* tradition that often cried out from certain students in the program. For me this was a unique experience and newfound knowledge that forced me once again to re-examine my primary identity and conversely, give appropriate attention to program changes for the future.

Perceptions are constantly and consistently stacked up against Spanish values, norms, over and below Deaf American values and norms. The following questions arose during the past five years: Why do non-Hispanic students tend to out-perform Hispanic students in the ASL/Deaf cultural domain? Why is ASL/Deaf culture a low priority for mastery by Hispanic students? What are the main variables that prompt this character in the majority of our Hispanic interpreter students? Why have the majority of our ASL, even interpreter teachers, been of non-Hispanic descent? Why do most Hispanic students attend to extended family needs at the expense of syllabus requirements? An Iberio-cultural tradition seems to hold sway.

The writer believes those constancies have had a foothold on the door of a *progress-prone* attitude inherent in the *Anglo-Protestant* tradition of Deaf cultural values. It challenges me to examine my actual identity. The fact that Hispanic students' performance levels are below those of non-Hispanics' could not be dismissed on an oversimplification of intelligence, socio-economic status, or education. It runs deeper, and I can sense it at the gut level. This observation lacks the blueprint by which I can construct an inclusive framework to identify the absent ingredients and build a corresponding avenue of passage across both cultures. My cultural attitude, inconspicuously, reflects a pro-Deaf culture to the detriment of the Hispanic culture of which I am a descendant. Who represents the Deaf community? Hold the question a second. It calls for inquiry. Is the Deaf community a compact one with equity of representation of all ethnic groups within? Why then are there so few models from the Hispanic members of that community? Why is resistance from the Hispanic student population so widespread in the program? The *Iberio-American* traditions do seem to reflect *progress-resistant* attitudes as a prescriptive cultural norm. That attitude seems to be a priority in cultural mediation and exchange; is it a barrier?

• Cross-Cultural Perceptions: Barriers?

It is logical to theorize that a high premium may be placed on the power of spoken Spanish within Hispanic families, because it is the medium in which children may carry on their traditional values: language, music, festivals, rules of social interaction, religion, and heritage. A spoken language has a veritable power base here. English is a spoken language that inherently has a lexical-borrowing morphological base compatible with spoken Spanish.

While ASL/Deaf cultural norms, per se, are vital for visual-spatial learners such as deaf children (I was one of them) in Spanish-speaking homes, it does not have any derivative element within the umbrella culture, therefore it faces greater resistance from family and interpreter students. Speechreading in one-on-one situations seems a more secure interactive context (of high-low context continuums) in which to facilitate communication from Spanish to English or vice versa rather than in sign language. Spanish is a spoken language with no diglossia of a coding system in America. English is spoken and may engage lexical borrowing of Spanish terminology; i.e. *compadres, dependencistas, chola, cholo, pachuco, sobrina, sobrino*, and others whereas ASL has yet to demonstrate such a capability except by fingerspelling, an extremely weak courier of cultural connotations. It invites by its own cultural nature, resistance. This is an important factor in the etiology of this field.

In my opinion, implications for "trilingual" Hispanic interpreters become evident when such students perform poorly on ASL and Deaf culture requirements of the course while experiencing an opposite effect in the Spanish culture requirements. The statement that future clients are "deaf first, Hispanic second," does not sit well with Hispanic students/graduates, even though the study of Deaf perspective and their language is the priority of the program for obvious reasons. An *Iberio-American* cultural attitude *does* influence the priority of language usage and integration for professional functions in powerful ways. It would not allow for cross-cultural mediation because there lurks a foreboding threat to cultural integrity. Can the ASL/Deaf culture perspective be subject to the Spanish cultural umbrella? If so, to what extent?

• A Call for Research, Scholarship and Publication

This program opens up a rich field of study specific to cross-cultural issues because evidently ASL and Deaf culture is another *Anglo-Protestant* tradition, as is English. On the opposite end of a cultural continuum is Spanish with an *Iberio-Catholic* tradition, even though students may practice another religion, and have no resources of a corresponding sign language/deaf cultural tradition to draw from. Nearly all the materials used in every class are non-Hispanic: the videotapes, literature, human resource and attitudes. Attitudes inherent to these three different traditions, I believe, do determine how a "trilingual" interpreter will acquire the necessary skills to function as a multilingual mediator. It also determines to what extent a Hispanic interpreter student will make him/herself vulnerable to cultural traditions that have been inculcated in them from infancy. Hispanic students have felt like second class citizens in every situation.

Ultimately, I am well aware that a deaf child will become a deaf adult. As such, the most convenient stress-free avenue of language exchange for these Americans must be ASL. In all humility, I consider myself proficient in both ASL and English, yet I experience cultural elements essential to my well-being that are neither of English nor ASL tradition. I am conscious that these elements are of Spanish origin. I can now empathize with Hispanic interpreter students, who resist the usage of Deaf values over the usage of their Spanish values. My perception that the value of ASL/ Deaf culture is regarded over and above the other two does not impact on the value of those two. This consciousness invites a major conflict of interest in the learning climate: a "love-hate" relationship exists thrice as complex as spoken English-Spanish!

Taking in the above observations, our program will require major modifications. Changes that require close attention to Spanish traditions which address cultural specific questions that were not considered when the program was implemented in 1993.

REFERENCES

Christensen, Kathleen M., and G. L. Delgado. *Multicultural Issues in Deafness*. White Plains, NY: Longman Publishing Group, 1993.

Hall, Edward T. *Beyond Culture*. New York: Anchor Books, 1989.

Harrison, Lawrence E. *The Pan-American Dream*. New York: Basic Books, 1996.

Van Cleve, John V., and B. A. Crouch. *A Place of Their Own*. Washington, DC: Gallaudet University Press, 1989.

Winfield, Richard. *Never the Twain Shall Meet*. Washington, DC: Gallaudet University Press, 1987.

19

Like other societies whose language has no written form, the Deaf community has a rich heritage of traditional poems, language games, and narratives of all kinds. Now that videotaping technology has made possible the creation of definitive texts of what were once performed only for live audiences, ASL artists are increasingly moving from folk traditions to high art.

Rathskellar

Some Oral-Traditional and Not-So-Traditional Characteristics of ASL Literature

Cynthia Lohr Peters

1999

Deaf American culture can be characterized as primarily—and paradoxically—an oral culture existing within a print-valorizing mainstream culture. The paradox derives from the culture's having a visual-kinetic vernacular for which there is no written form in general use. This vernacular is a face-to-face means of communication utilizing not the voice but the hands, face, and body. At work and at school, Deaf Americans use printed and manually coded English, but at home and among themselves, many use the visual vernacular, American Sign Language (ASL). Such a bilingual, bicultural matrix has resulted in a diglossic, or rather polyglossic, discourse that comprises a wide range of both "oral" (sign) and written expression including hybrid forms that feature an interanimation of two markedly different rhetorical traditions. It is the vernacular genres and forms of expression, as well as the hybrid forms, that are of particular interest here, for they display, interestingly enough, many of the characteristics of oral-traditional literature.

As has been the case with traditional oral societies around the world and throughout history, Deaf Americans exhibit to a large degree the immediacy of personal experience and the more intensive socialization of the world that is characteristic of traditional oral cultures. For most of the past two hundred years, Deaf Americans have been educated at state residential schools for the deaf and a small number of postsecondary institutions where, if they have not already done so, they acquire, more or less, sufficient competency in ASL. After secondary and postsecondary education, Deaf Americans frequently congregate for regularly scheduled conventions, festivals, clubs, school reunions, and team sports, and it is primarily by means of such gatherings that they pick up on the latest political, economic, and cultural developments within the culture. In the absence of readily available and inexpensive videophone technology and broadcast/cable television in ASL, it is largely by means of such gatherings, large and small, that the culture and its vernacular art forms are maintained and promulgated.

The vernacular literature of Deaf Americans is very similar to what we know or surmise about much of the oral-traditional literature of the past. For one thing, vernacular ASL literature is more of an "art for a people's sake" than an "art for art's sake." The literature in the vernacular is largely a collective, "orally" (via sign language) transmitted body of performative works. Although ASL works are increasingly recorded or even composed on videotape, many Deaf American storytellers, like the storytellers of old, still travel about and render stories and other vernacular art forms to comparatively small groups of people, frequently as part of some occasion such as a social gathering, ceremony, or festival. Drawing on a traditional stock of stories and other ASL art forms, an ASL artist can choose a story, art form, or even an original piece by another ASL artist, make individual modifications, and, at one time or another and in front of one or another group of viewers, render his or her own variant. An ASL storyteller, in telling a story to a group of viewers, does not just recite but performs to keep the interest and attention of the viewers, enacting one or more characters in a kind of semi-play, semi-mime, all the while conveying mannerisms, appearances, attitudes, and emotions. As renowned ASL storyteller Ben Bahan has expressed it, "The storyteller IS the story."[1] A good story told well and often is picked up by one storyteller after another, with the result that numerous variants have evolved through the years and throughout the country.

Many of the oral-traditional characteristics of ASL literature are evident in *Rathskellar*, produced and directed by Jonathan Kovacs, with Melissa Draganac as artistic director. Not an official product of the Theatre Arts Department or any other Gallaudet University department, *Rathskellar* was independently produced and staged during commencement week in 1999 in a small campus auditorium for members of the Gallaudet community. The action, ostensibly taking place in a student watering hole, featured twenty-one loosely connected performances pieces. The thread running through these performance pieces is the Rathskellar itself: the socializing that goes on at a campus pub as highlighted by "Tequila," "Salsa Dance," and "Party Time" and the opportunity such socializing affords for the display of ASL dexterity, as seen most particularly in "My Dream," "My Childhood," "Who Am I?" "Ice," and "Heart Surgery."

The twenty-one performance pieces in *Rathskellar* range from the traditional to the nontraditional, with many of the traditional forms incorporating modern, innovative features. For example, the drum song, often colloquially called "drum story" in the culture, is a genre at least half a century old, but the *Rathskellar* drum songs "Rain" and "Tequila" depart to some degree from the traditional genre. These two drum songs are more "song" than narrative, but the drumbeat and ASL lyrics make them characteristically Deaf American. In contrast, the A to Z performance pieces are more traditional in form and function. For a long time previous, anything making use of the English alphabet as the main structuring device had been labeled offhand-

A dance number from *Rathskellar*. Photo from the author's private collection, courtesy of Jonathan Kovacs.

edly as an "ABC story" or "ABC poem," but now, many of these are more appropriately called "A to Z mime," for they are not narratives or poems in the usual literary sense. *Rathskellar*'s "Beer," for instance, is an A to Z mime that does not simply evoke an experience—in this case, the act of drinking beer—but enacts it to a large extent. As for the more poetic forms, simply identifying a performance piece as "ASL poetry" fails to get the job done here, what with the more narrow prosodic delineations such as "ASL Poetry '5'" and "ASL Poetry '1'" (the latter case based on the relentless "1" alliteration in the ASL poem "Who Am I?") Another category represented in *Rathskellar* is the "face story," which proves to be a traditional ASL art form characteristically and expertly fusing mime, narrative, and comedy.

A traditional ASL form that may go back to the 1930s or earlier, the ABC story (in *Rathskellar* categorized as "A to Z mime") in particular is usually a quick performance piece that is highly constrained in its structure: the handshapes used to represent the letters of the English alphabet.[2] The ABC story/poem/mime is somewhat similar to an English acrostic, whereby each letter of, for instance, "mother" is the beginning of the first word or phrase in the line; but with an A to Z performance piece, all the letters of the alphabet are used. Just as the English alphabet has twenty-six letters and progresses from A to Z, the traditional A to Z art form usually has only twenty-six signs and likewise progresses consecutively from A to Z. For instance, the A handshape is a kind of fist with the thumb held close to the side, and if one wants to sign KNOCK ON DOOR, one utilizes the A handshape and mimes knocking on a door. An A can also be used on the chest in a circular motion to express regret or remorse (as in "I am sorry"); or each hand in the A handshape can be used to mime washing a car. Although the English alphabet as a structuring device might be considered quite restrictive, the versatility of the vernacular and the dexterity of a skillful signer can effectively overcome such a constraint.

A case in point: early on in the *Rathskellar* production, two performers render an A to Z mime, "Little Hamster," in a simulated impromptu collaboration, resulting in a story longer than twenty-six signs.[3] For the most part in this collaborative work, one performer goes through a few letters and then breaks off, passing the "story" on to the other performer, after which the first performer does a few more letters before passing it back. In effect, in "Little Hamster" the first performer begins with both hands held out in the A handshape face down and parallel to the ground, as if in a starting position. Her hands (still in the A handshape) then swivel as if they are turning the doorknobs of a double door, after which they rise and assume the B handshape of the two sides of the double door opening. As the door opens, the young woman reacts in surprise (each hand in the C handshape on the eyes) and consternation. In ABC reverse, she quickly closes the door (B handshape) and turns the doorknobs (A handshape). Thus what has happened so far is that first the young woman has gone through A, B, and C and then, in reverse, through C, B, and A. Such reversing or backtracking through the alphabet in this case provides a nontraditional twist on the traditional ABC story, which typically has a uniformly forward momentum through the alphabet.

At this point, the story is passed to the second performer, who begins with the sign ENTERPRISING using both hands in the A handshape. Enterprisingly, he PROCEEDS onward in his actions (B handshape). He LOOKS (C handshape), MOVES STEALTHILY (D handshape), and then breaks off, nodding to the young woman and passing the story back to her. Having the story passed back to her, the young woman repeats her A, B and C (although in doing the C handshape, the young woman acts less startled this time around), at which point she adds GOING UP SOME STEPS, using both hands in the D handshape, and, in another direction, GOES UP SOME OTHER STEPS, using the E handshape, where she LOOKS (both hands in the F handshape) in this direction and that direction. She next comes to some heavy curtains and pulls down on the drawstrings (G handshape), drawing the curtains open (H handshape), and then looks over questioningly at her partner (F handshape). The male performer gets another handoff here and pooh-poohs it all with YOU SCREAM "Eeeeeeee!" (E handshape), but IT'S NOTHING using both hands in the F handshape; IT'S JUST A LITTLE THING (G handshape), JUST A HAMSTER (H handshape). The young woman LOOKS WARILY (F handshape) and again DRAWS OPEN THE CURTAINS (G and H handshapes). The male performer here pulls out a knife (I handshape) and SLASHES (J handshape). Responds the young woman vehemently: KILLED!! (K handshape). The young man DRAWS HIS GUN (L handshape), first mimes a round object using the M handshape, and then mimes the barrels of the gun (N handshape, culminating in the O handshape). The young woman remarks with much savoir faire, WE'LL SEE, using the P handshape, which provokes the young man to shoot (R handshape prompted by triggering the gun: Q handshape). The young woman, realizing the danger she is in, mimes running (fists in the S handshape) to escape the BULLET MOVING IN HER DIRECTION (T handshape). She escapes but FALLS (U handshape), and although she manages to GET BACK ON HER FEET (V handshape), she is still very ANXIOUS (W handshape). Her anxiety is well founded, for the other performer PULLS OUT A KNIFE (X handshape). The young woman despairingly responds, WHY??!! (ending in Y handshape), but to no avail as he SLASHES (Z handshape). All through this duet, the two performers are not only narrating but acting out their roles as victim and predator in this dynamic ASL takeoff on the traditional "Haunted House" ABC story.

In contrast to this performance piece that is based on a traditional ASL art form, "Beer" is an innovative A to Z mime that more closely resembles a (humorous) lyric poem than a folk narrative.[4] Starting off this rather unlyrical lyric, the performer mimes a BOTTLE OF BEER, using the A handshape with the flat edge of the hand resting on the palm (in the B handshape). The signer then mimes the cap (C handshape), takes solid aim at it (D handshape), and, as if using an E-shaped bottle opener, removes it with much aplomb. Carefully holding the SLIM BOTTLE (using the G handshape now to mime it), the signer LAPS THE OUTSIDE OF THE BOTTLE (H handshape). ARE YOU JEALOUS? (going from the I to the J handshape), he asks rhetorically. The signer GAZES lovingly at the bottle using the K handshape, LICKS THE BOTTLE (L handshape), brings the L handshape to the lips, and fingerspells "Mmmmmmmm" in a satisfied manner. The signer then indulges in another kiss of the bottle (N handshape) and, using the O handshape on the mouth, guzzles down some more of the full-bodied liquid. The LIQUID GOES DOWN THE THROAT (P handshape), after which condensation from the bottle DRIPS–DRIPS (Q handshape). Using the R handshape to boost the liquid in the bottle and the S handshape to smack it, the signer tops the bottle off with the T handshape. And the bottle of beer is lovingly emptied, the amber liquid savored to the end of the alphabet.

All in all, "Beer" is not simply mime, not simply narrative, and also not simply poetry. It differs markedly from the usual indigenous lyric poetry, which characteristically treats of birds, flowers, the four seasons, the clock tower on the Gallaudet campus, the expressiveness of ASL, and similar lyrical topics. The subject of "Beer," in contrast, is a physical, rather mundane activity—the experience of drinking beer. Nevertheless, the subject is treated lyrically, if somewhat humorously: the liquid as collegiate ambrosia, the multidimensionality of its receptacle, and the multiphased, detailed act of imbibing. It is thus an unusual and wonderfully refreshing specimen of ASL art in the culture.

The slapstick "Heart Surgery," somewhat later on in the *Rathskellar* production, is a performance piece combining two traditional art forms in the culture: the generic ABC story and the "operation" skit.[5] The latter art form traditionally depicts surgery done to a deaf person in need of a definitive cultural identity, with such "surgery" typically involving the removal of audist objects such as a hearing aid or cochlear implant, a Walkman, and a CD from a patient's abdomen. Substituted for these audist objects during the "operation" are widely used Deaf American items such as an ASL videotape, a residential school banner, and an "I Love You" pin. *Rathskellar*'s

The "operation skit" from *Tales from a Clubroom,* by Bernard Bragg and Eugene Berg-man, performed in 1981 at the NAD Convention in Cincinnati. Photo courtesy of Bernard Bragg, from his private collection.

"Heart Surgery," however, departs from the traditional skit in incorporating a farcical A to Z narrative with more than twenty-six signs. The performance piece is set up when, as the ostensible Rathskellar patrons mingle on stage, one of them makes as if to slip and fall unconscious to the floor. Immediately, two of the female performers enact an ambulance coming onto the scene (one performer driving [A handshape] and the other one, behind her, using her hands to FLASH–FLASH–FLASH). They reach the accident victim and proceed to administer electroshock therapy (A hand-shape), but not before one paramedic bumblingly zaps the other in a kind of hilarious Laurel and Hardy routine. But look! The heart monitor (B handshape) is warning that the patient is dangerously flatlining (B handshape), prompting one of the para-medics to quickly rummage around inside a medical bag. She takes out a surgical mask and rather too briskly snaps it onto the other paramedic's face (C handshape). As she dons her own, it is grasped and pulled, the elastic band stretching to the breaking point. In gleeful retaliation, her partner lets go, and it springs back with a resounding smack (C handshape). Belatedly remembering the expiring patient, the two paramedics mime giving the patient a hypodermic injection (D handshape). Then, using the E handshape, the two paramedics industriously and, for once in sync, unbutton the shirt and lay it open (F handshape). From here on, the narrative continues from G to Z, at which point the patient revives and the monitor displays a strong, steady heartbeat (Z handshape), to everyone's immense relief. All in all, "Heart Surgery" skillfully and artistically fuses the traditional skit and the generic A to Z vernacular, taking the two art forms into the realm of entertaining narrative, ASL art, and slapstick.

Likewise, the 1–5–ch10–15 mime, "My Childhood," takes the traditional number story and comes up with a collaborative art form utilizing only the handshapes for one, five, ten, and fifteen. Depending on the ASL artist and the desired pattern, a "number story" can go from 1 to 10, 1 to 20, and onward or consist of any combination of even or odd numbers. The traditional number story, however, is never so introspective as "My Childhood" but typically takes as its topic an action theme, such as that of "Cowboys and Indians."[6] In effect, "My Childhood" begins with the handshape for ONE, with the signer enacting a little boy, pointing to himself and then making the one-year-old sign off the chin. Still using the 1-handshape, the performer mimes SQUARE OBJECT and TAPPING SQUARE OBJECT using only the two index fingers. AN ADULT APPROACHES, and he responds happily with the baby sign for MOTHER (with one finger on the chin—this is typical of the early signing of very young deaf children). The performer now enacts his mother gesturing, COME HERE, and he responds by pointing to himself, ME? He TOTTERS OVER excitedly (each forefinger like a leg moving but maintaining balance precariously) to a CAKE WITH A CANDLE IN THE MIDDLE, and HAPPY BIRTHDAY TO YOU is sung (like someone conducting an orchestra). Still using the 1 handshape, the performer enacts the little boy TOTTERING OVER TO THE CAKE and AT-TEMPTING TO FINGER OFF SOME ICING. Next enacting the mother, the per-former gestures and mimes, forefinger wagging, NO, NO, BLOW OUT THE CAN-DLE. Again enacting the child, the performer BLOWS OUT THE CANDLE WITH A PUFF and CLAPS HIS HANDS. From here on, all the signs are in the five-handshape, not the least of which is the AGE FIVE off the chin, the day and age the little boy opens a birthday box and takes out one book after another until he comes to a teddy bear. Still using only the 5 handshape, the performer as the little boy falls fast asleep cuddling the teddy bear, and the next morning he wakes up for the first day of school. He eagerly dresses, waves farewell, leaves the house, steps into the school bus, arrives at school, and walks down the hallway to his classroom. This continues to when the performer as a little boy reaches age ten, from which point on he uses only the 10 handshape. In the same vein, when the narrative/mime arrives at the point when the boy reaches age fifteen, the performer begins using fifteen-handshape signs exclusively. As the young man appears to look in a mirror, seeing himself as something in one mirror and something else in another mirror, the spot-light shifts to another performer who, looking into a mirror, offers the following soliloquy, a remarkable tour de force in which every sign alliterates on a single handshape, the "1."

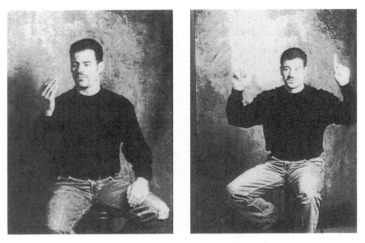

Jonathan Kovacs performing "Who Am I?" Left: looking in a mirror, the opening line of the poem. Right: SUCCEED, showing the alliterative "1" hand. © John Consoli.

WHO AM I?[7]

ASL	English
MIRROR (Looking–Action)	Looking at the mirror/talking to the mirror
WHO YOU? (at mirror)	Who are you?
THEY SAY ME HEARING	They say I am hearing.
WHO YOU?	Who are you?
THEM SAY ME DEAF	They say I am Deaf.
WHO YOU?	Who are you?
THEM SAY ME DIFFERENT	They say I am different.
WHO YOU?	Who are you?
THEM SAY ME SMART	They say I am smart.
WHO YOU?	Who are you?
THEY SAY ME STRUGGLE	They say I am struggling.
WHO YOU?	Who are you?
THEM SAY ME SUCCESS	They say I am succeeding.
WHO YOU?	Who . . . are . . . you?
Thinking/confused (Action)	Now I am confused!
FINISH (I've had it!)	That's it! I've had enough!
FIST HIT (hits mirror with both hands)	(Hits the mirror)
CRACK–CRACK	(Mirror cracks)
FALLING (mirror) PIECES	(Mirror pieces falling down)

(Picks up a mirror piece and says . . .)	(Picks up a mirror piece and says . . .)
(repeats pickup for each word)	(repeats pickup for each word)
HEARING?	Am I hearing?
DEAF?	Am I Deaf?
DIFFERNET?	Am I different?
SMART?	Am I smart?
STRUGGLE?	Am I struggling?
SUCCESS?	Am I succeeding?
(Looks back at mirror)	(Looks back at the mirror/talks to self)
WHO ME?	Who am I?
YOU SMART	You are smart.
WHO ME?	Who am I?
YOU SUCCESS	You are succeeding.
WHO ME?	Who am I?
YOU DEAF	You are Deaf.
(Looks at self)	(Finally understand yourself)
ME	I am . . .
TRUE	Truly . . .
DEAF	Deaf!

Upon the completion of this poetic capsule, viewers are passed back to the first performer, who resumes "My Childhood" with fifteen-handshape signs, indicating with alternating hands a mirror to one side and another mirror to the other side. Still using the fifteen-handshape, the young man insists on his cultural identity as a Deaf American and his right to use the visual vernacular, ASL.

In the indigenous literature, lyric poems are "personal" only insofar as Deaf American identity is concerned. While they seem self-referential (navel gazing), they actually are reflective of the circumstances of virtually all Deaf Americans and thus are community statements. When it comes to "My Childhood" and "Who Am I?" specifically, the two-world condition of Deaf Americans more often than not results in a double identity: on the one hand, the hearing world insists that a deaf person has a hearing impairment and needs to be rehabilitated and integrated; on the other hand, the Deaf world views a deaf person as being smart, capable, and differently oriented (i.e., visually oriented). The performer at the end of "Who Am I?" evinces this double identity in a dialogue with himself before a mirror, using predominantly one-handshape signs, alternating from one side to the other until the mirror shatters into myriad little pieces. Hence the message of this lyric and many other such lyrics in the vernacular literature is that not just this one Deaf American performer but deaf children as a whole think they are alone until they discover the Deaf world. The innovative combination of this theme and tone with the traditional art form is surprising but gratifying to Deaf American audiences.

Another traditional form in *Rathskellar* featuring a number of innovations is the drum story. The drum songs "Rain" and "Tequila" are ASL narratives, but each has a drum accompaniment. The culture has always had rhythmical performance pieces such as the "Boat, Drink, Fun, Enjoy" song performed by George Kannapell and caught on 8 mm film by Charles Krauel in the 1930s.[8] Beginning in the 1940s with the use of the big bass drum to communicate signals and plays during football games at Gallaudet University, the drum story or song came into being. One of the more widely known drum songs is "The Bison Song," the thrilling mascot song still performed today, and the drumbeat for this song has become so ingrained that it has been picked up and utilized in other songs and stories. Such a drum story or song is characterized by patterned, repetitive signing, done as if a drum were being rhythmically pounded—and in the case of *Rathskellar*, one actually is. Various drumbeats, from one-two-three-four to a slow one-two and quick three-four-five, can now be found in many vernacular forms in the culture. "Janitor" in *Rathskellar*, however, makes use of a drum accompaniment only in the "dance" refrain repeated after each "stanza" of the narrative. Four performers with long wooden poles render this narrative, with one narrating and then all four doing the dance refrain five times in all. During the dance refrain, the poles are tapped on end on the floor, three times to each side, after which the performers swivel and tap again three times. This pole tapping continues in diverse ways, but always to the beat of three. The narrative begins with the following stanza:

ASL	*English*
LOOK BOOK, REMINISCENCE	I remember with affection and sadness
LONG AGO, AGE TWELVE	A long time ago when I was twelve
JANITOR, FRIEND	A janitor who became my good friend.
Tap Tap Tap	Tap Tap Tap
Tap Tap Tap	Tap Tap Tap
Tap Tap Tap	Tap Tap Tap
Tap Tap Tap	Tap Tap Tap
WALK DOWN HALLWAY, CARRYING BOOKS	I walk down the hallway, carrying my books
WALK DOWN HALLWAY, CARRYING BOOKS	I walk down the hallway, carrying my books
THREE BIG BOYS APPROACH MENACINGLY	Three big boys approach menacingly.
RUN, STAND—BACK AGAINST WALL	I run and back up against a wall.
LOOK UP, SEE MOP HANDLE	I look up to see a mop handle.
JANITOR MOTIONS BOYS TO LEAVE	The janitor motions the boys to leave.
JANITOR MOPS FLOOR	The janitor begins mopping the floor.

HEY, THANK YOU			"Hey, thanks!"			
DEAF?			Are you deaf?			
YOU DEAF?			Are you deaf, too?			
FRIENDS			We become good friends.			

Tap	Tap	Tap	Tap	Tap	Tap	
Tap	Tap	Tap	Tap	Tap	Tap	
Tap	Tap	Tap	Tap	Tap	Tap	
Tap	Tap	Tap	Tap	Tap	Tap	

FUTURE, AGE THIRTEEN	Later on, I become thirteen years old.
JANITOR COMES, GIVES BOOK—DEAF HERITAGE	The janitor gives me a book about Deaf heritage.
READ/READ, KNOWLEDGEABLE	I read and become very knowledgeable.

Tap	Tap	Tap	Tap	Tap	Tap	
Tap	Tap	Tap	Tap	Tap	Tap	
Tap	Tap	Tap	Tap	Tap	Tap	
Tap	Tap	Tap	Tap	Tap	Tap	

THANKSGIVING, SIT, EAT	At Thanksgiving, we sit together and dine.
FOOD, DRINK, STORYTELLING	There is food, drink, and storytelling.
LEARN/LEARN, PILGRIMS AND INDIANS	I learn about the Pilgrims and Indians.
ABSORB/ABSORB, BECOME SMART	I keep learning and learning and become smart.

Tap	Tap	Tap	Tap	Tap	Tap	
Tap	Tap	Tap	Tap	Tap	Tap	
Tap	Tap	Tap	Tap	Tap	Tap	
Tap	Tap	Tap	Tap	Tap	Tap	

SNOWING, CARRYING PRESENT	It is snowing and I walk to the janitor's house with a present.
WALK/WALK, CARRYING PRESENT	I keep on walking, carrying my present.
AMBULANCE ARRIVES, FLASH/FLASH	I see an ambulance arrive at the house.
CARRYING PRESENT, WALK/WALK	I continue walking with my present.
PEER, CRANE, ANGLE TO SEE	I try to see what is going on.
JANITOR LYING ON STRETCHER	The janitor is brought out on a stretcher.
DOORS OPEN, STRETCHER PUT INSIDE	He is put into the ambulance.
AMBULANCE LEAVES, FLASH/FLASH	The ambulance leaves, lights flashing.
LOOK DOWN, PRESENT	In shocked disbelief, I look down at the present in my hands.
DROP PRESENT	And the present falls to the ground.

Tap	Tap	Tap	Tap	Tap	Tap
Tap	Tap	Tap	Tap	Tap	Tap
Tap	Tap	Tap	Tap	Tap	Tap
Tap	Tap	Tap	Tap	Tap	Tap

WALK/WALK CEMETERY	I visit the cemetery.
TOMBSTONES, TOMBSTONES	There are many tombstones there.
TOMBSTONES, WALK/WALK	I see more tombstones and keep walking.
READ/READ TOMBSTONE	I come to one tombstone and read the inscription.
SUN SETS	The sun begins to set in all its glory.
TREES, TREES, BIRDS, BIRDS	There are trees and birds everywhere.
LOOK AT TOMBSTONE	Deep in thought, I gaze at the tombstone.
RAINDROPS, RAINDROPS	Raindrops pitter patter.
RAINING/RAINING	Rain falls softly and steadily.[9]

As in "Who Am I?" and "My Childhood," "Janitor" treats of communal knowledge and heritage, of which the Deaf American janitor at the residential or public school with a mainstreaming program is symbolic. Although the performance piece itself is personal and lyrical, it speaks to all Deaf Americans.

Another feat of ASL dexterity is evident in "Ice," a face story—specifically, a performed narrative that takes an inanimate object, usually some round or square object, and anthropomorphizes it.[10] In this case, one of the *Rathskellar* performers enacts an ice cube, his or her face moving in a way to intimate that it is subject to outside forces and conveying feelings and reactions as a result. Basically, in "Ice" one performer kneels down on the stage and a second performer stands behind him. The performer who is behind is the one who is acting upon the ice cube. As he seems to act upon the ice cube, the other performer mimes the ice cube being acted upon. As the standing performer mimes filling up a large ice cube tray with water from a faucet, the other performer, using his head, arms, and hands, mimes the water pouring into the tray, filling the cubicles, swirling around, and then becoming quiescent. The standing performer mimes turning off the faucet and putting the tray into the freezer. The other performer's face shows the water freezing until it becomes solid and immovable. The tray is then taken out of the freezer, turned over, and banged against the table to loosen the cubes. One cube is picked up and deposited in a glass. As it is picked up and deposited, the kneeling performer mimes his head being grasped, lifted, and dropped into the glass, where it hits the bottom and bounces off the sides until it settles down. As soda is poured into the glass, we are treated to an enactment of the ice cube being submerged (the performer mimes his head being engulfed in water) and bicarbonated soda foaming over it. Then the liquid becomes still and the cube floats contentedly (the performer's head stops moving in motion with the water). But this is only temporary, for soon the standing performer mimes drinking from the glass, and as the glass is tipped, we see the cube moving in a downward and sideways direction as the liquid is imbibed (the "ice cube" performer leans to the right and uses his hands to mime the movement of the liquid). The cube flows very quickly downward and is taken into the mouth, after which it is moved around and tucked into the cheek. As the standing performer enacts biting down on the ice cube, the other performer mimes teeth (using his hands and fingers—one on top and one below—in the shape and action of teeth) biting down on his head. As the cube is bitten several times, the performer mimes cracks appearing in his face. Finally, the cube is ejected back into the glass, and the glass is set down on a table. As the liquid swirls, we see tears (or is it condensation?) streaming slowly down the kneeling young man's face. But the water becomes quiescent, and the cube comes to a contented rest.

In Deaf American culture, many works are collaborative enterprises, conceived and refined by more than one ASL signer or artist. Rarely are these performances listed along with the names of their creators or performers. Similarly, neither creators nor performers—actually one and the same—are listed in the *Rathskellar* program. This is because in vernacular ASL literature, authorship is not prioritized. The impermanency of ASL vernacular forms (aside from the few on videotape, and very few are on tape because of the very small market, which makes them correspondingly expensive) is similar to the impermanency of oral traditional works, as is the absence of any "definite," "formal," "original," or "authorized" version. Therefore, no prohibition exists against someone taking whatever can be remembered and doing a variation of it. This has continued down through the decades and throughout the country, with the result that many, many variants of a traditional narrative, skit, or other performance piece exist.

In addition, the *Rathskellar* production has a communal or collective appeal in that the embracing concept is that of the campus watering hole, popular as a gathering place in the middle third of the twentieth century. Originally located in the basement of the student union building at Gallaudet University (since moved to the top floor, unfortunately redesigned and renamed "The Abbey"), it was where students congregated, imbibed both alcoholic and nonalcoholic beverages, gave vent to pent-up academic (and literacy) pressures, and made merry with vernacular storytelling, jokes, mime, and other popular (and indigenous) forms of expression. A segment called "Rathskellar Memories" in the *Rathskellar* production highlights this history through collective storytelling, bringing on stage Chuck Bowie (a former Student Body Government [SBG] president now working in computer services) and Brenda Keller (an alumna now working in auxiliary services), both of whom reminiscence about their frequenting of the campus pub.

In reminiscing in "Rathskellar Memories," cast members and special guests discourse on stage as if carrying on a conversation among themselves. They position themselves so that the viewers can easily (and visually) follow the thread of talk and feel involved in the conversation, if only as "listeners." In one previous *Rathskellar* production, Sam Yates, a counselor at the Model Secondary School for the Deaf (MSSD) on the Gallaudet campus, recalled the establishment of the Rathskellar in the 1960s. Brenda Keller next described what it was like to congregate at the watering hole and luxuriate in the free-wheeling atmosphere, spiced with A to Z narratives and other ASL art forms. Then it was on to Chuck Bowie, who recalled the Rathskellar being closed, relocated, and renamed at the time he was SBG president in the 1980s. At the end of the reminiscing, the special guests were bid farewell, and they waved to all and sundry, including the viewers, as they walked off the stage. The whole presentation made for an interactive experience, including the viewers in the conversation and bidding farewell to them at the end.

To further promote interaction, the May 1999 *Rathskellar* production was staged in the student union auditorium rather than at the university theater, which packs a much larger audience. The student union auditorium is a smaller and more intimate theater with a lower stage and more casual seating arrangement. Such close proximity allows for more interaction, including good use of eye contact, which is necessary for effective ASL discourse. A good deal of the time the *Rathskellar* performers keep their eyes on the viewers during the production, often as part of whatever eye behavior is required at the linguistic level. Frequently, viewers in the first three or four rows feel as if the performers are signing directly to them. This makes for more interaction and intimacy and therefore fosters more of a collectivity, as opposed to the solitary activity that occurs in the hearing world in the writing or reading of a narrative or poem. The viewers at a *Rathskellar* production in this auditorium feel very much caught up in the performances and very much a part of the whole player-viewer community.

Rathskellar is actually not as interactive as a number of other indigenous Deaf American productions have been. Many indigenous productions go out of their way to include a good deal of interaction with the viewers. They endeavor in diverse ways to make the viewers feel a part of the production itself. For instance, *Institution Blues*, the 1993 SignRise Cultural Arts production in the Washington, D.C., metropolitan area, began with a protest rally whereby the protesters entered the auditorium from the back and marched down the aisles amid the viewers, waving their placards and pumping their hands. Upon arrival onstage, the protest rally leaders advanced to the front of the stage and brought the viewers into the protest. And the viewers joined in enthusiastically, many of them leaping to their feet and pumping their hands, "Keep the institution open! Keep the institution open!" Similarly, a Kappa Gamma fraternity production of *Vaudeville* in 1999 at Gallaudet University opened with a masked, hooded emcee striding across the stage and demanding of the viewers, "Who am I?" Before long, this fearsome character was leaping down from the stage and striding from one seat to another, caustically addressing and responding to various attempts at identification. A "Dry T-Shirt Contest" as part of this production ensured the viewers would prompt the (imaginary) visual applause meter. Such productions or performances, interactive as they are, can be likened to the oral-traditional literature of the past in that they are a co-creational effort—co-creational in that the emcee and viewers alike, as in the case of *Vaudeville*, are responsible for the end product. Such dramatic productions or performances have a significant amount of performer-viewer interaction, all of which leads to a collaborative, communal product.

Another characteristic of some oral-traditional literatures can be seen in the whole assemblage of twenty-one performance pieces in *Rathskellar*: the cobbling together or coming together of diverse elements and performances. The production is something of a Deaf American musical revue or variety show: a heterogeneous yet collective effort on the part of a fairly large number of cast members. It is true that musical revues and variety shows are also common in American culture as a whole, but this production is especially reminiscent of oral-traditional literature in its heterogeneity and collectivity. The production does not just have one performer or group following another but draws on an ensemble effort throughout the twenty-one performances. Not all cast members participate in all the performance pieces, but almost all of these pieces have at least two performers; it is rare for any one piece to have fewer than three performers. Even the A to Z mimes, which are traditionally done by a single performer, are here frequently done by two or more performers collaboratively. ("Beer" is a solo performance, but a few of the other players are grouped about the bar looking on.) Even when one performer is spotlighted at a particular point, viewers never have the feeling that this performer is hogging the stage and the spotlight. No one performer is identified and no one headliner is singled out for special attention, even though several, including the producer/director, Jonathan Kovacs, are especially effective and riveting (though this depends on personal preference and prior knowledge of the cast).

Despite being a musical revue, *Rathskellar* does not emphasize the aurality of music and song as a typical American musical revue or variety show does. The accent is instead on the visual and the tactile (i.e. the vibrations of the drumbeats and the special voice effects) rather than the aural. This does not mean that the production is utterly soundless—in fact, the drumbeats and the music are boomingly loud—but that it is instead oriented to the visual and tactile. The goal here is to showcase ASL, not to approximate a popular song's aural qualities. This contrasts with a period in the 1970s when many popular songs were done for or by Good Vibrations!, Rock Gospel, Musign, and other companies in a way to leave them still recognizable as the popular aural songs they were. Even when signed, they retained their aural features, for the signing, phrasing, and tempo were done to highlight the original musical score. By using body movements, the performers attempted to convey the pitch, tempo, and mood of the songs. It could be said that the music, with its wide-ranging scales, pitches, and tones, did not pass over into the visual realm well, although many Deaf Americans appreciated the translations. In contrast, in *Rathskellar*, the popular songs selected or originated have been drastically modified or created with ASL in mind, rather than the other way around. Those selected were chosen for how "ASL" they could be. As a result, sign communication and body movement incorporated as part of the "singing" are clear and appropriate to the beat and the vernacular.

Also, whereas in the 1970s various songs and musical numbers were signed for a particular musical program, this production mostly draws on the vernacular art forms of the culture. Many a *Rathskellar* number starts with an ASL vernacular form itself. For instance, in the case of "Janitor," Jonathan Kovacs took the traditional theme of the deaf school janitor and came up with a number of verses, each followed by a drum/dance refrain. The selection of signs is very careful, keeping to a minimum the number and diversity of handshapes, orientations, and motions in order to have a patterned and harmonious whole. The structured, rhythmic narrative has stanzas marked off by refrains involving rapping the floor with one and then the other end of a pole representing a broom or mop handle. This is augmented by patterned drumbeats; indeed, the narrative is structured in such a way as to take advantage of traditional drumbeats in the culture. Hence, the drumbeats tactilely reinforce and enhance the visual features.

This brings up the question of whether or not *Rathskellar* is literature. First of all, what is highly artistic in ASL discourse may not be seen by the traditional literary critic to be highly artistic or even literary when it comes to Western discourse. The ASL poem "Who Am I?" with its adept use of alliteration and enactment (Kovacs's body language and facial expressions are skillful and effective) and its provocative theme of split identity has an (ASL) aesthetics on a par with those of Western literature. However, some of the same aesthetics can be seen in "Motorcycle Ride," but here, while they are practiced in a way congenial to ASL discourse and culture, they would not be congenial to high Western discourse. The performance, which often depicts three performers physically "riding" on each other, would be considered "low" and common from the viewpoint of Western literature. Another example would be that of the drum song "Tequila," with its use of the drumbeat aesthetic in ASL discourse. Its use of visual rhyme based on the drumbeat is a high aesthetic in ASL, and it has a stirring effect on viewers. It would probably have as stirring an effect on the literary critic because he or she would find high aesthetics in it approximate to those of Western discourse. The "but" is: at the end of "Tequila," one of the performers announces—and this is natural and appropriate to the topic and the performance piece—that he needs to attend to a particular body function. Such a switch to the low and common is not well countenanced in conventional Western literature, but it is an integral part of ASL discourse and was no doubt a part of much oral-traditional literature in the distant past.

Other criteria more suitable for oral-traditional literature and for a visual-kinetic discourse should be considered when it comes to approaching *Rathskellar* and other ASL art forms. The ASL storytelling in the production is not actually storytelling or actually narrative; nor is ASL poetry actually poetry. The program book identifies or classifies particular ASL art forms as ASL stories, poems, and songs, but many are not actually stories, poems, and songs according to Western literary or musical conventions. They are more a fusion of performance (mime and dramatics), graphic arts, modern dance, cinema, and literature because of the nature of the visual vernacular and Deaf American culture itself. And indeed, the company for the most part avoids conventional Western literary classifications, utilizing instead more culture-specific labels for vernacular art forms such as "A to Z Mime," "ASL Poetry '5'," and "Drum/Story."

Therefore, from the viewpoint of the literary scholar *Rathskellar* is a mixture—a heterogeneity—that is not literature per se, certainly not literature as "well-wrought urn." Questions about the literary value of *Rathskellar* would probably resemble the ongoing debate about whether the African American *Cane*, a composite of narrative, poetry, and drama, can actually be considered a novel. This early twentieth-century masterpiece by Jean Toomer was long discounted because many readers and critics were not comfortable with its heterogeneity and apparent disunity. But like *Rathskellar*, *Cane* is an example of minority discourse—a minority discourse with oral roots. A minority discourse, particularly one having oral origins or underpinnings, can be very different from a literary discourse. Both *Cane* and *Rathskellar* should thus be examined in the light of their own cultural aesthetics rather than of those solely characteristic of Western discourse.

Perhaps most important, *Rathskellar* is communal literature. Like oral-traditional literature, it is more a discourse of the people than an art. It is a means of communal education, a means of letting a people know who they are and what life is all about (i.e., how they decide to view life). In such a discourse, vernacular art forms that are passed down from generation to generation and come together—as in, for example, a Literary Night or *Rathskellar* production—function like a cultural encyclopedia. So, too, were the Homeric epics something of a cultural encyclopedia for the ancient Greeks. It may seem presumptuous to compare a campus production by young Deaf Americans to the epics of Homer, but *Rathskellar* has a quality found not only in these epics but in the plays of Shakespeare, the novels of Cervantes and Rabelais, and other great early literature. This 1999 production touches on all of the following: the everyday, the low, the common, the high, the transcendent, and the noble. It combines the high artistic and the low popular. It speaks to everyone, both the individual and the community. *Rathskellar* is very much literature in many, if not all, senses of the word.

NOTES

Grateful acknowledgments to Melissa Draganac and Jonathan Kovacs for their assistance and permission to use the ASL/English transcriptions of "Who Am I?" and "Janitor."

1. E-mail correspondence between the author and Ben Bahan in March 1995.

2. It is not clear at this time just when ABC stories first materialized.

3. "Little Hamster" is the creation of Jonathan Kovacs and several other members of the *Rathskellar* company.

4. "Beer" was composed by the company under the guidance and direction of Jonathan Kovacs.

5. "Heart Surgery" was also composed by the company under the guidance and direction of Jonathan Kovacs.

6. "My Childhood" is another collaborative performance piece composed under the direction of Jonathan Kovacs.

7. "Who Am I?" and its English translation used by permission of Jonathan Kovacs.

8. *Charles Krauel: A Profile of a Deaf Filmmaker,* produced by Joe Dannis, directed by Ted Supalla. 30 mins., videocassette, Dawn Pictures, San Diego, CA, 1994.

9. "Janitor" is the original work of Jonathan Kovacs. The dance/pole refrains were choreographed by Fred Beam. ASL and English transcriptions by the author are used by permission of Jonathan Kovacs.

10. "Ice" was originated by Nancy Travis and expanded upon by Jonathan Kovacs.

Despite the potential for ASL literature of increasingly available and affordable videotape equipment, the lack of a written form continues to stymie ASL artists seeking publication in the mainstream venues of print media and live theater.

20

In Search of the Perfect Sign-Language Script

Insights into the Diverse Writing Styles of Deaf Playwrights

Willy Conley

1999

Unlike hearing playwrights of the English language who may occasionally incorporate dialect or second languages, deaf playwrights must work with the Deaf community's minority signed language, ASL, and its many dialects, as well as a range of signed English systems. They have the added task of considering the most accurate and efficient way of expressing this polyglot dialogue in written English, because ASL itself has no written form that is in general use among deaf signers. As a playwright who happens to be deaf, I struggle to find a standardized way to create specific sign dialogue on the page. And I agonize over whether or not my script will be understood by other theatre artists, let alone influential producers and directors.

What would help hearing theatre artists understand the inherent artistic, cultural, and linguistic elements when reading a script by a deaf playwright? Deaf playwrights are up against thousands of hearing playwrights when submitting plays for grants, fellowships, festivals of new works, LORT (League of Resident Theatres) /Equity theatres, and the like. With a stack of hundreds of scripts to go through, what hearing evaluator with limited or no knowledge of Deaf culture would want to read past the first few pages of a script filled with linguistic and cultural considerations such as Sim/Com, word-codes, English glosses, bilingual puns and double entendres, finger-alphabet play, and pantomime scenarios?

Script excerpts from a variety of deaf playwrights were collected in this essay to give the reader a sense of the diverse approaches to staging the signed dialogue of a play. The signing actor, in most cases the deaf actor, must analyze his or her role to determine how to develop the manual communication mode most appropriate to the character. The range of options includes: universal gestures, pantomime, American Sign Language (ASL) with a grassroots feel, ASL from a college-educated deaf family,

Signed English of a bilingual-bicultural background, Signed English of a strict English-language education via word for word signs, and "Signing Exact English," an encoding system for spoken English that uses signs in conceptually incorrect ways to transcribe all the prefixes, suffixes, contractions, and idiosyncrasies of the English language. One could go as far as Cued Speech, with its little hand codes around the mouth. And then there's Oralism, which uses no signs, and its sometimes valiant yet tragic attempts at speaking and lipreading. Oralism is not manual communication, although it comes with a whole set of dramatic choices and faux pas for the playwright or actor.

One may wonder why deaf playwrights with a sign language background would use English to express their visual, three-dimensional, mobile language in a script. To record sign language as stage dialogue on paper would be like drawing a card stack of animated figures that indicate movement in their arms, hands, and faces and then flipping through the cards like an old-fashioned peep show to read the signs. A deaf playwright may use videotape to develop a script, but that would require a cumbersome combination of expensive video-editing equipment, editing knowledge, and a considerable chunk of time to layer characters and signed dialogue into scenes, and of course, it would assume a "reader" who is fluent over the Deaf language continuum.

Videotapes have been used to record raw footage of improvisations that resulted in producing written lines in English. It is much easier to watch a videotape, rewind or fast-forward, and hit the Play/Pause button to jot down useful snippets of improvised ASL dialogue into English. Then the playwright can shuffle around the English dialogue and structure it into an industry-standard playscript format with a word processor. Perhaps someday visual recording and editing of sign language may be done with ease on a computer with CD-ROM or video-to-computer technology. A script program would have to be developed and standardized so that all deaf theatre artists are "on the same page" when receiving a published copy.

It is interesting to note that couple of ASL writing systems are available to deaf writers if they care to learn them and, more important, have any reason to believe that other theatre artists, deaf and hearing, have previous knowledge of these systems.

One such system is called SignWriting®, developed in 1974 by Valerie Sutton, a hearing dancer who created the Sutton Movement Writing. Originally, she created an arrangement of visual symbols as a way to learn ballet. Later, she developed a similar arrangement for recording a signed language. On the next page is an example of SignWriting, showing symbols of handshapes, movements, and facial expressions of American Sign Language.

If theatre artists are taught this system early in their lives so that it becomes second nature, it may be a viable scriptwriting option. To my knowledge, however, no deaf playwright today has used this system in his or her script—perhaps for good reason. Deaf playwrights would have to hope that current directors, designers, and actors nationwide know how to read these symbols.

An older writing system—the first known for ASL—was developed in 1965 by

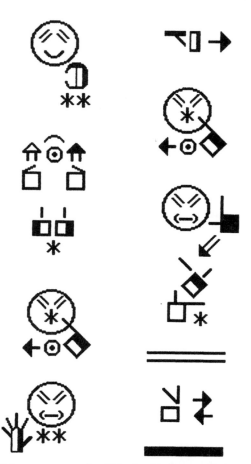

Sutton SignWriting®. This passage reads: "Cinderella lives with her stepmother and two stepsisters." http://www.signwriting.org/cind01.html, 9/5/99.

William Stokoe, Dorothy Casterline, and Carl Croneberg as part of their research in ASL. While the Sutton System is ideographic, Stokoe's team isolated individual ASL signs (just as spoken language can be broken up into word-sized units) and then assembled a complex system of symbols and diacritical markings that correspond to sign handshapes, orientation, and movement. The following are some examples:

$\emptyset \sqrt{A} \sqrt{A^{1\sim}}$ —"thunderstruck"
[ ] LL÷ —"generous"
$\cup Y_T{}^x$ —"mistake"

Again, playwrights would need to be able to read and write in this system as fluently as English speakers write English; likewise with the rest of the collaborative team of theatre artists. No existing script has been found using this technique.

The deaf community's flat rejection of these and other attempts to create a graphic system for ASL is an interesting story in its own right, but the fact remains that deaf playwrights universally document the sign language they envisioned in English. There is no better organized recording system for a playscript format available today.

In 1973, Gilbert Eastman, now Professor Emeritus of Theatre Arts at Gallaudet University, wrote a play called *Sign Me Alice*, based on George Bernard Shaw's *Pygmalion* and Alan Jay Lerner's *My Fair Lady*. He is perhaps the first published deaf playwright to tackle, comprehensively, the challenge of using English in a way to capture the essence of ASL and other sign systems in a playscript. For readers and actors, Professor Eastman developed a table of "word-codes" for the number of sign language modes that he envisioned in his comedy:

word . . . . sign of American Sign Language
w̲ord . . . . sign with letter [meaning fingerspelled letter from the manual alphabet]
w̲o̲r̲d̲ . . . . fingerspelled
word-word . . . . one sign
word/word . . . . repeated sign
word=word . . . . same sign, both hands
word+word . . . . different sign each hand
WORD . . . . gesture (generally understood)
"word" . . . . spoken word
[word] . . . . action or mime, conventional stage directions
*n̲ame . . . . sign for proper name
(S.C.) . . . . simultaneous communication [meaning signing and speaking at the same time]

Eastman also included a chart of initialized signs in the American Manual Alphabet, a few illustrations on how to sign the proper names of characters, and some illustrations of special sign vocabulary. In his notes, he gave suggested sign language mannerisms for some of the characters, such as stuttering with signs, signing and speaking at the same time, and signing in exact English word order with corresponding mouth movements (an artificial language he called Using Signed English— U.S.E.).

This is an excerpt from *Sign Me Alice* that shows how the word-code system looks on the page:

ALICE: [*to* TERRY] Woman mad.
TERRY: She right.
DR. ZENO: I̲ w̲ould r̲ather l̲ook a̲t a̲n i̲nterpreter w̲ith p̲roper E̲nglish. A̲pes gesticulate in a̲ c̲age *(points at* ALICE*)* just li̲ke t̲his one.
ALICE: YESYESYESYES
DR. ZENO: W̲hat i̲s t̲hat? I̲ ask you. You just sign "CCC" and "Sick you" and now "YESYESYESYES." N̲o wonder s̲he c̲an't r̲ise f̲rom h̲er place. W̲hy c̲an't the d̲eaf learn h̲ow to s̲ign E̲nglish. W̲hy c̲an't the d̲eaf? You see this c̲reature w̲ith h̲er bad E̲nglish t̲hat w̲ill k̲eep h̲er i̲n the d̲ark w̲orld. W̲ell, s̲ir, in six m̲onths I̲ c̲ould pass

her off as a lady at a convention ball. I could even get her a place as a teacher or secretary, which requires perfect English.

ALICE: What that you just say before.

DR. ZENO: I say I could pass you off as the First Lady.

ALICE: CCC *(to DR. YLVISAKER)* You believe?

As one can see, Dr. Zeno, the Professor Higgins character, strings together a lot of words coded as initialized signs, an absurd, artificial way of communicating that's nearly incomprehensible to deaf people in real life. Alice, the Eliza Doolittle equivalent, signs in a grassroots ASL manner, indicated by the use of broken English.

In 1993, I directed Don Bangs's script *Primetime Tartuffe*, an adaptation of the hilarious Molière play about a phony religious man named Tartuffe who infiltrates, cons, and almost wrecks the lives of an innocent family. What struck me the most about his script was the tremendous amount of time and energy that went into the English translation of the lines he created in ASL. On the left page of his script were the lines in English that corresponded to the ASL lines on the right page of the script. To record ASL on the page, Bangs created his own English glosses that he hoped would trigger the appropriate signs and ASL order in the minds of the actors and directors.

The following is a brief example of the left and right page script format that Bangs developed. In this modern adaptation, the character of Orgon was named Oscar.

English	*ASL*
TARTUFFE: Well, you see, I must protect my reputation. I don't want rumors running around about me having an affair with your wife, so, from now on, I will stay away from her.	TARTUFFE: Well, see, must protect my good name. Me don't want (same-down-circle) rumors about me (affair-affair) your wife, so, there on, me will avoid wife, (1-1-back-and-forth).
OSCAR: I don't care about those rumors. If you want to meet my wife, you can do that any time you want. If my family doesn't like it, that's just too bad. I encourage you to get together with my wife often.	OSCAR: No, me (nose-throw) rumors. You want (meet-meet) my wife often, (think-self). Will my family aggravated, fine, (blame-self). Me encourage (you-two) wife get together often.

The challenges for readers, directors, and actors are: (1) the obvious need to know ASL and (2) understanding Bangs's personal identification system between the ASL and the English glosses. For example, to indicate the ASL for Oscar's line "I don't care," Bangs wrote "(nose-throw)," which looks like a short mime of grabbing the nose and throwing it aside. This is indeed a variation of the ASL for that concept. But a deaf theatre artist with a different visual vocabulary might get confused by this description because there is another way of signing "I don't care" that uses the index finger pointed on the nose and turning it away in the opposite direction. If I were

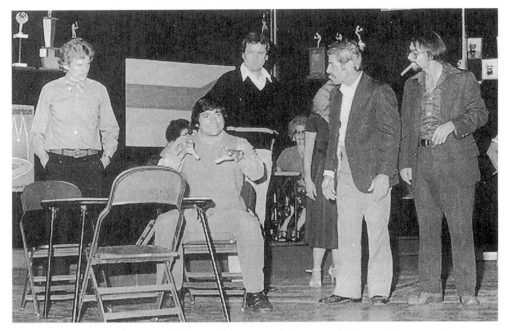

A scene from *Tales from a Clubroom*, by Bernard Bragg and Eugene Bergman, performed in 1981 at the NAD Convention in Cincinnati. Photo courtesy of Bernard Bragg, from his private collection.

making my own translation, I might write "(point-to-the-nose, flick out)." Like Eastman, Bangs includes an English glossary of his ASL intentions. Signing theatre artists would have to study the identification system; and once one is acquainted with it, the system becomes somewhat standard for those who return to work on other plays by Don Bangs.

At the other end of the language-description continuum we have Bernard Bragg, a world-renowned mime, actor, storyteller, and playwright who is deaf. When it comes to how to approach his scripts, his philosophy is to leave the sign language considerations up to the actors, particularly those fluent in ASL and English. If some actors are not fluent in English, then he expects them to be guided by signmasters. Bernard Bragg prefers to write scripts "in the plainest and barest English possible," at the same time reflecting the rhythm of ASL. He chooses relatively neutral dialogue so as not to confuse actors with idioms or figures of speech that would be foreign in ASL. He expects actors to be responsible for their own character interpretations, researching the part and being inventive with their sign language choices.

The following is a segment from his published play *Tales from a Clubroom*, cowritten with Eugene Bergman. This docudrama portrays a club gathering of deaf people from all walks of life:

LINDSEY: Why did you drop out of Gallaudet, or is it a secret?
BRANNON: Oh, no. I just got fed up. Just got the habit of not showing up on exam

days. Know what my grade record was? I was on the dean's list one year—all straight A's—and all F's the next year. Nope, I didn't freak out. (*She laughs harshly.*) I just had no patience. Everything the teachers said was so predictable. And the campus atmosphere was just too sophomoric for me. So here I am. I'm a computer programmer now and make twice as much as anybody else, except that low-life ABC card peddler.

LINDSEY: I see you don't want to become a member of this club. Neither do I. But I am curious to know why you keep coming here.

BRANNON: *(Ponders for a while)* It's a love and hate relationship. The larger world— the hearing world—shuts me out, but I loathe the gossip and banalities that prevail in the small, constricted world of the deaf. At the same time, I'm attracted to the deaf. Why? Because they represent my last human contact. In spite of, or rather because of, their bluntness and candor they somehow seem more human than the hearing.

In the above dialogue, there are no specific stage directions explaining to the actor how a line should be signed. It makes the script much easier to read, giving more focus to the dialogue and plot, yet leaving a lot of translation choices up to the actor. The translation could go in a direction totally against the playwright's intention.

As for hearing characters, Bragg writes the way hearing people would normally speak, with idioms and expressions. If they sign, it would be in an English word order, or they would sign and speak simultaneously, which he labeled Sim/Com in a play called *To Whom It May Concern* that he cowrote with Alek Friedman for a class at California State University at Northridge. The play is about twin brothers, one deaf and one hearing. They meet for the first time after being separated for twenty-five years and discover that they have led reverse lives.

ROBERT: *(to ROSEMARY)* Yeah, you and I can communicate, and you two can communicate. You and Alfred. So, maybe you and I can spend some time together, and then you and Alfred. But me and Alfred. We need you.

ROSEMARY—Sim/Com: No! No you don't. You don't need me, you can just communicate with me easily. I'm the best of both worlds. I can understand who each of you are underneath, and I can understand who you've both become. But who cares what I can understand. I'm just the *interpreter*. I'm a Band-aid. You won't talk to Ms. Parkers because you blame her for splitting you up, you can't talk to your parents because you blamed them for how they raised you. And you can't talk to each other because you refuse to accept the fact that maybe—*maybe*— your language isn't the only language. Guess what? I'm going to do the first thing I've done right since I got here. I'm leaving. Congratulations, Alfred. Your ASL is excellent. Congratulations Robert, you're an oral success story. God forgive me for breaking all the interpreters' rules . . . I don't want to sound like a teacher but I want to remind you of the famous quote: "Know thyself."

ALFRED: Wait—which one of us are you talking to—him or me?

ROSEMARY—Sim/Com: To whom it may concern. Goodbye.

(ROSEMARY *leaves.* ALFRED *and* ROBERT *are left on opposite sides of the room. The lights fade.)*

Sim/Com, an abbreviation for "simultaneous communication," is a controversial sign communication method that incorporates speech and signing at the same time. Usually, the signs follow the same English order as the speech, which sometimes annoys Deaf ASL users who have no residual hearing or speechreading skills. While both languages are juggled one of them usually gets fumbled or dropped. Yet its use is rampant in the deaf community. Many hearing family members and educators—whose first language is English—as well as deaf children from hearing families use Sim/Com. These children with their deaf peers sometimes go to mainstreamed public schools with a predominantly hearing student population. It is common to see scripts with deaf and hearing characters call for Sim/Com in the dialogue.

When I wrote a play called *The Water Falls*, I tried to take Sim/Com to another level. In this play about a deaf college student coming to terms with his hearing grandfather's suicide, I had the grandson character use Sim/Com to show him straddling the fence between the hearing world of his father and grandfather and the deaf world of his mother. I also used Sim/Com for several other reasons: (1) for double entendres in sign language; (2) to frame a word/sign or a line; (3) to reach a broader audience by having the language of the play come directly from the deaf actor's hands *and* mouth, not from some disembodied voice of a hearing actor or voice actor speaking on behalf of the deaf character.

An example of an attempt at a double entendre in sign language is when the grandson, Jed, in his mind calls forth his grandfather and reviews the events leading up to the suicide. In the excerpt below, the grandson's deaf mother has temporarily lost her capability to sign. She can express herself only through guttural, incomprehensible means. What she tries to say is between the brackets.

A scene from *The Water Falls*: Grandpop, played by Mike Deninger,

MOTHER: *(Enters, like in the beginning of the play)* Oohhaaaayyyyyyyyaahhhhhhhh uuuhhhhahhhhhielllllehhhhhhhhhhh . . .

[Your grandfather shot himself, Jed.]

FATHER: *(Enters)* Jed, can you come home? It would be good for your mother.

MOTHER: Oohhaaaayyyyyyyyaahhhhhhhhhuuuhhhhahhhhhielllllehhhhhhhhhhh . . .

[Your grandfather shot himself, Jed.]

JED: What?

FATHER: Your grandfather . . .

JED: WHAT? What happened?!

MOTHER: Oohhaaaayyyyyyyyaahhhhhhhhhuuuhhhhahhhhhielllllehhhhhhhhhhh . . .

[Your grandfather shot himself, Jed.]

FATHER: Your grandfather . . . uh . . . passed away.

(Exits, escorting MOTHER *away)*

JED: How?

GRANDPOP: *(fingerspells)* S-u-i-c-i-d-e. *(then signs)* Suicide.

JED: *(Pause; in a daze.)* I see *(signs "see" literally)*. Why Grandpop?

GRANDPOP: You see? You si? You sea? You C? U.C.? O, . . . U . . . C? *(the "O" handshape emphasizes the open mouth, the "U" handshape shows the double-barreled shotgun going into the mouth, and the "C" handshape indicates a chunk of the exit wound leaving the head)* What do you see?

JED: *(horrified)* See? I don't see anything. I'm just saying that I understand.

GRANDPOP: Do you understand?

Besides using the "OUC/Oh, you see?" double entendre, I was trying to frame the terribly graphic moment of how the suicide happened by using the fingerspelled letters of O, U, C.

In another scene in the play, I attempted to create a Freudian slip in sign language.

signing "OUC/Oh, you see?" (*a*) O/open mouth. (*b*) and (*c*) U/gun. (*d*) C/flying piece of skull. © Goodman/VanRiper Photography.

Again, the grandson is having a conversation in his mind with his grandfather after the suicide.

(GRANDPOP *goes to his slide projector case, opens it and lifts out a projector with a carousel tray of blank slides. The projector is set to project over the heads of the audience, in the aisle of the theatre, or on one of walls next to the audience. He takes out a long roll of electrical cord.*)

JED: What are you doing?

GRANDPOP: Work. *(Hands JED the cord.)* Go plug this in.

JED: Work? You've retired! *(signs with "R" handshape and arms crossed on his chest; the sign should look like the crossed arms of a dead person lying in a coffin. GRANDPOP gives him a hard stare.)*

I'm sorry I didn't mean that. It just came out like that. Honest! Retired, ha-ha-ha-ha. *(JED looks at the way he signed with the "R" handshape—straightens out the handshape and makes it with the palms crossed over his chest.)*

I had no idea that related to-to . . . you know. . . . I'll go find an outlet.

When I experimented with the word *retired* in my script, I wondered if hearing readers, directors, or producers would appreciate the intended visual double meaning of it in signs.

Shanny Mow's script *Counterfeits* was produced in 1995 by Cleveland Signstage Theatre at the Cleveland Playhouse. He has a script segment in which he envisioned how the dialogue could be done in mime beforehand. Mow, who tends to direct his own plays, once wrote, "As director, I always try to include a silent scene somewhere in the play where for a few minutes the audience gets the experience of depending totally on their eyes" (personal correspondence). The dialogue below merely served as a guide, and the actors were free to invent the pantomime and use as much time as needed.

Counterfeits takes place in the third year of the Civil War. Thomas, a Union soldier, captures Conroy, a Rebel, and a runaway slave. As fate would have it, both soldiers are deaf. In this scene the slave finds a skull in a trench one morning. Keep in mind that this dialogue is supposed to be expressed almost entirely in mime.

SLAVE: *(Points the skull to sleeping Thomas)* Northern? *(To CONROY)* Southern? *(To self)* Slave? *(Places skull down in front of CONROY, carefully like a peace offering.)*

My mother? Preacher? Big slaveowner? No matter. Skull white. White. Under skin, me white. Dead, we all white. White. Yet we different. Why? You hate me. You want kill me.

CONROY: This my land. I fight defend it.

SLAVE: Your land? I pick, pick cotton. I sweat, I bleed, I shed tears. Your land!

CONROY: *(Beat)* I fight be free.

SLAVE: Free? What is free?

CONROY: Me no speak. Me no hear. People treat me like dog.

SLAVE: Dog walk free. You walk free. I walk not free.

CONROY: My spirit bound, suppressed.

SLAVE: You feel rage?

CONROY: I feel rage. Me free yet not free.

SLAVE: You free yet not free.

CONROY: You understand?

SLAVE: *(Nods)* Free is peace, peace inside.

CONROY: *(Holding the skull up)* Under skin, we all deaf and dumb.

To get a glimpse at how Mow visualized the mime, look at Slave's line "You feel rage?" When describing the mime scenario in his mind, Mow wrote, "The actor would point to Conroy, then to his own heart, clutch his fingers and make an angry face, drop the face and look at who is trying to communicate with the deaf person; Slave would spit a word or two in voice: 'Rage, rage.' Conroy, being deaf can nod and repeat Slave's gestures, no voice, for his line: 'I feel rage' " (personal correspondence).

Aaron Weir, a deaf playwright and former artistic director of Cleveland Signstage Theatre, won an award in the one-act category of the Sam Edwards Deaf Playwrights Competition in New York City for his play *25 Cents*. The play deals with the hot issue of deaf peddlers, who are an embarrassment to hard-working members of the deaf community who feel they make an honest living with "regular" jobs.

In this script excerpt from *25 Cents*, Weir gave his dialogue some ASL essence with word repetition in the characters' lines. He drew upon the two-beat and sometimes three-beat rhythm of ASL signing and portrayed that by repeating specific English words two or three times.

MAN: Rejection, rejection, that's my life. You don't want the same. Anyway you're luckier than I.

BRIAN: Why?

MAN: You have TTY, you have telephone, "r-something" . . .

BRIAN: Relay.

MAN: Yes, relay. Now sign language is accepted everywhere. It's not like when I was young. You have a chance. It's too late for me.

BRIAN: Don't give me that pity–pity–pity stuff. I'm deaf too, remember. Sure I have a chance, but it's the same for all. It hasn't really changed that much. Hearing people still say, "Sign Language is so beautiful," or "Do you know how to drive a car?" or "Can you have children?" Wait . . . wait, this is one of my favorites, "Have you seen *Children of a Lesser God*? Such a nice movie." I want to scream in their faces, "I've lived it."

MAN: Hey, pity–pity–pity, remember. We both can talk–talk–talk . . . nothing changes for us.

BRIAN: Okay, okay, that's true, but your stories are different. They're good. It's important that we know that there was a past worth being proud of. Then hope is possible.

MAN: Before my hope was the same as yours. When I sit very, very quiet here and look for a long, long time across the park. Sometimes, if I stare past the crowds and trees long enough, I see deaf ghosts. Those ghosts are crying and grieving for what we lost . . . our signs bastardized, no love for one another, our culture destroyed by mainstreaming. . . . Those ghosts cry and cry, but if I look hard enough, I see past them, see Moses. Then I find the hope you talk about. But, not I only cry. We're like clowns. Hearing people, they laugh–laugh–laugh. We're silly clowns.

While the dialogue is readily comprehensible to a reader unfamiliar with ASL, the emotional charge of the topic is likely to be missed. It is no exaggeration to say that the depth of feeling toward peddling among deaf community members is similar to the feelings among African Americans toward slavery.

Another example of the need for cultural knowledge to understand the script occurs later on, in an exchange between Brian, the college student who befriends the peddler, and another deaf man, Harry, who went to the local deaf school. Harry is accompanied by his friend Kelly, a hard of hearing woman:

HARRY: Look at that. The college whiz kid and the old peddler, together. I can't believe. I'm gonna check this out.
KELLY: Harry, you agreed we'd go to the movies. We just have enough time to get there.
HARRY: Kelly this won't take more than a minute.
KELLY: One minute? You! Impossible. Don't start trouble, that's all.
HARRY: Ah, come on. (*Pulls her along with him. Steps behind the bench. Taps each man on shoulder at the same time. MAN reacts.*)
MAN: Moses? Oh, it's you Harry.
HARRY: Well, well, well. What do we have here. Teaching some tricks of the trade, old man?
BRIAN: Look, we're just talking.
HARRY: Talk! About what? There's nothing this old man knows that's worth talking about.
BRIAN: Oh, that's right! I forgot, Harry, the big "D." You've figured everything out.
HARRY: I don't need a college education to know what to do about deaf peddlers.
KELLY: Harry, let's go.
HARRY: Not yet. The whiz kid thinks he's got all the answers. Let's give him a real education.
KELLY: Here's what's real. We were going to the movies. Now we can do it together, or I can do it alone. Which is it?
BRIAN: Hey, Harry, that's easy enough to understand. Go to the movie.
HARRY: What's the problem with you . . . you and your lousy attitude.
BRIAN: Go somewhere and see if you can figure out my "so-called" problem.
HARRY: Well now, how about if I just become a quick study and tell you right now

what the problem is. But, first . . . we need some visual aids for the college kid here. *(goes over to MAN and frisks his coat pockets)*

MAN: Hey!

BRIAN: Harry, what the hell you doing now?

KELLY: Harry!

HARRY: *(finds what he is looking for and takes it from MAN's pocket)* Okay, class, Life 101 is now in session. Please observe what the professor has discovered. Ah, yes, the famous A–B–C cards. Let's see, yes, here we are. We'll take some class time to read the material: "HELLO! I AM A DEAF PERSON. I AM SELLING THIS DEAF EDUCATION CARD TO MAKE MY LIVING. WILL YOU KINDLY BUY ONE? PAY ANY PRICE YOU WISH. THANK YOU . . ." Then we turn it over and here's our ASL alphabet. *(goes to all three and shows A–B–C cards close to their faces)* Now if you look real close, you can see one simple word— W-H-O-R-E. *(throws A–B–C cards at BRIAN)* How can you socialize with scum like this? When I was little I would see him beg for quarters, 25 cents. Every day I live with the shame of your begging. What do you beg for now old man, one dollar, two dollars?

The subtle but cruel put-down in the line "Harry, the big 'D'" would not be understood outside the deaf community. Hard-core deaf people who consider themselves very deaf, totally involved in ASL and deaf culture, will identify themselves as *Deaf*, not deaf with the *d* in lowercase. The little *d* is for the oral deaf, the hearing-impaired, the late-deafened, or those not active in the deaf community. Here, a little nuance like this can speak volumes to deaf artists and audiences but easily be overlooked by outside script evaluators.

Michele Verhoosky's *The Middle of Nowhere* provides another example of cultural nuance, as well as an innovative solution to the technical challenges posed by hearing characters and audiences. Set in the 1960s, this coming-of-age drama is about inner journeys, family secrets, and—ultimately—triumphs. Jessie, a fifteen-year-old CODA (child of deaf adults), longs to move beyond the farm she lives on in The Middle of Nowhere, Ohio, with her deaf Nana and deaf mother, Emily. Jack, a hearing stranger she meets while waiting for a bus not expected to arrive for a few days, turns out to be not only well versed in the ways of the world outside The Middle of Nowhere but fluent in sign language as well. Could all this lead somewhere for this young girl looking for her own ticket out of town?

JESSIE: *(gloating)* I told you they made good chili. He thought we didn't have any place decent to eat around here. *(EMILY smiles, walks around to JACK's side, serves him the cake, resting her hand on his shoulder. JESSIE noticing, grows more boisterous, flirtatious.)*

JACK: I thought that, huh?

JESSIE: Well, words to that effect.

JACK: You're a fine one to talk! I didn't notice *you* going hungry.

JESSIE: What? You *told* me to get what I wanted!

JACK: A bowl of chili, a hamburger platter, *and* a chocolate shake?

EMILY: Jack's right. You ate *a lot*, Jessie.

JESSIE: I was *hungry!*

JACK: What do you think I am? Made of money?

JESSIE: *(sobering, guilt-stricken)* Oh . . . what, are you *broke?* I got some money upstairs. I was saving it for . . . oh never mind, I'd never have enough anyway. It's only five bucks but . . . *(Jumps up, runs to stairs.)*

JACK: *(voicing only, STASHU signing)* Jessie, wait! Jessie. *Jessie!* Where's your class? *(JESSIE halts, turns back to table.)*

JESSIE: *(voicing only, LEAH signing)* Huh? You saw it! Well, most of them. At the Big Boy.

JACK: *(reverts back to sign, STASHU voicing)* I *mean* . . .

JESSIE: I know what you mean. It was your treat and you wanted to throw your money around, and impress the socks off of me 'n Nana, and have everyone in the place eatin' their heart out wondering who the handsome devil we were having lunch with was. Right?

JACK: *(taken aback)* Uh . . . yeah. Yeah.

JESSIE: *(crowing)* And we sure did show them, didn't we?

NANA: We had a good time. A nice meal. The *salad* could be better, but . . .

JESSIE: And did you see the look on Darleen Werner's face?

JACK: Darleen?

JESSIE: Yeah! Darleen! You know—big hair, big chest, little sweater, little brain.

JACK/EMILY/NANA: Ohhh! *Darleen!*

(JACK snickers and signs a "D" by the nipples like swirling tassels. NANA and EMILY, giggling, mimic JACK.)

JESSIE: Yeah. That's her.

On Verhoosky's cast-of-characters page, she identifies Stashu as "age late 60's–early 70's (hearing)," Nana's departed husband who acts as a spiritual guide, and a voice and sign interpreter. Another spiritual guide/voice and sign interpreter is Leah, Nana's departed daughter in her early twenties who was previously deaf but now is hearing. This shows a good example of how shadow interpreting works. When there are hearing characters on stage who do not know sign language, a technique of informing the deaf audience what these people are saying is having a "shadow" on stage sign the lines. Verhoosky cleverly goes beyond the old black-clothed shadow interpreter technique by giving her shadows characters of their own, namely, Stashu and Leah, the spiritual guides. The technique works in reverse with voicing for a hearing audience when deaf characters use only sign language.

Regarding the signplay on the finger-spelled letter *d* on the nipples, for anyone who knows the manual letter *d*, it is easy to imagine its round nipple shape coupled with the protruding index finger that could be waved in circles alluding to a strip-teaser's pasties. But to grasp the full import of Jack's vulgar neologism, one must be conversant in deaf culture name sign traditions, which involve using a fingerspelled letter from the name somewhere on the body or gesturing a distinctive physical trait to indicate a person's name. In effect, Jack invents a vulgar new name sign for Darlene, and the snickering of the older deaf women, Nana and Emily, is in response to his manipulation of that tradition.

It goes without saying that in the theatre business, a script is just a blueprint for a play. In scripts written by hearing actors, one can see acting and voicing possibilities to explore during the rehearsal process. With scripts written by deaf playwrights, there is an additional layer of sign dialogue and movement, with all of its endless choices, added to the voice and acting possibilities. This maximizes the dramatic potential of a theatrical production.

In his introduction to Gilbert Eastman's book *Sign Me Alice and Laurent Clerc: A Profile*, George Detmold wrote, "The play makes clear sense as an English script; but the thousand little jokes, puns, and word-play are missing, as well as the lyric beauty of some passages, if the play is read simply as English" (2). This seems to be true of all the scripts written by the well-known deaf playwrights included here.

For those interested in reading or producing the scripts of these playwrights, their E-mail addresses appear below:

Donald Bangs: SignRise@aol.com
Eugene Bergman: ECBergman@aol.com
Bernard Bragg: Bernat83@aol.com
Willy Conley: Willy.Conley@gallaudet.edu or Plumpick@aol.com
Gilbert Eastman: Jungilea@juno.com
Shanny Mow: Shanmow@aol.com
Michele Verhoosky: MicheleL1@aol.com
Aaron Weir: Aaronweir@signstage.org

WORKS CITED

Bergman, Eugene, and Bernard Bragg. *Tales from a Clubroom*. Washington, D.C.: Gallaudet University Press, 1981.

Eastman, Gilbert C. *Sign Me Alice and Laurent Clerc: A Profile*. San Diego: DawnSignPress, 1997.

Stokoe, William C., Jr., Carl G. Croneberg, and Dorothy C. Casterline. *A Dictionary of American Sign Language on Linguistic Principles*. Washington, D.C.: Gallaudet College Press, 1965.

III

"The medicine that swallowed the patient"

Deaf Education

Graduation day at Gallaudet. © 1994 Willy Conley.

21

"Mainstreaming" or "inclusion," the practice of isolating Deaf children in public schools designed for the hearing, is endorsed by taxpayers, parents, speech therapists, and even disability activists, most of whom regard it as a bold new idea whose time has finally come. The truth is that hearing people have long wanted to disperse deaf children among neighborhood schools and long failed to listen to the claims of Deaf adults that segregated, residential schools and sign-language education best equip deaf children for life as Deaf adults.

The Associative Feature in the Education of the Deaf

George Wing

1886

Professor J. C. Gordon gives, in the April *Annals*, a "sketch of the principal theories of deaf-mute instruction, in connection with the public or common school system, which have been put to the test of experience for long periods in different lands and under a wide range of conditions." He confines himself strictly to his subject, historical review, but by analysis of the facts gathered he demonstrates that experiments based upon these theories have always failed and must necessarily fail.

A reader of Professor Gordon's article, mistaking its scope and purpose and giving the matter only cursory attention, would infer that his conclusions embrace attempts, under any and all conditions, to educate the deaf in association with hearing children. In effect, the article is a strong argument in favor of the segregation of the deaf in special schools, and throws discredit upon "the associative feature" as a factor in their education.

It is not my purpose to question any of Professor Gordon's conclusions. I would, rather, add to them the further conclusion drawn from my own bitter experience as a victim of an attempt to educate a deaf child in a public school, that such experiments are cruel and must be barren of good results, for no good results are possible in the face of the humiliation and discouragement of a deaf child in such surroundings.

Professor Gordon's array of the "inexorable logic of facts" leaves no room for anything but unqualified acceptance of his conclusions so far as he has made them apply, but he has not covered the whole subject by any means; there remains for discussion the broad inference that association with hearing children is of no value in the education of the deaf under any conditions. Experiments made under a "wide

165

range" of certain conditions have resulted in failure, but it does not follow that there are no conditions under which such experiments may be successful.

The great value of the association of the deaf with the deaf, as a factor in their education, is indisputable. It is true that it has been questioned by prominent theorists, but they have gone no further than expression of biased opinion. Those who have had opportunity to note the mental torpor of deaf-mute children when admitted to an institution, and to observe the quick awakening that follows, cannot for a moment doubt that without the stimulating and brightening effect of association the attempt to educate them would be well nigh hopeless.

It was my good fortune during my school days at Hartford to be associated in close companionship with a number of remarkably intelligent young men. No logic could convince me that my association with these young men was not of greater benefit to me as a factor in whatever education I have acquired than the sum of all other influences subsequent to the loss of my hearing. And it is certain that one and all of my school-mates would make the same acknowledgment as to their association with each other. Among these young men there was a constant "fusillade of discussion"; there was scarcely any subject pertaining to "heaven above, the earth beneath, or the water under the earth," that did not contribute material for disputation. Not unfrequently these discussions encroached upon the time that should have been given to their lessons, but it is undeniable that the mental stimulus and habits of independent study and investigation so acquired were as valuable to them as the grist of their daily tasks. With all these thronging memories, knowing so well that the development of intelligence and character in the subsequent lives of so many of these boys* was due in a greater degree to their association with each other than to their school-room work or even to the influence of their teachers, it fills me with astonishment to read in Institution Reports such assertions as these: "The less the deaf are associated with the deaf the better for them in every way," and "It would be better for a deaf child if he did not know that another deaf child existed in the world!"

Boy-like, these school-boys would settle, off-hand, questions of theology, politics, science, and what not with the utmost positiveness and to their immense satisfaction; but there was one question, often discussed, that ever remained to them an unfathomable mystery. Why was it that A., who lost his hearing when three or four years old, was possessed of an easy and natural flow of language not different from that of hearing boys of his age, while B., who lost his hearing a year or two earlier and was much superior to A. in mental calibre, was doomed to struggle with a load of "deaf-mutism," viewing the world of language all askew? It could not be A.'s memory of his childish prattle that made all the difference, for he had utterly forgotten it, and, in fact, had no more conception of sound than if he had been born deaf. Where was

---

* That this picture may not seem overdrawn, I give the names of well-known teachers who were my school-mates: Thomas L. Brown, Melville Ballard, Ralph H. Atwood, Amos G. Draper, J. B. Hotchkiss, Samuel T. Greene, William L. Bird, Henry W. Syle, Louis A. Houghton. Of these, five were my class-mates, three were younger boys in lower classes, and one a private pupil of Professor Bartlett's. Others not teachers, but as well known, could be mentioned.

the point of divergence and what the cause that carried them into channels of mental flow so sharply defined and so far apart? Teachers, when questioned, could give no answer but that A. was a "semi-mute" and B. a deaf-mute, which was merely begging the question. With all the material for investigation close at hand, and existing in ourselves, we could never find a solution of the problem.

Many years afterwards, I had occasion to take a long journey in company with one of my boyhood friends, a deaf-mute from birth. Both of us being teachers, much of our time was given to discussing methods of teaching, and we naturally switched off upon discussion of the problem that had bothered us so much in our younger days. He described to me the successive steps by which he had finally arrived at a clear understanding of written language. He said that during the greater part of his school days all the idea of language he had was that it consisted of words strung together without rule or reason. The study of language was, to him, no more in reality the study of language than memorizing complex chemical formulas and associating them with material objects is the study of chemistry. It never occurred to him to search for a clue to guide him through the mazes of language; he had no idea that any such clue existed. By prodigious labor he committed to memory a large number of model sentences associated in his mind with certain pictures. His original composition consisted either in reproducing his models or writing series of words as nearly like them as possible. Taking his models as a starting point, he would try, by a mechanical process of substituting words, to make his composition represent the picture in his mind. The process by which he arrived at the meaning of what he read was not so apparent; there was a good deal of guess-work and hap-hazard about it. Gradually he became less dependent upon memory and mechanical substitution, but his mental drift continued in the same direction. When he left school, for illustration, he was unable to understand why relative pronouns are used. He used relative clauses in his composition because he had been taught to write in that way, but he could not see why such sentences would not be just as correct and just as clear if all relatives were omitted. After some years he found himself looking at language from a different stand-point, and his difficulties vanished. He had somehow drifted out of the slough of deaf-mutism: with the majority of deaf-mutes the drifting is apt to be the other way.

This long conversation, a fragment of which I have imperfectly transcribed, seemed to throw a glimmer of light upon the question. It revealed with great distinctness the forced, unnatural process by which deaf-mutes acquire the understanding and use of written language. Subsequent observation and experiment have convinced me that this process is almost universal among congenital deaf-mutes.* Starting thus,

---

* I was inclined to doubt the correctness of my friend's recollection and of my own understanding of what he said, and, to test the matter, I tried a number of experiments. I select one of many of these experiments for illustration: Taking an absurd and misleading sentence written by one of my pupils, I submitted it to the criticism of a number of quite intelligent deaf-mutes who had been educated by the so-called "natural method." The sentence was as follows: "The little dog which barked at a box in the barn contained a cat." Every word in the sentence was familiar to them, and they had been drilled upon like constructions. Not one of them smiled; every one of them in forming a mental picture from the sentence located the cat inside the box instead of inside the dog! It was

with an impulse in the wrong direction, their course persists in that direction with gathering force. Those who have possessed hearing and speech in childhood, seemingly effaced from their recollection though it may be, have received an impulse in the right direction, and their course in this direction also persists with gathering force. Hence it is that some are doomed to an almost hopeless struggle in mastering the simple forms of expression, while others are carried along with the current, mastering the most difficult forms of language almost without effort.

The most important question in the education of the deaf is whether it is not possible to give the congenitally deaf an impulse in the right direction in their early childhood, and so direct their course that they may acquire the understanding and use of language by a natural process. Questions of school-room method are trifles in comparison.

When we examine our own mental processes, our introspection reveals that the current of our thought runs in two distinct channels. Inventing a terminology for the sake of brevity, I will call one channel the imaginative and the other the expressive. When we form a conception of any kind our thoughts run wholly in the imaginative channel. If we think of going a-fishing, for instance, we seem to see, as in a vision, the rippling waves, the dancing boat, our hooks and lines, and the thousand little details of what we may see and do. If we wish to communicate our thoughts to another, at once we shift into the expressive channel; sentences flow from our lips, or colloquial signs from our fingers, with scarcely more mental effort than is required to imagine the scene or event that we describe. Receiving a communication from another by the expressive channel, our thoughts take the imaginative channel almost without any effort of our will. Thus the two channels run side by side from earliest childhood throughout our lives. In the mind of the uneducated deaf-mute the expressive channel has no existence: he knows nothing of any means of communication but graphic and suggestive gestures—rough copies of the pictures in his mind. Of words or signs, as conventional representatives of thought, he has no conception. All his thoughts are pictures: he reasons, when he reasons at all, in a groping, uncertain way, and his mind grows stunted and twisted in a manner beyond the comprehension of any but those who have made his mental state the study of a lifetime. In this condition he is sent to school and the struggle to change his settled habit of mind begins. Not only has the expressive channel to be filled with language, but the channel itself must be created. The teacher's efforts to this end are not limited to digging and dredging in virgin soil, but obstinate stumps of habit must be slowly and patiently picked to pieces.

Under the manual system it is assumed that in the mind of the deaf-mute child the expressive channel is wanting, or, at least, that the faculty of expression is dormant. He is placed with others like himself. Communication with them is established at

plain that they took the meanings of individual words, dog—barked—box—barn—contained—cat, and by association of ideas and help from the prepositions, made a sort of mental hash of the sentence. Those who are inclined to share my original doubts are recommended to try like experiments.

first by means of crude significant signs, which gradually merge into a sign-language not different in its essence from other languages, wanting only inflections and order of collocation, which are replaced by suggestive gestures. By familiar use the significant character of signs is lost sight of and they become purely conventional, serving only to recall ideas, regardless of their significant origin, precisely as articulate words serve to recall ideas to hearing persons. The flow of thought in the expressive channel being thus established, it remains for the teacher to produce another form of expression, written language. This is the theory, but how different the practice! With the child who has learned to lisp some childish prattle in a foreign tongue before losing his hearing, the theory is carried to practical demonstration. The slender thread of his expressive faculty is picked up where he dropped it in his mother tongue, his mental powers are stimulated by means of the sign-language, and development of expression in written English proceeds apace. The congenitally deaf child is thrust at once into the school-room: he is forced to memorize and reproduce words and sentences before he can have any conception of conventional expression. He is persistently drilled upon empty forms disassociated from trains of thought. The impulse in the wrong direction thus given him gathers force as he proceeds, and intractable habits of study are formed which lead him astray.*

Under the oral system the development of the mental faculties is subordinated to the development of speech. It is assumed that with speech will come the power of expression, for "speech is expression and expression is speech." Years of labor are spent in mechanical drill upon vocal sounds, a process which results in permanently dwarfing the mental faculties.

Under whatever system the education of the deaf child is attempted, it is unquestionable that the best results depend upon the development of the faculty of expression in some form in early childhood. This development cannot be produced by school-room drill; it must be a spontaneous growth from communion of mind with mind. Efforts by means of lessons and exercises to force written or spoken language upon a deaf child, before the conception of symbolic or conventional expression, of which language wholly consists, takes possession of his mind, must be in a great measure fruitless. Such efforts are like trying to drive in first the blunt end of a wedge. Taking this postulate as a starting point, let us see by what means, if any means are attainable, the faculty of expression can be developed in childhood.

Manifestly, if speech can be used as a medium of such development it has immense

---

* As an illustration of these misleading habits—whose name is legion—I will relate some of my experience: When I began teaching I soon became aware that there was something radically wrong in the mental processes of my pupils. They were, for the most part, bright and industrious, but, making due allowance for their condition, the progress they made was out of proportion to their evident capacity. Having little experience I was for a long time completely mystified. Then I began to watch them in the evening study-hour. I discovered that two of them placed slips of paper upon the pages of their books and proceeded to memorize the lesson *line by line,* uncovering the lines as fast as "learned." One memorized between punctuation points, and so on. The process of committing lessons to memory was *absolutely divorced from association with meaning.* With "all the confidence of a new broom" I set to work to sweep this vicious habit out of existence. I might as well have tried to sweep back the sea!

advantage over other means. Can it be used? We have to deal with facts, not with theories or suppositions based upon impossible conditions. Starting with the child at home, much might, could, would, and should be done by wise and thoughtful parents and friends, but little *is* done. The mental condition of the deaf child when he enters an institution *is*, in nearly every case, deplorable. The environment of his home life does not favor the development required and does not produce it.* It is urged that parents should be educated to give their children preliminary training. An excellent idea, truly, but is it practicable? Can we overcome the facts that many parents are incapable; that of those who are capable the greater portion are engaged in a struggle for daily bread, and have no time to give to learning and teaching; that the few who are able and willing are so scattered that the difficulty and cost of reaching them would be enormous? Much may be, and indeed has been, accomplished in exceptional cases, but, in general, the hope for material results in this direction must be abandoned.

Can anything be accomplished by means of day schools in connection with the public schools, giving an environment of hearing children? Professor Gordon has effectually answered this question in the negative.

Can kindergartens for deaf children be conducted under the oral system with reasonable expectation that speech will develop under the skillful direction of teachers, and be freely used by the children in talking with each other? The fact that half a dozen years of patient drill on vocal sounds are necessary to produce bare articulation of words disposes of this question.

Shall we establish kindergartens under the manual system and let the children freely communicate by signs? This would be something like setting the blind to lead the blind. The advantage over the present practice of associating the little ones with the older children who have made some progress is not apparent,

In prescribing "environment of hearing children" as a remedy for the ills existing in the methods of instructing the deaf it is remarkable that the doctors have unanimously ordered that the medicine shall swallow the patient—in other words, that deaf children shall be "assimilated" by the mass of children in the public schools! Naturally all attempts to carry out their directions have resulted in disaster, and a remedy, excellent if properly administered, has fallen into disrepute. Environment of hearing children, to be of any help to the deaf, must be within the walls of special schools where it can be controlled and directed by trained specialists.

Educating the deaf is emphatically an experimental science. The carpenters' "rule of cut and try" is the only practical rule recognized in our profession; mere generali-

---

* The value of home environment, in the absence of means of communication other than crude pictorial signs, is well illustrated by an incident—a type of many—recalled by Professor Noyes on reading this paragraph. A deaf-mute boy, from a very intelligent family containing eight children, came to the Philadelphia Institution when fourteen years old. His ignorance was so dense that he did not even know that he was deaf or in any way different from his brothers. From mere imitative instinct he would address persons who noticed him with hideous inarticulate cries. Placed in conditions where his chaotic ideas could be arranged and formulated in a definite language, he developed rapidly and became a sensible, well-educated man.

zation and *a priori* argument go for nothing. The weaver of a web of theory, be it ever so fine, has no market for his goods unless the woof of his imagination has a substantial warp of facts. It is not difficult to prove a negative by an array of impregnable facts; the way is strewn with the failures of empirical experiment for a hundred years. Proving an affirmative is another matter. I will try to show some results of environment of hearing children properly applied.

Some thirty years ago Professor David E. Bartlett conducted a family school for both deaf and hearing children at Poughkeepsie, N.Y. This school was not established for the development of a theory; it was simply a private enterprise. Professor Bartlett's purpose was to build up a school for very young deaf children, and the association of hearing children was incidental. He was an enthusiast in the matter of early education,* recognized the value of association in a general way, but I do not find that he made a special point of the association of deaf with hearing children outside of family association. Upon the advantage of a medium of free communication between members of a family, to be acquired by the education of deaf and hearing brothers and sisters together, he laid great stress. His pupils numbered twenty-five or thirty, of whom at least half were hearing children. The enterprise, after a few years' trial, proved financially unprofitable, and was therefore abandoned.

Several of Professor Bartlett's former pupils have been for many years among my intimate friends and associates. Some of them are remarkable examples of deaf-mutes from infancy using written language with all the freedom and accuracy of educated hearing persons. One of them, a lady, deaf from birth, in relating her experience, said that she was sent to Professor Bartlett's school at nine years of age, and remained five years. Her room-mate and close companion for nearly the whole period was a hearing girl of her own age. No distinction was made between the deaf and hearing children, except in school-room exercises. There was no "oil and water" about the association of the two classes, no clannishness, but genuine comradeship. The sign-language was universally used, the hearing children, as a rule, being more expert than the deaf.** There was a tendency to use the manual alphabet in preference to signs. This lady attributes her remarkable facility in the use of language mainly to her learning at the start *to think in language*. Childish and imperfect though it was, the language she used was a *living* language. The words and sentences spelled with her childish fingers were spelled with the purpose of communicating thought, and the signs habitually used were representatives, rather than pictures, of thought, taking much of their cast and sequence from the mental habits of the hearing children. Thus

---

* "We propose in this course of education, at first, not so much to confine the little ones to a regular routine of exercises in school hours, as to teach them and accustom them at the table, in their little plays, walks, and amusements, and in the ordinary every-day occurring incidents of juvenile life, to express their thoughts and *learn to think in alphabetic language*, thus making the acquisition of language a matter of *early imitation, practice*, and *habit* as nature plainly indicates it should be." — *From Professor Bartlett's Circular*, Aug. 10, 1852.

** This statement should be taken with some qualification. The "expertness" of the hearing children probably did not consist so much in manual grace and skill as in their ability to make what they said interesting through superior information and mental training.

the entering wedge was driven and the way opened for the acquirement of education by a natural process.

Another is a lady who taught for several years in the Minnesota Institution. She is one of the few congenital deaf-mutes among my acquaintances who are thoroughly emancipated from deaf-mutism. I took it for granted that she was a "semi-mute"; in the course of an intimate acquaintance, extending over a period of ten years, I never observed any of the grammatical slips or queer solecisms to which even the best educated deaf-mutes are liable. In questioning her as to her recollection of Professor Bartlett's school, I was surprised to learn that she became totally deaf before she was a year old. She most emphatically declares that she traces the ease and freedom with which she uses language to her early instruction and association at Poughkeepsie.

Another of my acquaintances, a comrade of my school-boy days, became totally deaf when about six years old. He was placed in Professor Bartlett's care when seven years old, and remained until he entered a New England college. He is a finished scholar and a writer of great merit. His case is hardly in point, as he had the advantage of hearing and speech in childhood; but, making due allowance for this advantage and for unusual native ability, much remains to the credit of early instruction and association. His views, as to the value of association, are well expressed in the following extract from a private letter to me:

"I think my old schoolmates, as a rule, take larger and more sensible views than deaf-mutes trained in an institution. They are not so clannish, and their minds did not get into a rut at school. They think and feel as hearing people do. . . . I believe a distinct and powerful influence was exerted by the association, the admixture of hearing children, between whom and the deaf there was perfect equality in every respect, save where a difference was made absolutely necessary by the fact of deafness. Hearing and deaf children slept in the same room, sat at the same table, mixed together, sat side by side at the prayers (which were conducted in signs), and, in certain studies, they were together in the class, and *all* recited manually. . . . It was this association, I have no doubt, that contributed largely to make my schoolmates feel at home and at ease in hearing society—that enabled them to understand how hearing people view things, and to view them in the same way, naturally and habitually, not in a forced and foreign way."

Still another of Professor Bartlett's pupils I remember as a bright boy, remarkable for the clearness and precision of his use of signs. In written language he was, at the time I knew him, decidedly "lame." He did not "take kindly" to the change from Professor Bartlett's unsystematic methods to the logical and methodical ways of the teacher under whom he was placed. He was fonder of sketching and caricaturing his comrades and teachers than of study. In his subsequent life, however, he has developed remarkable talent in many ways. If success in life, the ability to "carve one's way to fame and fortune," is a criterion of success in educational methods, then this is a case of more than ordinary success in educational methods.

Pursuing inquiry further, and outside the range of my acquaintance, I do not find material for comparison with results in institutions. Few of the bright children, besides those I have mentioned, remained in the school longer than a term or two before they were transferred to institutions. It is impossible to judge with certainty as to the results in the cases of those with whom I have no personal acquaintance.

Many things have to be considered in estimating the benefits to these children from early instruction and association. Their own natural gifts and the efficient aid of intelligent and devoted friends have weight on one side; the want of system and the brief period under which the "associative feature" was tried should weigh on the other; but when the account is balanced a good deal remains on the credit side. Not the least weighty fact in this connection is that those of Professor Bartlett's former pupils who are capable of correctly weighing the benefits derived by themselves are positive in their belief in the value of the "associative feature."

In the course of thirty years' association with the deaf, I have encountered a number of cases of notable results of development in articulation by the congenitally deaf through association with other children, aided by wisely directed efforts of their parents and friends. I have never seen or heard of a person totally deaf from birth or infancy using to any practical extent speech acquired in an institution. The most remarkable case I have met is that of a life-long friend who became totally deaf when she was about a year old. She was placed in the care of an aunt, who taught her to speak, and by every available means induced other children in the family and neighborhood to talk with her. In this the child herself was a potent ally; her eager curiosity and desire to learn were never satisfied. She was not permitted to know anything of signs; even the use of crude gestures was discouraged. It was found impossible to give her any idea of connected written language, and, when she was fifteen years old, her father sent her to the Hartford Asylum, where she remained four years. Her ability as a lip-reader is phenomenal, and her power of modulating her voice is scarcely short of miraculous.

The term "expression," in the application I have given it, may need a more precise definition. I mean by the term the intimate association of ideas with words—spoken, written, or spelled—and, in some degree, with conventional signs. Conversely, the absence of the faculty involves either entire absence of association of ideas with words, or association so weak that words, even when well learned, do not call up ideas, nor do ideas suggest words, but require efforts of memory. This is the case with all deaf-mutes for some time after their education has commenced. There is some analogy between their mental state with respect to the words and sentences they have learned and that of a person who has just learned the telegraph alphabet. The learner may know every letter by sight and sound, yet the reading of a message is, to him, a difficult and laborious task. To a practical operator the rapid click of the instrument is as full of life and meaning as the spoken words he hears or the written and printed words he sees. It is natural for deaf-mutes, in learning their tasks, to dismiss from their minds the significations and relations of words, and to concentrate their efforts upon the reproduction of naked forms, because that process is, to them, the least difficult and laborious. Just here is the greatest obstacle in the way of the teacher. It may be surmounted or removed by great labor and skill, but the true way to deal with it is to avoid it. It can be avoided only by making the deaf child's first steps in the acquisition of language "a matter of *imitation, practice,* and *habit,* as nature plainly indicates it should be."

The conclusions I have drawn from the above facts and generalizations are:

1. That the best results in deaf-mute education are possible only through the development of the faculty of expression in early childhood.

2. That development of expression should commence before systematic attempts are made to teach written or spoken language, for such attempts, made before the conception of the nature of language finds lodgment in the deaf child's mind, tend to confirm and intensify his mental distortion.

3. That expression must be a natural growth from communion of mind with mind, not a creation of the teacher's art, and can be best developed in deaf-mute children by association with those in whom the faculty is already developed.

4. That the language of signs and the manual alphabet are the only practicable means of securing genuine comradeship and free communication between deaf and hearing children.

As to the practical question of means to bring about the association of deaf and hearing children in special schools for the deaf, it would be premature to say anything in this article. Before we can profitably discuss the means to an end, it must be accepted as a fact that the end is desirable. If it be generally admitted that the "associative feature" is of great value in the education of the deaf, the discovery of the means to the end will surely follow.

With regard to the effect upon hearing children of association with the deaf, all experience and opinion coincide in concluding that it cannot be otherwise than beneficial.

22

The best lipreaders are those who can normally hear speech and can therefore match visible mouth movements with meaningful linguistic units by way of (imagined) sound. That no hearing person would willingly depend on lipreading for communication should bring us to ask why Deaf people are expected to do so. Yet lipreading and the artificial production of speech were the goals of American Deaf education for almost three generations and are still widely endorsed as educational goals today.

The Attitude of the Adult Deaf towards Pure Oralism

Amos G. Draper

1895

The intelligent adult deaf favor every effort to preserve and improve natural speech. Those who have it know that it is priceless. Those who once have had it lament its loss. Those who never have had it feel their deprivation by contrast. Many among them perceive and regret that too little attention was paid to speech when they were pupils, and they rejoice at the change which is coming over all our schools in this respect. These are also the opinions of the deaf in regard to the treatment of defective hearing and to training in the art of understanding speech by sight. While, for reasons to be shown, the deaf are not given to expressing the above opinions, every one acquainted with large numbers of them knows that they do hold the same.

• The Deaf Oppose Pure Oralism

To the deaf, pure oralism means *that method of teaching the deaf which has speech and the understanding of speech by vision as primary objects; and endeavors to teach all the deaf to speak, and to teach them all branches of knowledge by speech; and forbids, and by all means in its power prevents, the use of a manual alphabet and of signs.* No fact is more observable with regard to the adult deaf than that they are unitedly opposed to this theory of teaching. Not only in America, but in countries where pure oralism has full or great sway, as England, Scotland, France, Italy, Germany, and Austria, the adult deaf make this opposition known by voice, pen, and public action, often in organized bodies. Not only former pupils of schools not pure oral, but also those of pure oral schools themselves join in this opposition. In a word,

175

it is practically the universal attitude of the adult deaf. The exceptions are individuals belonging to certain groups noted below.

• This Opposition Unfortunate

It is certainly unfortunate that the adult deaf thus oppose a method of teaching which has gained the support of many able and enthusiastic persons. It cannot be an inspiring thought to any honest teacher to feel that his pupils will condemn his method as soon as they reach years of discretion and experience in life. Therefore

• This Opposition Deserves Notice

The opinions of the adult deaf as to what is best for deaf pupils ought not to be ignored by those who profess to be unselfishly laboring for their good. They should be taken up and considered, and only dismissed when they are found to be not well based in reason and in experience. In order to understand the opposition of the deaf to pure oralism we must know what are the

• Causes of This Opposition

To set forth some of these causes is the object of this paper. If the causes are found to be trivial, then the claim of the deaf to be able to judge of their own needs may be dismissed, and the problem of educating them worked out without regard to what they now or soon will think and feel about it. But if the causes are found to rest solidly in reason and experience in life, then the attitude of the deaf can by no means be for long ignored or discredited. If it has truth to back it, or a measure of truth, by just so much it will in time have due effect. Let, first, the

• Causes Assigned by Pure Oralists

be noted. So far as appears, they are two in number. One is that the deaf are not capable of judging about their own condition and its best needs. This may be true of the deaf as pupils. It would be equally true of hearing pupils. But is it true of the adult deaf? On the contrary, does not personal acquaintance with them, as well as the work they are doing in the world, prove that they possess as good judgment in the affairs of life as other bodies of men in like circumstances? Why, then, should their judgment be reckoned of no value in this single direction? Do they not know where the troubles of life pinch them? Dismissing them with the remark that they do not is too much like giving the man with the tight boots a bland assurance that the pain is in his heel, and not, as his very soul asserts, in the infernal corn seated between his little toe and its neighbor. The second cause assigned by pure oralists is that the deaf are morbid. This was the one lately given by the principal of a pure oral school when a large number of her former pupils joined in a petition to the legislature praying for the establishment of a school which should give the deaf the freedom and advantages which they asserted lay in a combination of methods. This cause, if true, is still more mortifying to the adult deaf and their friends. Deaf children are probably more open to this charge than hearing. The hardships that caused their deafness probably affect the clearness of their minds. But does that diseased condition continue through life and sway the minds of the educated adult deaf? Let them be judged as before, by their works. Does not the work they are doing, the positions they fill, and the infrequency of their presence in asylums of any kind—in a word, the degree of their success in life—prove that they have minds as sane as those of their hearing neighbors in like conditions?

It will be observed that both the causes assigned by pure oralists can stand only by disparaging and discrediting the adult deaf, including their own former pupils, as a class generally incapable and diseased. This is certainly a melancholy conclusion. But may we not escape it—may not

• The True Causes

lie deeper, and make their assertion consistent with capacity and sanity on the part of the adult deaf? If we enter into their lives, may we not find that their opinions, like the opinions of other people, are the inevitable outgrowth of their experiences? It is in those experiences that this article seeks to find the true causes of the opposition of the deaf to pure oralism. The experiences will be largely given in the shape of concrete examples. Every one of these examples is "taken from life." Name, date, and place can, and, if it were consistent with kindness, would in each case be given. It may be objected that an example here and there proves little. The reply is that each example is a type—it can be duplicated over and over by the writer and by others familiar with the deaf. The first of the causes claimed as the true ones is

• The Frequent Inadequacy of Mechanical Speech

Pure-orally taught adults are generally accompanied in society by hearing associates, whom I shall designate as familiars. From long intercourse the deaf person and the familiar understand each other's peculiarities of utterance. Sometimes the familiar is a hired companion, but oftener he is a relative or friend. The relation is similar to that which exists between a deaf person and one who knows the manual alphabet, in that they are mutually initiated.

A lady, congenitally deaf, and having received the highest pure oral training, was at a country inn, in company with a familiar. The innkeepers were uneducated but observant. They afterwards described their impressions, one saying:

"They got along pretty well together. An' twuz wonderful! She couldn't hear, but she watched his face *clus* when he talked, and she understood a good deal what he said. An' *she couldn't talk nuther, but she made noises with her mouth* an' he could understand 'em, tew!" It will be observed that this is testimony of the highest character, since it is honest ignorance describing merely sense-perceptions.

Again, at an evening party, a lady visiting in the town and a stranger to most of the party said to a teacher of the deaf:

"Do you know Miss ———, of my town?" The teacher said he did not, and the lady went on:

"She was born deaf. I have known her from a child. She has just finished her schooling at ——— [naming one of the prominent pure oral schools], and is at home. I often meet her. She is very bright and pleasant." The teacher expressed his interest, and asked:

"How well does she speak?"

"Oh," said the lady, with a little *moue* and shrug, "I feared you would ask me that. The fact is her utterance is such that every one shrinks from speaking to her in a company, knowing that her reply will draw all eyes upon them." Here, again, the testimony is of the highest character, coming as it does from an educated person and given with the reluctance of a friend.

The effect upon the innkeepers and upon this lady gives fairly the effect upon the public of many cases of utterance by the congenitally deaf. But the point I seek to bring out by these examples is, *What is the effect on those deaf persons themselves?* Few, if any, of them can take many steps on the rugged path of life outside their schools before reaching the bitter conviction that their utterance is but a stiff imitation of human speech, unintelligible or disagreeable, or both, to most persons except their familiars. What, then, is the effect upon them? Can it be anything but disgust and discouragement with efforts to use their utterance except with familiars? Evidently not, if they are ordinarily sensitive. What will be their impulse? Inevitably they will pitch upon the pencil, a manual alphabet, or natural signs, as a more certain and less unpleasant means of communication to hearing people, and, quite as inevitably, human desires will impel them to seek the society of others who have the same or like disabilities.

When oral graduates come to this parting of the ways, there are three things that may keep them in the straight and narrow path of pure oralism. The first is wealth. A recent practical philosopher says that a good bank account is man's best friend, and the saying has special force when it comes to the deaf. In cases like the two above, if they have money they are sure to have associates who will bear with their peculiar utterance cheerfully, and if company palls or fails they still will have the independence and entertainment that money supplies. In a suburb of Boston, last summer, a lady told me of a neighbor living in a splendid house across the way. He was just come of age, and had become deaf a year before. He relied on lip-reading and writing, knowing nothing of other means of conversation. He was handsome and bright and she knew him well. I asked if he was happy. "Oh!" she exclaimed, her face wreathed in appreciative smiles, "he is rich. He has horses; paints a little;

has acquaintances in plenty; can go anywhere and do anything he pleases. Why! it makes all the difference in the world."

Again, suppose oral graduates have genius, or talent approaching it. Then, also, they will have the friends, or, failing them, the independence, higher and sweeter than that which money confers, flowing from absorption in delightful labors. They can feel with immortal Milton—

> Mid books and papers in my study pent,
> If this be exile, sweet is banishment.

Of such is Humphrey Moore, though he was never taught orally.

Lastly, when living in a large circle of relatives or friends who have enthusiastically adopted oral principles, oral graduates will be under little temptation to depart from them.

If an adult deaf person can be found preaching and practising pure oralism, he will almost surely be among one of these three groups. But how is it with the vast majority of the deaf whom no such happy lot befalls—who have neither the entertainments of wealth nor the resources of genius nor the happy immunity of a protected environment? How is it in cases like the following:

A married deaf couple were recently assaulted in a Boston tenement by a thief, while both slept. The man bravely rose up and beat off his assailant, and by cries aroused his neighbors and the police. Next morning the Boston daily papers described the couple in staring headlines as "deaf and dumb," "deaf-mutes," and said the neighbors mistook the cries for "dogs barking in the house." The Associated Press despatches to all centers again described the couple as "deaf and dumb." Now, this couple were graduates of a pure oral school. Why, then, all this prominence of dumbness? Did they or did they not use what speech the school had conferred upon them? If they did not, then it was useless to them in a supreme moment. If they did, then it was equally useless, for it was not understood by "the intelligent reporters" nor by the police—their uncouth utterances only conveyed the impression that they were "deaf and dumb." How long did it take this couple, after they left school, to discover that their speech was speech only to themselves and to those who bred them? What did they do then? They fell back on natural signs, and for sympathy they married one another. All these are natural inferences; they are also ascertained facts. One who has known them during and since their school days says "their education is very poor, and to get to an understanding with them one must be acquainted with the natural signs generally used by the pupils of that (the said pure oral) school." Is, then, the judgment of the deaf poor when they think that all the years of time, toil, and trouble lavished in the Sisyphean effort to endow this couple with speech would have been better spent upon their mental development? And is it without reason that the deaf, finding themselves in the pass this couple were in, or seeing their friends struggling through it, fail to be convinced of the truth of the recent, complacent, sweeping dictum that "oral methods are sufficient"?

The second of what are claimed to be the true causes of the attitude of the adult deaf is

• The Limitations of Lip-Reading

In an evening party of hearing persons in a metropolitan city was a lady entirely similar to the two above mentioned. She was accompanied by a familiar. The two practised pure oralism. The party was an elegant social affair, composed of the most refined and intelligent people of that city. It had nothing to do with the deaf. Now, when the familiar talked to the lady and she did not understand, he would frown, and shake his head, and by his manner chide her while he repeated—and the company stood by noticing it all with polite though forced composure. How did the lady feel during these episodes? If she was sensitive—she certainly is in the other respects—was she not keenly conscious of the fact that she was importing kindergarten features into that elegant company, and thus offending the first canon of good society, which is that all shall be consonant and none *outré?*

Again, in a summer hotel was a fourth young lady entirely similar to the three above and likewise supported by a pure-oral familiar. At breakfast one of the guests told how he had collected a tin can full of black-bass bait the night before but that some miscreant had pulled off the lid during the night and all his precious bugs, beetles, and frogs had scattered over land and water. All laughed. The young lady looked inquiringly at her familiar. The latter began to tell the story to her. The whole table ceased to ply knife and fork and watched the process and waited for the effect. Soon the familiar came to the word "frog," at which the lady stuck hopelessly. Then the familiar began the usual repetitions, frog—*frog*—FROG—FROG—FROG—*frog*—frog, and so on, *diminuendo ad crescendo, crescendo ad diminuendo.* But meantime there was no *diminuendo* in the emotions of the guests. *Their* part, beginning in interest and sympathy, mounted successively to suspense, pity, commiseration—until at last one merciful soul could stand it no longer, and, lifting a hand at her seat across the table, *spelled* to the lady f-r-o-g—and, presto! the lady's face grew radiant with comprehension, the familiar sought refuge in subsidence and perspiration, and the whole company dropped off the tenter-hooks with sighs of relief. Now, how did this lady—she is a true lady—feel, in and after such occurrences? Let all delicate and intelligent minds give answer.

The third cause of the attitude of the adult deaf claimed to be true is that in one to them most important direction

• Pure Oralism Denies the Deaf Chances of Employment

In schools using a combination of methods some adult deaf persons have almost always been employed. They have been cooks, scullions, hostlers, gardeners, seamstresses, matrons, monitors, supervisors, and teachers of every grade. Since the establishment of collegiate instruction among them, not a few have reached the highest places in the profession, being to-day teachers of the highest classes and principals of leading institutions. This they have done and are doing, not only with the approbation but by the choice of hearing principals and directors, who have deemed them better fitted to fill these places than any hearing persons then obtainable. Now, under pure oralism, all this must cease. It is one of the tenets of that creed that no deaf person should be employed in any school for the deaf in any capacity whatever. Pedagogy is the only one of the learned professions that is open to any considerable number of the deaf. Pure oralism would shut them out from it even more rigidly than they are shut out from medicine and law. It asks all deaf persons now employed as above to leave, and, moreover, to yield their support to a plan which shall bar out all deaf persons who might in time succeed them. Is not this asking much of the deaf? Ought not pure oralists to be able to show them most indubitable justification for such a request? Only one such showing might command success. If pure oralists could bring the deaf to see by their own experience in life that pure oralism makes the great mass of the deaf wiser, happier, and more prosperous than any other method or combination of methods, then, indeed, the deaf might fairly be called upon to vote to banish themselves and future generations of the deaf from the career of education and all its services. The deaf by no means consider that such a showing has yet been made in this or any other land.

The fourth cause claimed as true is that

• Pure Oralism Often Militates against Happiness

Happiness, after all, is the one end for which all mankind strives. The deaf are no exception to the rule. Happiness is the fruition of all one's tastes, desires, and faculties. Its largest factor is the enjoyment of social instincts. Under a combination of methods the adult deaf in a measure obtain it, both among the hearing and among themselves. In the intervals of daily toil they meet and enjoy social converse, wit and humor, dramas, debates, and intellectual and religious exercises of every sort. Oralists sometimes admit the value of these meetings. Said one of its prominent promoters, speaking of a certain deaf missionary among the deaf, "He is doing a good work. His efforts are helpful and his influence elevating; his lectures, too, are excellent—in fact, he is the Whitefield of the deaf." "Well," said I, "what will the deaf do for aid and comfort like this when you have abolished the sign-language?" "Oh," he replied, "we shall have to wait a long time for that"—a statement in which we perfectly agreed.

But the theory of pure oralism forbids the deaf such indulgencies. After educating the deaf man, it would have him live among the hearing alone. From a scientific standpoint its position may be sound. From that point the adult deaf should not assemble, much less form social friendships, far less marry. From that point, when pure oralism has polished each deaf person to its utmost and set each in his separate niche among the hearing, there should he stay, remote from, oblivious to those whom life affects as life affects him, as an island in the Pacific to an island in the Atlantic. That is science. But is science the whole of life? Shall we allow for nothing in the human being that is not scientific? Will the mass of these deaf persons so isolated be happy? Alas! no. Evidence accumulates with every sunset that they cry out with the poet:

> We are not cunning casts of clay!
> Let science say we are,—and then?
> What matters science unto *men*?

The deaf do look at their case from the cool pinnacles of science, but they insist, also, on viewing it from the warm precincts of religion, humanity, and love. More than five hundred graduates of pure oral schools met in Berlin last summer, and held exercises in the sign-language—this in Germany, a country that has done all that bureaucracy and autocracy can do to stamp out that language.

"Alas!" sighs an American pure-oral graduate, "we are mongrels, fitted to enjoy freely neither the society of the hearing nor that of the deaf." Another, one of the brightest of her class, says, "However intelligent, well educated, and deserving the pure-oral graduate may be, and no matter how good a conversationalist and lip-reader, hearing people in general will hold aloof from him." This she sets down to prejudice, whereas it is due to the same cause as the indisposition of those persons to converse by writing; they have learned that oral converse with the deaf is, like writing, a more or less limited and laborious process, and, moreover, involves, as writing does not, the element of uncertainty. Of this fact my note-book supplies many instances. The president of a university said of a congenitally deaf lip-reader, "I know she is an estimable person, but I shrink from meeting her in a company, because I am uncertain whether she understands me and am certain that I do not understand her."

It may be asked, would a training involving a combination of methods help the deaf in such cases? Infinitely, often. Last spring I was with a young lady who was well acquainted with the manual alphabet. We were in a large open car going to a lawn party that involved nearly two hours' sitting, and were closely girt by other persons invited to the same house. At first I read her lips by littles and in littles, but gradually we fell into real conversation, she spelling and I speaking. We talked of everything—books, politics, poetry, the scenery, our fellow-travelers, the coming party, and—ourselves. I had a capital time. If the young lady did not, she is capable of admirable deception. Had I been—instead of an ordinary one—the best lip-reader that ever lived, I could not have had, under like conditions, a conversation so perfect in range, freedom, spontaneity. It is simply a physical impossibility.

Again: last summer, at a seaside hotel was a young semi-mute with a hearing wife. He was sociable, and took part in much of the gayety about the place. His wife spoke to him habitually, but if he failed to "catch on" she instantly *spelled* the word that tripped him, and both were up and away at once. They were not conspicuous, and therefore not offensive. *That* was the combination of methods in real life.

Within a month, in an evening party at which I was the only deaf person, a gentleman and a lady among the guests came to me at different times of their own motion. One was a stranger. Both made the same remark—that they had noticed the celerity and ease with which my wife spelled to me; and they went on to compare it with the lack of those characteristics in the efforts of pure oralists to communicate which they had witnessed in society. One of them further described those efforts as "painful."

• Conclusion

The deaf believe in all wise efforts to preserve and improve natural speech and impaired hearing, and in training in the art of understanding speech by sight. They would in very many instances appear in support of this belief were they not placed on the defensive as against claims of pure oralists which they think aggressive in spirit, idealistic rather than practical, and not supported by their results, viewed broadly and apart from special cases. The deaf do not believe in long-continued efforts to endow the deaf-born with mechanical speech, except in rare instances. They believe that pure manualism is like a log, clogging many. They believe that pure oralism is like a bicycle—a very elaborate machine, highly praised by its makers, but quite unfit for rough roads, and extremely liable to have its tires punctured and otherwise to get out of order in seventy-seven different ways. They believe that a manually taught deaf man is all the better off if he has any modicum of speech. They believe that a pure-orally taught deaf man, even if he reads the lips like a prescient angel, is better off for knowing the manual alphabet. They believe that perhaps all the deaf, and certainly the vast majority of them, receive untold aid and comfort through the sign-language. They believe that three stout strings to the bow are better than one. They, in short, believe in a combination of methods.

Finally, in giving reasons for the faith that is in them, the deaf rest in part upon theories of pedagogics, but more upon what they have encountered and have seen their deaf friends encounter in the storm and stress of life.

23 | The Fable of the Ass Who Was Taught to Whinny

Warren Milton Smaltz

1921

There was once a farmer whom everybody called Uncle Sam. He was unusually successful in raising and training horses. His horses were the best trained, most intelligent, and altogether the most desirable horses to be found anywhere. Naturally he came to have more than local fame on this account. And as is to be expected, his horses were by no means unconscious of their own excellence. On the contrary, they grew quite vain and egotistical, and imagined every horse who was not born or bred under Uncle Sam to be more or less inferior and gauche.

As time passed, these horses developed among themselves a lot of faddists, reformers, uplifters, and philanthropists. For were they not the salt of the earth? And being so, was it not their heaven-set duty to teach all to be like unto them?

Wherefore it came to pass that one day Uncle Sam became possessor of an excellent ass, who was most diligent in his work, very modest in demeanor, and quite unassuming in his ways. "He looks lifeless and uninteresting, and his bray is certainly very unpleasant," said Uncle Sam to his neighbor, "but he can do more hard work than any two horses I have ever seen."

As soon as the horses had had time to recover from their surprise and disgust over the advent of the ass in their refined community, they took counsel among themselves as to the best course to pursue. They unanimously agreed among themselves that the poor ass, although very well able to work and earn his livelihood, was deficient in culture and the refinements of society. Accordingly, a number of the more charitably inclined faddists among them volunteered to undertake the task of educating the ass. Forthwith they acquired a new eminence as philanthropic educators. The other horses were also exalted at the thought of subscribing to charity.

Under the enthusiastic instruction of the horses the modest ass learned quite rapidly. First of all they taught him that to bray was a mark of inferior training. They declared that to whinny was natural and proper, because—well, just because. And to buttress this unassailable argument they reasoned that, in order to make his way in a world of horses, he must needs whinny as all good horses do. The ass modestly agreed that he was a perversion of nature, and that his bray was merely a "weed language," acquired probably from subsisting too much upon weeds instead of upon hay, the refined food of the horses.

As time passed he forgot entirely how to bray. But although he strove with might and main to whinny, his efforts sounded amazingly like a sneeze. In vain he contorted his face, strained his neck, and dilated his eyes and nostrils. The result was always a sneeze.

It was not a very great while before the horses became very properly disgusted. "See that miserable ass," said they. "We have donated large sums of money to charity in his behalf, and our most worthy educators have striven to improve him. Now see how the ungrateful wretch repays our kindness."

Uncle Sam also noted changes in his ass. Said he to his neighbor: "I cannot for the life of me understand what has come over that ass. He was formerly very docile and hard working, but now nothing seems good enough for him. And it is passing strange that he never brays anymore. Yesterday, while I was out in the fields ploughing with him, he turned around and gazed at me very queerly a number of times. Then he acted as if a blue-bottle fly was on his neck, and sneezed all the while. I sent for a veterinarian, but he left without doing anything, saying it was clearly a case for an alienist."

Thus it came about that the horses, in whom he had once awakened the divine sense of pity, now regarded him with ill-concealed disgust. His master, whose respect he had once held, now thought of him only with mystified worry. And his fellow asses, whom he occasionally encountered, treated him as a pariah, for was it not a known fact that he could not bray?

The moral of this fable may not be very clear, but it seems to be in some way concerned with oralism, and with the education of the deaf.

> Who never loved ne'er suffered; he feels nothing.
> Who nothing feels but for himself alone. — Young.

24

While the Deaf community widely supports state residential school educations for Deaf children, and Deaf adults cherish their own alma maters, no one is unaware of the schools' frequent failures to prepare Deaf children for college, work, and civic life.

The Graduate

Albert Ballin

1930

Today the deaf-mute graduates and goes into the world poorly equipped and prepared for the task of taking care of himself. During his life at school, every one of his actions have been regulated by rules designed more for the benefit of his teachers than for himself. He has so long been denied the right to think for himself that he is now an automaton with no initiative of his own. He is conscious that in leaving school he is "free," but he does not know what to do with his freedom. He is dazed. He feels like the long-term prisoner or slave suddenly liberated from captivity. With the habit of childlike dependence upon others bred into his soul, he seeks sympathy and help from his fellow-unfortunates. Usually he is guided to the parsonage of some Church for the Deaf, where the parson is a deaf man with a sympathetic understanding of his kind. After looking into the case with care, this good parson tries to find employment for the graduate, a heart-breaking task, because of the deep-rooted prejudice against employing deaf-mutes. Unless the graduate is more skillful than the average hearing man doing the same kind of work, it goes pretty hard with him.

The school he just left teaches several trades, such as tailoring, baking, printing, cabinet-making, carpentry, shoemaking, and a few others; but the methods taught are all so antiquated that the pupils are seldom able to handle modern tools or machines. The schools cannot be blamed for this, for industry is constantly introducing new machinery and methods, and the schools have not the finances to follow suit. The one I attended had a large printing equipment. It was set up over sixty years ago, and has been changed but slightly since then. The graduate from that shop had to begin as a "printer's devil," and learn all over again.

But a small percentage of the graduates follow the trades they learned at school. The majority, unless they have well-to-do relatives to help them, are half starved before they become proficient at a trade that does not call for the use of the English language.

A few deaf-mutes possess talent for highly skilled work like Commercial Art, Carving in wood, clay or marble, Architectural Drafting, Decorative Painting, Illustrating. This is found even among the most illiterate. But the poor devil is up against

186

it good and plenty if he is ignorant of English while working at one of these arts. Sometimes he is employed on trial. He receives in writing instructions as to what he is to do. Often he cannot understand them. If he turns to his fellow-workers for explanation, he finds that none of them know the sign-language, and therefore cannot help him. He scratches his head, makes wild guesses, and goes ahead, taking desperate chances. He makes mistakes. The boss tears his hair and kicks him out, vowing never again to employ another "dummy." This poor "dummy" then has to give up his cherished vocation, and wash dishes, help the janitor, scrub floors, or undertake some other form of menial labor.

Is it not a pity that he did not find a boss who could understand the sign-language? If he had, both might have prospered together happily. But, alas, such employers are as scarce as hens' teeth.

There are, today, many graduates from Gallaudet College working side by side at manual labor, with deaf-mutes from Russia, Poland, Germany, Italy, and other countries, who can scarcely scrawl their own names. They grumble at their lot, and ask, with wonder, what is the use of higher education, if all it fits one for is making bed-springs, auto tires, etc. Often the foreigner draws higher wages. Many of them never went to any school, but they did receive thorough training at some trade like tailoring, cutting garments, carving, engraving on copper, stone or steel, and similar trades that require extraordinary dexterity.

There are rare cases where genius, by sheer force of ambition, pride or unusual opportunities, overcomes all handicaps and rises in spite of, not because of, institutional life and training. It is also strange that most of the artists among the deaf are found in Europe, where schools for their kind are few and considered inferior to those in this country.

The deaf-mute does not wish to be an object for compassion. He craves neither pity nor charity. Should you be approached by anyone extending his hand to you for alms on account of his deafness, it is high time for you to yell for the police, for the chances are ninety-nine out of one hundred that the pan-handler is an imposter. The deaf-mute has pride and believes himself as good as any man alive. All he asks for, nay, *demands,* as his birthright, is to be respected and treated as an equal and be given an equal chance in this life. He does not want to be discriminated against because of his impediment.

25

What a deaf child needs most, both at school and at home, is free and easy communication, the ability to absorb cultural information by eavesdropping on adults and other children all day, every day. Without it, a decent education is impossible. This paper was presented at the Teacher Institute, Maryland School for the Deaf, by the president of the National Association of the Deaf.

The Deaf Adult's Point of View

Frederick C. Schreiber

1969

When Dr. Denton invited me to speak to you this afternoon, I felt like a seven-year-old turned loose in a candy store. And like a seven-year-old I soon discovered that with so many goodies available I was having difficulty in choosing a place to start and if I sampled them all I was in danger of getting a verbal tummy ache.

So I decided to stick to what I know best—the deaf adult's point of view. We find education of the deaf is a complex thing. There are times when we wonder if anyone knows what he is doing in this area. Our first question is—Education for what?

It frequently seems to us that the parents in particular are concerned with education for education's sake rather than what it is supposed to do for their children. Last Friday Dr. Ray L. Jones, of San Fernando Valley State College, in speaking on mental health problems of the deaf in Texas, quoted a poem which he said was typical of our approach to mental health and which, in my opinion, applies as well to education of the deaf. Unfortunately, I did not copy the poem but the gist of it had to do with the problems of the people who lived in a town adjacent a steep cliff.

Because they lived near a cliff, people were continually falling over it; and, faced with the decision of whether it would be better to build a fence by the cliff or place an ambulance down in the valley, the town decided to place an ambulance in the valley. Well, people still fell off the cliff, but the ambulance was there in the valley to cart them off promptly. When it was suggested that perhaps a fence on the cliff would be better, the response was Why? The ambulance down in the valley is giving adequate service. We may not be preventing our children from falling over educational cliffs but we certainly have the best ambulance service in the world.

We think parents of deaf children are the most dedicated, self-sacrificing and short-sighted people we know. This is because there has been so little contact with the adult deaf. While there is no doubt that education is a tremendously important issue,

188

the fact remains that your child will be concerned with education for but one-third of his life. What about the remaining two-thirds?

There are many problems facing the adult deaf today. These problems, unless they are taken care of, will be inherited by your children tomorrow. These problems vary widely, covering needs ranging from legal rights to socio-economic factors, and it is a fact that the deaf do not have the kind of people within their own ranks to cope with these problems. There are no deaf doctors, lawyers, public relations men or the like. However, since deafness is no respecter of persons, all these professions can be found among the parents, who can, if they will, do wonders in easing the pressures their children must eventually face. To do this, one must know what the problems are and to know the problems, one must know us. [. . .]

To get back to education—last year a superintendent of a midwestern school for the deaf wrote an article entitled, "Deaf Education—An Educational Miracle." In this article the Superintendent defends the low achievement of deaf school leavers as being an educational miracle and contended that to expect more from education was asking too much. The funny thing is—I agree with him, insofar as the topic goes. It is truly a miracle that the deaf get any education at all—but not for his reasons.

When a deaf child is born, his parents are advised to toss him into the sea of knowledge and let him sink or swim. The parents are told at the onset that because of his handicap he is the equivalent of a one-armed swimmer, so it is likely that the swimming lesson will be hard. They are further advised that since the child must eventually compete with swimmers with two arms, it would be necessary to hang a one hundred-pound weight around his neck, also, so that, if he doesn't drown, then his one arm will be twice as strong and therefore capable of doing the work of two.

This is the true miracle. It is a tribute to the deaf that they survive at all under such conditions. Lesser people would have gone under at the outset and most would have given up before long.

Recently a report on the use of Cued Speech referred to it as a crutch and implied that the use of such a crutch would be detrimental to the child. But what's wrong with crutches? The one-legged man used them to take his rightful place in society. He is not compelled to make his one leg serve unassisted in place of two. The blind are not required to see with their ears. Why must the deaf be compelled to hear with our eyes?

You have been told that if your children are permitted to use manual communication they will not try to talk, and sometimes this has been demonstrated to be true. This is ridiculous! Deaf children are human and they can see that the majority of the other children talk, so they have to try. Every parent has been exposed, at one time or another to a child's plaintive, "But mama, *everybody* does it." And for those who do not talk—Well, I have a story which may cast some light on the reasons.

When I was seventeen, I had a bad case of hives. As a result, my doctor put me on a diet for two weeks. This diet consisted solely of tea, toast, canned peaches and lamb chops. To make matters worse, at the time I was working as a bookkeeper in a restaurant, and it was real agony to stick to such a diet. At any rate the two weeks finally passed and on the fifteenth day I came home for lunch which was—you guessed it—lamb chops. I stormed out of the house ignoring my bewildered mother's plaintive, "I don't understand—you always liked lamb chops!" And I have never eaten lamb chops since.

Deaf children have had a steady diet of talk, talk, talk for nine or more years, whether they could or not. If fifteen days of lamb chops could do this to me, nine years of an enforced diet of speech could do worse. We'd like to know, too, why the insistence on speech anyway? What is in it that makes one think it is the end all of deaf education? Parrots can be taught to speak, so can mynah birds, but no one gets excited about that. Somewhere I read a short poem about a Deaf Child's Prayer. I have not found it again, but the last two lines went something like this:

> . . . the only words he knew,
> "a ball, a fish, a top, a shoe."

It was a cute poem no doubt, and I am sure many people were touched by it, but it filled me with rage to think that a child could have lived so long with a vocabulary of only four words—"a ball, a fish, a top, a shoe."

We are told we have to live in a hearing world and hence must talk. What's a *hearing world*, anyway? The deaf adult, whether he can speak or not, works with hearing people. He goes to the same doctors, patronizes the same stores as people who can hear and, depending on his ability to communicate, he has the same successes as his hearing peers. If living in a hearing world means social living, then ask some of these people who advocate "integration," when did they last have deaf people over to their house for cocktails or a dinner party. Even those of us who have excellent speech and better-than-average lipreading skills are rarely if ever asked.

I do not want to give the impression that I am against speech or lipreading. If I were, I would not be talking to you now. We all know that to be able to speak and read lips is desirable and should be sought after. We believe that every child should have the opportunity to learn to speak and read lips, just as we believe every child should have the opportunity to be another Van Gogh, or Beethoven, or Edison. But our first need is to be able to communicate.

Communication is not speech! You might say that it is not even language. You can communicate a lot with a wink, a hug, or a pat on the shoulder. You can express more displeasure with an angry shake of the head than with a two-hour lecture.

Neither is speech language. Speech helps convey language, of course. It is useful in communicating, also. But one can have speech without language, and one can communicate without either.

I see we have with us today Dr. McCay Vernon. Dr. Vernon is one of the people who has demonstrated a real understanding of the deaf. He has written many articles and offered many suggestions to parents as to how they can effectively cope with their problems. Invariably, he has suggested that parents get to know the adult deaf, to subscribe to our magazine the *Deaf American* and to learn as much as they can about the conditions under which we live. One thing I don't believe he mentioned, however, is what might be the basic reason for becoming involved with deaf adults: we are your children grown.

We can, in many instances, tell you the things your child would like to tell you, if he had the vocabulary and the experience to put his feelings and needs into words. We, too, had parents who went through all the anguish and indecision you face. We have experienced all the bewilderment, all the longing your child has now and some of us, if not all of us, can put these needs and wants into words. If I were your child, I would want to tell you my greatest need is to be able to communicate.

I need more than anything to be able to understand you and to make you understand me. I need to be able to sit with you and ask you why? To ask you to help me explore the universe around me. To understand the do's and don't of everyday living. These are hard things to learn; don't make them any harder for me than they already are. Give me the freedom to ask and understand in the easiest way possible—if there is an easy way.

Talk to me, yes, but give me the help that I get from signs and fingerspelling. Remember, I don't speak or lip read too well.

I want all members of my family, my father, my mother, my brothers and sisters to be able to communicate with me. I don't want to be a guest in my own house. I need to feel that I belong to you and you belong to me as well.

If you will use the simultaneous method, then use it all the time in the home. Aside from the fluency that it will give you from constant usage, I need to be able to *oversee* what my brothers and sisters normally *overhear*. I need the constant exposure to language that this can give. I need to know how third-person conversations are handled. I also need to be able to see for myself what happens to me within the family does not happen just to me—nor just because I am deaf.

Communication is my greatest need. Given adequate means of free and easy communication, I can acquire language and possibly speech as well. I will also acquire the things I need to know that are not formally taught in school and that will help me to grow up to be a well-adjusted citizen, able to handle the demands of the world around me.

I need to know, too, that you don't blame me for all the trouble I am causing you and that you aren't ashamed of me.

And I must say, as Executive Secretary of the National Association of the Deaf, that parents have every reason in the world to be proud of their deaf children. The NAD is the oldest national organization of the deaf in this country. 1980 will mark its first one hundred years. Today the name is somewhat misleading since, while it is called an association *of* the deaf rather than *for* the deaf, many of our members are people who can hear; parents, teachers, vocational rehabilitation counselors, among others. But since the administration of the association is in the keeping of deaf adults, the name has been retained. As an association, we try to better conditions for our members and future members: better educational opportunities and facilities, more employment, and the removal of discriminatory practices that exist as bars to employment. We help recruit personnel for professional training in areas relating to the deaf and serve as an information-and-referral center. Among the projects in which we are currently engaged are the national Census of Deaf People, a project which we expect to complete in 1972. We also have a Communicative Skills Program which conducts classes in signs all over the nation. In addition we have the Registry of Interpreters for the Deaf, all supported by federal grants. We have contracts for such things as evaluating general interest films for the Captioned Films program, and we have in-house projects, such as the Junior National Association of the Deaf, which is a school program designed to make our youth more aware of the responsibilities of citizenship and to develop leaders. Daily our office receives letters requesting information or asking for help with problems which cannot be taken care of by independent action. It is from this experience that I speak.

Your children have indomitable courage. They have and are standing up to burdens that have floored lesser men.

As our world grows more complex and the need for an adequate education becomes more acute, it is obvious that we need new miracles. The miracle of a fourth-grade education will not do. There are no jobs for fourth graders any more and, even if there were, they would not be the kind of jobs you would want for your child.

We believe that communication is the key to unlocking the potentialities of the deaf. And when we speak of communication we mean free and easy communication that will have the opportunity to grow as we grow, change as we change and continue to evolve until something develops that will be the best possible means we can devise.

This will not happen overnight. It may never come about at all unless the parents of deaf children accept their child's handicap and strive to give him the skills and strengths he needs to overcome this disability rather than try to make him an "imitation hearing man." You have such an opportunity here. I pray you make the most of it. It will take the best efforts of all of you, parents, teachers and counselors alike. And we want you to realize the whole world will be watching to decide for once and for all that it really is wiser to build a fence on top of the cliff rather than maintain ambulances down in the valley.

26

Deaf African American children in the South, like their hearing relatives and neighbors, were educated in underfunded, segregated residential schools, where academic success and high school graduation were often not possible. In addition, due to the much lower incidence of hereditary deafness in people of African, Asian, and Native American ethnicity compared to Europeans, students attending a school for the "Negro deaf" were consigned to very small social networks.

Black Deaf Students

Ernest Hairston and Linwood Smith

1983

Approximately two million Blacks have a hearing impairment serious enough to require special medical or educational services. Of this two million approximately 22,000 are profoundly deaf.

Early profound deafness is said to be the most severe handicap a child can have because he is denied the most vital developmental stimulus of all—the voice. Deafness is also a severe educational handicap. A glaring characteristic of the education most deaf school graduates receive is their low achievement and reading levels.

Historically and traditionally, the education of Black deaf children, as with Black children in general, has been of a second-class nature—a game in which they started late and are still trying to catch up.

When speaking of the education of Black deaf children, it is necessary to take a backward look in order to understand the present situation. In researching for information on education involving Black deaf children during the pre-integration days, we interviewed several of our older acquaintances to solicit their views on their educational background and what the system was like when they started out. We talked to "J" who was deafened by spinal meningitis at seven years of age, transferred from public school to a Southern school for the Negro deaf, and started all over again at grade one. He spent eight years in that program and, through luck, transferred to a private religious preparatory school. Even if he had stayed at the school for the Negro deaf a few years longer, he would not have graduated. "Graduation was something unheard of in this separate program for Blacks and was only known to happen in the dual system reserved for whites," he bitterly remarked years later. Not fully benefiting from the prep school because of his deafness, he moved to a Northern city and attended the school for the deaf there. At that school he received some vocational training, participated in sports, and got a reasonable secondary education. When asked what were some significant events affecting him that contributed to his success in life, he responded:

> While at the (Southern) school, I was fortunate to have had a deaf teacher who was very civic minded and with good insight into the needs and learning problems of the deaf students. This person happened to be white (Blacks were not hired as instructors at that school then) and very much dedicated to his teaching as were most of the teachers who were deaf. As I now recall, this teacher had a very touching and dramatic way of arousing self-awareness in the students and (awareness of) the world around them. This teacher was a great factor in my later curiosity about myself as a Black person in the world and my later interest in doing outside reading beyond that called for in class.
>
> While at the (Northern) school, the great civil rights movement was just starting to take place. Jackie Robinson had just broken into major league baseball, the U.S. Supreme Court had ordered the University of Texas to admit its first Black student, and other sweeping changes were taking place in our government. After classes I was reading just about every bit of news the civil rights movement made and felt a strong identification with it. This was a factor in my eventually applying for admission to Gallaudet College which theretofore had no Black deaf student in its program. My application was accepted but I failed to pass the examination for admission for the obvious reason that the school was reluctant to push, or to be a party in pushing for, integration at Gallaudet College by placing me in the class with the other college bound students from the school. However, after some protest and another try, I was fortunate to become the second Black student accepted at Gallaudet.

When last interviewed, "J" was a successful vocational adjustment instructor in a school for the deaf. And he had earned his masters degree the year before.

For more than a century and a half, deaf children have been educated in special schools in America, yet Black deaf children, especially those in Southern states, have been relegated to segregated schools, just as have their hearing peers.

Many Blacks have attended schools for the deaf for thirteen years or more, only to graduate with a second to fourth grade achievement level or less. This was especially true of the previously segregated schools in the South; however, the Northern schools have not done much better.

In the South, most of these schools were jointly for deaf and blind students and were called state schools for the "colored or Negro" deaf and blind, such as North Carolina School for the Negro Deaf and Blind, Florida School for the Negro Deaf and Blind. In the early 1950s, thirteen states were operating separate and segregated schools for the deaf. As late as 1963, eight states maintained separate facilities.

Gallaudet College, established in 1864 and the world's only liberal arts college for the deaf, did not open its door to Black students until about 1952. By 1964, Gallaudet's Centennial year, only a handful of Black deaf persons had graduated. Even though they were educated, professional, and admired by other Black deaf persons, most had no role model that they could emulate and were rarely encouraged to aspire to anything higher than classroom teaching.

A researcher at Gallaudet College's Learning Center (D. DeLorenzo) stated that Hume Le P. Battiste, Class of 1913, was the first Black deaf graduate of Gallaudet College. This caused controversy. Not the question of whether or not Battiste graduated, but whether or not he was Black. Some say he was Indian, some say Creole. Papers, however, seem to indicate that he was Black. If this is so, then other questions rear their curious heads. Did he "pass for white" in order to enter Gallaudet? Did Gallaudet knowingly admit a Black person when segregation was in force? If Blacks were admitted to Gallaudet in the early years, when did the doors close on them and why?

"T" is a counselor with a rehabilitation program in Indianapolis, Indiana, and for over thirty years was a volunteer para-professional with organizations serving the deaf and with community service agencies. During the same period, "T" worked at an electronics company. When we asked if he ever applied for college, he replied:

> The reason I did not go to Gallaudet College was because, prior to 1949, educational programs were segregated in Washington, D.C., which also included Gallaudet College. I was informed in my sophomore year at the Indiana School for the Deaf that Blacks were not allowed to go to Gallaudet. Four of us Black students did not know what to do after we learned this. Naturally, I lost interest in studying with no goals for which to aim. Going to Gallaudet used to be my number one goal since many ISD graduates went there.

Today, things are far different. Gains were made mostly through street demonstrations and court actions brought on by Blacks in general and their invaluable white sympathizers. Black deaf people played little or no role in such demonstrations, but reaped the benefits that resulted. When schools became integrated or desegregated, few if any provisions were made for the disadvantaged backgrounds and special needs of Black deaf children. At least, in segregated schools there is little if any identity problem, social discrimination, or "benign neglect."

In the late 1940s and throughout the 1950s, most schools for the Negro or colored placed strong emphasis on vocational training and skills and made certain most of their graduates were employed. The West Virginia School for the Colored Deaf and Blind, for example, prior to integrating with the West Virginia School for the Deaf and Blind in Romney, offered its students training in home economics, typing, tailoring, pressing (dry cleaning), beauty culture (hairdressing), barbering, and shoe repairing. "Programmed" is a better description than "offered" since students were placed in training programs according to grade, age, and mental ability rather than by aptitude and each student, no matter what his or her intelligence level, was allowed to try and become proficient in at least two vocations. For example, from age twelve to fourteen, it was tailoring and pressing for boys; typing, cooking, or sewing for girls. From fifteen to twenty-one, depending on when they graduated from school, courses were barbering, shoe repairing, or dry cleaning for boys and home economics and continuing beauty culture for girls. The West Virginia School for the Colored Deaf was located in close proximity to West Virginia State College, an all-Black college at that time, and most of the vocational teachers were also teachers at the college. For instance, the barber teacher, who taught at the deaf school, was also head of the barber college at West Virginia State; the tailoring teacher had his own shop near campus and taught at the deaf school from two to four in the afternoons, as most of the other vocational teachers did.

Four of six vocational instructors were master craftsmen and demanded quality work from their students. Consequently, when the students graduated, whether with a vocational certificate, diploma, or both, they had a marketable skill and were usually placed in employment shortly after. Most popular were barbering and tailoring for boys and beauty culture for girls. Some eventually became shopowners. Students in barbering and beauty culture were required to take the examinations of the State Board of Barbers and Beauticians. Upon passing, they received licenses to work for one year as apprentices and then as master barbers or beauticians. The state presented them with the tools of the trade.

In most of the other Southern states, schools for the Negro deaf and blind were usually near predominantly Black colleges from which many vocational and academic teachers and dormitory personnel were recruited. The Louisiana School was near Southern University, the North Carolina School was near Shaw University, and the Virginia School was near Hampton Institute. These schools prided themselves on their vocational training record; the academic side was also strongly emphasized, albeit less successfully. For example, the course of study at the West Virginia School for the Colored Deaf and Blind in 1951 was as follows:

Academic Program of the Deaf

The education of a deaf child presents much greater difficulties than that of the blind. It is the consensus of opinion that the training of a congenitally deaf child is the supreme challenge to teaching skills. When such a child enters school at five (5) or six (6) years of age, he is usually devoid of any concept of language. He frequently does not know his own name nor the names of any of the objects with which he has had contact. His only method of communication is by means of grunts, noises, cries, and simple gestures. He looks out upon a world that he sees and touches but cannot interpret to others nor have interpreted to himself through the common medium of spoken language. Soon after he enters school, he is also taken to a specialist in Charleston for an examination to determine the degree of his hearing loss. The audiogram, or chart of the loss of hearing in decibels, is kept on file as a guide in the child's training. His loss may be of a slight degree and thus his hearing can be improved by the use of a mechanical aid.

Thus, as the result of a lack of language caused by inability to hear the spoken word, the deaf child begins his school career at a great disadvantage. For two or three years the teacher labors unceasingly to give the little deaf child the rudiments of language before he can even reach the stage of the hearing child at the beginning of the first grade. This retardation of two or three years because of the language handicap can seldom be overcome. The deaf pupil throughout his educational career remains two, three, or more grades behind his normal brothers and sisters of the same age.

Two basic methods have prevailed in the education of the deaf. The one is the Oral Method and the other the Normal Method. There may be combinations of the two. However, the best schools of our country employ the Oral Method exclusively, and the time is not far distant when all the schools will follow that method. In the oral method, the deaf child is taught to make sounds, to speak, and to understand speech by reading the movement of the lips, jaws, and face. It is a long, slow, difficult process and calls for the utmost skill and patience on the part of the teacher. The manual method makes use of signs and fingerspelling. This is the universal language of the deaf and has come down through the years. The one serious drawback to this method is that so few normal persons understand the sign language.

This school has sought to use a combination of the two methods, with the emphasis placed upon the oral approach. The chief difficulty encountered has been the lack of teachers trained in the oral method. However, that situation has improved greatly in recent years.

Speech and language remain the important subjects for a deaf student throughout most of his school career. Therefore, fewer of the deaf than the blind have finished the high school course. The vast majority complete the eighth or ninth grades along with a vocation and are then able to make their way to success in life. The curricular offerings in the deaf department show some variations from those of the regular public schools.

The foregoing example is by no means the model that all, or even the majority of, schools for the Black deaf followed. Some schools, as stated earlier, did not even award certificates to some of their students. The most unfortunate aspect of this situation was that students with higher than average intelligence were deprived of or denied opportunities to achieve higher than a secondary education. A few, however, did manage to enroll in and graduate from Black public colleges. On the other hand, there were no available jobs to match their educational level.

On May 17, 1954, the Supreme Court ruled that the separate-but-equal doctrine (Plessy *vs* Ferguson) used to exclude Black children from public schools maintained for white children was unconstitutional. However, many school administrators sought to prevent Blacks from enrolling by stating that their schools were set up for "whites only" or that they were for the most part "privately" supported.

The Court did not require a deadline for desegregation efforts but did say that it should be carried out "with all deliberate speed." Problems immediately arose among schools relating to administration, the recruitment and integration of additional staff, and physical plants and transportation. With the desegregation of most of the Southern schools during the 1960s, Black deaf children were assimilated into previously predominantly white institutions. With their admittance into these schools, Black deaf children for the most part became cultural nonentities.

27

Forced integration of Deaf children into public schools puts warm bodies in the neighborhood classroom, but no Deaf person, child or adult, can ever be truly integrated in a group communicating by speech.

Who's Itching to Get into Mainstreaming?

Ben Bahan

1986

For a year I have had a bothersome itch that keeps teasing my foot. When I scratch it, it won't go away; it only gets worse.

I went to a podiatrist (a foot doctor), who examined me and declared there was nothing wrong with my foot. I was puzzled and decided I had to discover the culprit behind that itch. Recently I found my answer, though I still endure the itch.

I was reading the May issue of *Silent News* and discovered an article on Integration. Instantly my foot began to itch like hell. Ahh, there it was: I made the connection between my itching foot and mainstreaming. Now every time I confront that issue I will declare: mainstreaming, my foot!

• Resentment towards Mainstreaming

My feelings aren't mine alone. I feel they reflect the overall resentment the deaf community has towards mainstreaming.

The trend in education today is to integrate (another term for "mainstreaming") students with diversified backgrounds, races, and abilities. Deaf students are guinea pigs in a national experiment being conducted in laboratories (read: schools) across the country.

Before someone hands us official results from the mainstreaming experiment, we can safely state why mainstreaming works for some groups of people while it does not work for others.

• Go to the Zoo

In one sense everyone is into integration. You'll find evidences of it being imposed on almost every level of life.

199

Go to the zoo. You'll find most of the modern zoos have animals roaming around free and having their share of integration (my foot: scratch, scratch).

You hop on a tour bus to take a ride around the zoo (with interpreters one hopes, if integration is to take place). As the bus rolls on, the guide explains the philosophy behind this integrated zoo, that the animals roam about freely and are happy.

As you take a ride around the zoo, though, you can't help noticing that in the midst of the integration speech, the animals are hanging out with their own kind: lions with lions, giraffes with giraffes, and so on.

• Creating Social "Harmony"

Let's go back to the supposedly highly-intelligent animal, the human being. Humans deserve a round of applause for striving to create an integrated society. We know integration has had its advantage among people of diversified races. It creates, among young people, social "harmony" and the understanding that to be different isn't monstrous.

It should be understood that integration usually involves people of different color, but the issues of integration are more than skin-deep. There exists a variety of cultural and linguistic differences, which creates a different set of problems. Students may be integrated, but they still will choose to hang around with members of their own cultural/linguistic group.

• Integrating Abilities

The point is that integrating on the basis of race is very different from integrating on the basis of communication abilities. More specifically, integrating blacks and whites is not the same as integrating hearing and deaf.

We may be able to integrate successfully on a physical level with hearing people. One deaf student might have made it on a hearing high school field hockey team, being a very aggressive player, winning athletic awards.

But that same student is not completely integrated in terms of communication. That student will miss out a lot, in the locker room, in the bus to away games. That student's communication will probably be limited to the coach and a few selected players.

The system will consider the student's involvement in the high school and field hockey team as a successful form of integration. While inside that student, the person's inner well-being is disintegrating. The student's intellectual/social form of integration has not been met.

• Mainstreaming's a Mistake

I speak from observation and experience. I was "integrated" in the first few years of my schoolhood (kindergarten through second grade).

I felt I was physically integrate-able until I was transferred to a school for the deaf, where I discovered I could be integrated in many more levels: physical, social, mental, and spiritual. The key to integration is mutuality among peers and, above all, a complete communication environment.

Some people feel we should mainstream students when they reach high school. This is a big mistake. When students get to high school, they reach a period in life where they start to detach themselves from the nest of "home" and begin associating with peers.

In a hearing high school, the deaf teenager will face a lot of hardship to his/her mental, spiritual and social integrity, though the teen may have a few friends and participate, for example, on a field hockey team.

• Incompetent Interpreters

Many programs do detect the gap in communicative needs. So they compensate by hiring interpreters. That's great! My heart extends to interpreters because they assist us in tearing down barriers.

I have one major criticism of the programs: they use incompetent interpreters without proper training or with insufficient training and without certification. The overall appearance of mainstreaming programs looks good now, with someone moving his/her hands in front of a classroom of integrated students.

Beware of this deceiving look! The interpreter may not be interpreting everything: the deaf students will still miss out on the hearing students' vocal intonations, tones, and moods that are conveyed through the auditory channel.

Incompetent interpreters don't have the training to convey that. The supposedly-integrated classroom isn't possible, even with interpreters (skilled or unskilled) because so many things are missed.

One reason is the difference in input channels: deaf perceive by eyes, hearing by ears (in terms of language exchanges). This alone requires different pragmatic functions (ways and rules to express and receive information) which will need different paces to keep the integrated students involved in the classroom dynamics.

• Why Not Ask Us?

I want to throw in one hypothetical situation and one question. The deaf community on the whole (maybe some individuals, but not the whole community) was not asked its opinion and desire to integrate/mainstream deaf children in hearing schools.

We were just thrown into this situation by legislative acts performed by hearing people. If they sincerely want to integrate us, wouldn't it be sensible for them to ask us as a community if we wanted to be integrated and how we feel about this issue?

If integration is to work, it has to work first outside of the education establishment before we can bring it into the schools. It projects an artificial picture of what the world is really like. Deaf children graduate from school and go out facing the desegregated society and end up hanging around with other deaf people.

So much for integration.

Ohh, my foot! Scratch, scratch.

Deaf children who enter school monolingual in ASL must learn written English as a second language. Unlike hearing ESL students, however, Deaf children are regarded by the educational establishment not as budding bilinguals but as language-impaired.

28

The Real Meaning of "Hearing Impaired"

Angela Stratiy

1989

For centuries, hearing people in the field of education have labeled Deaf children (aka hearing-impaired, deaf mute, deaf and dumb, and hard of hearing) as retarded or delayed in their language development. Charts are frequently developed which compare the language development of hearing and Deaf children and adults. Frequently noted are the low scores of Deaf children and adults in the areas of negatives, conjunctions, question forms, verb conjugation, pronominalization, relative clauses, nominalization, and sentence completion.

As a Deaf teacher of American Sign Language (ASL) as a second language to hearing students, I thought it only appropriate for Deaf people to develop a chart noting the deficiencies of hearing students of ASL (aka severely to profoundly hearing, signing impaired, hard-of-fingerspelling, etc.).

Hearing students of ASL frequently have problems with usage. Syntactic errors include: (1) noun-verb pair discrimination (how often have you had to show blow-by-blow the difference between AIRPLANE with a short restrained double movement, and TO–FLY–BY–AIRPLANE with the single continuous movement?), (2) over generalization of sign usage (using the same sign for lose in TO–LOSE–A–GAME and TO–LOSE–A–CAT), (3) poor sign execution (WHY NOT? is often executed to look like two separate thoughts—WHY?? NOT??), (4) weak pluralization (did this student read one book for a long period of time or did this student read a number of books? Was the item shown to one person or was it shown to a crowd?), and (5) inaccurate temporal aspect (did s/he GO somewhere once or did s/he GO–*frequently* to a place? Did s/he CRY–*continuously*, or CRY–HARD?). This poor performance has led to the classification of many severely and profoundly hearing students as *sentence impaired*.

A less severe problem, but one that is common among ASL-as-a-second-language (ASLSL) students, is that of inappropriate or inconsistent time markers—a disability which we may refer to as *hard-of-timing*. Errors in this category include the failure to properly produce number incorporation in such semantic items as PAST–WEEK, EVERY–SATURDAY, and ALL–MORNING for example. In addition, hearing students do quite well with expressive fingerspelling, but score miserably on reading it (*hard-of-fingerspelling*).

Locus confusion, a common syndrome among the severely to profoundly hearing, frequently results in misenunciated and misperceived locatives. How often have you wondered when looking at your ASLSL students whether the event being described happened on the side, in front, or in back of the building? This syndrome also causes confused pronominalization.

It is difficult for a *pronoun deprived* hearing person to properly indicate or understand (1) who is speaking to whom, (2) pronouns including or excluding the signer (US–TWO, THREE–OF–THEM . . .), and (3) static location on referent nouns. This area of weakness is also reflected in numerous subject/object errors particularly when it is linguistically appropriate to use directional verbs which incorporate subject/object information. We might classify this type of handicap as *misinformed*.

Classifiers are another inherent weakness in the hearing ASLSL student. Due to *dexterity disability* and *sentence impairment*, a hearing person frequently errs in the selection of handshape when attempting to use classifiers. Such an error results in a toothpick being described as having the diameter of a telephone pole or a group of people moving in all directions rather than a mass of people gathered in one location. Another common error is the failure of ASLSL students to shift between real-world and abstract classifiers, resulting in the overuse and over-generalization of such classifiers as 1-CL (*person moving*) and 3-CL (*vehicle moving*). This error often results in an increased number of prayers by ASL teachers to Saint Vitreous Humor for opthomological strength. Since this serious deficit is so common to the profoundly hearing, we label those who suffer from this disability as *misclassified*.

It is the author's opinion that severely to profoundly hearing students produce fingerspelling with approximately 60 percent accuracy (second–third grade level), comprehend ASL at a rate of about 40 percent (fourth–fifth grade level), and produce ASL at about a 50 percent level of accuracy (second–third grade level)—an overall level of performance of second–fourth grade level—far below acceptable levels! It is time for Deaf people to unite and provide ASL and visual discrimination remediation clinics for these poor hearing handicapped individuals. Unless we do, teachers will continue to be hired who have only second to third grade Sign Language proficiency and deaf children will continue to suffer under their instruction.

29 Do We Continue This Tragedy?

Jack Levesque

1991

If you ever feel like getting into a nice, heated debate all you have to do is bring up the subject of how schools for deaf children ought to teach. We all love to take our battle-stances on one side of the "deaf-ed" fence. But whichever side we take, the kids we are arguing about are all the lucky minority.

Most deaf kids never set foot in a school for the deaf. There are approximately 75,000 deaf children in this country, and 55,000 are not enrolled in residential, state schools or large day class programs. At lease 41,800 are in "mainstreamed" programs with one or two other deaf children.

To me, this is my childhood nightmare multiplied by 40,000. My idea of torture, to this day, is to be the only deaf person (or one of two or three) held captive with hundreds of hearing, shouting, fast-talking people.

And, of course, the culprit of this horror is PL. 94-142.

If we want to see quality education for deaf kids, we must adhere to some new guidelines which were not considered when deaf kids were tossed into the general special education category. As it stands now, deaf kids are struggling along in mainstream programs that cannot possibly meet their needs. Consider these facts:

- Critical mass is crucial to the development of a deaf child into a well-adjusted adult. "Critical mass," meaning a pool of peers within which to form social and communicative bonds, should consist of at least eight to ten similarly aged school children who are at approximately the same functional level. Schools flunk this category if they think a deaf, non-signing five-year old, a signing twelve-year old, and a developmentally disabled, hearing, eight-year-old make up a peer group. Seventy-six percent of the programs identified flunk this category.
- Just as important as peers for the healthy development of deaf children are adult role models. There is no evidence of sufficient role models in 76 percent of "mainstreamed" programs. Some deaf kids have never seen a deaf adult and may fantasize that some day they will become hearing adults.
- Most, if not all, teachers of the deaf in these mainstream programs do not have

205

certification in deafness, but rather have certification in special education or are certified with "emergency credentials."

- Most, if not all, teachers in these programs lack the fluent communication skills in sign language to communicate at an adult level with their deaf student or students.
- Most, if not all, "interpreters" in these programs do not have certification and lack qualifications to interpret at an adult level.
- Most, if not all, teachers of these mainstream programs are overburdened with a variety of special education students or a very full class of hearing students and do not have time to provide extra attention and instruction to the deaf kids.

Given these facts, can anyone argue that this is the right way to treat these kids? Do we allow this to continue?

As you might guess, I won't sit by while those potential deaf leaders spend their days waiting for someone to tell them what's going on.

Congress is conducting oversight hearings on the Deaf Education Act taking place this fall. This is routine. What should happen is that the hearings include testimony describing the need for a revamp and asking the DEA to consider the following changes:

- Transfer all responsibility for deaf education to DEA, instead of PL. 94-142.
- Establish a Department of Deaf Education and staff it with qualified deaf administrators and a majority of qualified deaf employees.
- As in the Swedish model, turn to the deaf community for expertise, rather than the professional community. Currently, the professional community is considered to be the experts, and the deaf community serves as advisors. It should be the other way around. History, and the present-day record of deaf student achievement, should point out how disastrous that has been.
- Leave the business of education of the deaf to the deaf community.

This is only a start, but like our successes with the Gallaudet revolt and with the change of the California Relay Service from a giant to a David, we know we can change our world. Furthermore, we know that nobody but us can do it.

30

The Deaf community has a long and fascinating history of diglossia, whereby a vibrant, colloquial variety of what used to be called "the sign language" was used at home and in informal situations, while a variety rich in English loans and grammatical structures was preferred for formal or ceremonial situations, including the college classroom. Today, the names and prestige of ASL varieties have changed, but the diglossic situation continues much as it has over the past 150 years.

A Taboo Exposed

Using ASL in the Classroom

Clayton Valli

1990

Remarks like "You have to do more research on ASL" or "What is ASL? We don't know what its definition is" are common to researchers and these comments become like an echo, no matter how often researchers explain their findings. Since 1965, there has been much important research on ASL and bilingual education and many linguists, sociolinguists, and anthropologists have given their time to carefully explain their work about ASL and Deaf culture. Some examples include: William Stokoe (1972), "A Classroom Experiment in Two Languages"; Barbara Kannapell (1974 and 1978 respectively), "Bilingual Education: A New Direction in the Education of the Deaf" and "Linguistic and Sociolinguistic Perspectives on Sign Systems for Educating Deaf Children: Toward a True Bilingual Approach"; Carol Erting (1978 and 1986 respectively), "Language Policy and Deaf Ethnicity" and "Sociocultural Dimensions of Deaf Education: Belief Systems and Communicative Interaction"; Charlotte Baker (1978), "How Does 'Sim-Com' Fit into a Bilingual Approach to Education?"; Susan Mather (1987), "Eye Gaze and Communication in a Deaf Classroom"; Robert E. Johnson, Scott Liddell, and Carol Erting (1989), "Unlocking the Curriculum: Principles for Achieving Access in Deaf Education"; and Sam Supalla (1990), "Segmentation of Manually Coded English: Problems in the Mapping of English in the Visual/Gestural Mode." There is a large body of research. In general, it explains the natural language that Deaf people use daily and suggests that their language should be used in the education of the deaf to improve their cognitive skills and English skills, and to provide access to curriculum content. Nevertheless, today there is still controversy about ASL, especially at Gallaudet University. Every time the issue of ASL is brought up, every faculty member's face turns to stone and his/her breathing stops. Where is the respect for researchers? At this point, I don't see why I, as a sociolinguist, should continue to contend with resentful faculty members and teachers of the deaf. Instead of that, I will tell you what I, as a faculty member, see in the Gallaudet community.

In the Gallaudet community, discussion of ASL is frowned upon. To faculty members, using ASL in the classroom is as abhorrent as having Deaf students in the classroom. (The term, *Deaf*, refers to culturally deaf people who use their language, ASL, and who share attitudes, cultural values, and a way of looking at the world.) Their veiled terms such as Simultaneous Communication (SimCom), Pidgin Signed English (PSE), Signing Exact English (SEE), Sign Communication, Sign Language, and the like are used in order to satisfy all students in the classroom. They are more concerned about students who have not yet been exposed to "sign language" when they come to Gallaudet. Most of the students pick up ASL very quickly from their peers during the school year. All of my students who learned ASL upon entering Gallaudet regret not having learned ASL at the very beginning of their educational careers. The concern of the faculty members is a weak excuse. They can say these terms anytime with comfort, but they don't seem comfortable using the term, ASL. And an uncomfortable atmosphere is growing daily. For example, recently, the Faculty Senate, which is now committed to a working model of a bilingual (ASL and English), multi-cultural community, passed a motion in which the communication policy was changed from SimCom to ASL and English and the term for ASL, "American Sign Language (ASL), is to be used in an all-inclusive sense, even including signs expressed in English word order, with or without voice—in much the same way many deaf and hard of hearing people communicate among themselves and with hearing people."

Now, we researchers know that ASL is not ambiguous, and that it is as distinct from English as Japanese is distinct from English. That portion of the policy really hit me hard and I realized that to faculty members, "ASL" is anything you can use, including Signed English, SEE, SimCom, Cued Speech, MSS (Morphemic Sign System) or other systems combined together. Thus, "ASL" is used as yet another veiled term to avoid the real issues and in order to keep control. Indeed, the choice of terms is not random or accidental. The natural language, ASL is still denied as a teaching tool at Gallaudet University. Notice communication policy. Another veiled term. I never see any communication policy around schools, colleges or the government. Also in the Gallaudet University Faculty and Staff Directory, the term "ASL" is not mentioned at all. The Sign Communication Department, Sign Language Program, English Department, English Language Institute, Communication and Developmental Studies, Audiology and Speech, Cued Speech Program are listed, and more. The idea of using the Sign Communication Proficiency Interview (SCPI) for evaluating signing skills is still supported. "Sign Communication" is other veiled term meaning combination of ASL and English. If "Sign Communication" is used in the classroom, does it provide linguistic access and meet the students' needs?

"Sign Communication" is not reliable because it is not clear what its linguistic structure is, so how can each faculty member's signing skill be assessed? The federal government has the Foreign Service Institute (FSI) that has used the Language Proficiency Interview (LPI) for over twenty-five years. This is used for assessing employees' skills in foreign languages before they go to other countries to work. This idea of using LPI is being spread around the U.S. and abroad. The Linguistics and Interpreting Department at Gallaudet University has adopted the idea of LPI from the FSI and now uses it for graduate students, to assess their skills in a recognized language, namely ASL. I don't see any *"Communication"* Proficiency Interview being used anywhere in the U.S. or in other countries except at Gallaudet University. Indeed, language is much easier to assess than communication.

The behavior of denying the use of ASL is still found in many schools for the deaf. Over sixteen thousand residential, mainstreamed, and day schools in the U.S. don't use ASL in the classroom at all. What's going on? There are some graduate-level programs related to education for the deaf in the U.S. that don't mention much about ASL and deaf culture. One good example is the Department of Education at Gallaudet University. The plan for their Master's Degree in Parent-Infant Studies includes twenty-two courses totaling fifty-eight credits. Students are required to take courses such as Signing Exact English and Cued Speech. No ASL or deaf culture courses are required. These courses are not seen as important and the students who graduate spread this approach everywhere in the education for the deaf.

I have been teaching at Gallaudet University as a faculty member since 1985. I remember clearly when I was called for a job interview for a position as a "sign language" instructor. I wanted the job very badly because it had been my goal to become a teacher ever since childhood. I had a big conflict inside of me just before going to the job interview. My question was: Should I use formal ASL for the interview? I mean using ASL in a formal situation, not switching to PSE, "Signed English," or whatever it is called which Deaf people are encouraged to use. I have been working on separating two languages, ASL and English, when I use them, that is, signing in ASL, and writing and reading in English. Like other deaf people, I found myself tending to use a combination of ASL and English when I approached any formal situation. But I never felt comfortable with that. I picked up this method from my school. The classroom itself is formal in general and the method of combining ASL and English in classroom is used all the time. Now I am empowering myself to use ASL and English appropriately as separate languages. I decided to take a risk and use formal ASL for the job interview. I had a fear of being rejected because of that, but I went ahead with caution and planned to tell the interviewers why I was doing this, in order to educate others about ASL as a language. After the interview, I was in agony for at least one week. Surprisingly, I got the job. Two years later, I applied for a teaching position in the Department of Linguistics and Interpreting, and got the job. I have never forgotten most of the undergraduate students' startled faces on each first day of Introduction of ASL Structure, when I use ASL in the classroom. I understand that they don't expect it as most faculty members use SimCom or contact signing (the outcome of contact between ASL and English). The students are startled because the use of ASL in the classroom is still not openly accepted or acknowledged at Gallaudet. It is certainly not a priority. It takes a while for students to get used to using my ASL. However, at the end of every course, most students are inspired and wish that they had learned and used ASL long ago.

In Victorian England and America, all references to sex were forbidden. One did not refer to anatomy, except in veiled terms. Women did not have legs, they had limbs; they did not have breasts, they had bosoms. The forbidden words continued to exist, but were not mentioned in polite society. Likewise, today at Gallaudet community, Deaf people don't have ASL, they have sign communication; they are not Deaf, they are hearing-impaired. And many other policies exist only to cancel out the forbidden behaviors or terms. Such forbidden behavior is known as a taboo. The taboo that has been hidden for a long time now is being exposed in the Gallaudet community, as the controversy about ASL heats up.

How did the taboo of using ASL in the classroom come about? I have wondered about this question for a long time. I am still not sure but one possibility comes into mind: The Milan Conference of 1880. Teachers of the deaf from over the world came to the convention in Milan, Italy one hundred and ten years ago and had a debate over which method, sign language or oral, should be used for teaching deaf children in the classroom. The oral method won and the majority of teachers agreed that using sign language in classroom should be forbidden. Thus, the taboo was born. As years passed, more and more Deaf teachers lost their jobs and more and more Deaf people turned to different careers that are not related to deafness, except vocational training and houseparenting at residential schools. It is very ironic, of course, that the first president of Gallaudet, Edward Miner Gallaudet, had a Deaf mother (Sophia Fowler), was a native signer of ASL, and supported the use of ASL in the education of the deaf. Probably around 1970 the taboo began to be broken when the philosophy of "Total Communication" was introduced. It included gestures, speaking, reading, writing, drawing, wearing hearing aids, ASL and other communications. However, Total Communication changed and became like SimCom, and ASL was not used at all. ASL had apparently been used in spite of the taboo, but the taboo against discussion was what kept the information hidden. The system for the deaf education is still largely controlled by the taboo. Any teacher exposed to ASL or touched by a Deaf person thus becomes dangerous, just like in Polynesian society, where another taboo holds that it is dangerous for an ordinary person to touch the king. The idea of using ASL in the classroom is too dangerous for teachers, no matter whether ASL provides full access to curriculum content and no matter what the researchers are trying to say about the very rich linguistic structure of ASL as a language separate from English. It is a serious problem, especially at Gallaudet University. And as a result of the taboo, we Deaf people and especially Deaf children, are suffering.

31

Arguments for ASL-English bilingual education have been met for over a century now with various objections, founded perhaps for the most part on the unexamined and very mistaken assumption that fluency in a natural sign language prevents children from learning English. Some, less inclined to be kind, would say instead that the root cause was the fear of the hearing at losing their monopoly in the Deaf-Ed business. In any case, until Deaf teachers themselves resumed founding Deaf Schools (a thing they had not done since the early nineteenth century), the experiment went untried.

Deaf-centric Teaching

A Case Study in ASL-English Bilingualism

Cynthia Neese Bailes

1999

Educating deaf children in the United States has a controversial history rooted in extreme beliefs about language use in general and signed language in particular. Thomas Hopkins Gallaudet, a hearing minister whose son, Edward, became the first president of Gallaudet University, was instrumental in the establishment of the first school for deaf children in Hartford, Connecticut, in 1817. After a tour of fourteen countries in Europe, Gallaudet concluded that while there was no difference in the speech production of students from oral schools and schools using sign language, schools that employed signed language produced significantly superior students (Sacks, 1989). He persuaded Laurent Clerc, a young Deaf teacher from France, to return with him to the United States for the purpose of establishing this school. Twenty-four of the schools established in the nineteenth century following Gallaudet and Clerc's efforts were founded by Deaf individuals, many of whom Clerc had trained (Gannon, 1981). During this period, there were large numbers of Deaf teachers in schools for deaf children, with a peak of 42.5 percent in 1870 (Moores, 1996).

A swift paradigm change occurred in 1880 when the Second International Congress in Milan, Italy, voted to disallow sign languages in schools (Brill, 1984). Of the 164 delegates, only sixteen dissented, including the sole Deaf participant (Lane, Hoffmeister, and Bahan, 1996; Van Cleve and Crouch, 1989). The effect of this congress was profound and long-lasting in its promotion of an ideology of oralism, defined as the use of spoken language as a primary means of instruction, superior to signed languages in the education of deaf children (Lane, 1984; Nover, 1995). Lane (1984) measures this impact as follows:

In America, there were 26 institutions for the education of deaf children in 1867, and ASL was the language of instruction in all; by 1907, there were 139 schools for deaf children, and ASL was allowed in none. (p. 113)

By 1917, the number of Deaf teachers was reduced to 14.5 percent (Moores, 1996), and by the 1960s their numbers were fewer than 12 percent (Lou, 1988). Sacks (1989) holds the 1880 congress responsible for "a dramatic deterioration in the educational achievement of deaf children and in the literacy of the deaf generally" (p. 28). Despite this rapid and profound paradigm shift in the education of deaf children, the question of the merits of these changes was not often a point of discussion for professionals or policymakers (Brill, 1984). The English-only curricula that developed after 1880 were primarily the result of hearing educators' fears that the use of signed languages would preclude the learning of oral and written English (Barnum, 1984).

Another paradigm shift occurred in the early 1960s when William Stokoe (1960, 1978) offered empirical evidence that ASL was a language in its own right, with its own lexical and syntactical system. Stokoe's work spawned a series of linguistic studies that resulted in a renewed pride in the signed language by Deaf people. By the early to mid-1970s, arguments and proposals for bilingual education for deaf children emerged (Kannapell, 1974; Maher, 1996; Woodward, 1978). These proposals drew on principles of bilingual education designed for other linguistic minorities. Stokoe himself wrote a proposal for bilingual education in 1975, in response to a call for innovative ideas from the president of Gallaudet College, where Stokoe was an English professor. This radical proposal, titled "An Untried Experiment," suggested a bilingual, bicultural education implemented by Deaf people; that is, Deaf people would actually control the educational process for deaf children, including the teacher preparation programs (Maher, 1996).

The research on ASL by Stokoe and others did not immediately result in the inclusion of ASL in the education of deaf children. Rather, policies allowing signing in schools but lending preference to English-like signing and signing accompanied by speech emerged. It was not until 1985 that a handful of schools for deaf children in the United States began to move toward a bilingual philosophy (Nover, 1995; Strong, 1995). These schools, in promoting both ASL and English in the classroom, have come about as a result of a growing understanding of the role of ASL as a minority language in the lives of Deaf people (Strong, 1995). In this essay, I describe one such school. I make no claims that this school is representative of other bilingual schools for deaf children. Indeed, this school is a unique case, which makes it all the more intriguing for close study.

• ASL-English Bilingualism in a Charter School for Deaf Children

Metro Deaf School (MDS), the first charter school for deaf children in the United States, was the brainchild of a Deaf and a hearing teacher of deaf children and four families with deaf children in St. Paul, Minnesota. Established in 1993 for the purpose of providing bilingual education in grades K–8 and operated by a board of directors including teachers, parents, and community members, it has grown from a student population of thirteen to its current number of sixty-two (Amy Hile, personal communication). A majority of the teachers at MDS are Deaf, and all are fluent in ASL and English. These characteristics contrast sharply with the low number of Deaf teachers in typical programs serving deaf children (especially in the primary grades) and the typically low number of teachers fluent in ASL (Johnson, Liddell, and Erting, 1989; Lane, 1992). MDS's mission statement is communicated through two attractive brochures, one of which states:

> Metro Deaf School promotes academic excellence in Deaf Education using an innovative bi-lingual and bi-cultural approach. Our primary purpose is to help our students develop a sense of identity and pride as deaf persons while providing them the skills and knowledge to succeed in the larger hearing community.

The second brochure further states:

> Students are taught both American Sign Language and English. ASL, the natural language of Deaf and Hard of Hearing students, is the language of instruction. English is taught as a second language through a unique combination of signing, reading and writing methods.

At the time of my study (Bailes, 1999), MDS had a population of thirty-nine children in grades K–5. I focused on how teachers in the primary grades used ASL to teach English literacy. Four teachers, three Deaf and one a hearing child of Deaf adults, "coda," worked with a total of nineteen children in grades K–3.

MDS occupied two floors of a building within the city. (It has since moved to a larger location in St. Paul, due in part to its increased enrollment.) Grades K–3 occupied an open area and one closed area on the main floor. The open area was subdivided by partitions and small bookcases, which were filled with children's books. The classroom walls were literally covered with various postings, including illustrations of various concepts, word walls, and examples of the children's work. Each classroom had a small classroom library filled with children's books. The children chose freely from this library during sustained silent reading time. The school also had a library and media room on a lower floor. A computer room adjoined the primary-grade area, easily accessible to the students, and was frequently in use. The environment appeared relaxed and friendly. Each morning as the children arrived, the teachers greeted them and conversed for several minutes prior to beginning classes.

In this case study, I interviewed all four K–3 teachers, two team leaders, and three parents. I also observed in the classrooms of two teachers: Amy Hile's grade 2 and 3 reading classes and Estella Bustamante's grade 1 ASL-English classes. I also observed Amy and Estella in their team-taught ASL classes. I observed a total of ninety-six class periods taught by these two teachers, each period lasting approximately forty-five minutes. I further reviewed a variety of school artifacts. The study resulted in a description of principles and instructional strategies for using ASL to teach English literacy. The remainder of this chapter describes these principles and illustrates them with some of the instructional strategies used at MDS.

• Using ASL to Teach English Literacy: Principles for Instruction

In any given classroom, teachers operate with a set of principles or beliefs that drive their choices of teaching strategies. These beliefs may or may not be explicitly stated; indeed, a teacher may not be explicitly aware of a belief she carries. Those beliefs not articulated can be uncovered through direct observation of classroom practices. The beliefs I describe here are those that were articulated or demonstrated by the teachers I interviewed and observed at MDS. I illustrate each principle with a number of pertinent supporting strategies.

Principle 1: Deaf Teachers as Language Models

A fundamental principle at MDS was the importance of teachers as language models. To this end, all teachers were expected to be fluent in both ASL and English. Deaf teachers who were native or near-native users of ASL were the preferred teachers for grades K–3. These teachers would serve as models of ASL as a natural language, affording the children natural exposure to this language. Hearing teachers at MDS taught primarily in the older grades; the sole hearing teacher in the primary grades was a coda (child of Deaf adults) who was exposed to ASL from birth. Native ASL users were deemed important because most of the students at MDS were from hearing families and did not arrive with firm language foundations in either ASL or English.

Estella, the first-grade teacher, cited as ideal the fact that the majority of the staff at MDS was Deaf and fluent in ASL, and that the hearing staff signed well also. Fluency in ASL was considered an essential qualification for teachers in the primary grades. Fluency in English was deemed equally important. The participants repeatedly stressed in interviews the importance of Deaf teachers as language models for young deaf children. But this was not stressed at the expense of good teaching: although Deaf teachers fluent in ASL and English were highly valued as teachers, competency in teaching was given high value as well. Thus, being Deaf was not enough to warrant a teaching spot at MDS. The ability to teach in general and the ability to make distinct connections between ASL and English and to teach these effectively in particular were equally valued. Hearing teachers who were fluent in ASL and actively involved with the Deaf community were also valued. A Deaf parent of two Deaf children in the school summarized these sentiments, stating:

> I think, number one, we must look at the quality of the teaching. Secondly, we must look at if the teachers are Deaf. Deaf children need role models. I grew up with no models. . . . Deaf teachers have a way of looking at what a deaf child doesn't

Estella is a strong language model in both ASL and English for her first-graders. Photo
from the author's archives.

understand; they can see why and what the deaf child doesn't understand and adapt
to help the child.

Deaf teachers fluent in both ASL and English were considered powerful models to
their young deaf charges. Indeed, a hearing parent of a third-grader stated: "I think
it is important to have Deaf teachers. Especially for young children. . . . Young children need a natural language and a good model to learn it from. I feel this model
needs to be a Deaf person whose native language is ASL." She elaborated that both
hearing and Deaf teachers are important and that they work cooperatively to expose
the child to both ASL and English. At MDS, three of the four primary-grade teachers
were Deaf, two hailing from Deaf families. The third Deaf teacher developed ASL as
a first language at an early age at a school for deaf children. The sole hearing teacher,
who also had Deaf parents and learned ASL naturally from her parents at an early
age, is involved with the Deaf community.

In my observations at MDS, it was apparent that spontaneous conversation among
students and between students and teachers was abundant. The children appeared to
feel free to contribute and express their thoughts during discussions. Perhaps the
most telling example of this was when Estella's first-graders were preparing for a visit
from the president of the National Association of the Deaf (NAD). Estella, who is
active in the Deaf community and knowledgeable about its institutions, explained

Margaret confidently shares her ideas for improving the lives of Deaf people, using ASL, her first language. Photo from the author's archives.

the organization and the purpose of the visit. She encouraged the students to prepare to share with the upcoming visitor their vision of how the lives of Deaf people could be enhanced. The students were immersed in discussing their ideas, then writing and illustrating them, and finally sharing them with their peers. Six-year-old Margaret (all children's names cited here are pseudonyms), for example, wanted Deaf drivers to be able to use a telecommunication device (TTY) in the same way that hearing drivers use cellular phones. She thought this would be possible by putting a special TTY on the steering wheel. Tina wanted all videotapes and programs to be captioned. Sean had a myriad of ideas, including the idea of a visual intercom system. Margaret confidently shared first her ideas, then Tina's and Sean's in their absence, on the day of the visit. Margaret felt free to share her opinion of Sean's idea with this important visitor, stating:

> This one is crazy. The student's name is Sean and he wants many things, including an idea for a fire and tornado alarm. Because Deaf kids can't hear the alarm and sometimes can't see the alarm light, his idea is to run a wire from the alarm under our seats. If there's a fire alarm, the seats would vibrate and we'd zoom outside. That's so funny. The idea of having our seats vibrate is funny. That's Sean's idea.

Examples of such eloquence were abundant in the primary-grade classrooms I observed at MDS. And the teachers, team leaders, and parents expressed the belief that having teachers who are fluent in their natural language from whom the children could absorb the language and with whom they could converse easily was a key factor leading to the children's eloquence and active participation. Additionally, they expressed the belief that without this attention to first-language models, subsequent development of a second language would not be possible.

Indeed, as Estella prepared her first-grade students for the NAD president's visit, she led them into making direct ties between their ideas expressed in ASL and writing them in English. Estella prepared her students well for negotiating this transfer of ideas. Her classroom routine included daily confrontations with both languages, making transfers from one to the other. The children observed her as she read/signed from storybooks each day, translating from English text to ASL, frequently pointing to text, fingerspelling, and then signing in ASL, thus explicitly bridging the two languages. She immersed them in lessons that dealt with the grammars of both languages, making comparisons and applying what they learned in a variety of ways. Thus the children viewed Estella not only as a fluent user of ASL but as a literate Deaf individual who knew and valued the workings of English. Estella thus was a language model, not only of ASL but of the second language—English.

Principle 2: ASL as the First and Natural Language of Deaf Children

Teachers and parents at MDS stated a belief that ASL was the first language of the children, regardless of parentage and home language. Third-grader Adam's mother expressed these beliefs in the following statement: "It's normal to see Adam as a Deaf person using ASL as his [primary] language."

An underlying theme in this principle is that first-language development in ASL supports subsequent development in English as a second language. Adam's mother expressed this also when explaining what bilingual education meant to her, stating: "It means [Adam] is learning both languages. First, he learns ASL as a natural language. He must focus first on this natural language until he fully understands it, then transfer it over to the second language [English]."

In reflecting on their experiences in learning French, one teacher and two parents described their ease in learning French as a result of being able to transfer knowledge about languages based on their first-language development in English. They believed these experiences were directly related to the issue of teaching English to deaf children. Again, Adam's mother well summarized their sentiments, stating: "If a deaf child doesn't have ASL, how can we teach English?" Clearly, a strong belief shared by teachers and parents was that language development for deaf children centered on ASL; through a natural development of ASL as a first and natural language, it was fully expected that the children would learn English.

Thus it was unanimously stated that to learn English, deaf children must apply their knowledge of ASL as a first language. The children who arrived in school without fluency in ASL were believed to develop it naturally through interaction with adults and peers. They also were involved in a study of ASL in the same manner that hearing children in the United States study English, their first and natural language.

They subsequently applied their developing knowledge of ASL to the learning of English as a second language. The primary goal was the development of fluency in both ASL and English. ASL was maintained as the language of instruction and learning and, as such, was a means for access to written English.

Students who arrived at MDS without fluency in ASL and who were not exposed to fluent models of ASL at home, of which there were many, were perceived to experience barriers in their development in both ASL and English. In recognition of this, MDS has since opened a preschool, allowing the enrollment of children as young as age three. Approximately 90 percent of the children at MDS were from homes where ASL was not the native language. A majority of these children arrived at this school without having first acquired ASL as a native language, although some had exposure through frequent contact with Deaf adults in the community. Learning ASL at an early age was deemed important; yet the fact remains that many of the primary-grade students at MDS had not. Left open to interpretation, therefore, are questions regarding how to approach the development of ASL as a first language when the children did not develop this naturally at an early age, as well as the consequences of children not doing so.

Regardless of this debate and of their ASL background at an early age, MDS students were immersed in ASL for both social and instructional purposes. The children were greeted each day by their teachers, who casually conversed with them prior to the beginning of class. The teachers read stories in ASL daily; and as a regular part of storybook reading/signing, the teachers regularly engaged their students in short asides, to describe a word or concept or to discuss these further with the students. Incidental conversations took place repeatedly throughout the day, covering a broad range of topics. Third-graders were observed discussing the many variations of their names, for example, producing a myriad of possible nicknames for themselves and for their siblings, friends, and teachers. Amy joined this conversation and added more variations of names to the mix. One of the children noted that Amy's name did not have nickname variations, to which Elizabeth joked, "Well, she could choose between 'Am' and 'My.' " The children were bathed in visual language, and they clearly mirrored this exposure in their interactions with teachers and peers alike.

Principle 3: Using ASL to Build World Knowledge

The use of ASL to tap into and build world knowledge, including knowledge about ASL and English as languages, was a key theme at MDS. The importance of world knowledge for the development of English literacy was well recognized. Indeed, this is not unique to MSD, as the principle of utilizing background knowledge in reading and writing tasks is well documented in literacy and language arts texts (e.g., Reutzel and Cooter, 1998; Tompkins, 1998).

In expressing the belief that background knowledge is an important component of the reading and writing processes, the participants in this case study frequently implied that ASL was an essential medium for tapping into, building, and processing this knowledge. As one teacher expressed it:

> The students must have experiences prior to writing. When the students have experienced something, they can write about it. If they have discussed it, they can write. If they have developed concepts, they can read. One of my principles is that students must develop strong background knowledge—background in language and [general] background knowledge, too.

This teacher later carried this assertion further, lamenting the fact that many of the students came from homes where signing was not consistent, thus impeding their access to information:

> Most of the students here have hearing parents at home. They don't have Deaf parents. I feel that influences their opportunity to receive information. For students with Deaf parents, it's easy for them to receive information that the Deaf parents share. Not all hearing parents are able to sign all the time.

Thus, while it was recognized that world knowledge was important for successful reading and writing, it was also acknowledged that many students lacked this knowledge because of an impoverished language environment from an early age. Using ASL to tap into and build the students' knowledge of the world prior to reading and writing was a frequently used strategy. Bridges from ASL to English were often made by first engaging students in a discussion of a topic through ASL and then making connections in English writing by webbing their ideas on the board. ASL was viewed as the best medium through which deaf children could communicate their existing ideas as well as learn new ideas.

Amy stressed the notion that reading is difficult when students do not have background information about the topic at hand. She also lamented the information deaf children miss out on and the importance of constant exposure to information in order to build a strong base of background knowledge:

> Well, the kids miss a lot from the radio, for example. They frequently aren't privy to their parents' conversations or conversations at a restaurant. They miss all this. Honestly, they miss a lot, and I miss a lot, too. I feel I try to fill these gaps, but I can't do that 100 percent. I probably only fill in 30 to 40 percent of the information because I'm not a hearing person. So, I'm confronted with these kids and I need to fill the gaps. Sometimes I tell the parents that their kids have reading difficulty because they do not have enough background information. [Thus] I have to explain more than I would for a hearing kid.

Amy further deplored that she needed to fill in these gaps because "students arrive here with no background information; they don't develop this at home or in preschool." She attributed this problem to the students' lack of easy access to communication through a shared natural language.

The situational contexts of daily classroom interactions provided frameworks for

Amy to take advantage of concepts that emerged for the purpose of building background knowledge and encouraging speculation based on existing knowledge. During reading classes, for example, Amy frequently elaborated on concepts at hand in an effort to tap into and enrich her students' understanding of the world. Sometimes these events were planned and sometimes they were incidental. Amy appeared ever ready to make use of whatever context presented itself and swiftly grasped opportunities to do so when they emerged in her classroom. Inherent in the events I describe here was the easy use of a shared language, ASL. Through the use of ASL, Amy was able to facilitate discussions that served to foster the development and application of world knowledge, and more, this occurred as naturally as one would expect in a classroom of active young learners.

All this on the surface might appear to be merely good teaching practice. But it was Amy's apt and easy use of ASL that opened the door to a vast world of knowledge for her students. Amy made these ASL asides in rapid succession, barely diverting from the task at hand. She frequently peppered her explanations of concepts with analogies while tapping into and building the background knowledge of her students.

As an example, when reading *The Bravest Dog Ever: The True Story of Balto*, by Natalie Standiford, Amy's students were confronted with the concept of diphtheria, alien to them at the outset. Amy used analogies to build an understanding of a disease they are not likely to confront in their lifetimes but that was so important for them to understand within the historical context of the story. In the story, a reference was made to the spread of diphtheria, hence the urgent need for medication to save lives. Here Amy referred the students to a recent bout of flu that struck the school. She reminded the students of how a student came to school with the flu one day, and the next day, another student was out sick, and so on. She then explicitly compared this incident, which the students had witnessed, with diphtheria, relating in fluid ASL how the disease struck one person then another, one town and then another, until it reached the severity that provided the conflict of the story.

In conveying this concept, Amy masterfully utilized classifiers, which are specific handshapes and movements used to convey locations and relationships in ASL (Valli and Lucas, 1995). This graphic use of ASL allowed the students easily to visualize the disease moving from one individual to another. To assess and extend her students' understanding, she asked them to name other diseases that spread easily, and they responded readily with "sore throats" and "colds." In this context, through the use of a shared natural language, Amy was able to convey information about symptoms of these diseases and connect these concepts to the story at hand. She compared sore throats and colds to diphtheria and discussed how diseases spread, using classifiers to convey the concept of the diseases spreading and adding the accompanying urgency conveyed in the story about the spread of diphtheria. She went on to elaborate on the conflict of the story, telling how, as with colds, flu, and sore throats, diphtheria spreads quickly and, in its case, was deadly. She conveyed how the characters in the story wanted to prevent the spread of diphtheria, which led to the story conflict and events. This explanation took place in a matter of minutes. Such a deft and elaborate explanation would have been hard to convey had there been language barriers between the students and their teacher.

Amy's use of analogy was effective because she masterfully conveyed her comparisons through ASL. In doing so, she attempted to fill gaps in her students' knowledge by engaging students in ASL asides, where she compared new concepts the students were approaching with their existing knowledge. These asides were deftly woven into the fabric of her classes through an apt use of ASL. The students' eyes rarely strayed, and when they did, it was most likely to make comments about this new knowledge to their peers sitting beside them. Indeed, frequently Amy would begin her explanations, then allow the students to break in and work to integrate a new concept into their existing knowledge. Amy gave students leeway to interject their comments at the same time as she guided them by well-timed comments of her own that served to extend understanding.

Amy also stressed the development of background knowledge through storybook reading/signing. She read/signed to her second- and third-graders every day. Her reading was not a direct print-to-sign production, however. She read portions of the text silently, then fixed her gaze on her students and translated this text into ASL. This was a difficult undertaking, since ASL and English are distinctly different languages, requiring different modalities. Translating from English print to ASL necessitates not only a knowledge of both languages but the skill to translate from one to the other. Since the process of translating is quite complex, Amy usually needed to prepare prior to the actual reading/signing; not only did she need to know the gist of the story, she had to think through and rehearse how she would translate passages.

During these readings, Amy also frequently stopped to make asides in which she explained vocabulary, including English idioms, and concepts. She encouraged predictions and asked questions that required students to draw on their prior knowledge. She expanded on story concepts to bring students to a deeper understanding, often using known information to help students conceptualize new knowledge. When Amy began reading/signing the introductory chapter of a new book to her third-graders, she first pointed out that the introduction would provide valuable information to help them understand the book, explicitly calling her students' attention to the importance of background knowledge. While reading/signing a chapter from *Garbage Juice for Breakfast*, by Patricia Reilly Giff, to her second-graders, over a fifteen-minute period Amy stopped several times to attend to background knowledge. As an example: when she read/signed that it was "pouring down rain," she noticed Timmy, one of her second-graders, turn to his classmate Jason and ask, "What's that?" Amy promptly stopped to ask her students what she meant when she said "pouring down rain." The ensuing discussion fostered background knowledge about concepts related to rain as well as the use of English and ASL as languages. Travis, another second-grader, responded that, "a lot of water was coming down," and Amy built on this, fingerspelling "pour" with distinct emphasis, and described the density of the clouds and the water pouring out of them. She signed, "It was raining hard," with great emphasis, to illustrate a synonymous concept in ASL, this time signing with a repeated hard and downward movement to indicate the rain was coming down in

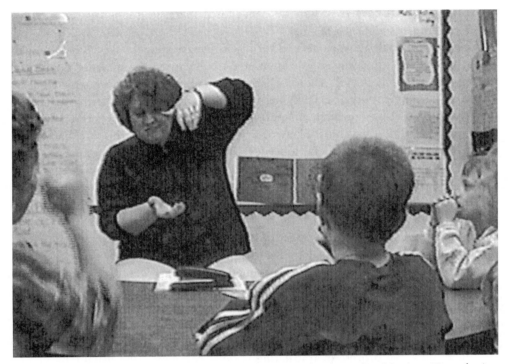

Amy frequently stops to explain concepts during storybook reading/signing. Here she is explaining the meaning of "pouring down rain." The English expression does not mean "to pour as from a large container . . ."

torrents. She allowed the students to interject their experiences at this point. Jason, for example, told about a time that "the water poured from his gutters so badly" his family "had to put up new gutters."

After the students briefly shared their experiences, Amy redirected them, twice explaining that when one signs, "It is pouring down rain outside," the person doesn't mean it is "raining lightly, but raining very hard." She then signed "pouring down rain" in a way that visually looked like water pouring from a bucket. In between her explanations, Timmy copied her signs, looking knowingly at Jason, expressing confidence in his newly acquired knowledge. The students then expanded on their knowledge once again, reflecting, for example, on how this "more likely happened in the summertime."

The discussion subsequently led to a question from Timmy that deviated from the storybook reading but was related to the context of rain. He asked Amy what "icy rain" and "rain that forms balls" was. Amy drew on Timmy's question to build the concepts of sleet and hail, fingerspelling both words and describing the concepts alternately and, on further questions from Timmy, affirming that hail comes in various sizes. Although sleet and hail were not directly related to the story at hand, Amy recognized and took advantage of this opportunity to build concepts based on

. . . but rather "to rain very hard." Photos from the author's archives.

the context of storybook reading. She not only recognized which concepts she needed to ensure her students understood, she knew instinctively there was no better time to address concepts than when students themselves posed the questions.

These asides were a natural part of the storybook reading/signing, seemingly expected by all, appearing to be almost a ritual. The students, despite their enthusiasm for elaborating on these concepts, were quick to get back to the story; Amy rarely had to remind them. Indeed, sometimes one of the students called his or her peers back to the story, anxious to move on. These asides during the course of daily storybook reading/signing were aimed at tapping into and building knowledge, and the students were often actively involved in the construction of this knowledge. While Amy frequently explained things to her students, she just as often involved the students in making meaning of these new words and concepts.

Principle 4: Promoting Metalinguistic Awareness and Knowledge of ASL and English

Students at MDS were encouraged to think about both languages, distinguishing between words and signs and identifying the similarities and differences between the ASL and English. Thus, the teachers promoted a metalinguistic awareness (Gleason, 1993) of these languages by leading the students to compare them explicitly. Expressed here was a belief that the children need to be able to identify, distinguish between, and use both ASL and English as separate languages. In applying this principle, the students were first to acquire a knowledge and understanding of ASL, albeit at varying rates. ASL then was considered to be their first language and was used to promote the knowledge and understanding of English as a second language. The teachers expressed a belief that, in this process, it is necessary to switch back and forth between languages, signing, fingerspelling, writing, and pointing to printed English. Indeed, fingerspelling was an important component of the process of comparing languages and was frequently used as a bridge between the two languages. In switching back and forth between languages, the teachers made explicit comparisons between the rules and structures of two languages. The teachers also led the students in expressing their growing understanding of the rules and structures of each language as well as in making comparisons between languages. Amy summarized the beliefs underlying this principle:

> When there are two languages, English and ASL, the students should be able to identify which language is which. They should be able to explain the differences between ASL and English, such as the rules. For example, in ASL there are eyebrow movements to mark questions; in English you have question marks.

Amy stressed that in learning English, these children need to compare the languages and note these differences.

To apply this principle, the teachers involved their students in parallel demonstrations and explicit comparisons of the two languages. In their study of ASL as a language, Estella involved the children in grades 1 through 3 in forming semantic webs, using one of forty-six handshapes. Here the students brainstormed signs using the handshape Estella presented to them, and a web was made of English words and phrases represented by these handshapes. In working on the handshape S one day, the students came up with signs for the following English words and phrases: *beat, motorcycle, shoes, rebel, car, work, umbrella, Superman, bicycle, canoe, fight, Sean* (name sign), *baseball, support, hot dog, climbing up a rope,* and *protect*. After the students finished brainstorming, they copied the words from the overhead transparency onto their own webs, then signed the English words and phrases individually to one of their teachers. In this way, Estella made the students explicitly aware of the English words and phrases they were conveying through ASL, thereby, acquainting them with similarities and differences in ASL and English. Here, the students were made aware that each language could convey the same meaning, but through a different mode, utilizing different parameters. "Protect" was conveyed in English, for example, by a written string of seven letters. In ASL, "protect" was conveyed by a sign with both hands utilizing the S handshape in a specific movement and location near the signer's body. In doing this, Estella led her students to an understanding of not only how the concept "protect" is conveyed in each language but also how differently it is conveyed in each language.

Estella used concrete symbols to represent the various language tasks her first-graders were encountering, in an effort to promote an awareness of the similarities and differences between ASL and English. She began the year by asking each of her students to make three visorlike hats, one marked "ASL" in huge letters, a second labeled "English," and a third "ASL-English/English-ASL." The first hat was used when the students worked primarily on ASL, the second when they worked primarily on English. The third was used when they were engaged in translating between the two languages. These hats hung on a hook just below the chalk board, within easy reach. Estella frequently began class explaining what they would be doing and then asking the students which type of hat they should wear. Once the appropriate hat was selected, Estella and the students wore their hats throughout the lesson. This gave a sense of importance to the business at hand. Estella states:

> When the students put on one of the hats, it is like putting a thinking cap on. When they put on the ASL hat, it signifies that now they are to think about ASL. Later they'll remove that and put on the English cap. So, in association with English teaching, this emphasizes that we are now focusing on English and gets the students thinking about that.

Estella involved her students in multiple tasks that required the comparing of the two languages, and in which they frequently wore hats to signify what they were doing. Indeed, Estella preferred to call her reading and writing classes ASL-English classes because she saw the task of reading and writing as negotiating between the two languages for her students. Sometimes in the middle of class, the focus would shift from one language to another, and they would then discuss this and switch hats. In choosing a hat, they had to understand the task before them and to identify which language was needed to complete the task. They made appropriate selections with little apparent difficulty.

One point for comparison that Estella incorporated during an early phase of these classes was verb tense. Estella first used a chart with a drawing of a person viewed from one side, with lines showing which area of the person's body is typically used in ASL to indicate each tense. This poster represented what Clayton Valli and Ceil Lucas (1995) define as the use of tense in ASL, that is, "an imaginary time line that runs perpendicular to the signer's body. The area near the signer's torso has a general meaning of 'present,' the area farther away has a meaning of 'future,' and the area over the shoulder has a general meaning of 'past' " (p. 114). After describing the "ASL rule" for verb tense and involving the students in examples of each tense, Estella then told her students that English also had rules for verb tense.

Estella explained these rules to her students over time and, as she did so, constantly made comparisons with ASL rules and usage. She asked the students to search for verbs from their many vocabulary lists posted in front of the room. They wrote the verbs they identified on strips of construction paper, which they posted on a "verb" bulletin board in back of the room. They then were asked to sign these verbs in multiple variations. As an example, the children signed the verb *go* in four variations, each utilizing different handshapes and movements. They signed the verb *play* using different classifiers, one indicating "playing for a long period of time," for example, and another indicating "playing all around the room." They then were asked to create short sentences with these verbs in ASL and subsequently to write the sentences in English on individual slate boards.

Sometimes Estella signed sentences and asked the students to write English translations on the slate boards or on large sheets of chart paper. This gave the students practice translating from ASL verbs, which, for example, do not add *s* to the third-person singular, to English verbs, which do. Over the course of several weeks, Estella, using fingerspelling to emphasize tense in English verbs, explained the "nuisances" among these verbs.

Estella read/signed "Kites Sail High," by Ruth Heller, using this story further to compare ASL and English verb usage. She began by asking the students what the title of the story was, to which Tina replied: KITE S–A–I–L HIGH. (In examples here, capital letters represent English glosses of ASL signs.) The following dialogue, shown here partially in translated English and partially in gloss, ensued:

ESTELLA: What does that mean? Translate the title to ASL. What do you mean by 'high?'
TINA: It means you hold the kite on a string and it is high up in the sky.
ESTELLA: Fine. The kite is high. What does the kite do?
MARGARET: It moves.
ESTELLA: It moves. That word *moves* . . . you said, "The kite moves." The English word to tell how the kite moves is *sail*. (Points to the word *sail* in the title.) S–A–I–L . . . KITE–SAIL–HIGH. Now, which would you say: MY DAD HELP ME KITE SELF MOVE–HIGH or MY DAD HELP ME KITE SAIL–HIGH?
MARGARET: The second example.
ESTELLA: Right. And it is the same with English. You have to match the appropriate words in English. K–I–T–E–S S–A–I–L H–I–G–H, not K–I–T–E–S M–O–V–E H–I–G–H.

Estella wrote, "Kites move high," on the board and continued, pointing to her sentence:

ESTELLA: Look at that sentence. It is not the way we say this in English.

She crossed out *move* and continued, stating that ASL has appropriate and inappropriate ways of signing this sentence as well and giving examples. As Estella proceeded with the reading/signing, she involved her students with explicit demonstrations and comparisons of ASL and English verbs within the context of the reading. She frequently called her students' attention to the printed text as they executed their signed translations. She was well aware that, in doing so, she was bridging the two languages.

Another strategy Estella used to promote metalinguistic awareness was translating English text to ASL. As an example: her first graders had previously read the book *I Like Me*, by Nancy Carlson. On a subsequent day, each took a turn at a reading a page and translating the text to ASL. After each translation, Estella would encourage the students to attend to English nuances and make sure they had translated accurately. She also encouraged them to come up with multiple variations of each translation. As an example, first-grader Tina began to translate English text by reading and signing simultaneously, signing word for word. Estella stopped her and reminded her to read silently first, then translate to ASL. Tina then read the page quietly to herself, looked up, and signed:

I #DO FUN THING WITH ME

(Some of the fingerspelling here would be categorized as loan signs, that is, fingerspellings that have been accepted as ASL signs. I use the symbol # prior to the sign, as in "#DO" above, to indicate these loan signs [Kelly, 1998].)

Tina read the next line, then looked up and signed:

I DRAW BEAUTIFUL PICTURE

Soon after signing, Tina noticed that *picture* is plural in the text and pointed this out to Estella. Estella then signed to all the students:

Now, look at the word *picture* and look at the picture in the book. Do you see many or one?

Sean responded that he saw "MANY," and Estella asked the students how they would translate this to ASL. Tina signed:

ME DRAW–DRAW–DRAW MANY PICTURE–PICTURE–PICTURE

Tina signed with movements to the right each time she signed "draw" and "picture" to indicate plurality. When Tina finished, Estella affirmed her translation, and Sean excitedly indicated that he had one of his own. He signed:

#OR ME PAINT ONE FINISH PAINT ONE FINISH PAINT–PAINT–PAINT EXPAND MANY

At this point, Estella pointed out to the students that the book did not say *many* but *beautiful*. She then modeled this translation, with movements to the right for each sign for *draw* to indicate plurality:

ME DRAW–DRAW–DRAW BEAUTIFUL PICTURE #OR ME DRAW–DRAW–DRAW PICTURE BEAUTIFUL

Next it was Sean's turn to read and translate into sign. Sean expressed to Estella at the outset that he was not confident with this task, preferring that Estella read/sign to them first and that the students read/sign later. Estella encouraged Sean to attempt the task, and he began to read. He pointed to the word *fast* and looked to Estella to supply its meaning. Estella pointed to the picture corresponding with the text and asked, "What is she doing?"

Sean looked at the picture and the text and attempted to translate: "SAYS ME LIKE . . ."

Estella's students attend to the nuances of ASL and English as they translate *I Like Me*, by Nancy Carlson, into ASL. Photo from the author's archives.

Sean shook his head and signed: "ME NOT UNDERSTAND."

Estella pointed to the text, and when Sean persisted in conveying uncertainty, pointed to the word *fast* and signed: "#OK F–A–S–T MEAN FAST."

Sean continued: "SAYS ME . . ."

Sean again looked at Estella, apparently unsure of himself. Estella pointed to the text and picture again and asked what the character was doing, to which Sean then signed:

ME FAST RIDE–BICYCLE ME FAST PEDAL ZOOM HAIR–FLIES–UP BIKE WHEEL–STAND

Margaret then signed her translation:

ME GET–ON–BIKE ZOOM FAST SILLY

Tina then signed her translation:

ME GET–ON–BIKE PEDAL FAST

Estella accepted all translations, and at the same time, she pointed out to Sean that the text and pictures do not show the character's hair flying up in the wind. She encouraged Sean to combine the text and pictures and translate to ASL accurately. Sean's "translation" perhaps reflected his growing comfort with the use of ASL to express his thoughts. He is a creative child and took creative license when executing his translations, and Estella was careful not to dampen his creativity or his apt use of ASL. At the same time, Estella bridged connections between what he signed and what was represented in the text.

Principle 5: Valuing Approximations in ASL-English

Approximations are "attempts to gain control of some process, knowledge, skill or understanding" (Mathie, 1994). Language approximations, then, refer to the attempts by children to apply developing knowledge to control usage. A young child's utterance of a phrase such as "Me go bye-bye" is an approximation and is considered within the realm of normal language development.

Providing a learning environment that allowed approximations in the development and use of both ASL and English was the fifth principle that emerged from the teaching at MDS. Empowering the children to develop and use both ASL and English was an underlying theme. The use of ASL in the school was deemed a means of fostering an empowering environment that was conducive to learning English. Interpreting how this empowerment translated into teaching practices, however, was problematic. Further analysis of actual classroom practices illuminated this principle further—by providing an environment that allowed for approximations as the children developed ASL and English skills, teachers empowered the children to approach competency in these languages.

Second-grader Susan's mother expressed a belief that the teachers at MDS "let the child be who she is; not forcing her . . . to be hearing," that is, to learn language from oral/aural modalities. Instead, she saw teachers allowing the children to develop language naturally through ASL—a mode she deems better suited for these children since it is visual. Adam's mother expressed a belief that teachers at MDS provide an environment that allows the child to "develop both languages [ASL and English], allowing for approximations." She stated that allowing approximations was important in order for the "students to be free to express their ideas without being limited by English."

Amy provided such an environment during an afternoon free-reading period, when the second-and third-grade children were expected to read self-selected books independently while eating their afternoon snacks. During these free-reading periods, which were fifteen to twenty minutes in length, the students could interact with books as they chose. Rather than read independently, the students began to form groups of two or more and read/sign to each other, mimicking Amy's storybook reading/signing strategies. Each of the second-and third-graders would sometimes choose a picture book and read/sign a page at a time in turn, an undertaking that did not immediately make sense to me as an observer. Watching these children over time, however, I realized that telling a cohesive story was not their aim. Instead, they were beginning to try out on their own the idea of sharing parts of a story with each other in a safe environment. In a sense, they appeared to be carefully toeing the waters before plunging in to read/sign whole texts.

As time passed, students began to read/sign whole books at a time, sometimes attending to the printed text and sometimes signing a story based on the pictures. Timmy, a second-grader, on one occasion read/signed to his classmates Susan and Jana from a chapter in the novel *The Wizard of Oz*, running his fingers along the lines of each paragraph and then signing what he had presumably read. According to Amy, Timmy was a struggling reader. Yet it was clear from observing him that he knew enough about the story to get the gist by skimming a paragraph at a time, and he could relate a reasonably accurate retelling (or translation, perhaps). Susan and Jana, his ready and ever-patient audience, provided him a risk-free environment to try out these approximations, which required him to read, or perhaps skim, portions of the story in English and then translate that portion into ASL.

During this period Amy allowed these exchanges to take place, recognizing that the children were "trying out" skills they had observed in their teachers but not yet mastered themselves. Amy continued to read/sign chapters from books to her students at regular times in the mornings, and the second- and third-graders utilized this free-reading time to mimic her. The students clearly deemed this a fun period. They did not have to be told what to do but had easily fallen into a routine. At the beginning of each free-reading period, they settled down with their snacks and quickly chose their books, formed groups, and decided how to take turns. Watching these children immersed in this activity, it was clear to me that they were taking their reading seriously. They were hard at work trying to make sense of books and conveying their understanding of this print with their peers in a shared language. Only once did I observe a student being corrected, and then only by a peer. Adam had chosen to readsign a nonfiction book on one occasion, and his classmate Benjamin chided him, stating that he had not readsigned a story. Adam retorted in a confident, matter-of-fact tone that Benjamin was right—his book was not a story but about something "real."

Free-reading time was but one situation in which the children at MDS could freely experiment with the use of ASL and English. Here they were approximating translations from English to ASL. Because Amy provided her second- and third-graders with such an environment, these children delved into books with unbridled confidence. Another strategy surfaced in Amy's third-grade reading class. After reading *The Bravest Dog Ever: The True Story of Balto*, the students were involved in a research project that required an ongoing process of negotiating between ASL and English in order eventually to conduct presentations to the whole school. The students began in pairs, signing and then writing research questions. This signing and writing required a translation from ASL to English. Barry and Brent agreed on the question: "SUPPOSE DOG DIE DO–DO." Having agreed, each boy translated the question to English. Barry wrote: "If dog dead what do?" and Brent wrote: "If a sled dog dies what would the sled dog driver do?" Barry attempted to convince Brent that he was mistaken in the use of *die*, arguing that *dead* was the appropriate choice. Neither boy

Adam and Berry negotiate their way between ASL and English as they conduct research about sled dogs. Photo from the author's archives.

changed his sentence, and Amy did not call attention to Barry's mistakes. Rather, the students were allowed to work together to frame their questions, research and expand on answers, and eventually construct posters as visual supports to their presentations. It was not until the final phases that Amy worked with the children on editing; thus, throughout this process, the children were allowed to approximate both languages. A direct result was that the children appeared to feel free to explore without fear of correction. Their enthusiasm for their topics was not stifled by fear of the red pen.

- ## ASL as a Means of Removing Barriers to Learning: A Deaf-centric Ideology

Amy and Estella are dedicated teachers committed to the teaching of English literacy through ASL. Both teachers are offspring of Deaf parents. Estella, a Mexican American, had six years of teaching experience, two of which were at MDS. Amy had taught at MDS for five years, the longest of any teacher there, and was also one of three team leaders. Both were members of the Board of Directors. These teachers taught in an environment that afforded them support as they grappled with what it means to be a bilingual teacher for young deaf children. From my observations, the children appeared to be immersed in an environment in which learning was accessible through the fluid use of ASL by their teachers. Fluency in both ASL and English were of prime importance at MDS, but this did not supersede the importance of good teaching. And these teachers consciously used strategies that engaged the children in both languages.

In this environment where teachers and children shared a natural language, the kind of interaction that is expected in a primary-grade setting was possible. Woodward (1978) stated, "No problem in communication occurs, if our way of using a language is not too different from the way of the person that we are communicating with" (p. 195). Yet the history of the education of deaf children is a history of language and communication barriers and of barriers to learning, because the use of sign language has been deemed detrimental to English literacy. MDS represents a unique setting in which the use of ASL as a shared natural language has broken down these barriers and, in doing so, *promoted* communication, language, and learning.

Ideology guides our perceptions of the world. It defines how we perceive normality. Parents of deaf children want nothing more than for their children to be "normal." There are different perceptions, however, of what it means to be normal. In an oral-based ideology, the definition of "normal" does not include D/deaf children; rather, it is hoped that these children will eventually become close replicas of hearing adults. The stance taken by K–3 teachers at MDS represents a "Deaf-centric" ideology, where being deaf is considered normal and educational principles and strategies take into consideration how the deaf child learns. Considering the child's need for full access to language, bilingual schools such as MDS use ASL as the language of instruction and learning. Knowledge of ASL as a first language is considered an important prerequisite for learning written English as a second language. In this ideology, the language and culture of Deaf people is incorporated within the school.

REFERENCES

Bailes, C. N. 1999. *Primary-grade teachers' strategic use of American Sign Language in teaching English literacy in a bilingual school setting.* UMI No. 9926724.

Barnum, M. 1984. In support of bilingual/bicultural education for deaf children. *American Annals of the Deaf* 129, 5: 404–8.

Brill, R. G. 1984. *International Congress on Education of the Deaf: An analytical history 1878–1980.* Washington, DC: Gallaudet College Press.

Gannon, J. R. 1981. *Deaf heritage: A narrative history of deaf America.* Silver Spring, MD: National Association of the Deaf.

Gleason, J. B. 1993. *The development of language.* 3d ed. New York: Macmillan Publishing Company.

Johnson, R., S. Liddell, and C. Erting. 1989. *Unlocking the curriculum: Principles for achieving access in deaf education.* Gallaudet Research Institute, Working Paper 89–3. Washington, DC.

Kannapell, B. M. 1974 (June). Bilingualism: A new direction in the education of the deaf. *Deaf American*: 9–15.

Kelly, A. B. 1998. The role of linguistics in Deaf Studies. Unpublished.

Lane, H. 1984. *When the mind hears: A history of the deaf.* New York: Random House.

———. 1992. *The Mask of Benevolence: Disabling the Deaf Community.* New York: Knopf.

Lane, H., R. Hoffmeister, and B. Bahan. 1996. *A journey into the Deaf-World.* San Diego, CA: DawnSign Press.

Lou, M. 1988. The history of language use in the education of the deaf in the United States. In M. Strong, ed., *Language learning and deafness*, pp. 75–98. New York: Cambridge University Press.

Maher, J. 1996. *Seeing language in sign: The work of William C. Stokoe.* Washington, DC: Gallaudet University Press.

Mathie, V. 1994. Making beliefs explicit: One teacher's journey. In B. Cambourne and J. Turbill, eds., *Responsive evaluation: Making valid judgements about student literacy*, pp. 28–35. Portsmouth, NH: Heinemann.

Moores, D. 1996. *Educating the deaf: Psychology, principles, and practices.* Boston: Houghton Mifflin.

Nover, S. M. 1995. Politics and language: American Sign Language and English in deaf education. In C. Lucas, ed., *Sociolinguistics in deaf communities*, pp. 109–63. Washington, DC: Gallaudet University Press.

Reutzel, D. R., and R. B. Cooter. 1998. Teaching children to read: From basal to books. 2d ed. Englewood Cliffs, NJ: Merrill.

Sacks, O. 1989. *Seeing voices: A journey into the world of the deaf.* Berkeley: University of California Press.

Stokoe, W. C. 1960. Sign language structure: An outline of the visual communication system of the American deaf. *Studies in Linguistics, Occasional Papers 8.*

———. 1978. *Sign language structure.* Rev. ed. Silver Spring, MD: Linstok Press.

Strong, M. 1995. A review of bilingual/bicultural programs for deaf children in North America. *American Annals of the Deaf* 140, 2: 84–94.

Tompkins, G. E. 1998. *Language arts: Content and teaching strategies.* 4th ed. Upper Saddle River, NJ: Merrill.

Valli, C., and C. Lucas. 1995. *Linguistics of American Sign Language: An Introduction.* 2d ed. Washington, DC: Gallaudet University Press.

Van Cleve, J. V., and B. A. Crouch. 1989. *A place of their own: Creating the deaf community in America.* Washington, DC: Gallaudet University Press.

Woodward, J. 1978. Some sociolinguistic problems in the implementation of bilingual education for deaf students. *Proceedings of the National Symposium on Sign Language Research and Teaching, USA*: 183–203.

IV | "Impressed with the value of character"

The Deaf Ethic

Mr. and Mrs. Ulmer in front of their new house and Chevrolet. From *The Silent Worker*, May 1950. By permission of the National Association of the Deaf, 814 Thayer Ave., Silver Spring, MD 20910; *www.nad.org*.

32

That Deaf peddler you bought an ILY key ring from at the airport last week has a long history of embarrassing the entire Deaf community; as the following antebellum letter to the American Annals of the Deaf and Dumb *shows.*

Vagrancy among Deaf-Mutes

H. M. Chamberlayne

1859

[The writer of the following communication is himself a deaf-mute. It is deeply to be regretted that there should be occasion for noticing this matter publicly. The facts and considerations presented by our correspondent, are worthy the attention of all deaf-mutes as well as of their instructors. We are happy to say that the educated deaf-mutes do as a body thoroughly disapprove of the vagrant course of life to which a few of their number addict themselves. Yet the character of the whole class is liable to suffer in public estimation, from the conduct of these few. The resolutions on the subject, adopted by the Convention at Jacksonville, reported in full in the Annals for October last, show how it is viewed by the instructors in our institutions.—EDITOR.]

Montrose, Near Richmond, Va., March 29th, 1859.
Samuel Porter, Esq.:
Dear Sir: I wish to inform the teachers of the deaf and dumb, through your useful periodical, that several northern mutes have visited Richmond and some other cities as vagrants. Indeed, my object in doing so is to call their attention to the fact that it is absolutely necessary for them to impress their pupils with the value of character.

The proprietor of a hotel informed us, not long since, that a mute, who assumed the air of a rich gentleman, after having been with him for some days, left for another hotel, and so on, till he had been at each hotel, when he took his departure for parts unknown without paying a cent! What think you of this?

The vagrants alluded to, whose names prudence forbids me to tell, were educated in various institutions, and were good mechanics after leaving school. They should have pursued their trades instead of a vagrant pedlar's life. One of them makes by far more money in two days than a deaf-mute teacher earns in a week; another, who has nothing to sell, begs money, or rather "lives upon the sympathies of his fellow-men."

Richmond is decidedly the resort of such visitors, as their misfortunes meet sympathy and assistance in money there speedily. But it will not be so any longer, as a mute resident has notified the Mayor of his wishes that he should cause all such

237

vagrants to be arrested. The other day I saw the following scrap in a city newspaper, which I send enclosed for your perusal:—

> ORDERED BACK. — ———, a mute from Brooklyn, N.Y., was before the Mayor, yesterday, as a vagrant. He presented a perfect embodiment of destitution, and stated in writing, that he had walked all the way from New York to this city. The Mayor informed him that he must return forthwith to Brooklyn, and then discharged him from custody.

Why should he have come over that long way on foot? Perhaps he had heard that the Virginians were hospitable, and would entertain a stranger. Vagabondism is like the poor moth that flutters around a candle till it scorches itself to death.

We often see mutes murmuringly contrasting their lot with that of the hearing. The endeavor would be senseless to devise means of opening their ears. *As they are*, they should submit gracefully to the will of Providence, or would be like "fools who would be beating their heads against walls of stone." We attribute their discontent to "the want of activity in moral and intellectual life." It is evident that industry is the source of contentment, and knowledge the source of happiness to mankind. Diogenes, although idle, was happy in his tub, because he was a great philosopher, and his brain was active; but one Diogenes is not enough for the world. Bayard Taylor never gets tired of traveling, because he is a man of observation. Cincinnatus never thought life a burden, because he was constantly hard at work, either in defense of his beloved republic or on his farm. It is the French philosopher (now dead), who says: "Laziness is a premature death. To be in no action, is not to live."

It is important that my unfortunate brethren should be impressed with the value of character. This is the first thing every body should endeavor to secure; it is better in beginning life to secure a reputation for probity and industry than to possess gold. Wealth may be lost, but character never. Character may be had by every one, if he desires it *in earnest*. Every man should reject any volunteer offer of money or any "free passage in public conveyances," with indignation; hold all displays of sympathy by money in contempt, like an ancient Roman in captivity; and lastly, learn diligently whatever he has a capacity to learn, and avoid idleness. I think it is Rochefoucauld who says: "Avoid, if possible, receiving an obligation which you have reason to believe you will never have it in your power to repay."

As to debt, every mute should be warned against going in debt; avoidance of debt his watchword. That many mutes are fond of wandering is well known; but they will find at the end that they have "paid dearly for the whistle." No man, who has not learned the old adage, can ever grow rich. "If you take care of the pennies, the pounds will take care of themselves."

Excuse this long note. Probably you may be able to dispose of it in a corner of the Annals without much inconvenience.

Yours truly,
H. M. Chamberlayne

33

The word childish *is commonly used by haves to describe have-nots, as though ascription of a character flaw would account for the latter's abject condition. In the Deaf World, the haves historically have been the hard of hearing, whose speech skills and residual hearing give them greater access to the goodies of the hearing world.*

Miss Martineau and Deaf-Mutes

Edmund Booth

1877

I have been reading portions of the autobiography of Harriet Martineau, recently deceased. She refers, among other matters, to her work on America, and thereby brings to my recollection an incident which I will relate.

It is known that at the time she was in America, now forty or more years ago, she was somewhat deaf, and used an ear-trumpet. The fact of partial deafness would naturally lead her to sympathize, at least to some extent, with deaf-mutes in case she came in contact with them, and from her remarks I judge it so occurred. She spoke of them, as a class, as over-praised and over-estimated, and described them as naturally "childish," frivolous, etc., adding that "mothers at least knew" the truth of her statement. I write from recollection, and the circumstances that followed fixed some of her words in my memory.

Now, what followed is this: Mr. Weld, the principal of the Hartford Institution, where I was then a teacher, came into my room, mentioned Miss Martineau's strictures, and said, "She has slandered the entire deaf-mute community," and proposed that I write an article in reply for some magazine. Those who knew Mr. Weld know that he was apt to be strong in his expressions when excited. As I had read Miss Martineau's work, and viewed it in a light different from that of Mr. Weld, I could not avoid a smile at his earnestness, and at what seemed to me the incongruity of his (and the general) opinion, when looked at in the light of daily practice; so the reply was left unwritten.

Miss Martineau told the truth. Of this I was satisfied from the first. But she did not go far enough, and tell the whole truth. She should have included in her sweeping charge of "childishness" and frivolity the entire hearing community also. Of course there are exceptions in both the deaf and the hearing class. They are both the same, the only difference being that one class has one avenue to knowledge closed. And here another thing must be taken into consideration.

At the time of Miss Martineau's visit, the time of study was limited to four years. The graduates of that day and the graduates now show a considerable difference in the degree of education and intelligence. There was no high class or college, no *Annals*, and no newspapers conducted by or for mutes. There was no clearly defined system of instruction in general acceptance and use. Some teachers, like Messrs. Weld, Clerc, and Peet, regarded language as a science, and tried to teach it accordingly. Others threw language at their pupils hap-hazard, pell-mell, as with a pitchfork.

What wonder that, after four years of such teaching as the latter, most of the pupils did not know the difference between a noun and a verb? Of course their use of language was miserable, except so far as they could remember the most ordinary phrases, and they would blunder even in the use of these.

There was another matter that was all wrong, and which contributed largely to the childishness and frivolity to which Miss Martineau alluded. When institutions for mutes were founded, the word was "charity." On this idea all appeals were made for assistance—state, national, and private. Governments and individuals who gave were impressed with that single idea, except those of the particular localities where the institutions were established or to be established. In such localities it was regarded as a business venture certain to pay. In that age men had not come to understand that what they called charity should be regarded as a matter of justice. Principals, teachers, friends, and the many-headed public of course talked of and to the pupils, and deaf-mutes generally, as though they were purely objects of charity. The tendency of this was to lower their self-respect. The fruit is not pleasant to contemplate.

But I said Miss Martineau should have made her assertions more sweeping, and should have included the hearing as well as the deaf. I have known two or three cases of hearing persons making statements similar to Miss Martineau's. You have only to look around, and you will understand that she ought thus to have gone further. Notice the everlasting political, theological, neighborhood, and other squabbles. Who can decide when the financial doctors disagree so widely? Is it strange that men of the higher mental and moral nature despise while they pity the world, or that Carlyle shuts himself in his den and growls? His saying, "Great Britain has forty millions of people, *mostly fools*," is a case in point.

Some years after the request by Mr. Weld—that I write a reply to Miss Martineau—I took occasion to convey my views to him on the word "charity," as then applied to deaf-mutes. I told him the word was a misnomer; that the laws of the land provided by taxation for all; that mutes and the blind could derive no benefit therefrom; that therefore special laws were necessary, and that mutes and the blind should of right, as a matter of common justice, be in school from the age of ten to twenty, or at least eight or ten years. Time passed, and now the idea is in practice, and the improvement is very great. Forty years have accomplished what I hoped for, and the teachers of to-day may be certain that forty years hence will see still further advances.

34 The habit of being prompt...

1902

The habit of being prompt in business engagements is one of the surest methods of winning success. Of course, this habit should be extended to all the affairs of life, but its usefulness in the world of business is more plainly apparent and of more practical value than in matters social.

A short time ago, the editor of the *Deaf-Mutes' Journal* wanted a half-tone of Rev. Dr. Gallaudet made from a photograph that he sat for only a short time prior to his death. In the first place, it was necessary to get a copy of the photograph. This was secured on a Saturday, when it was too late to place the order for a half-tone engraving. The following Monday was Labor Day, and the engraving establishment was closed. It was not until late Tuesday evening that he could see the engraver and urge the necessity of a quick job, as the cut must be used on Wednesday morning. The engraver, who is our deaf friend, Mr. Souweine, could not promise to have it ready in so short a time, but offered to do his best. Knowing Mr. Souweine's determination and energy, we felt pretty safe, and gave him the order. Next day he brought the engraving to us personally, having accomplished it in the short space of seven hours. As the work was done at ruling prices, he probably made nothing on it, so far as money profit is concerned. But he kept up his well-known reputation for good and prompt work, which is of more account to him than a small money profit, and which will result in future orders that *will* be profitable. We have no doubt but his success in his engraving business is in large part due to the qualification of being prompt, and never giving his promise without fulfilling it. Added to this he is careful and skillful, and an example of what a man of business should be.

The boy or man who is prompt and obliging, will do much to neutralize any natural shortcomings in other directions. No business man overlooks bad faith in his subordinates. He may endure with patience many blunders in the performance of tasks, but he will not tolerate tardiness and neglect.

One of the important phases in industrial training in schools for the deaf, is the inculcation of the habit of promptness. Anything which militates against this essential in industrial education, should at once be discouraged. A prompt boy is usually an attentive boy, and it is only by attentiveness that skill and ability is properly developed. The boys themselves seldom realize this, and it is the imperative duty of their instructors to impress it upon them. To be tardy and careless is the sure road to incompetence; but to be ready and punctual and attentive, is to walk on the plain road that leads to future success.

35

Deaf men and women seeking work have long been turned away by employers in virtually all industries, including the U.S. military. The sudden labor shortage induced by World War I, therefore, provided Deaf men and women with unprecedented employment opportunities—until the Great Depression returned Deaf applications to the waste basket. Typically, many Deaf people blamed their own shortcomings, specifically an allegedly deficient work ethic.

Finding Men for Jobs

B. M. Schowe

1937

To the average job hunter employment offices must loom like impregnable citadels which may be scaled only when the stars are inclined, and then only by means of arts as devious as anything that Jurgen knew. This reflection is inspired by some years of experience interviewing deaf applicants in an employment office, and more recently by the surveys of employment opportunities conducted by organizations of the deaf in several states.

A nation-wide study of the same subject was completed only a few years ago by the U.S. Office of Education. The information so collected, although slow in coming to light, must surely prove more comprehensive and useful than anything a limited state survey could hope to uncover. Nevertheless, the state organizations seemed to believe that an investigation conducted by amateurs could turn up information that would be worth the expenditure of considerable time and money.

The information these surveys reported proved interesting to read even though we may express a doubt that it has any practical value. Moreover, it should be noted in this connection that the dilettante survey business is not free from all possibility of actual injury to the cause of deaf employment in the long run. The employment office managers who have to bear the brunt of the investigators' barrages of questions may find their patience exhausted with the repetition of calls from different surveying agencies. When this happens, the only product of the survey will be to get a nuisance rating for deaf employment in general.

It seems clear that the state surveys were not organized for the straightforward purpose of gathering more reliable statistical data concerning employment opportunities. What these state investigators wanted was simply jobs for the jobless—here and now. Their surveys were more in the nature of quests for a magic formula that would (with a wave of the hand) transmute the dross of unemployment into the gold of wage-paying jobs.

The emphasis, as it so often is in cases of this kind, was all centered on finding out what was wrong with the other fellow, in this case the employment managers who had proved to be anything but lavish with jobs. Nothing was done, so far as the writer can learn, to discover how unemployed deaf people can be better trained and equipped for the responsibilities that go with good jobs.

Is it safe to assume that nothing save prejudice keeps deaf workers off the payroll? Is there anything that really can be done to improve the chances for deaf men and women to get—and keep—jobs?

There is, of course, some luck in landing a job. A man is fortunate indeed if he can arrive at the employment office on the particular day when his skills and abilities happen to be in special demand. But there is no magic in it. The employment manager, in fact, looks on the business of fitting men with jobs as something of a science. There are definite rules to be applied with skill and discretion. The man who "fits" will have little difficulty in getting a job. The question is: At what points then do the deaf fail to come up to requirements?

The writer is not, of course, an employment manager. It would be more accurate, perhaps, to say that he is an associate of employment managers. The association has been fairly constant since he was graduated from Gallaudet College in 1918. During a considerable part of that time he has worked in the employment office of the Firestone Tire and Rubber Company on special assignment and interviewed deaf applicants as a convenience for all parties, rather than because it was a part of his regular duties.

That gives his background in brief and it will not be difficult to understand his sentiment when he says that his natural sympathies are always with the deaf job hunter. He hopes to see him land his job, no matter who he is or what. The writer, in a manner of speaking, is the deaf person's advocate. Nevertheless, he cannot always recommend the deaf applicant for employment. And the reason he cannot always recommend employment is, in a large measure, the subject of this paper.

If we had time to attempt an exhaustive study of the subject, we might classify and cross classify under several different heads the reasons why deaf applicants are turned down. We cannot attempt a detailed classification within the limits of this paper. The reader, however, may do well to keep in mind that such an analytical organization of the problem is possible and that it would help to focus attention on essential elements.

Welfare workers will be concerned especially with rejections that develop out of misconception of the limitations which surround deaf workers and with arbitrary office rules that bar the way to jobs. The educator will be more particularly interested in training deficiencies, physical and mental, and also, perhaps, in temperamental defects. Neither will be touched in cases where deafness is *correctly* the reason for rejection. For we all recognize, the writer believes, that there are some barriers which we may not hurdle.

Every possible reason for rejection is of interest to the employment manager. He cannot afford to make errors on any account. And it is this fact that the people trying to improve deaf employment most often overlook. Yet the responsibilities and the mental attitude of the man who hires are elements of prime importance.

He is not infallible in his judgments certainly. Neither is he a careless trifler with the fates of people looking for work. But he does, of necessity, look at employment from the other side. While the rest of us are trying to find jobs, the employment manager is steadily looking for men qualified to fill the jobs he has, or expects to have in the near future.

In the very nature of things, it is impossible for him to rate stories of personal hardship or misfortune as valid qualifications for a job. Nearly everyone who passes through his office has a hard luck story and believes firmly that his own need is greater than that of any one else. But no scales have been perfected for measuring human needs. Jobs cannot be dispensed as prizes for the most heart-rending stories of personal misfortune. The nearest that the employment manager can come to an intelligent handling of this factor is to set up an office rule that men with a certain number of dependents will be given jobs first. Beyond that he cannot go in this direction. If you want to get a job, it is necessary to approach the man who hires with values a great deal more impressive than a first-class hard luck story.

What, then, are the values which are likely to be effective?

Taking deaf workers as a whole, there is probably no argument that will strike with such force as the contention that deafness is less of an obstruction to communication, and therefore a handicap to successful employment, than it is a ready-made opportunity for the foreman and factory supervision to establish the kind of relations with the worker which modern factory management has found to be so difficult in mass production industries.

We may safely concede that the new deaf worker is more dependent on special consideration from his immediate superiors than the beginner who can hear. However, a little extra patience and written instruction is not wasted if by that means the foreman can come to intimate personal contact with his man which is comparable to years of ordinary fair dealing in the case of most hearing workmen.

This is no mean item. Big industry is spending millions of dollars to this same end directly or indirectly, every year. The actual amount cannot be calculated because no one can say definitely where expenditures for this purpose begin, or exactly where they end. The fact is that big industry today is too distant and impersonal in its dealings with the individual workman and must depend on expensive "welfare" projects to win him over to an attitude of co-operative partnership. One large employer has announced that he will distribute up to 11 percent of wages each year on various projects, all more or less directly devoted to this general purpose.

Even when the money is spent, however, the result is not at all certain—for the sound and simple reason that dollars do not buy employee goodwill in the end. A bit of extra patience while breaking in a deaf worker is a far more reliable method.

That is why we may say that the deafness of a worker may prove to be the foreman's opportunity.

But if we can discern a possible advantage in deaf workers at this point, we should not let the novelty of it blind us to the fact that the whole thing hangs a bit precariously on the reactions of the deaf worker himself. The benefits are not automatic by any means.

First of all, the deaf worker must be alert. The special demand he may make on the factory supervision must be reduced to the minimum. Next, he must have the perceptions to recognize special consideration when he gets it, and the innate honesty to value it accordingly. His sense of appreciation must be well developed.

This last is an exceedingly delicate point. It touches on the whole philosophy and art of being deaf.

The deaf cannot approach life with an apology for existence. Servility is out of place. For self-justification the deaf are bound to believe that the world has a place for them. The special consideration which is sometimes necessary is little more than common courtesy. They are correct in believing that they have a right to expect it.

Nevertheless, even common courtesy carries an obligation. Courtesy must be met with courtesy.

That is simple clear—not to say trite and sententious. Yet what proportion of the product of our schools for the deaf go out in the world equipped to recognize its force and to live up to its implications? How many of them have a manner which would impress an employment manager with their ability to go into the shop and work harmoniously with the organization in spite of the various inconveniences to which they were liable?

In one factory with which the writer is familiar, deaf workers are employed on machines where gasoline-powered trucks occasionally pass at a good rate of speed directly behind the machine operator. If a worker leans back, as he sometimes must, or if he steps around his machine for any reason, he may find himself directly in the path of the truck.

A few days after one deaf worker started on these machines, he leaned back at the wrong time, and was bumped by the truck. His shirt was torn, and a long red welt appeared on his back.

In the investigation which followed, the deaf worker testified: "I was attending strictly to business. If the truck had not come along so fast, I would have seen it and kept out of its way." The truck operator reported: "I blew my horn. Everybody had moved out of the aisle and the way was clear. Then this fellow stuck his shoulder out in front of the truck."

Both men were quite right and the foreman faced what appeared to be an unavoidable accident hazard as long as he kept the deaf worker on the job. The foreman is wholly responsible for just such hazards and his superiors rate it a very important item. Under the circumstances he could scarcely be blamed if he decided to take the deaf man off this operation. In fact, if he did anything else, it would be because he gave the matter more careful attention than the facts seemed to justify.

And this last is what he did. He had had long experience with deaf workers and had high regard for their adaptability. His decision might be stated this way: "There is little or no danger of serious injury from trucks of that kind. When those boys are better acquainted there isn't even much danger that anyone will get bumped around. I'll caution them both and let it go at that for the present."

Now this is, at the very least, a broad-gauge view. It is not necessary for us to prove that the foreman was moved to special consideration because he knew that the deaf man would have a hard time getting another job. In any case the deaf worker was placed under a certain obligation. He had been the beneficiary of consideration that was rather more than fair after a defect in his own hearing equipment had got him into trouble.

Perhaps it is asking too much to expect the deaf worker to understand the nature of his obligation to the foreman under these circumstances. The foreman's problem and viewpoint are too obscure. But what of his obligation to the trucker for extra caution in the future? This is a matter of prime importance. The trucker certainly will expect some acknowledgment of his consideration. If he fails to get it, friction may develop which will cause the foreman to regret his generosity.

One need have no doubts about the deaf young man in this particular case. He had a winning way with him at all times and he won the friendly regard of the trucker in his normal stride.

Well and good! But does the reader, conversant with the foibles of the average deaf job hunter, have full confidence that any large proportion of them could have carried off the situation half so well?

Too many of them operate on the principle that they belong to an underprivileged minority and that the only way to preserve their self-respect is to face the world defiantly, or with callous indifference to the conventions and amenities of the majority. They are perfectly insulated against any recognition of the inconvenience their deafness may cause. They charge through life unmindful of the toes they tread on and can usually be found off in a corner whining that the world is in a conspiracy to deny them jobs.

We cannot pause here to take up the philosophy and art of being deaf. But we should recognize, I think, that a very delicate adjustment is required. There is no more profit in servility than there is in defiance. Somewhere between the two is the happy medium that brings, among other things, success on the job.

The bare fact that it is inconvenient to communicate with the deaf and sometimes hard to instruct them in their jobs is of less consequence to the employer, or employment manager, than the general understanding that they do not fit smoothly into the routine of employment office and factory. Their contacts with fellow workers are not merely a bit abnormal by reason of the unusual means of communication required. The slight abnormality is a minor consideration as long as there is no actual friction or antagonism in those contacts. The difficulty centers in the friction rather than in the abnormality itself. And it has been proved, I think, that most of the friction, if not all, can be avoided by deaf workers who have resources of character and training which enable them to smooth over the little irregularities which crop up.

Most employment men know that the deaf are reputed to have unusual manual dexterity and are less liable to distraction from the grind of repetitive processes. Some employment managers may be convinced that deaf workers, more often than not, are the stuff from which loyal, conscientious workmen are made. Still, the deaf applicant cannot be hired offhand, simply because he is deaf.

There may be half a dozen places where a new worker will be expected to answer when his name is called during the first few days before he is broken in and knows his way around. There will be no serious consequences if he does not answer, but too many minor irritations of this sort may mount up into major annoyances for foremen, fellow workers and everyone else concerned. It is necessary to be sure that the different functionaries along the line will give the deaf beginner due consideration, or that there is someone in the factory sufficiently interested to take the deaf man under his wing and smooth his path for the first few days.

To a certain extent, common courtesy is all that is required and this difficulty is more apparent than real. Nevertheless, it is necessary for the man who hires to have some assurance that supervision in the factory is ready to receive the deaf worker.

Accident hazards and possible conflict with compensation laws are the standard reasons for refusing to hire the deaf which are usually offered by employment managers who do not consider it worth their time to make a survey of operations to find the ones suitable for deaf workers, or to start looking for foremen who will not be averse to some special effort in order to get the deaf workers started. The hazards, however, more often than not, are merely excuses to cover up the general inertia.

It is a question, nevertheless, if the employment manager's responsibilities actually cover the obligation to take the steps necessary to admit deaf workers. And it is at this point that the government-paid employment agent for the deaf can really function effectively. There is a job of work for him which requires qualifications of the top ranking. He must be familiar with the deaf, their peculiar susceptibility to vibrations of various kinds and the sound signals which are, or are not, actual accident hazards. He must understand the arts by which the deaf minimize their disability. Finally, the ideal man for this work would have broad experience with industrial processes and employment problems in general.

A competent survey of a plant by such an authority would do more to open it up for deaf workers than unlimited hours of persuasion by a social service enthusiast.

Of course, the deaf applicant cannot be hired because he is deaf. Landing a job is strictly an individual business and the qualifications of the individual finally must govern. In addition, each applicant must run the gauntlet of a considerable list of office rules based on current employment policies in the different establishments. These last are governed by changing economic conditions and may vary from day to day. While they last, however, they are as inflexible as any rule in the book.

For example, no one cares to trifle with the rule that no out-of-town residents may be hired as long as there is anyone on the local relief rolls who can do the work. Hiring only men with dependents is a rule with obvious advantages under certain circumstances. Equally obvious is the necessity for changing the rules when all the competent jobless men in these classifications have been hired. Such rules are arbitrary, but they are not capricious as they sometimes appear to the man looking for a job.

Rules that are more or less capricious do make their appearance from time to time in certain establishments. Some employment managers will hire only men who come recommended by one of their reliable employees.

Taken together, rules of this nature are a formidable barrier. They explain many of the difficulties that the deaf applicant encounters and indicate a field where welfare workers and employment agents for the deaf can be useful. For, if employment agents were familiar with these rules, they could, in many cases, prevent the deaf applicant from running afoul of their provisions. And they could also make sure that the applicant's case was presented in the most favorable light. The deaf themselves lack the means for getting such information as easily as a hearing man would.

In the rubber industry, training, experience and education enter the problem only in the most general way. It is the physical equipment which is important. This does not mean that intelligence is unimportant. Quite the contrary. Nevertheless it is possible to train most men for the job if they have suitable physical equipment. This is true of employment in all, or nearly all, of the mass production industries. We are not dealing with an isolated phenomenon in this detail.

Too many of the deaf applicants are languid, cigarette sucking, hollow-chested youths whom one would not trust to rake the leaves in the front yard. A layman cannot help but feel that there is scant excuse for boarding schools such as we have in every state to turn out such an inferior product in a physical way. Thorough attention to physical education is easily possible under the circumstances and it would help to clear up a surprising amount of unemployment.

There is a young man in the writer's own experience who came to Akron while times were still quite bad and landed jobs with four different employers within the space of a year. Most of the jobs were temporary fill-ins, but they did help the boy to pay his way and even send home a few dollars.

As far as deafness is concerned this young man is no less deaf than half a dozen other young fellows about town who have not had a job for years. His education differed from theirs in no detail worthy of our consideration. But he was an upstanding young man, well muscled and alert. When one looked at him there was no difficulty whatever of conjuring up a picture of his doing valiant deeds with a pick and a shovel, or of giving alert attention to the more exacting requirements of machine operation.

He got the jobs.

The part that his physical equipment played in his relative success is obvious. Must we hold then that his vocational training in school was a total loss? The writer does not believe that any such conclusion is justified.

The main trouble of the employment manager is to find deaf applicants with the craftsmanship to handle a responsible piecework operation. This quality is even more rare than the right kind of physical equipment. It is not exactly the craftsmanship of the carpenter, the toolmaker, or the printer. It is the craftsmanship of all of them rolled into one—craftsmanship in the abstract, as it were. It implies familiarity and skill in the use of tools and machinery in general. More particularly, it demands established standards of workmanship and the ability to take hold and push through an assignment without too much waste motion.

A friend of the writer who is more familiar with conditions in the state schools is firmly convinced that standards of workmanship are the last things that a boy would be likely to get from his vocational training in these schools. Whenever there is an exacting piece of work to be done in the school's workshops, the instructor invariably does it himself, so he relates.

Regardless of the justification which must be accorded this criticism, it certainly is true that we have as much right to expect the schools to produce standards of workmanship as we have to look to them to turn out graduates with the physical equipment to hold down jobs. Here are primary objectives of the first importance which may have had less than their due share of attention in the years that the success of all educational endeavor was being measured by the language yardstick.

It is not the purpose of this paper to give the impression that there are five easy steps to employment—or ten steps or fifty, for that matter. The writer cannot claim that employers are actively in the market for deaf workers, even when they are perfectly equipped. Looking at it in the most favorable light possible, we must conclude that deafness is a deviation from normal which, if not actually fatal itself, surely will serve to multiply the consequences of a second or a third fault.

In effect, the deaf applicant marches up to his turn at bat in the employment office with one strike already called against him.

If he can show that he is competent, willing and alert, he may convince the employer that he should not be disqualified by reason of the one strike when certain jobs are to be filled. But there is only one way by which that strike can be canceled out. That is by means of a resounding hit when he gets a chance to show what he can do on the job in the factory.

What we do want is to try to make sure that the umpire in the employment office never gets a chance to call a second strike, or a third.

36 | The Development of Postwar Employment

B. M. Schowe

1944

There are about two hundred deaf workers on the Firestone payroll at this time and at least one fourth of them are women. With the turnover being what it is, it is probable that we have hired more than four hundred deaf workers since 1940. About twenty of our deaf people have seniority records running up to ten, twenty and thirty years or more.

The people on this work force come from California, Florida, Texas, Oklahoma, New York and South Dakota as well as from states nearer home. For about three years there has not been a day when we did not have jobs waiting for qualified deaf workmen. This means that we have just about scraped the bottom of the barrel and know the limit of possibilities for deaf workers under present conditions at least.

Aside from mere numbers, however, the feature in which we take great pride at Firestone is the diversity of occupation for the deaf. Of course, the bulk of our deaf workers are on semi-skilled production jobs. This includes steel fabrication, airwing and gunmount assembly, as well as the production of rubber goods. But we also have a scattering of skilled craftsmen on such jobs as line inspector for gunmounts, armature winder, precision grinder, printer, machinist and some others. In addition, we have several chemists, a draftsman and supervisors on airwing assembly. Seven of these people are salaried employees.

This will give an idea of the status of employment of the deaf today, in one establishment at least.

Among other jobs on which deaf workers are engaged at the Firestone Steel Products plant in Akron is the testing of oxygen tanks used for stratosphere flying. It is much like testing the inner tube of your automobile tire. Air is pumped into the tank and it is placed under water. One deaf worker, new to the job, fumbled with the tank valve while it was under water and the escaping air sprayed water in his face. The supervisor on the job explained what happened thereafter in a written report:

J. Ardmore working nearby laughed at him as did several of the other men. Burke, being a mute, did not hear the others laugh but did see Ardmore and thought Ardmore was making fun of him and motioned Ardmore to come on and fight.

Several blows actually were struck and the men had to be pulled apart by fellow workmen.

To the mind of the supervisor, the only way to explain the flareup was on the ground that Burke (which is not his real name) was a mute. Ordinarily, grown men do not fight over trivial mishaps like this one. Therefore, he reasoned, it must have been because Burke was deaf and did not hear the general hilarity that he took it as a serious personal affront.

The supervisor was not a psychologist and we need not accept his judgment as final. Still, it does seem reasonable to suppose that deafness entered into the picture at one point or another. The easy explanation would be that it was a show of temperament which somehow is mysteriously generated in deafness. But this sort of thing really helps not at all and it is a libel on the deaf as a class.

Burke's vanity was pricked by his mishap, certainly. But what was it that stung him to the fighting pitch? The situation was ludicrous and Burke unquestionably was intelligent enough to know that a laugh was in order at his expense whether he liked it or not.

If the men around him had been deaf like himself, would he have resented their laughter with his fists? Probably not. You have to learn to take it better than that in any and all of our schools for the deaf. Then it must be that the situation was colored in his mind by the fact that the men who were laughing at him were hearing men.

Now we have something into which we can sink our teeth. Burke felt that they were playing up his discomfiture, exaggerating his inexpertness—*because he was deaf*. His resentment was the instinctive reaction of his unrealistic attitude toward his own deafness. He injected his deafness into a situation where it was not logically a factor.

You may, if you choose, interpret this incident in some other way, but it would be a mistake to dismiss this interpretation too lightly. Over and over you will see this unrealistic attitude among the deaf in less dramatic situations. The pattern is familiar. Other workmen, they will tell you, are crowding them away from first place in line at the time clock—because they are deaf. Foremen are not assigning them to the best jobs every day—because they are deaf. Everything that goes against them is "because they are deaf."

Invariably, these same people who are most sensitive to imagined slights "because they are deaf" are the most insensitive to the inconveniences which their deafness does inflict upon others. They have no consideration for salespeople in stores and other public servants who must wait on them. They seem totally indifferent to the extra effort required of these salespeople to help them smooth over the unavoidable difficulties in the way of easy communication. Their unrealistic attitude toward their deafness cuts both ways. Subjectively, they are over-sensitive. Objectively, they are impervious and indifferent.

I am convinced that this is the source of just about one half of all the trouble we have with employment in general.

The wartime emergency has put all deaf workers to the test. It tends to magnify both their faults and their virtues. Now the time has come to take inventory. What of the whole record on balance? What tactics will be most effective as we square away for the next phase, the transition from war to peace?

The illustrated magazine *Folks* is published by the second largest corporation in the United States—General Motors—and is circulated to employees and customers. In the issue for March 1944, it carries the pictures of two fine appearing deaf workers and explains how these two men, together with ten others, have built up admirable work records in a certain division of the company.

This is just one outstanding exhibit among many which have been brought out by the wartime activity of deaf workers. The special beauty of this particular sample is that it bears the imprint of one of the best known corporations in the world, and it does not even hint at any mysterious techniques required for the successful training and employment of deaf workers. It indicates that these two deaf men went through the normal employment procedures and took over the job in their stride.

This last is an important consideration. Judged by this standard, much of the publicity we have had has been bad. The very numbers of deaf workers which we boast of in some plants may suggest that special techniques, special accommodations are provided. The average small employer might get the impression that it would be too difficult to duplicate these accommodations and he might be discouraged from trying to employ deaf workers.

It is worth noting that not all publicity is good publicity. With the best intentions in the world, some of the publicity put out by certain employers has seriously offended in this respect. It praised deaf workers effusively and, in the process, managed to convey the impression that some special magic was involved in their employment.

Nevertheless, observe the contrast with the past in this department. Until the present time the scraps of information about deaf workers in industry were few and far between. Little or none of it was in such form that it could be used to influence the employment policy of an employer who had no previous experience with the deaf. In the future we are going to have a wealth of information on the subject which has been published by leading employers, by organizations of employers and by several different agencies of government.

To illustrate, I have [. . .] an exhibit of material along this line. [. . .] The N.A.D. wants to build up a complete collection for future reference. Some of our wartime gains surely can be preserved in this manner.

There are several interesting research reports in this collection and the work along this line is continuing. In Pittsburgh, the Industrial Hygiene Division of the Mellon Institute is now conducting a further investigation into manufacturing operations which can be performed by workers with different kinds of handicaps. The project is designed chiefly for the benefit of disabled veterans, but all of us should profit from it in the end.

In place of prejudice and misinformation, after victory we can build our employment structure on a foundation of broad experience and well authenticated research studies that cover a surprising range of investigation.

Now, is there anyone who would like to puncture my balloon by pointing out that a miscellaneous collection of pamphlets like this is not going to make jobs when business goes into a tailspin?

My answer is that we must take up one subject at a time and the subject for today is limited to deaf employment. The only way we can rate our prospect intelligently is to consider what change there will be in our status after the war regardless of variations in the level of business activity. I have proceeded on that basis so far.

Of course, the volume of business and employment as a whole cannot be eliminated from consideration in actual practice. The only thing about it worth noting at this time, however, is that all this postwar planning we are doing surely must bear fruit of some kind. Some of it does appear to be trivial and much of it will be found to be useless after victory. But it is also evident that the basic principles of our economy have never had such a thorough overhauling in all history. We should not be disturbed by apparent conflict among the planners at this time. There is evidence of powerful undercurrents of purpose and these undercurrents all seem to bear toward the same objectives. It is reasonable to hope that at the proper time they will surge to the top in one more or less coherent program.

In any event, deaf war workers are not going to be thrown out in the street the moment this war is won. At the very least, the layoff of workers during the transition period will be under close Federal supervision and the employer could not cut loose from all responsibility toward them in a moment even if he wanted to. It is fairly certain that there will be benefits for displaced war workers who hold up their end of the load to the very end only a little short of the benefits which will be showered on returning veterans. There is no real need to concern ourselves about them at all. But it is a different story with respect to the deaf workers who have not been able to take advantage of their wartime opportunity to establish themselves as competent workmen.

A nation which has "social security" for its watchword cannot very well neglect them entirely. All the logic of the situation points in the direction of pensions, similar to the pensions for the blind, or else toward subsistence in sheltered workshops. It has been demonstrated clearly enough that some of the deaf people are totally incapable of maintaining themselves in the complexities of modern industrial society.

The spread between the best and the worst of our deaf workers is enormous and the pressure of postwar trends will be like a wedge. It will force the split steadily wider and deeper.

One of the first concerns of postwar planners of all description is the reduction of the war-swollen labor force to normal proportions. For a variety of reasons, this is necessary to bring the economy into balance. The Secretary of Labor mentioned it in her report for 1943 and it is, as of today, the official policy of the Federal Government.

Of course, industry itself does not normally look with favor on any proposal to reduce the labor force and perpetuate a scarcity of labor. But at this time there are other forces bearing on the employment policies of industry which will leave employers with very little choice in the matter. The vice-president of a large steel company summed it up this way:

> With the application of promotion, seniority, layoff and discharge provisions of union contracts throughout industry and the adoption of experience rating in unemployment insurance by a growing number of states, there is a clear trend in the direction of stabilized employment and decreased turnover.

In other words, employers in the future will feel impelled to tighten up their qualifications for employment for several different reasons. The old easy-come-easy-go method is out. Choosing a new employee under conditions which will prevail after victory will be just about as ticklish a piece of business as choosing a wife. Employers will have to be very sure they are getting the right man because, like a wife, he is likely to be around for a long time and it may be very expensive to get rid of him.

Taken all together, the signs are unmistakable. For deaf workers who can qualify, there will be a better understanding in industry and a wider range of opportunity than ever before. For those who cannot measure up to employment standards which have been advanced to a new high level, there will be nothing much in sight except pauperism and, perhaps, pensions or the sheltered workshop. The borderline cases, the marginal workers, will tend to disappear. They will either be *in* the labor force or else they will be *out* of it entirely. That is the prospect.

The pressure on the schools to bring all pupils up to the required level will be what you would expect under the circumstances. It will be all the more insistent because the dividing line between qualified and *dis*qualified deaf workers is not going to follow their I.Q. ratings very closely. Some pupils with poor school marks will make the grade as successful workmen, and some in the higher intelligence brackets will be found wanting. The line of cleavage will follow more nearly the level of the realism in their attitude toward their deafness.

Some deaf adults of rather limited mental attainment seem to have a knack for making themselves useful in industry, but the people with an unrealistic attitude toward their deafness are never conspicuously successful. These are the ones who are going to be hardest hit.

There is no direct line of attack on this problem. You cannot establish a Personality Department to match your Vocational Training Department. The solution will come indirectly through a conscientious effort to understand the implications and to identify the symptoms of an asocial attitude. At the same time, measures broadly designed to help equip the deaf youth for a place in this complex society will surely help to improve his attitude in a general way.

I think that safety clinics in our schools would help.

A few years ago while visiting the printshop in one of the schools for the deaf, I saw one of the pupils start to remove boxes of linotype slugs. The boxes were small, but heavy. He seized them with both hands and dragged them across the floor while walking backward. Now, I am not a safety expert, but you cannot remain long around an industrial establishment without becoming safety conscious and learning some of the elementary principles. It was apparent that this boy was a likely candidate for several different kinds of accidents.

It seems to me it would be a simple matter to have a series of safety meetings each year, six or eight perhaps, with an occasional lecture by the safety engineer from some nearby industrial plant. He might even offer to conduct the class on a tour of his plant and point out safety devices and the reason for the many safety rules which he had found to be necessary. Why is it that a workman may be severely disciplined for placing a milk bottle on a window ledge? The class also could be taught how to lift a weight without danger of rupture, and many other interesting facts of the same sort.

If no safety engineer were available, a member of the staff could take over the project with a little study and preparation. Upon completion of the course, the pupil should be equipped with a certificate which he could show to prospective employers.

I have also been much intrigued by the possibilities in the "Diploma of the Future" which was discussed in the *Vocational Bulletin* a few years ago. The "diploma" was a certificate of the graduate's rating on a battery of aptitude tests. The sentiment of the *Bulletin* seemed to be that the idea was rather impractical. Certainly it would not be simple or easy to put into practice.

The steel industry executive quoted a few minutes ago also stated that "increased emphasis is being accorded throughout industry to aptitude tests. . . ." Actually, few employers have done much about it so far and few personnel men know what it is all about. Nevertheless, a certificate showing the graduate's rating in comparison with the average for some control group of known capacities would mean something to any employer who could read. There would be other incidental benefits from a program of aptitude testing which are beyond easy calculation. Adventuring in this direction might pay unexpected dividends in the struggle to keep abreast of the swirl of economic events which will come after victory.

Within the limits of this paper, I have been able to give you only a sketchy outline of my theme and perhaps I have failed to establish some of my points. But if you have followed me thoughtfully so far, perhaps at some point you have felt the spark of exhilaration which I have felt as I faced the dimly perceived challenge of the future. A time is surely coming which will inspire the leaders of America to their highest endeavor. The rewards for success will be great and the penalties for failure will be severe.

To succeed in the hearing world, Deaf schoolchildren were taught to be cheerful, hard-working, and very, very patient with the hearing.

37 A Review of the Little Paper Family for 1944–45

Thomas A. Ulmer

1945

• A History of the Little Paper Family

In the years 1929 to 1935, Professor Irving S. Fusfeld, then editor of the *Annals,* published what he was pleased to term "A Review of the Little Paper Family." This review was greatly appreciated by the profession and it was decided to present another review, this time for the year 1944–1945.

To all accounts, credit for establishing the first paper in a school for the deaf seems to belong to the Ohio School when, in October, 1868, a paper was printed entitled *The Mutes' Chronicle.* Another paper, *Vis-a-Vis,* was also published at the Ohio School and ran concurrently with *The Chronicle.* The *Vis-a-Vis* was discontinued in 1886. The title of *The Mutes' Chronicle* was changed to *The Ohio Chronicle* in 1894. *The Kentucky Standard* came into being in April, 1874, and *The Virginia Guide,* then known as *The Goodson Gazette,* was started in December, 1874. The Georgia *Cave Spring Enterprise,* also seems to have started in 1874. It was not for the deaf children but was circulated among hearing people. *The Mute Journal of Nebraska; Michigan Deaf-Mute Mirror; The Silent Observer* (Tennessee); *The Gopher,* later the *Mute Companion* of Minnesota; all had their beginning around 1874–1876. In most cases, the title contained the word "mute" but these were all deleted later. Without exception, all of the papers were started as a means of instruction in printing, to keep the parents informed as to the general welfare and progress of their children, to keep the alumni in contact with their school, and to have an outlet for the creative efforts of the pupils.

It is difficult to say exactly when the term "Little Paper Family" was first applied to the publications prepared by our schools. The *Annals,* Volume 68, page 90, uses the term and it seems to have been in general use among the editors of the papers. Professor Fusfeld furnishes the following information:

> It was a term long in vogue when I [Fusfeld] came upon the scene. As a matter of fact, at meetings of the convention, it was customary for editors and superintendents to get together for at least one Little Paper Family Banquet.

The "Little Paper Family" is also known as "The Little Paper Fraternity," the latter term being coined by Professor Fusfeld.

During the past several years many of the papers have changed their format, the number of issues, and the number of pages. Another notable change was in the writers, many new names appearing among the contributors. These changes, however, did not affect the quality nor the contents of our Little Paper Family. As in the past, the articles dealt with questions concerning the education of the deaf, presenting problems and answers that were calculated to improve present-day conditions.

One of the major issues of the past year was the controversy between the National Association of the Deaf on the one hand, and the American Federation of the Physically Handicapped on the other. Prominent educators expressed their views as to the value of the two organizations. Another important issue discussed was the methods used in giving vocational training to our students and its value in the postwar period. In almost every instance it was pointed out that our schools were behind the times, that our shop language needed brushing up, and that our students should be given more time in the shops in order to learn that past performances help but it is the present ability and attitude of the worker that count the most. Many editorials expressed concern over the shifting deaf worker. Repeated warning was given that if the deaf did not fight to keep the working privileges obtained under the present labor shortage, the deaf would again be discriminated against and go through a period of unemployment.

There were so many interesting articles on topics of importance that it was difficult to select from among them. Space prevents the inclusion of them all. Those here included give a retrospect of the year.

• Introduction

In compiling this "Review of the Little Paper Family for 1944–1945" it has been the intent of the writer to record only those subjects dealing with the betterment of the education of the deaf. Many ideas were put forth but only a few have been selected for reproduction here. In some instances the author of the article is known and, where this is true, due credit has been given. In a majority of the quotations, the authors failed to sign the products of their pens. To them the compiler wishes to offer his apologies, and at the same time extend his thanks for the material supplied.

The Little Paper Family for the past year had many interesting articles. In making his selections from the different papers, the writer had several things in mind. First, he selected those articles that would prove of most interest to the educators of the deaf; and, second, he tried to choose those articles that contained worthwhile ideas and information.

The different articles have been arranged alphabetically under titles appropriate to the material contained in the article. Thus, all extracts dealing with finger spelling or manual instruction are listed under the heading "Manual Alphabet."

It is the hope of the writer that these articles will prove of interest to the reader. If the research worker and the educator of the deaf are benefited by this collection of opinions on the education of the deaf, the writer will have considered his time well spent.

• Athletics

Deaf athletes are still trying to make good in the major leagues. Zipp Newman of the *Birmingham Age-Herald* writes in *Baseball Digest* for October, 1944, that a young deaf man, Richard Sipek, will be given a try-out with the Cincinnati Reds of the National League. *The Hoosier*, Indiana, for November, 1944, reprinted the article and mentions that Sipek is a product of the Indiana School for the Deaf. There have been other deaf men in the majors, Luther "Dummy" Taylor with the New York Giants, and "Dummy" Hoy with the Cincinnati Reds, both teams of the National League. Sipek, so the account goes, has natural ability and deafness is no handicap to this cheerful, hard-working ball player.

> Sipek reports to the Cincinnati Reds next spring with a fair chance of sticking. He is a natural ball player, determined to become the first deaf man to play in the majors since "Dummy" Taylor was a New York Giant forty years ago.
> Sipek well rewarded the Barons for recalling him. He finished the season hitting 336 in seventy-four games and he was voted by the fans the most popular Baron, which placed his picture in the Baronial Hall of Fame.
> In all the history of the Southern league there never has been a more accurate throwing outfielder and this includes Tris Speaker and Joe Jackson. There have been many outfielders with stronger throwing arms than Sipek's good right, but none more accurate.
> Sipek is no sensational player. But he is steady, he has better than average speed, and he gets a good break on the ball and covers plenty of territory.

• The Deaf Teacher

Mr. Winfield S. Runde deplores the lack of deaf teachers in some of our state schools. Writing in *The Deaf Mississippian* for March, 1945, which copied the article from the *O. A. D. News* (Ontario Association of the Deaf News), he regrets the fact that the Ontario Department of Education will not hire deaf teachers.

> It is my understanding that there is in existance a policy regulated by the Department of Education, Ontario, which offers no opportunity whatever for highly educated deaf pedagogues to serve on the faculty of the Belleville School for the Deaf. I cannot see the wisdom of such a backward plan.
> During my long tenure as a classroom teacher I have had opportunity to observe and study the relative merits of both hearing and deaf pedagogues. Out of that experience and the innumerable contacts, I have formed convictions that I

sincerely believe are for the best interests of the deaf children in our public residential schools.

I believe that every school for the deaf, including state owned boarding schools and day schools, should have on its faculty one or several competent college-educated deaf teachers, depending on the size of the faculty. Contrary to the assertion of certain overzealous advocates of the oral method, who claim it to be the only method that should envelop the deaf child, the method that holds out to him the sole means of acquiring a normal education and restoration to the society of men, the deaf teacher and the educated deaf adults don't oppose the teaching of speech and lip-reading to deaf children. The fact is the educated deaf do encourage and believe in speech teaching for those deaf children who may profit by the method. But they also know that there are a great many children in our schools for the deaf who will never learn to enunciate intelligible speech. They believe that the sooner this fact is recognized in the lower grades and such children are accorded proper placement, viz., a change of method of instruction and approach—writing and free use of the manual alphabet—the better are their chances of acquiring language comprehension and usage.

The deaf teacher, by reason of his hard experiences and outside contacts—his struggles to master his handicap—becomes a great asset to our specialized educational system, and as such he is an inspiration to the pupils because they see in him the life that they themselves must lead. To be a success, to be independent, they see in the deaf teacher an example which they absorb and feel that they should emulate.

The deaf teacher sustains the noblest traditions of the teaching profession. He is scholarly; he continually searches for truths and more and more knowledge; he travels to far places to open to his mind vistas that he may translate in his life as a classroom pedagogue. He is loyal to his school and the sacred trust that is his responsibility. He is the heart and soul of his school because, naturally, his all is with those who look up to him for guidance and inspiration. They understand from contacts with him—they emerge into a realization of the hard road they may have to travel, so the sphere of the deaf teacher's influence ameliorates the harsh conditions of the life out in the world that eventually they must, as citizens, experience in the fearful struggle to successfully compete with normal men in the great and complicated hearing world.

The Gallaudet College trained scholarly deaf teacher—the kind of teacher who possesses the Godgiven native aptitude in his association with pupils and also the important proper understanding of pedagogical procedure and approach—is sought by the heads of schools for the deaf, educators who understand the needs and the rights of deaf children. These educators, these hearing leaders of American schools for the deaf, retain on their faculties the deaf teachers whom they regard as indispensable. There is today hardly a state school for the deaf in the United States that has not on its list of educators a fair quota of deaf pedagogues. And to these deaf teachers the heads of schools ascribe the success in preparing for college entrance pupils of ability so aspiring for higher education.

Hearing teachers of the deaf of long experience in the classroom, those who possess a consummate knowledge of the psychology and the needs of the deaf child, realize fully the necessity of inclusion of deaf teachers on the faculty.

In American schools for the deaf employment of deaf teachers today is increasing as the need of their services is recognized by the authorities. Schools that employ them stand high on educational achievement.

• Hearing Aids

[. . .] A great deal has been said on the value of hearing aids in the development of speech and learning in the deaf child. Some educators are strongly in favor of their use, while, to others, their help may be a bit doubtful. A Sub-Committee of the Committee on Problems of Deafness, under the direction of Rudolph Pintner, Ph.D., and Arthur I. Gates, Ph.D., and others, including Dr. Percival Hall, was chosen to investigate the value of hearing aids to the hard of hearing child in the public schools. This committee was started by the National Research Council in 1940. Interpretations of the findings were made by Doctors Stanton, Lorge and Gates, and the report, from which *Just Once a Month* for February, 1945, obtained material for summarization, was written by Dr. Stanton.

> In October, 1940, the National Research Council established a grant for investigation of the psychological and educational influences of the use of individual hearing aids by hard of hearing children with Dr. Rudolph Pintner, of Teachers College, as Director. A "Sub-Committee on the Value of Individual Hearing Aids for Hard of Hearing Children in School" was appointed, consisting of Dr. Harvey Fletcher, Director of Research of the Bell Telephone Laboratories; Dr. Edmund Prince Fowler, New York City; J. B. Kelly, Bell Telephone Laboratories; Miss Harriet F. Mc-Laughlin, Elementary Schools, New York City; Miss Estelle E. Samuelson, N.Y. League of Hard of Hearing; Dr. Percival Hall, President of Gallaudet College, Chairman. The report of this committee has been published recently.
>
> The purpose of this study was to determine in what way and to what extent the use of hearing aids helps the hard of hearing child attending regular public school classes.
>
> Over a period of 26 months hearing aids were provided for 52 hard of hearing children who were attending regular public school classes in Greater New York and Jersey City. The children were divided into two groups, a control group and an experimental group. They were tested at the beginning and at the end of the experiment to see what effect the wearing of the aid might have upon school achievement and personality. Careful case studies were made of 50 children and the speech of 74 children was studied.
>
> The number of hours the aids were worn by individuals varied from 100 to over 7,000 hours and there was little breakage.
>
> There were no statistically reliable differences between the experimental and control groups with respect to scores on the achievement test or the personality inventories.

There was no evidence of improved speech.

An analysis of interviews indicated a trend toward improvement in school adjustment and achievement and in social adjustment. Parents and teachers frequently remarked that many of the children seemed happier and less tense.

This report represents a first analysis and presentation of major findings and points clearly to the need of further investigations.

• Jobs

The Empire State News, as clipped by *The Western Pennsylvanian* of December 7, 1944, says that Mrs. John Koeper, of Schenectady, has been doing splendid work for General Electric in their Schenectady plant. They praise her work highly now that they need her. We wonder what they will do when the man-power shortage is eased?

General Electric, in the Schenectady plant, has just realized the value of employing the deaf. In a newspaper release, a Schenectady paper pictures Mrs. John Koeper, of Schenectady, who, although she has not worked outside her home in many years, has proven a valued worker. She assembles with deft fingers brittle nickel tubes from delicate pieces of mica and porcelain. Plant officials say her well-developed sense of rhythm and touch keep breakage of scarce materials surprisingly low. Her husband, John Koeper also deaf, has been with the American Locomotive Company for many years and holds a responsible position as Diesel engine inspector. He formerly was a pattern maker with the same firm.

Our hope is that these very same industrialists will remember this after the war is over and keep them employed instead of letting them off first when things slow down. Reports show that in some instances the deaf are still being discriminated against, most especially by army and navy officers who happen to be in charge of some plants and navy yards.

Michael Lapides, in *The North Dakota Banner*, which was reprinted by the *California News* for December, 1944, writes about the deaf in the post-war world. Deaf workers are in great demand at present due to the shortage of help. Will they be wanted after the war? That, he points out, is a question the deaf must settle for themselves.

A trend in the war effort that promises well for the deaf is now clearly enough defined by their excellent performance in war industries. They are engaged not only in turning out war production but also in the collective effort to win a bridgehead in the form of public recognition of the quality of their contribution to the war effort. They are concerned with the question as to whether industrialists, generally speaking, are aware of the fact that the vast majority of the deaf are making good in war production. A lack of the sense of awareness on the part of industrialists that the deaf can and do compete efficiently with normal persons, has been a very serious deterring factor in their lives. Such a resistance to the advancement of the deaf in commerce and industry has been their greatest handicap in the last few decades.

Superintendent Quigley, in *The Kansas Star* for December, 1944, is timely in his warning to the organizations for the deaf when he calls to our attention the help the returning veterans will receive from the Government's Bill of Rights. He points out that the deaf are not included in this bill, and after the war, it will be harder for the deaf to secure positions.

Events shaping up under the influence of the GI Bill of Rights will, it seems, have a profound effect upon the post-war employment of the deaf unless some action is taken to prevent it. The GI Bill of Rights provides for a vast amount of training, both academic and vocational, to benefit returned servicemen. The purpose is to fit these men for more rapid placement among the employed, and to give those who had begun college careers the opportunity to finish them, or at least to get back on their feet during the readjustment from military to civilian life. The deaf, being unable to serve militarily, do not come under the provisions of this bill. Thus, competition in field of employment will be increased so far as the average chance for the deaf person to get a job is concerned, and nothing is in sight to help him meet the competition, other than that heretofore provided.

Possibly this is a matter that can be worked out only among the deaf themselves. No one decries the Government's action in providing for the return soldier, so there can be no avenue of approach there. The deaf should analyze the situation from their own standpoint and do what they can now to forestall certain difficulties later. This is a matter of concern to all organizations of the deaf. The time is rapidly approaching when hundreds of deaf workers are going to be in need of consideration.

• Manual Alphabet

There is an interesting article on the manual alphabet, written by W. S. Runde, in *The New York Journal of the Deaf* for December, 1944. All employees of our state schools should be masters of the manual alphabet. Mr. Runde goes a step further and says that its use should be more general, making it available to hearing people in colleges, universities, and in other walks of life. The manual alphabet is in the *Handbook* of the Boy Scouts of America, being one of the tests that can be passed for advancement to a higher rank. Some of our schools are conducting classes in signs, among them being the California School with Mr. and Mrs. Vernon Birck in charge; the Michigan School with Mrs. Helen Stewart and Miss Julia Berg conducting the classes; Mrs. Georgiana Ulmer conducting classes in the Oregon School; and classes being held in Kansas, West Virginia, and Wisconsin.

The Manual Alphabet which 80,000 practically totally deaf people in the United States use in conveying thought—one to the other—is easily learned by hearing people. It is a graceful, convenient way to talk to the deaf and it should be used more and more. The best way to bring about its general use is to get the Board of Education of each city to require teachers in the grammar and high schools, and the colleges and universities to acquaint the students with the alphabet. Fluency in manipulating the fingers, rapidly and clearly, is not as difficult as it may seem to the uninitiated. A little practice will soon develop dexterity—and what a wonderful boon it would be to the deaf to meet every other hearing person who happened to be able to use the manual alphabet which to the deaf person really is a Divine gift that conveys to him (from the minds of others) those thoughts which, not going through the closed ears, come to his understanding mind by this wonderful Abbe de l'Epee invention!

. . . It may be mentioned that one lady of high connections in London, an oral advocate, told the writer that because of its ease of communication and gracefulness, the single handed alphabet is to the deaf what the spoken word is to the hearing, and that all deaf people should be able to converse by that means. (She evidently was thinking that in English schools for the deaf, only the oral method of communication is used.)

A class in Sign Language and finger spelling was set up at the California School November 20, under the auspices of the University of California Extension Division. The idea of getting the university interested originated with Superintendent Elwood A. Stevenson [of the California School].

Hearing people should not find it difficult to become proficient in the use of the single handed (manual) alphabet. It is, however, a very different matter in learning the sign language. Most hearing people who have a workable command of signs make stiff and even awkward gestures. The trouble is they learned signs from individuals, off and on.

. . . To understand the deaf pupil—to understand to the fullest—it is absolutely necessary to become versed in the use and understanding of signs. Without such knowledge the loss falls on the pupil. In that atmosphere day in and day out, because of inability to rise to frequent occasions where a knowledge of signs would enlighten them, the precious time lost is a calamity to the helpless deaf learners.

The manual alphabet, if some present day writers could see their plans carried out in toto, would become a national language, being used by everyone in the country, deaf and hearing alike. George Culbertson, writing in *The Cavalier* for February, 1945, expresses the idea that the deaf lose out in employment not because of their lack of skill, but because of the employer's displeasure over not being able to communicate with the deaf employee except by writing. Mr. Culbertson says that if everyone learned to use the manual alphabet much of the friction between the hearing and the deaf might be removed.

All too often we meet deaf persons who remark upon how hard it is to associate with hearing people, how distrusting of the deaf employers seems to be, and other emotings of like nature. Just as often we see much to the same effect. It occurs to me that efforts to effect a cure of this difficulty are practically non-existent in proportion to the magnitude of this common barrier.

I am very strongly convinced that the attitude of the hearing public to the deaf man is not so much one of distrust in ability as it is of just plain impatience. In the majority of cases the deaf man applying for work is rejected, not because the employer thinks him incapable of the time-wasting pad-and-pencil method of communication.

We must admit that the pad and pencil constitute a patience-trying nuisance not only to the hearing people, but even to the deaf themselves who must resort to their use. It is small wonder, then, that the deaf man, unless he is an extraordinary good lip-reader, seldom gets past the first interview for work, and just as seldom is welcomed to any social gathering of hearing people.

The only feasible and permanent cure is education. It has been tried to educate the deaf to this end—trying to make lip-readers of one and all of them. That has been proven to be impossible, and so the alternative is to work on the other end of the line and educate the hearing people instead. This cannot be done overnight. It would require a generation of time and cooperation on the part of the public school system the country over.

Incorporate the manual alphabet into the course of study of every public school. That sounds like a big order, and it is even bigger than it sounds. To accomplish such an end would require the co-operation of every national and loyal association of the deaf in the United States. But is it worth our every effort?

If every public school taught the manual alphabet to the pupils in an early grade, and reviewed it regularly through the higher grades, it would mean that in a few years of time there would be hundreds of thousands of young hearing people fresh from school who could spell on their fingers whenever and wherever occasion required it. In just one generation of time the position of the deaf would be almost entirely free from this restriction of impatience which we fight against today. In that time, a large percentage of the hearing people would have learned to use a handy medium of communication with the deaf. . . . They can be made to see this advantage at an early date and so add impetus to the desire to learn and to retain the use of the manual alphabet.

The idea can be sold. The public schools teach children to play with blocks, to cut out dolls, to draw maps, and to work with tools in order to teach muscular co-ordination of fingers and hands. Show me a single better exercise for muscular co-ordination of fingers and hands than the manual alphabet.

After all, the manual alphabet is not a "foreign language." It is as much a part of the English language as is the written alphabet or the written word. The sign language is a complete and separate language from English, but not so the manual alphabet. The average child of normal intelligence can learn the manual alphabet sufficiently well enough to go through it without mistakes after as little as from 15 minutes to half an hour of concentrated effort.

Some persons would have to be convinced that it would not be the deaf alone who would profit by this innovation, but the entire public as well.

Inauguration of the manual alphabet in the public schools now will not save the deaf from discrimination in employment in the near future, but it would be a very good innovation for the benefit of our children and grand-children.

- Sign Language

The Ohio Chronicle for January, 1945, carries a reprint from *The Deaf Lutheran*, written by O. C. Schroeder, in the November, 1944, issue. A meeting of the Ephphatha Conference was held at Omaha, Nebraska, on October 3. This conference of ministers to the deaf urged a uniformity and preservation of the sign language. Signs are a thing of beauty when used by the right people and ministers to the deaf make good ambassadors in the spreading of correct and beautiful signs. It is imperative that signs be made uniform throughout the country. Too often a school will invent local signs that cannot be understood by a person from another state. We should strive to make our signs uniform, and to do this the book on signs issued by Dr. J. Schuyler Long is again being published, this time by his daughter, Dorothy Long Thompson of 306 South 57th Street, Omaha, Nebraska. Every state school for the deaf should have a copy of this book in its school library and every school permitting its literary society the use of signs on the stage should provide the society with a copy.

> Twenty Lutheran ministers to the deaf and the blind, together with three members of the Synod's Board of Missions to the Deaf and the Blind, met September 29 to October 3 at Omaha, Nebraska, for their annual conference.
> Most of the essays delivered at the meeting treated matters pertaining to the signs used in preaching to the deaf. The conference is greatly interested in uniformity and preservation of the sign language, which is the natural method of communication of the deaf.

Wesley Lauritsen, on the editorial page of *The Companion* for January, 1945, encourages the study of two languages, English and the sign language. The sign language should be taught by masters, and the California School, with Mr. and Mrs. Vern Birck as instructors, is, with the cooperation of the University of California, doing its share to make the language of signs known to more people.

> The study of language is always interesting. It has been our privilege to study a number of languages including Danish, Norwegian, Latin, French, English, and the sign language. Each of these languages has some appeal. Our greatest interest has been in English and the sign language. Properly used, these two languages are as beautiful as anything can be and a source of pleasure and profit to the users.
> To appreciate these languages they should be properly taught. The man on the street who has been in school but a few years may understand English and use it fairly well, but there is no beauty in it to him. In the same way there is no beauty in the sign language as it is used by some people who have picked it up here and

there. To appreciate English, to appreciate the sign language, one should learn from masters.

• Conclusion

As long as our schools continue to edit their little papers, the improvement in methods of instruction is bound to continue. These papers are exchanged among the various schools, and sound principles of education are usually given a tryout before final judgment is passed.

There are weak places in our curriculum that must be strengthened. These weak places can be defined as: Reading, language, and vocational work. In reading an attempt must be made to build up better libraries in addition to the teaching of reading itself. In all three subjects the pressing need is more time and simpler methods of presentation. Vocational work, especially, deserves better treatment than it has been receiving. The equipment, in many shops, is out of date, or inadequate for the work intended. Shop language has also been found unsuitable for conditions in the work-a-day world. Modern machinery and modern ideas are necessary if our graduates are to be properly fitted for work in a competitive world.

It is evident that the controversy between proper methods of instruction still waxes strong. Some educators believe in one system, and some believe in another. Interesting articles have been written, extolling the strong points of each. The cloud hovering over the methods is beginning to clear away. Most educators now know, and admit, that the system should be adapted to the child, not the child to the system. Pure oralism has its points, and the combined system of speech and finger spelling also has its points. Sometimes the oral method is carried too far and time is wasted on speech that should be given to written language.

In some instances parents have been persuaded to purchase hearing aids through lack of sales resistance, and under the mistaken belief that a hearing aid will *cure* deafness. Such is not the case. No hearing aid now on the market will cure deafness. It is nothing but what its name implies—an *aid* to hearing. It is a crutch on which to lean, a device to help whatever hearing remains. In one or two instances a hearing aid has improved hearing, but in general it can be said that a hearing aid enables the wearer to understand speech more clearly and easily than would be the case without such an aid. No hearing aid should be purchased without advice from the nearest school for the deaf, and a competent ear specialist.

The use of signs should be permitted in all assemblies. To be useful, however, signs must be taught by competent instructors and not just "picked-up" at odd moments. Finger spelling, too, should be taught. It has been put forth that finger spelling should be made a regular part of the curriculum of the public schools and universities. This would be of much benefit to the deaf but a careful thinker will realize that public schools have a crowded curriculum and would find it next to impossible to include such a course.

"The Little Paper Family," next to the *Annals* and the *Volta Review*, plays a very important part in the education of the deaf. Workers in the field of the deaf realize their value and each month the issues are read with interest. Ideas that have proven their worth in one school are adapted to other schools, and all benefit from the interchange of ideas.

ACKNOWLEDGEMENT

The compiler of this *Review of The Little Paper Family for 1944–45* wishes to thank:

Dr. Powrie V. Doctor of Gallaudet College,
Mr. Marvin B. Clatterbuck, Superintendent of the Oregon School for the Deaf,
Dean Irving S. Fusfeld of Gallaudet College,
Dr. Clarence J. Settles, Superintendent of the Florida School for the Deaf and the
    Blind,
Robert M. Greenmun, instructor in the Ohio School for the Deaf,
Fred Krepela and Mrs. Georgiana Krepela Ulmer for their aid and criticism in
    preparing this paper.

38

The trappings of middle-class respectability are still a considerable motivating force in the Deaf World a half century after this address was delivered at the dedication of the New California School for the Deaf at Riverside by the president of the California Association of the Deaf.

Place of the Adult Deaf in Society

Toivo Lindholm

1953

Thank you, Dr. Brill, for the honor and privilege, on behalf of the California Association of the Deaf of saying a few words at this dedication of the new State School for the Deaf. The CAD is proud of having had a hand, little though it be, in the building of the school; in fact, many of the Southern California members were active on the project from the very inception. The CAD bespeaks a great future for the school, rivaling the great Berkeley school. This rivalry will be healthy.

The members of the Association and all other deaf people have reason to be interested, not only as citizens and taxpayers of the State, but being ourselves "products" of the State residential and city day schools for the deaf. Naturally we went through the mill and know whereof we speak. We are the prime examples of what the schools produce. Our parents were normal people, deeply grieved when we became deaf from sickness or accident. They were relieved, however, to find that the State provided facilities for the education of the deaf, so we could learn to be independent, self-supporting, respected citizens of the state, just like our own hearing sisters and brothers. They are interested in that their children be trained to return to society from which deafness has set them apart. The schools are interested primarily in training the children for life. Both sides are happy at the results.

I think we, the deaf, have proved this point of being self-supporting beyond the shadow of doubt. And the state has kept down its roll of "wards of the state," while adding us on its list as appreciative taxpayers. We are paying back to the state every penny it ever spent for our education, and more. And we never have asked, and never will ask, for special consideration in taxes or special benefits. We don't need them.

We, the deaf, come from all walks of life, rich and poor, all colors, race, creed, nationality. We learned our trade at school, which many of us follow through life; at that we learn industry, responsibility, adeptness of hand, and so forth. Generally speaking our employers appreciate our work and pay us wages on equal scale with normal people, and our hearing co-workers treat us on a level with themselves—

after they have assessed us and found we are human and like unto themselves in all respects except for our lack of hearing.

Many of us have positions of trust. Some of us are in the teaching and ministering professions. One man is an associate engineer in the Los Angeles City Hall, working on freeways. A few girls are doing clerical work in the civic centers of Los Angeles and San Bernardino. Many of us work for Douglas, Lockheed, AiResearch, and other equally important plants. Two are design engineers at North American Aviation Co. Many of us may be found in smaller places. Some of us own our own job printing shops, cleaning and pressing establishments, shoe repair shops. And we do well, thank you. Many of us are printers and linotype operators on big city dailies. And almost everywhere we are entrusted with the operation and care of expensive machines, and we do produce. We haven't just stepped in and taken over. It has taken time and patience to prove ourselves capable.

We, the deaf, marry and raise families of normal children, and many of us own our own homes. We go to church. We drive cars, and the California Bureau of Motor Vehicles will attest to our skill and care as drivers. Fact is, lacking the sense of hearing, and conscious of the defection, and because of public awareness of, and probe into, highway accidents, we take extra precaution when behind the wheel to keep our own records very good, indeed.

We, of certain denominations, own our own churches; we own a big clubhouse in Los Angeles which formerly was a Masonic Temple. We own one at Oakland, too. We belong to clubs, hearing and deaf, to political groups, to unions, to local, state and national associations. We attend conventions run by our kind. An example of the humanitarian work the deaf do among their kind is the L.A. Ladies' Sunshine Circle for the Deaf that has existed for thirty-nine years and to which belong about eighty-five ladies, not one of whom is hearing. An example of achievement done entirely by the deaf on a national scale is the National Fraternal Society of the Deaf, which is on the lodge system and handles life and sickness and accident insurance. Established at the turn of the century it has weathered the depression better than a majority of life insurance companies. Today its total assets are over three and a half million dollars. It has already paid out millions in death and sickness and accident benefits. And it grows at the rate of $11,000 a month or $130,000 a year, serving only the deaf of this country and Canada. As I said, it's run entirely by the deaf— and it has won recognition and citations for efficiency and soundness. This fraternal society sprang into being chiefly because of the practice of life insurance companies to charge deaf applicants 25 to 50 percent above par, thinking them only fair risks. The deaf through this society have since proved the life insurance companies wrong. Today the companies will take deaf applicants at par. And now we have about the same trouble with auto insurance companies through their agencies. The auto insurance companies do not themselves discriminate against us, but leave discretion in the matter with the agencies. It is the agencies we have to convince and the CAD and the NAD are working on them.

The CAD is affiliated with the National Association of the Deaf, Inc., also run by those who know their own kind. Organized in 1880 and incorporated in 1900, the National Association has looked after the welfare of the deaf on a national scale, and aided and abetted the state associations in the solution of many of their problems. To this group we are indebted for the splendid station we enjoy in life—outside of the purely educational side. The California Association, organized in 1906 and incorporated in 1914, enjoys a splendid record of achievement and service to the deaf. Today it owns its own Home for the Aged Deaf where residents may enjoy their declining years in the company of their own kind.

In the arts and crafts, some of us have reached the heights, so to speak. There are Cadwallader Washburn, eminent dry-point etcher, now past eighty, and living in Maine; Douglas Tilden, sculptor, some of whose creations still adorn San Francisco parks; Granville Redmond, California landscape painter; Howard Terry, poet and author of Hollywood, and others. In passing I want to say that on its campus the Berkeley school boasts one of Tilden's masterpieces, "The Bear Hunt."

Many of us attend Gallaudet, federally supported college for the deaf, at Washington, D.C., and some of us went to other higher centers of learning.

We deaf are sports loving, too. Close to one hundred clubs of the deaf in the land are members of the American Athletic Association of the Deaf. We have annual tournaments to pick the championship team. A few years ago Oakland entertained such a tournament; in 1955 Los Angeles will entertain. We have bowling teams and a few of us play golf, to say nothing of bridge, 500, and canasta. We have our little share of athletic greats—Bill Hoy, now ninety, a Cincinnati outfielder, uncle to Paul Helms of the Helms Bakeries; Luther Taylor, seventy-eight, pitcher for the New York Giants, under the great McGraw.

All this is on the bright side. I'm sorry if we seem to pat ourselves on the back a little too much. We have been told that we need better publicity, better public relations. I recall reading about somebody asking a blind man if the Braille he used was the same that the deaf used. We do try to go for more publicity and better public relations.

We do have our own problems—some of them black, indeed. We are human, born of human parents, living and working among human beings. As one educator of the deaf said: "There are good, bad, and indifferent deaf people." Some of us of course are weak and wander off the narrow path. Some of us are shiftless and peddle shoddy stuff for good money given by people out of misplaced pity. Deaf peddling would disappear if people would only discourage it. Some of us do break laws. We shouldn't ask leniency because of our handicap, but should receive similar treatment given other offenders. We are grateful such deaf people are in a very small minority among us, thanks to the wonderful training at such schools as this one.

It goes without saying that for the courage and fortitude with which we face the world and make good, we are indebted to many hearing people—our home folks and relatives, our old teachers, our friends and neighbors and co-workers, and to our local, state and federal lawmakers and administrators.

We thank God Almighty that we live in this land of freedom, schooling and opportunity which are accorded deaf citizens equally with more fortunate citizens. Isn't it any wonder that America is so great? Americans are far-sighted and progressive. Americans train their handicapped to take care of and support themselves.

Thank you, Dr. Simpson. Thank you, Dr. Stolz. Thank you, Dr. Stevenson and Dr. Brill. And to all our other friends, thank you, too. This from all the members of the California Association of the Deaf, and their friends, and the parents of deaf children, past and present, who call down the blessings of God upon you.

39

The notion that Deaf-owned or -managed businesses or organizations, including Gallaudet University, are de facto sheltered workshops for Deaf people who cannot make it in the hearing world is widely believed, even among the well-educated Deaf elite, but rarely acknowledged.

What Exactly Am I Supposed to Overcome?

Tom Willard

1998

Sometimes I wonder if I've managed to overcome my deafness yet, or if I ever will.

It's a hard question to answer, because I don't really know what it means to overcome one's deafness.

You would think I'd know the answer, since I work in journalism. Just about every article you ever see about people with disabilities focuses on their efforts to overcome their disabilities.

That's because most of the people who write for newspapers and magazines are able-bodied. They assume that having a disability is a negative thing. The idea of accepting and living peacefully with a disability is a concept they rarely consider.

So you end up with a lot of stories about people who won't let their disability stop them.

A list of current Associated Press articles on disability shows one story headlined, "Man overcomes deafness to teach students music." Another, headlined "Tumors in eyes don't stop 10-year-old from acting her age," shows that the "don't let it stop you" slant can be applied to any kind of disability.

It makes me wonder what the newspapers would say if they wrote about me. Have I overcome my deafness?

My mother certainly gave it the old college try when she first realized my hearing was a problem when I was a kid. She dragged me around to doctors, got me a hearing aid and gave me vitamins that made my ears turn red.

This was the 1960s, a time when it wasn't cool to be deaf. There weren't a lot of role models back then. Until I lost my hearing, my only experience with deafness occurred one Saturday afternoon when a peddler who said he was deaf sold me a flag lapel pin for 50 cents in a downtown store.

My hearing kept fading. My mom thought she would have to support me for the rest of my life.

Unless, of course, I could overcome my deafness.

Did I? Today I wear a hearing aid that makes noises noisier, but I've never considered a cochlear implant or lessons in speech and lipreading. Instead, I've pretty much accepted the fact that I'm deaf.

Did I fail to overcome my deafness by refusing to engage in battle with my failing auditory nerves? Was I wrong to accept my condition without a fight?

I've managed to do pretty well in spite of being deaf, and I think I'm a lot happier having accepted the fact that, for whatever reason, I'm destined to live my life as someone who is deaf.

I've had low-paying jobs in the hearing world where I was the little man on the totem pole, a quiet guy who just did the work and went home. And I've had high-paying jobs in the deaf world where I've directed some challenging and noteworthy projects and made a lot of interesting things happen.

Those with a "disability is bad" mindset would probably say that I had done a better job of overcoming my deafness when I worked in the hearing world, even if I was lonely and isolated and had a job that was turning my brain to mush.

And they'd probably look down at me for "taking the easy way out" by pursuing a career in the deaf world, even if it means that I'm doing important work that makes a difference to people.

Oh well. I'm happy and I don't think my inability to hear is anything that I need to overcome. I've adjusted to it, adapted to it and gone on with my life, just like everyone else.

If anyone has anything to overcome, I would say it's the people in the media. They are the ones who keep feeding the misconception that people with disabilities are not happy or whole until they have overcome their disability.

Instead, why not recognize that a disability often is a part of our lives, something that makes us who we are? Our ears may not work as well as we'd like, but we have nothing to be ashamed of and certainly nothing that needs to be overcome.

40

Historically, Deaf people and our organizations have fought against various outbreaks of governmental paternalism, such as tax-exemption proposals. That traditional stance, very effective in blocking entitlement legislation, changed radically in the mid–twentieth century, with the expected disastrous results.

Thoughts on the Effects of Provisions for the Deaf

David J. Kurs and Benjamin J. Bahan

1998

The Candy Store

As we entered the drugstore there was a long glass candy counter. The candies were arranged at the kids' eye level. There were rows of candies. One row had M&Ms, then the next row had other kinds of candies. It was very colorful. It captured my attention immediately as I walked in.

I saw it and said, "Ma, I want some candy."

My mother said, "You can't have some because we do not have money."

At that time my father had a menial job. So, money was really tight then. My mother would always say, "No," to everything I asked for. So, when she said, "No," I just accepted it as routine and thought nothing of it.

Less than a minute later, maybe 30 seconds later, my deaf brother, who is a little older than me by two years, tapped her on the shoulder and pointed to the candy counter. My mother immediately stopped everything and bought candy for my brother.

I was bewildered and hurt. I asked my mother, "Why?" Her answer, as usual, was: "He is deaf; he does not understand." (INTERVIEW, 2/25/97)

• Introduction

The aim of this paper is to discuss the social role a Deaf person acquires at birth. The social role the Deaf have at birth makes them natural receivers (Lane, Hoffmeister, and Bahan, 1996). We can make the inference that Deaf people are socially predetermined to be in need of provision by society at large by virtue of being deaf. That is, deaf people almost always fall into the role of receiving various provisions that are not normally given to others.

In discussing this particular issue, we draw from the real-life examples of a hearing family with a deaf child, as delineated in an interview, and reflect on how our society possesses the Western tendency of giving provisions and support to the needy. We examine an entire social complex where the deaf person is naturally guided toward the position of accepting provisions and falls into the provider-receivership complex by default.

• Life Story of a Family's Treatment of a Deaf Child as Seen by a
Hearing Sibling

We began by presenting an anecdote about a mother and her two sons at a candy store, taken from an interview with the hearing child (2/25/97). From this example and others to follow from the hearing brother's life, we can see that the parents treated them differently with respect to who was in greater need of provision. It will become clear that the deaf brother got favorable treatment. This difference appears to come from the parents' perception of deafness, which will be discussed in the section on social perspective. It should be noted that this story is not unusual.

In the case of the candy store, the culture of expecting provisions on demand is nurtured and established within the family. Now, when the family sends the child to a residential school, the culture of providing continues. As MJ Bienvenu recollects her school days:

> Growing up, who gave you school supplies? When I enrolled in school they gave me everything. I didn't ask for them or have to ask for them. They gave me pencils, paper, and erasers. But because I was a day student I had my own supplies and a briefcase. So many deaf kids go into schools entering into the relationship where they are constantly given things all their school lives. (INTERVIEW, 3/7/97)

The Cub Scouts

When I was young, I would attend Cub Scouts gatherings regularly. The following year I was ready to be admitted into the Boy Scouts. I brought home papers for my parents to fill out. Upon reading it they said, "No, you can't join the Boy Scouts." I was puzzled until they explained, "We will have to buy shirts for you."

You see, as members of the Cub Scouts, you did not have to have those issued outfits. But for the Boy Scouts you had to have an official Boy Scout shirt. So I ended my scouting days with the Cub Scouts.

My deaf brother, on the other hand, continued with the Boy Scouts for many years at the residential school he attended. And he rose in ranks until he was in the Order of Arrows. He received everything, you know, shirts, pants, a hat, a handkerchief, medals. He, also, went camping and everything. I am not even sure if the residential school paid for his outfit or my parents, but I clearly was denied opportunity to join the Boy Scouts because we are poor. (INTERVIEW, 2/25/97)

The system of provisions clearly has an effect on the hearing brother who learns he can win his parents' and family approval if he behaves in certain ways.

Winning Approval and Praise

I have learned as a child growing up that approvals and praise came pouring in from my parents and extended family whenever I helped my deaf brother. That, in turn, motivated me to encourage my brother to "depend" on me so I could have my parents' approval.   (INTERVIEW, 2/25/97)

The unequal treatment continued throughout their childhood and into their teenage years and then adulthood.

The Summer Job

As teenagers, we lived in a medium-sized town. My father had a good network of business friends. I remember one day I asked my father if he wouldn't mind asking some of his business friends to see if they'd hire me for part-time help.

My father's reply was a resounding, "No, you do it yourself. You need to learn independence."

It took me a while but I eventually found a part-time job to earn extra money. But, when my deaf brother came home from school for the summer, my father hustled and asked his business friends for my brother and found him a job. And that happened every year. When I pointed that out, his reply would always be, "It's different; he's deaf."   (INTERVIEW, 2/25/97)

The brothers go on to their own lives—they both marry and lead different lives. One Christmas, their father calls them both to a family meeting.

The Will

About 15 years ago at Christmas time, my father called up my deaf brother and me while we were at his house to have an important meeting on family matters. My father asked me to interpret. Naturally, I accepted the task. It appeared to be important so I set myself up in a position between my father and brother.

"I want to talk about the will," he began.

My father continued as I listened and interpreted. "I want my estate to be divided two ways: one-half of the money goes to the church, and one-half to you (pointing to my deaf brother). As for you (pointing to me), you do not need anything."

I was taken aback and thought to myself, "What's the point? I am your son, too." But I said nothing and continued interpreting.

To make things worse, my father added, "Because you (meaning me) are hearing, you will be the executor of the will. And make sure things are divided as instructed. Do you understand what I want?" I replied, "Yes."   (INTERVIEW, 2/25/97)

These examples prove that the experience of receiving provisions and engaging in the provider-receiver relationship lasts a lifetime. From these examples, one can understand how easily a Deaf person can get trapped into the "social-institutional-help" complex. Sadly, in this case, the hearing brother suffered, also. It should be pointed out that the entire situation did not stem from this Deaf person's demand that he should be treated favorably, but rather from his parents' pre-determined social perception (to be discussed later) of deafness.

As this discussion grows, some questions come into play. Does this pre-determined social arrangement make Deaf people susceptible and easily engaged in the receivership role? Are these roles transferable to other levels of receiving provisions (e.g., Supplemental Security Income [SSI], etc.)? Is the acceptance of provisions akin to that of falling into a vacuum created by society?

• The Phenomenon of Provisions

We argue that one who is the receiver early in life naturally evolves into one who actively seeks and fights to maintain provisions later in life. Another question comes about: How universal is this active-maintenance provider-receiver relationship?

In the book *Prospero and Caliban* by Mannoni (1993), the author details the psychological themes in the colonization of Madagascar by the French in the early twentieth century. Drawing heavily on Freud and Lacan, he attempts to make some sense of the relationship between the colonizer and the colonized, and in the process, introduces the concept of the dependency complex.

He provides the following example: he once took weekly tennis lessons from a Madagascar native. One week he went to the native for a routine lesson, but the native was not there. He asked around and discovered that the native was ill with malaria. So Mannoni procured some antibiotics for malaria, and the native subsequently became well. The tennis lessons resumed, and after one lesson, the native *told* Mannoni to get some new tennis shoes for him. Over time, requests like this became far more common. Mannoni concludes that since he was a European and thus in a superior position, the natives began to expect that the colonizers would give them provisions. From this, Mannoni created his dependency complex theory.

Mannoni sums up the natives' attitude as follows: "You have done something for me which you were under no obligation to do. Therefore I am yours, and you may command me, but on the other hand I expect you to look after me" (Mannoni, 1993, p. 10). In essence, we are seeing how the act of entering into the provider-receiver relationship may spring from how the dominant culture perceives the subordinates. It is interesting how the subordinates perceive the situation, actively engaging in this process by demanding provisions.

We argue that a parallel can be extracted when examining the relationship between the dominant hearing culture and the subordinate deaf culture. This interesting assumption may also be the fundamental principle underlying the expectancy of provisions from the hearing for the deaf. Is the relationship between the hearing and the deaf similar to that of colonizer and colonized? While many people have become critical of Mannoni's ideas, his ideas are consistent with the thoughts brought forth in this paper.

Provisions for the deaf are not limited to welfare money. These also include discounts on mass transportation fares, ski lifts, movies, and so on. By examining these provisions and deaf people's perspectives of them, we can understand more about how this role evolves. The following joke, taken verbatim from a widely circulated e-mail, accurately shows many Deaf people's perspective on SSI:

> One day Jesus came back to help handicapped people to be cured. He encountered a group of Blind people. He was surprised to hear that blind people can read by Braille, walk around with their canes or seeing dogs. He asked them if they want to be able to see. They replied, "Yes, of course!" He cured them. They jumped in a joyous manner. They threw their canes away. Some felt close to their seeing dogs and kept them anyway.
>
> Later Jesus entered a Paraplegic Convention. He was amazed to see people riding in electronic wheelchairs everywhere. He managed to get on the podium and announced that he could cure them and they could walk. Some yelled, "Yes." Some of them talked to each other, "Who in the hell did he think he was?" Jesus proceeded to cure them. At first, some tried to get up and walk. They succeeded. Others observed and managed to walk. Soon the whole building was filled with joyous screams and people walking around. The wheelchairs were left behind and forgotten by their former owners.
>
> Jesus entered the deaf clubhouse. He observed the Deaf people signing to each other. He was impressed with the beautiful ASL they used. He tried to call them to attention without any luck until one person blinked the lights for them to pay attention. Jesus thought to himself that it was a keen idea. He announced that he intended to cure them of deafness. Every deaf person said, "No! No! No!" He was surprised by their replies. He asked them why they didn't want to be cured. They said that they didn't want to lose SSI benefits.

Deaf people are able to laugh uproariously at this joke, but they shy away from forwarding it to hearing people. Does this reveal a skeleton in the closet—are we truly ashamed of our dependence on provisions? In *Journey into the Deaf-World* (1996), Lane, Hoffmeister, and Bahan argue:

> Members of the Deaf-World pay a high price for "going on the dole": their standard of living remains low; they forgo the psychological benefits that derive from working. . . . And they literally buy into the system which construes the salient difference between Deaf and hearing people to be an impairment possessed by Deaf people. (p. 347)

• A Predetermined Social Perspective

Our train of thought leads us back to the notion of "predetermined social perspective." If Deaf people are now paying a price for "going on the dole," then how was this social arrangement established in the first place? In this section we want to bring in various possibilities that lead to this predetermination and how that eventually becomes a relationship forged on dependence.

These "predetermined perspectives" might be derived from the overall perception of deafness as a pathology, which may be rooted in the Judeo-Christian tradition of saving the infirm and providing them with necessary help. While not everyone adheres to this tradition, it has trickled down into the consciousness of various social institutions over the course of time and become part of the systematic division of the "haves" and the "have-nots" in society. In the case of Deaf people, the "haves" (hearing society) see deaf people as part of the "have-nots" that is, they have a terrible affliction. This difference leads society to believe it is acceptable to view deaf people with pity (for example, the parents in the hearing brother stories), as evinced in their encouragement of others to be Good Samaritans by doing service toward deaf people. This encouragement comes in the form of praise—for instance, "You are doing good for poor deaf Alfred."

This culture of sympathy may very well be at the root of the system underlying the entire idea of provisions, leading to the idea that people will increase their self-gratification because they have helped the needy. This suggests that some people help the deaf out of a need for self-help or salvation, not out of pure altruism. In this frame of mind, even the praises are different when comparing the responses white hearing people give when they find out that a white hearing woman teaches in two different settings. When they learn the woman teaches at a black neighborhood school, their response is, "Wow, you must be brave." When they learn the woman teaches at a deaf school, their response is, "Wow, you are noble" (Lane, personal communication).

The principle of charity, which is deeply rooted in American culture, is shown in the desire to help poor people out of poverty, to help people with disabilities, and so on. Monetary or gift compensation is designed to alleviate the problems of the underprivileged or disabled: "Because they are deaf and they lack hearing, how can they survive on their own in this brutal world?" It follows that relations between hearing and deaf people can easily be seen by the former as charitable notions: hearing people do good unto deaf people. This spirit of doing good, in the end, turns into a business (see for example, Lane 1992). Agencies are set up to provide for deaf people. Even deaf leaders find it necessary to make money out of helping the deaf advance. This state of mind, along with the core belief that the deaf need intervention in their lives in order to succeed, ends up driving the social institutions into providing for deaf people, thereby initiating and perpetuating the provider-receiver relationship.

• "Because They Are There"

The next question we come to is: Why do Deaf people take SSI and ask for other entitlements? As mentioned earlier, there are discounts for deaf people on mass transportation fares, ski lifts, and even movies. In our interviews, the most commonly-given answer in response to taking these provisions was, "Because they are there." By taking these benefits, the deaf embrace the concept that "I am deaf, I have suffered; therefore you owe me."

In interviews with fourteen people from the metropolitan Washington, D.C., community, we discovered some things about the role Deaf people accept as receivers. For instance, to apply for SSI, some Deaf people advise others to "act very deaf." They are advised to build a wall between the Social Security administration and themselves; in doing so, they give up their intended status as a member of a linguistic/ cultural community and assume the label of "disabled." Yet, these very same people criticize Deaf peddlers for selling ABC cards. With peddling, you depend on pity to sell cards. With SSI, you depend on a certain perspective to receive benefits—a perspective that, in fact, is not far from pity.

We can see this perspective in the actions of the United States government. The crowning achievement of Franklin Delano Roosevelt's New Deal was the passage of the Social Security Act of 1935. It was well-intentioned, meant to help bail out those who were in need during the Great Depression. The New Deal evolved slowly into Lyndon B. Johnson's Great Society. During the 1960s the scope for welfare assistance exploded to the point that virtually every low-income American could receive benefits. Even today, the welfare budget is something that federal lawmakers are afraid to touch. Our desire to help others out of poverty or misfortune may have backfired on us in that these programs and attitudes all create a culture of entitlement without the receiver really asking for it or participating in the architecture of the fiscal and service structure. We suggest that welfare is a forged relationship between social phenomena and the human instinct for survival.

• Receivership by Default

Dependence spills over into every aspect of deaf people's lives, as in the story of the brothers. The parents' perspective set the tone for their children's lives. Deaf people are instantly placed at a disadvantage at birth, because they are immediately debilitated by the frame of mind society imposes on deaf people (as discussed in the section on predetermined social perspectives). What we see here appears to be the underlying human tendency to stratify. So, by default, the hearing-deaf relationship is that of dominator and subordinate. In an unwritten decree, by default of their being deaf, deaf people take the subordinate (receiver) position.

Is the tendency for those who are judged as socially inferior to gravitate toward the provider a result of social force or instinct? It appears the instinct for survival spurs deaf people to become attached to a provider. Eventually, the social phenomenon keeps them at it—once their needs are met, they just keep going at it. As a result, they get caught up in the entire service structure.

The dynamics within a family are the result of the greater dynamics of society as a whole. This establishes the child in the role of expecting provisions. This expectation is further confirmed as the child enrolls in school, where deaf students are taught how to fill out forms to apply for SSI and vocational rehabilitation. Some state vocational rehabilitation counselors will not serve clients unless they apply for and receive SSI, thereby encouraging them to enter the world with SSI. Golden Access Passports at National Parks are usually forced down deaf tourists' throats. In all, the act of expecting provisions just becomes a natural byproduct of the system to which deaf people have become accustomed. They are encouraged by the system to participate.

The irony lies in the fact that many deaf people wish to be freed from these bonds, but are extremely fearful of the threat of abandonment by the provider agencies. If the government abruptly stopped SSI and VR benefits, would the deaf revolt, wanting to initiate the provider-receiver relationship again and thus begin the circle anew? The people that we interviewed said there would be public outcries and protests if provisions were taken away.

• Conclusion

Predetermined social arrangements seem to make Deaf people susceptible and easily engaged in the receivership role. The acceptance of provisions is akin to that of falling into a vacuum created by society. This paper sets out to discuss the role contemporary society plays in shaping the lives of Deaf people. Many of the pitfalls have to do with society's perception of deafness, per se. The only way to reverse this trend is to increase awareness as Lane, Hoffmeister, and Bahan propose: "As society's understanding of the Deaf World grows, and Deaf people are increasingly given control of their own destiny, there will be fewer such double binds for the Deaf World to resolve" (p. 347).

This paper sets out to act as a preliminary stage for further research and discussion. We feel that this confronts an important issue in today's society, and by bringing this issue to the academic sector, we hope for further developments in regard to this topic.

NOTE

The authors wish to thank Robert Weinstock for his help in preparing this paper.

REFERENCES

Lane, H. (1992). *The mask of benevolence: Disabling the deaf community*. New York: Knopf.
Lane, H., Hoffmeister, R., and Bahan, B. (1996). *A journey into the deaf-world*. San Diego, CA: DawnSignPress.

Mannoni, O. (1993). *Prospero and Caliban: The psychology of colonization.* Ann Arbor, MI: University of Michigan Press.

41

Antifeminism in the Deaf community has always mirrored that of mainstream culture, but Deaf feminist responses here have traditionally been far more modest, Deaf women tending more toward identifying with the male-centered Deaf ethic of cheerfulness, hard work, and stringent conformity.

'Til All Barriers Crumble and Fall

Agatha Tiegel's Presentation Day Speech in April 1893

Katherine Jankowski

1999

In the fall of 1887, all eyes were on the group of six women who filed into the building where all students congregated on the first day of classes at the National Deaf-Mute College (the present-day Gallaudet University), the world's only liberal arts college for the deaf, located in the nation's capital. Gentlemanly propriety prevented prolonged gazes upon this group, yet restrained curiosity and excitement hung in the air. After all, this was the first group of female students at Gallaudet as part of a two-year trial. Prior to that, females had entered Gallaudet only sporadically from 1864 to 1868, although none stayed beyond her first year of college study.

The two-year trial did not occur without much previous heated debate. Even though colleges in the United States had begun enrolling women students more than fifty years prior to the trial at Gallaudet, reasons given for not admitting women at Gallaudet ranged from their being "lazy lady students" who had needed much help before they became discouraged and left college (Chase, 1881) to a lack of housing accommodations. One anonymous writer went so far as to state that "woman is the emblem of weakness and dependence . . . [and] cannot endure work to any lasting, available results" (X, 1878).

The proponents of coeducation, in contrast, rationalized that educated women were more engaging than noncollegiate women. Arguments were also made that coeducation at Gallaudet would put deaf education on the same level as colleges elsewhere that were already successfully serving women students.

The debate over coeducation at Gallaudet did not become heated, however, until academic year 1879–1880, with the announcement that Congress would award Gallaudet funds to build a new gymnasium (to become the present-day Peikoff Alumni House, fondly called "Ole Jim"). This followed the preliminary discussion at

284

the Fourth Conference of Executives of American Schools the same year about whether women students should be allowed to enter Gallaudet or whether a separate college should be established solely for deaf women. Edward Miner Gallaudet, then president of the National Deaf-Mute College, had evaded the question by suggesting that the discussion be put on hold until a future conference. The controversy surrounding the gymnasium lay in the fact that the administration chose to pursue funding for a new building as opposed to living quarters for women students.

This controversy brought coeducation back to the forefront and created the impetus for a fund-raising effort to establish a separate college for deaf women. Although this effort did not materialize, the outcome of such attention was the eventual two-year experiment at Gallaudet that began that fall day in 1887. The experiment produced several firsts and paved the way for permanent coeducation at Gallaudet. Alto Lowman, one of the six women who entered Gallaudet in the first year of the experiment, became the "First female graduate" in 1892 (*General Record*, p. 49). Agatha Tiegel, who was among the second group of female students entering Gallaudet in 1888, was recorded as the "First female B.A." by Gallaudet in 1893 (*General Record*, p. 72). Agatha also was the first woman graduate to earn the distinction of ranking first in her graduating class (*Thirty-sixth Annual Report*, 1893).

Even though the experimental status of women students at Gallaudet was permanently removed in 1889 (Jones, 1983), concern persisted among some educated deaf women that the education of deaf girls was not valued. This concern was perhaps best reflected in the rhetoric of Agatha Tiegel on Presentation Day at Gallaudet in 1893. Presentation Day was a formal ceremony in which graduating students presented an oration on a topic of their choice to the faculty and distinguished visitors. On this important day in 1893, Agatha Tiegel chose to deliver an oratory titled "The Intellect of Woman," the focus of this essay. This oratory is particularly intriguing because Agatha was undoubtedly addressing a predominantly male audience who were in a position to promote or hinder the progress of women at Gallaudet. The context of her oratory then raises the question of how her speech dealt with the particular historical situation and rhetorical challenges she faced.

• The Rhetor

Agatha Mary Agnes Tiegel was born on September 14, 1873, in Pittsburgh, Pennsylvania. She became deaf at the age of seven from spinal meningitis. For her, this was an especially traumatic experience, because she came from a musically inclined family that frequently gathered around the piano (Agatha, 1944). She later transferred her love of music to the reading and writing of poetry. Agatha was especially fond of the "musical" poets, such as Tennyson, Longfellow, Whittier, Scott, and Byron (Agatha, 1944).

Agatha began writing poetry when she entered Gallaudet at the age of fifteen. Prior to her admission to Gallaudet, she had attended public schools for most of her formal schooling, with the exception of two years during which she was a student at the Western Pennsylvania School for the Deaf (*General Record*, p. 72). When she entered Gallaudet in the fall of 1888, she was the youngest student and one of eight women students at the college.

Her experiences and those of the other female students during their ensuing years at Gallaudet appear to here been pleasant yet restrictive because of their gender. Living accommodations were among the enjoyable experiences. Because the campus in 1888 still did not have separate accommodations for its female students, President Edward M. Gallaudet moved his family to Hartford, Connecticut, in order to provide room for Agatha and her female classmates in his spacious home (Hanson, 1948). This was a bonus for the women, since they were "blessed" by Gallaudet's presence at mealtimes (Hanson, 1937). He was an excellent conversationalist with rare wit and an "outstanding authority and exponent" of sign language, of which he demonstrated a "thorough and graceful command" (Hanson, 1937).

Unfortunately, many restrictions were also placed on the women at Gallaudet, which clearly had an impact on Agatha. As she would say years later: "I was a very young girl at the time, and I resented that there might be any question of the right, the God given right, of my sisters and myself to take our places in the sun" (Hanson, 1937). Some of the restrictions placed on the women students included limited or no access to the clubs in existence, such as the Literary Society, Reading Room Club, and Saturday Night Club (Jones, 1983). These were not just social clubs. The mission of the Literary Society was to promote scholarly discourse and debate, and it had a small library. The Reading Room Club kept a collection of periodicals and newspapers, including those of schools for the deaf. (A nominal fee was charged for membership to this club.) The Saturday Night Club provided dramatic productions.

The women were granted honorary status to the Literary Society in 1888 (Van, 1888). After subsequent appeals to the society for full membership were denied, the women students went to the faculty for a final decision. The faculty decision against full membership was attributed to "the obvious impropriety of association of the young ladies with the young men on the same grounds that exists among the young men themselves" (W.B., 1890b). So the women were permitted only honorary membership and, as such, were allowed only to use the library (Jones, 1983). They were still not permitted to use the Reading Room Club collection, the main source of relaxation for the men. The women had to depend on the generosity of individual male members to lend them periodicals (M.M.T., 1891).

The Saturday Night Club produced plays that were performed only by men, even in female roles: "those of the sterner sex will don the skirts and stays . . . and will require the utmost care and delicacy in its rendition" (F.J.B., 1892). The faculty remained steadfast in their denial of women students in play productions with men until after the turn of the twentieth century (Burke, 1954). The segregation of the sexes was especially severe on the women, particularly since access for deaf people to general society was very limited in these days.

The insistence on segregation in clubs between men and women students prompted Agatha and the other women to establish O.W.L.S. (the present-day Phi Kappa Zeta sorority) in January 1892. O.W.L.S. was established to promote literary works,

Agatha Tiegel. Photo courtesy of the Gallaudet University Archives.

orations, debates, and performances. Agatha was elected the first president of the new organization.

Agatha accomplished other firsts as well. She became vice president of her senior class, the first woman to be elected class officer. When the *Buff and Blue*, the college student newspaper, was established, Agatha was elected one of its first three associate editors (Board of Managers, 1892).

Agatha also excelled academically, receiving perfect scores, called "ten-strikes," in subjects considered the most difficult, including Cicero, French, Butler's Analogy, moral philosophy, physiology, and German (W.B., 1890a; *General Record*, p. 72; M.M.T., 1892; and Wit., 1892), subjects that few people today attempt to study. During these days, "tens" were applauded and publicly noted. A reporter praised Agatha's ten-strikes in Cicero and physiology as "unusual" occasions (W.B., 1890a; and Wit., 1892). In addition, Agatha's ranking as first in the junior class was noted as especially remarkable, considering that she was only nineteen years old (M.M.T., 1892).

- The Audience

The audience in attendance of Presentation Day Exercises on April 26, 1893, during which Agatha Tiegel presented her timely topic, "The Intellect of Woman," likely included members of Congress, government and religious officials, distinguished visitors, the college administration and faculty, and fellow students. At that time, there was still an air of novelty about deaf college graduates, and that year more so with a deaf female valedictorian. The guest presenter, President Gilman of Johns Hopkins University, commented on this in his presentation, to a round of applause:

> Women are now admitted fully to its [Gallaudet's] advantage, and I am extremely glad, as I have no doubt you have been, to hear that the young lady who graduates to-day stood on a perfect equality with the most advanced students among the young men. Young women always excel where they have equal advantages in academic careers. (*Thirty-sixth Annual Report*, 1893)

No doubt, the audience was predominantly male and made up of potential "agents of change." They would represent a variety of viewpoints about the right of women "to take their place in sun" along with men, as Agatha would later say (Hanson, 1937). Although prior to the two-year experiment many men had been resistant to the notion of women attending Gallaudet, some of these opinions had shifted to support. J. Schuyler Long, a fellow student, was one who had changed his mind, but as is apparent from his autobiography, his support had little to do with his new fellow students' intellect:

> I was among the group of students who resented this invasion of their stronghold, and was outspoken in my opposition. I let the world know that I was not interested in co-eds. But Fate took hold of things. On the opening morning, coldly indifferent,

but somewhat curious, I sat in my accustomed place in chapel and watched the six candidates file in. Then the world changed. I sat up and took notice. I had seen something. In the line was a petite miss, with a long braid of golden hair hanging down her back. . . . I took back, abjectly, everything I had said or thought against co-eds. (Long, 1934)

Regardless of Long's self-serving conversion, there was still evidence of resistance to coeducation or to the free rein given to women on campus during these early years. For instance, some men would line up alongside the women, subjecting them to "a daily gauntlet of masculine curiosity" (College Heirlooms, 1895). At least one male student would stand "in prominent places" and "grin derisively" at them (College Heirlooms, 1895). Others considered the women "freaks" (College Heirlooms, 1895). The environment at times caused "fear and trembling" in the women whenever they had to encounter the "mocking crowd of boys in the halls" (Gallaudet College Alumni Association, 1900).

These viewpoints very likely represented those of the predominantly male audience that Agatha faced as she promoted her cause on April 26, 1893.

• The Presentation

As one of the first female graduates at Gallaudet and the first female valedictorian, Agatha had the prime opportunity to make an impact on her audience with her oratory, if she chose her rhetorical strategies carefully. This would be the time to educate the audience about the virtues of women and to promote a more vigorous recruitment of female students.

Agatha's credibility as a scholar and her popular personality were likely a positive influence on the audience. In addition to her scholastic acclaim, she had been described by her principal as "a girl of superior ability" and "quite ambitious" (Brown, 1888). She was also charming and personable. Described as the "life of the party," she was full of "sparkling vivacity and boundless enthusiasm . . . never at a loss for conversation or a witty remark" (Intellect, 1975). Faculty member E. A. Fay, a highly regarded professor and head of the Language Department, demonstrated his admiration for Agatha in a letter to her: "I shall always have the remembrance of your faithfulness, your devotion to your work, your love of all things true, beautiful and good; and the inspiration of it all will remain with me forever" (1893).

The qualities she demonstrated certainly established her credibility as a presenter according to the Aristotelian model of "ethos," or moral character of speakers. Since Agatha possessed the characteristics of "good sense, good moral character, and good-will" (Aristotle, 1982), she likely began her presentation with a high ethos that contributed to making her oratory persuasive and well received.

The presentation is fairly brief and is quoted here nearly in full. It begins by going right to the heart of the matter:

Gallaudet College, Class of 1893. Photo courtesy of the Gallaudet University Archives.

> The apparent inferiority of woman's intellect is to be attributed to many restrictive
> circumstances. We are so accustomed to behold her in a stage of development so far
> below her powers that we do not apprehend the full evil of these circumstances.
> (Tiegel, 1893)

She has identified the cause of the perceived inferiority of women as that of society.
Rather than pointing the finger to any particular groups of people, she has attributed
the problem to societal influences. Her strategy here is to join forces with the audience
of males to combat this "evil" that has permeated society. Her use of "we" illustrates
this collaborative strategy. Agatha also exhorts her audience to go beyond current
perceptions of women as inferior to elevate to ideals of what women can be, if
society's evil forces are overcome.

She then goes on to illustrate how societal influences are so pervasive that a
woman is marked before "she leaves the cradle," and thus, "her sex is a chain and
restraint" (Tiegel, 1893). The metaphor of "chain" is particularly striking and evokes
a comparable image of slavery, which is what Agatha intends. This metaphor is a
shocking contrast to the image that most men probably held of women in those days.
Her audience of men were far more likely to hold images of women as "meek and
docile" (Tiegel, 1893). The chain metaphor aptly destroys that image.

Agatha goes on to say that "in childhood, she [woman] is tutored in the idea that her role on the great stage of life is secondary to that of the brother who plays by her side" (Tiegel, 1893). Another powerful image is evoked here. The female child is allowed to play alongside her brother, but when she grows up, that "great stage of life" is granted to her brother, not to her. Again, she cites society as the influence that "tutors" the female child in her inherited role as that of the second-class citizen.

She then illustrates how societal norms advance the cultivation of "meek and social graces" at the expense of women:

> She is not expected to reflect for herself. . . . Marriage is held before her as the goal of her existence, and she sinks into a state of passive waiting. She loses her soul . . . her inherent talents are not exercised and grow rusty . . . for want of use; her real self lies dormant. She is content with superficiality in thought, attainments, and conduct and forgets that she is in the world to help it by action. (Tiegel, 1893)

Here, she portrays women in a different light. Contrary to societal expectations, and those of her audience, women are not content with their lot in life. She argues that women lose all sense of identity because society's only purpose for women is marriage. In society's perception, women exist solely to satisfy their husbands. For that role, it is not necessary to have any intellectual curiosity. Agatha challenges that perception and redefines the role of women. Marriage is not the sole mission of women. Rather, women share the same mission as men; they are on earth to accomplish something. And if women are, indeed, as responsible as men for achieving great things, then by that token, women need the intellectual challenge of higher education.

Next, Agatha states that society "exerts a powerful influence" by keeping women "in this condition, a rut has been made on the highway, and the wheel slips into it easily and glides along smoothly" (Tiegel, 1893). Again, she uses the strategy of metaphors. This was another strategy to point the finger at "society" and "tradition" that have created a "rut" that everyone follows without much thought. Thus, men have the power to control their destiny, and the highway represents the journey they choose to undertake. Women, however, can only follow the rut in the road laid out before them.

She goes on to argue that women are intellectually equal to men. It is the stimulation of the mind, which society expands or restricts, that makes the difference between women and men:

> There is no inferiority in intellectual capacity, but only neglect of use . . . [It has been] demonstrated in all ages by women whose independence has burst every fetter and won them recognition in the fields of science, theology, literature, politics, and art. . . . She [woman] has often restrained much of her greatness of intellect and soul, she will better do justice to her inborn powers when she has room and light in which to grow. (Tiegel, 1893)

Agatha once again uses the chain metaphor in her use of the word *fetter*. She evokes repeatedly the image of women as chained and restricted. She claims, however, that there is evidence that once women have been allowed to break free from those chains, they can accomplish great things. By stating that women have "inborn powers," she is making the case that it is society that restricts, not biology.

In a response to ideas for a separate curriculum, such as the cooking school for women debated only a few years earlier, Agatha swiftly banishes the idea:

> The idea is absurd that a special course of study should be selected different from the one pursued in the average college under the impression that such a selection would be better adapted to woman's needs and sphere in life. The agitation of this topic is merely the old current of prejudice against learned women turning itself into a new channel when its old one has been dammed up. (Tiegel, 1893)

Agatha effectively ridicules the idea of a separate curriculum, as well as any other idea that might be devised for women only, by labeling such strategies as prejudice. She has already redefined the role of women's presence on earth as that of actors rather than idle spectators. Hence, women need the same course of study as men, one that supports this new vision of women. Her use of the water current image supplies another metaphor that effectively creates the image of the strength of the ongoing prejudices against women. The strong current eventually is "dammed" up; women figuratively build dams to block the streams of prejudice. The currents do not die out, however. Rather, prejudice finds another form, a "new channel."

To close the door on the arguments for separate courses of study, Agatha declares, "No one has a right to say to a woman: 'In this path of knowledge shalt thou walk, and in no other.'" She alludes to religion here, using the "quote" as if it were a religious verse. She reinforces this in her next statement: "knowledge, like religion, admits of . . . no narrowing boundaries."

Agatha then reverts to the metaphor of chains and explicitly compares the treatment of women to that of slaves:

> To argue also, that a woman is not fit to be trusted with her liberty on the score of her emotional nature, her poor powers of logic and judgment, and other character-istics open to criticism, is to copy the fallacies of the opponents of emancipation, who used as arguments those very faults in slaves that slavery had produced. (Tiegel, 1893)

The theme of "woman as slave" was frequently used by women in their work for emancipation at that time. So powerful and effective was this metaphor that it persisted into the twentieth century, even though women could hardly be branded as slaves in later years (Japp, 1985). Agatha's use of the metaphor was, therefore, not only timely but a powerful tool.

Agatha then goes on to refute the claim that women should act and think like women:

> To cry out that she would be unsexed . . . over and above the peculiarities which pertain to a woman as a woman are her needs as a human being. She has her own way to make it in the world, and she will succeed or fail in whatever sphere she moves. (Tiegel, 1893)

To label women "unsexed" if they stepped out of the sphere designed for them by society was a strategy to keep them in their place. Indeed, women who dared to speak in public in the mid–nineteenth century were often labeled "masculine" or "unwomanly" (Campbell, 1989). Accordingly, if one's position was that women should "remain in their place," the logical reasoning to follow would be that there was no need for women to advance their learning. Agatha rebuts this position by raising women from "their" sphere to a universal one that embraces both women and men as "human." As "humans," women are equal to men and therefore have the same rights to higher educational attainment. In so doing, Agatha asserts the right of women to do what they want. They may fail, but it will be on their own terms.

She begins her concluding remarks by acknowledging that the changes made at Gallaudet have been a good start: "It is true that we have made a start in the right direction." She then cautions:

> But that start has been made very recently, and it is still too early to pass sentence on the results. There yet remains a large fund of prejudice to overcome, of false sentiment to combat, of narrow-minded opposition to triumph over. (Tiegel, 1893)

After she cautions her audience that the battle has just begun, she takes on a prophetic stance:

> But there is no uncertainty as to the final outcome. Civilization is too far advanced not to acknowledge the justice of woman's cause. She herself is too strongly impelled by a noble hunger for something better than she has known, too highly inspired by the vista of the glorious future, not to rise with determination and might and move on till all barriers crumble and fall. (Tiegel, 1893)

In her conclusion, she modifies her original stance that society is the evil that obstructs the intellectual advancement of women by asserting that society is too "advanced" to continue these practices. While she is predicting the future rather than stating the present situation, she is also challenging her audience. If her audience is truly progressive, then they will agree that women deserve equal justice. The strategy here is to urge her audience to align themselves with a "civilized" society rather than an "evil" one.

Also in her conclusion, she predicts that women will play a major role in influencing change because women themselves will continue their accession to justice until equality is achieved. With her closing, she has made the case for equality in every respect by prophesying that women will passionately strive for justice until "all barriers crumble and fall." And thus her oratory concluded that Presentation Day on April 26, 1893, at Gallaudet.

• Evaluation

The effectiveness of a presentation can be determined by a number of factors. Agatha's presentation demonstrated the potency of a combination of credibility, circumstance, and aesthetics. Having established her credibility with her peers, faculty, and administrators, she was in an excellent position to take on a controversial topic. She was uniquely qualified to present her cause, being the only female graduate in her class, having survived the trial period for women, and having earned the highest scholastic distinction in her class. She exemplified the Aristotelian characteristics of "good sense, good moral character, and goodwill" and was thus a trustworthy authority.

The circumstances were ideal for the promotion of her cause. As she would say years later (Hanson, 1937), she had chosen a topic on an issue that "burned [her] heart." Clearly, she had seized on the moment of her time to present a cause that she hoped to promote with a captive audience. By doing so, she had capitalized on the unique opportunity that the occasion had presented her.

The quality of aesthetics in Agatha's presentation is remarkable, particularly in two instances. Her use of metaphors is very effective in producing the visual images she chose to make her case. The use of metaphors can often be tricky, because if they are not well woven into the text, they can appear to be merely icing on the cake or superficial decorations. Agatha integrated her metaphors into her presentation so aptly that the desired result was likely achieved. The other quality is her use of arguments. She took several arguments against coeducation and refuted them one by one. She used metaphors and analogies to rebut claims that women were intellectually inferior, that women were not equal to men, and that women needed a separate course of study. She built up her claims by first elaborating on the evils of society, then building her case that women, given every opportunity, could perform equally to men, and finally proceeded to the main argument that all barriers should be thrown out.

Agatha Tiegel's "The Intellect of Woman" presentation clearly had a powerful impact, in large part because of the fusion of credibility, circumstance, and aesthetics.

• Conclusion

On graduation, Agatha went to the Minnesota School for the Deaf, where she taught for six years. She left her position to marry Olof Hanson, an internationally known deaf architect. Agatha never regretted her decision to leave her job, as she enjoyed a happy home life with her husband and children (Agatha, 1944). She continued to be active in deaf organizations and held several offices. Agatha continued to be widely respected, and at a 1948 Gallaudet alumni reunion, she was greeted with "applause ... almost to an ovation" (Andrewjeski, 1948). Her legacy also lives on. The O.W.L.S. literary society, currently known as the Phi Kappa Zeta sorority, that she established is still in existence at Gallaudet and has alumni chapters all over the United States.

Agatha Tiegel Hanson was clearly years ahead of her time. It is a tribute to her forward thinking that deaf women of today can "rise with determination and might and move on till all barriers crumble and fall."

REFERENCES

Agatha Tiegel Hanson: An editorial comment. 1944, December. *North Dakota Banner*, 54:1–2.

Andrewjeski, L. G. 1948. 20th GCAA reunion, June 1947, outstanding success. *Gallaudet Alumni Bulletin*, pp. 6–7.

Aristotle. 1982. *"Art" of rhetoric*. Translated by J. H. Freese. Cambridge, MA: Harvard University Press. (Reprinted from work published in 1926.)

Board of Managers. 1892, November 1. *Buff and Blue*, p. 1.

Brown, J. G. 1888, August 15. Edward Miner Gallaudet correspondence.

Burke, D. 1954, March. The history of drama. *Gallaudet Alumni Bulletin*, p. 2.

Campbell, K. K. 1989. *Man cannot speak for her: A critical study of early feminist rhetoric*. New York: Praeger Press.

Chase, W. K. 1881, May 26. A ladies college. *Deaf-Mutes' Journal*, p. 3.

College Heirlooms. 1895, March 5. *Buff and Blue*, p. 49.

Fay, E. A. 1893, February 23. Letter to Agatha Tiegel. Agatha Tiegel Hanson Papers. Washington, DC: Gallaudet University.

F.J.B., 1892, December 8. College chronicle: A Christmas pantomime. *Deaf-Mutes' Journal*, p. 2.

Gallaudet College Alumni Association. 1900. *Minutes and Proceedings of Association Meetings, 1889–1899*. Grinnell, IA: Waring Press.

General Record, N.D.M.C. (National Deaf-Mutes College) 1:49, 72.

Hanson, A. T. 1937. The Victorian era at Gallaudet. *Buff and Blue*, pp. 5–8.

———. 1948, June. Dr. E. Gallaudet sacrificed family for two-year coed experiment. *Gallaudet Alumni Bulletin*, p. 8.

The Intellect of Women. 1975, January. *The Lamp of Delta Zeta*, pp. 12–13.

Japp, P. M. 1985. Esther or Isaiah? The abolitionist-feminist rhetoric of Angelina Grimke. *Quarterly Journal of Speech*, 71:335–348.

Jones, N. C. 1983. Don't take any aprons to college! A study of the beginning of co-education at Gallaudet College. Unpublished master's thesis, University of Maryland, College Park.

Long, J. S. 1934, January 1. Joseph Schuyler Long, an autobiography. *Iowa Hawkeye*, p. 28.

M.M.T. 1891, October 22. College chronicle: The "Lit."—Our reading room. *Deaf-Mutes' Journal*, p. 2.

———. 1892, April 7. College chronicle: End of term "Exams." *Deaf-Mutes' Journal*, p. 2.

Thirty-sixth Annual Report of the Columbia Institution for the Deaf and Dumb. 1893. Washington, DC: Government Printing Office.

Tiegel, A. 1893, April 26. The intellect of woman. Delivered at Presentation Day exercises. Agatha Tiegel Hanson Papers. Washington, DC: Gallaudet University.

Van. 1888, October 4. College chronicle: Our various societies. *Deaf-Mutes' Journal*, p. 2.

W. B. 1890a, June 26. College chronicle: Closing exercises. *Deaf-Mutes' Journal*, p. 2.

———. 1890b, October 23. College chronicle: First literary meeting of "The Lit." *Deaf-Mutes' Journal*, p. 2.

Wit. [pseudonym]. 1892, December 29. College record: Examinations. *Silent World* (Philadelphia), p. 3.

X [pseudonym]. 1878, March 28. Correspondence: Female teachers. *Deaf-Mutes' Journal*, p. 3.

42

Often it seems that the highest praise the Deaf World can offer one of its own is to say that he or she made a constructive but exceedingly minor contribution to the hearing establishment.

Dummy Hoy

"Play Ball!"

James A. Nickerson

1999

One day in 1966, the year I turned nine, my father came up to me smiling, a book in his hand. The book was Lawrence S. Ritter's *The Glory of Their Times*, a compilation of reminiscences of men who played professional baseball in years ranging from the late 1890s to the 1930s. My father had it opened to the section on Sam Crawford, and it was there I first read of the deaf ballplayer William Ellsworth Hoy. Crawford, described elsewhere as "an educated man of great dignity and varied interests" (James, p. 59), was generous with praise and affection for his teammate from the 1902 Cincinnati Reds, saying that he should be, as Crawford himself was, in the Hall of Fame.

When my father gave me the book, I was at a crossroads in my career as a baseball fan. Growing up near Trenton, New Jersey, I often went with my dad to see the Philadelphia Phillies play in ancient Shibe Park, but it was with the Mets and Yankees that I placed all my nine-year-old passion. I was able to get a fuzzy reception from the New York television stations, the sound of which, I imagine now, would have driven any hearing person to distraction, and I watched both teams religiously, often keeping a scorecard on accounting paper my father would bring home from his job. The Mets were still awful then, and the heretofore mighty Yankees, along with my favorite player, Mickey Mantle, were beginning to match them in ineptness, to my growing and uncomprehending dismay. So when my father gave me the copy of *The Glory of Their Times* he had borrowed from the library, I was perhaps ready for greener pastures, so to speak. The book enthralled me as much as anything I can remember, with its eyewitness retellings of stories of how Germany Schafer once stole first base, the Merkle boner, the incredibly exciting climax of the 1912 World Series, and why Sam Crawford could (occasionally) hit Walter Johnson while his teammate Ty Cobb "couldn't hit him with a ten-foot-pole" (Ritter, p. 52). But it was to Crawford's reminiscences of Dummy Hoy that I kept returning. I had become deaf at the age of five as a result of a bout of spinal meningitis and at that time knew no deaf adults other than the parents of one of my classmates at the Willis and Elizabeth

Martin School, a school for the deaf in Philadelphia that stressed the oral method of instruction and frowned on the use of sign language. To be sure, I had read of "deaf heroes" such as Thomas Edison and Beethoven, and the film version of William Inge's *The Miracle Worker* had recently brought Helen Keller back to the attention of Americans, but for all intents and purposes my deaf community began and ended at the school door. To read of a deaf man who had excelled at the most prestigious occupation imaginable was an astounding and thrilling experience. My father, of course, tried to use Hoy's example as a practical lesson to demonstrate that I myself could expect success from hard work, while I, for the time being, took the narrower and more romantic view that maybe my dream of playing for the Yankees wasn't far-fetched after all.

Many, if not most, baseball fans have not only a favorite team but also a favorite player, and often a fan chooses a player with a similar background to root for. Today, Sammy Sosa is as wildly popular with his fellow Dominicans as his countryman Juan Marichal was in the 1960s. Mexican fans flocked to Los Angles Dodgers games when the great Fernando Valenzuela was scheduled to pitch. Jackie Robinson was unquestionably the most popular player among Black fans while he played, at least in 1947 when he was the only African American in the major leagues, and two decades previously Babe Ruth was extremely popular in the Black community, which may be explained in part by the common belief that he had African American ancestors. Hank Greenberg, in the updated edition of *The Glory of Their Times*, perhaps describes this phenomenon best:

> I realize now, more than I used to, how important a part I played in the lives of a generation of Jewish kids growing up in the thirties. I never thought about it then. But in recent years, men I meet often tell me how much I meant to them when they were growing up. It's almost the first thing a lot of them say to me. . . . When I was playing I used to resent being singled out as a Jewish ballplayer. . . . Lately, though I find myself wanting to be remembered not only as a great ballplayer, but even more as a great *Jewish* ballplayer. (Ritter, p. 330)

Being ignorant of the existence of a vibrant community of signing deaf adults, I didn't then realize that what Crawford described in the book was common knowledge for a great many people. As I recall those days, I find it interesting that Hoy existed for me solely as a deaf baseball player, as I gave no thought to his life off the diamond or even to his interactions with his deaf fans, of which he undoubtedly had a great many. I can remember my father coming up to me early one Sunday morning and saying, "It's a beautiful day. Why don't we go see Willie Mays play?" Although I then had the pick of the National League's best players, for the deaf during the 1890s and early 1900s, their star was Dummy Hoy, and deaf families, I am sure, flocked to see him play, not knowing when, if ever, another deaf player would appear on the scene. Ballparks then were much more intimate than they are now, and the deaf fans, sitting in their carefully chosen seats in the center-field bleachers, would have had conversations with Hoy, much as hearing players and fans have throughout baseball's history. Hoy died at the age of ninety-nine in 1961 (he lived longer than all but one major leaguer ever) and for many years was for many people a flesh-and-blood hero; even now he is the most famous of all deaf athletes. He had been a student at the Ohio School for the Deaf in Columbus and was active in the Cincinnati Deaf community after his retirement, so one can easily picture multiple generations of deaf fathers bringing their sons up to Dummy Hoy and saying, "This man was a great professional baseball player." In "The Amazing Dummy," Stephen Jay Gould portrays Hoy as a generous, well-spoken man, the kind of person who never lacked for friends and admirers. What Crawford had to say about Dummy Hoy was then, to the Deaf community at large, pretty much nothing more than what they had already known for sixty or seventy years. Nevertheless, I have no doubt that the familiarity of Crawford's story did nothing to lessen the joy they experienced at seeing a deaf hero get his due, and perhaps also in providing the hearing world a rare, if small, glimpse into the deaf world.

There is one thing Crawford said that I believe took the Deaf community by surprise and perhaps gave them the most joy and satisfaction. As Crawford tells it:

> Did you know that he was the one responsible for the umpire giving hand signals for a ball or a strike? Raising his right hand for a strike, you know, and stuff like that. He'd be up at bat and he couldn't hear and he couldn't talk, so he'd look around at the umpire to see what the pitch was, a ball or a strike. That's where the hand signs for the umpires calling balls and strikes began. That's a fact. Very few people know that. (Ritter, p. 54)

That *The Glory of Their Times* was and remains an enormously popular and influential book can be shown by the fact that, as Stephen Jay Gould points out, nearly all popular sources today credit Hoy with the introduction of umpire's ball and strike signs. The truth of the matter is, as such truths usually are, much less compelling. In 1909, Albert G. Spalding took it upon himself to discover the origin of these signs, and his conclusion was that their use was begun by a particular umpire in 1905. Given that, in 1909, Hoy had been retired for only seven years and many of his teammates, Crawford included, were still active, it is hard to believe that Spalding, who as president of the Chicago Cubs from 1882 to 1891 surely saw Hoy play many times, could have been kept ignorant of Hoy's real role in the matter, thus denying him his due. More recent research performed by the Hall of Fame could not improve on Spalding's conclusions. In a 1948 interview in the Deaf periodical *Silent Worker*, Hoy himself said that he taught his third-base coach how to inform him of the ball and strike call, and his obituary in the *Cincinnati Enquirer* makes no mention of the issue. To all this Gould says, "I suppose that the pathways of legend must conjure up stories to render the oddly contingent both purposeful and anecdotally touching—in short, to vest the origin of a general practice in a sensible and particular source" (Gould, p. 141). Although I don't like his use of the word *conjure* here, as Crawford's reminiscences of events that had occurred sixty years previous hardly put him in the same league as Parson Weems or Abner Graves, the elderly gentleman who in 1905 provided the myth of Abner Doubleday inventing baseball in Cooperstown, New York, in 1839 (in reality, Doubleday had absolutely nothing to do with it), the truth of this quote is hard to dispute, and once these stories have time to take root, they develop a persistent staying power. Moreover, given the fact that the story makes evolutionary sense, as Hoy *had* to be informed somehow of the umpire's call (Gould guesses that Hoy got the signals from teammates in the dugout), it is safe to say that as long as there are flesh-and-blood umpires, baseball fans everywhere will credit Dummy Hoy for originating the practice of umpires signaling the ball or strike call with their hands.

It is hard to overemphasize the importance of this myth to the Deaf community. Like the great majority of hearing people, deaf people tend to go about their lives in anonymity, and when, for whatever reasons, the world does take notice of a deaf individual, the attention of the Deaf community naturally focuses on this individual. This focus can be positive or negative but is almost never indifferent, as seen in the case of the deaf Miss America Heather Whitestone. At first, Whitestone's triumph was seen as a glorious verification of the ability of the deaf to succeed in whatever field they choose. Afterward, Whitestone, who was raised in an oral environment and came late to sign language, naively implied in an interview that it was better for deaf children to be raised in such an environment than to learn sign language and be raised within the Deaf community. To the Deaf community this was a betrayal, and her reputation among the Deaf has been irreparably damaged. As for Dummy Hoy, this focus has been only positive. For many present-day Americans, the only true meritocracy in our culture is to be found in professional sports; that Hoy, a deaf individual, excelled as a professional baseball player has been a point of great pride in the Deaf community. That he, in addition, played what was in their minds a integral role in establishing the game as it is known today is something to be cherished, in part because of the role this legend plays in keeping his memory alive for the world at large. I believe, however, that this story more than anything else serves the deaf baseball fan as a means of connecting with hearing fans. More than ten thousand men have played major league baseball in the twentieth century; that two or three of them happened to be deaf would be, to a hearing fan at least, not remarkable. For a hearing fan to learn that a deaf player was responsible for the umpire's ball and strike signals is something else altogether and provides that fan with an insight into Deaf mythology that has no parallel in his own culture. A deaf person who tells this story thus takes up a position of authority as a guide into Deaf culture for an eager and curious audience.

Ironically, it appears that this desire to give Dummy Hoy his just due as the inventor of the umpires' signals is precisely what brought the truth of the matter out. Around ten years ago, a group of Hoy fans sent a petition to the Hall of Fame's Veterans Committee with the intention of getting Hoy enshrined in the Hall of Fame. As Gould points out, instead of stressing his ability as a player, much of the emphasis was put on his supposed role in the origin of the umpire's ball and strike signals. As a result, when Spalding's research was uncovered, much of the force behind the petition was dissipated. I believe, as Gould does, that, whether or not the story is true, the emphasis should have been solely on Hoy's skill as a player. Whether or not this strategy would have succeeded is debatable. The Hall of Fame is a peculiar institution, in Bill James's words, "a self-defining institution that has manifestly failed to define itself" (James, p. 175). In his classic book *The Bill James Historical Baseball Abstract*, James, in an attempt to discuss the meaning (or, depending on one's point of view, the meaninglessness) of the Hall of Fame, compares the careers of Billy Herman and Buddy Myer, both second basemen from the 1930s, "probably the two best-matched Hall of Fame candidates that one could name" (James, p. 346). Going into considerable and eye-opening detail, James concludes by asking, "How in the world can you put one of those people (Herman) in the Hall of Fame and leave the other one (Myer) out?" (James, p. 346). James estimates that in 1986 there were 500 to 700 players at or above the level of the worst player in the Hall of Fame, in comparison with the approximately 225 players actually enshrined now. In considering whether or not Dummy Hoy belongs in the Hall of Fame, all I can say that he was a far better and more valuable player in his time than Henie Manush, who is in the Hall of Fame, was in his own time, and a lesser player than Hoy's contemporary Harry Stovey, who is not.

I would love to see Hoy enshrined in Cooperstown, but he was a genuinely a great player regardless of what the Hall of Fame has to say. Even now, nearly thirty-four years after first hearing of him, the picture I have of Dummy Hoy is not much changed from the one I received from Sam Crawford. A certifiable terror on the base paths, he stole 597 bases in his career, third highest number of all time when he retired after the 1902 season and even now, at the end of the 1999 season, the seventeenth highest of all time. As a hitter, he had a lifetime average of .287, a more than decent accomplishment in the dead-ball era he played in; he is still among the top one hundred players in lifetime runs scored (sixty-fourth) and triples (ninety-fifth). Because he played in four leagues from 1888 to 1902, it is difficult to assess his year-to-year statistics in relation to his peers, but a look at his record with the 1901 Chicago White Sox speaks volumes about his talent. That year, at the age of thirty-nine, he was third in the American League in runs scored, the year Napoleon Lajoie led the league with 145 runs to go along with his .422 average. It is hard for the layman to evaluate any player's efficiency on defense, much less that of one who played a hundred years ago, but that Hoy was a great center fielder is clear. According to Crawford, "even late in his career he was a fine outfielder. A *great* one" (Ritter, p. 53), and this is easy to see even now. That he had a great arm is evidenced from his being, in 1889, the first of three players ever to throw three base runners out at home plate from the outfield in the same game, and his great speed enabled him in 1897, at the advanced age of thirty-five, to lead National League outfielders in putouts and total chances per game.

Those players from the 1890s who are remembered now tend to be those who have been enshrined in the Hall of Fame, and it seems to me that many of these men, besides being fine ballplayers, were colorful characters with catchy nicknames. For example, two of Hoy's contemporaries who were comparable to him in playing style were "Wee Willie" Keeler, who "Hit 'em where they ain't," and "Sliding Billy" Hamilton, both of whom are in the Hall of Fame. Stephen Jay Gould has a theory that Hoy's deafness led to his being ignored and patronized by the sportswriters of his day, and he was, as a result, much less likely to be known to later fans, particularly Hall of Fame voters. It is a lazy man's conclusion to say that since so many great players are in the Hall of Fame, anyone who has not been enshrined in Cooperstown must not be a great player; this makes as much sense as saying that because F. Scott Fitzgerald never won the Nobel Prize, he was not a great writer. The 1890s were full of players such as Bill Lange, Pete Browning, Harry Stovey, and Dummy Hoy who went to the ballpark with the single goal of winning that day's baseball game and were exceedingly good at doing just that. That they went about their jobs without unnecessary flash or show, that they didn't catch the eye of important sportswriters, or that they, like Hoy, are virtually unknown today is irrelevant.

I have seen only one photograph of Dummy Hoy. Taken in 1888, it shows him standing in a photographer's studio in his uniform, a bat by his side and a pastoral landscape behind him. He looks as if he were wishing he could get out of there and go do what he did best, play baseball.

BIBLIOGRAPHY

Gould, Stephen Jay. "The Amazing Dummy." In *Forgotten Heroes: Inspiring American Portraits from Our Leading Historians*, edited by Susan Ware. New York: Free Press, 1998.
James, Bill. *The Bill James Historical Baseball Abstract*. New York: Villard Books, 1986.
Ritter, Lawrence S. *The Glory of Their Times*. New York: Quill, 1992.
Swope, Tom. "Eighty-six Year Old Dummy Hoy Still Likes Baseball." *Silent Worker* 1, 1 (September 1948): 27–28.
Ward, Geoffrey C., and Ken Burns. *Baseball, an Illustrated History*. New York: Knopf, 1996.

V | "Strengthening the spirit of clannishness"

The Deaf Community

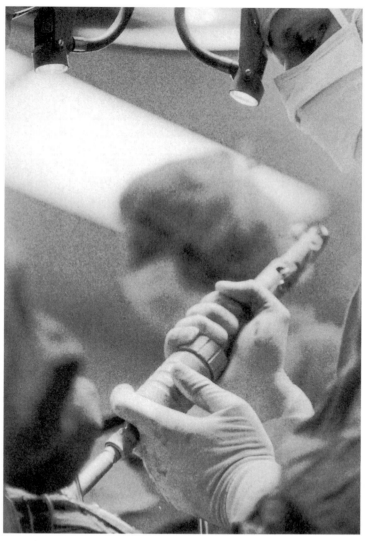

Care for a cochlear implant? Cranial excavation procedure. ©
Willy Conley.

43

The clannishness among Deaf people that the hearing have long found so off-putting, even insulting, might better be seen as the sincerest form of flattery: imitation. Like a postcolonial capital, the Deaf community mirrors and often exaggerates the faults of the still-dominant culture.

Racism within the Deaf Community

Glenn B. Anderson and Frank G. Bowe

1972

In the wake of a rising trend toward "Black Pride," a growing impatience with second-class citizenship, and a burgeoning militancy toward obtaining legal and social rights among black people, the black deaf have been overlooked. It is a cause for concern that extensive apathy and indifference continue to exist among professionals and laymen alike with respect to the gross under-education, mass under-employment, and severe social isolation of blacks who are deaf.[1,2] Fortunately, scattered efforts in various parts of the country give promise that the lot of the black deaf may be alleviated significantly in the decades to come.

The literature in deafness has begun to reflect the growing concern over special problems of the black deaf. At the Leadership Training Program in San Fernando Valley State College, two seminal papers—one by Ernest Hairston and John Bachman,[3] the other by Linwood Smith[4]—have explored characteristics of the black deaf population in Los Angeles and in the Watts area. The *American Annals of the Deaf* recently printed a review of the literature in this area.[1] Talks have been presented to the Convention of American Instructors of the Deaf[2] and to the American Psychological Association.[5] Symposia and panel discussions were held for the first time in 1972 at major conferences such as the PRWAD, ACB, and a conference on deafness at Gallaudet College.

Impressive as some of these activities might appear in contrast to the quiescence of just four years ago, they only scratch the surface of the total problem. This paper will concern itself with some of the many unmet needs of the black deaf population. Problems already considered in previous papers by the authors[1,2,5] will receive only passing attention here. The interested reader is referred to the earlier articles for additional information.

• Lack of Integration

Certainly it is no secret that there is relatively little integration of whites and blacks in the adult deaf community. Vernon[6] has noted that there was a smaller number and proportion of blacks in his Chicago project than might have been expected. He suggested that the lack of black representation at the staff level, with a resulting difficulty in communicating with black deaf persons through established channels, and the limited integration of blacks and whites in the Chicago deaf social stratum might have accounted for the low percentage of black deaf persons in the study. He also points out that few efforts have been made to account for the isolation of black deaf from white deaf, nor to understand the nature and consequences of this isolation as it pertains to the black deaf adult.

These manifestations of racism in the deaf community appear over a broad range of degrees. Certain remarks by George Ayers in a recent issue of *Journal of Rehabilitation* contribute to this orientation. He observes that: "Many whites fail to recognize, much less accept, the fact that racist attitudes have been institutionalized and transmitted generation to generation among their people. They can't see that forms of racism have ranged from unconscious to overt, benign to malignant." In this connection we might contrast certain forms of indirect discrimination with more overt manifestations.

On the one end of such a scale we find that black deaf persons do not learn of services available to deaf people in their areas because of their limited contact with professionals in the field and with the mainstream of deaf life.[4] Consequently they frequently do not take advantage of such services to the extent that the white deaf do.

Furthermore, there are numerous cases in which deaf clubs specifically deny membership to black deaf persons, or at least its members act in such a manner as to make a potential black member unwilling to join. In other situations' deaf clubs request athletic services of black deaf persons while refusing to grant them full membership privileges. For instance, in the Detroit area there are two major clubs for the deaf with a combined membership of over 250. The smaller club has a total of ten black members, all athletes. The larger club does not have black members, yet they admit black individuals for social events.

• Young People

It seems appropriate to include in this context a discussion of some typical problems a deaf Afro-American may face during the developmental stages of his growth toward adulthood. All too commonly many black parents are undereducated, victims of white oppression and of other social ills. They are often too overburdened with their own strength-sapping responsibilities of trying to survive and support their families to have the time and energy to facilitate the educational and personal development of their children.

One manifestation of this phenomenon is the extreme lack of preparation possessed by many black deaf children at the time of school entrance. While numerous white deaf children have benefited from pre-school education and home encouragement, too many black deaf children come to school lacking virtually any speech or language. Their often chaotic home environments give birth to a multitude of personality problems, general confusion, and total bewilderment with the unexpected challenge of formal education. Consequently, the educator must be knowledgeable and sensitive to the problems of children from inadequate home environments. Unfortunately, in the majority of the fifty-eight teacher training programs listed in the April, 1972 *American Annals of the Deaf Directory of Programs and Services*, courses in minority studies are not included as part of their curriculum. This lack of knowledge and sensitivity may in part explain why some of the aforementioned studies have indicated lower academic achievement among the black and other minority group deaf youth.

These conditions, combined with the educational implications of deafness, impose a tremendous barrier for an individual who is black and deaf. The poor communication skills that these persons develop[2] as compared with those of the average white deaf person, in many ways account for their being snubbed and rejected in the deaf social and cultural milieu.

In schools for the deaf, the black students learn very little about themselves, the problems of their people, or the contributions of their ancestors. They are exposed to texts oriented toward a belief in white supremacy. They learn that their ancestors were savages brought in from Africa for use as slaves in America. The many contributions of black Americans, with some isolated exceptions such as those of George Washington Carver, are glossed over if mentioned at all. The rise of the Black Panthers, the race riots, the black student demands and rebellions in high schools and colleges, the "Black Power" slogan, and countless other concepts and incidents are generally discussed from the white point of view, if indeed they are mentioned at all. The black student finds that he has no one to turn to understand these happenings. For example, the little available information indicates that there are fewer than twenty black deaf teachers in the schools for the deaf.

On the campuses of schools for the deaf, the black student often takes an active part in athletics. We feel it is one of the few areas in which he is permitted, even encouraged, by his background and environment to excel. Yet, he often is not able to participate actively in some of the other affairs enjoyed by his white counterparts in school. The senior author of this paper vividly recalls many occasions in which classmates reserved facilities for class functions, such as picnics and parties, which were closed to blacks.

• Summary

Racism in the deaf community is an issue that has received far too little attention from professionals and laymen alike. Hardly any literature exists regarding the race problems, the socio-economic and educational problems, the socio-economic and educational problems, and the needs of the black deaf community.[1] Attention must focus on the paucity of black deaf professionals and community leaders; on the lack of involvement by the black community in local, state, and national affairs of the deaf; the social isolation of black deaf persons; and the undereducation and under-employment manifest among this population.

In the past decade we have seen an increase in the provision of services to the deaf population. Stereotyping and discrimination by the hearing community are being attacked in a constructive manner. Similar efforts are needed on behalf of the most neglected segment of this minority group, the black deaf.

REFERENCES

1. F. G. Bowe, "Nonwhite Deaf Persons: Educational, Psychological and Occupational Considerations,"*American Annals of the Deaf*, Vol. 116, No. 3, 357–361, 1971.
2. F. G. Bowe, "Some Observations on the Education and Rehabilitation of Black Deaf Persons" (paper delivered to the 45th Meeting, Convention of American Instructors of the Deaf, Little Rock, Arkansas, June 28, 1971).
3. E. E. Hairston and J. Bachman, "A Study of a Segment of the Negro Deaf Population in the Los Angeles Area" (unpublished master's thesis, San Fernando Valley State College, 1967).
4. L. D. Smith, "The Hard-Core Negro Deaf Adult in Watts" (unpublished master's thesis, San Fernando Valley State College, 1971).
5. F. G. Bowe, "Educational, Psychological and Occupational Aspects of the Nonwhite Deaf Population" (paper delivered to American Psychological Association, Washington D.C., September 5, 1971).
6. In: R. S. Grinker, ed., *Psychiatric diagnosis, therapy and research on the psychotic deaf*, final report Grant No. RD-2407-s, Washington, D.C.: Social and Rehabilitation Service, 1969.
7. George E. Ayers, "The White Counselor in the Black Community,"*Journal of Rehabilitation*, April, 1970.

44

Community maintenance often takes the form of policing the boundaries: who is in and who is out; who is central and who is peripheral. Cochlear implants may be a genuine threat to Deaf culture (by reducing our numbers and by turning public opinion against those of us who want to keep our skulls intact), or they may prove to be just another kind of overhyped snake oil, like lipreading. Whatever the future reveals about the true significance of cochlear implants, their appearance on the borderland of the Deaf World has inspired a minirenaissance of Deaf activism.

GLAD Publishes Position Paper on Cochlear Implants

Carol Padden

1985

After eighteen months of meetings and research, the GLAD Ad Hoc Committee on Ear Surgery has completed a position paper on cochlear implants, the newest medical device for deaf people. Cochlear implants involve surgery to implant one or more electrodes in the inner ear which are connected to an outside device approximately the size of a hearing aid. The committee's first concern was the fact that until very recently, cochlear implants were used only with adults, but now very young children are being implanted with these devices. Are these implants safe for deaf children? Are they necessary? What do audiologists, doctors and other professionals think about this new development? The committee also wanted to know what the effects of the implant were on adults.

The committee is made up of members of the deaf community as well as professionals in the area of special education, language and communication: Samuel Block, former Board member of the National Association of the Deaf, Dr. Lawrence Fleischer, Professor of Special Education at California State University, Northridge, Joyce Groode, Assistant Professor of Special Education at California State University, Northridge, Dr. Tom Humphries, Associate Dean at San Diego Community College District, and Dr. Carol Padden, Assistant Professor of Communication at University of California, San Diego.

The committee gathered information about the medical aspects of cochlear implants and their present use in the United States. Almost all publicity about cochlear implants emphasizes the positive, but rarely mentions that many audiologists and doctors do not support use of implants with children. The committee found that most public information about cochlear implants is available only from clinics performing the surgery to place implants in the cochlea, or from brief newspaper articles; accordingly, the committee's first task was to interview individuals who were considering or had had the surgery, to review articles in medical journals, and to interview audiologists and medical ethicists. The committee also talked with an implant clinic staff about these concerns.

The report itself, in addition to an introduction framing the background against which the committee was formed, has four sections: (1) a brief description of cochlear implants and the surgery performed to place these devices in the cochlea, (2) common misconceptions about cochlear implants, (3) key issues about the devices and the surgery itself, and (4) recommendations.

The task of writing a report as a summary of the committee's investigations was clearly difficult. As stated in the introduction, "This document contains some basic information about cochlear implants, but we do not discuss in detail the medical aspects of the implant. Instead we have taken a different role: we want to direct attention to implications of the procedure . . . and to ask the public to re-examine the procedure in more careful and dispassionate ways." Consequently, "In order that the debate include the alternative views, we have taken strong positions."

• What Is a Cochlear Implant?

The first section contains a brief description of what the cochlea is, and what type of damage takes place when a device is implanted. There are two basic types of implants: single-channel and multi-channel, and clinics disagree about which type of implant is most effective. One of the leading clinics performing cochlear implant surgery, the House Ear Institute in Los Angeles, uses the single-channel device which implants only one electrode. Other clinics such as Symbion, Inc. in Salt Lake City, Utah, use the multi-channel device and argue it has better possibilities for sound variance than the single-channel device. But supporters of the single-channel implant say that their device is medically simpler; it does not have a "pedestal" or "plug" extending from behind the ear. Primarily because of its simplicity, it has been approved for use with children.

But in a recent issue of the journal *Ear and Hearing*, a prominent otolaryngologist from the Stanford University Medical Center raised many difficult questions about whether implants should be used with children. He argues that medical simplicity is not enough. Cochlear implants have not yet been demonstrated to be truly effective enough to support their use with children. The committee found that he is not the only one raising objections. Many audiologists share his concerns, but aside from a few articles discussing possible problems with implant surgery for children, there is very little publicity about this opposition.

• What Is the Quality of Sound with a Cochlear Implant?

The report also contains a discussion about what people with cochlear implants "hear," to quote: ". . . Does the implant restore hearing? The answer is no. This is one fact on which the clinics and researchers agree. The patients do not 'hear' in the same way as normal hearing people do. They must learn . . . to interpret electrical buzzes, pops and noises sent to the auditory nerve (via the electrode) as 'sound'." For adults who have lost their hearing, many say this is satisfactory replacement "sound." The committee also found that some patients "can identify environmental sounds, distinguish between male and female voices, and monitor their own voices," but human speech is still out of reach for most of them.

• What Is Involved in the Surgery to Implant the Device?

As for the surgery itself, many people think it is a simple procedure and the implant works like a hearing aid, but implanted in the ear. This is not correct. The surgery involves general anesthesia and drilling through the hard bone behind the ear, the mastoid bone. Also, in order to place an implant in the cochlea, the procedure destroys living tissue in the cochlea. Because of this destruction, implants are used only in "ears (which) . . . are already profoundly deaf." Doctors are uncertain how much damage can result from not only implant surgery itself, but also long-term damage to other areas of the ear. Possible complications include tinnitus, temporary facial paralysis, and otitis, but in one published report supporting the use of implant surgery with children, the authors say there have been no "serious complications," and one implant clinic staff assured members of the committee that there have been no cases of "permanent" but only "temporary" facial paralysis resulting from the surgery. But the committee was not able to find out "how long such cases last."

• Common Misinformation about Cochlear Implants

The next section addresses common misinformation being spread about cochlear implants by newspapers, doctors from clinics performing cochlear implant surgery, and others who are promoting use of the implants. Four major areas of misinformation were identified. The first common erroneous claim was: "the amount of increase in hearing which results from ear surgery and implantation has a direct relation to the quality of a person's life." The committee found that often publicity about the implants implies that a person's life will be "significantly enhanced" by small changes in level of sound perception. Apparently many adults who have received the implant, especially those who lost their hearing late in life, have found the implant valuable. But there are others who do not feel the same way. As stated, "The view that hearing, no matter how much (or how little), has the power to change social, political, economic or psychological conditions for the individual is simplistic."

The next two claims which the committee reviewed deal with misinformation about the implant. The public seems to feel that new technology and medical surgery is is far better than the much cheaper and conventional hearing aid. But Daniel Ling, a well-known educator of deaf children admits that "the single-channel implant provides little spectral information and probably less than would be available to a profoundly deaf child who is provided with appropriate amplification." An implant, including surgery, hospital costs and rehabilitation, can cost upwards of $12,000 compared to $600 for a hearing aid.

The committee then asked whether damage to the cochlea might preclude future technological advances which require intact ears and found that other doctors are asking the same question and expressing concern that we may be destroying children's ears for limited benefit.

Another common area of misinformation is the claim that cochlear implants improve reading skills. The report says that "There is no evidence to show that these devices have any relationship to improvements in educational achievement." In addition, the report states that "Being able to read is the consequence of different factors, including . . . understanding of grammatical structure of the language as well as other environmental factors such as child-rearing practices, cultural patterns and home environment. Awareness of a range of loud noises cannot make up for these complex factors."

- Issues

Six different issues were raised in the report. They are summarized here, but readers are encouraged to review the full paper for more detail. The first concerns the type of publicity that has come out of the public attention to implant surgery. In one newspaper article, an implant recipient was described as having miraculously avoided being hit by a car because of her implant. The committee felt that this type of publicity "conveys a mistaken impression that Deaf people are frequently the victims of car accidents . . . and implant procedures are needed to prolong their lives." The report goes on to say that "There is a subtle, yet clear impression (in the publicity about cochlear implants) that our lives are fraught with fear and unmitigated disaster."

The committee felt that implant clinics should take special care to avoid conveying such impressions to the press. It is true that the press will come up with its own interpretations, but this does not relieve the clinics' responsibility to make sure the media avoids negative publicity about deaf people.

Another issue about which the report raises concerns is whether "adult patients or parents of deaf children are always protected from unreasonable expectations from the ear surgery and implantation." Although there is often a disclaimer in the clinics' materials that "one must guard against unreasonable expectations about implants," the fact remains that there is high-pressure publicity about the successes of the implants and many claims are made about improvement of reading skills and speaking ability. The report gives another quote from the previously cited article in the journal *Ear and Hearing* which is worth repeating here:

> The pressures will be tremendous if my mail is any indication. Parents, and especially grandparents, who encounter enthusiastic testimonials for this new miracle, are going to get implants for their children. They will find the money. Implants offer hope beyond what educators of the deaf and audiologists are realistically able to promise. To be fair, the staff of the House Ear Institute are not promising miracles for their implants, but they are enthusiastically selling hope, and hope is a powerful commodity.

In connection to the "hope" which people seem to desperately want for their deaf children, there is a fact which many people fail to recognize. Implants do not restore hearing, thus implants in children "do not create a new group of hearing children, but create a special group of deaf children who, according to any assessment of hearing impairment are just as likely to need special education." The committee says that "from all information we have, children who receive the implant continue to need the services of teachers trained to teach deaf children, speech therapists, audiologists and special education." Two other authors in recently published articles have come to the same conclusion. The report says plainly: "It should be made clear to society that it will need to support both expensive procedures as well as rehabilitation because the (implant) procedure does not remove hearing loss."

The last issue discussed in the report concerns the varied impact of implants on the individual: "Not all Deaf people want the implant. The benefit in terms of improvement of quality of life is not uniform in the eyes of the recipient." In its interviews with recipients of implants, the committee found that they report "tremendous benefit and . . . have received emotional and psychological gain from having the implant." Many recipients of implant devices are typically adults who have lost their hearing late in life and still have memory or knowledge of sound. But other deaf individuals have abandoned use of their devices due to inconvenience or other reasons.

The committee expressed concern that the medical profession has little knowledge of, or ignores the different attitudes held by deaf people about their deafness, and consequently about implants. The report includes a short description of the different attitudes expressed by deaf people about implants.

The public seems fascinated with implants because it promises a modern, medical approach to a "problem" of hearing impairment, but the committee observes that deaf people vary with respect to how they view their "problem." Some do not view implants as "a tool to fix a defect, but to add to the repertoire of tools that an individual has available. Some individuals will choose to have such a tool, and others will not." The fact that an implant is irreversible is a factor influencing an adult's choice about whether to have an implant. But they are free to make their own choices. In the case of very young deaf children, the choice is made for them by someone else. Based on what is known (and not known) about effectiveness of implants, doctors, audiologists and deaf people have asked that implant surgery on children be seriously reconsidered.

In summary, the report takes some strong positions in order to force the debate to include all viewpoints, including those that are little-publicized. Medical technology is now the darling of the public; we read daily about new "breakthroughs," and publicity about artificial hearts is still in the forefront. But the public must seriously look behind the hype and the gloss and ask hard questions: (1) is the surgery really necessary? (2) is the public romance with medicine pressuring deaf people and children to have the surgery? (3) do the real gains of the implants justify the enormous expense of the medical costs, rehabilitation in addition to special education which is still required? and (4) most difficult, can we be assured deaf children receiving implants are really benefiting from them, or are they serving as an experimental pool?

• Recommendations

The report gives seven recommendations; they are printed here in entirety:

The committee recommends:

(1) That information be prepared based on accurate information about Deaf people and ear surgery and implantation and that all doctors, clinics, and hospitals, or others engaged in ear surgery and implantation be asked to voluntarily distribute this information to each and every person requesting information about ear surgery and implantation. It is further recommended that, if after a reasonable time, it is determined that voluntary compliance is not working, legislative mandate be sought to require the distribution of such information in this manner.

(2) That public forums be organized to identify concerns regarding ear surgery and implantation and that these concerns once identified become part of the informational effort above.

(3) That a consumer protection unit be established to explore product safety, product claims, consumer satisfaction, comparable worth of products, cost-benefit analysis and any other consumer concerns.

(4) That the monitoring and consumer protection units identify and publicize areas where questions about risks of ear surgery and implantation have not been answered and encourage research in these areas.

(5) That a special effort be made during all these recommended actions to reach the parents of young deaf children and provide them with accurate and complete information.

(6) That clinics performing implant procedures recognize and address negative media representations of deaf people as fearful, prone to disaster and in desperate need of the facility of hearing. The medical profession cannot in good conscience reap the benefits of public support of medicine and refuse to correct potential hysteria resulting from their efforts.

(7) That the FDA recognize the growing dissent among professionals, doctors and deaf people about the current practice of implants in children and return implant research on children to an experimental level until key questions about destruction of living tissue and invasive techniques in children are adequately answered.

45

As integration continues apace, the occasional valiant effort by a Deaf person or group to stage a cultural event on the Deaf community's own terms more often than not finds that event colonized by the hearing. (This practice will stop when the Deaf community ceases to provide English interpreters for the audio-dependent.)

Reflections on The Deaf Way

Bob Alcorn

1989

Now that several weeks have passed since the monumental occasion known as The Deaf Way, I feel the need to share my reflections on the conference with others. Many good things happened at The Deaf Way—many of the presentations dealt honestly with the oppression of Deaf people in various countries and made strong recommendations regarding steps to liberate Deaf people; several papers were presented sharing progressive ideas related to Deaf empowerment. A variety of interpreters were selected—including Deaf relay interpreters—who demonstrated a wide range of skills and they were appropriately placed where all could shine. There was a delightful variety of programming from formal presentations to workshops, plays to art shows. From the international Deaf Club to the hotel lobby encounters of long-time friends, there were thousands of Deaf people from all over the world all using their various sign languages and all coming to the common ground of visual-gestural communication when communicating across national boundaries.

There were many good things about The Deaf Way; however, I must also take note of some things that left me with an empty feeling in the pit of my stomach.

Was The Deaf Way really the Deaf *way*? The sign used for "way" in the sign version of *The Deaf Way* actually means *tendency, typical, characteristic of.* In my opinion, many of the workshops, papers, and presenters were NOT characteristic of the way Deaf people think, behave, or act. Some of the presenters were hearing Ph.D.s who talked about deafness, deaf education, and deaf people from an inadequate base of knowledge and/or information about Deaf ways, views, values, or beliefs. While a hearing person may know many things about Deaf culture, at a conference titled The Deaf Way, it seems more appropriate for a Deaf person who has lived the culture and who is a member of the cultural group to make such a presentation, rather than one who knows about the culture second hand. It is admirable for a woman who has been deafened after a long career as a professional actress and dancer to make a psychological and sociological adjustment to her new status of deafness, but it is NOT the Deaf way to perform tap dance, complete with costumes

316

in a review of famous types of tapology. It is nice that hearing educators who work with Deaf children wanted to talk about the latest educational methods, but isn't it time the hearing educators heard about Deaf education from the Deaf point of view? Is it the Deaf way to charge outrageous registration fees and then oversell a conference so that paying attendees cannot get a seat to hear the presentations made? I think not!

Likewise, many of the exhibits did not reflect the Deaf way of culture, life or attitudes. Are the Alexander Graham Bell Association, distributors of SEE books, or computers which assist hearing impaired people improve their speech reflective of Deaf people and their views? I think not!

Were the native dances performed by Deaf individuals truly reflecting the Deaf way within those countries or were they reinforcement for the oppression Deaf people continue to endure because they lack the freedom to develop their own art forms— apart from music, sound, and other remnants of hearing art forms?

I strongly urge the future planners of The Deaf Way to do a better job of screening presenters to insure that the genuine Deaf way is reflected in papers, presenters, and workshops. Use DEAF people, rather than deafened, hearing impaired, or hearing people to make presentations. Look at the topics of papers and workshops to determine whether they truly reflect the Deaf way before accepting those papers. Exhibits should be selected on the basis of their reflection of Deaf ways rather than on the basis of who could afford a $750 fee, and more Deaf exhibitors should be included. Deaf authors, producers, artists, and craftsmen should be featured if this is to truly be the Deaf *way*.

46

Community maintenance and boundary control often proceed by highlighting differences between Deaf people and all others, implying that for any given issue involving Deaf people, only Deaf people themselves have the requisite moral authority to define and decide. In most cases, that is exactly right.

Can Deaf People Survive "deafness"?

MJ Bienvenu

1991

This collection of essays [in which this article originally appeared] is entitled, "Perspectives on Deafness." And I'm sure many of you have heard of people who work "in the field of deafness." But let me ask you . . . what is *deafness*? I would like to quote from a short article by Charlie Rancke, printed in *TBC News* No. 9, December 1988:

> *Field of Deafness.* Hmmm . . . what does that mean? I have heard of other fields like veterinary science or horticulture or interpreting, but I haven't yet heard of the fields of animalness or plantness or languageness. . . . If one is an educator of Deaf students, is s/he involved in the Field of Deafness? or the Field of Education? If one is an interpreter, doesn't s/he work *for* Deaf people rather than in the field of their physical difference from hearing people? . . . Let's not apply pathological language to people who can't hear. You may be a specialist in your chosen field of education, counseling, management, whatever. And you may choose to work with and/or for Deaf people. I know one thing: that is *not* the Field of Deafness.

Can you imagine having a Field of Blackness, or a Field of Womanness? That is equally as ridiculous as having such a term as the field of 'deafness.' Yet these words have been allowed to describe the members of the Deaf[1] community. For a long time, people have patronized Deaf people, lamenting the loss of our hearing. Unfortunately, what the general public does not know is that we are not people with a loss, but that we are a cultural, minority group. It is time that we stopped being passive, and boldly declared our objections about how we are defined by non-Deaf people. No one can describe Black people except Black people themselves. Stokely Carmichael accurately asserted:

> It [definition] is very, very important because I believe that people who can define are masters. (Bosmajian, 1983)

318

It's about time we Deaf people declare who we are without having our community defined and described by non-Deaf professionals who more than likely have not taken one course in ASL or American Deaf Culture. Instead, they are well versed in the psychology of deafness, educating the deaf, audiology/speech therapy, etc. I'm sure most of you can fill out the rest of their medical course history, and imagine the textbooks they have written.

All too often hearing people, especially in the medical and educational systems, have regarded Deaf people as handicapped or disabled. People often ask me, "What is it like to be deaf?" I have always thought that was a strange question, kind of like asking what it's like being a PWA (person with AIDS) or what it is like having cancer. When looked at from a cultural perspective, of course, Deaf people are not victims of a disease. Yet, the people who hold a pathological perspective have vigorously sought ways to prevent and cure deafness; they have devised "intervention" programs for deaf children that begin at younger and younger ages. A recent ruling by the FDA now makes it possible for parents to determine the future of their deaf children by forcing cochlear implants into the skulls of infants.

While these people are busy trying desperately to make deaf people into hearing people, those of us who are culturally Deaf hold a very different perspective. Our immediate response is, "What do you mean when you talk about prevention, cure, and early intervention? Do you want to eliminate people like us from the face of the earth?" Rather than prevention, many Deaf parents want to have Deaf children. We are interested in passing on our rich heritage to Deaf children who are fine, just as we are fine. We do not want or need to become hearing in order to consider ourselves normal. For us, early intervention does not mean ear phones, amplifiers and training a child to appear as hearing as possible. Instead, a good early intervention program would offer deaf children and hearing parents early exposure to ASL and many opportunities to interact with Deaf adults. From our perspective, we are a minority group with our own language, culture and heritage.

The Gallaudet uprising focused much attention on Deaf people. Now, three years later, some organizations for the Deaf have started to identify with the disabled in order to have more political clout. I question that strategy. Although, as individuals, we may support the struggles of disabled people, we need to ask ourselves who benefits when we attempt to work in coalition with disability groups. Do we have the same goals? With the passing of the Americans with Disabilities Act, many of us were disappointed to be labeled "disabled" once again.

Those with a hearing loss who do not speak ASL, and who don't associate with Deaf people, would probably feel comfortable under the umbrella of the ADA; however, those of us who consider ourselves culturally Deaf are reticent to celebrate. The people who have accepted themselves as disabled are those who have truly lost their hearing—from advancing age, from injury, or from some kind of disease. However, many of us haven't lost our hearing—we were born deaf or were born with genes that would eventually lead us to become deaf. It is ironic that many Deaf

Awareness events I have been to try to educate the public about the negative label "handicapped," yet these same people rooted for the advancement of Deaf people's rights enveloped within the ADA.

I am a firm believer in the benefits of political action. I cannot help but wonder why we have not been able to introduce a bill specifically for Deaf people—who have the right to a TTY (please note that I use the term "TTY," not "tdd"),[2] a decoder, and interpreting services because we come from a different culture that speaks a different language. We do not have the same needs as the disabled, because they hear and speak English. Since most Americans speak English, they are more likely to understand and communicate with those who cannot see or walk. We can succeed on our own, as we have in the past, or by joining with other minority language groups. Our goals for education, and our concerns about oppression and lack of understanding are similar. Many Deaf people have also embraced the political scene as a cultural unit, organizing to obtain formal credit for ASL as a foreign language. How can we fight for official recognition of ASL and allow ourselves to be labeled "communication disordered" at the same time?

How we label ourselves is very important. I don't know many deaf people who would define themselves as "communication disordered," yet that is the term many social service agencies and schools use to describe the deaf population with whom they work. How many people do you know have called themselves "hearing impaired" rather than Deaf—and is there a difference? My dictionary defines "impaired" as "to make worse by or as if by diminishing in some material respect." In my computer's thesaurus program, synonyms listed for the word "impaired" are: ill, unhealthy, ailing, delicate, diseased, down, frail, indisposed, sick, sickly, suffering, unsound, unwell, and weak. Imagine all the negative connotations of the word people are using to describe us. We are people with our own language and culture, and we already have a way to describe ourselves—DEAF. Bosmajian also wrote:

> Self-determination must include self-definition, the ability and right to name oneself; the master/subject relationship is based partly on the master's power to name and define the subject. . . . While names, words and language can be and are used to inspire us, to motivate us to humane acts, to liberate us, they can also be used to dehumanize human beings and to "justify" their suppression and even their extermination. (Bosmajian, 1983)

After having described what we are not, allow me to talk about Deaf people in terms of who we are. There are books and videotapes recently made which accurately portray American Deaf culture (ADC). Padden and Humphries (1988) wrote *Deaf in America: Voices from a Culture*, an introductory view of ADC filled with basic information and very educational for people who have never met Deaf adults. Susan Rutherford (1984) produced a four-part videotape series, *American Culture: The Deaf Perspective: Deaf Folklore*. The tapes are both entertaining and instructional, and detail many parts of ADC. There is also a five-part videotape series developed by Betty Colonomos and myself, *An Introduction to American Deaf Culture* (1985–1988). The goal of this series was to educate people about the Deaf community. We explore who we are—as a cultural group—and help to eliminate the pathological perspective held by non-Deaf people as well as some misinformed and oppressed Deaf people.

Deaf people have their own language—ASL. Because we are an oppressed culture, people have often tried to *define* ASL. However, no language is definable, it can only be described—in terms of grammatical rules, how it works, how it is used, and so on. ASL is *not* derived from English, nor is it a generic term for any form of communication that uses the hands. There seem to be so many myths about ASL, I would like to take this opportunity to clarify some of the more glaring misconceptions.

Myth No. 1: ASL Has Free Word Order

In fact ASL has its own word order and structure. Most basic ASL sentences place the verb at the end. It is also a topic prominent language, which means that sentences begin with a marker (in the case of ASL, raised eyebrows at the beginning of a sentence shows area of focus).

Myth No. 2: ASL Forbids Mouth Movement

Actually ASL has many nonmanual modifiers, which serve as adjectives and adverbs, on the mouth. There are also specific lip movements which are found in ASL, different from English mouthing, which are not simply silent "pronunciations" of English words.

Myth No. 3: ASL Is a Picture Language

People are now beginning to realize how much complex grammar is on the face. Ursula Bellugi conducted a study to see if ASL signs were iconic, as many people claimed. She discovered that most ASL words she used for the research could not be correctly identified by non-Deaf viewers. Some words in ASL (about 15%) are transparent. Research (see Klima and Bellugi 1979) has shown that non-signers cannot figure out the meanings of most ASL signs, and can only see connections between signs and things when they are given the meaning beforehand. All languages, including English, have some vocabulary that looks/sounds like the things they represent (e.g. hum, hiss, hiccup, snore/sneeze/snout). There is also some obvious evidence that this can't be true: if ASL were merely a picture language, then why is it so difficult for intelligent hearing and deaf people to learn to use it fluently? This idea has been perpetuated by people whose bias holds that a legitimate language must be spoken; it came into use to prohibit signing among Deaf children and adults by those who favored the oral philosophy.

Myth No. 4: ASL Only Represents Concrete Ideas and Has Difficulty Representing Technical Terminology

I know many Deaf people who discuss love, religion, philosophy, education and politics in their language, ASL. English has no more than ten words to describe "snow," while some Eskimo languages have more than sixty ways to discuss unique varieties of snow. This does not mean that Eskimos have a more technical language than English speakers. It is a clear demonstration that language will provide an ample vocabulary to discuss what is important to its culture. If you think about it, you will realize that ASL has far more words related to the concept of "visual" than English.

In addition, because historically many Deaf people worked in printing shops, the vocabulary variety in this vocation is high. Similarly, because sports is highly valued in the Deaf community, words to discuss football, basketball, baseball and other sports are beyond count. In deaf classrooms in America, English is the language used for instruction, so it is understandable that ASL would borrow some English technical words, which are typically fingerspelled (until a new ASL word evolves). Likewise, Japan has borrowed a lot from English, and English vocabulary is mostly derived from words from other languages. As history shows, English was an oppressed language about eight hundred years ago, just as ASL is presently.

Because we are oppressed by an English-speaking society, we tend to be more protective of our language or insecure about using it. We sometimes unconsciously code-switch, which means we change our ASL to a form of signing which is influenced by English structure and meanings. Minorities in all cultures do this no matter how proud they may be of their own language. Some of us also code-switch to assist non-Deaf people in understanding us (see *An Introduction to American Deaf Culture: Group Norms*, 1987, for more discussion on this).

In addition to language, we also have norms and values unique to Deaf culture. Because hearing people do not know and understand our culture, they have sometimes labeled our behavior "deviant," "rude," and "tactless." We follow different rules—created and handed down from our own people. Cultural rules are not right or wrong; they are simply different. When someone acts "tactfully" in white, middle class American culture (AHC), a Deaf person might view this behavior as "tactless." A notable difference between American Deaf culture and AHC is that Deaf people place a strong value on group identity, while AHC strongly values individualism. As one example of cultural differences, it seems that most Deaf people, whether at work or home, prefer to leave their doors open. But non-Deaf people will often close the door to their office or bedroom for privacy. This is rarely done in ADC, as Deaf people assume something is wrong when they see a closed door.

Videotapes and books have described in detail some of the norms and values of Deaf people. Often people who are not Deaf react negatively to ADC, but this is to be expected. When we read something that conflicts with our own cultural values or norms, our ethnocentrism surfaces. People tend to believe their own ways are appropriate and all others are inferior. Another reason for the discomfort comes from the realization that what they thought about Deaf people all along was incorrect. We are not a group of people who need help nor are we a group of people who yearn to be hearing. I would also like to add that educators and those in the "field of deafness," as they call it, react with the most suspicion towards cultural information concerning Deaf people. Perhaps it is because they are deeply invested in keeping Deaf people dependent on them. People who are least involved in this area are usually more understanding and accepting of who we really are.

We have our own identity—*Deaf*. Others have tried to label us differently. People have called us "deaf and dumb," "deaf mute," and now people are labeling us "hearing impaired."

> The power which comes from names and naming is related directly to the power to define others—individuals, races, sexes, ethnic groups. Our identities, who and what we are, how others see us, are greatly affected by the names we are called and the words with which we are labelled. The names, labels, and phrases employed to "identify" a people may in the end determine their survival. (Bosmajian, 1983)

Since the drafting of Section 504, the government has tried to cluster different people into one group—Deaf, deafened, hard of hearing, elderly, disabled, etc. They wanted one word to describe us (despite the variety of needs); the result is the term "hearing impaired." If we accept this label to simplify the government's paperwork, I feel it will be a very *big* mistake. We are much more than people with a hearing loss. We must clarify ourselves until we are certain that everyone is aware that we are a distinct cultural group. As Bosmajian said, this label could very well determine our survival. We see ourselves as *Deaf* people (see Bienvenu, *TBC News* No. 18; Jordan, *TBC News* No. 21). The term "hearing impaired" is just as offensive to Deaf people as the word "girl" is to Women, "nigger" is to Black people, "faggot" is to Gay men, or "wops" to Italians. That is how offensive "hearing impaired" is in our culture.

We have all seen the statistics citing 20 million people with a hearing loss of some kind in America. I do not wish to overlook the majority of them. There are people who are hard of hearing (audiologically or attitudinally); people who advocate oralism and support this approach to communication in the classroom; and people who are deafened from trauma, disease or from advancing age. There are also heafies[3] who prefer to work with the ADA, with English transliterators, and although they were probably once members of Deaf Culture, they no longer share the values and beliefs that most Deaf people do. Representatives from each of these groups often speak for Deaf people, presenting their view of a unified community, confusing the general public. We must be clear in our message that there are indeed 1 to 2 million Deaf Americans who do not share the same language, norms and values as these "spokespersons."

We Deaf people need to work together to educate everyone about who we are, to help eliminate the pathological perspective of us which is subtly embedded in everyday conversations. We need to fight for recognition for ASL as a language, and Deaf people as a cultural group to be afforded respect. I am not saying we should forget that there are other groups of people with hearing losses. They have organizations such as Self Help for Hard of Hearing People (SHHH) to serve them. I believe that the public is capable of understanding that these separate groups among deaf people do exist in America. While some organizations (SHHH, A. G. Bell, TBC) are clear about which group they serve, the NAD and other institutions (e.g. Gallaudet, NTID) send confusing messages to the public. This fosters in-group fighting among D/deaf people that ultimately hurts everyone.

Let me close by saying that Deaf people are people who also live in America, who speak a different language, who have their own cultural values and norms, who recognize and identify themselves as Deaf and not disabled. We are tired of being oppressed, mislabeled, misrepresented and misunderstood. It is time to recognize and respect us as full citizens, not as some non-human entity called "deafness"!

NOTES

1. Many authors use capital "Deaf" to refer to those who are members of the American Deaf culture and lower case "deaf" to refer to the audiological condition.

2. I prefer to use the term *TTY*, rather than *tdd*. The term "telecommunications device for the deaf" implies that Deaf people need help communicating. It takes two people to hold a conversation, and one of them could be hearing. It seems to infer that no hearing people need/want access to Deaf people. So, "for the deaf" is inaccurate. Second, why not recognize and respect the term TTY, which is used and preferred by Deaf people? Some have argued that "tdd" refers to a smaller and portable model, but the same is true for "TV," which retained the name, even though the early models were not portable or computerized.

3. Heafies are people who may have attended a residential school and/or know ASL, but prefer to function and communicate as hearing people. They follow hearing norms and behave more like hearing people than Deaf.

BIBLIOGRAPHY

Bienvenu, MJ, and Betty M. Colonomos. 1985–1988. *An Introduction to American Deaf Culture* (five-part videotape series). *(1) Rules for Social Interaction; (2) Values; (3) Language and Traditions; (4) Group Norms; (5) Identity.* Silver Spring, MD: Sign Media, Inc.

Bosmajian, Haig A. 1983. *The Language of Oppression.* Lanham, MD: University Press of America, Inc.

Klima, Edward, and Ursula Bellugi. 1979. *The Signs of Language.* Cambridge, MA: Harvard University Press.

Padden, Carol, and Tom Humphries. 1988. *Deaf in America: Voices from a Culture.* Cambridge, MA: Harvard University Press.

Rutherford, Susan. 1984. *American Culture: The Deaf Perspective (a four-part videotape series) (1) Deaf Folklore; (2) Deaf Heritage; (3) Deaf Literature (4) Minorities within the Deaf Community.* San Francisco, CA: San Francisco Public Library/National Endowment for the Humanities.

TBC News Nos. 9, 18, 21. Riverdale, MD.

When community members fail to conform to community mores, they are in for some old-fashioned schoolyard ridicule. When a non-conformist is in a position highly visible to the hearing, however, he or she may actually be shunned, snubbed, excommunicated. Unfortunately, since the hearing world doesn't get to watch these public stonings, the technique is stunningly ineffective in silencing dissent and may actually be breeding an underground.

Cochlear Implants vs. Deaf Culture?

Kathryn Woodcock

1992

Cochlear implants are hearing aids. In the cochlea—a part of the inner ear—of a hearing person, sound waves are translated into nerve signals. Some types of deafness result from sound waves not reaching the cochlea, or the cochlea failing to make this transformation. In these types of deafness, advocates propose using a cochlear implant to bypass the malfunction.

Part of the device is a bundle of electrodes of different lengths, surgically implanted into the cochlea. A microphone and body-worn speech processor pick up the sounds from the environment. The speech processor determines which of the electrodes to stimulate to relay each specific sound. The electrodes, spaced at intervals along the cochlea, then apply electric current directly to the auditory nerve. The nerves transmit the signals to the brain, creating perception of sound of different frequencies. There is no advantage to a cochlear implant in deafness where the auditory nerve has been damaged.

Auditory therapy is an important component of the implant process, to teach the implantee how to interpret the new combination of "sounds." Many professionals and implantees will say that the auditory therapist plays a more important part than the surgeon, in assuring the success of the procedure. Therapy is thought to be easier—therefore, more likely to succeed—when the implantee remembers what speech sounds like, when the new sounds can be taught as counterparts to the old sounds. However, advocates also argue that early implantation of deaf children should be considered as a way to expose them to the spoken word, enable them to learn spoken languages, and develop better speech skills.

Many deaf adults claim cochlear implants, especially implanted in children, threaten Deaf Culture. It is reasonable to worry about threats to a culture that has been continuously challenged over the years. I argue that cochlear implants represent no such threat. We feel an insult when we see cochlear implants as a high-tech

325

statement that we are not good enough in our natural deaf state. However, I do not believe that this technology can ever be a threat to Deaf Culture. We must not be misled into a spurious argument that can only fragment us.

As an adult who became deaf progressively, I have a broad experience with the hearing world, with fifteen years of being hard of hearing, and with deafness. Although I have good speech and good English skills, my preferred method of communication, especially for reception, is American Sign Language, which I began learning at the age of thirty. Despite my late start, the "Deaf World" is where I find my friends, my recreation, and my only true sense of belonging. I appreciate (and exploit) the employment and commercial opportunities that the hearing world provides for me, but I am never able to relax with Hearing people, so I am not comfortable socializing with them. I have a fair amount of memory of sound. Sometimes, for example, I find a particular song running through my mind, or imagine what a person's voice sounds like when I read their captions on a TV program. But I am not interested in a cochlear implant for myself. If had a deaf child, I would not choose an implant for her. But I argue that the Deaf community's perception of cochlear implants as a cultural threat is misplaced.

• Deaf Culture

What is the basis for Deaf Culture? When I realized I was deaf, I enrolled to study ASL at the Canadian Hearing Society. As in many ASL courses taught by Deaf teachers, Deaf Culture is an important part of the course of study. Finding myself in a visual environment where I could receive information unhindered for the first time, I devoured my classes, and read as many books about Deaf history and culture as I could find. In addition, I was in the middle of my second term of ASL when the Gallaudet protest occurred. This was a dynamic time to become exposed to Deaf Culture.

My teacher explained that deafness plus acceptance of sign language and Deaf Culture would make a person a member of the culture. Hard-of-hearing people raised in ASL would be accepted as Deaf, while non-signing oral deaf people would not. Being "Deaf"—that is "culturally Deaf"—did not depend on how much a person could hear. This was reinforced by statements I found in my growing library on deafness: "People who are Deaf can have a range of hearing abilities from 'hard of hearing' to 'profoundly deaf,' and, conversely, there are people with severe or profound hearing impairments who do not participate in the community of Deaf people" (Padden and Humphries, 1988). Markowicz and Woodward (1978) suggested self-identification with the group and skill in ASL should be important criteria for labeling someone as Deaf. Surely, these considerations are true whether the person uses unaided hearing or a hearing aid. And surely it does not matter what physical form the hearing aid takes: body aid, behind-the-ear, in-the-ear—or implanted.

We know that many Deaf people use hearing aids, even at deaf clubs and parties.

This cannot be due to the sheer comfort of the earmolds! There seems to be subtle pressure from some Deaf people to give up hearing aids—sort of a Deaf-liberation equivalent to bra-burning. Despite this peer pressure, many Deaf people continue to use them because they find some sort of advantage to the sound they are able to hear using the hearing aids. However, as the peer pressure to discard hearing aids shows, there is prejudice in the Deaf community against any form of listening. At this point in my progressive hearing loss, I can usually still hear a firm, multiple knock on the door of a quiet room. Several times, this has earned me suspicious glances and even overt queries as to why I am present in a deaf group. I can't hear a fire engine siren at twenty feet! I can't understand speech without lipreading—or, preferably, ASL interpreting. But because I can hear a door knock in a quiet room, my entitlement to the Deaf label is challenged. This is absurd.

Padden and Humphries (1988) spent a chapter discussing the "uses," recreational and otherwise, of sound in the Deaf world. But appreciation of sound, and using the sound to hear language are two different things. That is why it does not conflict with membership in the Deaf Culture.

- Opposing Views of the Implant, Accurate and Inaccurate

There are uninformed people among both advocates and opponents of implants. The oversights of each group are most evident and aggravating to the other. The arguments, rather than convincing the opposing group to the preferred point of view, merely raise already acute sensitivities.

Three-quarters of the Deaf people in my unscientific opinion-sampling identified concerns about the safety of the surgery, and particularly about the integrity of the skull after an implant, whether the fitness to participate in active sports was jeopardized (active sports being highly valued in the Deaf culture). They viewed the cochlear implant as a largely experimental procedure with unproven safety or efficacy. Most of these concerns could be resolved by simple question and answer from the professionals, if only the Deaf adults trusted the professionals.

I believe what really concerned the Deaf people I spoke with was the interpretation of implantation as proof that hearing people want to eradicate deafness and, by implication, wish that they—Deaf people—didn't exist. That's a pretty difficult message to accept equably. By the time these Deaf people have reached adulthood, I suppose they are weary of being told they should be more like hearing people. I am not aware of any major initiatives to provide support groups for deaf adults to deal with these pains in a constructive way. In the absence of other therapeutic outlets, it seems that these demons are combated by opposing contemporary incidents of what they recall as oppression from their own past. However, rather than eliminating the messages that tell deaf youngsters that deafness is "no good," the hearing "establishment" now offers the cochlear implant, which goes a step beyond the old hearing aids. It consists of being surgically altered on account of being defective. To the deaf adult who carries the hurts of his own childhood, this is escalation of a self-esteem war which he is struggling not to lose. How can professionals gain the trust of Deaf adults when this is perceived as their main message?

Some advocates for implantation of children believe that the implant will restore or impart the ability to hear, or significantly enough of the ability to hear, to allow the child to function in the hearing world, avoid the perceived "confines" of the Deaf world and live a "better life." It is not surprising that Deaf people who oppose implants, who are proud of their culture and satisfied with their lives, would interpret this motivation as somewhat insulting. They believe that parents make this decision too hastily, unfairly characterize Deaf adults as failures unworthy of their child's emulation, remain ignorant of the richness of Deaf Culture, paying only lip-service to consideration of a deaf-positive upbringing for the child. If they interpret the motivation as a statement that "My child will succeed in the hearing world, because she will not be a failure like these signing Deaf adults," they may not be misinterpreting the intent; I have actually been told this by one parent of one already-implanted deaf child under two years of age.

Some deafened adults hope that an implant will restore the lifestyle they formerly enjoyed, replete with music, the charming prattle of toddlers, and whispered sweet nothings, and allow them to avoid having to make major changes in response to becoming deaf. The majority of deafened adult members of ALDA—the Association of Late-Deafened Adults—responding to an invitation for anonymous comment indicated that they were uninterested in cochlear implants. They exclaimed "stop pathologizing my deafness!" "it wouldn't do anything my body aid can't do," and "I'm afraid it is just another instrument of denial." A deafened audiologist: "[to state that] we know by the end of an assessment, that a good implant candidate will hear more with the implant that with hearing aid(s) . . . is at best grossly unethical, irrespective of the fact that it is totally false."

However, among the implanted ALDAns responding, the majority believed their implant was "worth it," even though some were not as impressed as they expected to be. One happy implantee added "it does not make you a hearing person" and emphasized that an implantee could still be a proponent of and participant in Deaf Culture. One ALDAn responded to a skeptical editorial: "I would think you would be more encouraging to those of us who choose this 'alternative to deafness' which is what the implant actually is . . . You seem to be pointing at a refusal to accept deafness as the sole reason for most adults taking the opportunity that has presented itself to hear again." Another spoke out: "For me, choosing an implant was easy, because I fought deafness all the way" (excerpted from *ALDAcon III Reader*, 1991). My subjective impression has been that the most "functional implantees"—those who can communicate best and seem to be happiest—are those who have added an implant to a full complement of skills for coping with deafness—including a deaf-positive attitude and acceptance of sign language.

While it can create the perception of sound, a cochlear implant does not make a person become "hearing." With the cochlear implant and good rehabilitation, the deaf person might be able to function in the hearing world as a hard of hearing person. This might mean that Hearing people are unaware that the person is deaf with an implant, but it doesn't mean that the person can function without difficulty. Unfortunately, I learned as a hard of hearing person that "passing for" hearing is a greater advantage for one's hearing associates than for oneself. It enables them to "forget" to keep their lips in view, leave meeting room lighting adequate, and so on. They excuse their lack of consideration with what they believe is a compliment: "you have such good speech." My ability to pass for hearing ensures that I don't impose much on the hearing people, allows them to convince themselves that I really am fitting in, participating as much as I would if I were hearing or they were all deaf. In fact, I have enjoyed much more "access" in the hearing world, including accommodations that ensure that I really do understand and can participate, when I made my deafness more obvious. This has included using ASL interpreters and occasionally feigning a "deaf accent," dropping my "perfect speech." I regret that I only learned this recently. For two decades, I directed a great deal of my intellect to lipreading, situational reconnaissance, mind-reading, and dominating conversations in order to pass for hearing, instead of applying it to concrete achievements.

The second way that hearing world success disadvantages the deaf youngster is that they may not have occasion to come into contact with the Deaf World at all. Succeeding academically is only part of growing up, and in many other ways, the oral-success deaf child is not just like her hearing contemporaries. Until I met another deaf person for the first time when I commenced sign language classes at the age of thirty, I thought I was utterly peculiar in so many ways when in fact I was merely behaving in characteristic "Deaf" ways. Feeling "normal" is an important emotional strength. Passing for hearing may hinder opportunities to discover this other point of reference that awaits in the Deaf world. Like deaf adults with their emotional baggage from deaf schools, my personal dread is that parents of implanted children will convince themselves that the child is not deaf, but indeed can function as, hearing, and another child will go through the waste of intellect and access that I did.

Amidst all the controversy, it is easy to lose sight of what the real decision is: what are the potential rewards, what are the costs, and does the balance between them make it worthwhile to me to have an implant?

Some comments published about evaluations of the twenty-two-channel cochlear implant in children are: "Children are able to *detect* conversational level sounds, including speech, at comfortable loudness levels when wearing the Nucleus implant. *Some* children can identify everyday sounds such as car horns, doorbells, and birds singing. The perception of speech *may* also be improved. Although the implant does not restore normal hearing, words *in small sets* can be identified by *some* children, and *a few* children can recognize words in conversation, without lipreading. Lipreading also is improved for *some* children when using the implant" (emphasis added) (Steve Staller, Ph.D., in *Soundings*, a newsletter published by the Cochlear Corporation, July 1990).

A careful reading of the paragraph reveals that the benefits are limited. The first thing we should notice that this honest description comes from a supporter of implants for children. It does not seem as though the manufacturers are trying to pull the wool over the eyes of deaf people or parents. I don't see aggressive recruitment or implants being misrepresented as a means to fully reverse deafness. If there are misunderstandings or unrealistic expectations about the implants, they arise in the marketplace. Hearing or deaf, when there is something that is important to us, we "hear" what we want to "hear." The manufacturers and professionals involved with the implant programs obviously believe that the limited rewards are worth the costs of the procedure. But then, so do many people who have already had or requested implants.

We must respect and recognize that the limited benefits might be completely satisfactory for the person making the decision about an implant—deaf adult or deaf child's parent. Most implantees have increased ability to hear environmental sounds and lipread better. Just as I find it useful to hear door-knocks, some people might find environmental sounds and enhanced lipreading to be adequate payback for the prospect of surgery, therapy, expense, wires and a body aid, and potentially prodigious consumption of batteries.

Maybe this is because they have been informed of all the facts and truly don't find the surgery and therapy too burdensome. Or they may be assuming very certain and very high rewards. We do know that people tend to differentiate themselves from others: I can drive above the speed limit and I don't consider myself to be "asking for" a collision, but when someone else does it, he is a menace on the road. This "self-other" phenomenon colors much decision-making. Nobody requesting the surgery assumes their implant will be a failure. There are some implantees who are phenomenally successful, able to recognize spoken words blindfolded. People who fiercely want implants for themselves or their children will tend to assume or at least hope that their case will be another success.

This is supported in part by the tendency for testimonials and personal-experience articles to be written by people who are pleased, if not overjoyed, with their implants. The article "How Can I Keep From Singing?" (Clickener, 1989) gives an example of a person who can hear very well with her implant, who can even understand perfect strangers over the telephone, whose next aspiration is to restore her appreciation of music.

• Deaf Protectionism

Deafened adults in their support groups share stories of becoming deaf and being rejected and criticized by their local Deaf communities as "not really deaf," "not deaf enough," "Think-Hearie," "hard of hearing," and so on. Through the process of becoming deaf, we lose membership in the hearing group, but the Deaf group won't let us in. Deaf outsiders arriving in a new community are similarly marginalized until they have proven their membership (Padden and Humphries, 1988). The same thing can happen to orally-educated deaf people past the age of majority deciding to explore the Deaf world. An oral upbringing, let alone the former ability to hear, is rarely the decision of the person. Yet the Deaf community treats this as a transgression, if not a threat. And we have the future generations of children being implanted today, who will likely suffer this same shunning as a result of a decision made by their parents, not themselves. Shunning (by brushing off and not befriending) or outright excommunication (by denial of the "deaf" label) is the punishment. The transgression seems to be the violation of some of Deaf culture's value structure that says sound and speech have no value.

This value seems only to have protectionist intent. Valuing sign language, visual art forms, deaf history and heritage, eye contact, unobstructed sight lines, and illumination are "deaf-positive" values. Disdaining sound and spoken language is "hearing-negative," enhancing deaf status only by discounting the status of the hearing. In my opinion as someone who has discovered the Deaf world after fifteen years of being hard of hearing and a couple of years as deaf—oral, by default—the Deaf world does not need to denigrate the hearing world to be a treasure for all deaf people.

There are only two main explanations that I have heard from deaf people who are not part of the Deaf world: "They won't let me in" and "We live in a hearing world." I think the first reason reflects narrow-mindedness on the part of the deaf communities. The second reason reflects short-sightedness on the part of the person making the excuse. Even those who are passionately committed to Deaf Culture live in a hearing world. Even if they work among deaf people all day, they still shop at hearing grocery stores, buy gasoline at hearing service stations, and have to call hearing fire departments and ambulances when emergencies arise. We do live in a hearing world. But each of us really "lives" in only a small part of it. Some of us live in the Jewish world, the rural world, or the bodybuilding world. We make our friends from those people who are most like us and who make us feel most comfortable about ourselves. Choosing to accept the Deaf world and make it one's "home" is no more denial of the real world than it is to have mostly women friends or vegetarian friends. Whom we are able to interact with is different from whom we prefer to interact with.

A successful cochlear implant can assist the implantee to interact more effectively with hearing people. The implant does not need to preclude finding one's social and recreational needs better met in the Deaf world. However, this will certainly be the case if the Deaf community continuously insults or ignores those who dabble in the "other" world.

Deaf pride has grown considerably since the days of signing under the table. If the Deaf community was proud and welcoming instead of proud and defensive, it could grow even further apace. Suppose the Deaf community said: "We are confident in the merits of our culture and our Deaf values. We believe that anyone who is deaf will find something of great value among us. And we welcome any new members to our culture. Regardless of whether you might have been hearing or hard of hearing in the past, your present deafness makes you a brother or sister to us. Whether you chose it for yourself, or whether your parents chose it for you, your use of amplification (hearing aids or implants) and your use of speech to communicate with hearing people outside the Deaf world does not threaten us, because what we have is truly the best."

The message I wish the Deaf community would send to other deaf people (oral, deafened, implanted) is: "What we have is good, and we think it could be good for you." Instead, the message it seems to send is: "What we have is good, but you aren't good enough for us."

• Summary

The cochlear implant does not represent a threat to Deaf Culture. What is a threat is the Deaf community's overeagerness to reject prospective members just because they used to hear, because their parents chose an implant for them, because they find environmental sounds useful, etc. This protectionism doesn't make Deaf Culture strong; it perpetuates its marginality in the eyes of the hearing world, and makes every one of its interests automatically an "outside" point of view. And ironically, this works against the credibility of the very campaign that is foremost in many deaf communities today: discouraging parents from premature decision-making about pediatric cochlear implants. The Deaf Culture would be wise to realize that it has a lot to offer without having to oppress or malign other backgrounds or points of view. If it were more welcoming, many more people would use that freedom to choose a home in it.

REFERENCES

ALDAcon III Reader. 1991. Chicago IL: Association of Late-Deafened Adults.

Clickener, P. A. 1989. "How can I keep from singing?" *SHHH*, July/August. Bethesda, MD: Self Help for Hard of Hearing People, Inc.

Markowicz, H., and J. Woodward. 1978. "Language and the maintenance of ethnic boundaries in the deaf community." *Communication and Cognition* 2: 29–38.

Padden, C., and T. Humphries. 1988. *Deaf in America: Voices from a Culture*. Cambridge, MA: Harvard University Press.

Staller, S. 1990. "22-channel implant approved for children." *Soundings*, July. Englewood, CO: Cochlear Corporation.

48

Borrowing strategies and language from the Civil Rights movement of the 1960s seemed like a good idea to many Deaf people hoping to shore up community morale, regain lost autonomy, and create a collective Deaf voice in the national arena during the 1980s–90s. Unfortunately, this strategy has led not to increased rights, recognition, or respect for Deaf people but rather to cultural co-optation as usual.

Into Their Own Hands

The Deaf President Now Protest and Its Consequences

Sharon N. Barnartt and John B. Christiansen

1996

In March, 1988, at Gallaudet University in Washington, D.C., the only liberal-arts university for deaf students in the world, there occurred a week-long protest which came to be called Deaf President Now (DPN). On a college campus which had seldom, if ever, before experienced disruptive collective action, protesters closed down the university, demanding, among other things, that a deaf president be appointed instead of the newly chosen hearing woman. The protest received a large amount of attention from the media, which generally supported the protestors. Within eight days, the board of trustees of the university had agreed to all of the protestors' demands.

Based upon research we and colleagues conducted,[1] in this chapter we present a different version of the events of DPN than has been reported in most media accounts (see, for example, *Gallaudet in the News*, 1988). We argue that to call DPN a "student protest," as most of these accounts have done, presents too simple a picture of a set of very complicated actions.

Unlike most studies of incidents of collective behavior, we examine both the events of the protest and its consequences. We suggest that the consequences of DPN have lingered beyond what might have been expected by most analysts of collective behavior. The DPN protest provides an example of a single, short collective action which has been followed by a substantial number of apparently related collective actions. We show that the DPN protest has affected the deaf community so profoundly that it is experiencing the beginning of a new social movement: That community has changed from being somewhat passive and apolitical to one mobilized for both traditional political action and nontraditional collective action. However, there are also some ironies which appear in the long-term consequences of DPN. These include the lack of involvement of most of the DPN protestors in subsequent collective actions, the lack of mobilization of current Gallaudet students for collective action, and the relatively small number of significant changes at Gallaudet University itself.

• Collective Behavior and Its Consequences

Collective behavior is action which occurs outside of the usual social structural context and in which mobilization for action is on the basis of beliefs (Smelser, 1962: 8). Collective behavior is not within the realm of normally expected social action; thus it has enormous disruptive potential. Fads and social movements are examples of long-term collective behavior; protests, riots, and panics are examples of shorter-term collective actions.

Protests such as DPN are likely to occur when powerless groups attempt to secure immediate responses to grievances or demands (Piven and Cloward, 1979; Lipsky, 1968; Oberschall, 1973; Rose, 1982).[2] Formerly powerless protesters gain power from the use of disruptive means—power which they formerly did not have and usually could not get from the less disruptive processes which comprise "politics as usual" (Meyer, 1993). While protests may be seen as rational responses to grievances, words such as joy (Fantasia, 1988), ecstasy (Murphy, 1987), and delirium or madness (Zolberg, 1972) are also used to describe what happens during a protest.

Protests are explosive, disruptive, joyous . . . and gone. Or are they? Although our knowledge of the consequences of collective behavior is perhaps less than we would like (Tarrow, 1991), some authors (e.g. Freeman, 1988; Fantasia, 1988; Oberschall, 1980, 1988) have suggested that an initial incident of collective behavior may increase the probability of subsequent collective actions.[3] This increase in "action mobilization" may occur through the dissemination or diffusion of the "repertoire of action" which develops during the initial collective action. A repertoire of action may include ideas; networks of relationships (Zolberg, 1972); collective identities (Gamson, 1992; Klandermans, 1992; Mann, 1973); actors, symbols, or rhetoric (Barnartt, 1993); and frames and frame extensions (Snow et al., 1986). Alternatively, subsequent incidents of collective behavior may occur because an initial episode of collective action changes the "political opportunity structure"— those social and governmental structures which encourage or discourage social and political changes in a society (Tarrow, 1993)—so as to make subsequent collective action more likely.

Our research on DPN suggests that, since 1988, there has been an increase in action mobilization in the deaf community, coupled with a diffusion of the repertoire of action seen during DPN, and there has been a change in the political opportunity structure. We begin by explicating the events of DPN itself. We continue by discussing the ways in which the increase in action mobilization, the diffusion of the repertoire of action and the change in the political opportunity structure have manifested themselves as consequences of DPN.

• The Events of DPN

The Deaf President Now protest began soon after Elizabeth A. Zinser, a hearing woman, was selected by the board of trustees to be the new president of Gallaudet University on Sunday, March 6, 1988. This selection occurred despite an intensive lobbying campaign, aimed at the search committee and the board of trustees, advocating the appointment of a deaf person. Some of this lobbying was done by deafness-related organizations, such as the National Association of the Deaf (NAD), which sent letters and lists of apparently qualified deaf persons to the board. In addition, after Gallaudet's previous president announced his resignation in August, 1987, a number of articles and editorials appeared in deafness-related publications (such as the *NAD Broadcaster*) urging the appointment of a deaf president. Some lobbying was also done by hearing faculty and staff members at Gallaudet, and even Republican presidential candidates Robert Dole and George Bush got involved by sending letters in support of a deaf president to the search committee.

The advocates who ultimately had the most impact on the events of DPN were six young deaf men (most of whom were Gallaudet alumni) who called themselves the Ducks. Among other things, they attempted to pressure the search committee and the board of trustees by organizing a rally in support of a deaf president on March 1. They also identified several student leaders and attempted to convince them of the importance of having a deaf president. This was necessary because, although extensive support for a deaf president emerged during the protest, most Gallaudet students and faculty were relatively apathetic about the appointment of a deaf president prior to the rally.

The announcement of Zinser's selection was not made by the board itself but by the university's public relations office, which had preprinted flyers available for distribution to those who had gathered on campus awaiting word of the decision. Several hundred people, including students, faculty, and members of the Washington, D.C. deaf community, had come to the campus on that Sunday afternoon because they expected the board to select one of the two deaf finalists. This expectation was especially strong among those, such as the Ducks, who had been working for months to try to convince the board to select a deaf president.

As it happened, one of the Ducks was in the public relations office at the time the board made its decision. He picked up a handful of the flyers and rushed to another part of the campus where another member of the Ducks actually made the announcement to the waiting crowd. The crowd was upset with the board's decision, and many were incensed that the board had not even bothered to come to the campus to announce or explain its decision. Angry speeches on campus and in the middle of the

336 | *Sharon N. Barnartt and John B. Christiansen*

busy street which borders the campus culminated in a march to the hotel several miles away where the board of trustees was meeting.

At the hotel a small group of protesters met with the chair of the board of trustees, Jane Bassett Spilman, and a few other members of the board to express their dissatisfaction with the board's decision. It was during this meeting that Spilman was reported to have said, in a comment picked up by many media reports, that deaf people were not ready to function in a hearing world.[4] After the meeting she addressed a crowd of several hundred people who were still at the hotel, but nothing was resolved. Meanwhile, others in the crowd had become impatient and had marched on to the White House, several blocks away. Spilman did, however, agree to meet with the protesters the next day in order to explain the board's decision.

During the night, protesters decided to close down the university by barricading all but one of the six entrances to the campus with their cars. Early on Monday, March 7, the protesters formulated their four demands. These included the resignation of the newly appointed president and the appointment of a deaf president, the resignation of the chair of the board of trustees, no reprisals against the protesters, and the appointment of a deaf majority to the board of trustees.

After an emotionally-charged meeting between the board and members of the campus community on Monday afternoon, it became clear that the impasse would continue. Spilman, using an interpreter, had begun the meeting by attempting to explain the board's decision. She was interrupted when a faculty member walked in front of her and signed to the crowd that the board had refused to reconsider its decision. Hundreds of people walked out in disgust and marched to the Capitol, about a mile away.

The protest picked up momentum throughout the week. Deaf students in several residential schools engaged in sympathy protests, and many deaf people rushed to Washington to join the protest. Offers of help and statements of support came from local labor unions, national organizations of deaf people, and congressional representatives. Unsolicited donations poured in, and a week of meetings, marches and the continued closure of the university ensued. Media coverage of protest events was extensive and sympathetic and included appearances by one of the student leaders and the new president on national news programs such as "Good Morning America," "The MacNeil/Lehrer Newshour," and "Nightline."

On Thursday evening, March 10, in the face of massive pressure from the deaf community, the new president resigned. Protesters marched to the Capitol on Friday, and on Sunday the board of trustees agreed to the protesters' demands. I. King Jordan was appointed as president of the university, and a deaf man was selected as the new chairperson of the board of trustees when Spilman resigned. There were no reprisals against the protesters, and a task force was established to study the composition of the board of trustees, which now has a deaf/hard-of-hearing majority. (For a detailed description of DPN, see Christiansen and Barnartt, 1995.)

• Action Mobilization Prior to DPN

The process of mobilization for collective action has been suggested to occur in three distinct phases: those of consensus formation, consensus mobilization, and action mobilization (Klandermans, 1984, 1988). The first two are concerned with beliefs, while the third focuses on behavior. Consensus formation is the "unplanned convergence of meaning in social networks and subcultures," while consensus mobilization is "a deliberate attempt by a social actor to create consensus among a subset of the population" (Klandermans, 1988). Both imply attitudes but not action, nor even necessarily a willingness (yet) to participate in action. Action mobilization, on the other hand, is "the process by which . . . a social movement calls up people to participate" in collective actions such as protests (Klandermans, 1984).

Prior to DPN, there had been some consensus formation and consensus mobilization in that part of the deaf population which calls itself Deaf,[5] but there had been minimal action mobilization. In other words, there had been almost no instances of collective behavior by members of the deaf community. Since DPN there has been a huge increase in consensus formation and mobilization as well as in action mobilization.

Before 1987, consensus formation focused on enhanced pride in being deaf and in being a part of a community with a unique language and culture. During the latter part of 1987 and the first few months of 1988, attempts at consensus mobilization had begun around the need for a deaf president for Gallaudet. This could be seen, for example, in articles that appeared in the *NAD Broadcaster* and other deafness related publications (Christiansen and Barnartt, 1995). However, those attempts at consensus mobilization were not strong enough to produce agreement on this (or any other issue) within the deaf community at that time.

Prior to DPN the deaf community as a whole had not experienced action mobilization,[6] except for a few localized protests on issues of interest to deaf people and conducted by deaf people (Gannon, 1981). It is true that some deaf people had been involved in collective actions in 1977 during which protesters occupied HEW offices in several cities demanding promulgation of regulations for the Rehabilitation Act of 1973 (Johnson, 1983; Shapiro, 1993); however, this was not just a deafness-related issue, and most of the participants were persons with other types of disabilities. Although several lawsuits were filed by the National Association of the Deaf, particularly after it established a legal defense fund in the mid-1970s, there had been no large scale, disruptive collective actions on deafness-related issues before DPN.

• Action Mobilization since DPN

Protests are explosive and short, frequently leaving no groups, leaders, or adherents who could coalesce into a new social movement. But this protest has been different. DPN was a single successful protest which has been followed by substantial numbers of subsequent, albeit less explosive, protests, as well as by other types of traditional and nontraditional political action. Since DPN there has been an explosion of action mobilization, as incidents of collective action have occurred around a number of issues and in a large number of locales. There has been a process of diffusion in which both the form and the content of DPN have spread within the deaf community (and, to some extent, to the larger disability community). This diffusion of the success of DPN has started a cycle of protest in the deaf community.

There have been protests at residential schools for deaf students in which the protesters have explicitly linked their demands to those at Gallaudet. For example, at the Wisconsin School for the Deaf in November 1991, students protested the insufficient numbers of deaf staff members, especially dorm counselors. Their demands—that the dean of students be removed, that half of the staff be composed of deaf people and that there be no reprisals against protesters—were reminiscent of DPN demands, and media coverage of the protest made the linkage clear (Kenyon, 1992). After two days of protest, all of these demands were met. Other protests, with similar actions and similar issues, have occurred at the Mississippi School for the Deaf, as well as, at the college level, at Gallaudet's "sister school," the National Technical Institute for the Deaf (NTID), a unit of the Rochester Institute of Technology (RIT).[7]

Protests in other locales have also focused on deafness-related issues. Issues in these protests have included the funding situation or threatened closing of residential schools (Maryland, Washington state, New Jersey, Oregon and Michigan), the appropriateness of an ASL-based curriculum (South Carolina) or mainstreaming (Colorado), the composition of a residential school's governing board (Maryland), the use of hearing actors to portray deaf characters in films (New York City and Washington, D.C.), and issues of television access in emergency situations (San Francisco).

Some of these actions explicitly harkened back to DPN. For example, a flyer from early 1989, encouraging people to attend a rally regarding hearings on the reauthorization of PL 94-142,[8] said,

> Why March 1st? Because on this day, exactly one year ago, Gallaudet students protested for their next president to be deaf. It is on this one year anniversary that we feel we should make the impact to call attention to the LRE [least restrictive environment] issue!

Other collective actions harkened back to DPN in neither demands nor tactics but still represent types of collective behavior seldom seen before in the deaf community. In Maryland, mobilization regarding state legislative issues has focused on funding for the state telephone relay system and a video caption access bill which, had it been successful, would have required that all videotapes sold or rented in Maryland be closed captioned. Additionally, in 1993, a coalition of organizations was formed to represent groups concerned with deaf and hard-of-hearing issues from all parts of the deaf community. Called the Consumer Action Network, it is particularly important because some of the constituent organizations had never been united prior to this time. The group's first chair, Roslyn Rosen, linked the coalition to DPN when she said it was significant that the organization was "born exactly 5 years after the deaf rights movement, alias DPN." The group, she said, was formed for purposes of "proactive legislative efforts"—although not, presumably, for purposes of disruptive collective action (Christiansen and Barnartt, 1995).

While all of these efforts did not take the form of disruptive collective action, they still represent a much greater awareness of the political process than existed before DPN. The two issues of greatest importance at this time are issues not covered by the Americans with Disabilities Act (ADA): the accessibility of visual media, including commercial videos, and the continued viability of residential schools.

Ironically, one locale which appears largely exempt from the collective action mobilizations which have been occurring in other areas of the country since DPN is Gallaudet itself. The only protests on campus since DPN have been small ones related to the English language requirement[9] and to student access to parking. This is true despite that fact that two events have occurred which seem as if they should have mobilized large-scale student discontent. One was the alleged asphyxiation of a student by campus security guards in November 1990 after a struggle in the student union. The other was the acquittal of those guards two years later. The death failed to produce more than a quiet and not completely successful one-day boycott of classes; the acquittal produced no action at all.

Several groups have experienced action mobilization. One group is comprised of those who participated in the DPN protest. While not the instigators of the protest, they were faculty or staff members who played important supporting roles. Several of them have emerged as leaders of collective actions which have taken place in Maryland and elsewhere. Another group is young people who, at the time of DPN, were too young to participate in it and who really stood to gain no direct benefit from it. They are now older and are initiating student protests at residential schools and at NTID.

A final, somewhat more diverse, group is "conscience constituents," those who support a social movement's demands even though they do not stand to benefit in any way (McCarthy and Zald, 1990). There are several examples of the mobilization of conscience constituents subsequent to DPN. After one protest at NTID, the hearing student government president of RIT put several of the deaf students' demands onto the agenda he presented to the student body, presumably adding significantly to the power of those demands. A more influential group of conscience constituents which has been mobilized consists of members of the boards of trustees or analogous decision-making bodies of residential schools for deaf students, who have appointed at least seventeen deaf superintendents since DPN.[10]

Ironically, several groups of potential collective actors have not been mobilized. One group includes the four student leaders of DPN. These four have retained the respect of the deaf community they gained during DPN, but they have gone to graduate school, started careers and families, and, with only one exception (Solomon, 1994), have not been known to have participated in subsequent disruptive collective actions. Another group is the other student protesters, who are also not participating in protests or other types of collective behavior. Although many students at the time felt that DPN changed their lives, it apparently did not do so in a way which engendered further participation in protests. A third group is the young men who comprised the Ducks—while they appear to be doing well for themselves professionally, they have only rarely participated in any of the subsequent collective actions undertaken by members of the deaf community.[11]

• A Spiral of Mobilization in the Deaf Community

One might be tempted not to place too much emphasis upon the protests which have occurred, since they do not represent the mobilization of the entire deaf community. However, as discussed above, the deaf community, which had seldom participated in disruptive collective actions before DPN, has begun to participate in collective action in a way which it never did before 1988.[12] We suggest that this "spiral of mobilization" (Klandermans, 1988) may represent the beginning of a new social movement.

Some might think this somewhat ironic, since there is already a movement for disability rights, within which a deaf rights movement might fit. However, in the eyes of the deaf community, this is not the case (see, for example, White, 1994). The DPN protest was not planned, instigated, or in any other way caused by the disability rights movement; neither were disability rights advocates involved at the beginning, although some offered statements of support as DPN events progressed. In general, the disability rights movement has been somewhat fragmented into groups representing different disabilities (Johnson, 1983; Scotch, 1989).[13] The split between deaf activists and activists within the disability rights movement is so great that there are policy issues on which they have taken opposing positions. Most recently, this has been true for the issue of mainstreaming. A rift developed between members of the deaf community and Judy Heumann, the highest ranking person with a disability in the Clinton administration,[14] who said that separate education for children with disabilities was "immoral." This is a position with which many deaf community leaders strongly disagree.[15] The split between deaf activists and disability rights activists may also have occurred because architectural accessibility and communications accessibility are very different issues. Mobility accessibility and personal care attendants are of primary interests to disability activists (Berkowitz, 1987), while for those who are deaf or hard-of-hearing, communications accessibility, including the provision of personnel (such as interpreters, notetakers or relay operators) and assistive devices (including hearing aids, FM or audio loop systems, closed or real-time captioning systems, and flashing light warning systems), is the primary accessibility issue (Barnartt et al., 1990).[16]

Despite this fragmentation, DPN has been hailed by disability rights activists as a victory for all persons with disabilities.[17] Through its contribution to the ADA (Altman and Barnartt, 1993), this may be true. However, DPN has not contributed to a noticeable lessening of the split between the movement for deaf rights and the disability rights movement. In fact, it may have exacerbated it, as activism in the deaf community, around deafness-related issues, has escalated.[18]

• Explaining Action Mobilization in the Deaf Community

Why have many people in the deaf community become mobilized for collective action since 1988? For one thing, DPN has retained a huge amount of "symbolic visibility." It continues to be mentioned frequently both inside and outside of the university. Within Gallaudet, DPN is extolled in publications used for internal and external fund-raising efforts (Barnartt and Christiansen, 1992). Outside of the university, the protest continues to be mentioned favorably in many places, including the *Congressional Record*.[19] It has become part of deaf community lore and is often mentioned in publications read by deaf people around the country. Recent books about deafness (Benderly, 1990; Lucas, 1991; Sacks, 1990; Lane, 1992; Luczak, 1993) have tended to mention DPN in glowing terms, whether or not it is relevant to the subject of the book.

In addition to the symbolic visibility of the protest, the man who was appointed as the first deaf president of Gallaudet, I. King Jordan, has retained a nation-wide visibility which few university presidents enjoy. He is present at many events which involve disability. In the summer of 1994, for example, he sat on the podium with President Clinton, Vice-President Gore, their wives, and a few others at a White House celebration of the fourth anniversary of the Americans with Disabilities Act.

This symbolic visibility has contributed to two aspects of the action mobilization which has occurred. Despite the fact that many deaf people know about the role of the nonstudent participants such as the Ducks in DPN, a "mythology" about DPN as a *student* protest has persisted. It is thought that the students at Gallaudet did it once; therefore students at other schools can repeat their actions. Thus, there has been a diffusion of the role of "collective actor" from Gallaudet students to other deaf students.

Additionally, DPN is widely seen as a protest which can be emulated because its *success* can be repeated. Knowledge of the success of the protest acts to enhance the consensus formation and mobilization which had begun in the deaf community before 1988. As mentioned above, at that time, consensus was beginning to be formed over goals such as having a deaf president for Gallaudet. But because the type of action used in DPN (a disruptive protest) was so successful, it has suggested a strategy which could be used again to try to attain other goals. DPN's overwhelming success has led to further collective actions which might not have occurred if DPN had been less successful or had been a complete failure. Thus, diffusion of the feeling of success has been a factor in mobilizing the deaf community (Barnartt, 1994).

A third part of the answer to the question of why members of the deaf community have been mobilized is related to the way the issue was framed (Snow et al., 1986) during DPN. Throughout the protest, the choice of a university president was framed publicly as a civil rights issue, rather than as either a student rights issue or a disability rights issue.[20] The framing of the issue as one of civil rights was used by

Elizabeth Zinser in her resignation statement, and it has been used in references to the protest in the *Congressional Record*. That framing was so important that it played a role in the passage of the ADA (Altman and Barnartt, 1993), as was noted by Justin Dart, who, in 1992, in the name of the Bush administration, presented Gallaudet students and faculty with the Distinguished Service Award of the President of the United States for their contribution to the passage of ADA (Christiansen and Barnartt, 1995).

DPN began a process known as "frame extension" (Snow and Benford, 1988). In a frame extension, one frame (e.g., that of civil rights) is extended from a group such as blacks, to whom the frame had already been applied, to another group, such as women, older people, or deaf people, to whom the frame had not yet been applied successfully. Frame extension can occur as a result of collective action or other means.

One result of this extension of the frame of civil rights to deaf people was that it encouraged deaf people to feel a sense of relative deprivation when compared to other groups to whom the frame of civil rights had previously been extended. Deaf people appear to be thinking that with the extension of the frame of civil rights to deaf people should come some of the tangible gains, such as equal employment or antidiscrimination laws, a lessening of prejudice and discrimination, and an improvement in socioeconomic status and life chances, which have occurred for other groups to whom the frame had previously been extended. In other words, members of the deaf community appear to be trying to put teeth into the frame extension which they felt they had won in 1988. They are now fighting harder than before for what they perceive to be their civil rights. Because there are significant omissions in the ADA which affect deaf people (Barnartt and Seelman, 1991), deaf people feel that there are still civil rights left to be fought for, and they are now mobilized for the collective actions which they feel are necessary for that fight.

Finally, because of its apparent role in the passage of the ADA (Altman and Barnartt, 1993) and its role in the passage of other legislation such as the Telecommunications Act of 1990 (Christiansen and Barnartt, 1995), DPN may also have caused a change in the political opportunity structure. As noted earlier, the political opportunity structure includes those social and governmental structures which encourage or discourage social and political changes in a society. The change we have seen in the political opportunity structure is that it has become less politically acceptable to deny rights and privileges to people with disabilities. This change has caused some deaf people to become more willing to make demands, since it has become more likely that their demands will be met.

For all of these reasons, we suggest that DPN began a cycle of protest which we could also call a "revolution of rising expectations." Because of the original success of DPN and the frame extension which it inspired, members of the deaf community have become much more willing to engage in disruptive collective action now than had been true in the past.

• Conclusion

DPN only lasted for one week, but it was a collective action with significant long-term impacts. Its impact on the institution toward which it was directed was perhaps more mixed and less profound than many of its participants expected. It did not dramatically change objective indicators of university health such as numbers of applicants, registered students, or federal or alumni contributions (Barnartt and Christiansen, 1992). However, it may have led to changes in sign language policies, the creation of a Department of Deaf Studies, small increases in the number of deaf faculty, staff, and administrators, and recent increases in private contributions (Christiansen and Barnartt, 1995).

Although it may seem somewhat ironic, we suggest that the impact of DPN on the deaf community has been much more profound than its impact on the university. The hope engendered by the protest has had a mobilizing effect which appears likely both to continue and to exacerbate the split with other disability activists. If this action mobilization continues, and if the results continue to be as successful as those from DPN, the ultimate impact of DPN will have been enormous.

NOTES

1. The colleagues, whose assistance we gratefully acknowledge, include Paul Higgins, Richard Meisegeier, Barbara White, Pat Johansen, and Bonnie Gracer. Data collection included participant observation of many of the events which occurred during DPN as well as over fifty unstructured, in-depth interviews, conducted primarily during the spring and summer of 1988, with participants at all levels of the action. The interviews lasted from one to eight hours, and, with a few exceptions, were video- or audio-taped (depending upon the hearing status of the interviewee) and transcribed. We conducted additional unstructured interviews in 1992 with participants who had been interviewed previously as well as some who had not. We also collected reports from Gallaudet offices and information from an electronic bulletin board entitled "Telephone For All" (TFA), which disseminates news of deafness-related events.

2. A protest may be part of a social movement and so be called a "campaign" (Kleidman, 1993; Marwell and Oliver, 1984), or it may not. DPN was not a campaign because it was not part of an existing social movement.

3. The long-term consequences of a protest, in contrast to longer-term types of collective behavior, are likely to be unintended, since the intentionality of a protest is focused upon its short-term goals (Kendrick, 1991; Marx, 1988).

4. It now appears that she did not actually make this comment, although many continue to believe that she did (see, for example, Solomon, 1994). Rather, she apparently used a "double negative" and was, for whatever reason, misunderstood (Christiansen and Barnartt, 1995).

5. The use of the capital D in Deaf was a deliberate attempt begun by Woodward (1972) to distinguish those who saw themselves as culturally deaf from those who saw themselves as being audiologically deaf (Padden and Humphries, 1988).

6. Other actions, which do not fall under the definition of collective behavior, such as

lawsuits, tended to be initiated by parents or other interested parties (Altman and Barnartt, 1993).

7. The first protest demanded better sign language skills for faculty. The second, called "Campus Access Now," included demands for more pay, TTY's on campus and better sign language skills among the support staff.

8. Originally enacted in 1975, and formerly called the Education for all Handicapped Children Act, the Individuals with Disabilities Education Act (IDEA) is the law which has been interpreted to mean that children with disabilities should be educated in a school with non-disabled students, which is assumed to be the "least restrictive environment."

9. Some students objected to taking courses in what they feel is not their "real" language, which is American Sign Language.

10. One of the recent appointees said that the relevant decision-making body visualized a "clenched DPN fist" while they were deliberating. While he may be engaging in wishful thinking, it is also possible that he is correctly reflecting the continued symbolic visibility of DPN.

11. This is consistent, for example, with what is known about activists from the Free Speech Movement at Berkeley who remained politically leftist but inactive after 1964 (Abramowitz and Nassi, 1981). It is also in the tradition of 1960s activists such as Jerry Rubin and Eldridge Cleaver who became somewhat conservative and nonprotesting members of society.

12. A small amount of evidence, such as increased membership in NAD (Rose and Kiger, 1994), suggests that consensus mobilization is also increasing. It is not, however, a clear enough trend to counter Barnartt's suggestion (1994) that action mobilization has occurred in the absence of consensus mobilization.

13. There are several explanations for this split. One is that deaf people themselves stigmatize other persons with disabilities (Johnson, 1983). Another is that the medical community divided disability groups therapeutically and therefore politically (Zola, 1983).

14. She is Assistant Secretary for the Office of Special Education and Rehabilitative Services in the Department of Education.

15. See, for example, Stewart (1990) and Lane (1992). Recently, another coalition, called ACTION (Action for Children to Ensure Options Now), was formed to address this issue— providing yet another example of the deaf community's new willingness to engage in political action.

16. It is also an issue for which the cost implications differ, since interpreters or real-time captioning create on-going costs, while architectural modifications necessary for mobility accessibility tend to be one-time costs (Barnartt et al., 1990).

17. See, for example, Zola (1992) and Shapiro (1993).

18. This leads to the somewhat paradoxical possibility that the movement for deaf rights may become a "countermovement" (Meyer and Staggenborg, 1994) to the disability rights movement. That is, the movement for deaf rights may respond in opposition to the disability rights movement instead of in concert with it, as might be expected.

19. See, for example, the *Congressional Record* for March 22, 1988; March 13, 1991; and March 10, 1992 (Barnartt and Christiansen, 1992).

20. Within the deaf community, however, the protest issue was framed as "the end to oppression by hearing people" (Christiansen and Barnartt, 1995).

REFERENCES

Abramowitz, S. L., and A. J. Nassi. (1981). "Keeping the Faith: Psychosocial Correlates of Activism Persistence into Middle Adulthood." *Journal of Youth and Adolescence* 19(6): 507–523.

Altman, B., and S. N. Barnartt. (1993). "Moral Entrepreneurship and the Passage of the ADA." *Journal of Disability Policy Studies* 4(1): 22–40.

Barnartt, S. N. (1993). "Frame Extension and the Passage of the ADA." Presented at the Society for Disability Studies Annual Meeting, June, Seattle, WA.

———. (1994). "Action and Consensus Mobilization in the Deaf President Now Protest and Its Aftermath." Pp. 115–134 in *Research in Social Movements Conflict and Change*, Vol. 17, edited by L. Kriesberg, M. Dobkowski and I. Wallimann. Greenwich, CT: JAI Press.

Barnartt, S. N., and J. B. Christiansen. (1992). "Symbolic Visibility: The Deaf President Now Protest Four Years Later." Presented at the Society for Disability Studies Annual Meeting, Rockville, MD.

Barnartt, S. N., and K. Seelman. (1991). "Meeting the Costs of Communications Accessibility: Will ADA Help?" Presented at the Society for Disability Studies Annual Meeting, Oakland, CA.

Barnartt, S. N., K. Seelman, and K. and B. Gracer. (1990). "Policy Issues in Communications Accessibility." *Journal of Disability Policy Studies* 1(2):47–63.

Benderly, B. L. (1990). *Dancing without Music*. Washington, DC: Gallaudet University Press.

Berkowitz, E. (1987). *Disability Policy: America's Programs for the Handicapped*. New York: Cambridge University Press.

Burstein, P., and W. Freudenburg. (1978). "Changing Public Policy: The Impact of Public Opinion, Antiwar Demonstrations, and War Costs on Senate Voting on Vietnam War Motions." *American Journal of Sociology* 84:99–122.

Christiansen, J. B., and S. N. Barnartt. (1995). *Deaf President Now: The 1998 Revolution at Gallaudet University*. Washington, DC: Gallaudet University Press.

Fantasia, R. (1988). *Cultures of Solidarity: Consciousness, Action and Contemporary American Workers*. Berkeley: University of California Press.

Freeman, J. (1988). "Resource Mobilization and Strategy: A Model for Analyzing Social Movement Organization Action." Pp. 167–189 in *The Dynamics of Social Movements*, edited by M. N. Zald and J. D. McCarthy. Boston: University Press of America.

Gallaudet in the News. (1988). Washington, D.C.: Gallaudet Office of Public Relations.

Gamson, W. A. (1992). "The Social Psychology of Collective Action." Pp. 53–76 in *Frontiers in Social Movement Theory*, edited by A. D. Morris and C. M. Mueller. New Haven: Yale University Press.

Gannon, J. (1981). *Deaf Heritage: A Narrative History of Deaf America*. Silver Spring, MD: National Association of the Deaf.

Johnson, R. A. (1983). "Mobilizing the Disabled." Pp. 82–97 in *Social Movements of the 60's and 70's*, edited by J. Freeman. New York: Longman.

Kendrick, J. R. (1991). "You Don't Always Hit What You Aim At: Evaluating the Peace Movement of the 80's." Presented at the American Sociological Association Annual Meeting, Cincinnati.

Kenyon, R. (1992). "Sign It Loud, I'm Deaf and I'm Proud." *The Milwaukee Journal* (April 5):5–13.

Klandermans, B. (1984). "Mobilization and Participation: Social-Psychological Expansion of Resource Mobilization Theory." *American Sociological Review* (49):583–600.

———. (1988). "The Formation and Mobilization of Consensus." Pp. 173–196 in *International Social Movement Research*, Vol. 1, edited by B. Klandermans, H. Kriesi and S. Tarrow. Greenwich, CT: JAI Press, Inc.

———. (1992). "The Social Construction of Protest and Multiorganizational Fields." Pp. 77–103 in *Frontiers in Social Movement Theory*, edited by A. D. Morris and C. M. Mueller. New Haven, CT: Yale University Press.

Kleidman, R. (1993). *Organizing for Peace: Neutrality, the Test Ban, and the Freeze*. Syracuse: Syracuse University Press.

Lane, H. (1992). *The Mask of Benevolence: Disabling the Deaf Community*. New York: Alfred A. Knopf.

Lipsky, M. (1968). "Protest as a Political Resource." *American Political Science Review* 62: 1144–1158.

Lucas, C. (1991). *Sociolinguistics of the Deaf Community*. New York: Academic Press.

Luczak, R. (1993). *Eyes of Desire: A Deaf Gay and Lesbian Reader*. Boston: Alyson.

Mann, M. (1973). *Consciousness and Action among the Western Working Class*. London: Macmillan Press Ltd.

Marwell, G., and P. Oliver. (1984). "Collective Action Theory and Social Movement Research." Pp. 1–27 in *Research in Social Movements, Conflict and Change*, Vol. 7, edited by L. Kriesberg. Greenwich, CT: JAI Press, Inc.

Marx, G. (1988). "External Efforts to Damage or Facilitate Social Movements: Some Patterns, Explanations, Outcomes and Complications." Pp. 94–125 in *The Dynamics of Social Movements*, edited by M. N. Zald and J. D. McCarthy. Boston: University Press of America.

McCarthy, J. D., and M. N. Zald. (1990). "Resource Mobilization and Social Movements: A Partial Theory." Pp. 15–42 in *Social Movements in an Organizational Society*, edited by M. N. Zald and J. D. McCarthy. New Brunswick, NJ: Transaction Books.

Meyer, D. S. (1993). "Peace Protest and Policy: Explaining the Rise and Decline of Antinuclear Movements in Postwar America." *Policy Studies Journal* 21(1):35–55.

Meyer, D. S., and S. Staggenborg. (1994). "Movements, Countermovements, and the Structure of Political Opportunity." Presented at the American Sociological Association Annual Meeting, Los Angeles.

Murphy, R. F. (1987). *The Body Silent*. New York: Henry Holt.

Oberschall, A. (1973). *Social Conflict and Social Movements*. Englewood Cliffs, NJ: Prentice-Hall.

———. (1980). "Loosely Structured Collective Conflict: A Theory and an Application." Pp. 45–68 in *Research in Social Movements, Conflict and Change*, Vol. 3, edited by L. Kriesberg. Greenwich, CT: JAI Press, Inc.

———. (1988). "Protracted Conflict." Pp. 45–70 in *The Dynamics of Social Movements*, edited by M. N. Zald and J. D. McCarthy. Boston: University Press of America.

Padden, C., and T. Humphries. (1988). *Deaf in America: Voices from a Culture*. Cambridge: Harvard University Press.

Piven, F. F., and R. A. Cloward. (1979). *Poor People's Movements: Why They Succeed, How They Fail*. New York: Random House.

Rose, J. (1982). *Outbreaks: The Sociology of Collective Behavior*. New York: The Free Press.

Rose, P., and G. Kiger. (1994). "Intergroup Relations: Political Action and Identity in the Deaf

Community." Presented at the Society for Disability Studies Annual Meeting, Rockville, MD.

Sacks, O. (1990). *Seeing without Voices*. Berkeley: University of California Press.

Scotch, R. K. (1989). "Politics and Policy in the History of the Disability Rights Movements." *The Milbank Quarterly*: 67, suppl. 2, Part 2:380–399.

Shapiro, J. (1993). *No Pity: People with Disabilities Forging a New Civil Rights Movement*. New York: Random House.

Smelser, N. (1962). *Theory of Collective Behavior*. New York: The Free Press.

Solomon, A. (1994). "Defiantly Deaf." *The New York Times Magazine* (August 28): 38+.

Snow, D. A., and R. D. Benford. (1988). "Ideology, Frame Resonance and Participant Mobilization." Pp. 197–217 in *International Social Movement Research*, Vol. 1, edited by B. Klandermans, H. Kriesi and S. Tarrow. Greenwich, CT: JAI Press, Inc.

Snow, D. A., E. B. Rochford, Jr., S. K. Worder, and R. D. Benford. (1986). "Frame Alignment Processes, Micromobilization and Movement Participation." *American Sociological Review* 51 (August): 464–481.

Stewart, L. (1990). "Deaf Children and the Regular Education Initiative: A View from Within." *Exceptional Children* 39(2):13–17.

Sztompka, P. (1988). "The Social Functions of Defeat." Pp. 183–192 in *Research in Social Movements, Conflict and Change*, Vol. 10, edited by L. Kriesberg and B. Misztal. Greenwich, CT: JAI Press, Inc.

Tarrow, S. (1991). *Struggle, Politics and Reform: Collective Action, Social Movements, and Cycles of Protest*. Cornell University: Western Societies Program Occasional Paper #21 (2nd edition).

———. (1992). "Mentalities, Political Cultures and Collective Action Frames: Constructing Meanings through Action." Pp. 174–202 in *Frontiers in Social Movement Theory*, edited by A. D. Morris and C. M. Mueller. NewHaven: Yale University Press.

———. (1993). Social Protest and Policy Reform: May '68 and the Loi d'Orientation in France. *Comparative Political Studies* 25 (January): 579–607.

White, B. (1994). "Yes, There Is a Deaf Culture." Presented at the Society for Disability Studies Annual Meeting, Rockville, MD.

Woodward, J. (1972). "Implications for Sociolinguistics Research among the Deaf." *Sign Language Studies* 1: 1–7.

Zola, I. K. (1983). "The Evolution of the Boston Self Help Center." Pp. 143–153 in *A Way of Life for the Handicapped*, edited by G. Jones and N. Tutt. London: Residential Care Association.

———. (1992). "Is the Cup Half Empty or Half Full? Reflections on the Role of People with Disabilities in the Formulation of Disability Related Research." Presented at the Conference on Furthering the Goals of the ADA through Disability Policy: Research in the 1990's, Washington, D.C.

Zolberg, A. (1972). "Moments of Madness." *Politics and Society* 2 (Winter): 183–207.

49

Are the Deaf obsessed with the hearing? Deaf businesses install answering machines for voice calls only, figuring that Deaf customers will always call back later or use the relay, while the busy hearing person demands smooth and instantaneous service. Young people who grouse about their hearing teachers' mangled syntax and spoonerist howlers are gravely cautioned against Hearing-bashing. Intelligent Deaf consumers frequently seek the advice and approval of the interpreters they hire. What kind of grip do the hearing have on the Deaf psyche, anyway?

Of Deaf-Mutes, the *Strange*, and the Modern Deaf Self

Tom Humphries

1996

His task was not simply one of moving toward the requisite largeness of soul and faith in the value of his experience. He first had to seize the word. His being had to erupt from nothingness. Only by grasping the word could he engage in the speech acts that would ultimately define his selfhood. Further, the slave's task was primarily one of creating a human and liberated self rather than of projecting one that reflected a peculiar landscape and tradition. His problem was not to answer Crevecoeur's question: "What then is the American, this new man?" It was rather, the problem of being itself.

—Houston A. Baker, Jr. (1985, p. 245)

In writing of the autobiographical acts of southern slaves, Houston A. Baker, Jr. described a process in which slaves began to talk and to write about themselves not as property but as human. The process is one of creating a self out of "nothingness" as Baker characterized it. Slaves could neither talk nor write about themselves except as it was done by the slaveowner. And in that sense, slaves did not exist. Existence, or being, came about only when slaves could begin to imagine for themselves a separate being from the one created for them by the slaveowner and to find the words to talk about themselves in this new way.

Deaf-mutes of the nineteenth and the first half of the twentieth century had a similar task. Considered at different times in history in various parts of the world to be nonhuman, or at the least, incapable of that which constitutes humanness, deaf-mutes could testify to the difficulty of imaging (as well as imagining) oneself and one's entire subset of humanity into existence. Surrounded by powerful ideas of others that they were less than human, how could deaf-mutes conceive of themselves as anything more? They were not beings in the sense that humans are beings, but rather, exotic life forms patronized, experimented on, and excluded by humans from human society.

The evidence of history tells us that people who hear and speak regard people who do not hear as speechless and voiceless in both the literal and figurative sense. In imagining Deaf people, others have, throughout history, understood that deaf-mutes neither could say anything nor had anything to say. Deaf-mutes, in suffering this silencing by others, also suffered a denial or silencing of the self. Like illiterate slaves, for whom the only traditions of talk and writing available to them were those of the slaveowner who did not consider them as beings, the deaf-mute had only the traditions of people who hear to emulate.

To have the word, or rather, to have language and traditions of language use such as the ability to tell stories about yourself and, then, to use the word to create a self that is more than the distorted reflection of a hearing people is the task that deaf-mutes have faced in bringing us to this point in history where Deaf people are as confident and certain of their place in humanity as they have ever been.

Yet, this is not saying much. The modern age for Deaf people did not begin until the 1970s. The voice of Deaf people from earlier eras is different in important ways. For one thing, the voice of Deaf people of the modern age is one of cultural explicitness and self-consciousness and a centeredness around a signed language that is not reflected in previous images of the Deaf self. However, the level of tension within communities of Deaf people across the country reflect that, as always, there is no peace or serenity among ourselves about who we are. "What is American Sign Language (ASL)?" "What is Deaf culture?" "Am I Deaf or deaf?" Deaf people ask these pointed questions of each other, of scholars, and of themselves. There are no answers, of course, because the questions themselves are born of evolving images of self and self-representation.

To understand the transition of a Deaf self into modernity, one must trace the development of these images of self and figure out how to alter conventional interactional patterns between Deaf and hearing people that would rapidly become dysfunctional to some extent. This chapter attempts to explain the differing theories about Deaf people held by others and by Deaf people themselves and how hearing and Deaf people account for each other. The problem of coming to voice for Deaf people is also an important aspect of the transition and is explored. Questions of authenticity (what/who represents the true Deaf self), the growing need of Deaf people to compel others to listen, and an insistence on telling their own story rather than allowing others to tell their story back to them are all central to the emergence of a new voice for Deaf people. Differences between Deaf and hearing people's ideals and concepts of being (and well-being) are also important and are examined here.

And, finally, Deaf and hearing people's existence in proximity to each other in this new age is not without conflict. How are conflicts played out now that the rules are different? Conflict and coexistence are reflected in discourse that we find within each group and in the interaction between groups. This chapter offers some examples of ways of categorizing this discourse and closes with some considerations for how interaction may need to be shaped for Deaf and hearing people to work successfully together.

• A Theory of Self Proposed by Others

It is the nature of human culture that the entirety of the person is accounted for in some way and that there are explanations for variation from the configuration of the "complete" being. Thus, hearing Americans, and hearing peoples of many other cultures, account for Deaf people among themselves in terms of disability or dysfunction. This is the theory that was for many, many years the only one allowed to exist both among hearing people and Deaf people. Deaf people were what hearing people theorized they were. Their accounting of themselves was the accounting of others. The Deaf person's image of self was the image of the hearing person rendered— languageless, speechless, unhearing, cultureless, and *strange*. Strange, not in the sense of "weird" but, as Spiro (1990) indicated, unknowable:

> But if the members of any group G cannot meaningfully and intelligibly translate the cultural concepts of any other group into their own concepts, then for G, other groups are not only strange; *they are fundamentally and irreducibly strange* [italics added]. In short, for G, any other group is . . . wholly Other, unknown because unknowable. (p. 52)

Deaf people were unknowable but not uncategorized and undefined. Theories of deaf people abound among people who hear. And in the failure to know, the impossibility to know, hearing people permitted no other theory that Deaf people might have had of themselves to compete. The first theories that Deaf people have had about themselves were those of others. (If Deaf people are Other for hearing people, then hearing people are most certainly Other for Deaf people.)

Because hearing people could not know us, we could not know ourselves. Because the concept of the self was so much a variation of the hearing self, there could be no Deaf self that was any different. How could any Deaf person have a self different than what was imposed? It was unimaginable. There were no other possibilities. Deaf people were just what hearing people said they were.

Like the forces that stripped African slaves of their language and religion, their image of being, and made them pieces of property by pure force of the White man's imagination, Deaf people's self was that imagined by the other. They were even strange to themselves. They identified themselves and described themselves just as the hearing people among whom they lived did. In what other voice could they speak except the hearing person's voice? What resistance is possible when one cannot imagine another self?

How difficult it must have been to Jean Massieu to "defend" his educability (Lane,

1984). How difficult it must have been for John James Flournoy (1856), who advocated for a deaf state in the 1850s, to tolerate the constraints of living a life like a hearing man (without hearing) while being denied a place among hearing men. How difficult it must have been for George Veditz in 1913 to try to convince an unheeding world that signed language was worth preserving. How difficult it must have been for generations of deaf-mutes to live the life of the strange.

• The Deaf-Mute and the Self: Strange but True

If being defined by others made deaf-mutes' image of themselves into something exotic and unusual, something special in the sense that they were savants, then it was this very image that bound them together and led to competing images. For in making deaf-mutes, society threw them together in groups. Out of these groups grew communities and from these communities came remembering. Once remembering began, a competing self began to form and grow. Remembering and reminding, selecting and creating, defining and redefining, remembering and reminding, it took on its own energy. Deaf-mutes in communities, large and small, took the strange and made it unremarkable.

To compete with an identity of languagelessness, deaf-mutes maintained "the sign language" and used it for everyday communication and to remember and remind. To compete with a society that openly discussed their undesirableness in the genetic pool, they procreated and recruited other deaf-mutes into their communities, rejoicing in each lost deaf-mute found and saved. Seeing themselves as incapable of *culture*, they raised their own children in a culture ever becoming richer and richer, stronger and stronger. Deeming themselves not worthy of learning, they never forgot the knowledge of their community from generation to generation. Thinking themselves incompetent to participate in the institutions of society (religion, art, sports), they formed parallel institutions, deaf clubs, athletic organizations, church missions, and literary societies. Being told they were afflicted, they healed themselves by embracing the *strange* and thus made themselves whole.

Hearing people, supremely self-confident in their images of themselves as complete and untouchable and equally confident of the incompleteness of deaf-mutes, were a powerful force. Ideas about the nature of "man," boosted by the sheer numbers of people who hear and a consciousness that could see no other consciousness, were constants in the lives of deaf-mutes. Deaf-mutes, overpowered, accounted for themselves in two ways: first as what hearing people said they were, and second as they were able to "invent" themselves over time and generations. If cultures are in some sense inventions, then hearing people invented themselves and deaf-mutes, deaf-mutes invented themselves and hearing people. Each had to account for the other.

What was the difference, then, between hearing people and deaf-mutes in this respect? The answer to this is that whereas hearing people accounted for themselves as complete and deaf-mutes as deficit, deaf-mutes accounted for themselves as complete and incomplete and for hearing people as complete. This is quite a difference. The deaf-mute self, in its duality, was a marvel of reconciliation. In the same sentence, deaf-mutes could both denigrate and praise their "sign language" (Padden and Humphries, 1988), talk of themselves as uneducated and unintellectual in very educated and intellectual ways, and feel alienated from community while building strong and vital deaf-mute communities. They knew themselves to be strange but could be true to a vision of themselves as unaffected, unmarked, and normal.

This is sometimes quite explicitly stated as in the following from a column called "Glimpse from the Past" that appeared in the January 1994 issue of the *NAD Broadcaster*, the house organ of the National Association of the Deaf.

> From the Silent Worker, January, 1954, Vol. 6, No. 9, Page 11
>
> We note, too, that there is frequent reference in the press, over the radio, and on TV, about "normalizing the deaf" by restoring them to society. All of this is well-meaning, of course, but it is getting rather monotonous, to say the least.
>
> In the first place, the deaf are about as normal as the fellow next door. True, he may be able to enjoy life a bit more due to his hearing and his fluent speech, but we think the deaf individual can give him a close race for all-around happiness in the enjoyment of life. (p. 15)

In the second paragraph, there is a grudging admission that hearing people are better. But deaf people are normal. This kind of doublespeak has been a way of reconciling these disparate beliefs about the self and is quite common in Deaf people's talk (Padden and Humphries, 1988). But reconciliation in talk does not necessarily mean a reconciliation in the self. It may be a way to explain the conflict of self, however, to allow the two views to coexist within the individual without ripping him or her apart.

• The Modern Deaf Self

The reconciliation continues among Deaf people of the 1990s. Competing accountings still coexist. Hearing people for the most part still hold to their accounting of deaf people as flawed. Some things have changed, however. There is some re-inventing going on that talks of the sign language as American Sign Language and a concession that, perhaps, it is a language after all. There is a sense that the communities of Deaf people might actually be rooted in culture and ethnicity.

Deaf-mutes are no longer "deaf-mutes" or "the deaf" but "Deaf people" just as "Negroes" are no longer "negroes" or even "Blacks" but "African American," and "girls" are no longer "girls" but "women." For Deaf people, there has been a great rejection of hearing people's accounting of Deaf people. The old dual accounting of incomplete/complete exists, but it is increasingly politically incorrect to acknowledge it. Deaf identity is now defined very sharply and debated in explicit terms. Individual by individual, we are deciding who is Deaf and who is not based on a new public, and as yet, fluid, prototype. Everyone who was Deaf before is still Deaf, but, nevertheless, we are putting each other to the test applying criteria of authenticity that are hard to pin down exactly but that are rigorously applied.

For example, is a deaf person who went to a hearing public school, transferred to a residential school for deaf children for the last two years of high school, learned ASL beginning at the age of fifteen, and is now a student at Gallaudet University *really* Deaf? Many Deaf people debate the answer to this. Another common question among Deaf people recently has been, "What is ASL?" We are asking what the sign language is and getting lots of different answers. Yet, with a few natural changes in vocabulary, the sign language continues to be used as it has been for generations. Why do we ask ourselves this type of question? It is as if a questioning and cleansing must take place before we can trust those things that we are. The modern Deaf self must search its collective memory and make sure that we have forgotten the self created by others and have remembered the "real" sign language and the "real" Deaf self.

When once the only public definitions of the Deaf self were those of doctors, audiologists, educators, and psychologists, now public definitions of the deaf self are those of anthropologists, ethnographers, and Deaf people themselves. The modern Deaf self is about identity, cultural identity but also about public face and otherness.

Public face is the way that we wish others to see and think of us. In "seizing the word," the writers of the slave narrators began to exert a public face that sprang from their own minds, not from the minds of others. Deaf people of the 1960s and 1970s not only began to redraw their public face in a different image but to do something equally important. They reached a stage that other peoples in similar situations had also encountered: "For black women our struggle has not been to emerge from silence into speech but to change the nature and direction of our speech. To make a speech that compels listeners, one that is heard" (hooks, 1990b, p. 337).

To compel listeners, yes. A self cannot exist if it is not heard. Deaf people have had to create voices, learn to hear their own voices, and now it remains to compel others to listen.

Perhaps it is too strong to say that deaf-mutes both literally and figuratively had no voice. Literally, many deaf-mutes could speak aloud. And, figuratively, there were individuals who "spoke out" in a voice that seemed lifted out of the modern age. What Massieu, Flournoy, Veditz, and some others had to say certainly resonates today (Padden and Humphries, 1988). But it cannot be denied that for the great majority of deaf-mutes, they could only speak of themselves and their social condition in the voice of the other, hearing people. This was the same as having no voice at all, or worse, of having a voice that belied one's own humanness. And even if they did speak in a different voice, it could not be heard.

The presence of a new and different voice and the dominance of this voice over the voice of the other has been an important change in Deaf people's lives. But it is an artifact of another change: Deaf people's relationship to otherness. To speak in the voice of the other, to possess a self that was the creation of the other, was the fate of deaf-mutes. But if deaf-mutes internalized the other and made it their own self-image, then what Deaf people are doing today is establishing a new relationship with the other. Much of the deaf–hearing tension that has sprung up over the past few years has been about control of institutions such as schools and colleges and social service agencies. But a great deal of the tension has been about who speaks for Deaf people and the type of self that is portrayed by this speech. The conflict that grows out of this struggle is, in turn, about separation of the self from other.

In the beginning, when Deaf people of the 1970s were trying to make sense of a new self-consciousness, there was a heavy reliance on changes in the way hearing people were talking about them. The subconscious knowledge that deaf-mutes had about themselves, that they were a cohesive and close-knit group of sophisticated signers who shared a history, began to converge with descriptions of them by others. Others began to talk about deaf-mutes as a language minority and as a community with an ethnic experience. The science of hearing people, notably linguistics and anthropology, began to talk about ASL as a language and Deaf people as a culture. Working with their own changing vision of themselves and hearing people's new theory of them, Deaf people's new self emerged. However, it was still in many respects the other who defined.

In the 1970s and part of the 1980s, it was still the researchers and the voice of researchers, most of them hearing, who defined Deaf people's image of self. Deaf people's relationship to the other was still the same as it always had been. Hearing people became caught up in the rush to redefine Deaf people. Scholars and nonscholars alike rushed to embrace the ideal of equality and equivalence between Deaf and hearing cultures, ASL and English, and Deaf person and hearing person. For hearing people, defining deaf-mutes in the way that they did was part of hearing people's process of self-definition (Lane, 1992). How could a Deaf self-definition not be influenced by the great power of this change among hearing people? Dominated for centuries by the voice of the other, Deaf people had no problem now in adopting the new language of the other in talking about themselves. Only now the other had adopted a new story, one that reflects the story Deaf people have always tried to tell themselves but have been unable to sustain without internal and external conflict. It remained for Deaf people to go one step further and recognize that true voice means not telling back the stories of others about themselves:

> No need to hear your voice when I can talk about you better than you can speak about yourself. . . . I want to know your story. And then I will tell it back to you in a new way. Tell it back to you in such a way that it has become mine, my own. Re-writing you I write myself anew. I am still author, authority. I am still colonizer, the speaking subject and you are now at the center of my talk. (hooks, 1990a, p. 343)

Thus, the modern Deaf self has come to this. Not stopping at the "telling back" of their story by hearing people, they have placed distance between the Deaf self and other. But it has not been easy, and confusion and tension still reign. Deaf people debate Deaf people about who we are and what we are. Deaf people dispute hearing people about who we are. The distance is necessary because the internalized other still remains within each of us, threatening to dominate once again.

• Differences

The differences between Deaf and hearing peoples' theories about each other are quite real, and not imagined. How do the competing accountings that Deaf people and hearing people have of themselves and Deaf people differ? A few of these differences are discussed here.

Ideals of Completeness

What constitutes completeness? For hearing people, Deaf people are incomplete beings. Through this cultural filter, Deaf people will always be one down on hearing people. Nowhere are these ideals so explicitly evident than in the languages of Deaf and hearing peoples. In translating from language to language, and in particular from ASL to English, meaning is attempted to be equated, and often it reveals the gap between perceptions and the realization that there are no equivalences. There is no word in English to refer to Deaf people that does not carry a meaning that is foreign to Deaf people themselves. The idea of disability or lacking something is so attached to the English words used for Deaf people (*deaf, hearing impaired, hard of hearing, communicatively handicapped*, etc.) that there is simply no escaping it. On the other hand, there is little possibility of translating Deaf people's name for themselves into English. *The people* or *us* may began to convey the meaning but lacks the richness of the true meaning of the sign (often translated as *deaf*) that Deaf people use for themselves (Padden and Humphries, 1988).

The English names for Deaf people are tied by history and perception to ideas of incompleteness, and it is difficult for English speakers to totally change from using the word *deaf* to mean someone with a hearing loss to an alternate meaning of someone of a particular community and worldview. Deaf people have no such problem, except in the sense that they are aware that their sign for themselves (glossed as DEAF) has the meaning of "hearing loss" for many people. To actually denote this meaning in the sign, Deaf people have to establish a context, alter the sign itself to be a little more explicit, or change it to another sign that is more specific to the meaning of hearing loss such as signs glossed as DEAF (2 hands) or EAR-SHUT.

Further, to describe a Deaf person, English speakers have little recourse to other vocabulary. The most common phrase, "can't hear," assumes again a dysfunction. Less offensive, but still loaded, is "doesn't hear." This is not the way Deaf people think of themselves and, as a description, it only reinforces the opposing sensibilities of Deaf and hearing peoples.

The Value of Being

One of the most difficult perceptions that both Deaf and hearing people have to deal with is the nature of the *being* that is the Deaf way of being. Because hearing people begin with an ideal of incompleteness in regard to Deaf people, is Deaf people's world an equal one? Are Deaf people, instead, marvels of adaptation? Have they adjusted to their condition in amazing ways? Do they sign because they cannot speak? Are they examples of the plasticity of the human being? Have they risen from the ashes of hearing people? It is one thing to see Deaf people as incomplete beings; it is another to believe there are other possible worlds, of equal quality and value.

To come to being, the deaf-mute certainly had to wrestle with the notion that all being begins from a single prototypical hearing human. If this is the way being begins, then yes, Deaf people are the descendants of a hearing Adam and Eve. Yet, what if Deaf people are not descendants of a hearing Adam and Eve but taken directly from the clay itself? What if they sign because this is the language of their community, no more special or exotic than English to a hearing American? What if the Deaf self sees hearing people as *strange* in the same way that hearing people view Deaf people? What if Deaf people are as supremely confident of the originality of their biology as hearing people are? Two sets of views of what constitutes the nature of being Deaf reveal crucial differences between Deaf and hearing people. For hearing people, the characteristics of their theory of Deaf people, rooted in a theory of incompleteness, are:

1. Contrastive/oppositional (hear/don't hear, speaking/mute, complete/incomplete, self/other)
2. Pathological (having physical and developmental conditions, needing medical intervention or prosthetic intervention, behavior is related to condition)
3. Adaptive (sign, use prosthetic interventions, adapt resources, use special procedures, systems, and technology)
4. Esoteric (noble, special, think without language, visual world, miracles of adaptation, needing to be taught and brought to life)

These can be compared to views Deaf people have about themselves:

1. Contained (self-knowing, having community, whole, complete)
2. Marked/unmarked (one with Deaf people but immersed among others, at risk)
3. Descendant (recipients and transmitters of ways of being, language)
4. Experiential and aesthetic (having moral imperatives and value systems based on experience that define a good life for themselves and the children, possessing concepts of beauty and ethics defined by experience, abstract creators)

These differences reveal the difficulty that hearing people may have in overcoming a deep-rooted sense of unequal worlds when it comes to Deaf people.

The Concept of Wellness

Others may never completely be able to let go of an idea that there is no naturalness to being Deaf. For these people, the Deaf self will always be housed in a body that does not work, is not well. In this regard, the distance between how Deaf people view their bodies and how hearing people view Deaf people's bodies makes the Deaf self unknowable to people who hear.

Two ways to approach the concept of wellness that are very instructive in understanding the distance and difference between Deaf and hearing peoples are: (a) the competition for ownership of Deaf people's bodies and (b) the relationship of the pathology of the body to the self.

Who owns the Deaf person's body? Do hearing parents own it for the first eighteen years at least? Do educators hold it in trust for parents for most of this time also? Do doctors and other medical intervention personnel such as audiologists and speech therapists own it more than Deaf people themselves?

We are all familiar with the artifacts of the competition for Deaf people's bodies. Speech and hearing science, surgical procedures, faith healing, immersion techniques such as oral and mainstream education, brain studies, and so on. At no time, even to the present, have Deaf people, as a group, been in control of their bodies. Individual Deaf people on reaching adulthood sometimes manage to take control sufficiently to preserve their bodies in an image of wholeness, and insofar as they are able to do this, they have hope of attaining and maintaining physical well-being. But do others even know that ownership of Deaf people's bodies is an issue?

If Deaf people have had difficulty with others owning their bodies more than they do themselves, they have had even more of a struggle formulating a self that is not an extension of this nonfunctioning body. Would a mentally ill Deaf person's illness disappear if he were not deaf? Are there unique sets of psychological phenomena that attach themselves to people who do not hear?

This debate over whether there is a "psychology of the deaf" (Lane, 1992) is not about whether there is a paradigm that we call a mentally "well" deaf person and another paradigm that we call an "ill" deaf person but how these concepts of wellness and illness interact with a pathology called a "hearing loss." In hearing people, concepts of wellness and illness are associated with socialization, heredity, trauma, and even brain chemistry. Women have had certain psychological attributes related directly to their biology. Gay men and lesbians have also had attributes associated with their biology. In women, their biology was thought to dictate emotions, moods, and sometimes mental illness. In gay men, the converse was thought to be true; a psychological condition caused biology to go haywire. In Deaf people, a biological condition is thought to dictate social behavior, personality types, moral development, and maturity development among other things (Lane, 1992).

For deaf-mutes, the self as given to them by others started out unwell. The self was that of a hearing person without hearing. A self that was made alien by virtue of being unable to hear speech and other sounds and ultimately, made uncentered by being marginalized by the people who controlled their bodies. The deaf-mute self could only be made well again by "adjusting" to the fact of a loss and the place others made for him or her in their society. The modern Deaf self struggles with marginality but is centered, sometimes subconsciously, sometimes consciously, in a complex and schematic knowledge of self and the world (D'Andrade, 1990) unimaginable to those who see Deaf people as disabled.

Thus, an understanding of centeredness and wellness in Deaf people can only be approached by hearing people when hearing people no longer see Deaf people as extensions of their own biological imperatives. An African American is not a non-White person, a woman is not a nonman, and a Deaf person is not a nonhearing person.

Ideals of Solidarity

The place of the other in relation to the self in deaf-mutes was sometimes so close that the two were confused as one. The modern Deaf self is more distant from others' models of the Deaf self. Solidarity, or the stressing of the same in the same-but-different approach to intercultural contact, may threaten the modern Deaf self that is not far removed from a self proposed by others at this point in history. What this means is that in intercultural interactions, there is sometimes a natural tendency for one party to break down differences, to assert sameness, to assume that despite cultural differences, underneath the skin, we are all the same. It is this assertion of the sameness that is threatening to the Deaf self because most Deaf people are still struggling with or can remember what it was like to be totally dominated and defined by others. As is often the case in interethnic interaction (Scollon and Scollon, 1982), distance, rather than solidarity, may be desired by Deaf people and demonstrated in very active ways including aloofness, avoidance, and hostility in encounters with hearing people.

This is evident in the growth of "deaf only" activity in the past decade. Retreats, conferences, caucuses, and other such attempts of Deaf people to get together with themselves to the point of explicitly excluding hearing people are symptomatic of a need to let Deaf people be Deaf people without worry of influence from or accommodation of hearing people's needs. Some see this as separatism, but it is far from that. Separatism, is a particular ideology that is not normally reflected in these types of meetings except when separatism, itself, is the issue. These attempts for Deaf people to take their own counsel are not separatist activities but, rather, are strong acts of marking of distance between Deaf and hearing people that Deaf people feel are necessary to their well-being. That this offends many hearing people is an indication of the difference in perception of the goal of interaction between Deaf and hearing people.

Although hearing people may think that Deaf people's goal is to be included in society, it is more likely that Deaf people's goal is one of maintenance of boundaries between cultures and a search for accommodation that allows the Deaf person to remain true to the self. When acted out in dramatic ways such as deaf only gatherings of Deaf people, solidarity is challenged and distance becomes so real, that an uncomfortable tension arises. Solidarity between Deaf and hearing people that seems to be highly valued by hearing people and often sought in friendships, mixed marriages, cross-cultural counseling, and psycho-therapy may not, in Deaf people's view, be a desirable or realistic goal given the nature of the history of dominance by the other in Deaf people's lives. This is not to say that strong relationships do not develop between Deaf and hearing people but that deference (discussed more fully in a later section), not solidarity, is the most likely path to successful and lasting understanding between Deaf and hearing people at this point in history.

• Conflict and Coexistence

Given these differences and Deaf people's own internalization of these differences, conflict is a possibility and a reality both within Deaf people's community and with others outside the community. Coexistence between Deaf and hearing people rests very strongly on reconciling these differences. As was mentioned earlier, the deaf-mute self was built on the assumption that the necessary reconciliation would happen *within* the Deaf person. Deaf people had to find ways to explain things and talk about things that gave hearing people their due. Hearing people were for the most part unconscious of Deaf people's ingenuity in maintaining within themselves two wholly different theories and, thus, finding ways to maintain coexistence with hearing people.

But the modern Deaf self is less interested in maintaining this type of duality. Conflict is pushed outward into the space between Deaf and hearing people, and hearing people are asked to confront differences on a conscious level. The modern Deaf self does not make the differences go away.

There are many ways that Deaf and hearing people act out the fundamental conflict over self. Here is a sampling:

1. Naming of Deaf people. Should they be called deaf or hearing impaired? Is hard of hearing okay?
2. Differing views of competence to control own institutions. Examples: The fight for a Deaf president at Gallaudet University, the push for Deaf directors and superintendents of schools and organizations, Deaf majorities on Boards of Directors, the "of, by, and for the deaf" political movement.
3. Struggle over control of the lives of deaf children. Examples: How will they be educated? Which language? Which culture? Who will teach them? Should young children be surgically implanted with electronic devices?
4. Argumentation over status inequality of ASL/English and Deaf people's/hearing people's culture. Examples: Legislative proposals for official recognition of ASL, demands for ASL interpreting as opposed to signed English interpreting.
5. Discriminatory/reverse discriminatory practices. Examples: Job descriptions that favor Deaf people versus job descriptions that favor hearing people, "hearing people need not apply" attitudes, hearing people can't teach deaf culture perceptions, "we would like to hire a Deaf person but we can't find any qualified for the job" rationales.

Many of the ways that Deaf and hearing people act out the conflict over the Deaf self are played out in specific kinds of language and talk:

1. Accusatory talk that includes oppressor/oppressed, colonizer/colonized, power-less/empowered visions of blame and of "us" versus "them."
2. Challenge talk that tests the other's belief system. Example: "If you had a pill that would make you hearing, would you . . . ?" "If you think it's okay to operate on deaf children to make them hearing, then it must be okay for Deaf people to operate on their hearing children to make them deaf."
3. Routinized expressions of problematicity or "griping" about the other. Examples: Complaints about lack of competence in ASL or in English, or "Deaf people have no tact," or "How will you get a job if you don't learn English?" or "You don't understand Deaf people."

Much of this conflict comes about because subordination and status inequality are not tolerable to a rising middle class of Deaf people. As the middle class of Deaf people grows, and it was quite small until the middle of the twentieth century, so do the ideals and expectations of the group, thus increasing the likelihood of conflict. As more and more hearing people become aware of the changing status of Deaf people, there is much more possibility of conflict because many do not accept the underlying assumptions about language and culture that are the foundation of the new Deaf self.

Deaf people have to a large extent always maintained parallel lives while living with others (Padden and Humphries, 1988). But this has been quite a subconscious process, and coexistence in the past was built on Deaf people's acquiescence and accommodation to the self-imagining proposed by hearing people. With Deaf people less and less likely to accommodate and the modern Deaf self still in the process of imagining itself, some new models of Deaf–hearing interaction will inevitably evolve.

• Interactional Considerations

Earlier it was mentioned that solidarity, or the emphasizing of the sameness of Deaf and hearing people, threatens the new Deaf self. Yet there is a need to find some commonality or mutual knowledge of the other between Deaf and hearing people so that successful interactions can take place. Everyone wants to know which interactional pitfalls to avoid.

The establishment of difference is a strong current in Deaf–hearing interactions at this point in history. Everyone wants to see a difference. All of us want descriptions of how Deaf people's culture is different. In fact, difference is demanded. An example, for years there was a strong push in research on ASL to find that it was very different from English (in word order, for example). If this difference could not be found, then ASL was not a language, but bad English. The fact that ASL has basically the same word order as English (as do many other languages) has taken a long time to finally be accepted.

For another example, Deaf people have felt compelled to emphasize that their world is visual whereas hearing people's world is auditory. Deaf people see, hearing people hear. There is little to actually say about this difference, but there *must* be a difference.

The reason for this insistence that there must be a difference is because the old deaf-mute self is very much a presence in U.S. society. In order to legitimatize the new Deaf self, difference must be clear and must be articulated in ways that differences between other groups may not have to be. It was said earlier that to seek sameness, commonality, or solidarity in intercultural interaction between Deaf and hearing people may not be a realistic strategy at this particular time in Deaf–hearing relations.

The obverse of solidarity in discussions of interethnic communication is deference (Scollon and Scollon, 1982). Deference, a type of politeness system that recognizes the autonomy of Deaf people (and hearing people for that matter) and assumes a low power differential between Deaf people and hearing people, seems to be the type of interactional strategy that is better suited for the context in which Deaf and hearing people find themselves today. Increasingly, over the past decade, Deaf people have found ways to tell hearing people to "back off," to stop defining Deaf people, and to stop tampering with Deaf people's bodies. They have not always been polite about it. But the sentiment, regardless of how strongly it has been expressed, has been clear: Distance is needed.

This is not to imply physical distance but a distancing of wills, self-images, and voice. There needs to be an acknowledgement in the interaction that there is little power differential between the two parties to the interaction as well. The relationship of hearing people to deaf-mutes was one of dominance and acquiescence, one of great power on the part of hearing people and powerlessness on the part of deaf-mutes. Status equality is one way to reduce power differential. In intimate kinds of interactions, such as teaching, counseling, or psychoanalysis involving Deaf people as the student or the client/patient, control of the context of the interaction may be one of the ways that Deaf people try to attain status equality.

There are several ways that Deaf people may attempt to gain control. One of these is to control the placement of "the problem." Gone is the old deaf self taking responsibility for communication failure or misunderstanding of purpose. The problem is not that the Deaf person is deaf (and, thus, having problematic communication, language, and psychological profiles). The problem instead is the hearing persons lack of ASL fluency, lack of understanding of Deaf culture, lack of experience with Deaf people, lack of knowledge of how hearing people oppress Deaf people, or lack of solutions that work for Deaf people.

Another way might be to control language use. By insisting that the communication used in the interaction be in ASL, the sense of comfort and ease is shifted to the Deaf person and the burden of second language communication or reliance on a sometimes less than fluent ASL interpreter is shifted to the hearing person. If there is to be a struggle with language equality, let the hearing person, not the Deaf person as in the past, make the effort and try to maintain a sense of power while doing so.

Controlling language use is most commonly seen in Deaf people's attempts to have hearing people learn ASL rather than some signed English system, in attempts to have ASL as the primary language used in meetings and conferences, in pushes for interpreters to use ASL, and in attempts to require that teachers and therapists be fluent in ASL. But it is also evident when Deaf people choose not to adapt their signing or communication style in an attempt to be understood by hearing people. The decision to stay with ASL and normal conversational style in ASL rather than code switch to a contact language or to use speech involves a new relationship between Deaf and hearing people. It implies that there is no longer a basis for it always being the Deaf person who adapts his or her language in a communicative interaction between a Deaf and hearing person.

Related to this are the high expectations of an interpreter in terms of being able to move between ASL and English without the Deaf person having to adapt his or her language use. Control of language use has taken on such an edge that many hearing signers and interpreters find themselves, to their acute embarrassment, being judged on their ASL competence using a more exacting standard. Pressure to be competent in ASL or use an interpreter who is competent in ASL is very much a part of the landscape between Deaf and hearing people at this point in history.

Yet another way to achieve status equality (and sometimes skew it in favor of the Deaf person) is to control the moral high ground in the relationship. One of the side products of the emergence of the modern Deaf self is that hearing people are supposed to and, in fact, may actually feel guilty for the way that Deaf people have been and are treated in society. A sense of moral superiority, whether real or imagined, is a very powerful weapon in the hands of many Deaf people. In some contexts, Deaf people may try to achieve control by relying on the hearing person's feeling that hearing people deserve whatever Deaf people want to dish out at this point. This makes Deaf people feel confident that they can get away with "bashing" hearing people. Indeed, hearing people have a problem of knowing when and how to challenge Deaf people's bashing and their sometimes incorrect and ideologically suspect statements about hearing people in general.

Historically, hearing people have held the moral advantage because of the "good works" that they do with people who do not hear. Every deaf-mute knew that everything that hearing society made available to them was an act of kindness. Harlan Lane (1992) referred to the "mask of benevolence" behind which hearing people have injured Deaf people while professing to "help" them. Another way to look at this, however, is in the way that hearing people make themselves morally superior by being the ones who are helping. To share or even to claim the moral high ground, Deaf people speak often in the language of the oppressed minority. The discourse between Deaf and hearing people at this time seems filled with such phrases as "discrimination," "oppression," "inequality," and more recently "audism" (Humphries, 1977). Once the moral high ground shifts, the interaction takes on a different context, and control is attainable for Deaf people.

What do we do now? To change the context of the interaction and to attain some equality of control, both parties in the interaction need to view the interaction as an intercultural interaction. This involves placing the problem in the context of the different languages, communicative intents, and worldviews involved in cross-cultural discourse, not in the Deaf person or the hearing person. Neither Deaf people nor hearing people are necessarily skilled at intercultural interactions, and, so in formal relations such as teacher–student, counselor–client, or therapist–client, it may be up to the professional to obtain the sensitivity and skill required to avoid breakdowns in intercultural communication.

It is possible that controlling the context of the interaction between Deaf and hearing people is more likely to produce results intended or hoped for by Deaf people just because Deaf people may feel more in control of possible outcomes. Solutions proposed by others are often not possible solutions in the eyes of Deaf people (Padden and Humphries, 1988). For Deaf people, ownership of the solutions may be more important for the moment than the actual results. An argument can be made that this is the way it should be, that this is the stage of the process of coming to voice in which Deaf people happen to be. Gaining control may be paramount at this particular time in history.

In summary, the strength of relationships that need to be built between Deaf and hearing people depends largely on several things: acknowledgment of differences; deference to each other's need for autonomy; acknowledgment of a struggle to find a new balance of power after a long history of inequality; a new paradigm of control in cross-cultural relationships, especially in regard to language and communication; and, finally, the modern Deaf person's ability to see hearing people as having solutions that don't remind them of or return them to the deaf-mute life of the past. It is this last aspect that is crucial. Deaf people have to choose to believe and trust in the possibility that hearing people may be able to help them without couching the help in a defunct ideology of the strangeness of Deaf people.

• Competing Illusions

Is Deaf culture an illusion, an extension of the pathology, an adjustment to being without hearing? It is easy to dismiss "culture" as a delusion of Deaf people. After all, the whole idea of culture and of a modern Deaf self can be made moot by the elimination of the hearing loss, can it not? Perhaps, but as we approach genetic selectivity, are we not each of us possibly moot? The biomedical discourse of the past that describes not a whole Deaf people, but a suffering deaf-mute people is a much more terrible delusion than any image Deaf people might create for themselves. Only through control of the image of the self can Deaf people make the *strange* normal.

REFERENCES

Baker Jr., H. A. (1985). Autobiographical acts and the voice of the southern slave. In C. T. Davis and H. L. Gates, Jr.(eds.), *The slave's narrative* (pp. 242–261). New York: Oxford University Press.

D'Andrade, R. (1990). Culture and personality: A false dichotomy. In D. K. Jordan and M. J. Swartz (eds.), *Personality and the cultural construction of society* (pp. 145–160). Tusca-loosa: University of Alabama Press.

Flournoy, J. J. (1856). Mr. Flournoy to Mr. Turner. *American Annals of the Deaf and Dumb,* 8, 120–125.

———. (1858). Reply to objections. *American Annals of the Deaf and Dumb,* 10, 140–151.

Glimpse from the past. (1994, January). *NAD Broadcast,* 16 (1). 15. Silver Spring, MD: National Association of the Deaf.

hooks, b. (1990a). Marginality as site of resistance. In R. Ferguson, M. Gever, T. Minh-ha, and C. West (eds.), *Out there: Marginalization and contemporary cultures* (pp. 341–343). Cambridge, MA: MIT Press.

———. (1990b). Talking back. In R. Ferguson, M. Gever, T. Minh-ha, and C. West (eds.), *Out there: Marginalization and contemporary cultures* (pp. 337–340). Cambridge, MA: MIT Press.

Humphries, T. (1977). *Communicating across cultures (deaf/hearing) and language learning.* Unpublished doctoral dissertation, The Union Institute, Cincinnati, Ohio.

Lane, H. (1984). *When the mind hears.* New York: Random House.

———. (1992). *The mask of benevolence.* New York: Knopf.

Padden, C., and Humphries, T. (1988). *Deaf in America: Voices from a culture.* Cambridge, MA: Harvard University Press.

Scollon, R., and Scollon, S. (1982). *Narrative, literacy and face in interethnic communication.* Norwood, NJ: Ablex.

Spiro, M. (1990). On the strange and the familiar in recent anthropological thought. In J. W. Stigler, R. A. Shweder, & G. Herdt (eds.), *Cultural psychology: Essays on comparative human development* (pp. 47–61). New York: Cambridge University Press.

Veditz, G. (1913). *The preservation of the sign language* [film]. Silver Spring, MD: National Association of the Deaf.

50

Discussions of cochlear implants and genetic "therapy" that are couched in terms of reproductive control, eugenics, ethnocide, and Adolf Hitler generally upset and embarrass Deaf people, who do not want to be seen as lunatic-fringe radicals, paranoid conspiracy theorists, or, worse, Luddites. That much of this discussion has been articulated and published by a hearing man (Harlan Lane) contributes to the Deaf tendency to censor such discussions. Yet a great deal of historical evidence both supports the connection and suggests that the outcome of widespread childhood implantation and genetic tinkering may be the same as that of Hitler's racial hygiene policies: the destruction of the Deaf community.

The Hearing Agenda II

Eradicating the DEAF-WORLD

Harlan Lane, Robert Hoffmeister, and Ben Bahan

1996

Because the hearing agenda for Deaf people is constructed on the principle that members of the DEAF-WORLD have a disability, and because our society seeks to reduce the numbers of people with disabilities through preventive measures, hearing people have long sought ways to reduce the numbers of Deaf people, ultimately eliminating this form of human variation and with it the DEAF-WORLD. The chairman of a National Institutes of Health planning group acknowledged this in a 1993 interview with the *New York Times*: "I am dedicated to curing deafness. That puts me on a collision course with those who are culturally Deaf. That is interpreted as genocide of the Deaf."[1] Two measures that would reduce the numbers of Deaf people and are actively pursued today in many lands are eugenics and cochlear implant surgery on young Deaf children.

• Reproductive Control of Deaf People

Hearing efforts to regulate childbearing by Deaf people have a long history which has not yet ended. Prior to the Enlightenment, Deaf scions of wealthy families, especially women, were frequently sequestered in religious institutions; this not only ensured their chastity, it kept them out of sight: if one child was known to be Deaf, other children would be less marriageable. Indeed, it was this practice of sequestering Deaf children in religious institutions in sixteenth century Spain that led Ponce de León to develop, at the monastery of Oña, the first recorded method of teaching the Deaf to speak.[2] With the beginnings of education for Deaf people as a group in eighteenth century France, Deaf boys and girls were not only strictly segregated in schools (a common, if less rigorous, practice with hearing children), but also Deaf girls were sent, on graduation, to special asylums with the explicit purpose of preventing their circulation in society at large.[3] Laws refusing primogeniture to Deaf-mutes, laws restricting consanguineous marriage, and laws specifically prohibiting or discouraging Deaf marriage, all had the effect of discouraging Deaf people from marrying and reproducing.[4] Such laws reflected values in society at large and presumably reinforced efforts by hearing parents to discourage their Deaf children from marrying and reproducing.

Before the advent of residential schools for the Deaf, marriages of Deaf people were relatively rare.[5] When scattered Deaf children gathered in residential schools, Deaf marriages were facilitated through increased contacts. Many educators were vigorously opposed to Deaf marriages, however, and they vigilantly kept boys and girls separated, while urging celibacy on the pupils.[6]

The stated goal of the movement for oral education of Deaf children that arose and flourished in the second half of the nineteenth century was not so much to enable Deaf people to speak with their neighbors, shopkeepers and the like; nor was it to facilitate their learning written English. In fact, the stated goal was not primarily educational at all. It was to discourage reproduction by Deaf people by discouraging their socializing and marriage.[7] The founder of this movement in the U.S., Samuel Gridley Howe, superintendent of the Perkins Institution for the Blind, appeared before a Massachusetts Legislative Commission in 1867 to support the establishment of the first oral school for the Deaf in America, the Clarke School. Howe assailed the network of state residential schools for the Deaf, which, he contended, fomented intermarriage of these defectives. "You would discountenance association between deaf-mutes?" the commission chairman asked. "Entirely," Howe replied, "but mind you, I would not discountenance association between them and other persons. I would endeavor to prevent the effects of their infirmity by bringing them into relations as close as possible with ordinary persons so that their infirmity should be, so to speak, wiped out of sight."[8]

In the following decades, more oral schools were founded while others abandoned ASL in favor of spoken English. Again, an explicit motive was the regulation of Deaf reproduction. For example, in the heated debate over a Nebraska law, which required the state residential school for the Deaf to use oral methods only, the president of the National Education Association weighed in with this support of oralism: Deaf people who sign "tend to segregate themselves from society—to intermarry. [They are] freaks, dummies."[9]

However, Deaf schoolmates intermarried whether their residential school used ASL or English. More stringent means of separation would be required to keep them apart. That meant boarding them at home and instructing them in small classes to minimize contact. This was the aim of the day-school movement, which began in Wisconsin in the late 1800s and was championed and funded in part by Alexander Graham Bell.[10] Day schools, Bell told Wisconsin lawmakers, allow "keeping deaf-mutes separated from one another as much as possible."[11] He warned of the dangers of Deaf congregation at the state residential school. An 1894 attempt by educators to expand the day-school law and reduce class size to four or five Deaf pupils provided that "congenital deaf-mutes of opposite sexes shall be kept apart as much as possible and marriage between them discouraged."[12] The next major day-school movement began in Chicago. The Chicago Board of Education similarly declared that day schools were valuable because they prevented Deaf intermarriage and the production of Deaf offspring.[13]

Hearing people have embarked on direct as well as indirect programs to restrict Deaf reproduction. In this century, there have been movements in the United States and in Germany, for example, to sterilize Deaf people by law and to encourage Deaf people in voluntary sterilization. The legal initiative in the United States had limited success, but its well-publicized pursuit led untold numbers of Deaf people to abandon plans for marriage and reproduction or to submit to voluntary sterilization, and untold numbers of hearing parents to have their Deaf children sterilized.[14] Alexander Graham Bell, head of the Eugenics Section of the American Breeders Association (later the American Genetics Association), laid the groundwork for such efforts in his numerous statistical studies and censuses of the Deaf population in the United States and, especially, in his 1883 *Memoir upon the Formation of a Deaf Variety of the Human Race*, which he printed privately and distributed widely. Moreover, he presented this broadside against Deaf culture and Deaf intermarriage to the National Academy of Sciences on his election to that body, giving the false impression that it was sanctioned by the academy and was scientifically valid. In *Memoir*, Bell warned that "the congenital deaf-mutes of the country are increasing at a greater rate than the population at large; and the deaf-mute children of deaf-mutes at a greater rate than the congenital deaf-mute population."[15] Bell attributed the problem to signed language, which "causes the intermarriage of deaf-mutes and the propagation of their physical defect."[16] The Eugenics Section prepared a model sterilization law and promoted it in the nation's state legislatures; it called for sterilization of feebleminded, insane, criminalistic, deaf, and other "socially unfit" classes.[17] By the time of the German sterilization program, some thirty states in the U.S. had sterilization laws in force. However, none of them specifically included Deaf people.

It is difficult to find a rationale for Bell's actions, and for those of other advocates for reproductive regulation of Deaf people, if they are taken at face value. The tables of data in *Memoir* show that only one percent of the pupils in Bell's sample had two Deaf parents; hence it was evident that if all Deaf couples in the U.S. stopped reproducing entirely, either through birth control or sterilization, there would be an insignificant reduction in the Deaf population. For the same reason, it must have been evident to him and other advocates of day schools, oral education, and other measures to discourage Deaf socialization, that such measures, even if totally success-ful, would have a trivial impact. A statistical study of the Deaf population conducted with funding from Bell showed that there was no greater likelihood of a Deaf child if both parents were Deaf than if only one was, and that Deaf married Deaf three-fourths of the time no matter whether the partners attended manual or oral schools, residential or day schools.[18] All of this must have been known by Bell and other eugenicists.

Consequently, the purpose of the eugenics movement with respect to Deaf people, of the measures aimed at discouraging their socialization, intermarriage and repro-duction, could not have truly been to achieve those goals, which were largely una-chievable and would be ineffective if achieved. Instead, the purpose must have been to reinforce a certain social construction of Deaf people, one that was linked to the construction of people with impairments such as feeblemindedness and to a particular non-infirm establishment with its own authorities, legislation, institutions and profes-sions. Moreover, the eugenics campaign marked the DEAF-WORLD as an important social problem requiring expertise, one that had been previously overlooked, much to the danger of society. In this respect, the claims-making closely paralleled the movement to awaken society to the dangers of mentally retarded people in our midst. We may surmise that, as psychologists and superintendents of institutions for the feebleminded stood to gain from the recognition of the newly discovered social problem of mild retardation, so a competent authority that stood to gain from the construction of Deaf people as a newly-discovered menace was the burgeoning orga-nization Bell had founded, the American Association to Promote the Teaching of Speech to the Deaf. In 1969, this association, now known as the Alexander Graham Bell Association for the Deaf, republished Bell's *Memoir* without disclaimers, still warning stridently of the "calamitous results to their offspring" of Deaf intermar-riage.[19]

The eugenics movement as it concerned Deaf people worldwide has received regrettably little study.[20] When National Socialism came to power in Germany, fully forty organizations of the Deaf in Berlin were combined into two; the treasuries of the original organizations were confiscated; the Jewish Deaf Association was prohib-ited, and Jewish members of all other Deaf organizations were expelled. Teachers of the Deaf advocated adherence to the hereditary purity laws, including the sterilization of congenitally Deaf people. Deaf school children were required to prepare family trees, and the school reported those who were congenitally Deaf or who had a Deaf relative to the Department of Health for possible sterilization. Leaders of the unified Deaf organization and the Deaf newspaper, themselves late-deafened, endorsed the sterilization campaign.[21]

The German sterilization law that went into effect in 1934 provided that: "Those hereditarily sick may be made unfruitful (sterilized) through surgical intervention. . . . [Among] hereditary sick, in the sense of this law, is the person who suffers from . . . hereditary deafness."[22] The census of 1933 showed forty-five thousand "deaf and dumb" persons in a total population of over sixty-six million. An estimated seventeen thousand of these Deaf Germans, a third of them minors, were sterilized. In nine percent of the cases, sterilization was accompanied by forced abortion. An additional sixteen hundred Deaf people were exterminated in concentration camps in the 1940s; they were considered "useless eaters," with lives unworthy of being lived.[23] As in the United States, the medical profession was the certifying authority for forced sterilization. And as in the United States, the overriding purpose may have been to reinforce their authority in the solution of perceived social problems.

In 1992, researchers at Boston University announced that they had identified the "genetic error responsible for the most common type of inherited deafness."[24] The director of the National Institute on Deafness and Other Communication Disorders (NIDCD, one of the National Institutes of Health) called the finding a "major breakthrough that will improve diagnosis and genetic counseling and ultimately lead to substitution therapy or gene transfer therapy." Thus a new form of medical eugenics applied to Deaf people was envisioned, in this case by an agency of the U.S. government. The primary characteristics of Deaf people with this genetic background are numerous Deaf relatives, signed language fluency, facial features such as widely spaced eyebrows, and coloring features such as a white forelock and freckling.[25] For such characteristics to be viewed primarily not as normal human variation in physiognomy, coloring, etc., but as a "genetic error," some of the common features must clearly be construed as signs of a disease or infirmity. In fact, according to a leading medical geneticist, the "sole detrimental feature" of the syndrome is that some of these people are Deaf.[26] Within the culture of the DEAF-WORLD, then, this cannot be a disease.

In the director's statement to the press, there were several explicit claims. In short, he claimed a major breakthrough that would enhance diagnosis and genetic counseling and lead to genetic engineering. There are further claims implied by his statement: this human variation is a disease and hence should be avoided; society's interest in avoiding it outweighs any individual or group's desire to continue it; medical research such as the institute supports has led to this achievement, and the public's investment in its research is justified in part by these developments; the competent authority in these matters is medical authority.

In its *National Strategic Research Plan* issued the same year, the NIDCD points out that at least half of all children born Deaf or who become so early in life are Deaf by virtue of heredity. The strategic plan continues: "The insertion of genetic material into cells to prevent or ameliorate hereditary hearing impairment may soon become a possible treatment option."[27] The foundation of the hearing agenda for the DEAF-WORLD on a disability model could not be clearer. Since all forms of human variation are genetically determined, but the genetic causes for only some of these are actively sought, the pursuit of such genetic causes tells much about how that variation is construed as a social problem. Federally funded research in the U.S. is currently seeking to uncover the hereditary basis for some people being Gay, others Deaf, and for an alleged intellectual inferiority of Black Americans. Research on the genetics of heterosexuality, hearing, and Caucasian intelligence, such as it is, reflects quite a different construction of those social groups.

The NIDCD explicitly addresses this issue in its strategic plan, where it acknowledges that "many Deaf individuals believe that deafness is not a disorder but a culturally defining condition."[28] Because the statement makes this a matter of individual belief among Deaf people (whereas it is a tenet of Deaf culture), and because the statement makes no mention of what hearing people believe, there is the implication that the authors of the statement and other such authorities have a different and perhaps more objective view of the matter. The statement goes on to say, however, that the NIDCD respects "the cultural integrity of Deaf society." What construction of Deaf people would allow the institute logically to support eugenic measures for limiting the membership of the DEAF-WORLD, all the while respecting the cultural integrity of Deaf society? The institute planners were willing to acknowledge, it seems, that there was a problem, but that was as far as they were prepared to go. Elsewhere in the report, the institute's commitment to a single, underlying construction of all people with limited hearing is as clear as its name: It calls for genetic research to improve diagnosis, counseling, and gene therapy, all with a view to reducing the numbers of children who enter the DEAF-WORLD. On the face of it, it is unethical to seek to prevent a "culturally defining condition." Is genetic counseling available for mixed-race couples? For homosexual prospective parents? For what culturally defining conditions is it available?

The main reason that issues like gene therapy generate strong feelings and invite pronouncements by various leaders and organizations is not because of direct practical consequences. Rather, they reveal underlying and conflicting constructions of Deaf people. Similarly, surgeons and audiologists in the lead to surgically implant young Deaf children discourage parents from allowing their children to use signed language. For example, a 1992 manual on the management of implanted Deaf children steers parents away from schools that use Total Communication as follows: "Most implanted children who used TC prior to implantation will always depend on sign to some degree and many will never develop the skills to communicate without it."[29] Such advice is given not because of any evidence that signed language would detract from the child's learning English (indeed, the available evidence points to the contrary), but because the child with a surgically implanted prosthesis is the archetype of a certain construction of Deaf people, while the signer is the archetype of a diametrically opposed construction. Thus to sign is symbolically to negate the construction of Deaf people that has motivated the costly surgery, and the efforts of the surgeons, audiologists, speech therapists, special educators, and others.

• Cochlear Implant Surgery on Deaf Children

The most sorely contested issue in the collision between the DEAF-WORLD and medical professionals is the growing practice of surgically implanting cochlear implants in Deaf children. [. . .]

Ethical Problems with Cochlear Implant Surgery

It must be an unparalleled event in medical history for organizations of adults to raise such an outcry against medical intervention for children like themselves. Cochlear implant surgery on young Deaf children encounters serious ethical problems that have not received widespread discussion and thoughtful exploration. We want to focus on the ethics of cochlear implant surgery with, specifically, children born Deaf, because they comprise about nine out of ten children who could be cochlear implant candidates, [. . .] and because the issues are more sharply drawn in their case.[30]

The challenges to ethical decisions about surgically implanting children born Deaf cluster around four themes. These are risk/benefit ratio; cultural values in conflict; surrogate decision-making; and ethnocide (that is, cultural genocide):

Risk/benefit ratio: Apart from the risks associated with surgery and anesthesia, cochlear implantation of children poses several primary risks: The combination of implant surgery and post-surgical oral/aural rehabilitation may leave the implanted child substantially languageless for several years.[31] The medium and long-term effects of cochlear implants on the child's language acquisition, social identity, psychological adjustment and mental health are unknown, and these may be compromised in varying degrees. Full participation in the language and culture of the Deaf-World will undoubtedly elude many implanted children as they develop, but they may also be unable to participate fully in spoken language and hearing culture. We simply do not know the outcome of the implantation. When it comes to potential benefit there is considerable consensus that, with children born Deaf, acquisition of spoken language is the significant benefit desired. However, there is *no* conclusive evidence yet of that benefit, and if it exists, we are unable to predict which children will receive it. Consequently, although more than a thousand children have been implanted, the treatment remains highly experimental. If experimental medical treatments of children can be justified ethically at all, it is only in the setting of a small, highly controlled long-term study.

Cultural values in conflict: As implants are perfected and more research is conducted, the risk/benefit ratio seems likely to improve. We want to consider the ethical issues if the implant did, in fact, offer a substantial opportunity to acquire spoken language. Three serious ethical challenges to implantation of children born Deaf remain. Is the possibility of acquiring some spoken language a benefit that would justify the surgery? Suppose one viewed children born Deaf as suffering from a gravely disabling condition; then the potential benefits loom large compared to the risks. Now suppose one viewed children born Deaf as exhibiting merely another form of human variation, like small stature; then the risks loom large and the benefits small. The opposing perspectives on Deaf people were nicely drawn by the founder of Gallaudet University, Edward Miner Gallaudet, and by Alexander Graham Bell. Addressing a professional conference, Gallaudet stated that education had transformed being Deaf from a calamity to "little more than a serious inconvenience" and, stopping to brush his bald pate, he added, "something like baldness in fly time." Bell, on the other hand, when challenged on the importance of speech to the Deaf, replied: "I am astonished. I am pained. To ask the value of speech? It is like asking the value of life!"[32]

It is a tenet of Deaf culture that Deaf people do not have an impairment merely by virtue of limited hearing. Deaf children in general are healthy, and it is unethical to operate on healthy children. The hearing parents and professionals insist that the Deaf child is not healthy and has a major impairment; it is a tenet of their culture that it is bad to be Deaf. How do we decide the ethical dispute when two cultures disagree on the wisdom of a surgical procedure because of fundamentally opposed values? Under certain restricted conditions, it does seem possible for one culture to ethically overrule the other. Thus, members of one culture might intercede when torture or murder is permitted in another culture. Is American culture thereby justified in interceding in Deaf culture? Implants are not a life or death matter. Nor are Deaf children caused suffering by the failure to provide them with implants. No one claims that Deaf parents are guilty of neglect of their Deaf children by refusing them implants. Since these special conditions do not apply, shouldn't the parents and medical personnel respect the values of Deaf culture as they demand that the members of the Deaf-World respect their values? If so, how can they justify implant surgery on their born-Deaf child?

If the young Deaf child has not yet had an opportunity to acquire the language and values of Deaf culture, do the values of Deaf culture have standing in this matter? We have argued [. . .] that a child born Deaf is as surely a member of the Deaf cultural minority as a child born Black is a member of the Black cultural minority. That is, their life trajectories can be deflected, but the potential they have to enter into their respective cultures travels with them. If the child born Deaf is in principle a member of the Deaf-World at birth, then do the parents have a moral obligation to respect the wishes of the Deaf-World in this matter, even if they disagree with them given their own cultural background? How much of an obligation to respect the values of the Black community do white parents incur who have adopted a Black child?

Surrogate decision-making: The decision to perform implant surgery on the Deaf child is made *for* the child who, as a minor, is considered temporarily incompetent to make that decision. It is the surrogate's responsibility to make decisions which will promote the patient's well-being, as that well-being would be understood by the patient.[33] Parents cannot know with certainty what their individual child would decide if able to make the implant decision but they do know the next best thing— what adults born Deaf like their child would decide. Such adults refuse the implant for themselves and protest its use with children.

There are, moreover, three considerations that challenge surrogate decision-making by hearing parents for their Deaf children. First, there is the problem of communication. The presumption for parents to be surrogates is that they care deeply about their children and know them and their needs better than others do.[34] No one doubts that parents of Deaf children are devoted to them. However, it is primarily young, largely languageless children who are implanted, so there are uncommon obstacles in the way of parents satisfying the presumption that they know their Deaf child's character and needs well. With older children who were born Deaf, parents might try to determine their child's wishes, but their inability to communicate in signed language and the natural desire of children to please their parents are serious obstacles.

Second, there is the problem of conflicting values. Parents should be especially cautious in weighting their views of childhood implantation more heavily than the views of the Deaf-World, because they are naturally advocates for their language and culture, but their child, when adult, will likely be an advocate for the language and culture of the Deaf-World.

Third, there is the problem of informed consent. Parents frequently cannot give informed consent to the operation because they know no Deaf adults and have no information about what growing up Deaf, with or without an implant, involves. They neither know the alternatives to surgery, nor the likely outcome of the surgery. Given these facts, it is unclear how their consent can be informed. Yet to perform the surgery requires the child or the surrogate to give genuinely informed consent.

It would seem, then, that the parents have an ethical obligation to give great weight to the negative views of the Deaf-World about childhood implants. However, they also have an obligation to do what they believe to be in the best interests of their child. Which should weigh more heavily in their choice, the belief that a certain surgical procedure is in the best interests of the child, or the knowledge that the child, as an adult, would likely disapprove of the surgery? Because parents are making the decision for someone else, the benefits of the surgery must outweigh the risks by a larger margin than if adults were making that decision for themselves.[35]

Ethnocide: The program of childhood implantation has as a primary goal to permit Deaf children to acquire the majority spoken language in place of the minority signed language they would have acquired. If this goal could be achieved on a wide scale, the consequence, however unintended, would be *ethnocide*, the systematic blocking of a language minority from coming into its own and from pursuing its way of life. Such actions are widely considered to be unethical. Contemporary ethical standards with regard to the treatment of such minorities are captured in part in the United Nations Declaration of the Rights of Persons Belonging to National or Ethnic, Religious and Linguistic Minorities. Article 1 calls on states to protect and foster the existence and identity of linguistic minorities (among others). Article 2 affirms the right of such minorities to enjoy their culture and use their language, and to participate in decisions on the national level affecting their minority. Article 4 asks that states take measures to ensure that persons belonging to minorities have adequate opportunities to learn the minority language. In addition, as several Deaf organizations have pointed out, the United Nations Convention on the Crime of Genocide prohibits forcibly transferring children from a minority group to another group.

A member of a cochlear implant team who wrote to the *Atlantic Monthly* after its June, 1993, cover story on "Deaf: The New Ethnicity" acknowledged that ethnocide is indeed the likely consequence of programs of cochlear implantation and that he (or she) is contributing to ethnocide: "The cochlear prosthesis on which I have worked for years with many other scientists, engineers and clinicians, will lead inevitably to the extinction of the alternative culture of the Deaf, probably within a decade."[36] The author likens Deaf culture to Yiddish culture and concludes, "Both are unsustainable." Is is self-indulgent nostalgia to want to protect Deaf culture and Yiddish culture, or do we all have an ethical obligation to do so? If ASL speakers or Yiddish speakers want to protect their culture, but other groups have an interest in seeing them disappear, how do we decide the ethical dispute?

It may clarify our ethical thinking on this issue to examine the arguments while supposing cochlear implants were able to do what they cannot do now, namely deliver close to normal hearing for most patients. In that case, the risk/benefit ratio would be more favorable (for example, the risk of remaining languageless would be smaller); the assumption that the implanted child would disapprove as an adult would likely be false, since the formerly Deaf child would probably be acculturated to his or her parents' culture; and the interests of the child, as parent and child would see them, would be pitted against the interests of the language minority. Do parents have an obligation to consider the rights of the concerned minority as well as the interests of their own child? Are parents acting ethically if they promote school desegregation by busing but refuse to have their child bused? Suppose these are white parents who have adopted a Black child? Are the parents required ethically to consider not only the interests of the community and their child, but also the views that Black parents of a Black child would have in the same situation? Suppose the parents believe that Black parents might give even more weight than they do to desegregation. Should they allow that to tip the balance in favor of busing their child?

Leading audiologists and otologists state that they respect and wish to preserve Deaf minority language and culture. Thus, for example, the director of childhood implant research at New York University Medical Center, Dr. Noel Cohen, has written: "We have uppermost in our minds not to harm let alone destroy the deaf community; not to do damage to deaf culture."[37] Otology and audiology want to provide implants to Deaf children who they believe need them, but also to protect Deaf culture. Are these two goals compatible?

Here's our view on these issues. Our experiences with Deaf people have led us to view being born Deaf as a form of human variation that does not require medical intervention. More important, Deaf people themselves, who surely must know whether they have a grave impairment, say they do not. Consequently, the risks of childhood implantation would have to be much smaller than they are, and the benefits much larger, before the risk/benefit ratio would ethically justify surgery (and post-surgical rehabilitation). We know of no acultural set of values (unless it be a value on reducing human suffering or death) that one can use to choose between competing cultural claims with regard to the ethics of some surgery. Therefore, we believe that the values of Deaf culture should be decisive in childhood implantation of Deaf children. We expect that Deaf children have many of those values, such as being attuned to the visual world and preferring signed language, and will acquire many more as they mature. Thus parents who make a surrogate decision for them should choose in accord with the values of Deaf culture. Finally, we believe it is unethical to restrict a language minority from coming into its own. Each cultural group demands that others give it their moral backing in defending the flourishing of its language and culture, and thus its members should feel obliged to reciprocate.

As we have seen, Deaf groups and hearing parents and professionals frequently have different views about the wisdom of cochlear implants for young Deaf children, even though they share the same principal goal—to contribute to the welfare of the child. The fundamentals of this disagreement on the means by which to assure the Deaf child a fulfilling life in hearing society is centuries old. U.S. Deaf scholar Tom Humphries has summarized it as follows: "There is no room within the culture of Deaf people for an ideology that all Deaf people are deficient. It simply does not compute. There is no 'handicap' to overcome. . . . Deaf people have a vision of integration [in the hearing world] that is different from what hearing people envision for them. Deaf people see a grounding in the culture and signed language of the Deaf community in which they live as the most important factor in their lives. Integration comes more easily and more effectively from these roots."[38]

The insistence of culturally Deaf people on their normalcy, and their resistance to using a prosthesis, oblige those who still view Deaf people only in a pathological light to take account of Deaf language, culture, and pride. To avoid this, some implant advocates have sought to dismiss the Deaf point of view by attributing devious motivations to Deaf people's protests against implant surgery on children.[39] More subtly, however, the advocates of implantation merely exclude Deaf people from the discussion. The message is: The parents have the rights, and the hearing professionals have the knowledge, so the views of Deaf people are simply of no concern. For example, although there is wide agreement that most implanted children will remain "severely hearing-impaired" and will continue to rely on manual communication, none of the five childhood implant conferences to date in the U.S. has had a single Deaf speaker.*

How are Deaf organizations to respond to this exclusion while acting in the best interests of the child and the community that child will likely join? Deaf leaders understand that their discourse of normalcy is marginalized by the more dominant discourse of medical authority. They rarely have an opportunity to talk with decision-making parents, while doctors and audiologists have privileged access. They do not have an opportunity to talk to doctors, who systematically exclude them from their programs. Speeches at Deaf congresses affirming the normalcy of Deaf culture are not reported in the national presses. These Deaf communities therefore have faced a choice: to remain silenced, or to force others to listen.

* Ben Bahan addressed the Sixth Symposium on Cochlear Implants in Children in 1996, when the original book in which this article appeared went to press.

What is the purpose of implant manufacturing and of childhood implant surgery? We are told that it is to remedy a serious social problem or set of problems. There is the problem of the child acquiring language, the problem of communication and special education, the problem of the child's learning a trade or profession, and so on. However, it is instructive to observe how people who are intimately familiar with growing up Deaf in a hearing world raise a Deaf child. They are not normally organized toward the solution of problems more than any other parents; they simply expect that their child will acquire language, communicate with them, go to school, and acquire a trade or profession and so on. They do not seek the services of professionals such as audiologists and ear surgeons. This contrast calls our attention to the source of the claim that a social problem exists: It is the very professionals devoted to remedying the problem who promote the claim. Does the implant then exist for the problem, or the problem for the implant? Note how the very existence of implant surgery creates a link that has not existed before, between the ear surgeon and the Deaf child.

Hearing parents could (and some do) construe the advent of their Deaf child in quite a different light, not as a social problem, but as a joyful event that makes an unexpected language demand of them. All children, Deaf and hearing, are able to acquire a full language naturally. They are apparently best able to do it in the first years of life, when caretakers need merely expose them to an accessible language. The hearing parents of a Deaf child usually cannot fulfill this parental role without first learning a manual language, or introducing into the family people who know a manual language, such as Deaf friends or employees. Later, parents may seek help in socializing their child from teachers, child-care workers, scout leaders, clergymen, and relatives; at this early stage they can benefit from the help of culturally Deaf people.

Even parents who are decided on implantation for their child might be wise to follow this strategy, thus avoiding formative years in their child's life during which there is no substantive communication and no exposure to language structure. There is reason to think that children who are given a rich signed language environment may have an advantage learning some spoken language with or without an implant. Perhaps the very limited achievement in language learning of prelingually Deaf children with implants is partly the result of their being deprived of language during the first two years or more of life. This matter has not yet been studied. Nor, as we have said, are there studies in progress concerning the long-term risks and benefits of childhood implantation. These should have high priority. More research and better implants, which are certain to come in time, may bring all concerned parties closer to agreement on the scientific issues. What will remain, however, is the profound difference between Deaf and hearing cultures in the construction of being Deaf, and therefore disagreement on the ethics of childhood implant surgery.

NOTES

1. Pride in a silent language, 1993.
2. Plann, 1993.
3. Lane, 1984.
4. Berthier, 1837.
5. Winzer, 1993.
6. Gallaudet, 1891. Cited in Winefield, 1987.
7. Lane, 1996.
8. Cited in Lane, 1984, p. 326.
9. Cited in Van Cleve, 1984, p. 209.
10. Cf. Lane, 1984.
11. Bruce, 1973, p. 393; Van Cleve, 1993.
12. Wisconsin Phonological Institute, 1894.
13. Van Cleve, 1993.
14. Johnson, 1918.
15. Bell, 1883, p. 216.
16. Bell, 1883, p. 216.
17. Lane, 1993, p. 287.
18. Fay, 1898.
19. Ruben, 1991.
20. Biesold, 1993.
21. Muhs, 1995.
22. Peter, 1934.
23. Higgins, 1993; Ruben, 1991.
24. BU Team, 1992; Gene that Causes, 1992.
25. Fraser, 1976.
26. Fraser, 1987.
27. National Institute on Deafness and Other Communication Disorders, 1992.
28. National Institute on Deafness and Other Communication Disorders, 1989.
29. Tye-Murray, 1992, p. 64.
30. Allen, Rawlings, and Remington, 1994.
31. Lane, 1991.
32. Quoted in Lane, 1984.
33. Grodin and Glantz, 1994, p. 85.
34. Grodin and Glantz, 1994, p. 94.
35. Grodin and Glantz, 1994, p. 97.
36. Doomed ghetto culture, 1993.
37. Cohen, 1994, p. 19; Tyler, 1993.
38. Humphries, 1993, pp. 6, 14.
39. Balkany and Hodges, 1994.

REFERENCES

Allen, T. E., Rawlings, B. W., and Remington, E. (1994). Demographic and audiologic profiles of deaf children in Texas with cochlear implants. *American Annals of the Deaf.* 138, 260–266.

Balkany, T., and Hodges. A. (1994). Misleading the deaf community about cochlear implantation in children. *Annals of Otology, Rhinology and Laryngology, 103,* 148–149.

Bell, A. G. (1883). *Memoir upon the formation of a deaf variety of the human race.* Reprinted, 1969. Washington, DC: Volta Bureau.

Berthier, F. (1837). Lettre sur les difficultés au marriage des sourds-muets. *Le sourd-muet et l'aveugle, 1.* 190–195.

Biesold, H. (1993). The fate of the Israelite Asylum for the Deaf and Dumb in Berlin. In R. Fischer and H. Lane (eds.). *Looking back: A reader on the history of deaf communities and their sign languages* (pp. 157–170). Hamburg: Signum.

Bruce, R. V. (1973). *Bell. Alexander Graham Bell and the conquest of solitude.* Boston: Little Brown.

BU Team (1992, March). BU team finds genetic cause of Waardenburg syndrome. *Deaf Community News*, March.

Cohen, N. (1994). Cochlear implants in young children: Ethical considerations. *Annals of Otology, Rhinology and Laryngology, 103,* 17–19.

Doomed ghetto culture (1993). (Letters to the editor of the *Atlantic Monthly* reprinted). *Deaf Life,* 6, 33.

Fay, E. A. (1898). *Marriages of the deaf in America.* Washington, DC: Volta Bureau.

Fraser, G. R. (1976). *The causes of profound deafness in childhood.* Baltimore: Johns Hopkins.

———. (1987). Hearing loss: Genetic causes. In J. V. Van Cleve (ed.), *Gallaudet encyclopedia of deaf people and deafness* (pp. 20–23). New York: McGraw-Hill.

Gene that causes (1992, February 18). Gene that causes Waardenburg's Syndrome. *New York Times.* 141, B7, C2.

Grodin, M. A., and Glantz, L. H. (1994). *Children as research subjects.* New York: Oxford University Press.

Higgins, W. (ed.) (1993). La parole des sourds. *Psychoanalystes,* 46–47, 1–216.

Humphries, T. (1993). Multicultural issues in deafness. In K. M. Christensen and G. L. Delgado (eds.). *Multicultural issues in deafness.* White Plains. NY: Longman.

Johnson, R. H. (1918). The marriage of the deaf. *Jewish Deaf,* 5–6.

Lane, H. (1984). *When the mind hears: A history of the deaf.* New York: Random House.

———. (1991). Cultural and disability models of Deaf Americans. *Journal of the American Academy of Rehabilitative Audiology.* 23, 11–26.

———. (1993). Cochlear implants: Their cultural and historical meaning. In J. Van Cleve (ed.), *Deaf history unveiled.* Washington, DC: Gallaudet University Press.

———. (1996). Who are hearing people? In N. Glickman and M. Harvey (eds.), *Culturally affirmative psychotherapy with Deaf persons.* Hillsdale, NJ: Lawrence Erlbaum Associates.

Muhs, J. (1995). Followers and outcasts. The history of Berlin's Deaf community under National Socialism (1933–1945). Unpublished manuscript, Berlin Deaf Club.

National Institute on Deafness and Other Communication Disorders (1989). *National research plan.* Bethesda, MD: National Institute of Health.

————. (1992). *National strategic research plan for hearing and hearing impairment and voice disorders. NIH pub. 93–3443.* Bethesda, MD: National Institutes of Health.

Peter, W. W. (1934). Germany's sterilization program. *American Journal of Public Health,* 24 (3), 187–191.

Plann, S. (1993). Pedro Ponce de Leon: Myth and reality. In J. Van Cleve (ed.), *Deaf history unveiled* (pp. 1–12). Washington, DC: Gallaudet University Press.

Pride in a silent language (1993, May 16). *New York Times,* 22.

Ruben, R. J. (1991). The history of genetics of hearing impairment. *Annals of the New York Academy of Sciences,* 630, 6–15.

Tye-Murray, N. (1992). *Cochlear implants and children: A handbook for parents, teachers and speech professionals.* Washington, DC: Alexander Graham Bell Association.

Tyler, R. (1993). Cochlear implants and the deaf culture. *American Journal of Audiology,* 2, 26–32.

Van Cleve, J. V., (1984). Nebraska's oral law of 1911 and the deaf community. *Nebraska History.* 65, 195–220.

————. (1993). The academic integration of deaf children: A historical perspective. In R. Fischer and H. Lane (eds.), *Looking back: A reader on the history of deaf communities and their sign languages* (pp. 333–348). Hamburg: Signum.

Winefield, R. (1987). *Never the twain shall meet: The communications debate.* Washington, DC: Gallaudet University Press.

Winzer, M. A. (1993). Education, urbanization and the deaf community: A case study of Toronto, 1870–1900. In J. Van Cleve (ed.), *Deaf history unveiled* (pp. 127–145). Washington, DC: Gallaudet University Press.

Wisconsin Phonological Institute (1894). *Improvement of the Wisconsin system of education for deaf-mutes.* Milwaukee: WPI.

51

To hearing feminists, Deaf feminism sometimes seems a trifle genteel. One explanation is that, like African American women, Deaf women have traditionally found pervasive sexism somewhat less an immediate problem than the discrimination that affected the whole community. Another explanation is the filter-down lag in new ideas reaching insular populations. But on the whole, Deaf feminism is a lot like the traditional Deaf community itself: cheerful, hard working, and generous of spirit. (By the way, as this book was going to press, I was undergoing an experience eerily similar to that of "Tina.")

Deaf Women Now

Establishing Our Niche

Martha A. Sheridan

1999

Tina, a thirty-six-year-old divorced Deaf woman and mother of two small children, works as an accountant for a bookstore chain in a large Midwestern city. Two months ago Tina was diagnosed with breast cancer. She is distraught and frustrated over her medical care. Tina's doctor, like many physicians in private practice, distrusts sign language and refuses to provide sign-language interpreters for her. The doctor insists on writing during their appointments, and communication between them is therefore superficial and strained. Tina is confused and does not fully understand the course of treatment that her doctor wants to undertake. She is unsure of her legal rights to sign-language interpretation and is not aware of resources available to assist her.

Tina is in need of child care during her hospitalizations. She is geographically separated from her parents and sisters. She moved three hundred miles away from her family with her ex-husband, who is also Deaf, when they got married five years ago, since both of them had found work in that area. Tina's parents and sisters never learned to sign, and Tina views their communication as stressful. Tina believes her family has difficulty accepting her deafness. In any case, without comfortable communication, her family could not be of much help to her. Since the divorce, Tina's ex-husband has cut off all contact with her and the children.

The only Deaf certified public accountant in her state, Tina is aware of professional organizations but has never joined them because the benefits of conferences and meetings would not be accessible to her. She wishes that she had access to professional networking and mentoring opportunities with others in her profession.

She would like to advance in her career but experiences many attitudinal and communication barriers to advancement in her current place of employment, where she works in isolation from other employees.

The staff at the day-care center where Tina sends her children cannot communicate with Tina and behave as though they doubt her ability to raise her children. They are not aware of the capabilities of Deaf parents. Concerned that her children's day-care center will think she is not able to care for her children because of her illness and their lack of sensitivity to her deafness, she is working very hard to develop a support network and to maintain stability for her children in this crisis. She does not want the ignorance of the staff at the day-care center to lead to unwarranted reports to child protective services and removal of her children from her care because she is a Deaf single mother. After all, she has heard rumors of such things happening.

Tina's Deaf friend Kathryn, who teaches in a Deaf education program in her state, has agreed to provide Deaf awareness training for the staff of the day-care center. This arrangement gives Tina a sense of relief. She and her friend are also networking with a local Deaf church to arrange for consistent evening care for the kids while Tina is hospitalized. So much support has come from this Deaf church that two Deaf women have recognized the need for a day-care program to be established for Deaf children and children of Deaf parents. They are looking into college training programs that will prepare them to establish their own business in this field. The contacts and support that Tina is gaining through this Deaf community network are providing her with information on resources related to her rights in medical settings as well.

Tina is no different from any other woman in her desire for appropriate medical care, good communication with her doctors, and the opportunity for professional and personal support and networking. The difference for Tina is that because she is Deaf, she has been denied access to the social supports that other women of her education and means often take for granted. Tina's story also depicts the resourcefulness of the Deaf community for mutual aid and problem solving.

This story gives us some idea about the unique issues that Deaf women may confront at various points in their lives. Incorporating feminist values and treating the Deaf community as a social minority, I examine the professional literature on Deaf women; critique existing theoretical approaches and their value as a basis for service provision; and discuss the social status of Deaf women both within and outside the Deaf community, the strengths of Deaf women, and the current state of affairs in the professional service arena. I end with recommendations for enhancing the quality of life for Deaf women.

• Feminist Visions

As I use the term, *feminism* envisions gender equality and the removal of stereotypes and barriers through a commitment to change in society (Van Den Bergh and Cooper, 1986). Achieving gender equality involves the removal of dichotomous standards for gender roles and power. Feminism accepts that the process by which we achieve change is as important as the change itself and that by taking matters into our own hands we can redefine our issues, remove the labels assigned to us through renaming, and develop our own strategies and processes for empowerment. Feminism sees the individual and the environment as interacting and mutually influencing. This implies that the behaviors, lifestyles, attitudes, and philosophies that individuals adopt have the ability to influence society just as society, in turn, influences individuals. This chapter illustrates the utility for and the inherent value of feminist principles in the community of Deaf women.

- ## The Social Status of Deaf Women

In the last three decades, civil rights legislation such as the Americans with Disabilities Act and the Rehabilitation Act of 1973 was expected to liberate people with disabilities. Largely, this legislation has enhanced independence, access to higher education, and the quality of life for Deaf people, but it has not eradicated discrimination. A lack of access to social, medical, legal, educational, psychological, and occupational support continues for Deaf women today. In addition to the discrimination that Deaf women face outside the Deaf community in the areas mentioned above, Deaf women may confront a number of stereotypes that exist within the Deaf community.

From a cultural perspective, the Deaf community functions as an ethnic minority community. Like other ethnic minorities, the language and culture of Deaf people have historically been oppressed. A major difference between the Deaf community and other ethnic minority communities is the near absence of a multigenerational aspect, with no more than 10 percent of Deaf children having Deaf parents.

Deaf culture has traditionally held very conservative views of appropriate gender roles and occupations for women (Egelston and Kovolchuk, 1975; MacLeod-Gallinger, 1991; Wax and Danek, 1982). In a 1981 article on the isolation that Deaf women experience with regard to mainstream women's networks, Becker and Jauregui stated that Deaf women had been almost untouched by the social change that had begun to occur for women in relation to stereotypes, attitudes, roles, and relationships: "The deaf community reflects the most traditional and conservative attitudes our society holds about women, attitudes that are perpetuated by the communication barrier created by deafness" (1981, p. 250). Similarly, women interviewed for an article published in a 1993 issue of *Gallaudet Today* stated, "Equal rights for Deaf women, as for women within other minority groups, have lagged behind those for Deaf people in general" (Shettle and Johnstone, 1993, p. 8). These interviewees nevertheless observed advancements by Deaf women into nontraditional fields such as science, math, and medical and mental health fields.

Traditionally, Deaf women have aspired to conventionally female careers, thus maintaining a lower socioeconomic status. Deaf women have a higher participation in the labor force than women in general but lower earnings, and they generally are in lower-skilled positions (MacLeod-Gallinger, 1991). Deaf women tend to marry

Deaf men (Moores, 1987), and Deaf women's higher participation in the labor force may be related to greater need for family income (Wax and Danek, 1982) due to the generally lower earnings of the Deaf men they marry. While the educational attainment of Deaf women and men has increased, the lag in occupational attainment of Deaf women relative to Deaf men continues to be statistically significant (Barnartt, 1997). Most of the research cited above was conducted in the last two decades. Additional research is needed to revisit and reevaluate the status of Deaf women today.

Deaf women's needs are seen as primarily related to information and access (Weinrib, 1988). As Tina's story illustrates, lack of access to information restricts Deaf women's options, and the role models and emotional and social supports that other women take for granted are often not available to Deaf women.

Tina's story is an example of how Deaf women tend to turn to Deaf peers for support and advice (Becker and Jauregui, 1981). The amount of support available from Deaf peers depends largely on the geographic area. Large metropolitan areas provide a large Deaf community, where there is ample opportunity for Deaf women to network with each other. Often separated from our families of origin by communication and geographical barriers, the Deaf community makes up for the lack of family support and communication (Schein, 1989). A system of reciprocity often exists in communities such as these, where Deaf women assist one another with child care, transportation, information, and support in times of physical or emotional crisis. Deaf women who are members of ethnic minority groups experience even greater isolation and may be more hesitant to seek out available resources (Becker and Jauregui, 1981). In contrast, smaller, more rural areas often do not provide this type of opportunity. The fewer options for socialization in these smaller Deaf communities increase the closed, "small-town" dynamics and tighten the personal, professional, and political boundaries of the members. Concern about anonymity and confidentiality in these smaller communities often prevents members from seeking assistance.

- Service Provision

It is likely that women who are Deaf, and minority Deaf women to an even greater extent, will face extensive bias in their attempts to access health, mental health, legal, and social services. Many practitioners interpret differences as deficits, and Deaf people are no strangers to the experience of such ethnocentric attitudes. Complicating the experience of Deaf women is the fact that many providers of health, mental health, legal, and social services are not communicatively accessible. Even when these professionals have conquered their biases against women or minorities, they must find a way to provide communication access and services that are culturally appropriate and affirmative based on Deaf culture. Tina's story is just one example of the rampant discrimination in health care against people who are Deaf.

Women tend to be higher users of medical services than men. Thus, Deaf women may be more likely than Deaf men to experience frequent discrimination in health care with providers who refuse effective accessible communication, which for many Deaf women is the provision of sign-language interpreters. In addition, we experience increased stress from discrimination and from the time-consuming and emotionally draining search for accessible providers. Finding an accessible provider often means we have to travel greater distances for services. Anecdotal evidence suggests that many Deaf women have chosen to use practitioners outside their health plans who are accessible, rather than use providers covered by their insurance plans who are insensitive to their communication needs. This results in Deaf women absorbing higher expenses for medical services from uncovered providers. All of these complications in health care access may cause a delay in treatment for Deaf women and may limit our choice of providers.

The incidence of physical and sexual abuse against Deaf women may be higher than among the general population (*Deaf Life*, 1994). This may be partially due to perceptions of Deaf women as vulnerable and as safe targets due to communication barriers. This perception of Deaf women is perpetuated by the stereotypical depiction of Deaf women as passive victims in films such as *Johnny Belinda* and *In the Company of Men*.

Deaf women face additional frustrations over and above those that many women face in the largely male legal system. Farrell (1994) exemplified this frustration and injustice in her discussion of the communication barriers that Deaf women confront in reporting physical and sexual abuse and harassment. Some recently assaulted women are not able to negotiate the tedious request processes for qualified interpreters, while others fear having to use this third party to file complaints of such a personal nature. The cohesiveness of the Deaf community limits a survivor's chances of maintaining confidentiality in the reporting process (Weinrib, 1988). And as always, miscommunication can easily occur through poor interpretation or attempts at writing (Farrell, 1994).

When Deaf women are physically or sexually assaulted by Deaf men, the cohesiveness of the Deaf community contributes to a fear of ostracism that often prevents Deaf women from reporting the assault and obtaining needed support (Weinrib, 1988). In addition, there has been so much discrimination and stigmatization of Deaf people in general and Deaf women in particular that survivors of physical and sexual assault fear further prejudicing the public and closing what few doors are open to them if they come forward (Farrell, 1994). To complicate matters, rape crisis centers are often inaccessible to women who are Deaf. In a survey of 413 rape crisis centers in the eastern United States, Block (1999) found that generally service providers express an interest in becoming more accessible to Deaf women and admit they are not knowledgeable about Deaf culture. Rape and domestic violence prevention and awareness information has traditionally been unavailable to Deaf women (Weinrib, 1988). Designers of prevention and awareness literature and audiovisuals typically are not aware of the lower English literacy levels of Deaf women and the need for signed and captioned materials.

The traditional approach to meeting the needs of Deaf women who are survivors of sexual assault has been for existing domestic violence and rape crisis programs to receive training in Deaf culture and increase their accessibility to Deaf women. This approach has had some success, but today Deaf women are taking matters into their own hands. A model program providing culturally accessible and appropriate services to Deaf women who are survivors of sexual assault and domestic violence was developed in 1986 by a Deaf woman, Marilyn Smith, in Seattle, Washington. This program, Abused Deaf Women's Advocacy Services (ADWAS), which is Deaf oper-ated, responds to the unique cultural issues inherent in providing services of this nature to Deaf women. Language and communication accessibility is also modeled by this Deaf-operated program. Many English words, especially those related to crime, have no exact equivalents in American Sign Language. Programs such as ADWAS are designed to work with this and other types of language and communi-cation realities of Deaf women. ADWAS assists in the development of programs based on their model in other cities throughout the United States by training Deaf women to establish and provide these services.

• Strengths of Deaf Women

Perceptions of women and minorities have improved dramatically over the last quar-ter of a century. Women, along with racial and ethnic minorities, have been major players in these social changes. Deaf women have also been active in these social changes, but their contributions and their lives have been largely overlooked and have not been celebrated outside the Deaf community.

While recognizing the barriers that society has constructed, and in keeping with the feminist values discussed above, Deaf women have organized against these obsta-cles, both within existing Deaf organizations and on their own. Through the organ-izing efforts of Deaf women, a women's caucus of the National Association of the Deaf was established in 1982, and three years later Deaf Women United (DWU), a national organization of, by, and for Deaf women, was formed. Focusing on advo-cacy, education, and outreach for Deaf women, DWU provides Deaf women with an opportunity for networking, for personal growth and empowerment, and to enhance the quality of their lives. The organizing efforts of Smith and her colleagues at ADWAS are further testimony to the strengths of Deaf women.

Smaller-scale organizing within the Deaf community is popular as well. In metro-politan Washington, D.C., a group of about ten Deaf women decided to form their own women's support group. This group has met monthly for fifteen years. They determine their own membership and agenda and take turns hosting the meetings in their homes. This group has stayed together through the achievements, life changes, and crises of all of its members. Tina's story also illustrates the value of mutual aid inherent in the community of Deaf women. Tina's resourcefulness, her persistence, and the responsiveness of the Deaf community to her needs are typical of the strengths that Deaf women and the Deaf community present. The feminist principles of self-help, social activism, sharing of resources, and sharing of responsibility are all inherent strengths of the community of Deaf women.

• Research and Theory Issues

In the last two decades, women's issues and issues unique to minority women have received increased attention in the professional literature. This literature has aimed to educate and sensitize professionals to the service needs of women in general and minority women in particular. A review of the professional literature, however, reveals a critical gap pertaining to Deaf women in both the general professional literature and in journals geared to professionals in deafness.

This author conducted a literature search on Deaf women in 1995 in preparation for a presentation on this topic. At that time, only four articles focusing on Deaf women were found in the professional literature. Two of those articles were in sociological journals (Becker and Jauregui, 1981; Egelston and Kovolchuk, 1975) and two in journals for professionals in deafness (Cook and Rosset, 1975; Staudder and Long, 1990). While the first three focused on issues of isolation, career advancement, and gender role attitudes exclusive to Deaf women, the last focused on a comparison of gender-role attitudes of deaf and hearing men and women. Other articles were published in Deaf community periodicals (e.g., *Silent News, Deaf Life*), conference proceedings, locally circulated manuscripts, and general periodicals. A search of articles published between 1995 and 1999 reveals that the dearth of literature on Deaf women in professional databases continues. Only one article devoted exclusively to the service needs of Deaf women could be found (Merkin and Smith, 1996) in a professional journal.

Traditionally, theorists who aspire to understand the development of Deaf people have examined existing developmental theories and attempted to adapt them to fit the experiences of people who are deaf. Schlesinger's (1972) application of Erikson's (1959) psychosocial model is an example of this. One problem with these types of applications is that many of these traditional developmental models have their own flaws, including gender bias. But no developmental model based on hearing people can be fully adapted to any Deaf person, and at present, we have no theories specific to the development of Deaf people regardless of gender, race, ethnicity, or the hearing status of their family members.

• A Commitment to Change

We can begin to transform the social inequities that Deaf women have endured through a commitment to understanding, confronting, and changing these conditions and to celebrating the strengths and achievements of Deaf women.

We can commit to changing our visions of research, policy, and practice and our

Four Deaf women: (left to right) Dr. Gina Oliva, Dr. Barbara White, Dr. Linda Lytle, and Dr. Martha Sheridan enjoy their semiannual bike outing in metropolitan Washington, D.C. Photo from the author's private collection.

personal stereotypes. We need to recognize that enhancing the quality of life of any individual calls for an examination of the social environment and change in the social and political conditions that contribute to oppression. The cause of these conditions is not personal but social. We need to challenge existing systems, establish new priorities, and take responsibility for personal contributions to social change. Tina's personal commitment and the commitment of her peers to her empowerment can lead to social change for her as well as for a whole community of Deaf women and others in their lives.

Deaf women should have their own voice in what programs and strategies they would like to undertake to achieve social change. Thus the following recommendations are just a starting point.

Community education programs for Deaf women on issues such as assertiveness, recognizing and responding to sexism and discriminatory practices, women's rights, health care issues, leadership skills, job skills, relationship issues, and parenting can do much to empower Deaf women (*Deaf Life*, 1994). Workshops for Deaf men also can help them develop an awareness of women's perspectives (*Deaf Life*, 1994) and participate in positive social change that affects their lives. Community advocacy workshops can provide Deaf women and men with the skills they may need to effect social change in policies and programs.

Education has always been empowering for populations who have experienced oppression. Scholarship funds should be made available for Deaf women and men to obtain college and graduate degrees in professions that are committed to social change, such as social work, and in nontraditional careers. Mentoring programs aimed at their retention in postsecondary programs would also be supportive.

In medical, mental health, and social service arenas, funding should be available to create materials and resources that are accessible to Deaf women. Culturally affirmative health, mental health, and crisis programs need to be established. Deaf women should be involved in the planning and provision of these services. Courses in Deaf culture and American Sign Language should be offered in university medical and nursing schools. Deaf organizations should prioritize advocating against discrimination in health care policy and laws that give protection to the medical profession and not to Deaf patients.

Deaf women should be encouraged and supported in authoring and publishing books, articles, and plays. Newspaper and television news reporters and journalists should be contacted about the positive accomplishments, attributes, and strengths of Deaf people. These efforts can counter stereotypical or damaging media influence.

Opportunities should be provided for Deaf women to participate in career advancement training, mentoring, and networking programs. Establishing local chapters of Deaf Women United would give Deaf women a vehicle for these opportunities. Deaf Awareness Month events should highlight the achievements of Deaf women.

Deaf women should be involved in all phases of research processes, including determining a research agenda and in the interpretation and presentation of data. We should advocate for the inclusion of research and articles by and on Deaf women in professional journals. We need to produce our own developmental theories that consider the diversity of Deaf people, including gender, which can then form the basis for service provision for Deaf women.

Finally, Deaf girls and their parents need to have strong Deaf women role models. Deaf schoolchildren should be encouraged to consider nontraditional careers, and curricula should not reflect gender bias. Family mentoring programs that include Deaf women provide opportunities for children who are Deaf to develop positive self-images and visions of their futures.

REFERENCES

Barnartt, S. 1997. Gender differences in changes over time: Educations and occupations of Adults with Hearing Loss, 1972–1991. *Journal of Disability Policy Studies* 8:7–24.
Becker, G., and J. Jauregui. 1981 (July). The invisible isolation of Deaf women: Its effect on social awareness. *Journal of Sociology and Social Welfare* 8:249–262.

Block, R. G. 1999. Rape and the deaf survivor: Agency perceptions of available and accessible services. Unpublished master's thesis, Gallaudet University, Washington, D.C.

Cook, L., and A. Rosset. 1975. The sex role attitudes of Deaf adolescent woman and their implications for vocational choice. *American Annals of the Deaf* 120:341–345.

Deaf Life. 1994 (November). 7, 5:24.

Egelston, J., and L. Kovolchuk. 1975. Deaf women: A double handicap in career development. *Social Science Record*, 25–26.

Erikson, E. 1959. *Identity and the life cycle.* New York: International Universities Press.

Farrell, M.H.J. 1994 (June 20). Silent screams. *People Weekly* 41:36.

Holcomb, M., and S. Wood. 1989. *Deaf women: A parade through the decades.* New York: Knopf.

MacLeod-Gallinger, J. 1991. *The status of Deaf women: A comparative look at the labor force, educational and occupational attainments of Deaf female secondary graduates.* National Technical Institute of the Deaf, Rochester, New York

Merkin, L., and M. Smith. 1996 (Summer). A community based model providing services for deaf and deaf-blind victims of sexual assault and domestic violence. *Sexuality and Disability* 132:97–106.

Moores, D. 1987. *Educating the Deaf: Psychology, principles and practices.* 3rd ed. Boston: Houghton Mifflin Company.

Padden, C. 1996. From the cultural to the bicultural: The modern Deaf community. Pp. 79–98 in I. Parasnis, ed., *Cultural and language diversity and the Deaf experience.* Cambridge: Cambridge University Press.

Schein, J. D. 1989. *At home among strangers.* Washington, D.C.: Gallaudet University Press.

Schein, J. D., and M. T. Delk. 1974. *The Deaf population of the United States.* Silver Spring, MD: National Association of the Deaf.

Schlesinger, H. 1972. A developmental model applied to problems of deafness. Pp. 7–29 in H. S. Schlesinger and M. P. Meadow, *Sound and sign: Childhood deafness and mental health.* Berkeley: University of California Press.

Sexual abuse: How can we stop it? 1993 (May). *British Deaf News* "Sign on": 1.

Shettle, A., and M. Johnstone. 1993 (Spring). Shattering the glass ceiling. *Gallaudet Today*: 8–17.

Staudder, L. K., and G. Long. 1990. A comparison of sex role attitudes of hearing and Deaf young men and women. *Journal of the American Deafness and Rehabilitation Association* 24:7–10.

Van Den Bergh, N., and L. B. Cooper. 1986. *Feminist visions for social work.* Silver Spring, MD: National Association of Social Workers.

Wax, T. M., and M. M. Danek. 1982. Deaf women and double jeopardy: Challenge for research and practice. Pp. 176–196 in A. Boros and R. Stuckless, eds., *Deaf people and social change.* Vol. 4. Washington, D.C.: Gallaudet College.

Weinrib, A. 1988. Impaired shelter for violence: Child abuse and battered women. *Silent News* 68:56.

52

The Deaf community is not known as a hotbed of sensitivity to other minority cultures, and to outsiders, it can seem stunningly hegemonic in its disregard for deaf children's ethnic backgrounds. But if the maintenance of a distinctive minority culture is heavily dependent on its language, as it seems to be, and if Deaf children have access to only one natural signed language, it is not surprising that Native and Hispanic communities lose their deaf children to the Deaf World.

Contemporary Native Deaf Experience

Overdue Smoke Rising

Valerie L. Dively

1999

Native deaf and hard of hearing peoples and their experiences seldom receive attention in deaf education or in Deaf community circles or, more important, in plans for improving contemporary Native Deaf education. Ethnography, the study of a specific cultural group of people and their ways of life, is used here as a step toward allowing the smoke of contemporary Native Deaf experience to rise from various Native communities' hearths in the Americas.

This ethnographic study is based on videotaped and transcribed American Sign Language (ASL) interviews between myself, the Deaf ethnographer with European American and Native heritages, and five Deaf people with Native heritages in the United States.

In addition to the taped interviews, I have had opportunities to observe and interact with Native Deaf people over the last four years and have had a fourteen-year friendship with a Rappahannock Deaf man, one of the five Native Deaf informants in this study. From these experiences, two cultural themes emerged: (1) limited participation of Native Deaf people in a Native community's ceremonies, powwows, and other events; and (2) difficulty among Native Deaf people in maintaining a Native identity in the non-Native U.S. Deaf communities.

• Native Deaf and Hard-of-Hearing Population in the United States

Gallaudet Research Institute's *1989–1990 Annual Survey for Hearing Impaired Children and Youth* (Center for Assessment and Demographic Studies 1990) indicates that the demographics of Native deaf and hard of hearing children in the United States as a whole are parallel to the 1990 demographics in the four states with the largest Native hearing population (Arizona, New Mexico, Oklahoma, and California). The survey indicates approximately 60 percent of Native deaf and hard of hearing children obtain deaf or special education. Based on the survey, the fifteen highest-ranking states in number of Native deaf and hard of hearing children are presented in Table 1. The *1995–1996 Annual Survey for Hearing Impaired Children and Youth* (Center for Assessment and Demographic Studies 1996) also is included in Table 1 as a more recent survey on the demographics of Native deaf and hard of hearing children in the United States There are no demographics available on the overall U.S. Native deaf population. A direct investigation of the demographics of Native deaf and hard of hearing people and school-age children who rely on visual cues for communication hence is needed to bring a better overall picture of the U.S. Native deaf population. For example, Alaska is the state with the fifth largest Native population, yet it is not included in the two surveys' lists of fifteen states with the largest numbers of Native deaf and hard of hearing children. It is be important to know why this is the case.

In 1990, approximately 685,000 Natives, or 35 percent of the Native population in the United States, lived on Native land such as reservations, rancheros, trust land, and Native Alaskan villages. In 1980, 37 percent of Native people lived on Native land. Employment opportunities, a main factor in this trend away from Native land, have resulted in increasing numbers of Native people moving from rural to urban areas (Sorkin 1978). This essay's ethnographic interviews indicate that Native Deaf people are likely to live in or near a major city with a Deaf community and in geographical locations where there are better employment opportunities.

• Literature on Contemporary Native Deaf Experience

Literature on Native deaf and hard of hearing people, especially contemporary Native Deaf experiences, is severely limited. Along with this ethnographic study, the literature that is available on Native deaf and hard of hearing experiences needs to become more comprehensive and be made accessible to Native deaf and hard of hearing people and their Native communities, so that future generations of Native Deaf children can have better means and opportunities for learning to live as Native Deaf people. Following is a summary of literature on contemporary Native deaf and hard of hearing people.

Eldredge and Carrigan (1992) presented four case studies in which they used art therapy to assist Native Deaf men living in the southwestern parts of the United States in expressing their views of self in relation to their community and society. The

TABLE 1
Native Population in the United States

Native population, 1890–1990

Date	Size	Change from Previous Decade
1890	248,000	
1900	237,196	−4.5%
1910	276,927	16.8%
1920	244,437	−11.7%
1930	343,352	40.5%
1940	345,252	0.6%
1950	357,499	3.5%
1960	523,591	46.5%
1970	792,730	51.4%
1980	1,366,676	72.4%
1990	1,959,234	37.9%

Source: Thornton 1987: 160; U.S. Bureau of the Census 1990.

Ten Reservations with the Largest Native Population, 1990
(in thousands)

Diné, AZ, NM, UT*	143.4
Pine Ridge, NE, SD*	11.2
Fort Apache, AZ	9.8
Gila Rive, AZ	9.1
Tohono O'odham, AZ	8.5
Roseburd, SD*	8.0
San Carlos, AZ	7.1
Zuni Pueblo, AZ, NM	7.1
Hopi, AZ*	7.1
Blackfeet, MT	7.0

*Includes trust lands.

Source: U.S. Bureau of the Census 1990.

Ten States with the Largest Native Population, 1990
(in thousands; rank in 1980 in parentheses)

Oklahoma (2)	252
California (1)	242
Arizona (3)	204
New Mexico (4)	134
Alaska (6)	86
Washington (7)	81
North Carolina (5)	80
Texas (9)	66
New York (11)	63
Michigan (10)	56

Source: U.S. Bureau of the Census 1990.

15 States with the Largest Native Deaf Children Population,* 1989–1990, 1995–1996 *(in individuals)*

1989–1990		1995–1996	
AZ	57	NM	60
NM	36	AZ	45
MN, OK	24	MN	19
CA	21	OK	16
NC, WI	17	NC	14
ND	16	CA	13
OR	15	OR, WI	12
LA, SD, WA	11	ND, SD, UT	11
MT	10	LA, MI	10
MI	7	WA	9
TX	6	MT	7

*For above tabulations, if a child was reported as having a multi-ethnic background, e.g., "Native" and "European American" were checked, this child is not shown in this table under the "Native" count.

Source: Center for Assessment and Demographic Studies

case studies included one Pima Deaf man, one Yagui Deaf man and two Diné (Naya) Deaf men. The conclusion of the case studies indicates that "the expected themes of self-identity, concern for family, personal power, and relationship with the community were not the basis of most participants' artwork or discussions. Rather, the most important expression" in their art work seemed to be their connection with their Native cultures (Eldredge and Carrigan 1992). Eldredge and Carrigan, this study's two investigators, who both have Native heritages, suggest that the participants' lack of reference to their Deaf culture probably was due to the fact that there was no communication barrier during the art therapy, as both the investigators and the participants all were fluent in ASL.

Eldredge (1993) provided a description of comparative cultural values of Native Deaf people, Native communities, and the European American hearing community based on three case studies of her counseling work with Native Deaf clients who lived in the southwestern parts of the United States. The case studies focused on a twenty-six-year-old Yagui Deaf man, a thirty-five-year-old Hopi Deaf woman, and a twenty-eight-year-old Diné Deaf man. Eldredge also provided a framework for identifying potential conflicts, which may have an impact on a counseling setting in which a client is a Native Deaf person, and offered practical suggestions for making counseling interventions culturally affirmative, such as openly addressing the issue of European American–Native relationships and Deaf-Hearing relationships; evaluating the degree of multicultural fluency or acculturation of a Native Deaf client; and being open to allowing other family members to participate in the counseling session.

Davis and Supalla's (1995) study of a Diné family in Arizona, Johnson's (1994) study of a traditional Yucatec Maya village in Mexico of approximately four hundred hearing people and fourteen deaf people, and Kakumasu's (1978) study of an Urubu' community in Brazil all indicate communication in Native signed languages that differ from ASL. These signed languages for communicating with Deaf people also differ from other Native tribes' and nations' signed languages.

Like other ethnic Deaf communities where diversity is ever present, the Native Deaf community comprises Native deaf and hard of hearing peoples from many different cultural groups, who have various educational experiences. Such variation includes the following: (1) attending a hearing Native school; (2) attending an educational program with a stress on acquisition and production of spoken English (oral education programs); and (3) attending a residential school for the deaf with ASL as a main communication mode. For the purpose of this ethnographic study, however, I focus on a group of five Native Deaf people whose primary or preferred language is a natural signed language such as a Native signed language or ASL.

• Ethnographic Interviews

In this essay, the informants' names, except for the Rappahannock informant, have been changed to keep their identities confidential. Michael Byrd, the Rappahannock informant, is a close friend of the ethnographer and was also interviewed by a part-Cherokee Deaf woman for *TBC* (The Bicultural Center) *News* (Massey 1992). Byrd thus permitted his identity to be known in this study. Table 2 contains general information on the informants' (1) Native tribe and/or nation, (2) residency, (3) onset of deafness, (4) relatives and sign systems, and (5) age when each first acquired a natural signed language.

All the informants except Michael were born and raised on a federally recognized reservation. Michael was born and raised in a Rappahannock community in Virginia. This Native community is not yet federally recognized but is recognized by the state.

TABLE 2
Informants' General Background

Name	Native Tribe and/or Nation & Residency	Onset of Deafness	Relative Use Sign System	Age When First Acquired a Signed Language
Art	Akimel O'odham; born and raised on the Gila River reservation in AZ; currently lives in a major AZ city	probably born deaf	few immediate family members use home signs and gestures; one Deaf distant cousin uses ASL	age 4 when first acquired ASL at a residential school for the deaf
Holly	Hopi; born and raised on the Hopi reservation in AZ; currently lives in a major AZ city	born hearing; became deaf at age 2 1/2	one sibling is a certified ASL interpreter; other immediate family members use home signs and gestures	age 3 when first acquired ASL at a residential school for the deaf; also indicated that she knows some Hopi Sign Language
Denna	Diné; born and raised on the Diné reservation in AZ; currently lives in a major AZ city	born hearing; became hard-of-hearing at age 3 or 4	family members use home signs and gestures	age 11 when first acquired ASL at a residential school for the deaf
Dan	Diné; born and raised on the Diné reservation in AZ; currently lives in a major AZ city	born deaf	father, brother, and possible other immediate family, plus Deaf and hearing relatives outside the immediate family, use Diné Sign Language and/or ASL; other relatives use home signs and gestures	at birth when first acquired Diné Sign Language; age 10 when first acquired ASL at a residential school for the deaf
Michael	Rapahannock; born and raised in a Rappahannock community in VA; currently lives in the Rappahannock community, with frequent travel to cities	prior to age of 2 or 3; probably born deaf	one sister uses a signed contact language	age 7 when first acquired ASL at a residential school for the deaf

Each informant was born and raised in a hearing family. Art and Holly attended a residential state school for the deaf during all of their schooling. Denna and Dan, the Diné couple, attended a residential school for the deaf during some of their elementary schooling and all of their secondary schooling. Michael spent most of his elementary schooling and all of his secondary schooling at a residential school for the deaf. The informants living in Arizona all graduated from the Arizona School for the Deaf and Blind, Tucson, Arizona. Michael graduated from the Virginia School for the Deaf and Blind, Staunton, Virginia. All the informants were in the twenties-thirties age range, and I was in the thirties age range, during the time the interviews were conducted. All the informants, with the exception of Art, are college educated. Art was taking some continuing education courses during the time of the interviews.

The ethnographic interviews with Native Deaf informants living in Arizona were conducted in April 1994. The ethnographic interview with the Rappahannock Deaf informant was conducted in February 1995.

All this study's interviews were conducted with the informants on a one-on-one informal basis, with the exception of the interview with the Dine' couple, in which there were two informants and myself as the ethnographer. This interview with the couple, like the other interviews, was conducted on an informal basis. A comfortable or convenient setting for the interview was agreed upon by all the participants. After introductions and informal discussion, I gave each informant an opportunity to share his or her Native Deaf experiences in the family, in Native Deaf and hearing communities, in school, and in non-Native Deaf and hearing communities.

• Results: Cultural Themes in Native Deaf Experiences

All the interviews with the five informants confirmed two main themes: (1) there is limited participation by Native Deaf people in a Native community's events, such as ceremonies and initiations; and (2) it is difficult being a Native person in non-Native Deaf communities, for instance, educational programs for the deaf and hard of hearing. In spite of all the difficulties they have had as Native Deaf individuals, all the informants indicated they were proud of who they were as Native Deaf people and proud of their Native heritages. All indicated that were they to have children, they want their children immersed as much as possible in their Native communities. All the informants indicated that they want to continue to be involved, as much as they can, in their Native communities in such ways as visiting relatives and attending ceremonies and powwows. All indicated excitement over the establishment of the Intertribal Deaf Council, as it provides an opportunity to interact with and support one another as Native Deaf people. Lastly, the informants gave recommendations for ways of supporting the acquisition of a Native identity when raising Native Deaf children and regarding Native deaf education.

Acquisition of a Native Culture

Of the five informants, Denna, with some hearing abilities, apparently had the least difficult time acquiring a Native culture, as she had the ability to communicate in a spoken Diné language with the assistance of gestures and home signs. Communication was most effective on a one-on-one basis. She was the only one of the three informants with whom the ethnographer discussed initiation(s) who had completed the initiation(s) for becoming a woman with a new or adult name. Art apparently had a more difficult time than the other informants in terms of acquiring a Native culture, as he knew little about his Akimel O'odham culture.

Holly

Holly acquired much of the Hopi culture through her mother, older sister (also a certified ASL interpreter), and hearing Hopi men who know and use Hopi Sign Language to interpret during Hopi ceremonies and other events. She also read literature on the Hopi culture to help her better understand her culture. Holly was deeply disappointed to learn that she could not have either her sister or the men with Hopi Sign Language skills present to interpret during her initiations, due to the Hopi customs. She observed that deaf boys apparently have a better chance to officially become men than deaf girls to become women, as deaf boys can have men with Hopi Sign Language skills present to interpret during their initiations.

Holly could not consider returning to live on the Hopi reservation, as it would be very lonely for a Hopi Deaf person on the reservation with inadequate communication means and social interaction. Also, only a few Deaf Hopi lived on the reservation. She preferred to live and work in a city with a Deaf community. Now married to a part-Native Deaf man, Holly was determined to have her hearing baby exposed to and acquire the Hopi culture as much as possible and thus planned to visit Hopi relatives and participate in the Hopi community more frequently.

Dan

Dan acquired much of his Diné culture through observations and through communication with Deaf and hearing relatives through gestures, home signs, Diné Sign Language, and ASL skills. Several times he missed an opportunity to go to an initiation due to his being away at the residential school for the deaf. He kept in touch with his relatives on the Diné reservation. He would consider moving back to the Diné reservation if he could have a job near or on the reservation. If not, Dan indicated he would consider settling down on the reservation when he retires from work.

Denna

Denna preferred to live and work in a city with a Deaf community near the Diné reservation. If she lived on the reservation, she would be lonely due to limited social opportunities and the task of taking care of one of her grandmothers and tending the sheep. She explained that she did her part in undertaking these tasks from age 8 until age 23 and now it was her siblings' and other relatives' turn to undertake these tasks. She nevertheless continued to be involved in her Native community by visiting relatives and attending the community's ceremonies and other events, as she was proud of her Diné heritage and culture.

As a very young child, Denna had a severe head injury from an accident and was eventually healed through a medicine man and his prayers and through her mother's prayers. She was able to acquire details of this experience from her mother at a later age. Denna obtained this information in one-on-one conversations with her mother and grandmother through her first language, aural/vocal Diné language, and through gestures and home signs.

Denna stated, however, that she preferred ASL as a primary language and a Deaf community for socialization. This preference clearly indicates that she could not participate fully in her Diné community as a hard of hearing person. She and her husband, Dan, both wanted to have their hearing children immersed in the Diné culture and go through the initiations for becoming a woman or man. They thus were fortunate to have jobs just a couple of hours' drive from their reservation, in a city with a Deaf community.

Art

Art, a single Akimel O'odham man, knew very little about his Akimel O'odham culture, traditions, and customs, as he did not have a person on his reservation who could communicate in ASL and assist him with his acquisition of the culture. He indicated that he also did not have adequate written English language skills to read or write well, despite the fact that English is the primary language of most of his immediate family members. Therefore, his main source of communication with his family was through a few home signs and gestures. Most of his other relatives spoke in their Native language, while other relatives spoke in English. A severely limited communication system thus existed between his family members and him. Having a non-Native hearing interpreter for a European American signed language would not help with his acquisition of the Akimel O'odham culture, as his people would not feel comfortable talking about their culture in front of a non-Native person.

Art currently lives in a major Arizona city for Deaf socialization purposes, as there was no means of communication for him on his reservation. He has a distant Deaf cousin living on his reservation but rarely sees him, as this cousin stays at home most of the time and does not go out for socialization. Art indicated he was proud of his Akimel O'odham heritage, and he wished to have access to his culture's stories, traditions, and customs. He occasionally attended powwows and other Native events on the Gila River reservation.

Michael

Michael, a single Rappahannock man, was much exposed to his culture through his paternal grandmother, an esteemed elder in his Rappahannock community, and through his family, especially his sister who uses a signed contact language. During childhood days, he frequently was taken by his paternal grandmother to powwows and other Native events. This grandmother made sure to expose him to the Rappahannock culture as much as possible. She thus provided him literature on the Rappahannock community's history, traditions, and customs, as he could read in English, his family's primary language. When he was growing up, it did not occur to him that he was significantly different from non-Native peoples until he entered a residential state school for the deaf. He had thought everyone's ways of life were similar.

It was not until he decided to return to the Rappahannock community, after completing all college courses except two, that he began to realize he wanted to live in the Rappahannock community. He missed not being in his Native country, as he had been outside the country most of the time during his many years of European American deaf schooling. Ever since returning to his Rappahannock community, Michael has become secure and confident in who he is as a Rappahannock Deaf man. He continues to be involved in the Rappahannock community. He also is active in Intertribal Deaf Council. In addition, he frequently travels to cities where there is a Deaf community for both socialization and employment, providing consulting services on Native Deaf peoples.

Acquisition of Native Names

In spite of the fact that Holly and Dan each have at least one hearing relative who can communicate in a signed language, they were not able to participate much in their Native communities and their ceremonies, initiations, and other events. They were deeply hurt and embarrassed at still being called by their baby names in their communities' aural/vocal Native languages (Hopi and Diné) since they have no means of completing their initiations in order to acquire an adult name. Both Holly and Dan apparently understood their families' and Native communities' good intentions in this matter. Denna acquired her adult name in Diné after completing an initiation. The interviews with Art and Michael did not contain information regarding their participation in initiations to become a man or woman. Michael mentioned, however, that during a trip with a group of approximately thirty Native people of different tribes and/or nations to an international gathering in Paris several years ago, he acquired a Native name from a medicine man through his sister's interpreting service. He felt deeply honored and humbled at the same time with this giving of a Native name, as it reconfirmed, in a special way, his identity as a Native person.

Native Identity in a Non-Native Deaf Community

All the informants indicated that they had a difficult time with their Native identities during their school years. Four informants experienced trauma when they were sent away from their Native communities to a residential state school for the deaf, which provided no assistance in preparing them for the experience of immersion into a non-Native culture, especially the European American cultures whose values and ways of life were very different from those of their Native cultures. Holly did not remember much about being sent away to a residential state school for the deaf, as she was a very young child of three years old. She had learned that she was ill during the first two weeks of her being away, probably due to different weather conditions.

Holly

Holly stated she was still not wholly comfortable with her Hopi culture traditions and customs, as she was sent away to a residential state school for the deaf at age three and lived with an European American hearing family who had signed language skills. During school breaks and summertimes she returned to the Hopi reservation, which was approximately a ten-hour drive from the school. She thus was more familiar with the European American cultures than with the Hopi culture. She accepted herself as a Hopi Deaf woman with European American cultural values, but she said that in her heart she will always be a Hopi, no matter what.

Holly understood her parents' difficult dilemma in sending her to a distant residential state school for the deaf at a very young age. She was grateful to them for this, as she acquired ASL and her education there. She stated that she would face the same dilemma if she has a deaf child, as she would want her child or children raised around and exposed to the Hopi culture. She was fortunate to be surrounded with Native Deaf students during all of her schooling years, and their presence and friendship helped reassure her Native identity. Also, she was not the only person at the school with Native physical features that European Americans tended to stare at.

Dan

With Diné Sign Language and home signs as his first language, Dan first attended a hearing school on his reservation when he was almost eight. His family did not know anything about deaf education or about the existence of a residential state school for the deaf. A school counselor at the hearing school then recommended that Dan's parents contact the local BIA (Bureau of Indian Affairs) office for consultation on their son's education program as a deaf child. This office strongly recommended that Dan be sent to a residential state school for the deaf. His parents sent him to this school when he was ten.

When Dan first arrived at the residential state school for the deaf, he had no idea that he had to stay there during most of the school year. He was waiting for his father to come to pick him up after the end of the first day of school. But his father did not come, nor did he come back as the days passed. Dan found himself in a different culture, with a signed language different from that he had acquired from his Deaf and hearing relatives. Dan could not communicate much at the school and thus broke down and was deeply hurt for a long time. Also, he did not think it was fair that his hearing brother was able to commute to a nearby school from their family home while he had to stay at a distant school.

Dan soon noticed that there were Native Deaf students at the school and met them. He became good friends with a Native student who helped him adjust to the school life and acquire ASL, as most of the other Deaf students signed too fast for him. He thus was always grateful for this friendship and for other Native and non-Native Deaf friendships during his school years. Having a Native Deaf male roommate during his school years helped secure his Native identity. After a lively discussion with his wife, Denna, over how many Native Deaf students attended their residential state school for the deaf during their school years, they eventually agreed it was approximately fifty Native deaf students. They figured it out based on the fact that nearly all Native students were living on the school campus and usually rode in a bus from the school to their Native communities during the long breaks or holidays and summertimes.

Denna

Denna, just before the age of six, had been in a school with a spoken English environment. (Denna described this experience very briefly and immediately moved on to other stories during the interview; the interview thus did not provide adequate information on this school's educational program for hearing and/or deaf children.) She was very frustrated in school as she could not communicate well in an aural/vocal English environment, since she grew up only speaking her first language, spoken Dine' and had no English language skills. She once had to stay in the same grade level twice due to poor class performance.

Later, a local BIA office strongly recommended that Denna be sent to a residential state school for the deaf in Arizona. Her grandmother did not want her to be sent to this residential school for the deaf at all as the school was too far away from their Dine' reservation. But the local BIA office continued to advise her grandmother that it was important for Denna to be educated at such a school and that they would provide her clothes and take care of other expenses. The grandmother, though not happy about it, eventually agreed to send Denna to the deaf school. Denna was eleven when she first enrolled in the school.

At first Denna's experience in the deaf school was traumatic, as she felt out of place. Everyone was signing too fast for her to acquire ASL easily. Moreover, a dorm counselor had cut off her beautiful long hair soon after her arrival at the school because this counselor did not want to braid her hair daily. Denna eventually picked up ASL signs and found herself happy to communicate in ASL and be with Deaf friends, especially Native Deaf friends and students. In addition, she enjoyed the freedom from her grandmother's stern control on the reservation. Denna finally learned to read and to write in English; she had not been able to learn English in the previous school.

At the school, Denna preferred to interact with Native Deaf students during mealtimes and free time, as they shared similar experiences in life. When she had to have a European American Deaf girl as a roommate, she felt she could not be herself, as she had to be tolerant of this girl's European American ways and values. Thus she always preferred to have a Native Deaf girl as a roommate. She was fortunate to have Native Deaf friends during all her years at this school and stated that she could not imagine how she would have survived the school if she had been the only Native Deaf student.

Art

Art was four when he first attended a residential state school for the deaf. At first he felt very awkward and scared, as he had never met a Deaf person, nor did he know a Native signed language or ASL. He also was scared of being surrounded by many European Americans, as he had never experienced this prior to entering the school. As he began to acquire ASL through his interactions with Deaf students, he adjusted to the school life. He interacted with both Native and non-Native Deaf friends and students. Like the previous three informants, Art was very much relieved when he found out he was not the only Native Deaf student at the school.

Art particularly enjoyed attending a local Native Deaf club established by a European American hearing person in Tucson, Arizona, to provide some Native Deaf awareness and educational activities and socialization. He was disappointed when this club ceased to be active because most Native Deaf people eventually lost interest or commitment to the club. He would have been able to keep in touch with Native Deaf friends more often if he had had better means of transportation.

Michael

Michael's schooling experience as a Native student with non-Native people was not pleasant. This was in part because many people were doubtful of his being a full Rappahannock or Native, as he did not seem, in their eyes, to be a typical Native person, such as a Plains Native. At first he attended a hearing school with an emphasis on art education when he was around four years old; then he was sent to an African American segregated residential state school for the deaf when he was seven. He did not acquire ASL until he enrolled in the latter school, and he acquired more at another residential state school for the deaf later in life. When the state discovered both schools were still segregated even though the federal integration law had been in effect for some years, it immediately ordered the schools to integrate. Michael was placed in the second school, a former European American segregated residential school for the deaf, during high school, since the first school's deaf education program ended at the eighth grade. He explained that African Americans considered him to be a mixed-blood or light-skinned African American with African and European American heritages, whereas European Americans considered him to be an African American.

His self-esteem and Rappahannock identity thus were severely affected for a long time. He often needed assurance from his family that he indeed was a full-blooded Native boy. He agreed that if other Native Deaf students had been present during his schooling, he would have had a less difficult time with his Native identity. He was the only Native Deaf student in either of the two schools during his time of schooling. Also, he explained that he later understood his family's dilemma over whether to send him to a distant, non-Native residential state school for the deaf, since they did not want him sent to a school outside their Rappahannock community. Now, Michael shows his certificate card (an identity card provided to Native peoples for the evidence of their Native heritages) as proof of his Rappahannock identity and heritage to people who doubt or question his Native identity.

Informants' Recommendations

All the informants except Dan and Denna found the question about the raising and education of Native Deaf children difficult but beneficial and important. The interview with Denna and Dan was interrupted by an electrical blackout caused by a severe thunderstorm in the area where they lived. I thus did not have an opportunity to ask them about the raising of Native Deaf children. They did mention, however, that they were envious of their residential school's present students, as they go home one whole week—really ten days—per month instead of just two long breaks during the school year. This modified academic-year schedule helps the present students maintain family and cultural ties and provides opportunities for them to participate in their families' and communities' activities and events.

Holly

Holly immediately answered the question about raising and educating Native Deaf children by highly recommending that Native hearing families learn a signed language for communicating with their deaf children. After a discussion on the issue of Native families' taking ASL classes, Holly suggested Native hearing families move to a city temporarily for that purpose, as most Native hearing families on a reservation would have difficult gaining access to ASL classes. She also recommended that Native Deaf children be placed in a residential state school for the deaf. She stated that she would face a difficult dilemma if she lived in a place far away from such a school. She feels, however, that she would still be likely to send her Deaf child(ren) away to the school.

Art

Art was at a loss when asked this question, as he apparently had never given it much thought. He therefore offered only one recommendation: that he did not want Native Deaf children to go through an experience similar to that he had with his family. He did not know his Akimel O' odham culture well, nor could he communicate well with his family and his people. In Art's experience, a written language was not an effective means of visual communication, as he could not read or write in English well enough to communicate with his family members. Therefore he believed that a language used with Native Deaf children for primary communication needs to be a visual, person-to-person (not written) language, such as a Native signed language or ASL.

Michael

Michael took time to ponder the question, as he felt it required more than a simple answer. He then had several recommendations: (1) materials and texts in schools need to be changed in order to remove cultural biases and to enhance cultural sensitivity and awareness (since school materials and texts still tend to be based on European American viewpoints and values); (2) educational programs for the deaf need to provide all Deaf children general information on various cultures, including

Native cultures; (3) Native families with Deaf children should be responsible for teaching their Native Deaf children about their cultures and ways of life; and (4) Deaf education should be bilingual—ASL and English—and multicultural, with attention and respect paid to all cultures (Latinos, European Americans, Native peoples, Jews, African Americans, and so on).

• Summary and Conclusions

The informants' Native Deaf experiences, in spite of their being constantly exposed to and surrounded by European American communities and ways of life, reconfirmed the existence of Native Deaf peoples in the mainland United States. All informants maintained fierce ties to their Native heritages, their Native communities' traditions and customs, and continued to walk on paths as *Native* Deaf people. They had not just become part of the overall U.S. Deaf population but viewed themselves as Native Deaf people. The informants' basic needs, as indicated in the interviews, were: (1) to be able to communicate in a natural signed language, for instance, Native signed languages or ASL, and to have their Native families learn and communicate in a signed language; (2) to be in a deaf educational program with some Native Deaf students; (3) to be well prepared for learning other cultures and their values and ways of life, especially European American cultures, prior to attending a deaf educational program with a majority of European American teachers, staff, and students; (4) to have time and opportunities to participate in and fully comprehend their Native communities' interpreted ceremonies, initiations, and other important events during their precollege school years; (5) to have opportunities to participate in their Native communities' interpreted ceremonies and other events during their lifetimes; and (6) to socialize with Native and non-Native Deaf people after graduating.

To meet the above basic needs, individuals in Native communities must have access to Native signed language or ASL classes and interpreting services. Some Native communities could set up their own Native signed language or ASL programs, where some of their own Native Deaf people would be ideal candidates to obtain training to become signed language instructors. This way, the communities could have instructors with the same Native heritage as the students and therefore learn a signed language and be comfortable discussing their Native traditions. If this is not possible, Holly's suggestion perhaps is the next best thing—for some families to take ASL classes in a non-Native continuing education program in a community or university in or near their Native community. Also, the Native communities need to investigate ways to have some of their own people become Native signed language or ASL interpreters. It would be extremely significant for Native individuals to become interpreters in their communities, as Native peoples tend not to be comfortable communicating with one another in the presence of a non-Native interpreter.

Michael recommended multicultural education for educating Deaf children of different cultural groups, including Native communities, so as to enhance cultural sensitivity and awareness among Deaf children of different cultural groups. Sonia Nieto's definition (1996:307–308) of such a multicultural education in a sociopolitical context is adopted here as follows:

> Multicultural education is a process of comprehensive school reform and basic education for all students. It challenges and rejects racism and other forms of discrimination in schools and society and accepts and affirms the pluralism (ethnic, racial, linguistic, religious, economic, and gender, among others) that students, their communities, and teachers represent. Multicultural education permeates the curriculum and instructional strategies used in schools, as well as the interactions among teachers, students, and parents, and the very way that schools conceptualize the nature of teaching and learning. Because it uses critical pedagogy as its underlying philosophy and focuses on knowledge, reflection, and action (praxis) as the basis for social change, multicultural education promotes the democratic principles of social justice. The seven basic characteristics of multicultural education in this definition are:
>
> > Multicultural education is *antiracist education.*
> > Multicultural education is *basic education.*
> > Multicultural education is *important for* all *students.*
> > Multicultural education is *pervasive.*
> > Multicultural education is *education for social justice.*
> > Multicultural education is a *process.*
> > Multicultural education is *critical pedagogy.*

It is hoped that further studies on Native Deaf peoples and new directions of education will contribute to a deeper immersion into a Native culture and a Native Deaf identity for future generations of Native Deaf children. That way, more and more smoke will rise from Native Deaf hearths among the Native communities across the Americas.

NOTE

This paper could not have been completed without the help of Michael Byrd, Jeffrey Davis, Nancy Owens, Patty Hughes, Clayton Valli, Margaret Hodges, and Shawn Mahshie. Funding for this study was provided through the small grants fund, Gallaudet University, Washington, D.C. Finally, I want to give special thanks to the Native Deaf informants for their participation in this study.

REFERENCES

Center for Assessment and Demographic Studies. 1990. *1989–1990 Annual Survey of Hearing Impaired Children and Youth*. Washington, DC: Gallaudet Research Institute.

————. 1996. *1995–1996 Annual Survey of Hearing Impaired Children and Youth*. Washington, DC: Gallaudet Research Institute.

Davis, J., and S. Supalla. 1995. A sociolinguistic description of sign language use in a Navajo family. In *Sociolinguistics in Deaf Communities*, edited by C. Lucas, 77–106. Washington, DC: Gallaudet University Press.

Eldredge, N. M. 1993. Culturally affirmative counseling with American Indians who are deaf. *Journal of American Deafness and Rehabilitation* 26, 4:1–18.

Eldredge, N. M., and J. Carrigan. 1992. Where do my kindred dwell? Using art and storytelling to understand the transition of young Indian men who are deaf. *Arts in Psychotherapy* 19:29–38.

Frishberg, N. 1987. Home signs. In *Gallaudet Encyclopedia of Deaf People and Deafness*, edited by J. V. Van Cleve, 3:128–131. New York: McGraw Hill.

Groce, N. E. 1985. *Everyone Here Spoke Sign Language: Hereditary Deafness on Martha's Vineyard*. Cambridge, MA: Harvard University Press.

Hirschfelder, A., and M. K. de Montano. 1993. *The Native American Almanac: A Portrait of Native America Today*. New York: Prentice-Hall General Reference.

Johnson, R. E. 1994. Sign language and the concept of deafness in a traditional Yucatec Mayan village. In *The Deaf Way: Perspectives from the international conference on Deaf culture*, edited by C. Erting, R. Johnson, D. Smith, and B. Snider, 102–109. Washington, DC: Gallaudet University Press.

Kakumasu, J. 1978. Urubu Sign Language. In *Aboriginal Sign Languages of the Americas and Australia*, edited by D. J. Umiker-Sebeok and T. A. Sebeok, 2: 247–253. New York: Plenum Press.

Klima, E., and U. Bellugi. 1979. *The Signs of Language*. Cambridge, MA: Harvard University Press.

Lucas, C., and C. Valli. 1989. Language contact in the American Deaf community. In *The Sociolinguistics of the Deaf Community*, edited by C. Lucas, 11–40. San Diego: Academic Press.

Massey, C. R. 1992. An interview with Michael Byrd, Deaf Native American. *TBC News* 47: 1–4.

Nieto, S. 1996. *Affirming Diversity: The Sociopolitical Context of Multicultural Education*, 2d ed. White Plains, NY: Longman Publishers.

Sorkin, A. L. 1978. *The Urban American Indian*. Lexington, MA: Lexington Books.

Thornton, Russell. 1987. *American Indian Holocaust and Survival: A Population History since 1492*. Norman: University of Oklahoma Press.

Umiker-Sebeok, D. J., and T. A. Sebeok, eds. 1978. *Aboriginal Sign Languages of the Americas and Australia*. Vols. 1 and 2. New York: Plenum Press.

U.S. Bureau of the Census. 1990. American Indian tribes with 1,000 or more American Indians for the United States 1990. In *United States Department of Commerce News*. Washington, DC: Economics and Statistics Administration. CB92–244.

Washabaugh, W. 1986. *Five Fingers for Survival*. Ann Arbor, MI: Karoma.

53

The Deaf community's rather heavy policing of any tendencies toward positive attitudes to speech and hearing often sends offenders into exile in the hearing world. A few brave souls fight back. This essay derives from a two-hour, videotaped discussion by Phil and Myrna ("Mo") Aiello about their new cochlear implants. The discussion was conducted with the editor in a combination of ASL and signed English in the spring of 1999, in Dean Dillehay's conference room on the Gallaudet campus. Although the passages selected for translation/transcription here focus chiefly on Phil's more typical experience and are therefore written in the first person as his story, much of the information and many of the reflections on identity and the Deaf community came from Mo.

Cochlear Implants and Deaf Identity

A. Philip Aiello and Myrna Aiello

1999

I was born "hearing" and became deaf at the age of three months from spinal meningitis. You might as well say I was born deaf, since at three months I hadn't learned anything through the ear. My parents didn't realize I was deaf, however, until I was three years old, and when they found out, they didn't know what to do. In those days, hearing parents didn't have the kinds of resources that they do today. They went to doctors asking for help and finally found one who told them about a school for the deaf, New York PS 47, that trained deaf children to speak and provided for them to live at home and interact with their parents and local community. I went there until I was sent to a hearing school in fifth grade because of my good speech. I used a hearing aid, which, in those days, was a big box worn on the chest. During that year, I was constantly teased by the kids in my new school. They called me "deaf," they called me "dumb"; it was very upsetting and frustrating for me. My parents told me to ignore them, explaining that they didn't understand, and said I shouldn't let their ignorance disturb me.

When I was in the eighth grade, we moved to New Jersey. At the time of the move, my parents were worried about my going to a new public school without additional support, because leaving New York and coming to New Jersey meant a new environment, a new culture for me, and they didn't believe I could cope with any more frustration. My parents decided that we should visit the New Jersey School for the Deaf and meet with the superintendent. When he talked with me and understood my speech well, he told my parents that I didn't belong in a deaf school and should be sent to a regular public school. He believed that I could function in a public school if my parents would get someone to come once a week to tutor me. That's what happened through eighth grade.

I remember very well how the teasing in eighth grade was worse than it had been in New York. But I also remember that in one of the classes I took, when many of the other students had problems doing the work and had to ask for help, the teacher pointed to me and said, "He's doing the work without asking a lot of questions and he can't hear, yet you others are complaining." I remember being surprised at that. Through high school, I continued to be very frustrated because I was the only deaf person in the school. I participated in sports—football, baseball, basketball—and tried very hard to go out on dates with girls. I did get one date but never dated again because it was such a bad experience. It's funny to look back on it now, though. I had asked the girl out to a basketball game, and after the game the students all got together for music, sodas, smoking. Later, I walked her home. It was dark. The girl talked constantly as we walked. Every time we got under a streetlight, I could see her lips. Then I would scurry along with her up to the next streetlight and say, "What did you say?" and she would talk and talk. I just couldn't get her to understand or accept the fact that I couldn't understand her in the dark because I had to see her lips. When we arrived at her house, she said, "I had a nice time with you, but I don't think I want to go out with you again because I can't communicate with you." I was humiliated. So I never dated again through high school.

When I was a senior, I applied for college, but one hearing college after another turned me down. It was never because of my scholastic record but because I couldn't hear. They were afraid that with freshman and sophomore classes of two hundred or three hundred students, the professors didn't give individual attention and I would never make it through. Then the high school counselor found out about Gallaudet. We visited the campus, and when I saw everybody signing, I couldn't believe my eyes. My mother was shocked. "No way!" she told me, "You'll lose your speech. After all these years of speech training, you'll come to Gallaudet and start to sign, and you'll lose your speech." I promised her I would continue speaking and pointed out that there was a hearing and speech center on campus. And so it was decided that I would enroll at Gallaudet.

Coming to Gallaudet was a culture shock for me. At that time, of course, I didn't know how to sign. Again, I was an outsider to the culture and people were teasing me: I "thought like a hearing person" (using the sign THINK HEARING), I signed like a baby, and so on. But after about six months, I was able to sign pretty well.

After graduation, I went back out into the hearing world to work, where communication was always somewhat frustrating. There were problems with co-workers and meetings. This was 1966, and in those days there were no interpreters, no captioning, no ADA, nothing. We had to fight our way through. Even at Gallaudet there were no interpreters, and if a hearing professor couldn't sign, well, that's what we got. Of course, today, it's different. But back in those days, going to training sessions and meetings was very difficult. I always had to ask someone to please take notes for me because I couldn't hear, but people either weren't willing or didn't know what to do.

In the meantime, I became more involved with the Deaf community here in the Washington area and was very active in Deaf advocacy issues, helping deaf people set up organizations and get recognition. The advocacy work went pretty well because the hearing community, thanks to Gallaudet, was becoming more aware of and responsive to Deaf needs. Then I got involved with AT&T's Special Needs Program. I was responsible for helping people with disabilities in the workplace—deaf, blind, limited-mobility people, wheelchair users, and so on. In that capacity, I met a great variety of people, and that's how I first met people with cochlear implants. The first people I met with CIs were people who became deaf at a later age. They seemed to hear pretty well with the implants, and I thought to myself, "Right, well they were hearing before, and now they've got some hearing back—that's good for them."

At that time, 1990, it never occurred to me that I might be interested in an implant myself. I started to meet a few Deaf people who had CIs but were afraid to tell anyone because of the Deaf community and culture. They were afraid of losing the respect of their friends and not being accepted anymore. I listened to what they were saying, and I thought about it. I asked them, "Can you hear?" And they said, "Yes! I can hear birds, I can hear cars." The more people I met, the more interested in implants I became. But still I had to wonder. One man from California had been deaf all his life until he got the implant at age forty-five. After six months, he was able to understand his mother on the phone, at least a few words. I thought, so what? Many deaf people can understand their own mothers without lipreading. My question was whether one could communicate with strangers, hear their voices when they come up and talk with you, and I was really curious.

At that time, around 1990, the requirements for implant recipients were stricter and I didn't qualify, so I more or less put it out of my mind. In 1991, Mo and I went to the SHHH [Self-Help for the Hard of Hearing] convention in Baltimore, where I was to set up an exhibit for a special access program for people who were hard of hearing, and where we were to give a lecture. We were the first Deaf people to give a signed lecture at SHHH, and what was interesting was that although we were signing and voicing at the same time, many of the hard of hearing cochlear implant people couldn't understand us and had to use an oral interpreter or real-time captioning. It was very disorienting to us because, like all Deaf people, when we lecture, we need eye contact and expect the audience to watch us. When they all directed their gaze off to the side, to the captions, we felt like we were talking to an empty room. For them, captions were more important than looking at the person who was lecturing. That experience made me wonder about the value of implants and the culture conflict.

In 1997, however, several people with implants made very positive impressions on me. They all told me that they could converse with other people and listen to music without any difficulty and could understand words without lipreading. All said their lives had been enhanced and were more enjoyable. I said to Mo, "I want a cochlear implant," but her response was "What for? Accept yourself for what you are, the man I married." She realized later that she was afraid of change. Anyway, one of the CI users was able to interpret the lyrics to songs during a dance, with all that background noise, and told us that she got the implant specifically because she loved music. I watched with total amazement and wanted to be able to do the same. She convinced Mo to let me go ahead with it, and the two of us decided to go and learn more about CIs at the Johns Hopkins support group.

There were almost fifty people there at the support group, and we met one Deaf person, a Gallaudet graduate, who had just got an implant six months before. She could understand a lecture with her back turned. We were struck by that, and by the stories of other Deaf and late-deafened people and how their lives were changed after their cochlear implants. They talked about which organizations supported implants and which were opposed. SHHH and AGB [Alexander Graham Bell] fully supported the concept but the NAD [National Association of the Deaf] was fully against implants for children. So I decided to stand up and explain to the group that I was from the Deaf community and was a member of the NAD. I said it was true that the NAD has its reservations about how well the implants work but that they are concerned mostly about implanting young children. I explained that I, myself, was considering getting one if they really performed as everyone claimed they did, and that I would work with the NAD to see if they would reconsider their position. I met a cochlear implant surgeon who told me that I was the perfect candidate for an implant because I spoke very well (which was fortunate!). The surgeon said that I met the qualifications because my decibel loss was just above the new cutoff and because my word discrimination was less than 40 percent—in fact, only 15 percent. I was thrilled and became even more interested.

Mo still didn't support my getting an implant but she felt that if I really wanted it, I should go for it. I felt that it was one thing for hearing people to be able to hear again what they had heard before, but what about us born-deaf people? I wanted to find out. Also, I learned that two men I went to Gallaudet with had implants. One had lost his hearing gradually through high school until he was profoundly deaf, and the other was deaf-blind. Both could use the telephone now.

When I made the decision to get an implant, Mo advised me to tell my friends before the surgery rather than after. That way, I would know in advance whether they were real friends or not! About fourteen of us got together one night and I told them I had an announcement to make that might have a big impact on them and so on, but they told me to quit beating around the bush and just tell them what I had to say. Their response to my announcement was stunned silence, but after a moment, they all agreed that if that was what I wanted, I should go for it. They said they were my friends and were there for me, and that it didn't bother them at all, which really surprised me. Then I made the announcement to my family, especially to my children. Now, my oldest daughter is Deaf, my second daughter hearing, and I have two younger daughters, both hearing. I told them that by getting an implant, I hoped to be able to hear more than I could with a hearing aid. My oldest daughter was totally against it, totally, and she told the story all over the Deaf community, how much she was against her father getting an implant. My third daughter was against it, too, but only because of the risks involved with the surgery. The night before the surgery was very emotional for me because I asked the family to come together, but my oldest daughter refused. I explained to the others that the implant wasn't going to work overnight and I would need their continuous support.

So I went ahead and had the surgery in June 1998. It went very well, as expected, but I had to wait at least four weeks before activation of the implant, to give the surgical area time to heal. During the four-week waiting process, my expectations were low due to past experiences with hearing aids. At the time of activation, I was nervous; I didn't know what to expect. The first thing I heard was the implant electrodes warming up. The next thing I heard was someone saying, "Hello." It was Myrna. I was shocked to hear her. They started testing my hearing by asking me to repeat sounds, and I was able to do it on the first try. The first few days were overwhelming, so many sounds that I'd never experienced before and couldn't identify. The sounds of my own footsteps on the hospital floor, the traffic outside—it was just crazy. The sound of rain, the noise of the engine turning over when I started the car, my own voice, which I now realized was very deep. Driving home, it started to rain hard, and noise of the rain on the car was unbearable. My God, I wondered, is that what hearing people hear? At home, everything echoed. I missed the clarity of my hearing aid, although I realized that it was only because that was what I had been used to for so many years.

Two weeks after the surgery, we went to the NAD convention in Texas. The friends I had already told about my implant warned me to be ready to face criticism. I was on the convention program with a workshop on implants, but no one suspected that I had one myself. I would bump into people I knew from all over the country and would be standing around chatting with them when they'd notice the wire coming out from behind my ear. As we'd talk, they'd try to peer behind my head, looking really puzzled as though they were thinking, "Can't be!" They'd be very polite and finish the conversation, but then they'd run tell their friends, "Hey, look at Phil, he got an implant!" and everyone in the room would turn and stare at me. People began to keep their distance and avoid talking to me. Or they'd come up behind me and make noises that I didn't recognize and then go off and tell their friends that the implant didn't work. I'd tell them that I'd only had the implant for two weeks and to give me some time, but their attitude was that once you got the implant, you suddenly became hearing. So that's when I realized the major misconception about implants. People thought that getting an implant would turn you into a Hearing Person.

The CI workshop that year was the first time implants had been discussed at an NAD convention, and it was a hot issue. The workshop had been scheduled for a small room but had to be moved to a bigger one to accommodate all the people who wanted to attend. More than 250 people showed up, and even with the bigger room it was standing room only. There were four speakers at the workshop and I was the last one. I didn't know how to introduce myself, so I just started by asking how many of the people in the room knew me. Many hands went up. "For those of you who know me," I asked, "am I the same since my implant, or am I different?" They all responded that I was the same, that implants didn't change the person in any way, not in personality or behavior. I told them that I was there, in the Deaf community, and wasn't going to be leaving to join some other cultural group. I explained that I got the implant because I was curious whether I would be able to hear more with it than with a hearing aid and that, yes, I could. I told them that I had a dream of being able to communicate over the telephone one day. I told them that the key word here was *respect*. We need to learn to respect a person's desires, because if we don't, naturally they're going to leave the Deaf community. The more Deaf people are resistant, the more we will lose people and our culture will be diminished. If we don't respect people, they'll join other organizations that do. I explained to them that an implant will *never* make a person hearing. Certainly, *I'll* never be hearing; I'll *always* be Deaf. The implant works for me up to a point, but that doesn't mean it will work for everyone.

After the workshop, a number of people came up to me and told me they'd been considering an implant but were afraid of disapproval and of losing their friends. One response to my implant that had a big impact on me was when one person came up to me and said, "You're a traitor to the Deaf community." Again, the idea was that I had "become hearing." I was very angry but tried to respect the feelings of others. Another person actually told me that even though he had known me for years, he never realized how sick I was! I said, "Okay, so I'm sick." A third person asked me how I kept myself sanitary since I couldn't shower with the implant. I explained to him that you remove the external part just like a hearing aid before you get into the shower, but he couldn't understand how I could do that with a hole in my head! There are so many misunderstandings about implants. People refuse to learn or to keep an open mind about it.

You sometimes see analogies with racism. People say that for a Deaf person to get an implant and become hearing is like a black person bleaching himself white. It's best just to ignore remarks like that. You also see analogies with Hitler once in a while, and people use the word *genocide*. But that's all part of the big misconception that implants make a person hearing. It's just not true.

In general, the community has a major problem with labeling people. You're hard of hearing; you're Deaf; you're hearing impaired; you're oral; you're ASL. But we're all Deaf. You wear hearing aids; you have an implant; you're low vision; you're Usher's syndrome; and so on and on and on. This labeling has just got to stop. It's nothing new, of course, because it's always been the case that people who are hard of hearing or use hearing aids and who speak well have felt rejected by the community. A person I know who works here signs fluent ASL and is Deaf, of course, but happens to be one of these people who can hear well with a hearing aid, use the phone, understand 65 percent of what people say. And still, no matter how many years she's been involved with the Deaf community, she still feels that she's not accepted, not part of the community. People say, "She hears so much, she thinks like a hearing person," using the sign THINK HEARING. What more can she do? People with that label, THINK HEARING, are seen as a threat to the Deaf community. Anybody who can hear well or speak well is a threat, for some reason. This isn't Deaf culture. It's just the behavior of some people and probably derives from all the anger that's out there. Hard of hearing people who speak well tend to be successful, and when people see that, they wonder, "Why? We're brothers (or we went to the same school, or whatever), but he's successful in the hearing world while I'm stuck here without a decent job." Of course they're angry. But why wouldn't anyone want to grab the chance to increase his or her hearing?

With children who have had implant surgery when they were very young, the implant is normal for them. When they grow up, some continue to benefit and some don't, but they have a choice whether to continue using the implant or not. We've meet some young people who got their implants years ago and don't use them now, but you have to understand that back then, the technology wasn't really great. Now, the technology has improved so much, it's amazing, and the success rate of children with CIs will be much greater from now on than it was in the past. All our statistics are based on those old models, but we're in a new generation of implants now. It's true that many Gallaudet students stop using their implants while they're here, but the same is true for hearing aids. When students arrive with hearing aids and discover that everyone on campus signs, they figure they don't need their hearing aids anymore and just stick them in a drawer. Four years later when they graduate and go out into the world to work, they start wearing them again. It's the culture here on campus that makes hearing aids, and implants, not important. Of course, with implants, there's also the fear among students that they'll be picked on. They want to be accepted so they hide their implants and identify as Deaf. Naturally, they want to conform.

It's interesting to compare implants with hearing aids. We have a number of friends who use hearing aids and do very well on the telephone, can talk to hearing people without lipreading. Are they "not Deaf"? No one says to the person with hearing aids, "You're not Deaf, you're not part of the community." Why is it any different with implants? If some Deaf people can understand speech with hearing aids, well, I want the same, and for me that means an implant. The big question here is how the community identifies who is in and who is out. I remember back in the days when hearing aids were big boxes worn on the chest, people wouldn't accept them, they would reject anyone wearing one. But over the years, the behind-the-ear hearing aids became part of us, and today a high percentage of people use them just to hear environmental sounds. Nothing wrong with that. So instead of fighting cochlear implants, we should welcome people who have them. They'll always be Deaf.

54 | Signing Off

Bruce A. White

1999

A flip quip made famous by I. King Jordan is "Deaf people can do anything except hear." This statement was presumably not intended to be taken literally, for we can all think of endeavors or occupations deaf people would fail at (even *with* the mediation of an interpreter), such as providing the voices for an animated cartoon or movie. Whether this example strikes some as frivolous is irrelevant; the point is whether deaf people, who have been steered into occupations deemed appropriate for them for hundreds of years, *can* do anything they want to. Perhaps the statement was meant to be taken as an idealistic platitude. However it was intended, the message may be less inspirational than cruel. Since the 1988 Deaf President Now uprising and Jordan's tumultuous appointment as president of Gallaudet University, no other deaf person has, to my knowledge, become a college or university president. Thus Jordan, a role model for many of the students at Gallaudet, continues to be the only member of a lonely club, which makes him the exception that proves the rule: deaf people *cannot* do everything except hear.

Perhaps we are being unreasonable, even uppity in expecting to have more than one deaf president at one of the approximately fifteen hundred colleges and universities throughout the United States. Perhaps we could more reasonably expect to have at least 750 deaf professors (the equivalent of one deaf faculty member at every other campus) scattered across the country, especially if we count those at Gallaudet? But since even at Gallaudet deaf professors are a minority, and since there are, at most, only a dozen professors known to be deaf at other campuses across the country, maybe the best we can hope for is approximately a hundred. The question is when.

Advocates for women's rights have for many years cited the need to break through the glass ceiling in professional and corporate organizations. In 1999 a woman became the first of her sex to head a Fortune 100 company, and she is only the third woman to head a Fortune 500 company. Women were not enfranchised in the United States until 1920, so it has taken nearly eighty years since then for a woman to reach the pinnacle of corporate success. Will it take deaf people eighty years following Deaf President Now to see comparable achievements? It may very well take longer than that, because deaf people contend not only with glass ceilings but with glass walls as well—communication remains a daily barrier and struggle.

Recently, when a deaf candidate for an administrative position in academia was going through the interview process, she was asked whether an interpreter would have to go along with her for off-campus travel. Such a question is, of course, not appropriate and deserved no answer, but after that awkward moment the interview grew strained. A comparable moment arrives all too often when a deaf applicant seeks employment. If she possesses extraordinary skills in speaking and lipreading, then the odds of receiving a chance to demonstrate her abilities rise markedly; otherwise, the "we'll give you a call" parting is more likely than not a farewell.

How controlling are the minimal expectations of an audist society when it comes to economic opportunities for deaf people? Recently there was a news article about young women in Jamaica who bleach their faces for economic gain—the lighter they are, the better they believe they will do both socially and economically. How different is this from the increasing use of cosmetic surgery to sculpt one's physique in order to be more competitive in the financial and meat markets? Deaf people who bleach their speech are perhaps hoping for similar benefits. Those who subject themselves to the high-tech version of the ancient practice of trepanning—done formerly, perhaps, in the futile hopes of gaining a mystic "third eye" and now done in an effort to obtain a third ear—are simply pursuing elective surgery with electrical ramifications. In the past people mutilated themselves for clairvoyance—now they do it not for clairaudience but from a desire to increase the din of fleeting sound by a few decibels. It is only a matter of time, however, before the Human Genome Project will be completed, and every parent will be able to ensure that any genes responsible for deafness are identified. We will move from body sculpting to gene sculpting, and taxpayers will no longer need to fund the offensively named National Institute of Deafness and Other Communication Disorders.

In the preface to *Seeing Voices*, Oliver Sacks, who participated in the DPN march to the Capitol, remarks that few people are likely to be interested in the lives of deaf people. Most of his readers are probably unaware that philosophers in the eighteenth century were fascinated by "deaf-mutes" and their acquisition of language. We have been subjected to varying degrees of neglect and exploitation throughout history, and perhaps only others like us can know us for who we are. Montaigne refers in a tantalizingly brief and casual manner to seeing signers; as famous as Montaigne is, though, most of us, given the ability to travel back in time four hundred years, would push him aside and run after those anonymous signers, asking for news and where they're from. To future scholars in a perfectly audist world, however, Montaigne's allusion will be simply another footnote in their version of the history of deafness.

Such a future history might touch upon, for example, the etymology of the word *absurd*: laughable, ridiculous. The hearing scholar may note that *surdus* (dull, deaf, insensible) is the Latin root, but will he understand what this etymology implies about how the hearing viewed deaf people? Will he wonder why the behavior of deaf people trying to communicate with the non-deaf was considered futile and foolish? Will he posit as an explanation the tiresome amount of patience and accommodation necessary on the part of the hearing to communicate with those thought to be incapable of eloquence?

This future reference work may also point out that the official seal of Gallaudet

Official Seal of Gallaudet University, depicting the
finger alphabet letters E, P, H, P, H, A, T, H, A. By
permission of the President, Gallaudet University.

University (perhaps long since converted to a minimum-security penitentiary) included the fingerspelled exhortation *Ephphatha*, "Be opened." This is from Mark 7,
in which Jesus makes the deaf hear and the dumb speak. Will the contributor of the
article on Gallaudet University observe that this motto might have been more appropriate for cochlear implant clinics than for a university of deaf students, especially
given the context from which this exhortation is taken? Worse still, in Mark 9:25,
Jesus says to a boy, "You dumb and deaf spirit, I command you, come out of him,
and never enter him again." This short passage has probably caused more suffering
and heartache for deaf people in the last two thousand years than any other single
text; but it is unlikely that future writers, in a world without deaf people, would
venture such a statement.

Similarly, the contributor on the psychosocial problems of deaf people may note
that the classic treatises dealing with the pathological behavior of the deaf repeatedly
cited anger, paranoia, self-centeredness, immaturity, and other negative traits. The
contributor probably won't hazard the opinion that those traits were perfectly normal responses to oppressive and destructive family and social forces; that being
sullen, angry, depressed, or withdrawn was a consequence of coping strategies, not
an inherent character flaw.

The contributor of the article about deaf people in the media will undoubtedly list
the many books, TV shows and movies, theatrical performances, and studio films
featuring deaf people. The fact that a deaf woman played the role of Cordelia in
King Lear in the nation's capital in 1999 may be mentioned—but as an example of

416 | *Bruce A. White*

what? An indication of the access deaf performers and audiences had, or a trendy packaging of a four hundred-year-old play? Will this contributor suggest that there might in fact have been a regression in how deaf people presented themselves and were portrayed by others? What progress is evident from *A Deaf Mute Howls* to *What's That Pig Outdoors?* What will be said about the fact that portrayals of deaf people in film and on TV ranged from the pitiful to the fanciful, from Sarah in *Children of a Lesser God* to the improbable character in the TV series *Reasonable Doubts*, who is able to lipread around corners and through the heads of speakers facing away from her?

Before the world of deaf people as we really are becomes an artifact of history, our best recourse may be to enjoy the hard-won opportunities we do have, cherish our deaf family, friends, and colleagues, and celebrate ourselves whenever we meet.

Further Reading

Arlene Blumenthal Kelly

CULTURAL SOURCES

Becker, Gaylene, and J. Jauregui. 1981. "The Invisible isolation of Deaf Women: Its Effects on Social Awareness." *Journal of Sociology and Social Welfare* 8, 2: 249–262.
Describes how double-discriminated Deaf women are in sociological terms.

Carmel, Simon J. 1987. "A Study of Deaf Culture in an American Urban Deaf Community." Unpublished dissertation, American University.
Explores how members in three different clubs for the Deaf in a Midwestern state construct "culture."

Croneberg, Carl. 1965. "The Linguistic Community." In *A Dictionary of American Sign Language on Linguistic Principles*, by William C. Stokoe, Carl G. Croneberg, and Dorothy Casterune, 297–311. Silver Spring, MD: Linstok Press.
Offers one of the earliest descriptions of Deaf people as a linguistic minority group.

Doe, Tanis M. 1993. "Exploring Gender with Deaf Women and Their Hearing Sisters." Unpublished dissertation, University of Alberta, Edmonton.
Probes how Deaf Canadian women and their hearing sisters define "gender."

Erting, Carol. 1994. *Deafness, Communication, and Social Identity: Ethnography in a Preschool for Deaf Children*. Burtonsville, MD: Linstok Press.
Originally a dissertation investigating how Deaf and hearing parents and Deaf and hearing teachers of preschoolers define deafness, language, communication, and social identity.

Erting, Carol, R. Clover Johnson, Dorothy N. Smith, and Bruce D. Snider, eds. 1994. *The Deaf Way: Perspectives from the International Conference on deaf Culture*. Washington, DC: Gallaudet University Press.
An international compilation of papers on history, culture, and language presented at the Deaf Way Conference.

Higgins, Paul C., and Jeffrey E. Nash. 1987. *Understanding Deafness Socially*. Springfield, IL: Thomas Publishers.
Deaf people described from a sociological perspective.

Holcomb, Mabs, and Sharon Kay Wood. 1989. *Deaf Women: A Parade through the Decades.* San Diego: DawnSignPress.
The only known compilation of birth/death dates and significant contributions of Deaf women.

Jacobs, Leo M. (1974) 1989. *A Deaf Adult Speaks Out.* Washington, DC: Gallaudet University Press.
Ahead of his time, Jacobs describes the variations within the Deaf community.

Jankowski, Katherine A. 1997. *Deaf Empowerment: Emergence, Struggle, and Rhetoric.* Washington, DC: Gallaudet University Press.
Originally a dissertation proposing the power of rhetoric among Deaf people through Stokoe's pioneering research on ASL linguistics and how this research engendered a sense of empowerment.

Kannapell, Barbara. 1993. *Language Choice–Identity Choice.* Burtonsville, MD: Linstok Press.
Originally a dissertation eliciting viewpoints on language and identity among Deaf college students.

Ladd, Paddy. 1993. "Deaf Consciousness—How Deaf Studies Can Improve the Quality of Deaf Life." *Deaf Studies III: Bridging Cultures in the 21st Century Conference Proceedings.* Washington, DC: Gallaudet University.
Written through a British lens, offering how Deaf Studies can promote cultural awareness.

Lane, Harlan. (1992) 1999. *The Mask of Benevolence: Disabling the Deaf Community.* San Diego: DawnSignPress.
Explores the gap between the Deaf culture and the hearing society, including the ethics of cochlear implants.

Lane, Harlan, and Ben Bahan. 1998. "Ethics of Cochlear Implantation in Young Children: A Review and Reply from a Deaf-World Perspective. *Otolaryngology–Head and Neck Surgery Foundation* 119: 297–313.
A defense of the Deaf position on cochlear-implanting deaf children.

Lane, Harlan, Robert Hoffmeister, and Ben Bahan. 1996. *A Journey into the DEAF-WORLD.* San Diego: DawnSignPress.
An introduction to the Deaf historical, cultural, and linguistic experiences.

MacLeod-Gallinger, J. E. 1992. "The Career Status of Deaf Women: A Comparative Look." *American Annals of the Deaf* 137, 4: 315–325.
Career struggles and achievements among Deaf women.

Padden, Carol A., and Tom Humphries. 1988. *Deaf in America: Voices from a Culture.* Cambridge: Harvard University Press.
One of the earliest works describing Deaf lives as related by Deaf individuals.

Parasnis, Ila, ed. 1996. *Cultural and Language Diversity and the Deaf Experience.* New York: Cambridge University Press.
Akin to the Padden and Humphries 1988 book, offering more stories from Deaf individuals, including a chapter by Francois Grosjean describing bilingualism.

Preston, Paul. 1994. *Mother Father Deaf: Living between Sound and Silence.* Cambridge: Harvard University Press.
Originally a dissertation surveying various experiences of hearing children of Deaf adults.

Rutherford, Susan D. 1988. "The Culture of American Deaf People." *Sign Language Studies* 59: 129–147.
Offers a brief overview of Deaf culture.

Sacks, Oliver. 1989. *Seeing Voices: A Journey into the World of the Deaf.* Berkeley: University of California Press.
The Deaf experience through the lens of an eminent neurologist.

Singleton, Patti Moos. 1994. "Leadership Style, Personality Types and Demographics: Profiles of Deaf Female Administrators in Educational Programs for Deaf Students." Unpublished doctoral dissertation, Gallaudet University, Washington, DC.
A survey of Deaf female administrators that shows how leadership and personality types emerge.

Turner, G. H. 1994. "*How* Is Deaf Culture? Another Perspective on a Fundamental Concept." *Sign Language Studies* 83:103–123.

Andersson, Yerker. 1994. Comment on Turner. *Sign Language Studies* 83: 127–131.

Bahan, Ben. 1994. Comment on Turner. *Sign Language Studies* 84: 241–249.
Turner questions the validity of "culture" among Deaf People, and both Andersson and Bahan respond to Turner's question.

Wrigley, Owen. 1996. *The Politics of Deafness.* Washington, DC: Gallaudet University Press.
Pushes the need to theorize the culture of Deaf people.

Wilcox, Sherman, ed. 1989. *American Deaf Culture: An Anthology.* Silver Spring, MD: Linstok Press.
Deaf people write essays on their thoughts and experiences of being Deaf.

HISTORICAL SOURCES

Albronda, Mildred. 1980. *Douglas Tilden: Portrait of a Deaf Sculptor.* Silver Spring, MD: T. J. Publishers, Inc.
A rare look into the life of famed Deaf sculptor Tilden, whose works can still be seen in the city of San Francisco.

Atwood, Albert W. 1964. *Gallaudet College: Its First One Hundred Years.* Lancaster, PA: Intelligencer Printing Company.
The first hundred years of Gallaudet College.

Baker, Charlotte, and Robbin Battison, eds. 1980. *Sign Language and the Deaf Community: Essays in Honor of William C. Stokoe.* Silver Spring, MD: National Association of the Deaf.
Written as a Festschrift presented to Stokoe as a surprise at the one hundredth anniversary of the National Association of the Deaf convention in Cincinnati.

Barash, Harvey J., and Eva Barash Dicker. 1991. *Our Father Abe: The Story of a Deaf Shoe Repairman.* Madison, WI: Abar Press.
The Life of Abe Barash, a Jewish Deaf man, described by his hearing children.

Baynton, Douglas C. 1996. *Forbidden Signs: American Culture and the Campaign against Sign Language.* Chicago: University of Chicago.
Describes the conflict between oralism and manualism in Deaf education in the context of nineteenth-century intellectualism.

Christiansen, John B., and Sharon N. Barnartt. 1995. *Deaf President Now! The 1988 Revolution at Gallaudet University.* Washington, DC: Gallaudet University Press.
The beginning and duration of the Deaf President Now! movement, including the involvement of the Ducks, a group of young Deaf men who planted the seed for this revolution.

Fay, Edward A. 1896. "An Inquiry concerning the Results of Marriages of the Deaf in America." *American Annals of the Deaf* 41 (1896): 22–31.
During an era when eugenics was valorized, Fay investigates whether Deaf-Deaf marriages produce Deaf offspring and discovered that it is not the case. This research, financed by Alexander Graham Bell's organization, set the precedent for the "10 percent–90 percent formula," where 10 percent of Deaf Americans are born to Deaf parents and 90 percent of Deaf Americans have hearing parents.

Fischer, Renate, and Harlan Lane, eds. 1993. *Looking Back: A Reader on the History of Deaf Communities and Their Sign Languages.* International Studies on Sign Language and Communication of the Deaf 20. Hamburg, Signum Press.
A compilation of historical essays on Deaf lives from all over the world.

Gallaudet, Edward Miner. Written, 1895–96. Published, 1983. *History of the College for the Deaf, 1857–1907.* Washington, DC: Gallaudet College Press.
The first president of Gallaudet College describes the first fifty years of this institution, including how General Postmaster Amos Kendall donated his ninety-nine acres to begin the Columbia Institution for the Deaf and Dumb.

Gannon, Jack R. 1981. *Deaf Heritage: A Narrative History of Deaf America.* Silver Spring, MD: National Association of the Deaf.
The first summation of Deaf American history, including the establishments of all the schools for the Deaf in the United States.

Gannon, Jack. R. 1989. *The Week the World Heard Gallaudet.* Washington, DC: Gallaudet University Press.
A coffee-table book offering various pictures taken during the Deaf President Now! movement.

Groce, Nora. 1985. *Everyone Here Spoke Sign Language: Hereditary Deafness on Martha's Vineyard.* Cambridge: Harvard University Press.
Relies on interviews and secondary historical documents offering a glimpse of the sign-language community on Martha's Vineyard.

Katz, Charles N. 1995. "A Comparative Analysis of Deaf, Women, and Black Studies." In *Deaf Studies IV: Visions of the Past—Visions of the Future. Conference Proceedings,* 133–148. Washington, DC: Gallaudet University Press.
Offers parallels in the formation of Black, Women's, and Deaf Studies as academic disciplines.

Kelly, Arlene B. 1998. "A Brief History of the Field of Deaf Studies." *Disability Studies Quarterly* 18, 2: 118–121.
Spiraling off Katz's 1995 article, this offers further insights on the formation of the field of Deaf Studies as an academic discipline.

Lane, Harlan. 1984. *When the Mind Hears: A History of the Deaf.* New York: Random House.
A semifictionalized first-person account of Laurent Clerc, the Deaf Frenchman who came to America in 1816 with Thomas Hopkins Gallaudet to begin the education of Deaf children.

Maher, Jane. 1996. *Seeing Language in Signs: The Works of William C. Stokoe.* Washington, DC: Gallaudet University Press.
The only biography of William C. Stokoe, who proposed in 1965 that the language of Deaf people is analyzable.

Mather, Susan M., and Cathryn Carroll. 1995. *Movers and Shakers: Deaf People Who Changed the World.* San Diego: DawnSignPress.
Famous and infamous Deaf people.

Moore, Michael S., and Robert F. Panara. 1996. *Great Deaf Americans: The Second Edition.* Rochester, NY: Deaf Life Press.
Famous Deaf Americans.

Van Cleve, John V., and Barry A. Crouch. 1989. *A Place of Their Own: Creating the Deaf Community in America.* Washington, DC: Gallaudet University Press.
The historical emergence of the Deaf American community.

Young, Betty A. 1997. *A Chain of Love..* Bloomfield, CT: P & S Services Company.
Chronicles the life of Alice Cogswell and how she inspired the 1817 establishment of the Connecticut Asylum for the Education and Instruction of Deaf and Dumb Persons.

LINGUISTIC SOURCES

Battison, Robbin. 1978. *Lexical Borrowing in American Sign Language.* Silver Spring, MD: Linstok Press.
Originally a dissertation describing ASL in depth, particularly finger spelling.

Cooper, Sheryl B. 1997. "The Academic Status of Sign Language Programs in Institutions of Higher Education in the United States." Unpublished dissertation, Gallaudet University, Washington, DC.
Spiraling off Newell's 1995 dissertation that surveys the status of sign language programs in American institutions of higher education.

Johnson, Robert, Scott Liddell, and Carol J. Erting. 1989. "Unlocking the Curriculum: Principles for Achieving Access in Deaf Education." Gallaudet Research Institute Working Paper 89-3. Washington, DC: Gallaudet University.
A controversial working paper stressing the importance of using ASL in the education of Deaf children.

Kanda, Jan, and Larry Fleischer. 1988. "Who Is Qualified to Teach American Sign Language?" *Sign Language Studies* 59: 183–194.
Offers ten criteria that sign-language teachers should possess.

Kelly, Arlene B. 1991. "Fingerspelling Use among the Deaf Senior Citizens of Baltimore." In *Communication Forum 1*, edited by Elizabeth A. Winston, 90–98. Washington, DC: Gallaudet University.
Describes how and when Deaf senior citizens of Baltimore use fingerspelling.

Kelly, Arlene Blumenthal. 1995. "Fingerspelling Interaction: A Set of Deaf Parents and Their Deaf Daughter." In *Sociolinguistics in Deaf Communities 1*, edited by Ceil Lucas, 62–73. Washington, DC: Gallaudet University Press.
Explores how a Deaf child of Deaf parents acquires fingerspelling and how this acquisition promotes English reading skills.

Long, Joseph Schuyler. (1909, 1918) 1952. *The Sign Language: A Manual of Signs*, Iowa City: Athens Press.
The first known American documented manual on sign language.

Newell, William J. (1990) 1995. "A Job Analysis of Teaching American Sign Language." Doctoral dissertation, Greenwich University. University Microfilms, Inc. no. LD 03041.
How the job descriptions of ASL teachers are alike and different in various American institutes.

Petitto, Laura A., and P. F. Marentette. 1991. "Babbling in the Manual Mode: Evidence for the Ontogeny of Language." *Science* 251: 1397–1536.
Dyads of Deaf infants of Deaf parents, hearing infants of Deaf parents, hearing infants of hearing parents, and Deaf infants of hearing parents show how similar the rate of language acquisition is among the first three dyads.

Pinker, Stephen. 1994. *The Language Instinct: How the Mind Creates Language*. New York: HarperCollins.
How language works, how children learn language, how language changes, and how the brain reckons language.

Shroyer, E. H., and D. W. Holmes. 1982. "Sign Language Classes—The 'In' Thing in Colleges and Universities." In *Proceedings of the 1980 Registry of Interpreters for the Deaf Convention*, 75–80. Silver Spring, MD: RID Publications.
One of the earliest known research findings on the phenomenon of sign-language classes that explores such courses offered in American colleges and universities.

Stokoe, William C. 1960. "Sign Language Structure: An Outline of the Visual Communication Systems of the American Deaf." *Studies in Linguistics* 8. Buffalo, NY: University of Buffalo.
With a belief that a component of a culture should be analyzed, this proposes a study of the language used by Deaf people.

Stokoe, William C., Carl G. Croneberg, and Dorothy Casterline. 1965. *A Dictionary of American Sign Language on Linguistic Principles*. Silver Spring, MD: Linstok Press.
A groundbreaking document that describes ASL as an analyzable language.

Valli, Clayton, and Ceil Lucas. 1992. *Linguistics of ASL: A Resource Text for ASL Users*. Washington, DC: Gallaudet University Press.
Offers a lucid look at the linguistics of American Sign Language.

Permissions

Excerpts from J. J., Flournoy, Edmund Booth, et al., Correspondence in *American Annals of the Deaf and Dumb 10* (1858): 40–160.

Albert Ballin, "Coming to California," from *The Deaf Mute Howls* (Los Angeles: Grafton, 1930): 105–15.

Frederick C. Schreiber, "What a Deaf Jewish Leader Expects of a Rabbi," in Jerome D. Schein, *A Rose for Tomorrow: Biography of Frederick C. Schreiber* (Silver Spring: National Association of the Deaf, 1981): 63–67. Reprinted by permission of the National Association of the Deaf, 814 Thayer Ave., Silver Spring, MD 20910; www.nad.org.

Tom Willard, "How to Write like a Hearing Reporter," *Silent News* (August 1993): 2. Reprinted by permission.

Jack Levesque, "CBS Hurt Deaf Children with 'Caitlin's Story,'" *DCARA News* (December 1992)/January 1993): 2. Reprinted with permission of Deaf Counseling, Advocacy and Referral Agency.

Elizabeth L. Broecker, "Who Speaks for the Deaf Community? Not Who You Would Think!" in Anita B. Farb, ed., *Who Speaks for the Deaf Community? A Deaf American* Monograph, vol. 47 (Silver Spring: National Association of the Deaf, 1997): 7–9. Reprinted by permission of the National Association of the Deaf, 814 Thayer Ave., Silver Spring, MD 20910; www.nad.org.

Gilbert Eastman, "From Student to Professional: A Personal Chronicle of Sign Language," in Charlotte Baker and Robbin Battison, eds., *Sign Language and the Deaf Community: Essays in Honor of William C. Stokoe* (Silver Spring: National Association of the Deaf, 1980): 9–21. Reprinted by permission of the National Association of the Deaf, 814 Thayer Ave., Silver Spring, MD 20910; www.nad.org.

Ernest Hairston and Linwood Smith, "Black Signs: Whatever Happened to the Sign for 'CORNBREAD'?" in *Black and Deaf in America: Are We That Different?* (Silver Spring: T. J. Publishers, 1983): 55–56. Reprinted by permission of Ernest Hairston.

MJ Bienvenu, "Reflections of American Deaf Culture in Deaf Humor," *TBC News* (September 1989): 1–3. Reprinted by permission of MJ Bienvenu.

Carol A. Padden, "Folk Explanation in Language Survival," in David Middleton and Derek Edwards, eds., *Collective Remembering* (London: Sage, 1990): 190–202. Reprinted by permission of Carol Padden.

Jack Levesque, "Let's Return ASL to Deaf Ownership," *DCARA News* (November 1990): 2. Reprinted with permission of Deaf Counseling, Advocacy, and Referral Agency.

Ceil Lucas and Clayton Valli. "What Happens When Language Come in Contact" [excerpt], in *Language Contact in the American Deaf Community* (San Diego: Academic Press, 1992), 9–14. Copyright © 1992 by Academic Press. Reprinted by permission of the publisher.

Tom Willard, "I've Had Enough of the I-Love-You Sign, Thanks," *Silent News* 25, 1 (January 1993): 2. Reprinted by permission.

Ralph Sedano, "Traditions: Hispanic, American, Deaf Culture: Which Takes Precedence in Trilingual Interpreter Training?" in Anita B. Farb, ed., *Who Speaks for the Deaf Community? A Deaf American* Monograph, vol. 47 (Silver Spring: National Association of the Deaf, 1997): 45–47. Reprinted by permission of the National Association of the Deaf, 814 Thayer Ave., Silver Spring, MD 20910; www.nad.org.

George Wing, "The Associative Feature in the Education of the Deaf," *American Annals of the Deaf* 31 (1886): 22–35.

Amos G. Draper, "The Attitude of the Adult Deaf towards Pure Oralism," *American Annals of the Deaf* 40 (1895): 44–54.

Warren Milton Smaltz, "The Fable of the Ass Who Was Taught to Whinny," *Silent Worker* (21 February 1921): 155.

Albert Ballin, "The Graduate," in *The Deaf Mute Howls* (Los Angeles: Grafton, 1930): 58–62.

Frederick C. Schreiber, "The Deaf Adult's Point of View," in Jerome D. Schein, *A Rose for Tomorrow: Biography of Frederick C. Schreiber* (Silver Spring: National Association of the Deaf, 1981): 54–58. Reprinted by permission of the National Association of the Deaf, 814 Thayer Ave., Silver Spring, MD 20910; www.nad.org.

Excerpted from Ernest Hairston and Linwood Smith, "Education: Black Deaf Students," In *Black and Deaf in America: Are We That Different?* (Silver Spring: T. J. Publishers, 1983): 9–19. Reprinted by permission of Ernest Hairston.

Ben Bahan, "Who's Itching to Get into Mainstreaming?" *Deaf Community News* (July 1986): 2. Reprinted by permission of Ben Bahan.

Angela Stratiy, "The Real Meaning of 'Hearing Impaired,'" *TBC News* (November 1989): 1–2. Reprinted by permission of MJ Bienvenu.

Jack Levesque, "Do We Continue This Tragedy?" *DCARA News* (August 1991): 2. Reprinted with permission of Deaf Counseling, Advocacy, and Referral Agency.

Clayton Valli, "A Taboo Exposed: Using ASL in the Classroom," in Mervin D. Garretson, ed., *Eyes, Hands, Voices: Communication Issues among Deaf People*, A *Deaf American* Monograph, vol. 40. (Silver Spring: National Association of the Deaf, 1990): 129–31. Reprinted by permission of the National Association of the Deaf, 814 Thayer Ave., Silver Spring, MD 20910; www.nad.org.

H. M. Chamberlayne, "Vagrancy among Deaf-Mutes," *American Annals of the Deaf and Dumb* 11 (1859): 86–89.

Edmund Booth, "Miss Martineau and Deaf-Mutes," *American Annals of the Deaf and Dumb* 22 (1877): 80–83.

["The habit of being prompt . . ."], *Deaf-Mutes' Journal* (16 October 1902): [2].

B. M. Schowe, "Finding Men for Jobs," *American Annals of the Deaf* 82 (1937): 105–16. Reprinted by permission of the *American Annals of the Deaf*.

B. M. Schowe, "The Development of Postwar Employment," *American Annals of the Deaf* 89 (1944): 350–58. Reprinted by permission of the *American Annals of the Deaf*.

Excerpts from Thomas A. Ulmer, "A Review of the Little Paper Family for 1944–45," *Ameri-*

can Annals of the Deaf 90 (1945): 284–329. Reprinted by permission of the *American Annals of the Deaf.*

Toivo Lindholm, "Place of the Adult Deaf in Society," *The Frat* (December 1953): 5, 9. Reprinted by permission of the National Fraternal Society of the Deaf.

Tom Willard, "What Exactly Am I Supposed to Overcome?" *Newswaves* (March 1998): 12. Reprinted by permission of *Newswaves.*

Benjamin J. Bahan, and David J. Kurs, "Thoughts on the Effects of Provisions for the Deaf," in *Deaf Studies V: Toward 2000—Unity and Diversity* (Washington, D.C.: Gallaudet University, College of Continuing Education, 1998): 295–304. Unrevised conference paper, reprinted by permission of Gallaudet University, College of Continuing Education.

Glenn B. Anderson and Frank G. Bowe, "Racism within the Deaf Community," *American Annals of the Deaf* 117 (1972): 617–19. Reprinted by permission of the *American Annals of the Deaf.*

Carol Padden, "GLAD Publishes Position Paper on Cochlear Implants," *GLAD News* (Summer 1985): 11–16. Reprinted by permission.

Bob Alcorn, "Reflections: The Deaf Way," *TBC News* (October 1989): 3. Reprinted by permission of MJ Bienvenu.

MJ Bienvenu, "Can Deaf People Survive 'deafness'?" in Mervin D. Garretson, ed., *Perspectives on Deafness*. A *Deaf American* Monograph, vol. 41 (Silver Spring: National Association of the Deaf, 1991): 21–25. Reprinted by permission of the National Association of the Deaf, 814 Thayer Ave., Silver Spring, MD 20910; www.nad.org.

Kathryn Woodcock, "Cochlear Implants vs. Deaf Culture?" in Mervin D. Garretson, ed., *Viewpoints on Deafness*. A *Deaf American* Monograph, vol. 42 (Silver Spring: National Association of the Deaf, 1992): 151–55. Reprinted by permission of the National Association of the Deaf, 814 Thayer Ave., Silver Spring, MD 20910; www.nad.org.

Sharon N. Barnartt and John B. Christiansen, "Into Their Own Hands: The Deaf President Now Protest and Its Consequences," in Paul C. Higgins and Jeffrey E. Nash, eds., *Understanding Deafness Socially,* 2d ed. (Springfield: Charles C. Thomas, 1996): 135–52. Courtesy of Charles C. Thomas, Publisher, Ltd., Springfield, Illinois.

Tom Humphries, "Of Deaf-Mutes, the *Strange,* and the Modern Deaf Self," in Neil S. Glickman and Michael A. Harvey, eds., *Culturally Affirmative Psychotherapy with Deaf Persons* (Mahwah, N.J.: Lawrence Erlbaum, 1996): 99–114. Reprinted by permission.

Excerpted from Harlan Lane, Robert Hoffmeister, and Ben Bahan, "The Hearing Agenda II: Eradicating the DEAF-WORLD," in *A Journey into the DEAF-WORLD* (San Diego: DawnSign Press, 1996): 379–407. *A Journey into the DEAF-WORLD,* by Lane, Hoffmeister, Bahan, copyright 1996, reproduced with permission, DawnSignPress.

Index

This index includes only those names and subjects pertinent to the Deaf World, and therefore excludes hearing people other than those with wide reputations in Deaf America (e.g., Lon Chaney is in, Napoleon out). **Bold** indicates a subject, names in *italic* indicate an author's contribution to the present volume, and numbers in parentheses indicate a silent reference.